C000182635

Sources of Value

Sources of Value is a comprehensive guide to financial decision-making suitable for beginners as well as experienced practitioners. It treats financial decision-making as both an art and a science and proposes a comprehensive approach through which companies can maximise their value. Beginners will benefit from its initial financial foundation section which builds strong basic skills. Practitioners will enjoy the new insights which the eponymous *Sources of Value* technique offers – where value comes from and why some companies can expect to create it while others cannot. The book also introduces several other techniques which, together, spell out how to combine strategy with valuation and an understanding of accounts to make a fundamental improvement in the quality of corporate financial decision-taking. *Sources of Value* is written in a readable conversational style and will appeal to those already working in companies as well as those studying on a business course.

Simon Woolley is a Fellow of Judge Business School, University of Cambridge and Managing Director of Sources of Value Ltd. He has had a long career with the oil major BP, working in a number of roles related to investment valuation and financial training, culminating in the position of Distinguished Advisor – Financial Skills.

Sources of Value

A Practical Guide to the Art and Science of Valuation

Simon Woolley

CAMBRIDGE
UNIVERSITY PRESS

CAMBRIDGE UNIVERSITY PRESS
Cambridge, New York, Melbourne, Madrid, Cape Town, Singapore, São Paulo, Delhi

Cambridge University Press
The Edinburgh Building, Cambridge CB2 8RU, UK

Published in the United States of America by Cambridge University Press, New York

www.cambridge.org
Information on this title: www.cambridge.org/9780521737319

First published 2009

Printed in the United Kingdom at the University Press, Cambridge

A catalogue record for this publication is available from the British Library

ISBN 978-0-521-51907-6 hardback
ISBN 978-0-521-73731-9 paperback

Contents

Figures

Preface

The content, style and potential readers of this book

Why should you read this book?

This book has some unique things to offer. It is about the subject of economic value and how this can be used to make better financial decisions within companies. Many other books do this but there are three things that make this one special:

1. It is a deeply practical book that delivers techniques and skills which will be of immediate use within a corporate environment. I claim this with all of the confidence which follows from my 36 year career with the oil major BP PLC. Although the fundamental reliance on discounted cash flow is the same, the approach recommended by this book adds up to something which is significantly different from that suggested by the current standard textbooks on the subject.
2. It introduces a technique which I call Sources of Value. This technique provides a new way of thinking about where value comes from and has the potential for very wide application in the formulation and implementation of successful strategies. The Sources of Value technique offers a way of adding a quantifiable edge to strategy concepts which are otherwise more often limited to qualitative consideration. In this way, Sources of Value creates a clear link between strategy and value.
3. It introduces a way of structuring accounting data that I call the abbreviated financial summary. This way of setting out accounting data makes a clear and obvious link between the economic value of individual projects and a company's overall accounting results. By adding this link between accounts and value to the previous link between strategy and value one can integrate what are usually treated as the separate business skills of accounting, finance and strategy.

Although the book draws heavily on my experiences, it is not just a book about the oil industry. I have written it for use in a wide range of industries – wherever significant investment decisions are made in the service of the goal of shareholder value. This book should even be of use beyond this sector because in the final section I look at decision-making when economic value is not the main objective. So those working in governments and charities, for example, should also benefit from reading this book.

Who should read this book?

I have written this book for two distinct audiences. These are what I term **'beginners'** and **'existing practitioners'**. Their needs at this stage are very different but I address this by including, as the first part of the book, a financial foundations section written specifically for beginners. I will consider the needs of these two groups next.

A good starting point for **beginners** is the saying that even the longest of journeys starts with just a single step. This, of course, is true, but if you only ever learn to walk you will probably never get anywhere really interesting. Learn to drive and then think where you can get to!

This book offers to beginners a 'quick start' to learning about how companies can make better financial decisions.[1] It offers to teach what I think of as 'the language of business'. By working through the first section of this book, beginners will speed along the initial stages of what, for me, has been a career-long journey towards understanding the financial side of business. Learn the language of business and then you too will have given yourself the possibility of joining in the running of a business with all the rewards that this can bring.

I anticipate there will be many people who will fall into my 'beginners' category. They will include new graduates who have just started on their career in industry. They will also include people who may be several years into their career but who have not yet learned how the financial side of business works. They will perhaps be on the point of switching from a technical to a financial/commercial role. They may even already have risen to management positions but will have limited financial understanding. What the beginners have in common is a weak understanding of the way financial records are prepared and how financial decisions are taken. I will assume that, at the outset, these readers have absolutely no financial knowledge. In most cases this will

[1] My analogy with driving prohibits me from calling the financial foundations section a 'crash course' although this is really what it is.

understate their skills but in my experience it is best for beginners to start from scratch rather than from some assumed position of basic awareness.

Beginners who are lucky enough to receive formal training would typically gain their financial skills by attending what is called a 'finance for non-financial managers' course. A more thorough approach would be to attend an MBA course or something like that. Many beginners, however, are simply expected to 'pick up' their skills on the job. This book cannot attempt to rival the in-depth teaching which the more thorough courses can offer. It can, however, offer a huge reduction in the time that is needed in order to get up to speed financially and, furthermore, individuals can achieve the learning on their own if they so wish. My experience tells me that time is a key constraint and many beginners remain exactly that simply because they can never find the time to give themselves the vital financial foundations. This book should remove that excuse for ignorance.

The financial foundations need to be quite broadly spread. They must cover accounting, strategy and finance. My aim for the first section of the book has been to offer a 'one-stop-shop' that covers what I consider to be all of the necessary skills that could transform, say, an intelligent but financially unaware chemical engineer into an individual who would function well in a planning or commercial project development role in any company. A great advantage of the one-stop-shop approach is that learning can be much more efficient with, for example, case studies being shared between chapters and developed as the book progresses. The alternative for beginners would be to study each foundation subject separately. This would take a lot more time and would miss the opportunity to share case studies.

The financial foundation section should get my beginners up to speed and upon completion of it, they can then consider themselves as though they were existing practitioners ready to start the main two sections of the book.

Existing practitioners could be doing a range of jobs right up to running a company. They will certainly know about things like profit and NPV. They will be well aware that in theory all positive NPV projects are beneficial for shareholders but they may well wonder why their company's investment policy is not simply to invest in all positive NPV projects. If they have attended a business school they may also be wondering what to do with all of the skills they have gained concerning setting the cost of capital. My expectation is that the links which I will demonstrate between accounts, value and strategy will leave this group of readers more satisfied that their learning was worthwhile and can be used to support 'real world' decision making.

Individuals who are already in this group will certainly not need to work through all of the financial foundation section. I could simply invite them to join the book at the start of the second section but there are some aspects of the way I look at finance that I believe need to be spelled out clearly. So I have provided a reading guide for practitioners at the end of this preface. This guide maps out a very quick path through the financial foundation chapters in order to highlight the points which I think existing practitioners need to review before they start on the main sections.

The focus in the book is on investments by companies. I would highlight two other distinctive areas which are briefly covered but which are not considered to be primary objectives. These concern how banks and other financial institutions make their lending and investment decisions and also how financial decisions are taken in 'not-for-profit' organisations such as state run medical and educational institutions or charities. Both of these topics will be covered but only in a relatively light-touch way.

What is in the book?

The book is in three main sections. The first has already been mentioned and is a financial foundation course for beginners comprising five so called building blocks as follows:

The five financial building blocks

1. **Economic value.** An introduction to the economic value model which provides the main theory on which this book is based. The model utilises the concept of the time value of money. Through this, sums of money that we anticipate will become available at different points in the future can be converted into the common currency of their equivalent value today. This in turn allows rational choices to be made between alternatives.
2. **Financial markets.** This section will summarise the two sources of finance that are used by companies, namely debt and equity. An understanding of these will provide one of the two key inputs to the economic value model, namely the time value of money. This section will also introduce the concept of treating the decision about how to finance an asset separately from the decision whether or not to invest in it in the first place.

3. **Understanding accounts.** The basic financial information within a company is captured in its accounts. This section will explain the key conventions that are adopted in preparing accounts. It will then show how accounting data can be restated in a format that I call the abbreviated financial summary. This provides an ideal way of computing the other key input to the economic value model, namely future cash flow.
4. **Planning and control.** Good financial decisions can only be taken within the context of a company with a sound planning and control system that can allow the vital feedback loops to be created between how companies plan and how they actually perform. This building block will explain the main planning and control processes and how such a feedback loop can be created. It will also stress the importance of setting appropriate targets and summarise a handful of key strategy tools and techniques which are needed later in the book.
5. **Risk.** The future prospects of a company are not certain. In this section, key statistical principles and techniques are explained including in particular the concept of expected value. The section will also introduce the concept of portfolio diversification. This provides one of the cornerstones of the theory of corporate finance. The section finishes with a summary of the different types of risk which should help provide a framework for risk analysis.

Each building block also contains a number of individual work assignments. These offer the chance to practise the techniques which have been explained and are a vital contribution towards transforming individuals from beginners into practitioners. Suggested answers are provided at the end of the book. These should be read by all beginners including those who decide, for whatever reason, not to attempt the exercises themselves. They form an important part of the overall learning offer.

The five building blocks are presented in what I consider to be their logical order. They do, however, interact a lot and so the foundation course is only completed when the final block is done. At this point, approximately one third of the way through this book, readers should feel able to join in the financial conversations that take place within companies and elsewhere and also to carry out some basic numerical analysis.

With a sound foundation in place, my analogy for the second main section of the book is that it provides three pillars which, between them, support the platform on which major financial decisions are made. A good decision is, in my view, a blend between judgement and rational analysis. The financial techniques described in this book will provide the rational analysis part of any good decision. These pillars are as follows:

The three pillars of financial analysis

1. **Modelling economic value.** This chapter provides an essential starting point for the consideration of value within a corporate environment. It should help individuals build the necessary spreadsheet models which will support value analysis. It also proposes a set of discounted cash flow conventions which could be adopted by any company as its standard evaluation methodology. A standard approach is essential if rational choices are to be made between competing projects because otherwise, decision-makers can easily be mislead by NPV differences which are purely a function of methodology and not the fundamental characteristics of competing projects.
2. **Sources of Value.** We are now ready to meet the eponymous Sources of Value technique. This starts by asking the question 'where does the NPV come from?'. The answer to the question allows one to build a bridge between the calculation of value and the strategic concepts which are used in the formulation of strategy. It gives an ability to calibrate the main assumptions which underpin our financial analysis and allows us to focus on the key reasons why our investments are expected to create value.
3. **What sets the share price?** The third pillar deals with the valuation of companies and with the implications of value being set by the present value of anticipated future cash flows. These implications range quite widely and go a long way towards explaining the performance of companies that is seen by their ultimate owners, their shareholders.

The new platform that we will have reached is not intended to cover everything that can be learned. It should, though, provide a sound working base that will allow significant financial analysis tasks to be undertaken. Readers who complete this second section should feel themselves well equipped to take a leading role in some important financial studies and, through the Sources of Value technique, to introduce some new and challenging thinking into their work place.

In the final section we will consider some more advanced skills. These chapters support the concept of judgement based on rational analysis. The philosophy is that it is only when one understands the limitations of our theories that one can really grasp how important executive judgement is in the making of good decisions. The theories are there to help make good decisions but they must be applied with the appropriate dose of real-life experience. What we can learn from the advanced sections is that this application of judgement does not negate the theories. Understand them properly and you realise that they require it. These three advanced skills areas that I will cover are:

Three views of deeper and broader skills

1. **Cost of capital.** This gives a deeper analysis of this topic and a consideration of alternative approaches to the setting of the appropriate time value of money. It also considers some of the implications of the theories for the way that risk is incorporated into decision making.
2. **Valuing flexibility.** Flexibility has a value which can be hard to capture in typical spreadsheet models as these tend to project the future as being simply a linear path from the present. In reality we can make choices which can allow us to enhance value. This chapter proposes a relatively simple discounted cash flow based approach to placing a value on flexibility.
3. **When value is not the objective.** We finish with a chapter which should broaden our skills. Governments and charities, for example, both work to different sets of rules. In this section we will consider how the techniques described can be adapted to such situations. This chapter is included as it should help us understand the actions of others and also because it allows us to understand better the strengths and weaknesses of the economic value model.

How should you approach reading this book?

As promised earlier in this preface, here is a guide for readers who are already well skilled in financial matters and who are reading this book to add some specific new skills. I hope that there will be many such readers because the book introduces what I think are several new techniques that I know from my experience are not a typical part of current practitioners' toolkits. Readers who do not consider themselves already skilled should skip ahead to the 'ready to learn' section now.

The simplest piece of guidance for skilled readers is to move quickly through the financial foundations section remembering it was written for beginners. I suggest that you give each of the five foundations a quick skim rather than simply skipping them altogether. The reason for this is that I do introduce some specific ways of doing things that I will apply later in the book. Also, several of the case studies are drawn on again later in the book.

My summary for you of these first five chapters and where you should focus your quick review is as follows:

- **Economic value.** There should be nothing new for you here. Just spend a couple of minutes glancing at the sections on project evaluation starting on page 14 with NPV and project evaluation through to the end of page 17.
- **Financial markets.** The initial summaries of debt and equity should be entirely familiar to you. The section on how these combine to give the cost of capital should be of more interest and I suggest you read the second half of it starting on page 53 with the Modigliani Miller proposition and ending with the conclusions on page 58.
- **Understanding accounts.** The first part on accounting basics can be skipped but I do suggest you read part 2 on the abbreviated financial summary (pages 74–79). This is because I use a particular way of structuring accounting data and it is important that you are aware of this.
- **Planning and control.** I think you can afford to skip the first three parts but I suggest you do read all of part 4 on words and music starting on page 125. You should be aware of most of what is covered but I do think some of my approaches are novel. I am assuming that you are already familiar with Michael Porter's work on value chain analysis, the five forces model and competitive strategy. If you are not, you should read pages 116–123.
- **Risk.** Most of this section will be familiar to you. I suggest you should read the section in part 1 on sensitivities starting on page 156 and the sections in part 3 on managing risk and the U-shaped valley starting on page 171. These are all important and may contain some new ideas. You may also want to look at my classification of risk as this may help by giving some checklists. This starts on page 172.

Since I cannot know exactly what a skilled practitioner already knows I do suggest that you read all of the second and third sections of the book. The chapters are set out in what I think is a logical order but I would excuse an impatient expert who leapt straight to page 258 to read first about Sources of Value!

Ready to learn!

I hope this outline has given all readers a fair overview of the book that follows. If it has intrigued you, then read on. If it does not sound like what you want then put the book down because from now onwards I will assume that all readers are keen students who commit to learn. Good luck, and enjoy the journey to financial skills!

Acknowledgements

My desire to write this book had been growing over many years. I must now give my thanks to all those who have helped me to transform a dream into reality. The most important acknowledgement must go to the institution that I call 'BP' for it was my career with this company which gave me the experiences on which the book is based. My colleagues may not realise it but their interesting questions and their appreciation of my teaching formed two great contributions to my deciding, eventually, to write this book. Hugely important also was the wide range of experiences which working for BP gave me.

With these general words of thanks in place I do now want specifically to recognise a few people who were especially influential in the journey which has resulted in my writing this book.

I benefited greatly from the teachings given to me by many people and in particular I would like to single out Eric Edwards and Ken Holmes who gave me my initial grounding in, respectively, finance and accounts. Special thanks also go to Brad Meyer who taught me a lot about how to be a teacher when my career reached the point where teaching rather than being a technical expert became my primary role.

Next I must acknowledge two people who planted two key ideas and two expressions in my mind. The most important idea and expression was that of Sources of Value itself. This came from Ray McGrath who was a colleague in corporate planning in the 1980s. A few years earlier it was Richard Preston who introduced me to what he called the abbreviated financial summary way of structuring accounting data. In both instances it has been my role to take an original idea and show how useful it can be, to codify its potential use and, now, to publicise it widely.

Several senior BP managers have supported me during my career but I must single out Dr John Buchanan who, ultimately, rose to be BP's CFO. We seemed to have our career paths joined together from the middle of my career onwards as I worked for him in supply, corporate planning, chemicals and finally in finance. He always gave me trust and support. Most importantly, it was he who invited me to 'do something about financial skills across all of BP'. It was this challenge which led, ultimately, to this book.

My final colleague to thank is Professor Don Lessard of MIT. He is associated with BP through what we call the Projects Academy. This is a high-quality executive education joint venture designed to enhance the ability of BP's senior project managers. Don invited me to lecture on Sources of Value to the BP classes and I found my conversations with him, and the seven lectures which I gave, inspirational. They, and the enthusiastic support from several of his MIT professorial colleagues whom he invited to my lectures, were the final step in giving me the confidence to write this book. I must finish with a big 'Thank you' to my wife Margaret who has been a huge help during the final proof-reading stage and who has had to put up with my obsession with this book over the previous two years.

Section I

The five financial building blocks

CHAPTER

1

Building block 1: Economic value

Summary

This chapter will provide the first of the five building blocks that are necessary in order to understand the language of business and play an active part in financial decision taking in a company. It is in four parts. The first part introduces some basic theory concerning the time value of money. In part 2 we will move into the practical realm of calculating value. Part 3 will work through three case studies in order to demonstrate further how the value technique can be applied in practice. Finally, part 4 will set several work assignments. It is anticipated that readers will work through these examples themselves. Specimen answers along with some additional comments on issues raised are given in Appendix I at the back of this book.

Part 1: The basic question

Would you rather receive $100[1] now or $100 in one year's time? The rational answer to this question is to take the money now.[2] If, however, the offer

[1] This book is intended for an international audience and so there is an inevitable question concerning what currency to use in any examples. Throughout the book the default currency in examples will be the US dollar. I have to ask readers for whom this is not their normal currency to swap, in their minds, references to US dollars to references to their own currency. Unless an example refers to two or more currencies I do not intend readers to take account of any currency conversion issues.

[2] It is possible to invent scenarios where the logical answer might be to take the money later, but these will concern unusual situations. For example, a scenario where two people are held at knife point and expect to be asked to give up all their possessions. One says to the other, 'Can I pay you back that $100 that I owe you?' The logical reply here might be to ask for the money later! I only say 'might be' because if you were insured you might think that taking the money now was the smart thing to do.

This is the first and last time in this book that I will invent an extreme example that apparently disproves a simple and generally true assertion. Business, in my view, is not a pure science and rules have exceptions. Part of the skill of business is to know when to trust to a rule and when to realise that the old adage that 'the exception proves the rule' must be applied.

concerned the choice between \$100 now but an anticipated \$200 in a year's time, many, but not all, would be prepared to wait. In principle, for a situation such as this there is a sum of money that you anticipate in the future which will just compensate you for giving up the certainty of receiving money now.

This simple question of money now versus money later is at the heart of most financial decisions. Take for example the decision to invest in a new piece of machinery. How should an organisation decide whether or not to invest money in the hope of getting more back later? What about the decision to sell a business? This concerns receiving money now but then giving up the uncertain flow of cash that the business would have generated in the future. In this section I will set out an approach which can be adopted to give answers to such questions. It is called the economic value model. Through it we are able to make rational choices between sums of money at different times in the future.

This economic value model has its most obvious uses in companies that are quoted on stock markets because it allows decision making to be clearly aligned with the best interests of shareholders. It is, however, of more general use. It makes sense for individuals to consider important financial decisions from this perspective. It is also used in the public sector. A good example comes from the UK. Here, HM Treasury's so called Green Book sets out the recommended approach for appraisal and evaluation in central government. This too, applies the economic value model albeit that it uses an alternative name for it, namely 'discounting'.

The time value of money

Let us return to the question of an individual deciding between \$100 now and \$200 a year later. How do you think the decision would be made? If you were faced with this question, what factors would you want to consider? Please think also about whether you would consider yourself typical of others. Can you see how different categories of people and different situations could lead to different decisions? Now think also about a similar transaction only this time where an individual was borrowing \$100 today but had to repay \$200 the following year. How do you think he or she would decide about this?

My guess is that the longer readers think about these questions, the more possible answers they will come up with. There are, however, likely to be some generic categories of answers. One category will concern the financial situation of the individual to whom the offer is made. Is he/she desperately short of money or will the cash simply make a marginal improvement in an already healthy bank balance? The second category of answer will concern the risks associated with the offered \$200 in the future. Just how sure are you about this sum of \$200 in a year's time? Is this a transaction with your trusted rich Uncle Norman or your fellow student Jake who you know is about to go off backpacking around the world and is seeking a loan to fund the purchase of the ticket for the first leg of the journey? Uncle Norman *will* pay whereas Jake will do so only if he can afford it! Then, when it comes to borrowing money, categories of answer are likely to concern things like the use to which the money will be put, the alternative sources of cash and, crucially, the consequences of failure to repay.

So we can see there are many reasons why the exact trade off between money now and money later may change. In any situation, however, there should be a sum of money in the future that balances a sum of money now. I will call the relationship between money now and a balancing sum of money in the future, the time value of money.

Quantifying the time value of money

The time value of money can be quantified as an annual interest rate. If the initial sum of money (traditionally called the principal) were termed P and the interest rate were r% then the balancing sum in one year's time would be:

$$\text{Balancing future sum} = P \times (1 + r)$$

In the \$100 now or \$200 in a year's time example above, the implied annual interest rate is 100%. Had we felt that a 15% time value of money was appropriate we would have been indifferent between \$100 now and \$115 in one year's time.

Quoting the time value of money as an annual interest rate creates a common language through which investments can be compared. If we did not express things in a common way we would face the practical difficulty that we could only compare investments that were over the same period of time. In this section we will consider the formula which governs how the time value of money works. We can then use this formula as one means of quantifying what our time value of money is.

Readers will hopefully be familiar with the difference between compound interest and simple interest. With compound interest, when interest is added it then counts towards the balance that earns interest in the future. With simple interest the interest is only paid on the original sum. So with compound interest at 10% an initial investment of $100 grows to $110 after one year and $121 after two years. By contrast, with simple interest it only grows to $120 after two years. The extra $1 in the compound interest case comes as a result of earning interest on interest.

The time value of money works exactly like compound interest. This is because with each year of delay the sum of money we anticipate in the future has to grow at the time value of money. The formula for it is:

$$FV = PV \times (1+r)^n$$

Where:

PV is the sum of money now (termed the present value);
FV is the balancing sum of money in the future (termed the future value);
r is the time value of money expressed as an annual percentage;
n is the number of years in the future that the balancing sum will be received.

This means that if we can decide on the future value that balances a present value a given number of years in the future, we can calculate the implied time value of money. So, for example, if we know that in a particular situation we are indifferent between $100 now and $112.5 in three years' time we could calculate our time value of money as 4.0%.[3]

This book will devote a lot more attention to the topic of setting the time value of money in later chapters. It is sometimes called different things such as the cost of capital or the discount rate. At this early stage in our journey towards financial expertise, however, all that is needed is an acceptance of the principle of the time value of money and that this works exactly like compound interest. This principle holds that for any situation there is a balancing point where future expectations are just sufficient to justify investing today. The balancing point is characterised by the position where a decision maker is indifferent between a sum of money now and a sum of money later. Once we have identified a balance, we can back-calculate from it the implied time value of money.

Armed with this time value of money we could then assess similar trade offs that involved different amounts of money and different time periods. We could, for example, use this single time value of money to apply to any offers

[3] Don't worry if the maths behind this looks a little complex at this stage. We will have plenty of opportunities to learn how to do the sums as this chapter progresses. For the time being, if you are not sure you could have calculated the 4% figure, simply check it is right by doing the sum $100 \times 1.04 \times 1.04 \times 1.04$.

from our rich Uncle Norman while we would probably have a different, and almost certainly higher, rate for any offers involving backpacking student friends like Jake.

The concept of value

The value concept allows us to translate any sum of money at one point in time into an equivalent amount at another time such that we would, in theory, be exactly indifferent between the two sums. One initial point to stress is that to count as 'a sum of money' in this context, the money must be immediately available to spend.[4]

So the concept of value refers to an equivalent amount of money that can be spent. It needs to be qualified by adding a reference to when the money can be spent. Hence present value refers to money that can be spent now while future value is money that cannot be spent until some time in the future. The term future value only has precise meaning when it is made clear exactly when in the future the money is available.

The time value of money formula allows us to convert future sums of money into their equivalent now. We have already introduced a special name for this. We call it the present value. We have defined the present value of a future amount of cash as the amount that we would be indifferent to receiving today compared with the future amount given all of its particular circumstances.

Using value to take decisions

So if value is the equivalent of cash in hand at a specified time, then present value is cash in hand now. Now the nice thing about cash in hand now is that it is very easy to count. Furthermore, if offered two amounts we can say that we would always prefer the greater amount. Contrast this with two different values, one corresponding to one year ahead and the other two years ahead. How could we decide between these? It would not be right simply to compare the two amounts and select the larger. The value approach is to convert each future value into its present value and then compare these. So when we are

[4] Cash is only really of use if you have it available to spend. If you want to test this statement out, try telling a bus driver who asks you to pay the fare that you have the cash but it is at home. This simple scenario will, hopefully, illustrate the difference between owning money and having money immediately available to spend. The value calculation only takes account of money when it is available to spend.

faced with two possible alternatives, if we were to express both in terms of their present value we would have a very simple way to make decisions:

Always select the option with the highest present value.

It is important to note the reference to using *present* value when making decisions. Would it be correct to make decisions based on maximising value at some point in the future? For example, what about a decision rule that required one to select the option with the highest value at the end of the current year? What do you think?

Well, the general answer is that such a decision rule would not be a good one although there is a special circumstance when the answer could be that it was.[5] There are two reasons for future values not being a safe basis for decision taking. First, there may be different cash flows between now and the point in time being considered and second, the time value of money may be different.

The point about different cash flows is fairly obvious. Suppose you are choosing between two options that offer either $150 or $100 at the end of this year. Your first thought will be that $150 is better. But suppose this option requires you to spend $50 now in order to gain the right to the $150 later while the $100 option requires no initial investment. In this situation the $100 option would clearly be preferable. The discount rate point is also quite simple. If the $150 was very risky compared with the $100 we might associate a higher value today to the low risk $100. Note, however, that when the clock has moved forward to the end of the year, we should take decisions based on what would *then* be the present value but today we take decisions based on value today, i.e. present value.

Taking stock and defining some terms

We have seen how money now is preferable to money later. We have associated the term *time value of money* with the concept of an amount of money receivable in the future such that we are indifferent between it and the alternative amount of money now. We have introduced the term *value* to emphasise the difference between money owned and money that is available to spend. Finally, we have seen how *present value* can be used as a financial decision making tool and we understand the distinction between this and any *future value*.

[5] This special situation is where the options being considered have the same time value of money and the same net cash flow between the present and the point in time in the future where you are assessing value. In this situation one could adopt a rule of maximising a future value.

I will give this approach a name and call it the *economic value model*. The economic value model gives a means of calculating the present value of any option or situation.

The following picture shows how it works.

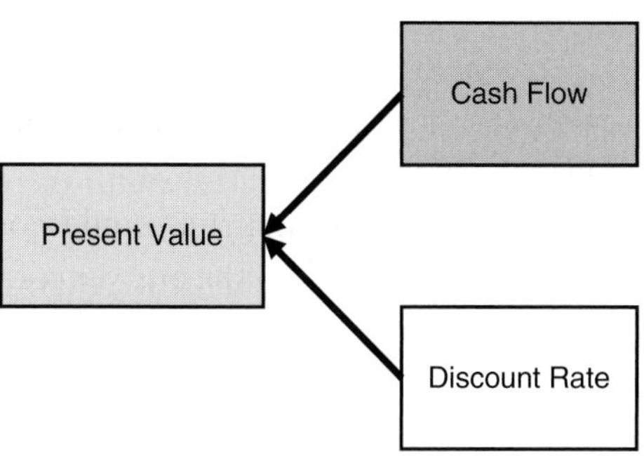

Fig. 1.1 The economic value model

There are a few more bits of jargon to learn:

- The process of adjusting a future cash flow to its present value equivalent is called *discounting* or *discounted cash flow analysis*. The abbreviation *DCF* is also used.
- The *time value of money* can also be called the *discount rate* or the *cost of capital*.[6]

One important aspect of the economic value model concerns the way that it treats the cost of any money that is used. This is allowed for via the discount rate and so any finance charges such as interest are not deducted from cash flow since to do so would serve to double count them. The basic principle is that one considers the cash flows which are required or generated *before* any finance charges are allowed for. We will return to this point later in the book.

The power of present value lies in two things first: in its intuitive and computational simplicity and second in how it provides a link between decision taking and how companies are valued. We will deal with both of these points later in this book. At this stage all we need to know is that values are things that can meaningfully be added up and that it is generally accepted that the market price of an asset is set by its value calculated via the economic value model.

[6] The term discount rate is obviously related to the concept of discounting. The reason for using the term cost of capital is not obvious at this stage in the book. For the present, please just accept it as all will be explained later.

For the remainder of this chapter we will concentrate on using the model to make simple financial decisions.

Part 2: Calculating present values

Now that we have some basic theory in place we can move to the more practical topic of calculating value. The following sections will introduce some simple approaches to calculating net present value.

Given the importance of present value it makes sense to rearrange the time value of money formula so that present value is the subject. Hence:

$$PV = \frac{FV}{(1+r)^n}$$

Note that the formula works irrespective of whether we are dealing with cash inflows or cash outflows. A cash inflow is given a positive sign while an outflow is negative. The objective is always to choose the option with the highest present value. A positive number is higher than a negative one and a small negative number is higher than a large negative number. So if we have a commitment to pay \$100 now but are given the choice of paying \$120 in three years' time we can choose which option is better once we know our time value of money. If our rate was 7% the calculation would look like this:

Immediate payment

$$PV = -\$100$$

Delayed payment

$$PV = \frac{-\$120}{(1.07)^3}$$

$$= \frac{-\$120}{1.225}$$

$$= -\$97.96$$

In this case we can see that the highest value is –\$97.96 and so we can conclude that delayed payment is the better option.

Up to now we have only worked with whole numbers of years. It is easy to conceptualise the idea of, say, $(1.07)^3$. What should we do if the payment was, say, two years and ten months into the future? Well, the formula works for non-integer values of n as well. Ten months is 0.833 of a year so the equation would be $(1.07)^{2.833}$. The arithmetic might appear a little complicated to those who are not familiar with mathematics but today's spreadsheets and even many calculating machines can make the calculation easy. The spreadsheet formula 1.07^2.833 tells us the answer is 1.211. So the present value would be –$120 ÷ 1.211 or –$99.07. So we could conclude that it would still pay to elect for the late payment option, but this time the present value benefit of doing so has reduced from $2.04 to $0.93.

Introducing the idea of discount factors

We can make a useful simplification if we introduce the idea of a *discount factor.* A discount factor is the amount by which you must multiply a future value in order to compute its present value. The equations are:

$$PV = FV \times DF$$

where DF is the discount factor calculated as:

$$DF = \frac{1}{(1+r)^n}$$

In the days before spreadsheets and electronic calculating machines, financial analysis depended on so-called discount factor tables. These listed the discount factor for different values of r and n. They can still be useful for doing quick calculations without having to fire up a spreadsheet. An example follows:

Discount factors – year-end cash flows

	Number of years into the future – n									
r	1	2	3	4	5	6	7	8	9	10
1%	0.990	0.980	0.971	0.961	0.951	0.942	0.933	0.923	0.914	0.905
2%	0.980	0.961	0.942	0.924	0.906	0.888	0.871	0.853	0.837	0.820
3%	0.971	0.943	0.915	0.888	0.863	0.837	0.813	0.789	0.766	0.744
4%	0.962	0.925	0.889	0.855	0.822	0.790	0.760	0.731	0.703	0.676
5%	0.952	0.907	0.864	0.823	0.784	0.746	0.711	0.677	0.645	0.614
6%	0.943	0.890	0.840	0.792	0.747	0.705	0.665	0.627	0.592	0.558
7%	0.935	0.873	0.816	0.763	0.713	0.666	0.623	0.582	0.544	0.508
8%	0.926	0.857	0.794	0.735	0.681	0.630	0.583	0.540	0.500	0.463
9%	0.917	0.842	0.772	0.708	0.650	0.596	0.547	0.502	0.460	0.422
10%	0.909	0.826	0.751	0.683	0.621	0.564	0.513	0.467	0.424	0.386

From the table we can see that the discount factor corresponding to 7% over three years is 0.816. So in our delayed payment example above the present value of delayed payment is:

$$-\$120 \times 0.816 = -\$97.92$$

The small difference of 4 cents between $97.96 and $97.92 is due to a rounding effect because the example table only shows discount factors to three significant figures.[7]

One particular feature of discount factors which should be immediately obvious is the way that the discount rate becomes increasingly important as one considers sums of money that are further into the future. The discount factor does not change much as you look down the one year column but there are big changes in the year 10 column. Every year of delay reduces the present value factor by a further amount of $(1 + r)$.

Another point to note is the reference in the title of the table to year-end cash flows. The discount factors have been calculated on the assumption that the first cash flow occurs a full year into the future. There are many occasions when this is exactly what is required. There are also, however, situations when it is not. The most common of these is when dealing with annual plans.

At the time the plan was formulated the present would be the beginning of the current financial year. The cash flow shown in the first year of a plan will usually be earned across the full year ahead. So would it be right to treat it as though it happened all at the end of the year? Surely not. It is usually a more accurate representation if the cash flows in a plan were all considered to happen in the middle of each year. The discount factors for the various years in a plan then become $1 \div (1 + r)^{0.5}$, $1 \div (1 + r)^{1.5}$ and so on. In pre-computer days this was a bit of a chore but with a spreadsheet it is quite simple to do these sums. We will explore this timing effect further in the second and third examples in part 3 below.

Introducing annuity factors

An annuity is a fixed sum payable at specified intervals, typically annually, over a period such as the recipient's life. How much might one have to pay in

[7] The 'correct' number, to the nearest cent, is $97.96. One has to get used to small differences if tables, as opposed to mathematical formulae, are used. It always pays to understand the limits of accuracy of any answer. The usual situation is that one cannot be very sure what the exact time value of money should be and so worrying about a few cents caused by rounding errors is usually a waste of time!

order to buy one of these? If we apply the present value formula you would expect to have to pay the present value of the future receipts.

We can see from the discount factor table above that a single payment of $100 in a year's time is worth $95.2 if the time value of money is 5%. If we receive $100 a year for two years the present value will be $95.2 + $90.7 (i.e. $185.9). So if we produce a second table where the discount factors are added across we will have a table that tells us the worth of an annuity for any given number of years and discount rate. This is done in the following table.

Annuity factors – year-end cash flows

	Present value of 1 per annum for *n* years									
r	1	2	3	4	5	6	7	8	9	10
1%	0.990	1.970	2.941	3.902	4.853	5.795	6.728	7.652	8.566	9.471
2%	0.980	1.942	2.884	3.808	4.713	5.601	6.472	7.325	8.162	8.983
3%	0.971	1.913	2.829	3.717	4.580	5.417	6.230	7.020	7.786	8.530
4%	0.962	1.886	2.775	3.630	4.452	5.242	6.002	6.733	7.435	8.111
5%	0.952	1.859	2.723	3.546	4.329	5.076	5.786	6.463	7.108	7.722
6%	0.943	1.833	2.673	3.465	4.212	4.917	5.582	6.210	6.802	7.360
7%	0.935	1.808	2.624	3.387	4.100	4.767	5.389	5.971	6.515	7.024
8%	0.926	1.783	2.577	3.312	3.993	4.623	5.206	5.747	6.247	6.710
9%	0.917	1.759	2.531	3.240	3.890	4.486	5.033	5.535	5.995	6.418
10%	0.909	1.736	2.487	3.170	3.791	4.355	4.868	5.335	5.759	6.145

The numbers in this table are called *annuity factors.* They can be particularly useful for doing quick calculations such as investigating how much we could afford to spend in order to generate a given saving that will last for a number of years. So, for example, from the bottom row, eight years column we can see that if you spend anything less than $5.335 in order to generate eight annual savings of $1 then you can justify making the investment if your discount rate is 10%.

Finally, in relation to annuity factors, note that as one looks further and further into the future the extra value from an additional year decreases. In fact, the factor converges on a figure of one divided by the discount rate. We will learn why later in this book. For now we can simply note that this provides a very useful way of calculating the present value of a sum that will be maintained for ever with the first payment happening in one year's time. You simply divide it by the discount rate.

Introducing the concept of net present value

We are now ready for the most important section in this chapter. This concerns the concept of *net present value* or *NPV* for short. We have shown how any sum of money can be adjusted to its equivalent in present value terms. So if we think of a project as a series of cash flows, we can adjust all of these to their present value equivalent. The total of all of these present values, some of which will be positive and some of which will be negative, is called the net present value of the project. The word 'net' is added in order to make it clear that the value being quoted is the net of inflows and outflows not just the value of inflows ignoring the investment cost.

NPV is the primary focus of this book and readers will learn more about why this number is so important as they progress through the chapters. For the time being it should be evident that the NPV of a project represents simply another way of stating the value test of whether it is worthwhile going ahead with it. A positive NPV means that overall you are getting more present value back than you have invested. So if you are considering just a single project you know that in principle it is worthwhile as long as the NPV is zero or greater. It should also be clear that if you have to choose between projects you should always choose the highest NPV alternative.

NPV and project evaluation

Many financial evaluation decisions concern projects. These decisions are typically of the type 'is it worth spending this much money in order to generate what will hopefully be a stream of positive cash flows into the future?'

Projects can be thought of as having a value profile, as illustrated in the following chart. This plots the cumulative present value of the cash flows associated with a project. The perspective of the chart is that it shows the present value of the money invested in, and taken from, a project. On the x axis we show the point in time being considered. In a typical project the initial cash flows are negative. This means the line immediately goes below zero. Once the investment phase of the project is over (i.e. after two years in the example shown in the chart) it should start to generate positive cash flow. This means the cumulative present value line starts to rise. If the project is worthwhile it will finish up with a positive NPV. That is to say the line will finish above the present value equals zero axis.

A close inspection of this chart will reveal that the curve goes downwards in the final year. What might the cause of this be? Well, the line goes down because a cash outflow is anticipated in the final year. There may, for example, be some clean-up costs associated with the project or some costs for laying staff off.

We can observe from the chart that it takes about eight years before the initial investment is recovered and the cumulative present value returns to zero. The point when the cumulative present value returns to zero is referred to as *discounted payback*.

The exact shape of the curve will be a function of both the anticipated cash flows and the discount rate. The particular project that was chosen had assumed a 10% discount rate. If we lower the discount rate the NPV will rise and discounted payback will occur earlier. Increasing the discount rate will

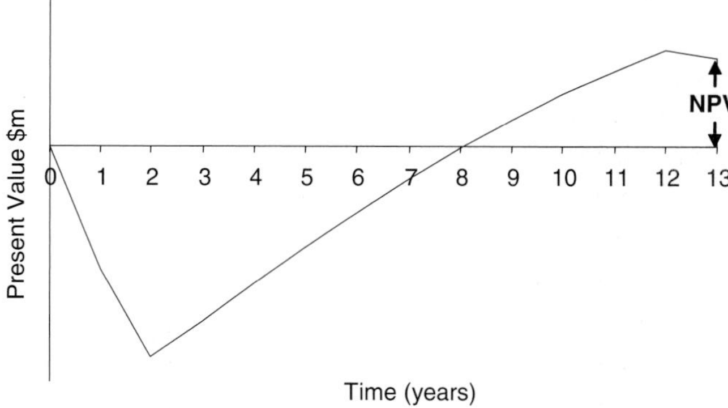

Fig. 1.2 Typical value profile for a project

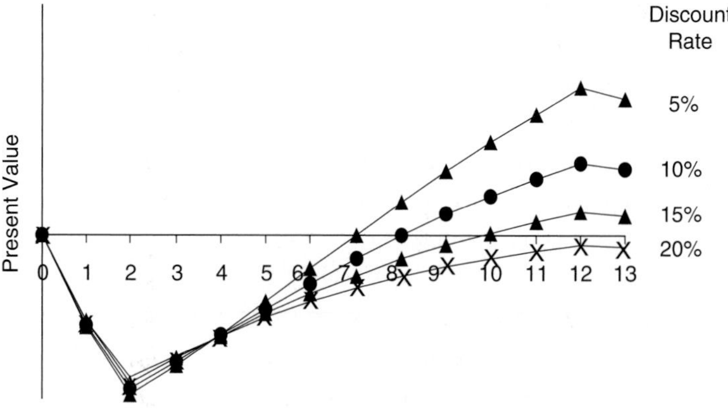

Fig. 1.3 Effect of discount rate on present value

lower NPV and delay discounted payback. The following chart shows how, for this hypothetical project, the profile of cumulative present value changes as the discount rate is changed.

The first point to note with this chart concerns how the lines get further apart as we move into the future. This illustrates how the effect of discounting becomes amplified as the time period increases.

We can also see that as the discount rate is increased so the discounted payback point increases. We can also see how there must be a discount rate for this project which results in it having a zero NPV. Extrapolation suggests this rate must be about midway between 15% and 20%. The discount rate which results in a zero NPV is referred to as the *internal rate of return* or *IRR* for short. The concept of the discount rate which causes a project to have a zero NPV is an important one and will be returned to later in this book.

Real life project evaluation

So far we have defined our decision rule as 'always select the option which maximises NPV'. Now with a project, where the choice is to invest or not to invest, one could imagine the decision rule becoming 'invest in all positive NPV projects'. Indeed, this is what the theory of value would tell us to do. There are, however, practical reasons why most companies do not adopt this approach.

The first concern is that resources are often limited. The resource that is limited may be people to implement projects or money to invest in them. Either way, a company may not be able to invest in all positive NPV projects. It may need to choose between two worthwhile options. There are also issues concerning risk. It is very rare for a project to be concerned only with certainties. Some projects may be so big that the risks associated with them could have severe impacts on the company.

How can these considerations be reflected in decision making rules? This is a very big question. At this stage we will consider the simplest answers. More will emerge as we progress.

What is necessary is to look beyond just NPV. There are a number of other factors which between them can help to paint a fuller picture of the relative attractiveness of a project. These are summarised in the table below. We will then illustrate how they can be applied in the practical examples section that follows.

Summary of additional economic analysis required for projects:

Indicator	Brief description
Internal rate of return (also called *IRR* or *DCF return*)	This is the time value of money which, if applied, would cause the project to have a zero NPV. It can give some idea of how big the 'safety margin' is between the project and economic break even where it has a zero NPV. It also aids comparison between projects of different size. Generally speaking, the higher the IRR the better although this approach can introduce significant biases which will be discussed later.
Discounted payback	This is how long it will be before the initial investment is recovered and the positive cash flows have been sufficient to build back to a zero NPV. It is where the line in the value profile chart crosses the x axis. This gives another indication of risk in how long one has to wait before the project has paid back its initial investment. The idea is that the longer the wait then, all other things being equal, the greater is the risk. Again, this is a useful concept but it has the drawback that it ignores cash flows after payback.
Investment efficiency	This is a 'bangs per buck' measure which states how much value is created per unit of constraint. So if money is the limiting factor, the efficiency might be NPV per dollar of initial capital cost or it could be NPV divided by the maximum negative NPV shown on the chart. If engineering capability was the constraint, the efficiency could be NPV per engineering man year utilised. This concept is most useful when there is a clear and obvious constraint and investments must be prioritised.
Sensitivities	These are calculations of the project outcome under different assumptions. Sensitivities give the answer to questions of the type: 'what if?' They are an essential part of any project appraisal. The problem with them concerns deciding when to stop, as there are always so many things to consider. Each sensitivity will have its own NPV, IRR, discounted payback and investment efficiency.

The first three items are what I term 'economic indicators' for the main case. These complement the primary economic indicator which is NPV. The final item makes the point that many cases need to be investigated in order to understand the effect of different assumptions. Each new case will have its own set of economic indicators.

Part 3: Practical examples

I will now take the economic value model and show how it can be applied in three different situations. I will use these examples to show how the economic indicators can add further insights on top of what is achieved by simply considering value.

Example 1: Uncle Norman's birthday treat

Uncle Norman talks to you on your 15th birthday. This is the generous offer that he makes:

'Everybody can have just one special birthday. You know that on that day you will get a super present from me. Do you want this to be on your 16th, your 18th or your 21st birthday? The longer you wait, the more you will get and on your other birthdays I will still give you your usual $500. At 16 you can have $10,000 but wait until you are 18 and this will be $12,500. If you wait until you are 21, I'll give you $16,000.'

Which should you choose if your time value of money was 10%?

The first step is to calculate the cash flows for the various options. These will be as follows:

Special day	16th birthday	17th birthday	18th birthday	19th birthday	20th birthday	21st birthday
16th birthday	**$10,000**	$500	$500	$500	$500	$500
18th birthday	$500	$500	**$12,500**	$500	$500	$500
21st birthday	$500	$500	$500	$500	$500	**$16,000**

The next step is to calculate the appropriate discount factor. The cash flows are all exactly one year apart and the first is in one year's time. This means we can simply take the factors from our discount factors table above. We then multiply the various cash flows by the discount factors to calculate their present values:

	16th birthday	17th birthday	18th birthday	19th birthday	20th birthday	21st birthday
Discount factor	0.909	0.826	0.751	0.683	0.621	0.564

Present value of cash flows (= cash flow × discount factor)

16th birthday	$9,090	$413	$376	$342	$310	$282
18th birthday	$455	$413	$9,388	$342	$310	$282
21st birthday	$455	$413	$376	$342	$310	$9,024

All that remains to be done is to work out the present value of each of the three options. This is simply the sum across each row. The results are:

16th birthday option: NPV $10,813
18th birthday option: NPV $11,190
21st birthday option: NPV $10,920

This analysis shows a priority order of 18th birthday, 21st birthday and finally 16th birthday. There is not a lot of difference in the numbers so one might well want to test the model a little further and in particular, to test what is driving the decision.

The above table has been computed line by line using discount factor tables. This approach was adopted in order to make the various steps absolutely clear. It is, however, generally preferable to build a spreadsheet model to carry out any analysis. This allows one to avoid small rounding errors[8] and, more importantly, allows one to carry out 'what if?' tests.

Two key assumptions to investigate concern the discount rate and the present on non-special birthdays. For example, a higher time value of money would favour the 16th birthday option. This is because the 16th birthday option gives you the large sum of money earlier and increasing the time value of money is giving the signal that money in the future is relatively less attractive. We can use a trial and error approach[9] to find what time value of money makes the 16th birthday option exactly equivalent in present value to the 18th birthday option. It turns out that at a discount rate of 12.39% the 16th and 18th birthday options are each worth $10,486. At any rate above this, the

[8] A spreadsheet model of the Uncle Norman's birthday treat scenario shows that the correct NPVs (to the nearest dollar) are:

16th birthday option: NPV $10,814
18th birthday option: NPV $11,193
21st birthday option: NPV $10,927

[9] The goal seek function can also be used if one wants to find the answer as soon as possible. I recommend, however, that when you are investigating such a situation you should adopt a trial and error approach. This gives a much fuller picture of how the decision you are investigating is influenced by changes in the assumptions.

16th birthday option should be preferred. This has shown how the internal rate of return calculation can be used.

Increasing the present you receive on non-special birthdays tends to favour the 21st birthday option because it means that the relative increase in present given for waiting goes up. With a 10% time value of money any default birthday present in excess of $1,924 would result in the 21st birthday option coming out on top. Since this number is a lot bigger than the current standard birthday present you would probably decide that thoughts about possible higher regular birthday presents should not influence your decision.

It is also possible to use this example to illustrate the concept of incremental cash flow analysis. So far we have considered the three options as independent alternatives. We considered all three on their own merits and decided which was the best.

Another way of doing the analysis would have been to start with a base case and test the impact of alternatives against this. The base case could have been to go for the 16th birthday option. There would then have been two alternatives to consider: what would the *incremental* cash flows have been had you selected the 18th or the 21st birthday options?

The cash flows would have looked like this:

Special day	16th birthday	17th birthday	18th birthday	19th birthday	20th birthday	21st birthday
Base case cash flow	$10,000	$500	$500	$500	$500	$500
18th birthday option:						
incremental cash flow	–$9,500	nil	$12,000	nil	nil	nil
21st birthday option:						
incremental cash flow	–$9,500	nil	nil	nil	nil	$15,500

The incremental NPV of the 18th birthday option would be:

$$-\$9,500 \times 0.909 + \$12,000 \times 0.751$$
$$= -\$8,635 + \$9,012$$
$$= \$377$$

While the 21st birthday option's incremental NPV would be:

$$-\$9,500 \times 0.909 + \$15,500 \times 0.564$$
$$= -\$8,635 + \$8,742$$
$$= \$107$$

These are exactly equivalent to the answers obtained in the first section of this case study. The only difference is that now we are considering the impact of incremental changes against a given base case (the 16th birthday option which has an NPV of $10,813) whereas the original analysis was of three stand-alone cases. One can think of the 18th birthday option as being like an investment. You invest $9,500 on your 16th birthday and receive back $12,000 two years later. This investment is giving you a return of 12.39%.[10] This is another way of thinking about what the IRR means.

This very simple scenario has illustrated one of the most important features of the value concept. This is the way that values can be added up. The value of the 18th birthday option is exactly equal to the value of the 16th birthday option plus the incremental value of the 18th birthday option compared with the 16th birthday option.

I refer to this effect as the principle of additivity. Economic value is additive. I would expect this to be self evident to many readers. After all, value is like cash in hand and cash in hand can be added up. It is nevertheless worth dwelling a little on this fact that values add up. It means that one can deconstruct a value calculation into its component parts and add up the value of each component. The value of a project overall will always equal the value of its component parts however you decide to divide them up. One of the key tricks of good financial analysis is to identify good ways to divide up value in order to gain useful insights. We will devote a lot more attention to the useful ways of dividing up value later in this book in the section on Sources of Value.

Not all things add up in the easy way that values do. Take for example the concept of the internal rate of return of a project. Recall that this is the discount rate which, if applied, would result in a zero net present value. In the case of the 18th birthday option compared with the 16th birthday option we have seen that this return is 12.39%. There are many situations where it is the return on investment that is most important. One example would be when comparing the performance of two different investment funds. Returns, however, cannot be added up. The 16th birthday option does not have a return because all of the cash flows associated with it are positive. Nor does the 18th birthday option, yet put the two together and the incremental investment does have a return.

[10] $9{,}500 \times (1.1239)^2 = 12{,}000$.

Example 2: A grand design

This example concerns a property development company. Its business involves identifying old homes that can be knocked down and replaced with new ones. In simple terms the development company buys a house and applies for permission to re-develop. Once permission is granted it demolishes the old house and builds a new one which it then sells.

We will build a simple economic value model of this business in order to investigate what the final selling price must be as a function of various assumptions if the business is to earn at least its required return.

In our model we will use the following input assumptions:

Plot price – $	1,450,000
D & A expenses – $ per year	50,000
D & A period – years	2.0
Demolish & build cost – $	850,000
Build time – years	1.0
Selling price – $	3,000,000
Cost of capital – %	8.0%

Plot price is the cost of purchasing the old house. D&A refers to the design and approval stage. The assumption is that during this period money is spent at a fairly steady rate. If there are no delays this can be a fairly short time but if objections are raised then lengthy appeals processes can result. If the approval is quick then architects' fees are the main component but if appeals start then legal fees go up. For simplicity this stage is modelled as incurring a fixed amount per year with the D&A period also being an assumption.

The other assumptions should be self evident. The D&A expense and the demolish and build expenses will be modelled as though the full cost is incurred in the middle of the phase concerned.[11]

The model looks like this:

Times (measured in years from today)	
Plot purchase	0.0
D&A	1.0
Build	2.5
Sell	3.0

[11] Hence with the assumptions as stated above the D&A expense is modelled as a total of $100,000 which occurs 1.0 years from the plot purchase date; the demolish and build cost of $850,000 is treated as though it occurs 2.5 years into the future and the final house sale is 3 years into the future.

Table (*cont.*)

Discount factors	
Plot purchase	1.000
D&A	0.926
Build	0.825
Sell	0.794
Cash flows	
Plot purchase	–1,450,000
D&A	–100,000
Build	–850,000
Sell	3,000,000
Present value cash flows	
Plot purchase	–1,450,000
D&A	–92,593
Build	–701,228
Sell	2,381,497
NPV of build project	137,676

So we can see that, based on the current assumptions, there is an NPV of $137,676. This means that provided we were happy with the assumptions we would be content that the project was worthwhile. We might well reflect on the relatively low NPV in relation to the initial cost of the plot. If we were constrained by the money available to purchase plots then our investment efficiency would be calculated as NPV divided by purchase price. The figure for this project is just 9.5%. We might also consider the delay between initial plot purchase and obtaining permission to build. A ten month increase in this would result in a slight negative NPV.

This project is one where there are many cash outflows and just one positive cash flow at the end. We should appreciate that this means the impact of any increases in the discount rate would be negative. If we were to increase the discount rate to 11% the project would have a very small negative NPV. This shows that to the nearest 0.1%, the IRR is 11%.

Our original purpose was to calculate what the required selling price was for any given set of assumptions such that the project would achieve a zero NPV. A spreadsheet model will make this type of calculation quite simple. So, for example, it would show that:

- For the base case assumptions the break-even selling price is $2,826,568.
- An increase in the initial purchase price of $50,000 would mean the selling price had to rise by approximately $63,000 to achieve a break-even NPV.

- A decrease in the D&A time of half a year (and hence also the associated D&A cost) would mean the break-even selling price would fall by approximately $100,000.

These are the kind of insights which should help anybody with responsibility for the project not only to decide on the simple question of 'go' or 'no go' but also to identify ways of making the overall economic result better.

We will return to this example in the next building block when we want to illustrate the impact of borrowing money to finance a project.

Example 3: Paving the way to the future

In this final example we will investigate a more typical project. This involves a heavy initial investment followed by several years of positive cash flows. The investment is in building a factory that manufactures paving slabs. The investment will cost $10m in the first year and $8m in the second year. The new plant comes on stream at the beginning of year 3 and will then operate for ten years. In the year after closure there will be a net negative cash flow as clean-up costs and redundancy payments are expected to exceed the resale value of the land. When the site is operational the key assumptions will concern sales price, sales volume (measured as a % of maximum sales capacity) and operating costs. In order to simplify things we will ignore inflation, tax and also timing effects related for example to any credit period given to customers. Cash flows will all be assumed to occur mid year.

Our assumptions are as follows:

ASSUMPTIONS								
Year 1 capex $m		10						
Year 2 capex $m		8						
Capacity		1,500,000						
Selling price $ per slab		5.00						
Inflation rate		0%						
Year	0	1	2	3	4	5	6	7
Sales rate – % of maximum		0%	0%	70%	75%	80%	85%	90%
Fixed costs $m		0.8						
Variable costs $ per slab		0.75						
Shut down cost $m		2						
Cost of capital		10%						

Note that further assumptions are made concerning the sales rate. This is maintained at 90% throughout the remaining operating period which is years 3–12. Shutdown happens in year 13.

The resulting cash flow model looks like this:

Year	0	1	2	3	4	5	6	7	8	9	10	11	12	13
Sales				5.3	5.6	6.0	6.4	6.8	6.8	6.8	6.8	6.8	6.8	0.0
Fixed costs				0.8	0.8	0.8	0.8	0.8	0.8	0.8	0.8	0.8	0.8	0.0
Variable costs				0.8	0.8	0.9	1.0	1.0	1.0	1.0	1.0	1.0	1.0	0.0
Capex		10.0	8.0											
Close down cost														2.0
Cash flow		−10.0	−8.0	3.7	4.0	4.3	4.6	4.9	4.9	4.9	4.9	4.9	4.9	−2.0

The next step is to convert the annual flows into present values:[12]

	0	1	2	3	4	5	6	7	8	9	10	11	12	13
Cash flow		−10.0	−8.0	3.7	4.0	4.3	4.6	4.9	4.9	4.9	4.9	4.9	4.9	−2.0
Discount factor	1	0.953	0.867	0.788	0.716	0.651	0.592	0.538	0.489	0.445	0.404	0.368	0.334	0.304
Present value cash flow		−9.5	−6.9	2.9	2.9	2.8	2.7	2.7	2.4	2.2	2.0	1.8	1.7	−0.6
Cumulative present value	0	−9.5	−16.5	−13.6	−10.7	−7.9	−5.2	−2.5	−0.1	2.1	4.1	5.9	7.5	6.9

The NPV of the project is the number in the far right hand column of the cumulative present value row, i.e. $6.9m. The other economic indicators are as follows:

- IRR – 18%;
- discounted payback – beginning of year 9;
- investment efficiency – 38%.[13]

Many sensitivities can be calculated. For example, zero NPV cases would be:

- sales price of $3.96 per slab;
- fixed costs of $2.1m;
- capacity of 1,135,000 slabs per year.

[12] I have used mid year discount factors. For the first year the figure is $1 \div \sqrt{1.1} = 0.953$. For subsequent years the factor is the previous year's factor divided by 1.1. Note also that I refer to a year 0 in the cash flow model. To be strictly correct this is not a year. It is better referred to as 'time zero' which is then present.

[13] In this case investment efficiency is NPV per unit of initial investment, i.e. 6.9/18.

Note that at this stage these sensitivities are purely arithmetic calculations which show the impact on the result of flexing a single assumption in the spreadsheet. One of the key skills of business concerns the ability to assess assumptions. So, for example, a wise manager would understand how lowering the selling price might well result in higher sales. For the present at least we have a model that will allow the value impact of changes in assumptions to be assessed.

Finally, note that this example was used to provide the cash flow data for the value profile chart shown earlier in this building block. It is important that readers should have a good understanding of this chart as we will be returning to it again later in the book. I suggest, therefore, that readers for whom this chapter has been their first introduction to the idea of NPV analysis for a project should return to the chart on page 15 and remind themselves of how it is constructed and how it can help to illustrate NPV, discounted payback, investment efficiency and IRR.

Part 4: Individual work assignments

1. If your cost of capital is 10%, what is the present value of $100 in one year's time?
2. By how much would this change if your cost of capital was (a) 5% and (b) 15%?
3. What is the present value of $100 in ten years' time if your cost of capital was (a) 5%, (b) 10% or (c) 15%?
4. An investment offers the potential to earn $10 per annum for the next five years with the first cash flow being in one year's time. If your cost of capital is 12% what is the maximum amount you should be prepared to pay for the investment?
5. The discount factor and annuity factor tables given above only cover a limited range. Extend them to cover a wider range that can still fit on a single sheet of paper. For example, discount rates going from 1% to 15% and a longer time horizon covering, say, 1–20 years plus also columns for 25, 30 and 40 years. Do this for both mid-year and end-year cash flows. If you are able to, print these tables out on both sides of a sheet of paper and get it laminated as a reference sheet.
6. An investment of $100 will yield you a cash flow of $15 for every year into the future with the initial cash flow being in one year's time.

a. If your cost of capital is 12%, how much value does the investment make?
b. How many years will it take before your investment has earned back at least its cost of capital?

7. Your engineering team can only cope with one further investment next year and you have to choose from three possible projects. Project A involves a capital spend during the year of $20m and will then generate cash flows of $8m per annum for the following four years. Project B involves a capital spend of $7.5m and will then generate cash flows of $2m per annum for each of the next ten years. Project C involves a capital spend of $36m and will then generate cash flows of $11m for each of the next five years. Your cost of capital is 12% and it is now the middle of the present year (so end year discount tables can be applied).
   a. Which project would you recommend?
   b. Are there any circumstances which would make you change this recommendation?
8. You own a retail outlet that you expect to generate cash flows of $1m pa for each of the next four years but then you expect sales to fall dramatically when a relief road for the town is opened. Your current expectation is that you will close the site when this happens and that your sales proceeds net of remediation costs will be $0.5m. Your cost of capital is 12%. It is the beginning of the year and the retail site therefore has 4 years of economic life left. You have just received an offer of $3.6m for the site. Should you sell? How would your answer change if your cost of capital was (a) 5% or (b) 15%?
9. Build a spreadsheet model to investigate the following project. It is 1 January and your time value of money is 8%. The capital cost of the project is $20m and this will be spent during the current year. There will then be ten years of operation. In the first of these years the cash flow will be $2m; in the second it will be $3m. During years 3 to 9 of operation the annual cash flow will be $4m but in the final year this will fall to $1m. For the initial evaluation assume no closure costs. What is the NPV, IRR, discounted payback and investment efficiency? Investigate also what capital cost increase would cause the project to have a zero NPV. Finally, identify what closure cost incurred at the end of the project life would cause a zero NPV.

CHAPTER

2

Building block 2: Financial markets

Summary

This chapter explains briefly where companies get their money from and what it costs. In the first part we will consider debt, which is how people will choose to invest in a company if they do not want to take any significant risks. In the second part we will consider equity, which is invested by people who are prepared to take higher risks in return for the chance of greater rewards. In the third part we will consider how to allow for the cost of these two very different types of finance and how to link this in to our calculation of value. In this part we will also meet the idea of separating investment decisions from financing decisions and also the perhaps surprising presumption that if you have a good project, then money should always be available to finance it. The final part will contain the individual work assignments, answers to which are to be found in the Appendices at the end of the book.

The purpose of this building block is to provide the necessary background for individuals who are considering investment decisions inside companies. In particular it will give a basic understanding of where the cost of capital comes from and why we treat financing decisions separately from asset investment decisions. Although some insights may be gained regarding how to make one's personal investment decisions, this is not the main intention. Indeed there are good reasons why companies and individuals should adopt very different approaches to financial decision making.[1]

[1] Two key reasons are that individuals have only a limited amount of money available and will also have very different attitudes to risk.

Part 1: Debt, an initial overview

Debt can take many forms and tends to be given different names[2] but its fundamental characteristics always remain that:

- the lender (typically a bank) considers it to be **low risk**

while the borrower takes on the obligations:

- to pay **interest;** and
- to **repay the principal** according to an agreed repayment schedule.

There are two sides to the transaction: the borrower and the lender. From the perspective of the lender, debt is expected to be a low or even a no risk investment. In recognition of this the interest rate tends to be relatively low. If there is some risk that the interest or the principal will not be repaid then the lender will charge a higher interest rate. Lenders typically lend to lots of borrowers and they look to their overall portfolio of loans to give a sufficient return to cover any under-recovery on a particular loan.

The best example of what would be considered a no risk loan would be a short term loan to the US government. It issues instruments called T bills which are, in effect, borrowings by the US government from lenders. The reason they are considered risk free is that the US government can always print more money in order to repay them. The so-called 90 day T bill is sold for a small amount below its face value of $1,000. This amount represents interest since the full $1,000 is repaid after 90 days.

Debt is not low risk to borrowers. This is because debt carries with it the legal obligation to make repayments. So if a company cannot repay a loan the lender can apply to the courts and, in the limit, force a company into liquidation for failure to repay. We will see later on in this building block how debt increases the risk of the equity in a company. To borrowers, debt is a high risk but low cost source of finance.

Loans can be for more or less any period. It is possible to borrow money for just a single day and equally possible to borrow for, say, 20 years. The interest rate on a loan can either be fixed at the time the loan is taken out or it can be what is called floating. In this case the interest rate will be set at a fixed premium or discount to some benchmark interest rate. The overall level of interest rates is set through a complex interaction between governments, central

[2] For example, in addition to debt it can be called borrowing, gearing, leverage, a mortgage, an overdraft, a loan, a bond, a bill, a note.

banks and market forces. This means that interest rates change over time and so floating interest rates can rise and fall over the period of a loan.

The ultimate source of debt finance is individuals and companies who want to invest but who do not want to take risk. Where does this money come from? Well, it can come from many sources. Think, for example, about money set aside to pay your future pension. Most people would want to be sure that at least a part of their pension was absolutely secure. Think also about short term saving which you might make for a particular big purchase which you anticipate making as soon as you can afford it. Again, it is likely that you would want to accumulate the money without being subject to the risk of losing it. As a result of structural factors such as this there is a huge potential supply of money available to those who can offer risk free investments.

Banks and other financial institutions act as the middle men between those who want to invest without taking risk and those who want to borrow. Banks will devote a lot of attention to understanding what is termed the creditworthiness of the companies and individuals that they lend to. Banks will also attempt to do everything they can to minimise the risks that they take. For example, they will reserve the right to take possession of your house if you fail to repay your mortgage.[3]

For the remainder of this section we will look into various aspects of debt in a little more detail. The aim is to paint the picture of debt that it is a convenient and highly flexible source of finance that can be tailored to the specific needs of borrowers or lenders thanks to the workings of the financial markets.

How to value debt

Debt is something that can be bought and sold. So banks can and do on-sell their rights to loans. The value of a loan can be calculated using the economic value model.[4]

Let us consider the example of a two year loan with interest at 4%. So if you borrow \$100 you would pay \$4 of interest at the end of the first year and then a further \$4 of interest at the end of the second year along with the \$100

[3] The so-called subprime mortgage crisis which hit the USA in 2007 was a consequence of lenders paying insufficient attention to downside risk and making loans which may well not be repaid in full even if houses are repossessed.

[4] The origins of the economic value model lie in the fact that debt is valued this way. The logic is that something which works for debt should also work for other riskier investments but should simply offer a greater return in order to make it worthwhile taking the extra risk.

original principal. The cash flows are $4 after one year and $104 after two. If the discount rate is 4% then the present value of the payments is exactly $100. Now suppose that interest rates fell to 3% immediately after the loan was made and that the loan was at a fixed interest rate. The payments to be made will remain as $4 and then $104. If these are discounted to the present at 3% we can calculate the present value of the payments as $101.9.[5] So from the perspective of the lender, the debt will have risen in value by $1.9 as a result of the fall in interest rates. Had interest rates risen then the value of a loan would have fallen.[6]

The implication of this valuation method is that floating rate debt will trade 'at par'. That is to say, it should always be worth its face value.[7] This is because it will always be discounted at the prevailing interest rate. Hence a loan of $100 can always be sold for $100. By contrast, fixed rate debt will rise and fall in value as interest rates go down and up.

Fixed or floating rate?

The interest rate is one of the key levers that can be used to control an economy.[8] Governments and/or central banks have various means at their disposal to control interest rates and the announcement of, say, a quarter percent rise or fall in the rate is quite common. So, which is best for borrowers or lenders, fixed or floating? Clearly, if either has a reliable crystal ball that will indicate the future direction of interest rates then this should be followed. But what should those who are not clairvoyant do?

The answer depends on the circumstances of the individual or company concerned. To explain why, we need go back to our understanding of the purpose of debt and how it is valued. The purpose of debt from a lender's perspective is that it should be low or no risk. Now we need to think about exactly what this means.

[5] The calculation is best done, in my view, by starting with the final year cash flow of $104. Discount this by one year by dividing by 1.03. This gives $100.97. The $4 cash flow in the first year can now be added to this figure to get to $104.97. This is now discounted for one year by dividing by 1.03 to arrive at the present value of $101.91.

[6] If interest rates rise to 5% the calculation would be as follows: $104 ÷ 1.05 = $99.05. Add the year 1 cash flow of $4 to get to $103.05. Now divide by 1.05 to get to the present value of $98.14. The debt has fallen in value by $1.86.

[7] I am assuming that the underlying creditworthiness of the borrower does not change.

[8] The basic principle is that governments want to encourage steady economic growth and stable low inflation as opposed to what might be termed boom and bust. If economies need stimulating then interest rates are reduced in order to stimulate new investment. If economies are in danger of overheating, interest rates are increased in order to reduce spending.

If lenders know when they want the interest and principal repayments to be made then a fixed rate loan can give them absolute certainty. So in our 4% example, if a lender knows that he wants to get back $4 next year and $104 in two years' time and interest rates are 4%, then lending $100 at 4% fixed is the no-risk way to achieve his objective. Suppose, though, that the lender did not know exactly when he wanted the money back. We know that a lender does not have to wait for the loan itself to be repaid because he can always sell it. How could a lender always be sure he could sell his loan for its face value and thus recoup his capital? The way to achieve this would be to lend at a floating rate.

Borrowers see a different picture. From a borrower's perspective it is fixed rate borrowing that is certain whereas floating rate borrowing brings the risk that the interest rate charge might increase. The balance between the two is set by competitive forces. At any point in time supply and demand reach a balance through small changes in the relationship between fixed and floating interest rates. Financial markets are ideally placed to achieve this because money is so easy to buy and sell compared with physical commodities such as oil or copper. If one considers averages over a long period, floating interest rates tend to be slightly lower than fixed rates. At any point in time, however, it is perfectly possible for floating rates to be higher than fixed. This would happen when the view of financial markets was that floating rates were at a peak and would soon fall.

Long term or short term?

Consider now the period of a loan. It is quite easy to think of borrowers needing to match the period of the loan to the life of the asset which they wish to purchase. It is also reasonable to think that lenders would be happy to consider a loan as being risk free as long as the period of the loan was no longer than a conservative estimate of the life of the asset. If, for example, you need a loan to buy a house you can feel quite comfortable about repaying it over, say, 25 years. By contrast, most people would not want to borrow for over three years to buy, say, a laptop computer because it may well be obsolete before they had repaid the loan. One way to reduce risk on a loan is to match the period of the loan with the life of the asset.

In an undeveloped economy, lenders and borrowers would have to seek each other out. It would be a great challenge to find the match between the lender who wanted to lend at, say, a fixed rate for 20 years and the borrower who wanted to borrow the same amount on the same terms. Into this gap step the financial institutions such as banks! They act as financial intermediaries between lenders and borrowers. If there is more demand for long term borrowing than potential supply, then banks offer lenders a slightly higher interest rate in return for lending long term. A balance is struck and, as economists put it, markets are cleared.

The general picture is that companies like to borrow over relatively long periods in order to achieve some certainty of repayment obligations as they finance what they see as their long term growth. Lenders, however, see having their money tied up for a long period as being somewhat more risky. So lenders typically require a premium in return for lending long term. The exact premium depends on market forces and it can even change sign in some situations.[9] The evidence is that over a long period lending long term has attracted a premium compared with lending short term.[10] This is consistent with the view that lenders normally require a premium for lending long term.

Interest rates and inflation

Inflation is the steady erosion of the purchasing power of a unit of currency caused by increases in prices. One can think of interest rates as having two components. One component concerns the desire of lenders to be compensated for the effect of inflation. The second offers a so-called real return.

This seems quite an intuitive model. If it were to hold then the numbers would work together like this:

$$(1+\text{inflation})\times(1+\text{real return})=(1+\text{nominal return})$$

So, for example, if the rate of inflation was 10% and the required real return was 2% the nominal interest rate would be 12.2%. Note that because the numbers are multiplied together rather than simply added, we finish up with the extra 0.2% on the nominal interest rate.

This model goes a fair way towards explaining the historical trend in interest rates.[11] It is also intellectually appealing as one can feel comfortable with a model that states that lenders are compensated for inflation. We do, however, need to treat it with caution. Interest rates tend not to respond to inflation

[9] For example, when short term interest rates are considered to be close to a peak it can appear cheaper to lock in a lower rate for a long period. Only the passage of time will allow one to be absolutely sure which was cheapest.

[10] Over the period 1925–2000 the return on a dollar invested in 90 day US T bills was the equivalent of 3.8% pa. By contrast, the return on 20 year US government bonds averaged 5.3%.

[11] Over the same 1925–2000 period, US inflation averaged 3.1%.

changes in the simple way that the above model would suggest. There are some fairly obvious reasons for this. For example, consider how investors do not know what future inflation will be and that governments use the interest rate as a lever to control inflation. So we should think of interest rates as having a link to inflation but not being tied to it.[12]

Interest rates and exchange rates

Each currency will tend to have its own interest rate. So, for example, at the beginning of May 2007 the short term interest rate in the USA was 5.23% while the comparable rate in Japan was just 0.57%. Would borrowers be better off borrowing in Japanese yen? This is a question that only the passage of time can give a definitive answer to because the answer will depend on what happens to exchange rates. So one can only know with hindsight whether or not dollar or yen borrowing was cheaper.[13]

Financial markets, however, will provide an immediate indication of which currency it is best to opt for. This is because these markets will allow currencies to be exchanged not just immediately but also at any date in the future. The answer that emerges from the markets will be that at any point in time it should not matter which currency you borrow in since the forward exchange rates will exactly compensate for interest rate differences. This is because if the rates did not exactly balance, people would be able to make a profit for no risk. Money would be invested in search of the profit and this would quickly eliminate the opportunity. This effect is referred to as arbitrage.

The numbers work like this: suppose \$1 will purchase 119.24 yen today; and that 90 day interest rates are 5.23% for US dollars and 0.57% for yen. We can compute the 90 day interest rate from the annual interest rate thus:

1 year interest rate	= 5.23%
Hence quarter year interest rate[14]	$= (1 + 0.0523)^{0.25} - 1.$
	= 1.283%
Similarly, quarter year yen rate	= 0.142%

12 The exception to this being for any debt that carries a formal link to inflation. Some government borrowing is structured in this way; for example, index linked savings offered by the UK government which pay interest at a rate equal to inflation plus a specified premium.

13 We would need to know the exchange rate on each occasion that an interest or principal repayment was made.

14 Remember that because interest rates work through compound interest as opposed to simple interest one cannot simply divide the annual interest rate by 4 to get to the quarterly interest rate. One has to find 1 plus the interest rate raised to the power 0.25 and subtract 1.

So $1 today will become	$1.01283 in 90 days' time
Likewise, ¥119.24 today will become	¥119.4093 in 90 days' time

These two amounts must be the same thanks to the principle of arbitrage.

Hence the forward exchange rate[15] must be	= 119.4093 ÷ 1.01283
	= ¥117.90/$

This means that a low interest rate is simply a signal that on the forward exchange markets a currency will be strengthening. The low interest rate can be expected to be offset by a higher cost of repaying the loan.

The answer to the question of which currency to borrow in comes from common sense rather than the financial markets. If a company wants to speculate then by all means take a view on which currency will be the cheapest and borrow in that currency. However, if a company does want to speculate, why set the amount of speculation by the amount of money that it wishes to borrow? Borrowing should be thought of in the context of the way that it will be repaid. So if borrowing will be invested with a view to generating a flow of US dollars, then borrow in dollars. If the investment will yield yen, then borrow yen. Hindsight may prove this to have been wrong, but no blame can be attached and hindsight is equally likely to show that the decision was favourable.

How lenders minimise risk

Lenders will do everything they can to minimise risk up to the point where they drive away a potential customer that they wish to satisfy. Lenders will be looking for what they term security. Security means confirmation that interest and principal will be paid on time. It can take many forms. The greater the security the lower the risk on the loan and hence the lower the interest rate can be.

Clearly the amount of effort devoted to assessing creditworthiness will be a function of the size of the loan. Major loans will be subject to large what are called due diligence exercises. These will assess the risks associated with a loan. This can be an eye-opening experience as banks focus on what can go wrong with a particular situation. They do not just look at the most likely outcome, they look at worst case scenarios. Banks will also have to limit their own exposure to particular risks. They will, for example, probably set a limit on the amount of money they lend in any particular country or industry sector.

[15] i.e. the exchange rate set today for a transaction that will take place in 90 days' time.

The due diligence process is such that a bank will usually enquire what a loan is to be used for. It will want to satisfy itself that the use will generate sufficient cash to make the required repayments. It will want protection against downside risks materialising. This will probably mean it will want confirmation that insurance is in place. It may well want the right to move in and sell an asset if repayments are not made.[16] This right to sell another asset may well go beyond the asset that was purchased with the original loan. Banks may want a separate guarantee from a third party.

A vital factor concerning security is that it is not like a chain, where strength is set by the weakest link. Security of a loan is set by the strength of the strongest item of security. This means that financially strong companies which are prepared to put the full weight of their assets as security will find it very easy to borrow. The banks will not need to go through a detailed due diligence exercise if a strong borrower is providing security.

When a company seeks to borrow money the terms recourse and non-recourse often crop up. The term recourse refers to the extent to which the lender can look beyond the assets that were funded by the original loan. Full recourse would mean that a company places all of its assets as security for a loan. This reduces the risks associated with a loan and hence reduces its cost. Thanks to the strongest link effect, a company with little or no existing debt will always find it very easy to borrow provided it is prepared to offer lenders full recourse to its balance sheet. By contrast, a non-recourse loan is structured such that the funding is secured just by the asset concerned. Loans such as this are generally more complex to set up and cost more.

Credit rating agencies

The credit rating agencies are companies whose business is assessing the potential risks taken by lenders when lending to companies. The main two are called Moody's and Standard & Poor's. These companies make independent assessments of companies and also of specific debts of companies. They do this by awarding a so-called credit rating.[17]

The rating means that individual lenders do not need to carry out such detailed due diligence studies and hence can help bring down the overall cost of debt as a source of finance. I have summarised below the credit rating system used by Standard & Poor's.

[16] e.g. banks sell your home if you default on your mortgage.

[17] Clearly companies have to make necessary financial disclosures to the rating agencies to allow such analysis to be completed.

AAA An obligation rated triple A has the highest rating assigned by Standard & Poor's. The obligor's capacity to meet its financial commitment on the obligation is extremely strong.

AA An obligation rated 'AA' differs from the highest rated obligations only to a small degree. The obligor's capacity to meet its financial commitment on the obligation is very strong.

A An obligation rated 'A' is somewhat more susceptible to the adverse effects of changes in circumstances and economic conditions. However, the obligor's capacity to meet its financial commitment on the obligation is still strong.

BBB An obligation rated triple B exhibits adequate protection parameters. However, adverse economic conditions or changing circumstances are more likely to lead to a weakened capacity of the obligor to meet its financial commitment on the obligation.

BB An obligation rated 'BB' is less vulnerable to non-payment than other speculative issues. However, it faces major ongoing uncertainties or exposure to adverse conditions which could lead to the obligor's inadequate capacity to meet its financial commitment on the obligation.

B An obligation rated 'B' is more vulnerable to non-payment than obligations rated 'BB', but the obligor currently has the capacity to meet its financial commitment on the obligation. Adverse conditions will likely impair the obligor's capacity to meet its financial commitment on the obligation.

CCC An obligation rated 'CCC' is currently vulnerable to non-payment, and is dependent upon favourable conditions for the obligor to meet its financial commitment. In the event of adverse conditions, the obligor is not likely to have the capacity to meet its financial commitment on the obligation.

CC An obligation rated 'CC' is currently highly vulnerable to non-payment.

C A subordinated debt or preferred stock obligation rated 'C' is currently highly vulnerable to non-payment. The 'C' rating may be used to cover a situation where a bankruptcy petition has been filed or similar action taken, but payments on this obligation are being continued.

D An obligation rated 'D' is in payment default. The 'D' rating category is used when payments on an obligation are not made on the date due even if the applicable grace period has not expired, unless Standard & Poor's believes that such payments will be made during such grace period.

This gives a sliding scale between the strongest companies in the world (Exxon would be an example) and those in default. Ratings in the triple A to triple B range are regarded by the market as investment grade.[18] Many investors are limited to investing in only investment grade securities. So lending to companies in lower bands would not be possible by companies subject to such limitations. The term 'junk bonds' is the colloquial description for such high risk lending. We will return to the question of exactly how secure the various categories are in the fifth building block, which deals with risk.

Two advantages of debt over equity

The picture so far might well appear to be that debt exists because of a need to offer low risk investment opportunities. Debt may be high risk to companies but this is compensated for by its low cost. We will complete this section with a reference to two particular benefits that debt has over the alternative source of finance which is equity. These are the availability of tax relief and the relative flexibility of debt.

In many tax regimes, interest is an allowable expense as one calculates taxable profit. This means that for a company that is paying tax, the incremental cost of debt is reduced by a factor equal to one minus the tax rate. This effect is referred to as the tax shield. Typical tax rules do not provide an equivalent tax shield for equity.

The flexibility of debt is reflected in the fact that it is usually possible to borrow or lend marginal amounts literally on a daily basis. This means that a company can balance its books by borrowing or lending each day. It simply is not practical for a quoted company[19] to balance its books via its issued shares. Companies cannot tell exactly what their daily cash balance will be. This is because they cannot control exactly when their customers pay them. The best way to cope with this unavoidable variability in cash holding is to finance a company, at the margin, through debt.

If a company wants 'no debt' it has to hold sufficient cash to cover the worst position in, say, a year and then accept that on every day except one it will have money sitting in the bank at the end of the day. A simpler solution is to

[18] Ratings from 'AA' to 'CCC' may be modified by the addition of a plus (+) or minus (–) sign to show relative standing within the major rating categories.

[19] i.e. one that has shares that are traded on a stock exchange.

negotiate an overdraft facility that permits borrowing up to an agreed level whenever it is required. If a company has no other debt then a bank will see this as a great opportunity.

Conclusion

So the picture of debt is that it is a company's 'flexible friend' which allows the chief financial officer to balance the books each day. There is a huge availability of money wanting to be invested in low risk situations. The laws of supply and demand set a fair price for this money which may be low risk to lenders but is high risk for borrowers. The cream on the cake for debt is that it also brings with it a tax shield.

Part 2: Equity, an initial overview

The fundamental characteristics of equity are very different from those of debt. From the investor's perspective it brings:

- risk;
- ownership; and
- potential high reward.

From the company's perspective it brings:

- anticipations of the need to pay future dividends but no commitments; and
- issues related to ownership and control.

A company that wishes to invest in a risky project and that has no spare money available will need to raise at least some of the cost via issuing new equity. This is because no matter how big the anticipated NPV, there is almost bound to be some associated downside risk and so bankers will not want to lend the full amount since this would expose them to some risk. All projects need some equity cushion in order to cover their downside risk. This means that a company that lacks the financial resources to implement a new project will have to sell new shares to investors in order to fund its growth.

Selling new shares is the only point at which a company actually raises money from share sales. All of the subsequent share sales that take place, typically via stock exchanges, are just deals between investors from which the company gains no direct benefit. Companies that issue equity have to facilitate these sales by, for example, issuing new share certificates each time a share is sold. The ongoing cost of this is, in effect, part of the overall cost of equity that a company must bear.[20]

Shares will have attached to them ownership rights in the company. These rights are, however, only limited in how they apply. The usual situation will be that:

- if a company pays a dividend then it is paid in equal amounts per share;[21]
- if a company is liquidated then any residual money left after all other creditors of the company have been paid in full is shared among the shareholders on a per share basis; and
- shares also give voting rights for things such as the appointment of the main officers of the company such as the directors and for changes in the rules under which a company operates.

The implications of this approach are that if an individual owns, say, 1% of a company and that company has $100 in cash available then he is not actually able to require the company to give him 'his' $1. The money belongs to the company and he simply owns a share of the company. The directors of the company will be empowered to ensure that the company's resources are used in an appropriate way and so could require the money to be invested in a further project rather than be paid out.[22]

Why would investors invest with so few rights? They do so because of the potential for limitless upside which comes in return for a downside risk which is usually equal just to losing any money already invested. So if a company is successful then huge returns can be generated. Clearly, not all companies are successful but the average return gained by investors in equity is several percentage points above those earned by investors who simply invest in debt.[23]

[20] Fortunately, thanks to IT and companies that specialise in providing the necessary service, the annual cost of maintaining a market in a company's shares is not too great. It does, however, represent a continued and unavoidable addition to the cost of equity.

[21] It is possible to have ownership models where different dividend rights apply to different categories of share but we will not consider these special situations in this introduction to equity.

[22] Directors must act in the best interests of the company overall but they will have some latitude in defining exactly what this is.

[23] We can return to the data on the US stock market for the period 1925–2000. Over this period the risk-free rate (i.e. the average return on 90 day US T bills) was just 3.8%. By contrast, the average return from investing in the equity of large companies was 11.0% while the return from investing in small companies was 12.4%. (This additional return was probably a reflection of higher risk in small companies.) The difference between the risk-free T bill rate and the average return on equity investments in large companies is referred to as the equity risk premium.

Unlike debt, shares do not have a fixed repayment date. Dividends are paid out as and when a company believes it appropriate so to do, but the main capital is retained within a company until it is liquidated. Investors who want to get their money back earlier can only do so by selling their shares. Many companies are listed on a stock exchange in order to facilitate buying and selling of their shares by investors. A stock exchange listing is not, however, a requirement for equity. There are many private companies that are still funded via equity but where the shares are not available for general sale.

Companies will often start as private companies whose shares are owned by a restricted number of individuals. At some stage, however, the company may outgrow its owners in that it may need access to more equity funding that the current owners are prepared to make available. In such a situation the owners may well decide to 'go public' by seeking a stock exchange quotation and floating new shares for sale to the public. This will bring in the necessary money but it does mean that ownership is diluted. A family can do more or less what it likes if it owns all the shares in a company but once the public become involved, the obligation to act in the best interests of the shareholders as a whole can restrict freedom of action. In effect, going public can result in a loss of full control even if only a minority stake in a company is sold.

We now have a basic understanding of equity. In the remainder of this section we will consider in more detail the question of how to value equity using the economic value model and also look at some issues related to the issue of new shares.

The value of equity

Equity investors receive their financial return in the form of a stream of dividends while they hold their shares plus the value of the shares themselves when they are sold or the company is liquidated. The usual expectation is that the share price will grow over time so shareholders tend to think of their return as being the sum of dividend plus share price growth. How, though, do the shareholders decide what the share price is likely to be when they decide to sell?

When a sale is made a new buyer has come into the picture. He too will be looking for a stream of dividends plus share price growth and, thanks to competitive forces, should have to pay the value of a share when they buy it. So provided all shareholders apply the same time value of money and there is a competitive market in the shares of a company, the share price should be the present value of all future dividends.[24]

If we simplify things such that a single dividend is paid each year then the value of a share would be as follows:

$$\text{Share value} = \frac{D_1}{(1+CoE)} + \frac{D_2}{(1+CoE)^2} + \frac{D_3}{(1+CoE)^3} + \ldots$$

Where:

D_1 is the divident paid in one year's time and so on; and

CoE is the cost of equity (i.e. the appropriate time value of money).

If we make one further set of simplifying assumptions, namely that the dividend grows at a fixed rate of g per year starting from a dividend of D which has just been paid, we can then carry out some algebra to work out what a share should be worth (we will call this V, short for value).

$$V = \frac{D\times(1+g)}{(1+CoE)} + \frac{D\times(1+g)^2}{(1+CoE)^2} + \frac{D\times(1+g)^3}{(1+CoE)^3}\ldots$$

Now multiply both sides of this equation by (1+CoE) and we get:

$$V\times(1+CoE) = D\times(1+g) + \frac{D\times(1+g)^2}{(1+CoE)} + \frac{D\times(1+g)^3}{(1+CoE)^2}\ldots$$

The right hand side of this equation can be simplified by extracting the term (1 + g). We then see that:

$$V\times(1+CoE) = (1+g)\times\left(D + \frac{D\times(1+g)}{(1+CoE)} + \frac{D\times(1+g)^2}{(1+CoE)^2} + \ldots\right)$$

Now note that all of the terms to the right of the final expression are exactly the same[25] as the original equation for V. This means that:

$$V\times(1+CoE) = (1+g)\times(D+V)$$

[24] The sum can either be done for ever into the future, which is referred to as a perpetuity valuation, or to a point at which it is assumed the company is liquidated. However, since the liquidation value should equal the value of the future cash flows that the remaining assets should produce, this too should give a value equal to the present value of the stream of dividends to perpetuity.

[25] This is true provided the growth rate g is less than the cost of equity.

Hence

$$V + V \times CoE = D + V + g \times D + g \times V$$

Which simplifies to:

$$V = D \times \frac{(1+g)}{(CoE - g)}$$

This is an extremely useful formula allowing almost instant share valuation. It does not matter if you do not follow the derivation, what matters is the equation itself. To value a share all you need is a set of assumptions about three things: the dividend, the growth rate and the cost of equity. With no growth one gets an even more simple relationship that value is equal to the dividend divided by the cost of equity. We first met this equation in the first building block, now we should understand its derivation.

The term $D \times (1+g)$ is equal to the anticipated dividend receivable in one year's time. Hence the equation states that a share should be worth this anticipated dividend divided by cost of equity less growth.[26] I refer to this relationship as the perpetuity valuation formula. It is also called the Gordon Growth model in recognition of its original 'inventor'.

There is one final rearrangement of the formula which I like to make. The dividend divided by the value is what is termed the dividend yield. This means that:

$$\text{Cost of equity} = \text{dividend yield} + \text{anticipated growth}$$

The cost of equity is the return an investor requires and it is achieved through a combination of dividend yield plus growth. When written this way the equation is almost self evident.

The relationship between dividends and funds flow

The valuation formula which we have just derived is based purely on dividends paid. We now need to consider the relationship between dividends and a company's actual generation of cash. The directors of a company are allowed, subject to certain rules,[27] to declare any dividend they consider

[26] Once again, remember that a valuation is only as good as the assumptions on which it is based. In this case the key assumptions concern constant growth to perpetuity and a constant cost of equity.

[27] These rules are set by the prevailing company law. The usual rule is that dividends can only be paid out of profits that have already been earned. So if more cash is available than the accumulated profit

appropriate. So if a company is valued based on its dividend, why not always pay as high a dividend as possible in order to achieve the highest possible value?

The answer is that shareholders can see through such a simple approach. If shareholders think a dividend is not sustainable then they will not be prepared to assume that it is actually paid out for ever into the future. The value they will place on the company will be lower than this would have implied.

Shareholders will even place a value on a company that is paying no dividend at all simply because they believe that at some stage in the future the company will pay a dividend. Microsoft was an extreme example of this. It managed to build a huge market capitalisation[28] before it ever paid a cash dividend. Its first cash dividend was paid in 2003 by which time it had generated a cash holding of almost $50bn.[29]

What was happening was that shareholders were buying shares in the anticipation that at some stage in the future, dividends would be paid out. So shareholders, as they set the share price, were looking beyond the actual dividend to potential dividends. In Microsoft's case, the shareholders knew there was $50bn in the bank and also all of the worth of the existing Windows suite of software. The implication had to be of huge dividends in the future.

A simple way to think about a future dividend is to assume that cash held by the company can either be paid out now or invested in a new project. If money is invested in a new project then this will simply defer the dividend because the project will return ever more money in the future. Indeed, if the project earns a return equal to the time value of money then the present value of that future cash will exactly equal the dividend that is foregone today in order to fund the project. So paying a dividend or investing should both yield the same value. If the project earns above the cost of capital then retaining the cash will create more value than paying a dividend and not investing in the project.

Cash raised from new share sales tends to be a significant source of finance only for new or very fast growing companies. For most other companies the main source of finance is the existing flow of cash generation. This is usually referred to as retained earnings. It might be tempting for established

this cannot be paid out as a dividend. Situations such as this can occur when companies stop growing and see their need for capital start to fall.

28 Market capitalisation is the aggregate value of all shares that have been issued.

29 This was a highly unusual position and was probably at least in part a function of Bill Gates' lack of need for cash.

companies to consider that they have three sources of finance: debt, equity and retained earnings. This would be wrong because companies belong to shareholders and should always consider that retaining earnings means paying lower dividends to shareholders and that they are already the owners of the company. Hence there are just two sources of finance.

Do dividends matter?

The answer to this question can be either yes or no. At the most obvious level, dividends matter because, ultimately, a company is only worth the present value of its future dividends. Dividends don't matter because a company is valued on the assumption that its cash resources already belong to shareholders. This is equivalent to assuming that the payment of a dividend simply moves money from one account of a shareholder (money held by the company) to another (money held directly by the shareholder).

Dividends don't matter only when shareholders trust the management of a company to invest their money wisely. If shareholders think that cash can be reinvested by a company and earn an NPV of zero or more then the shareholders would, logically, be happy to see this happen even if it meant a company paying no dividend today. In theory, if a company has cash equivalent to, say, $1 per share then if it pays this out as a dividend or retains it to invest in a zero NPV project, value to the shareholder is unchanged. The share price will fall by exactly $1 when a dividend is paid but the shareholder will be indifferent to this because they will have received $1 in cash.

Reality is more complex than this for several reasons. Some shareholders like to think of their dividend as being money available to spend whereas the shares themselves must not be touched. Some shareholders are taxed differently on dividends compared with capital gains. There are also transaction costs to consider.[30]

The view that I hold is that dividends are about signalling and about trust. So:

- a company that pays a high dividend is signalling successful cash generation coupled with relatively low opportunities to reinvest in the business;
- a company that retains its profits and pays a low or even no dividends is signalling confidence in future growth;

[30] The theory says that shareholders should be indifferent between a dividend of $1 per share and a share price $1 per share higher. However, if the shareholder needs the money and has to sell shares he or she will incur costs in so doing.

- a company that pays no dividend because of low profits is signalling that it is in trouble but that at least it recognises this;
- a company that pays a dividend despite doing badly is signalling that it expects to get better soon;
- BUT, if companies lose the trust of their shareholders, the signalling fails.

Issuing new shares

When a new company is formed it issues shares to its founding shareholders and they gain an interest in it that is proportional to this investment. At the outset, the company will hold exactly this amount of money and so, in the absence of any other information, it will be worth the money that has been put in. If, however, the company is expected to invest this money wisely and earn above its cost of capital then it will be worth not just the initial sum invested, it will be worth this plus the NPV anticipated on its investment. Whatever the final share price is, however, value is shared, pro rata, among all shareholders in proportion to their original investment.

What happens the next time a company wants to raise new equity in order to invest in NPV positive schemes? How can it avoid the risk of diluting the existing shareholders' value when it issues new shares?

One way to do this is via what is termed a rights issue. A rights issue is an offer to sell new shares to existing shareholders for a price which is below the current price. It is a clever way of ensuring that when a company needs additional equity finance it does not dilute value for existing shareholders. It can seem counter-intuitive that issuing shares for below their value can be the right thing to do. The point to remember, though, is that a company belongs to its owners. So if you own, say, 1% of a company and are given the chance to buy a 1% share in an underpriced issue of new shares you will still finish up owning 1% of the company and having paid your 1% share of the new money that is raised. The way that rights issues work is probably best illustrated through a practical example.

Suppose a company currently has 100m shares in issue and they trade at $2 per share. Market capitalisation is $200m. Suppose also that the company needs to raise $50m to finance a major new project. One way of doing this would be to allow existing shareholders to purchase one further share for just $1 per share for every two shares currently held. This would raise $50m and the company would then have 150m shares in issue. If we assume that the $50m was going to be invested and earn just the cost of capital then the overall value of the company would increase from $200m to $250m. The share price would fall from \$2 per share to \$1.67. A shareholder who used to hold two shares worth \$4 would have invested a further dollar and would now own three shares worth \$5. So for such a shareholder, value would have been maintained.

Now suppose that instead of issuing 50m shares for \$1 each the company issued 100m shares for \$0.50. Our shareholder with just two shares would still invest an additional dollar and would now own four shares. The company would still be worth a total of \$250m but because there were now 200m shares, the share price would be \$1.25 per share. The shareholder would own four shares worth \$5 and value has been maintained.

Suppose that a shareholder did not want to invest any more money in the company. A further feature of a rights issue is that the right to purchase new shares is usually tradable. So a shareholder who did not wish to invest any further cash could sell his right to purchase cheap shares. What would a buyer pay for the right to buy a cheap share? The answer must be that the price for a right must be related to the discount between the rights issue price and the price at which the shares will trade after the rights issue. In the second situation above where the issue price is \$0.50 per share we have calculated that the share price after the rights issue would be \$1.25 per share. So the right to purchase one new share in this situation must be worth \$0.75. Our hypothetical shareholder owned two shares and so has two rights to sell. He would receive \$1.50 in cash and still own two shares that would now be worth \$2.50 in total. Once again, value has been maintained.

What we have demonstrated is that a rights issue allows value to be maintained without having to worry what the selling price of the new shares should be. If instead of issuing shares to existing shareholders, shares are sold to new shareholders then the price charged is of considerable importance for the current owners.

Conclusion

Equity is investment that takes risk. The upside potential is great but there is also the possibility of loss. The return on equity comes in the form of dividends plus share price growth but because share price growth is a reflection of future dividends, ultimately it is the stream of dividends that really matters. We have also seen the importance of trust when it comes to understanding dividends.

Debt may be very useful, but companies can survive without it. Equity, however, is essential for companies because they must have at least some in order to provide a cushion against risk. Equity also gives control but once it is widely held the value of control is reduced because a company must be run in the best interests of all of its shareholders.

Part 3: Introducing the cost of capital

We are now ready to consider how debt and equity interact and to learn the implications of this for setting our time value of money.[31] In the first section the approach was, in effect, simply to assert that there must be a time value of money which would govern how trade-off decisions could be made between money now and money later. We introduced the idea that this rate could also be called the discount rate or the cost of capital. Now that we know where the money comes from, we can put some more logic behind our decisions concerning what this rate should be. With this knowledge we can understand why, rather than using the term 'time value of money', we should refer instead to the cost of capital or CoC[32] for short.

The cost of debt is easy to understand. It is the interest rate that the banks charge on a loan. As we have already seen, if loan cash flows are discounted at the interest rate we will find that the present value is equal to the amount borrowed.

The cost of equity is not so clear cut. We have seen that the cost of equity for any particular share should be equal to the dividend yield plus the anticipated growth in the share price. But how can we know what is the anticipated share price growth? What we do know is that, in logic, the cost of equity must be higher than the cost of debt because from the perspective of the investor, equity is higher risk. Investors do not take on higher risks unless they think they will receive higher returns.

We will shortly introduce the simplest of models to describe how this requirement for extra returns to compensate for extra risk might work. Armed then with a cost of debt and a cost of equity we can see how the CoC should simply be the weighted average cost of the two sources of finance.

[31] Please remember that this is just a foundation course! We will be looking at this topic in much more detail later in this book.

[32] The term CoC is short for the cost of capital and is usually pronounced 'cock' although it can be pronounced 'cee – oh – cee'. There are two similar terms. CoE refers to the cost of equity and perhaps confusingly is usually pronounced 'cee – oh – ee'. Finally, the term CoD refers to the cost of debt. I have heard this referred to either as 'cod' or 'cee – oh – de'.

At this stage it might look as though the cost of debt and the cost of equity would be decided upon through two separate and independent calculations. This is not, however, how things work. The key principle for this section concerns how debt and equity interact. We will learn how risk is concentrated on the equity portion of finance and how a vital implication of this is that the cost of equity will change every time the amount of borrowing changes.

The capital asset pricing model

The capital asset pricing model (CAPM[33] for short) suggests that there should be a simple linear relationship between risk and required return. The model was proposed in the 1960s by three economists led by William Sharpe. A particular feature of the model concerns how they chose to define risk. We will come back to this point in the final building block which deals specifically with the question of risk. For the time being, however, we can make some good progress if we simply accept the concept of a linear relationship between risk and required return.

The model is summarised in the following chart. The basic idea is that the line which specifies required returns is the straight line between the risk-free rate and the return required by investors who invest in a portfolio of all the shares on the stock market.

The particular jargon of the model is as follows:

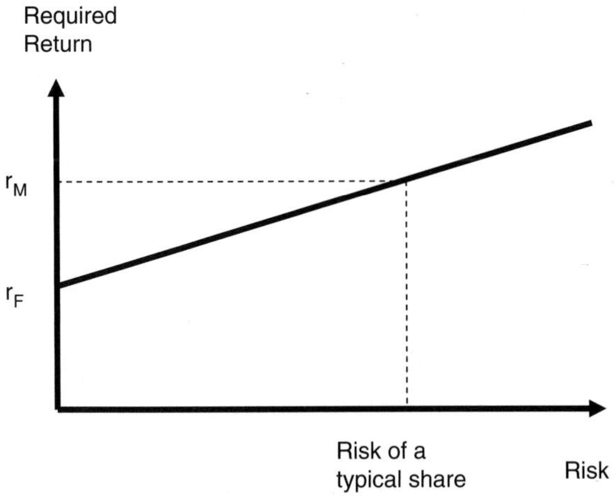

Fig. 2.1 The capital asset pricing model

[33] Pronounced 'cap em'.

- the risk-free rate is referred to as $r_{F;}$[34]
- the return required by investors who invest in a portfolio of all the shares on the stock market is referred to as $r_{M;}$
- the line linking these two points is referred to as the security market line;
- risk is characterised by a term given the Greek letter β (beta). This is explained later in this book.

There is some clever economic thinking behind why the line has to be straight but we do not need to concern ourselves with this. All we need to know for now is that there is an accepted way of linking required return to risk and that this comes through CAPM.

Armed with CAPM we can calculate the cost of equity for any particular situation. We can then combine this with the cost of debt in order to calculate the CoC. The expression WACC,[35] short for weighted average cost of capital, is used for this because the calculation weights the two costs in proportion to the amount of money provided. We will see what the WACC numbers should look like soon, but first we have to consider one more piece of theory. This concerns how the risk inherent in equity changes with the level of debt.

Risk is carried on equity

Debt represents a fixed obligation for a borrower. In any year, the amount of money left over for the equity shareholders will equal the total cash generation less this fixed obligation. Anything which increases the fixed commitments must mean that the remaining variable commitments will be more exposed and that, in the limit, there is a greater chance that the company will run out of money. Now think about the fact that we can never be certain what a company's future cash generation will be. This is what we mean when we say that cash flows are risky. The combination of uncertain cash inflows and fixed flows due to borrowing serves to reduce the amount of equity that is needed but it increases the volatility of the residual equity returns. This is best illustrated through a simple example:

Practical example – how debt makes companies more risky
This example develops the scenario first introduced as the Grand Design (example 2) in the first building block. It concerns a plan to purchase land and then develop a house for subsequent sale. Suppose that instead of funding all of the

[34] For the US market the risk-free rate is generally considered to be the interest rate on 90 day US T bills.

[35] Pronounced 'whack'.

project from a single source, it was financed by a blend of debt and equity. Say that the development company borrows a specified percentage of the original cost of the plot and repays this loan along with all accumulated interest when the house is finally sold.[36]

The revised assumptions follow. The new assumptions concern the borrowing as a percentage of the plot price and also the cost of debt.

Grand Design – with finance

ASSUMPTIONS	
Plot price – $	1,450,000
D & A expense – $ per year	50,000
D & A period – year	2.0
Demolish & build cost – $	850,000
Build time – years	1.0
Selling price – $	3,000,000
Cost of capital – %	8.0%
Borrow as % plot price	80.0%
CoD	5.0%

The initial cash outflow for the investor on the land purchase is reduced by 80% but in return there is a need to repay the loan plus interest out of the sales proceeds. Now readers should recall from the previous building block (page 9) that the need to exclude finance effects from cash flows was stressed. This example will help to explain why this needs to be done by illustrating what happens if the instruction is ignored.

The revised financial model makes the following adjustments in order to incorporate the effect of finance on the project:

- A debt repayment factor is calculated. This calculates the amount of money necessary to repay the loan and the principal. It is equal to one plus the interest rate raised to the power of the number of years between land purchase and the final house sale.
- The cash flows are referred to as equity cash flows in order to distinguish them from cash flows before any financing effects.
- The plot purchase is now net of the borrowing and is calculated by multiplying the purchase price by one minus the borrowing percentage.
- The sales proceeds are shown net of the loan repayment.

[36] This would be quite a normal thing for a property company to do and a bank would consider a loan for, say, 80% of the cost of the land to be pretty low risk as long as it had the additional security of a mortgage on the land.

The revised model is given below.[37]

CALCULATIONS	
Times (measured in years from today)	
Plot purchase	0.00
D&A	1.00
Build	2.50
Sell	3.00
Discount factors	
Plot purchase	1.000
D&A	0.926
Build	0.825
Sell	0.794
Debt repayment factor	1.158
Equity cash flows	
Plot purchase (net)	–290,000
D&A	–100,000
Build	–850,000
Sell	1,657,155
Present value cash flows	
Plot puchase	–290,000
D&A	–92,593
Build	–701,228
Sell	1,315,503
NPV of build project	231,682

With no debt the project generated a total amount of cash of $600,000 and after we allow for the time value of money, the NPV was $137,676. So we can see that the NPV appears to have risen by almost $100,000 as a result of including finance.

Is the project a better one? The answer appears to be 'yes' but we cannot answer this question properly without thinking about risk. At present the numbers have been calculated without changing the CoC. The equity cash flows have been discounted at the same 8% rate as was used in the original calculation. Is the situation for the investor equally risky after borrowing is included?

With no debt, the project returns the original cash that was invested as long as the selling price for the house is at least $2,400,000.[38] After debt is included this cash break-even selling price rises to $2,582,845. There must therefore be a greater

[37] Note that I checked the model gave the original answer when I set the assumed percentage of borrowing to zero. A check such as this should always be carried out when models are adjusted.

[38] The original project involved a total cash outlay of $2,400,000 and was expected to return $3,000,000. After we include borrowing and its associated interest cost, the initial cash outlay to purchase the

chance of an investor not even getting his or her money back if the project is partly financed via debt than if there is no debt. By contrast, if the selling price rises above the assumed $3,000,000 the relative returns per dollar invested are much greater after borrowing is included.

Hence we must conclude that the two situations are not equally risky. Perhaps, therefore, the change in NPV is simply down to our having ignored this change in risk when we assess the two ways of looking at the project.[39]

What this example has done is provide a practical illustration of the reason why debt is called gearing or leverage. This is because debt serves to magnify risk exactly as a lever or a set of gears can magnify a force. When things go well, debt magnifies a positive return. When things go badly, debt makes the residual equity return even worse.

The clear conclusion must be that it would be wrong to apply the same cost of equity to the two situations, one with debt and one without. The scenario with debt must justify a higher cost of equity than the one without. The question, though, is how much higher? In order to do this we need to introduce another piece of theory.

The Modigliani Miller proposition

I introduced the idea that values can be added up in the Uncle Norman example in part 3 of the first building block. We can now see a perhaps unanticipated spin-off from this and also meet two more famous names in the history of corporate finance. This time the names are Modigliani and Miller or MM for short. They started with the principle that you can slice up the value of a project however you like but should always come back to the same overall value provided, as one might put it, the process of slicing does not in itself consume value.

I think of this as being like a law of conservation of value. MM realised that this conservation of value should work for liabilities as well as assets. The liabilities of a company concern how it is financed. The so-called MM proposition 1 postulates that the value of a company is independent of how it is financed.[40] It is hugely important for how we carry out economic evaluations.

land falls to just $290,000 but the total outlay after one includes the need to repay the loan and the interest charge rises to $2,582,845.

39 Risk has been ignored because the same discount rate is being used and discount rates should be a function of risk.

40 This is provided there are no tax implications and that the financing choices do not result in changes in the company's other investment decisions.

If value is independent of how an activity is financed then the $100,000 increase in NPV that we described in the Grand Design project above cannot be right. All that we had done to the project was introduce some debt. We know that the debt must have made the residual equity cash flows riskier. So now we have a means of quantifying what the impact on the cost of equity must have been. According to MM's proposition 1, the cost of equity must have changed by exactly the extent necessary to ensure that value is conserved. We can use our spreadsheet model and the goal-seek function to discover that if a discount rate of 13.4% is applied to the equity cash flows with all other assumptions as above then the NPV becomes $137,676 and value is maintained.

So we have an answer to our question. In this particular situation where the appropriate CoC to apply to pre-finance cash flows was 8%, the act of borrowing 80% of the cost of the land means that the appropriate discount rate to apply to equity cash flows is 13.4%. Now since the only way of calculating the figure of 13.4% was first to do the analysis pre finance, surely there is an obvious lesson here? Surely we should simply evaluate all investments in a way that ignores how they are financed.

The consequence of MM's proposition 1 is a huge simplification in how we carry out our financial analysis. We do not need to bother with identifying the cost of equity and the cost of debt separately. These change every time the level of borrowing changes. We can use the CoC which should remain unchanged. What is it that sets the CoC? It is the riskiness of the underlying cash flows before any financing effects.

The indivisible finance pool

There is another way of thinking about how financing decisions impact on the CoC that I find quite intuitive. This way is to consider the concept of an indivisible finance pool. Company finance can be thought of as coming from a single source, the indivisible finance pool. This is topped up from time to time with debt and equity but once the money is in this pool, it is not possible to distinguish between a dollar that originated as debt and a dollar that originated as equity.

If a company were to allow one project to benefit because it happened to need money at exactly the same time as it borrowed money it would be unfair to other projects if it was allowed to claim that its cost of finance was low. This is because the other projects would then have to suffer the much higher cost of equity when, in reality, they were all part of the same company. The security for all of the company's debt is provided by all of its assets. So surely the benefit of debt's apparent cheapness should be shared by all of the assets.

This indivisible finance pool approach leads one to the same answer. Analysis should be carried out such that decisions on asset investments are taken independently from the way that they are financed.

There are, however, one or two conditions to all of this and these will be considered next. These relate to what happens if money is limited or if risks are too big. After that we will be ready to finish the section with a look at an estimate of what the CoC for a typical company might actually be.

Precondition 1: What if money is limited?

Most individuals who read this question would probably wonder why the words 'what if' and the question mark are included. Individuals are used to living with only a finite amount of money. We learn how to run our lives with only a limited amount of cash. We make choices. Even governments, with all the money they have available, are forced to make choices.

Should companies do the same thing? Should a company make a decision about one investment opportunity by considering the alternatives? In particular, how would a company take decisions if it only had enough money to invest in one more project but it had available two good positive NPV alternatives? If this were the situation then surely the value of one project should only be considered relative to the value of the next best alternative that would have to be foregone?

MM had foreseen this problem. This is why they added the caveat which I included as a footnote 40 to the MM proposition 1 section. I pointed out that the proposition only held if the investment did not result in changes in the company's other investment decisions. If a company were to be short of money then investing in one project would stop it investing in another and so this condition would be breached. So do real world factors such as shortages of money invalidate the basic approach?

Corporate finance theory gets round this particular problem by invoking a useful and, I believe, quite reasonable principle that the financial markets will always fund a good project.[41] Suppose a company genuinely had two good positive NPV projects that it could invest in but only had enough cash

[41] I wrote this sentence before the onset of the so-called liquidity crisis which has followed on from the subprime mortgage crisis. The potential seriousness of this is that if companies cannot raise finance even when they have good investment opportunities, the implications are very severe in that companies will be unable to invest and economic growth will stall.

to invest in one. Well, in that situation the company could go to the financial markets and raise new equity to finance the second project. The picture that we should have is that the markets have a huge pool of money invested in anticipation of earning just the CoC. This is what investors expect to get whenever they invest in a company share. So if there is a better opportunity available it is only logical to believe that the markets will fund it.

So the investment appraisal approach is built on the presumption that there is never a shortage of funds to finance what the market considers to be good projects. We should note both the reference to this being merely a presumption and not a statement of absolute fact, and also the words 'what the market considers' to be good projects.

Companies in general and the sponsors of projects in particular can often adopt a rather optimistic view of the prospects for their project. Markets tend to be more dispassionate. They also can be more aware of risk than people close to a project. These differences may well explain why some companies are capital constrained even though they think they have positive NPV opportunities open to them. So just because a company thinks it has a good project does not mean that we assume it will always be financed. What we assume is that if the market believes a project has a positive NPV, it will fund it. As I have already noted, I consider this to be reasonable. It also greatly simplifies investment appraisal since otherwise we would have to allow for the opportunity cost of funds in our analysis and not just the CoC.

Precondition 2: What if risks are too great?

We have, in effect, through precondition 1 discounted the possibility of a company running out of money. It is harder to deal with the situation where a project is too risky for a company to undertake it. We have already described equity as a cushion to protect against risk. If a project encounters a severe downside risk then two things might happen. First, the project itself might suffer and second, the problems with the project may cost so much to put right that this interferes with the good operations of the remaining assets of the company. Now if, for any reason, a company becomes short of money it has to start operating in a different way. It has to operate in a way that will destroy value relative to the situation before it became short of money. It may, for example, be forced to sell an asset simply to generate the cash to repay a bank loan. It may choose to cancel good projects for fear of having to go to the markets to raise further cash. Suppliers may demand immediate payment for goods which could exacerbate the financial problems. Investors will start to lose faith that the NPVs they anticipated from other projects will actually materialise. The bottom line of this situation is that the company finds it hard to raise cash exactly when it needs it and a vicious circle is started.

Insurance is a simple way around this problem. However, many large projects are simply too large to insure. This means that a small company may simply be unable to finance a very large project. This situation can go a long way to explain why size is so important in some industries. The oil industry is a good example. Companies have to be big in order to be able to spread their risks.

So the limit to the application of the theories that we have been developing concerns the capacity of a company to take on risk. The way to think about equity is that it acts as a cushion against risk. A project needs two things. First, the physical cash to pay for its development. This cash comes from both debt and equity. Second, a project needs enough equity to protect it should events turn against it. Sometimes the original equity that was provided to fund the development is sufficient but in some very risky investments companies need additional equity if they are to proceed with a project. We will not be considering this point any further at this stage but we will return to it later in the book because it is very important. All that we need for the present is the awareness that in some instances companies need large amounts of equity simply to protect against possible future downsides.

Estimating the cost of capital

We are now ready to take a first look at how to estimate the cost of capital (CoC) for a typical company. We will carry out a very rough exercise simply to get an order of magnitude feel for things.[42]

The CoC comes from the cost of equity and the cost of debt. We know from CAPM that the cost of equity for a typical share is equal to the risk-free rate plus the equity risk premium. We have been told that for the USA, the risk-free rate at the time this chapter was first being written was 5¼%.

What should the equity risk premium be? This is a more difficult number to estimate. We know that over the period 1925–2000 the additional return earned through investing in shares in large US companies compared with the risk-free rate was 7.2% (see footnote 23). Some approaches would use this

[42] In most companies the task of estimating the CoC will fall to the finance department. The aim of this section is simply to give a rough indication of how the numbers might look. In principle, each company will have its own views on the CoC and these should be followed rather than the rough estimate which we will now calculate.

number as an estimate of the required return. For reasons that will be outlined in the more detailed study of the CoC which will follow in the final part of this book, I believe that a figure of 5% for the equity risk premium is more appropriate. If we use this figure then the cost of equity must be 10.2%.[43]

The cost of debt is what companies pay on their borrowings less the associated tax relief. Companies will be paying the risk-free rate plus a premium to allow for the fact that they are not risk free and that they will probably be borrowing long term. Let us assume this premium is 2% and that tax rates are about one third. The after-tax cost of debt will therefore be 4.8%.

A recent article in the *Journal of Applied Corporate Finance* suggested that the average level of debt held by US companies was just below 30% of the total value of debt and equity.[44]

In this case the WACC for an average large US company to the nearest percentage point would be 9%. Furthermore, thanks to MM proposition 1, it should not matter what level of gearing a particular company adopts, the CoC should remain at about 9%. This will hold as long as the company does not take on too much risk which typically means as long as it limits its debts to what are considered to be affordable levels.

I should stress that this is only a very rough number to get us started, so to speak. I will be looking in much more detail at how the CoC should be set later in this book in the first of the three views of deeper and broader skills. Readers will need to wait until then to find what is my best estimate of the CoC.

Conclusions

Although the CoC is an average of the cost of debt and the cost of equity, thanks to the Modigliani Miller proposition 1 we can assume that, within a reasonable range of borrowing levels, the exact mix of debt and equity does not matter. Provided a company does not over-reach itself, its CoC is set by the risks inherent in its assets. This allows us to separate our decisions on which assets to invest in from the subsidiary decision of how to finance them.

We can carry out our investment analysis on the assumption that funds will always be available for good projects. This means that we do not need

[43] Note that at this stage I am showing numbers to a spurious level of accuracy of the nearest 0.1%. I will round the numbers only at the end of the calculation because, in my opinion, any numbers are accurate at best to the nearest one percentage point.

[44] The article was 'What is the Market Value of a dollar of Corporate Cash' by Pinkowitz and Williamson, published in the Summer 2007 edition of the *Journal of Applied Corporate Finance*. The authors have confirmed that this ratio is based on the market value of shares and the market value of debt.

to allow for the opportunity cost of a project which might be turned down because another was approved.

Finally, we need to be aware that risk may complicate things not only because of the need to have a cushion against the downside but also because we have not yet considered exactly how risk is defined in the CAPM.

Part 4: Individual work assignments

1. What is the best way to invest if your primary concern is to minimise risk?
2. Which source of finance should a new company use if it is intending to go into the oil exploration business?
3. If a 90 day US T bill was sold for $982 what (to the nearest 0.1%) would the US risk-free rate be?
4. If the dividend yield on a share is currently 2% and the market consensus is that this dividend will grow at 5½%, what cost of equity does the market appear to be using for this company?
5. A company currently pays a dividend of $3.75 per share. It appears to be subject to the same degree of risk as a typical large US company and so we decide to apply the time value of money that was calculated in the 'Estimating the cost of capital' section above. What would the share price be in the following situations?
   a. If the dividend was expected to grow at a steady rate of 4% into the future;
   b. If the dividend was expected to decline by 10% pa into the future;
   c. If the dividend was expected to grow by 5% a year for the next ten years but then growth would decline to 2.5% pa;
   d. If the dividend was expected to grow by 20% for each of the next five years and then growth was expected to fall to 5% pa.
6. A company takes out a loan of $100m at a fixed interest rate of 6%. It will repay the loan in four equal annual instalments starting at the end of the second year and interest is paid at the end of each year. (a) What will the pre-tax cash flows associated with the loan be? (b) If the corporate tax rate is 33.3%, how will this affect the after-tax cash flows?
7. Now consider the loan described in question 6 from the perspective of the lender.

a. If interest rates remain unchanged what would the loan be worth to the lender just before the end of the first year (i.e. just before the first interest payment has been made)?
b. What would the loan be worth immediately after the first interest payment has been made?
c. If interest rates fell by 1% what impact would this have on the answers to questions (a) and (b)?

8. The central bank of the hypothetical country called Lightvia aims to maintain real interest rates of 2.5%.
   a. If inflation is averaging 26% what will the nominal interest rate be?
   b. The Lightvian currency is the dia and the current exchange rate is 235 dia/$. If the interest rate on US dollars is 5.6% what would the future exchange rate be for dia/$ in one year's time?
9. A company is planning to raise further equity through a rights issue. It has 575m shares in issue and the current share price is $10.87 per share. The company wishes to raise $750m of new equity and the decision is taken to launch a 1 for 5 rights issue.
   a. What price would the new shares have to be offered at?
   b. What would be the anticipated share price after the rights issue if the market thought that the cash raised would be invested in zero NPV projects?
   c. How much cash would an investor who owned 1,000 shares expect to receive if he decided to sell his rights in this situation?
   d. What would this investor need to do if he wished to maintain the same amount of money invested in the company?
   e. What would be the answers to questions (a)–(d) if the market anticipated that each dollar invested by the company would generate an NPV of $0.40?
10. A company is planning to buy a high-temperature moulding machine that will manufacture kitchen utensils. The machine will cost $2.5m and the company is seeking a bank loan of $2.0m to help fund this purchase. The remaining $0.5m will come from a cash injection from the company's owner. How would a bank view the security on this loan and how might it respond to the loan request in the following situations?
    a. The company was a new start-up and had no other assets at the present time.
    b. The company already had two similar machines and a four year track record of profitable growth. These machines had been purchased thanks to loans which were guaranteed by the founder's rich uncle.

Loan repayments were being made on schedule but $1m was still outstanding.

c. The company was as outlined in (b) above but following the recent sudden death of the rich uncle, the owner had inherited $4m.
d. The company owns several similar machines and also a factory building worth $3m and currently has no debt.
e. The company is as outlined in (d) but the lender has just learned that although the facts presented are true, the company only recently repaid a $3m overdraft from another bank.

11. The chief financial officer of a company is contemplating whether to recommend that it should declare its first cash dividend. The company was floated on the stock exchange four years ago and since then has retained all of its profits in order to fund its growth. The company has been very successful and has just paid off the initial overdraft that it had. It has no other debts. The plan for next year, however, shows that the business operations will not generate any cash owing to the capital investment budget using all of the anticipated cash flow from operations. Summarise the main pros and cons for declaring a first cash dividend.

CHAPTER

3

Building block 3: Understanding accounts

Summary

Accounting and economic value are often considered as separate subjects. They will typically be taught in different classes on an MBA course. This foundation section, however, covers both topics. The book will not teach you to become an accountant. The aim is to build just a minimum understanding of accounts such that individuals will be able to do three key things:

1. Join in with conversations on accounting topics such as those which surround publication of accounting results.
2. Understand the link between accounting results and the economic value model.
3. Use a simplified set of financial statements that I call the abbreviated financial summary to produce accounting based cash flow models.

The building block is in four parts. In the first part we introduce some basic ideas concerning accounts and in particular introduce the three main accounting statements. These are the:

- income statement;
- balance sheet; and
- cash flow statement.

The main focus will be on the accounts for wholly owned operations although the complexities that tend to follow when activities are not all wholly owned will also be explained. In part 2 we will learn how to restructure the basic accounting data into a more useful format which is better aligned with the concept of economic value. I call this format the abbreviated financial summary (AFS) and we will use this to work with the numbers and learn how the various accounting statements are 'wired' together. Part 3 will concentrate on two main case studies in order to demonstrate how the technique can be applied in practice. Finally, part 4 will set several work assignments in order to reinforce learning.

Part 1: The purpose of accounting

Accounting can be defined as the process by which financial information about a business is recorded, classified, summarised, interpreted and communicated.[1] What financial information would you want if you were the owner of a company? At an absolute minimum you might want to know how much cash you had. Would this tell you enough, do you think?

I suggest the answer should be 'no'. If all you knew was how much cash was held you could make things look better simply by delaying paying the bills. This does not mean that you would not want to know how much cash you had since you need cash to pay the bills. It means you need to know more than one thing. At the least I suggest you need to know the following:

- how 'well' you are doing;
- what assets you own and what you owe to others; and
- how much cash you are generating.

So we can anticipate that, as a minimum, accounting statements would provide this information. This first part of the Understanding Accounts building block will explain briefly how this is done and while so doing, will introduce some key accounting concepts.

Before we start our investigation of accounting we need to understand an important point. The accounting approach was not primarily designed in order to support calculations of economic value. Accounting predates the economic value model. The aim of this building block is to learn how to use accounting data in order to calculate value. I think this is the right thing to do. An alternative would be to design a new data system that directly supported value calculations.[2] As I will show in part 2, this is not necessary since accounting-based data can be quite simply re-structured in order to provide the basic input for value calculations.

[1] I am grateful to Wikipedia for these words.

[2] This data system would probably have to be run in parallel with the traditional accounting system since not everybody wants to use the numbers in order to calculate value. The way I see it, there is no escape from accounting-based numbers. The tax authorities, for example, are concerned with collecting tax and they have set their rules to apply to accounting-based results.

How 'well' is a business doing?

This question almost seems too simple to bother asking. Surely, one might think, it is just a question of seeing how much revenue is coming in from sales and knowing how this figure compares with the costs incurred in generating the sales. But exactly when does a sale count as a sale or a cost count as a cost?

Think first about a business selling something. In some instances the point of sale is pretty obvious. In a shop the purchaser offers his or her money and the shopkeeper accepts it. A sale is made. But what if the sale is made on account? Is the sale made when the goods are taken or when the account is paid? What about an agreement to purchase a cargo of crude oil to be loaded in, say, two months' time with payment due 30 days after loading? In this situation there are three possible points at which the sale could be deemed to have been made.[3] What about the sale of a service that is delivered over a period of time with payment via, say, two lump sums, one before the first service is given and the other after the service has been fully delivered?

Clearly we need some conventions regarding when sales revenue is recognised as such. This concept of revenue recognition is the first accounting convention that I want to introduce. To me it is one of the most important principles that underpin the accounting process.[4]

For the sale of physical items the usual approach is to deem a sale to have been made at the point when ownership changes. So, for example, if I look at the sales contract for my Dell computer, this states that ownership passes from Dell to the consumer at the later of the time of delivery or the time of full payment. Since Dell usually requires payment at the time of order this means that the usual situation is that a sale 'counts' as a sale not when the money changes hands or when the order is placed but when the product is delivered. This is the normal approach and not something special associated with Dell. It is what would be done in the case of the crude oil sale that I referred to in the paragraph above. So, as far as I am concerned,[5] the first thing to know about a set of accounts is that the line called 'sales revenue' for a period is not the cash received in that period, it is the sales value of products delivered in that period.[6]

[3] These three points are when the sale is agreed, when the cargo is loaded and when the oil is paid for.

[4] In this chapter I will concentrate on four main accounting principles. In addition to revenue recognition I will cover the matching convention, valuing assets at cost and the principles of consolidation.

[5] I must stress that I am not a qualified accountant and this book does not attempt to teach accountancy. The aim is to provide a minimum level of understanding of accounts suitable for general use in a business career.

[6] More complicated conventions are required in situations where the sale is of a service rather than a physical item. This book will not go into any detail on this topic other than to say that the approach

Now the other half of knowing how well a business is doing concerns knowing what costs it has incurred. The difference between sales revenue and costs will be the result. Once again, one is faced with a question of when to count a cost as a cost. Take the case of Dell supplying a computer to a customer. Recall that Dell's sales revenue in any particular period comes from computers delivered. However, Dell will have to take delivery of component parts in order to assemble its computers. By definition, this is in advance of the sale being made. Should Dell deduct from sales revenue the costs actually incurred during a year or does it show the costs associated with the sales that it makes? This is where a second accounting principle comes in. This is the principle of matching. Where possible, costs are matched with sales.

This means that the costs for a year are not simply the costs incurred during a year, they are the costs associated with the sales made during a year. Now not all costs can be directly associated with particular sales. An example would be what are called overheads, such as the cost of a head office. Costs such as this are apportioned on a time basis to the relevant accounting period. So, for example, consider the payment of the rental on an office block. Suppose this was paid via a lump sum once a year and this was paid each November. In the quarterly accounts for the final quarter of the year would all of this charge be shown as a cost because it was paid in that quarter? No, the charge shown would be just a quarter of the annual payment representing the appropriate proportion for that period.

Now an accountant uses the term profit to describe how well a business is doing. The accounting statement that shows how profit is derived is called the income statement or the profit and loss account (often shortened to P&L). So now we understand that profit is not a measure of how much cash a business has generated. Profit is the difference between sales made in a period and the associated costs. So what happens to the bills that are paid during a year but, because of the matching principle, do not get charged as costs? To answer this question we need to consider the second key accounting statement.

What does a business own and what does it owe?

This question is answered in what is generally called the balance sheet.[7] I need first to get the question of why it is called a balance sheet out of the way.

is generally conservative and designed to recognise sales revenue over the period of delivery of the service.

[7] I use the expression 'generally called the balance sheet' because it can be given other names such as 'the statement of financial position'. In all cases, however, there will be two sets of numbers that balance each other. These tend to be called the two sides of the balance sheet or the assets and the

A balance sheet not only shows what a business has invested in, it also shows where the money invested in the business came from. We know from the previous chapter that the normal way a company is financed is such that the money will have come from issue of new shares, from retained earnings or from bank borrowing. The balance sheet is given this name because, by definition, money must have come from somewhere. So if you detail where it comes from and where it goes to, there must be a balance.

We are now ready to go through the main components of a balance sheet. I will try to describe these in general terms but I do have to warn that at present different countries apply subtly different accounting conventions and terminologies. There is a drive to produce a single internationally accepted way of producing accounts but this has yet to deliver an agreed result. Good progress has been made and there is a set of International Financial Reporting Standards that applies across the EU. This is called the IFRS approach. In the USA, however, what are called 'US generally accepted accounting principles (US GAAP)' apply. Unless and until a worldwide standard is adopted we simply have to learn to live with the ambiguities of multiple names and multiple conventions.

Summary of the main components of a balance sheet

Component	Brief description
Fixed assets	These are investments intended to benefit the company over many years. In accordance with the matching principle the cost is not all charged against profit as soon as it is incurred. The general principle is that the number shown in the accounts will be what is termed the net book value. Do not confuse this number with economic value! An asset is initially put on the balance sheet 'at cost'. The cost is then gradually charged against the profit over the estimated asset life. This charge is termed amortisation or depreciation. A typical way of assessing the charge is called the straight line method. This simply divides the total cost by the estimated asset life in years and charges this amount each year.[8] Another common method is to spread the cost out on a per unit of anticipated production basis. This would be a good approach in, say, a mining business where there is a set amount of mineral to produce. Net book value will be the original cost less accumulated amortisation/ depreciation.

liabilities. The number that balances will be either the total assets of the company which will equal the total liabilities or the net assets of the company which will equal the shareholders' equity. At this introductory stage I suggest you don't bother too much about these differences. Just be aware that different conventions do exist and that you always need to check the detail and make sure when comparing two different businesses that the accounts are shown in the same way.

[8] This is referred to as the straight line method because a plot of the net book value of the asset over time will form a straight line starting at its original cost and finishing at zero.

Table (*cont.*)

Component	Brief description
	The main categories that you will come across are: • *Property, plant and equipment.* The term is, hopefully, self explanatory and refers to the physical assets of a company such as buildings, manufacturing facilities and equipment. These assets can also be called tangible assets. • *Intangible assets.* Long-term assets where there is not an obvious physical item to see. For example, the right to explore for oil. • *Goodwill.* This is where an asset has been purchased for a price above what can be termed its fair market value. Any excess is termed goodwill. 'Why might you pay above fair market value?' you might ask. Well, perhaps in anticipation of earning greater profits in later years – this situation often arises when one company is purchased by another. • *Investments.* This can cover several different things; for example, where a company owns a share of another or where a company makes a long-term loan to another. • *Other.* There can be other assets which are long-term in nature such as advance payments, or pension fund surpluses.
Current assets	The term current means items that are expected to be dealt with within one year. The main categories that you will come across are: • *Trade receivables.* This refers to money owed to the business by its customers. We have already learned that a sale counts as a sale when delivery is made even though the customer might not yet have paid. This is where the money owing is shown until it is actually received. Note that the UK term for receivables is debtors. • *Prepayments.* Money paid out by the company in advance of the cost being charged. An example would be the office rental referred to above. • *Inventories.* This refers to stocks of, for example, raw material, partly made product and unsold final product. All of these are shown at cost. So in the Dell computer example above, the costs of parts purchased by Dell to make a computer that has not yet been delivered would be shown as a part of the company's inventory. • *Cash and other securities.* Money held in the bank or in short-term financial instruments is shown in this category. • *Other.* Once again it is often necessary to utilise the catch-all category of 'other'. This could, for example, refer to the portion of a long-term loan by the company to a third party that is repayable within one year of the balance sheet date.
Total assets	This is the sum of fixed assets, and current assets.
Current liabilities	The equivalent to current assets, only this time for money owed by the company that must be repaid within one year. The main categories will be: • *Trade and other payables.* Money owed to suppliers. In the UK the term creditors is used. • *Accruals.* This refers to bills which the company expects to receive but which have not yet arrived. It is an important part of the matching convention that companies allow for such charges even though they do not need to make actual payment until an invoice is received.

Table (*cont.*)

Component	Brief description
	• *Short-term finance debt.* Any loans that are repayable within one year are shown here. • *Other.* The seemingly unavoidable catch-all for any other sums charged but not yet paid for but expected to become payable within a year.
Non-current liabilities	This refers to amounts of money owing over the long term and not repayable within the next year. Main categories are: • *Finance debts.* Long-term borrowing. • *Provisions.* Allowance for future liabilities that are charged against profit now but where the actual bill will be received some long time in the future. A typical example would be an allowance for cleanup/closure costs. If an asset is expected to incur costs when it is finally closed then the matching principle requires these costs to be spread over the asset's life rather than be left until the actual closure. The charges made in each year are built up as a provision on the balance sheet. When the actual costs are incurred the provision is reduced accordingly. • *Minority interests.* This occurs in situations where assets are not all wholly owned. The term minority interest refers to the net book value of assets that are owned by others. This is explained later in this part.
Net assets or total equity	Total assets less current and non-current liabilities will equal the net assets of the company. This is also referred to as equity or shareholders' equity.

So now we have a description of what the various items in a balance sheet will be.[9] Readers should have noticed several references to the idea of items being shown in the balance sheet 'at cost'. This, to me, is the next important accounting principle that all users of accounts must understand. The 'at cost' principle means that a balance sheet will only show what a company has spent in order to produce assets. It will not show what they may be worth when sold. In effect, profit can only be earned when a sale is made.

Showing assets and liabilities 'at cost' on the balance sheet is also the way that accountants can make their matching convention work more simply. We have seen that items purchased in order to make a product are not charged against profit until the product is sold. The way that this is achieved is through showing the so-called work in progress as an asset on the balance sheet that is valued at cost. The accountants can then include all costs incurred in purchasing raw material during the period as costs and adjust for the fraction that is unsold by adding back the work in progress at the end of the year. A similar adjustment is made at the start of the year with the closing work in progress in effect being added to the cost of raw material purchases.

[9] We will consider a real balance sheet in part 3 below.

At this stage I would not be surprised if some readers who are unfamiliar with accounting concepts would be thinking that there is a lot to learn and that they might well wonder why things are done this way. There will be plenty of opportunities to play with the numbers later in this part and the answer to the question 'why?' may become more apparent when the third accounting statement is introduced.

How much cash is being generated?

The third accounting statement should be the easiest to understand. It explains the movement in cash during the period. The starting point is the calculated profit. We know that profit is not equal to cash so what is necessary is to make a series of adjustments that will convert it into cash. These adjustments are linked to the balance sheet and they will be explained in this section.

Now I remember many years ago sitting through a rather long and somewhat boring lecture that taught me why accounts work the way that they do. I will not attempt to repeat this explanation in this book. My view is that to speak the language of business one does not need to know why everything in a set of accounts works the way that it does, one just needs to know that they do work and what the various calculations are that have to be done.[10] It turns out that there is a lot that you can do with a set of accounts even if you don't fully understand why a balance sheet will balance or why the relationship between profit and cash is what it is.

We already know that a company's economic value is set by its anticipated future cash flow and not simply by its future profit. So understanding the bridge between profit and cash flow is clearly vital. Well, the bridge works like this. Anything that serves to increase the total assets of a company must be deducted from profit while anything that increases current and non-current liabilities acts as an addition. Finally, any dividends that are paid will clearly reduce cash. The profit, plus additions to total assets less deductions and dividends paid will equal the change in cash.

There are some useful ways that the various changes in assets and liabilities can be grouped together in order to describe the relationship between profit and cash. These are explained in the table below which suggests three steps which, between them, create a bridge between profit and the net change in cash during a period.

[10] There are many things in life like that, my computer being a prime example. I can become quite skilful at using it even though I don't really know how a silicon chip works.

The steps from profit to cash flow

Step	Brief description
Operating activities	This first step concerns the day-to-day business activity of the company and how much cash this generates or requires. The first adjustment to profit concerns the amortisation charge. This charge is a way of spreading the cost of an asset over its useful life and does not impact on cash. So amortisation is always added back to profit as one attempts to move from profit to cash flow. There may well also be other non-cash charges that are included in the profit and loss account such as any provisions for asset abandonment. The net change in these provisions needs to be added back to profit.[11] Next we have to deal with what is called working capital. Working capital is the net balance of current assets and current liabilities. I suggest that it is best to think of working capital as being the money that is tied up in the day-to-day running of any business. The key elements have been explained above. The one change that is necessary is to exclude cash from current assets. We do this because our aim is to calculate what the change in cash must have been in the light of all the other accounting data. If working capital increases during a period then this requires funding and so any increase is deducted from the profit in order to calculate net cash flow. If working capital decreases during a period then the reduction is added to profit in order to calculate cash flow. An alternative way of thinking about working capital is to treat the profit for the period and all of the working capital at the start of a period as sources of cash. The working capital at the end of the period is a requirement for cash.
Investing activities	This step concerns adjusting for the impact of long-term investments made by the company. We can recall that long-term investments are not charged against profit in the year in which they are made; instead, their cost is spread out over the estimated life of the asset through a charge that is called amortisation or depreciation. We have already seen how to adjust for this amortisation effect in the operating activities adjustment outlined above. This investing activities adjustment stage is where the cash cost of the investments is incorporated in our calculation of cash flow. In most simple situations all that is necessary is to deduct the cash that is invested in fixed assets during the period. This spending is usually referred to as capital expenditure or capex for short. In more complex situations one can also have to deal with asset sales. Should any assets be sold this will also impact on cash flow. If an asset is sold for more than its book value then the surplus will be treated as a profit.[12] So if all that one wants to do is calculate the correct net cash flow one has to add back to profit just the book value of any assets sold. In order to get a fuller and more accurate picture of the distinction between cash flow from operating activities and cash flow from investing activities it is necessary to strip any profit on asset sales out of operating activities and include it all as part of the investing activities category.

[11] The net change is calculated as the sum of any new provisions made during the period less any actual cash expended on items that have previously been provided for. This will equal the change in the provision which is shown on the balance sheet.

[12] If an asset is sold for less than book value then a loss will be incurred and this loss will reduce profit.

Table (*cont.*)

Financing activities	This category covers the net effect of any changes in long-term borrowings and any cash raised through the issue of new shares or any spend on repurchasing existing shares. Dividends paid are also included here because, unlike interest on debt, dividends do not reduce profit.

These three steps allow one to build the bridge between profit and cash and so complete the third main accounting statement. By convention all cash inflows are shown with a positive sign while cash outflows are negative. The bridge between profit and cash is then:

Cash flow[13] = profit + operating activities + investing activities + financing activities

Dealing with assets that are not wholly owned

So far this section has implicitly assumed that all assets are 100% owned. This provides a good starting point for understanding accounts but life is not that simple! The various conventions that are applied in order to produce accounts for companies that own shares in other companies are referred to as the principles of consolidation. A set of accounts that looks beyond the so-called parent company's holdings of shares in other companies through to the underlying assets and activities would be called a set of consolidated accounts. These principles of consolidation represent the final element of accounting mystery that the uninitiated need to grasp in order to gain a basic understanding of accounts.

One might imagine that if a company owned just a given percentage of another company then that percentage of all of the financial numbers would be shown in the consolidated accounts.[14] I am afraid, however, that this is not what is usually done. Accountants make a big distinction between activities that are controlled and activities that are not. Control typically comes with ownership. In many companies if you own just one share more than half of the issued shares then you can force through a vote and so legally have control. In some companies, however, the articles of association set different rules concerning control such as requiring, say, a two thirds majority to change strategy. In such a situation, 60% ownership would not bring control.

[13] Cash flow is the change in cash during the period.

[14] For example, if you own 20% of a company, why not show in your accounts 20% of the company's sales, costs, assets, liabilities, etc.? If this approach is adopted it is referred to as proportional consolidation.

The table below gives a brief summary of the main principles of consolidation. It describes how a holding company will show in its consolidated accounts the results of a company in which it holds any given degree of ownership.

Basic principles of consolidation

Extent of ownership	Accounting treatment
100%	This is the simplest situation. All items are shown as they are.
Control but not full ownership	In the income statement, 100% of sales and costs are shown. One deduction is made for the so-called minority shareholders' share of net profit. Likewise 100% of the various balance sheet items are shown with one deduction representing the minority shareholders' share of equity.[15]
Substantial ownership but not control	The holding company's share of net income will be shown as a single line item called, typically, earnings from associates. The balance sheet will show just the net investment again as a single line. This will equal the original investment in the company plus the share of any retained earnings since the share was purchased.[16]
Low ownership[17]	All that will be shown is dividends received (contributing to the income statement) and the original investment at cost as part of the balance sheet's fixed assets section.

There is a lot of logic behind these various principles of consolidation but they do mean that full and accurate interpretation of accounts requires some skill. In particular it is necessary to know what principles of consolidation have been applied and what ownership category each investment fits into.

The principles of consolidation can lead to situations where accounts can be open to some degree of manipulation as some items can become what is called 'off balance sheet' or a small change in ownership can result in a large change in reported sales revenue. So for example, debt in a company of which a holding company holds a one third share will not appear on the holding company's balance sheet. If two other companies also own one third of this company then none of its debt will be reported.

[15] This does mean, for example, that a company may own just three quarters of a company but will have to show all of its debt on its balance sheet and all of its sales revenue as sales.

[16] So the sales revenue of a company that is, say, 40% owned will not be shown in the consolidated accounts of the holding company. All that will be shown is the 40% share in net income. The retained earnings will be equal to the holding company's share of net profit less any dividends received.

[17] This refers to situations where the shareholding is less than 20%.

Dealing with forex effects

A final complication to mention at this stage concerns the effect of foreign exchange rate changes. These effects can be categorised into two types – realised and unrealised. A realised gain (or loss) is something that has an actual impact on cash flow while an unrealised effect does not impact on cash flow.

To illustrate the two types of effect, consider the personal decisions surrounding purchase of foreign cash to take on holiday. Suppose you were an American planning a visit to London to compete in the London Marathon in April 2007. You decide that you must travel with, say, £1,000 to cover hotel and other living expenses. Suppose that you initially decided to visit London in July 2006 when the exchange rate was about $1.85/£. You could have decided to purchase the currency then or you could have waited until the date of departure. Had you waited, we now know that the dollar fell over this period to about $2.00/£. So from a US$ perspective, waiting would have resulted in a realised loss of $150.

Now suppose that our American did in fact buy the currency in July 2006 at the same time that he entered the race. How would this American view the currency that sat in his safe in August when the rate had weakened to $1.90 or in October when it had strengthened back to $1.85 again? I suggest the American would have considered any notional gains or losses as unrealised because they have no impact on cash flow.

A similar situation surrounds the impact of exchange rate changes on accounts. Some changes do have a real impact on cash flow and these effects are incorporated into the reported profit for the period. By contrast, effects that simply impact on the rate at which balance sheet items are translated into the holding company's currency of accounting are deemed to be unrealised. They do affect the reported balance sheet but not the reported operating profit.

These consolidation and foreign exchange effects represent an unavoidable complication. We cannot ask that the world only allows full ownership of companies or that no changes in exchange rates be permitted. So we just have to live with the complications that follow. My view is that they are an unavoidable complication rather than a fatal flaw in accounts. They go a long way towards explaining why it takes so long to become a qualified accountant but should not represent an impossible barrier to an unqualified person's reaching a sufficient understanding of accounts to play a substantial part in the financial decision making in a company.

Part 2: The abbreviated financial summary

Distinguish between investing and financing

So far in this building block we have looked at accounts the way that accountants prepare them. We now need to introduce a different way of presenting the numbers in order to align them more closely with the steps in a value calculation. The key change concerns the principle of separating investment decisions from financing decisions which was introduced in Building Block 2.

Consider first the accounting concept of profit. Accountants will subtract any interest charges in order to arrive at a net income figure but they do not deduct any dividends paid. This means that the reported net profit is heavily influenced by decisions about whether to finance with debt or equity. If we turn to the balance sheet, the accounting definitions of current liabilities will include any finance debts that are repayable within one year. So once again, a financing decision will be having an important impact on a set of accounts. Finally, think about the cash flow statement. By definition this sets out to explain the movement in cash during a period. As has already been explained, a well funded company can always borrow more money and so can always increase its cash holding through a purely financing decision. Hence the movement in cash is in principle a combination of financing effects and the cash flow effects which we need to identify in order to calculate value.

The necessary restructuring steps are explained below:

Adjusting accounts to exclude financing effects

Accounting statement	Changes required
Income statement	Any interest charges must be excluded. So net profit will be after tax but before any interest charges. Since interest charges can usually be offset against tax it is necessary also to adjust for this effect. This is done by adding back not only the gross interest charge which is shown in the accounts but also any associated tax relief.[18]

[18] So if, for example, the interest charge was $100 and the tax rate was 35% both the interest charge of $100 and the associated tax relief of $35 would be excluded. So the tax charge shown in the adjusted accounts would be $35 higher than reported in the actual accounts. Another way of thinking about this would be to think of interest being paid net of tax relief.

Table (*cont.*)

Balance sheet	Significant changes are required. The aim is to structure the balance sheet such that all assets and liabilities related to the underlying business activity are on one side of the balance sheet while the other side depicts the various sources of finance. The balance sheet will balance, but on a different number which is called capital employed. I suggest that readers should refer back to the first table in this part and decide for themselves which items would be considered to be business related and which are finance related. My answer is that the fixed assets and current assets are business related with the exception of any cash that is held.[19] So too are most of the current liabilities such as accounts payable and accruals; however, short-term finance debt is clearly a financing item. So capital employed is fixed assets plus a series of items which together are referred to as working capital. These are current assets less cash and less the non-finance related current liabilities. This capital employed will then balance with the total finance that is provided.[20] Note, however, that since we are considering business decisions and not how the necessary financing is arranged, we generally only need to look at what I term the business side of the balance sheet.[21] The term the asset side of the balance sheet can also be used.
Cash flow statement	The first thing to do is to recognise that the term cash flow needs to be changed because, understandably, cash flow refers to changes in cash and we want to calculate something different. What we want is the cash change that we would use in order to carry out a value calculation, that is to say the change in cash before any financing effects. I use the term funds flow for this in order to distinguish it from cash flow. Funds flow is equal to: • net profit before finance charges calculated as above; • plus amortisation charged in the period plus the net change in any other balance sheet provisions less any increase in business related working capital;[22] • less capital expenditure.[23]

[19] Complications can be caused by cash holdings because in reality cash is generally part financing and part business related. I usually treat cash as part of the financing activity of a company. As such, cash does not count towards my definition of capital employed, rather it serves to reduce the debt (which strictly speaking should therefore be called net debt). There are, however, some situations where it is more appropriate to treat cash as a business asset. If this is considered to be the case then cash does form a part of capital employed and debt is not shown as a net number.

[20] The total finance provided is net debt plus provisions, minorities' interests and shareholders' equity.

[21] One occasion when we would need to consider the financing side of the balance sheet would be when we want to look at the value of just the shares in a company, for example as part of an acquisition.

[22] i.e. the current assets and current liabilities that are shown on the business side of the balance sheet.

[23] Capital expenditure should be net of the impact of any divestments.

Introducing the abbreviated financial summary

Now that we have restructured the numbers to strip out financing effects we are ready to move to what I consider to be the key workhorse of financial analysis. I call it the abbreviated financial summary (AFS). It comprises four stages that between them will calculate the economic value of any activity using accounting data. These four stages are:

1. The income statement adjusted to exclude the effect of interest charges.
2. The asset side of a balance sheet.
3. The funds flow statement.
4. The value calculation.

So an AFS will look like this:

A first look at an AFS

	Detail
Income statement	• start with sales revenue • deduct all costs including tax but excluding interest net of associated tax relief • finish with net profit before finance charges
Balance sheet	Show just the asset side of things: • fixed assets • plus working capital[24] • equals capital employed
Funds flow statement	• profit before finance charges • add back non-cash charges (e.g. amortisation) and the net change in any other balance sheet provisions • deduct any increase in working capital • deduct net capital expenditure • equals funds flow. Note that the way the numbers work is such that funds flow will also be equal to net profit less the increase in capital employed.
Value calculation	Value comes from: • funds flow • times the relevant discount factor • which gives the present value of the funds flow • adding the present values gives the cumulative present value Net present value is the final number in the cumulative present value row when the project or business is complete.

There are two final things to add in order to complete the AFS. These are set out below.

[24] Recall that working capital is equal to current assets excluding cash less current liabilities excluding short-term debt.

Adding more detail to the income statement

In most respects the AFS does what it says. That is to say it represents a good way to simplify a set of accounts.[25] There is, however, one key way that I recommend a set of published accounts should be analysed in more detail. This concerns the distinction between fixed and variable costs.

Published accounts simply detail total costs and it is rare to see the distinction made between fixed costs and variable costs. Theory has it that variable costs are directly related to sales volume while fixed costs are largely unaffected by the exact level of sales. The advantage of separating these two items out is that one can then build a financial model which will more accurately allow for changes in sales.

In reality there is a spectrum of fixed and variable costs between some costs which are absolutely fixed and some which are fully variable while many are somewhere in the middle. Take, for example, what in the USA would be called a gas station while in the UK would be called a petrol station. Each gallon (or litre in the UK) of fuel will have a basic cost to the oil company. This is quite clearly a variable cost. Meanwhile the operating costs of the service station will be substantially fixed. If, however, a decision is taken to extend opening times in order to win more sales then is the increase in costs a fixed cost or a variable cost? Well, the answer depends on what you are doing the calculation for.

The approach I recommend is to show as variable costs only those costs which are variable in response to small non-strategic changes in sales volume. Sales revenue less these variable costs gives a figure that is called the contribution.[26]

It is also useful to subdivide the remaining costs into those which involve actual cash outlays and those such as amortisation which are non-cash in nature. So the income statement part of the AFS will then be as follows:

	Sales revenue
less	*variable costs*
equals	contribution
deduct	fixed costs
deduct also	*amortisation and other non-cash fixed costs*
gives	profit before tax
less	*tax*[27]
equals	net profit

25 To illustrate the need to simplify consider the fact that the three main accounting statements in BP PLC's 2007 accounts amount to 114 separate lines of financial data.

26 Short for contribution towards overheads and other costs.

27 Remember that this tax figure is tax on operations which is the total tax charge plus any tax relief gained owing to interest payments.

Note that the term NOPAT is often used to describe this net profit number. This stands for net operating profit after tax.

Include one key financial ratio

There are many financial ratios. These can be very useful as ways of comparing the performance of different companies that will be of different size. Examples include profit as a percentage of sales or debt as a percentage of equity.

From a value perspective one ratio stands out above the others. This ratio is called the return on capital employed. It is generally referred to as ROCE, in which case it is calculated as profit as a percentage of year end capital employed. It can also be calculated as the return on average capital employed. It would then be termed ROACE and would be profit as a percentage of the average of opening and closing capital employed. This second approach is preferable in my view.

The ratio wins, in my view, for two main reasons. First, because its calculation methodology strips out financing effects. The profit number that is used is profit after tax but before interest while the capital employed also excludes financing impacts. Second, as will be explained later in this book, the ROACE of a business is also a rough proxy for the IRR that it is gaining on average on all of its investments. So in order to be creating value, a business needs to achieve over time a ROACE of at least its CoC.

Why do it this way?

We are almost ready to move into part 3 where the focus will be on the numbers. My experience tells me that a real understanding of accounts will only come to those who know how the numbers work together. So working through part 3 is vital. No single number on the AFS can ever change on its own. There is always an interaction with something else. So part 3 will provide the opportunity to learn how the numbers are all 'wired' together.

I could understand it if readers who are new to accounting felt at this stage that they wished accounting would go away! The economic value section (in my admittedly biased view) seems so much simpler. Why do we have to learn about accounts? I accept that this is a valid challenge. It is particularly relevant to this book since I wrote at the start of this building block on Understanding Accounts that accounting and economic value are often considered as separate subjects.

I believe that there are great benefits to be had if one links the two subjects together. These benefits are:

- Accounts provide the medium for financial communication between companies and shareholders. Shareholders are presented with accounting-based information and then, in effect, asked to judge from this what the business is worth. So if shareholders are doing this, then it is reasonable to ask management to understand the same set of issues.
- Accounts provide a basic data system within any company. A company has to produce accounts because the law requires it to do so. It could, if it wished, build a second data system that was not based on accounting-conventions and that directly supported value-based decision making.[28] There would, however, be considerable additional costs involved in this and users would still have to learn the rules and conventions by which this different system works. Using an existing data system is more efficient.
- Related to this point is the fact that the planning and control system within a company is almost bound to be based on accounting data so looking at projects in this way will mean that it is easier to monitor their subsequent performance.
- Information on competitors tends to be available mainly in accounting format. So relative performance needs to be judged using accounting-based data.
- By preparing our estimates of project cash flow in an accounting format we can reality test our projections against a company's track record of performance.
- Finally, it takes only a few adjustments to accounting data to get the necessary data to support value calculations so this is overall a much simpler approach to follow.

Now I have gone over these arguments because I want to stress at this stage the importance that I attach to the particular way that I structure accounting data in order to highlight the link to value. As this book progresses I will show how various insights can be obtained provided financial data are structured in the standard format dictated by the AFS. The starting point is the simple awareness that accounting data can be restructured to highlight the correct cash flow number for a value calculation. Much more will follow later.

[28] For example, it could build a management information system that only dealt with cash.

Part 3: Practical examples

This section will deal with the numbers rather than the underlying concepts. The first step is to understand how each line on an AFS is calculated and how they interact. We will then work through a few simple examples concerning how individual accounting items are calculated and then move on to two worked examples. This will include a study of a real set of published accounts.

How the accounting numbers interact

I refer to the way that the accounting numbers interact with each other as the AFS wiring diagram. This is described below:

The AFS wiring diagram

	Calculation method
Income statement	Note that calculations refer to a period of time such as a year or a quarter.
Sales revenue	• In a simple single-product situation the calculation is sales volume times unit price. In more complex cases the sales revenue for each individual product line is summed.
Variable costs	• Variable cost per unit times number of units sold.
Contribution	• Sales revenue less variable costs.
Fixed costs	• The sum of all cash fixed costs that are charged in the period. This could be modelled as a single number or as the sum of several budget items which together cover all the fixed costs of running the business.
Amortisation	• The sum of amortisation (also called depreciation) and the change in provision for any other non-cash charges.
Pre-tax profit	• Contribution less fixed costs and amortisation.
Tax	• The tax charge for the period.[29]
Profit	• Pre-tax profit less tax.

[29] I will not attempt to describe how taxes are set. This is a complex subject beyond the scope of this book. Each country has its own method of setting taxes and this method can be changed from time to time. It is always necessary to get specialist tax advice as regards how to assess the tax that will be payable. Note also that the figure is the tax charge for the period and not the tax paid. The adjustment to get to tax paid is done as part of the payables calculation. Finally, note that the tax charge should be the tax on operations. This will typically be higher than the overall tax charge owing to tax relief on interest.

Balance sheet	Note that calculations for the balance sheet will refer to the situation as at the end of the period concerned.
Fixed assets	• The net book value of all long-term assets. This is equal to the opening fixed assets[30] less amortisation (from above) plus capital investment (see below).
Accounts receivable	• The total amount owing by customers to the company at the end of the period. Usually calculated from the sales revenue figure based on an assumed average number of days of sales outstanding.[31] Any pre-paid costs are also included as part of the overall accounts receivable.[32]
Inventories	• The sum of the book value of the stocks of raw materials, intermediate and final products and any stores (such as spare parts). The book value is assessed based on the cost to the company and not the assessed sales value if this is higher.[33]
Accounts payable	• The total amount owing to suppliers and others plus any accruals for bills that are related to this accounting period but that have not yet been received. Note that the payables would include any tax that has been charged in the income statement but that is unpaid at the end of the year.
Working capital	• The net of accounts receivable plus inventories less accounts payable
Capital employed	• Fixed assets plus working capital
ROACE	Return on average capital employed is profit as a percentage of the average of opening and closing capital employed.
Funds flow statement	These numbers refer to the flows during the period under study.
Profit	• From above.
Amortisation	• Add back amortisation from above.
Working capital	• Deduct the increase in the working capital number on the balance sheet during the period.
Capital investment	• Deduct the capital investment during the year. Any asset sales would be netted off. Note that the capital investment is needed in order to calculate the fixed assets on the balance sheet.
Funds flow	• Profit plus amortisation less the working capital increase less capital investment. Note that funds flow should also equal profit less the increase in capital employed in the period.

[30] i.e. the fixed assets from the previous year's balance sheet.

[31] So, for example, if there are 30 days of sales outstanding the year end accounts receivable would be 30/356 times the sales revenue (always assuming that sales are level across the year).

[32] A key aim of the AFS is to reduce the amount of data such that it can be more readily understood. Fitting data onto a single page is, in my view, a major prize that is well worth the cost of some aggregation of lines of numbers and consequent loss of detail.

[33] Note that should the assessed sales value of any inventory be lower than cost then the stock value on the balance sheet would be shown at this lower level and the difference in value would be included as a charge in the income statement.

We will now illustrate the AFS first through some calculations of individual lines and then through two full examples.

Simple calculations

Fixed assets and amortisation

A company spends $10m on building a chemical plant which it anticipates will have a useful operating life of 20 years. What will the amortisation charge be and what will be the net book value (NBV) of the asset after seven years of operation?

The amortisation will be the cost divided by the estimated operating life. This is $0.5m pa. The net book value of the asset will decline by this amount each year. So at the end of seven years of operation the NBV will be $6.5m.

Accounts receivable

A company has an annual turnover of $12m. It gives 45 days of credit to its customers, all of whom pay on time. What would its accounts receivable be? How would this answer change if you were told that the company sold Christmas novelties and its financial year ended on 31 December?

The simple calculation of accounts receivable would assume sales were level across the year, i.e. $1m per month. So the accounts receivable would be $1.5m. If, however, sales were all in the run-up to Christmas and the financial year end was 31 December the full amount of annual sales would remain unpaid for at this time and so the accounts receivable would be $12m.

Accounts payable

A company incurs total costs of $36m each year. One third of these are related to staff salaries, one third to office rental and one third to purchase of general supplies. Salaries are paid at the end of each month. The rent is paid annually at the start of each year while the general supplies are bought on account with payment due one month after receipt of the invoice for the previous month's supplies. What will be the accounts payable figure at the end of the year?

The salaries are always paid by the end of each month and so will not feature as accounts payable. The rental will be the same as it is paid in advance. So payables will relate just to the $12m of general supplies. At the end of each month there will be one invoice received and awaiting payment and one invoice not yet received but which must be allowed for. So the accounts payable will be $2m.

Inventories

A company sells about 1,000 tonnes of product per month. It holds 15 days of raw material stocks. This raw material costs $200 per tonne. The company also holds 15 days of finished product which it will subsequently sell for $400 per tonne. The cost of the manufacturing process is assessed to be $30 per tonne. What will be the value of its inventories?

The raw material inventory will be 500 tonnes. It will have cost:

$$500 \times \$200 = \$100,000$$

There will also be 500 tonnes of finished product that cost $200 + $30 per tonne to manufacture (i.e. raw material cost plus manufacturing cost). So it will have cost:

$$500 \times \$230 = \$115,000$$

The inventory will therefore be shown in the accounts at $215,000. Note that the potential sales value of the finished product is not used unless for some reason this is less that cost.

Effect of inflation on working capital

A company sells the same volume of goods each year and has a consistent policy regarding payables, receivable and inventories. Its year-end working capital is as follows:

Accounts receivable	$200,000
Inventories	$100,000
Accounts payable	($50,000)
Net working capital	$250,000

If the company continues to sell the same volume of product and to incur the same costs, what will the working capital level be at the end of the year (a) if there is no inflation and (b) if inflation of 10% pa hits all costs and revenues?

With no inflation the working capital will remain unchanged at $250,000. If there is inflation of 10% which impacts all costs and revenues then all working capital items will increase by this amount and so the net working capital will also rise by 10% to $275,000.

Stripping out financing charges

A company's income statement shows the following:

Profit before tax and interest	$10,200,000
Interest charge	($1,300,000)
Tax charge	($3,115,000)
Net income after tax	$5,785,000

What would be the net profit when financing charges are removed?

We need to calculate the implied tax rate. This is equal to the tax charge as a percentage of the profit before tax but after interest.

$$\$3,115,000 \div \$8,900,000 = 35\%$$

So the tax relief associated with the interest charge is $455,000. The resultant income statement excluding finance charges will be as follows:

Profit before tax and interest	$10,200,000
Tax charge	($3,570,000)
Net income after tax	$6,630,000

Effect of making a payment in advance

A company pays its insurance premium of $85,000 for the coming year just before the start of the year in order to ensure that its insurance remains valid at all times. What will be the impact of this on the income statement and the balance sheet for the current year?

We follow the matching convention and so do not include the insurance charge as a cost in the current year. We have, however, paid the bill and so we show it as a prepayment which forms part of the current assets. This increase in current assets serves to increase year end working capital and so it reduces funds flow. Note, however, that we would have included the insurance premium which was paid one year earlier as a cost in this year's accounts.

We should now be ready to move to our two case studies.

Scaffolding example

This example concerns a business opportunity to set up a company and run it for five years. It is simplified compared with the full detail which should be investigated in real life, the aim being to show just enough detail so we can see how each line of the AFS works without getting bogged down in excessive number crunching. So, for example, we will be ignoring inflation effects.

The idea is to form a company which will provide and install scaffolding. The business model is very simple. The owner plans to purchase a large quantity of scaffolding and then offer this for rental. The service will include installation and removal but the owner will subcontract this work to locals who own their own lorries and are skilled scaffolders but who cannot afford to own their own scaffolding. This installation cost will therefore be a variable cost for the new company. The business will store the scaffolding on some spare land at the corner of a farm where the owner lives. This land is available at no cost.

The full set of business assumptions are set out below. The aim is to build a financial model of the following situation and use this to investigate the effect of different assumptions in order to assess the potential viability of the business.

Scaffolding example: business assumptions

Initial cost of scaffolding – $m	4
End of project scrap value of scaffolding – $m	1
Inventory required – $m	0.1
Fixed costs – $m per year	0.2
Sales growth rate	5%
Average sale value per contract – $	1700
Estimated number of sales contracts in first year	1000
Install and remove cost per contract – $	350
Tax rate (tax is paid the following year)	0.3
Average credit period given to customers – days	45
Average credit period received from suppliers – days	15
Current year (it is December at present)	2007
The business will commence in January next year	
Number of years the business will operate	5
Cost of capital	12.0%
Assume that tax is charged on the accounting profit	

The AFS provides, in effect, a template for financial analysis. All that one has to do is fill in the numbers! My version is given below. I suggest that readers should first review this table and check they understand how the numbers are working together. Note, for example, how fixed assets change each year and how the amortisation is added back to profit as we calculate funds flow.

Note also how it is the change in the balance sheet working capital that is subtracted from profit as we move towards funds flow and not the total working capital. Once familiar with the approach, readers should then confirm their understanding by attempting to build their own spreadsheet model and check this against my answer.

My model shows each of the five operating years as well as a column for the initial purchase of scaffolding and a column to show the closure of the business after year 5. This then allows one to apply the correct discount factor to these significant flows of money. One could have included the initial purchase of scaffolding as part of the first year of operation but this would miss the fact that the initial money is paid out immediately. At the end of the assumed operating period for the company the working capital returns to zero as the final customers pay their bills, the inventory is liquidated (I assume it is sold for what it originally cost) and the remaining bills are paid. The largest bill is the tax charge for the final year of operation.

One important point to notice is that if one adopts the accounting approach it is not necessary to carry out a separate calculation of when things like tax will actually be paid. This is a big advantage of the AFS approach. Provided you are happy to study just the funds flow within a period and you do not want to bother with the exact date on which each payment is made then all you need in order to calculate funds flow are the accounting-based figures for the period including the opening and closing balance sheet. There is no need to carry out a separate calculation of when individual items are paid.

The final step of the AFS is to use the funds flow line as input to the value calculation. In this case I have used mid-year discount factors for the five year operating period with the initial capital investment being spent at the end of December 2007 and with shutdown assumed to be at the end of the final year of operation.[34] I have chosen to round the figures in the AFS to the nearest \$0.1m. Some precision is lost but the result is a simpler presentation.

[34] Note the way that I have used separate columns for the start-up and shutdown. This is to allow me to give them the correct discount factor to allow for their exact timing. By building a model in this way it is possible to model assumptions more accurately. You do, however, need to beware of using the IRR function with any models which do not have simple annual cash flows. If you ask the spreadsheet IRR function what the IRR of the funds flow line is it will show 14.8%. The goal seek approach shows 18.1%. The difference is due to the implicit assumption with the IRR function that each cash flow is one year ahead of the previous one. So it would be as though the capital investment were in the middle of 2007 and the residual value in the middle of 2013. This would serve to spread out the project over a further year and clearly, if this were true, the IRR would fall.

Scaffolding example: AFS

	2007	2008	2009	2010	2011	2012	2013
Income statement							
Sales revenue		1.7	1.8	1.9	2.0	2.1	
Variable costs		−0.4	−0.4	−0.4	−0.4	−0.4	
Contribution		1.4	1.4	1.5	1.6	1.6	
Fixed costs		−0.2	−0.2	−0.2	−0.2	−0.2	
Amortisation		−0.6	−0.6	−0.6	−0.6	−0.6	
Pre-tax profit		0.6	0.6	0.7	0.8	0.8	
Tax		−0.2	−0.2	−0.2	−0.2	−0.3	
Profit		0.4	0.4	0.5	0.5	0.6	
Balance sheet							
Fixed assets	4	3.4	2.8	2.2	1.6	1.0	
Accounts receivable	0	0.2	0.2	0.2	0.2	0.3	
Inventories	0	0.1	0.1	0.1	0.1	0.1	
Accounts payable	0	−0.2	−0.2	−0.2	−0.3	−0.3	
Working capital	0	0.1	0.1	0.1	0.1	0.1	
Capital employed	4	3.5	2.9	2.3	1.7	1.1	
ROACE		10.2%	13.4%	18.5%	26.8%	42.6%	
Funds flow							
Profit		0.4	0.4	0.5	0.5	0.6	0.0
Amortisation		0.6	0.6	0.6	0.6	0.6	0.0
Working capital		−0.1	0.0	0.0	0.0	0.0	0.1
Capital investment	−4.0	0.0	0.0	0.0	0.0	0.0	1.0
Funds flow	−4.0	0.9	1.0	1.1	1.1	1.2	1.1
Value calculation	Set up						Close down
Funds flow	−4.0	0.9	1.0	1.1	1.1	1.2	1.1
Discount factor	1.000	0.945	0.844	0.753	0.673	0.601	0.567
Present value funds flow	−4.0	0.8	0.9	0.8	0.8	0.7	0.6
Cumulative present value	−4.0	−3.2	−2.3	−1.5	−0.7	0.0	0.6

The AFS provides, in effect, a financial plan for the business. We can see that \$4m is needed as the upfront investment and that, based on the assumptions, the business then generates approximately \$1m per year. The crucial four words of course are 'based on the assumptions'. Any calculations like this can only ever be as good as the assumptions which underpin them. A well-built model will allow all of the key assumptions to be tested.

The final section of the AFS is a value calculation. From it we can see that the NPV is \$0.6m and that discounted payback is more or less exactly at the end of the assumed five year period of operation. In effect, the business pays for itself over this period and the scrap value of the scaffolding is what contributes the NPV.

Finally, have a look at the ROACE line. What conclusions can one draw from this? Well, at this stage I would say, 'not many'. This is because we are dealing with just a single project and ROACE is not a particularly meaningful indicator for single projects. It becomes much more useful when studying the performance of companies with many operations so that the accounts show an average snapshot. I will return to the question of ROACE in the following building block when we deal with planning and control issues.

Real life example: Corus PLC

We will now take a real set of accounts and see how these can be put into the AFS format. I have chosen to show the company Corus PLC. This was a major steel producing company which was acquired by the Indian company Tata Steel in April 2007 following a takeover battle. As the takeover price is known we can see what valuation was put on the company by a willing third party buyer and compare this with the price before the takeover was mooted. This will provide some interesting insights in a later part of this book.

First, however, we will see how to convert a real set of accounts into the AFS format. The published accounts of the Corus Group are set out below. I obtained them from the Corus website.

Corus PLC published accounts

INCOME STATEMENTS	**2005**	2004
For the financial period ended 31 December	**£m**	£m
Group turnover	**10,140**	9,332
Total operating costs	**(9,460)**	(8,670)
Group operating profit	**680**	662
Finance costs	**(132)**	(129)
Finance income	**31**	13
Share of post-tax profits of joint ventures and associates	**1**	21
Profit before taxation	**580**	567
Taxation	**(129)**	(126)
Profit after taxation	**451**	441
Attributable to:		
Equity holders of the parent	**452**	447
Minority interests	**(1)**	(6)
	451	441

Table (*cont.*)

BALANCE SHEETS	**2005**	2004
At 31 December	**£m**	£m
Non-current assets		
Goodwill	**83**	85
Other intangible assets	**56**	39
Property, plant and equipment	**2,820**	2,793
Equity accounted investments	**95**	109
Other investments	**113**	66
Retirement benefit assets	**157**	311
Deferred tax assets	**172**	174
	3,496	3,577
Current assets		
Inventories	**1,954**	1,732
Trade and other receivables	**1,512**	1,363
Current tax assets	**21**	19
Other financial assets	**85**	–
Short-term investments	**–**	11
Cash and short-term deposits	**871**	589
Assets held for sale	**3**	–
	4,446	3,714
TOTAL ASSETS	**7,942**	7,291
Current liabilities		
Short-term borrowings	**(384)**	(379)
Trade and other payables	**(1,844)**	(1,742)
Current tax liabilities	**(79)**	(117)
Other financial liabilities	**(38)**	–
Retirement benefit obligations	**(5)**	(18)
Short-term provisions and other liabilities	**(117)**	(141)
	(2,467)	(2,397)
Non-current liabilities		
Long-term borrowings	**(1,308)**	(1,063)
Deferred tax liabilities	**(126)**	(137)
Retirement benefit obligations	**(436)**	(455)
Provisions for liabilities and charges	**(116)**	(122)
Other non-current liabilities	**(46)**	(26)
Deferred income	**(65)**	(33)
	(2,097)	(1,836)
TOTAL LIABILITIES	**(4,564)**	(4,233)
NET ASSETS	**3,378**	3,058
Equity		
Called up share capital	**1,697**	1,696
Share premium account	**173**	168
Statutory reserve	**–**	2,338
Other reserves	**283**	201

Table (*cont.*)

Consolidated reserves	**1,199**	(1,378)
Equity attributable to equity holders of the parent	**3,352**	3,025
Minority interests	**26**	33
TOTAL EQUITY	**3,378**	3,058
	£m	£m
CASH FLOW STATEMENTS	**2005**	2004
Operating activities		
Cash generated from operations	**939**	578
Interest paid	**(115)**	(104)
Premium received on issue of new loans	—	8
Premium paid on redemption of Eurobond	—	(9)
Issue costs of new loans	—	(15)
Interest element of finance lease rental payments	**(1)**	(2)
Taxation paid	**(166)**	(93)
Net cash flow from operating activities	**657**	363
Investing activities		
Purchase of property, plant and equipment	**(423)**	(310)
Development grants received	**2**	–
Sale of property, plant and equipment	**49**	37
Purchase of other intangible assets	**(29)**	(12)
Purchase of other fixed asset investments	**(35)**	(12)
Loans to joint ventures and associates	—	(1)
Repayment of loans from joint ventures and associates	—	6
Purchase of subsidiary undertakings and businesses	—	(17)
Net cash acquired with subsidiary undertakings and businesses	—	6
Investments in joint ventures and associates	—	(5)
Sale of businesses and subsidiary undertakings	**29**	95
Sale of joint ventures and associates	**3**	2
Dividends from joint ventures and associates	**9**	4
Interest received	**30**	12
Sale/(purchases) of short-term investments	**11**	(5)
Net cash flow from investing activities	**(354)**	(200)
Financing activities		
Cash inflow from issue of ordinary shares	**6**	1
New loans	**3**	558
Repayment of borrowings	**(19)**	(503)
Capital element of finance lease rental payment	**(1)**	(1)
Dividends paid	**(22)**	—
Net cash flow from financing activities	**(33)**	55
Increase in cash and cash equivalents	**270**	218
Cash and cash equivalents at beginning of period	**557**	340

Table (*cont.*)

Effect of foreign exchange rate changes	**(2)**	(1)
Cash and cash equivalents at end of period	**825**	557
Cash and cash equivalents consist of:		
Cash and short-term deposits	**871**	589
Bank overdrafts	**(46)**	(32)
	825	557

The first point to note is the sheer quantity of data. There are something like 90 lines of financial data. It is understandable that there are a lot of numbers because the operations are complex and so there is a lot to report. The AFS approach is ideal for a simple company that owns 100% of all of its assets and where complications related, for example, to long-term provisions such as for pension funding are not involved. I will, however, now show how to simplify the accounts into the AFS format. Later on in this book I will show how to use this to assess the value of the company.

We start by putting the balance sheets into the AFS format. This involves going through line by line and putting each number in the published balance sheet into the highly simplified AFS balance sheet. The purpose of this is both to simplify the numbers into a consistent layout that will facilitate subsequent financial analysis and, more importantly, to strip out the impact of financing.

The AFS only has a limited number of lines and one often has to apply some judgement as regards exactly where to put each number. I recommend an approach that is based on the application of the spirit of the AFS approach rather than attempting to write long lists of rules regarding where to place each number. The key questions concern the difference between financing activities and the day-to-day business activities of the company. The big items are usually fairly clear and, to be honest, the smaller items can create a lot of work but they tend not to be crucial in a valuation. The approach I recommend for a beginner at the art of understanding accounts is to have a go and then review your answer with somebody with more experience.

The exact order in which one does the analysis does not really matter as the three accounting statements interact with each other and the picture is only complete when the final statement is finished. My recommendation, though, is to start the analysis with the balance sheet.

Fixed assets are meant to represent the long-term investments of the company. I chose to put the first five lines of numbers here (goodwill, intangible assets, property plant and equipment, equity accounted investments and other investments). Hence fixed assets are £3,167m in 2005 and £3,092m in 2004. There are two remaining items listed as non-current assets. These are retirement benefit assets and deferred tax assets. I noted that there were equivalent numbers on the non-current liabilities side of the balance sheet. I decided therefore to treat the net of all of these items as a long-term liability that was related to how Corus was financed and so I excluded these numbers from my fixed assets numbers in the asset side of the AFS.

Next we need to identify the various items that together comprise the working capital. The accounts receivable will be the sum of the trade and other receivables, current tax assets and assets held for sale. This is £1,536m in 2005 and £1,382m in 2004. Inventories in this case are very simple as this number can transfer directly from the published accounts. The accounts payable number will be found within the current liabilities section of the balance sheet after one has excluded the items that relate to financing activities. In this case the financing items are referred to as short-term borrowings and other financial liabilities. These total £422m in 2005 and £379m in 2004. There is also the retirement benefit obligation of £5m in 2005 and £18m in 2004. These need to be treated in the same way as the long-term liabilities with the same name on the balance sheet. So we finish up with the accounts payable number being the sum of trade and other payables, current tax liabilities and short-term provisions and other liabilities. The numbers are £2,040m in 2005 and £2,000m in 2004.

So now we have all of the numbers to complete the AFS balance sheet which is as follows:

	2005	2004
Fixed assets	3,167	3,092
Accounts receivable	1,536	1,382
Inventories	1,954	1,732
Accounts payable	(2,040)	(2,000)
Net working capital	1,450	1,114
Capital employed	4,617	4,206

One could normally stop the analysis at this stage since the aim of the AFS is usually to focus on the asset side of operations. For completeness, however, I will show both sides of the balance sheet. This will assist later in this book when I will calculate what shares in Corus might be worth. The other side of the balance sheet concerns how the business is financed. The items on this side will be finance debts, provisions, minority interests and equity.

Finance debts are the net of short- and long-term borrowings and the cash and financial assets numbers. The figures are:

	2005	2004
Long-term borrowings	1,308	1,063
Short-term borrowings	384	379
Other financial liabilities	38	—
Cash and short-term deposits	(871)	(600)
Other financial assets	(85)	—
Net debt	774	842

Notice that because we are dealing with liabilities here, the cash holding appears as a negative. This is because it serves to reduce the overall level of net debt. The intention at this stage is simply to prepare the numbers and not to comment on this but I would certainly note that the end 2005 cash holding looks large. It is the equivalent of about a month's sales revenue.

Provisions will be the net of a lot of figures including the retirement benefit assets and liabilities and also the deferred tax numbers. The full reconciliation is given in the footnote below.[35] The minority interest and the equity are exactly as given in the balance sheet. So the financing side of the balance sheet looks like this:

	2005	2004
Net debt	774	842
Provisions	465	306
Minority interest	26	33
Equity	3,352	3,025
Capital employed	4,617	4,206

We can finish our analysis of the balance sheet by confirming what each of these lines represents.

- Net debt is the bank borrowing net of any cash holding.
- Provisions are an accounting allowance for costs which will not have to be paid until some time in the future but which have been charged already because they do relate to current activities. Good examples are provisions for abandonment of an asset or for paying future pensions.

[35] For 2005 the number is 5 + 126 + 436 + 116 + 46 + 65 – 157 – 172 = 465.

- Minority interest is the allowance made for when assets are not wholly owned. If, for example, a company owns 90% of another company then 100% of all of the balance sheet items is shown with just a single adjustment to allow for the outside ownership of 10%.
- Equity is the residual book value that belongs to shareholders. Equity will increase each year with any retained earnings (i.e. any profits that are not paid out as dividends) and also with any new shares that are issued. Share buybacks would reduce equity.

We are now ready to deal with the income statements. Although our aim is mainly to focus on performance during 2005, it is usual to show the previous year so that any trends in the numbers can become apparent. Indeed, full analysis in my view requires at least three years of historical data and preferably five.

The top line of the published income statement (the group turnover which is another name for sales revenue) goes directly into the AFS. Ideally we would then show variable and fixed costs but this information is not available from the published accounts and so we can only show total costs. We also want to show the amortisation separately but this too is not stated. We can, however, back-calculate the implied figure from the balance sheet and funds flow statements. This is because the closing fixed assets should equal the opening fixed assets plus the capital investment less the amortisation. So as soon as we know the capital investment we will be able to calculate the amortisation.

We can now move down the income statement and strip out the interest charges and their associated tax relief. The net of finance income and finance costs is a charge of £101m in 2005 and £116m in 2004. These costs will almost certainly have resulted in a lower tax charge and so we need to adjust for this. If no better information is available[36] one assumes that the average tax rate for the company will have applied. The average tax rate is simply the tax charge as a percentage of the pre tax profit.[37] In the case of Corus the tax charge was a consistent 22.2% of pre tax profit in both 2004 and 2005. That the numbers are the same is almost certainly a coincidence. So we can calculate that the associated tax relief due to the net finance charges in 2005 was £22m and in

[36] One will not usually find better information but it is always possible that you will be provided with additional data that show finance charges net of associated tax relief and if this is available then obviously you would use it.

[37] This is only an approximation because the tax charges will usually have been incurred as a result of quite complex tax rules often from several different tax jurisdictions. So the average tax rate will not actually have been the rate at which tax relief was gained on the actual finance charges. There is, however, nothing more accurate that can be done unless the company is kind enough to publish the actual figure.

2004 was £26m. The published figure for tax paid needs to be increased by this amount as part of the process of stripping out finance charges.

So at this stage the AFS income statement numbers look like this:

	2005	2004
Sales revenue	10,140	9,332
Costs	(9,459)	(8,649)
Pre-tax profit	681	683
Tax	(151)	(152)
Profit	530	531

Now we turn to the funds flow statement. The cash flow statement in the published accounts is not a lot of help in producing this. This is because in this case it only shows cash generated from operations as a single figure and we do not know how this is built up. We are forced to carry out some back-calculations of what the numbers must have been. We can do this because we know that funds flow will equal the profit less the increase in capital employed over the period. Since capital employed increased by £411m, the funds flow in 2005 must equal £119m.

We can identify the capital investment from the cash flow statement. It is shown in detail as the main part of the investing activities section. Again this is somewhere where we need to apply judgement as regards what to include but in this case I consider that the capital investment will be the net of all of the investing activity lines from purchase of property, plant and equipment down to sale of joint ventures and associates.[38] For 2005 the figure is £404m while for 2004 it was £211m. The big increase was mainly due to higher investment in 2005 and a significant sale of a business in 2004.

We can also identify the working capital increase during 2005 from our AFS balance sheets. It is £1,450m less £1,114m which is £336m. Note that since we do not have a balance sheet for 2003 we cannot calculate the working capital change during 2004.

Finally, we can now calculate what the amortisation must have been. We know that the fixed assets on the AFS increased from £3,092m in 2004 to £3,167m in 2005. This increase of £75m means that amortisation must have been £75m lower than capital investment. So amortisation was £329m.[39]

[38] We want to net because for the purposes of the AFS, capital investment is the net of investments less divestments. A single number is shown in order to achieve simplicity and as few numbers as possible.

[39] When one is forced to back-calculate an item such as amortisation you have the advantage that you know that your AFS is absolutely bound to reconcile with the funds flow calculated from profit,

We can now complete the full AFS for Corus. There is no point showing the 2004 data as we cannot complete the funds flow statement. We will now also adopt the usual convention of allowing time to progress forwards as one moves from left to right. For some reason accounts often show the current year as the first column. We have copied this approach as we have gradually converted the accounting data into value based AFS data.

Corus PLC AFS

Income statement	2004	2005
Sales revenue		10,140
Costs		(9,130)
Amortisation		(329)
Pre-tax profit		681
Tax		(151)
Profit		530
Balance sheet		
Fixed assets	3,092	3,167
Accounts receivable	1,382	1,536
Inventories	1,732	1,954
Accounts payable	(2,000)	(2,040)
Net working capital	1,114	1,450
Capital employed	4,206	4,617
ROACE		12.0%
Funds flow statement		
Profit		530
Amortisation		329
Working capital		(336)
Capital investment		(404)
Funds flow		119

There are no particularly unusual features in this AFS. The numbers paint a picture of a company that is growing (capital employed increases by about

amortisation, working capital change and capital investment equalling profit less increase in capital employed. There are times when you are provided with all of the numbers separately in the accounts. My experience has shown me that when this happens you may not always get exactly the right answer! This is usually due to things like exchange rate effects. I tend to calculate what the unexplained difference is and then decide whether it is small enough to ignore or whether it is a sign that I need to do more analysis either to find what mistake I have made (the more likely cause) or to find what has caused the accounts to have this apparent blip. If you get stuck, this is where you need to call for help from a more experienced analyst or a qualified accountant.

10%) but that can fund this growth out of its own cash generation (i.e. the funds flow is positive). The ROCE of 12% is good but not particularly high.

It is also worth reflecting on the difference between the top line (sales revenue) and the bottom line (funds flow). Roughly 99% of the sales revenue is utilised within the company. The contribution to value of 2005's funds generation is just £119m. It is clear that better things are anticipated in the future because Tata Steel paid £6.2bn to purchase the equity in this company. We can return to how this price might be justified later in this book. The point to make at this stage is that funds flow is usually the small difference between two large numbers. This is why valuations can never, in my view, be precise. A small error in one's forecast of either cash inflow or cash outflow will lead to a relatively large change in value.

Part 4: Individual work assignments

Carry out the following exercises and then review your answers against the specimen answers given at the end of this book.

1. A company spends $10m in 2005 and $6m in 2006 building a new depot. It estimates that its useful life will be 25 years. The company starts trading in 2007. What will be the amortisation charge in 2006 and in 2007?
2. The same company anticipates cash fixed costs in 2007 of $10m and variable costs of $10 per unit sold. It expects to sell 1 million units per year for a price of $25 per unit. It is taxed at 30% and the tax authorities allow fixed assets to be depreciated at the same rate as is used in the accounting books. At this stage assume that all transactions are paid immediately with cash except the tax charge which is paid in the middle of the following year. Prepare an AFS for 2007.
3. Now allow also for the following working capital effects and show via an AFS what the impact of working capital is on funds flow. Customers pay for their purchases on average 45 days after receipt. Bills are paid on average after just ten days and the depot will hold a stock equivalent to three months of product (which is valued at variable cost).
4. To complete this exercise now produce a financial summary for the years 2005–2009. Assume that in 2008 and 2009 sales volume grows by 5% pa while inflation causes all costs and the product selling price to rise by 2% pa.

5. Finally, return to the scaffolding example. As a result of further studies the potential owner of the business realises that she has left out the following items:
   - The business will require insurance. This will cost $125,000 pa and will be paid in advance of each year.
   - The initial plan omitted any allowance for a salary for the owner who would run the company. The owner decides she should receive $100,000 a year and that this will be paid monthly at the end of each month.
   - A rental charge of $25,000 pa will be made for the land that will be used. This will be paid in four instalments at the start of each calendar quarter.

What is the impact of these changes on the NPV of the project and what selling unit price would be necessary in order exactly to offset the changes and maintain NPV?

CHAPTER

4

Building block 4: Planning and control

Summary

This building block is all about planning and control. It will explain what documents to expect and summarises some key concepts and techniques. It will also show how the numbers which we have learned to calculate for individual projects come together to form the overall results for a company. It is, however, just an introduction to the topic. Furthermore, the focus is on planning and only those aspects of control that are directly related to economic value. My aim, as with the other building blocks, is simply to get my readers who started as beginners up to speed so that they can join the existing practitioners in the main sections of the book.

I must stress at the outset that when it comes to planning and control, it is up to individual companies to decide what processes they want. There are good reasons for companies to adopt different approaches in this area. In particular, the fact that although the shareholder value objective is common across companies, the nature of business can be very different. So, for example, some businesses are growing fast while others may be shrinking; some have many customers while some have only a few; some have a long time cycle while others have to respond quickly to changes.

Differences such as these do mean that when it comes to planning and control, there are several right answers and even within a company, the right answer will evolve over time. This makes it a much harder subject to get right. In this book I can prescribe with confidence a standard approach to calculating economic value. This is because, in my view, all value calculations are the same. When it comes to planning and control, however, it is less easy to offer a simple template that all can follow.

Nevertheless, my view is that making good choices about the focus of the planning and control system is a key success factor for a company. So too is the way that companies ensure implementation of their plans. This is why I include planning and control as a building block. What readers will need to do as they read this section is adjust the general approaches to their specific situation. I believe that everything I cover is necessary but the relative importance of one component or concept compared with another will primarily be set by the specific situation of the company concerned.

The building block will comprise five parts. In the first part I will describe what I suggest should be the main components of a planning and control system. I will, for example, introduce the idea of the need for a strategy and a plan and explain the differences between them. The second part covers various concepts such as the planning cycle and the importance of setting the right targets. Then, in part 3, I will summarise a few key planning techniques. I selected these because they are all important to the understanding of the Sources of Value technique which will be introduced later in the book. The fourth part is called words and music. It is about how the strategic concepts (the words) should link to the financial performance numbers (the music). This is a very practical section and relates to how the numbers link together and how to value plans. It is here that I will show how to use the AFS approach to understand the relationship between individual projects and company level performance metrics such as ROACE and the dividend payout ratio. This section will conclude by showing a simple way to value a business. The final part will, as usual, contain the individual work assignments.

Part 1: The main components

Strategy

A strategy should set out the overall direction of an organisation and indicate how it expects to win. Some companies operate in a single line of business and so for them, strategy is simply about how they will beat their competitors. I use the term business strategy to refer to how an operation seeks to beat its competitors in a single line of business. Many large companies operate in more than one business area and so for them there is also the question of corporate strategy to consider. Corporate strategy concerns the choice of what businesses a company should be in and how to organise and manage them. The distinction between how individual businesses beat their competitors and how groups of businesses come together to form corporations is important but the terminology which describes it is much less so. Hence my nomenclature of business strategy and corporate strategy will not necessarily be followed in all companies but the basic ideas should be.

A document entitled 'Strategy' can serve two different purposes. It can be there in order to facilitate the discussion of strategy among the top leadership of a company or it can be there in order to advise the full workforce of the chosen direction. The former will emphasise the various options that are available while the latter may not mention choice at all. I will distinguish between these two purposes by referring to the former as a strategy discussion while the latter is the agreed strategy.

The main purpose of an agreed strategy is to guide the organisation in general and decision-makers in particular, as they make their choices. So, for example, if a company wants to grow, then its strategy should indicate where it expects that growth to come from. The strategy, in effect, tells the organisation where to go and look. The strategy should also indicate the fundamental basis of competition because a strategy that says simply 'This looks like a good place to go, so let's go there' is unlikely to be a winning one. Success is usually contingent on having a good place to go and having a better way of getting there than others.

Business strategy discussions start with an analysis of the nature of the business that you are in. Issues such as the size of the market; its growth rate; the competitors; and what strategies they are following, are all covered. So too is the question of the balance of power between the suppliers to the sector, the players within the sector and the customers. Major risks such as technology change or new regulations are also considered. When combined, this analysis paints a picture of the relative attractiveness of the sector under consideration.

The next stage of a business strategy discussion is to analyse the position of the company within its sector. What are the strengths and what are the weaknesses? How can the strengths be maintained and exploited and how can the weaknesses be corrected? It is out of the answers to these questions that strategic choices will emerge. The company could do this or it could do that. It is rare for there to be an obvious future path which is self-evidently better than all others. A good strategy discussion will highlight the main choices and make an on-balance recommendation. Choices should be guided by economic value. A good choice is one that serves to maximise value compared with alternatives.

When it comes to the corporate strategy questions of 'What businesses?' and 'How to organise and manage them?', there are many more choices to be made and the choices are harder. For example, when considering what businesses to be in it is not just a question of choosing the best. It also concerns how businesses can fit together. For example: do they utilise similar technologies?; do they share customers?; do their risks offset each other? Then there is the question of how to organise and manage the chosen businesses. There can be choices here, for example about the balance of power between global brands and national operating companies or about the power of functions versus the power of business units. The corporate strategy discussion is the vehicle through which decisions such as this should be made.

The question of communication is vital. A strategy may, for good reasons, be kept secret. For example, it may be wise not to alert your competitors about your impending change of direction or the new way in which you will go about beating them. However, it is important that the necessary people are told about the strategy so that they can organise their work accordingly. The more people who can be advised of the strategy, the greater the organisational alignment that can be achieved. There is, however, a significant distinction between what is necessary in order, on the one hand, to facilitate a senior-level discussion of what the strategy should be, and on the other to advise the organisation of the chosen course. This latter statement of strategy should ideally be very simple so that everybody can remember it.[1]

Another way to think about strategy is to think about what can go wrong and then invoke strategy as the means of avoiding these perils. In business your competitors are always striving to beat you. Nothing stays the same. So companies need to change simply to preserve their standing in this competitive environment. Small actions taken early can avert large problems coming up later. The analogy of a hand on the tiller of a boat is often made. Strategy can be like that hand. It is the strategy that calls for a business development team to be set up that builds the presence in a new market that, in years to come, will become a major contributor to the continued health of the company.

A strategy should be enduring. So a full strategy discussion need not take place each year. A simple annual confirmation that strategy remains on track may be all that is necessary. No strategy can, however, last for ever. Sooner or later one of two things will happen. Either goals will be achieved or events will have turned out in a way that negated the assumptions on which strategy is based. At such times a new strategy is needed.

[1] A Head of Planning that I once worked for had a simple rule: if it won't fit on a page, it is not a strategy. There is a lot of force in this as long as it is only applied to the communication of strategy after it is agreed and not to its original formulation.

Companies that are always changing their strategies will be considered to be poorly managed but, equally, companies that do not change despite real world events are also liable to be termed failures. Any decision concerning a change in strategy is crucial. I do not favour an approach which sets in stone the dates for strategy review. I believe that this should be a chief executive/board-level decision with the only fixed requirement being an annual review of whether strategy remains on track. It is quite clear that failure to implement an agreed strategy should be grounds for calling a strategy review. Unexpected success should also be a signal for a review since there may well be more opportunities available than had been envisaged.

Long-term plan

If the strategy sets out the overall direction, the long-term plan (LTP) sets out the detailed route plan for the first stages of the journey. Ideally it should cover a long enough period in order to see at least the first year of what success will look like. So if the strategy calls for a three year transformation then the LTP would cover at least four years. If, however, success was a very long way off then a five year LTP might be acceptable.

The LTP should always include financial projections but it can also cover the requirements for other key resources such as skilled people. It should set out the anticipated path that will be followed and set milestones along this path so that progress can be monitored. For example, if a strategy calls for a development team to be established with a view to building a position in a new market, then milestones would specify the date when the team was formed, when new market entry was anticipated, how many outlets were anticipated and the estimated market size and share after, say, the first two years of operation.

A feature of LTPs is that they will focus on what might be termed a success case. This is to say that those putting forward plans will always put forward a plan that shows how they will succeed. It is unrealistic to expect much else since a manager who put forward a plan that showed failure would almost certainly be replaced on the grounds that he expected to fail. A good LTP will recognise risks and alert readers to the downside possibilities but a degree of bias is always to be anticipated. Corporations may well, therefore, need to aim off when they add up the LTP submissions of their various units since the likelihood is that aggregate performance will be lower.[2]

[2] We will look at how this aiming off can be done in the final building block which covers risk.

A key difficulty with any LTP concerns the impact of variables outside the control of line management. In many cases this will include the selling price and/or the margin on sales. Each company will have to decide whether the LTP should be an estimate of what the next few years will look like or whether the plan should normalise for uncontrollable variables. Whatever choice is made, the company will then need to understand the consequences of that approach and not try to pretend that one set of numbers can do all things.

Consider, for example, an oil company preparing its LTP. Should the company prepare the plan based on its best estimate of what future oil prices will be or should it plan on the basis of a fixed oil price even if it knows that such stability will never materialise? I tend to favour an approach where the major variables are held constant across the period of the LTP. The reason for this is that it is then possible to identify any underlying trends without these being swamped by the effect of an assumed oil price change. The problem, however, is that the actual numbers can then become divorced from reality.

One important point to make about any LTP concerns what I call flow-through. The LTP should be updated each year. Flow-through is how year 5 of this year's plan should be year 4 of next year's plan and ultimately should become the current year. There can be a tendency to treat each new LTP as a new plan. This then means that it is only the first year's performance that is ever monitored. I believe that it is vital that performance monitoring should consider flow-through factors in order to ensure that the long-term promises are actually delivered.

In some companies a planning timetable may be adopted that sees the LTP completed in mid-year or perhaps three quarters of the way through the year. The theory behind this is that at this time the organisation is less stressed. It can help to avoid cramming everything into the financial year-end period so that longer-term issues can be given more time. The disadvantage of this approach is that an organisation may seem always to be planning and never leaving business units alone to get along with implementing their strategy. Once again, there are no unique right answers, just things that work well in a particular situation but may not in others.

The financial projections in an LTP will provide a basis for assessing the value of a business. We will see how to do this later in this building block. The fact that the LTP contains sufficient data to allow a business to be valued will mean that it should always be treated as confidential and/or as containing price-sensitive information.[3]

[3] Price-sensitive information is a specific term related to information which might impact on the share price. It must be treated as confidential and those in possession of price-sensitive information are

Annual plan

The annual plan can simply be the first year of the LTP or it can be a separate document if it is prepared at a different time or by a different part of the organisation. The point is, though, that the annual plan sets out what will be done in the coming year.[4] This will then form the basis for any variance reporting once actual results become available.

The annual plan for a company should in effect represent the summation of a series of plans and/or budgets for the various parts of that company. In principle one should be able to trace a flow of anticipated delivery all the way from the company plan down to individuals' personal objectives. The plan should normally be approved shortly before the start of the year in question. It will often serve as a vehicle for granting top-level approval for operating budgets.

The annual plan will always contain financial projections and will highlight some financial outcomes as targets. These targets may well be formally linked into the company's pay system. The annual plan should also contain many non-financial targets which are expected to be delivered during the coming year. The inclusion of a target in the annual plan serves to stress its importance. This means that the plan will spell out what is important during the coming year. Like the LTP, the annual plan will also be a confidential document as it will contain price-sensitive information.

Performance reports

The management of a company will require various performance reports throughout the year. One purpose of these will be to ensure that the company is on track and to give early warning of variances so that any necessary corrective actions can be taken. There is likely to be a hierarchy of such reports. Individual managers will all require reports to ensure that their particular part of the organisation is on track.

An organisation that was operating well would find that if very senior managers asked for a particular report then they would discover that a more junior manager was already receiving it. There can, however, be times when the perspective of senior management differs from that of line managers. The leadership act of a senior manager's calling for a report should send a signal to the organisation of the importance of this topic. So if it is not currently

subject to what are termed insider trading rules which limit their ability to trade in shares of the company concerned.

4 The company's financial year as opposed to the calendar year will usually define the dates for the start and finish of the year in question.

under regular review, this will need to be reconsidered. This highlights a second function of a performance report, namely the way that the report points towards what is important.

Accounting results

All companies are legally required to produce accounting results and to file these regularly with the relevant authorities. Major stock exchanges tend to require quarterly results to be published while the default elsewhere tends to be for annual results.

Major corporate scandals such as Enron have led to increased legislation around accounting results and filing incorrect results can now be a criminal offence. Understandably therefore, company directors have a great incentive to ensure that accounting results are correct. This therefore is a major concern of all staff who work in this area.

I believe that the planning and control system which a company develops should pay important attention to the headline numbers in any set of accounting results. The system should not, however, be exclusively concerned with planning the accounting results. It will, for example, need to cover a far wider range of issues than just the financial numbers. It may also select some financial metrics that are designed in a unique way to suit the company and that do not necessarily follow strict accounting conventions.

Accounting results are always treated as being price-sensitive information until they are published. At this point they are deemed to be known by all. There is, however, always a wealth of additional detail that is not published and this remains confidential.

Controls

Companies need a suite of controls. These will range from ways of ensuring that cash is not stolen through to confirming who has the authority to approve what expenditure. These controls are all important but I consider most of them to be beyond the scope of this book.

One key control is, however, particularly relevant to this book and it concerns the approval of capital expenditure. Most companies will have rules concerning who has authority to approve capital expenditure and will require specific documentation to be completed. I will refer to the investment approval documentation as the finance case for an investment and I will call those who are authorised to approve such a document decision-makers. Each project will also have a sponsor who is the manager who formally puts the finance case forward for approval and an analyst who actually prepares the financial numbers and writes the finance case. Although I will use language which treats these roles as being held by individuals, they may well be taken by committees and teams. Once again, this is an area where companies will exercise choice.

Initiatives

The final component of a planning and control system that must be mentioned is the ubiquitous 'initiative'. An initiative is a special effort devoted to achieving a particular goal. Companies, particularly big ones, always have initiatives under way.

Cynics tend to link initiatives to the latest management fad or to a successful sales call on a senior executive by a firm of management consultants. This picture may be true in some instances. I, however, am a strong believer in the need for initiatives. I see them as the way that change is brought about.

Organisations need to change but change is almost always difficult. There is a concept called organisational inertia that suggests that if a company is progressing in a certain way then this acts like inertia and it requires an effort to overcome this. I prefer to think about change through a medical analogy. I think of organisations as having a natural immune system which makes change difficult.[5] The immune system has to be lowered to allow change to take place. The aim of the initiative is then to help lower the immune response which would otherwise stop a change taking place.

The trick with initiatives is to launch the right number. Too few will mean that a company does not change fast enough. Too many can create a phenomenon called by some 'initiative overload'. When this happens so much attention is devoted to change that there is never actually enough time to implement it. The choice of initiatives should therefore be a senior-level prerogative. They should, however, link back to the strategy since it is this which sets overall direction.

Nomenclature

I do need to finish this part with a note of caution about nomenclature. I have on several occasions warned about how individual companies will develop

[5] An example of the immune system is a department that is so busy preparing its reports that it cannot send people away on the training course that, ultimately, will improve skills and speed up the process.

their own planning and control processes. These individual differences will include giving items their own names. I have adopted the names that I think are best for describing each part of my recommended approach. Readers will need to be prepared to meet things like 'strategy' or 'long-term plans' under different names.

Some companies, for example, make a distinction between what they call a vision and a strategy. With this approach, the vision concerns where a company is heading and a strategy concerns how it will get there. I think it is better to treat the two together as being the strategy but I cannot say that the alternative approach is wrong and I am right. I just have to warn readers to expect complications like this.

Part 2: The main concepts

In the first part we met the half-a-dozen or so main documents in the realm of planning and control. We must now turn to the question of how these are connected together. Up to now the components have been explained in their logical order with strategy coming first. In reality it is most likely that everything will be happening at once. Once a company has been started it is never possible to go back and address strategy from the perspective of the proverbial clean sheet of paper. This part will consider some important concepts which need to be considered as companies decide how to design their overall planning and control system.

The planning cycle

One could perhaps envisage an approach to planning that looked like this:

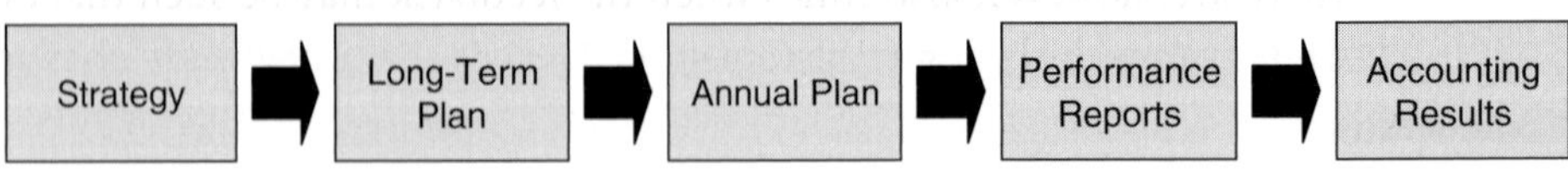

Fig. 4.1 From strategy to actuals

This is the logical flow of the main components of the planning and control system. You start with a strategy and ultimately it becomes reality. There is, however, a fundamental flaw in this approach. What do you think that is?

Well, this approach lacks any feedback loops. If everything went exactly according to plan then one could simply move from left to right as time passed. The chart above would be OK. In reality, events intervene and companies do better or worse than expected. A well-run company will respond to this information in an appropriate way. It is this ability to respond to events that is lacking from the strategy-to-actuals approach characterised above.

It is important to allow events to have the appropriate degree of influence. This leads to the idea of the 'Plan, Do, Measure, Learn' planning cycle which is summarised in this picture.

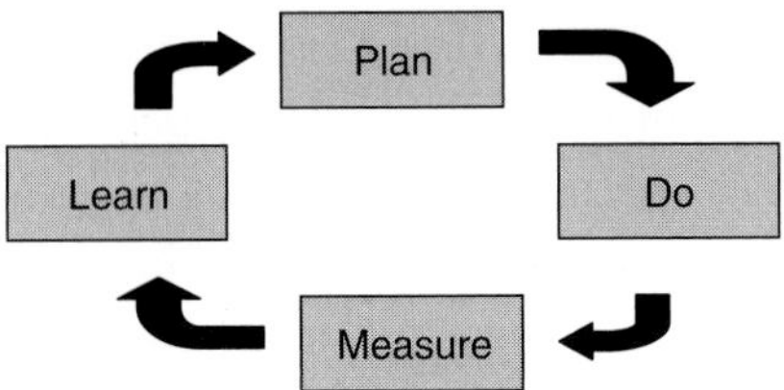

Fig. 4.2 Plan, Do, Measure, Learn

The basic concept is that planning should not be carried out in a vacuum. It needs to be informed by events. A plan should be formulated and then implemented. Actual results should be observed and learnings from these incorporated into new plans. This cycle need not wait until the following year. A good manager will adjust actions immediately in response to events.

Look again at the initial from-strategy-to-actuals picture and think how far back the feedback needs to go. Should feedback just concern the annual plan or should it perhaps impact on strategy?

My answer to this question is that it all depends. There are times when a good manager will say that a small gust of wind must not be allowed to divert the company from its strategic intent. Short-term results may be disappointing but the strategy remains valid and must be steadfastly implemented. There are, however, also times when the feedback may be such that even the strategy must be brought into question. Decisions about what to change in the face of unanticipated events are a vital challenge that managers must face.

Consider the situation of a company that generates slightly more cash than anticipated. On the face of it this is a good thing. One should, however, enquire into the cause. Is it, for example, a result of a small improvement in the short-term trading environment or is it perhaps due to the failure to set up a new business development team? The dollar impact on the current year's cash flow might well be the same, but the effect on strategy could be fundamentally different. There could be any number of reasons why a business generates more cash than anticipated. Management must apply judgement as to how they react. There can be learning opportunities even when results are exactly in line with plan. The confirmation of what can actually be delivered may give greater comfort about future plans.

The Plan, Do, Measure, Learn planning cycle does create a new risk. This is what is often termed 'analysis paralysis'. It is possible to carry out so much analysis that an organisation, in effect, grinds to a halt. Once again, judgement needs to be used to ensure that the effort involved in creating feedback loops is repaid through improved performance.

Some situations are simple enough to allow them to be freed from the usual Plan, Do, Measure, Learn approach. These may be permitted to follow the much simpler Do, Learn, Do approach. This involves starting and then learning as you go. This can be a good way to do things when risks are small or when speed is of the essence. It is, however, much more risky and is not usually recommended for anything major.

Top-down and bottom-up

These terms are often used in relation to planning. A top-down plan is one that is prepared from high up in an organisation. It tends to set out what senior managers think can be achieved. By contrast, a bottom-up plan is one that has been prepared in full detail involving all those parts of the company that will contribute to it.

As usual, the two approaches have their own advantages and disadvantages. Top-down is simpler and much less demanding on an organisation. Top-down is also the best way to deal with secret projects or projects that are likely to meet internal resistance. Bottom-up is more likely to win organisational commitment and will probably be a better reflection of the current trading environment.

WYMIWYG

WYMIWYG stands for 'what you measure is what you get'.[6] I have already alluded to this concept when I explained how senior managers can signal to an organisation what is important to them by requiring performance

[6] I pronounce it 'wi me wig'.

reports on particular topics. I believe that this is a vital concept and that senior managers need to pay great attention to choosing the right things to measure.

The WYMIWYG effect is obvious when a company sets up a bonus system that rewards achievement of particular financial goals. If a bonus is paid for achieving sales targets then this is what should be expected. The sales force will go out and win sales with little regard to how profitable they are. If a company wants to focus on profitable sales then it had better set a bonus system that rewards this.

The WYMIWYG effect goes way beyond the bonus system. Most staff will want to impress their managers since this is the most obvious route to promotion. So if a manager asks for a report on something, staff will assume this is important and that they can impress their managers by ensuring the report shows an improving trend. They will therefore devote their limited time to maximising performance measured against whatever yardsticks their managers choose to apply. It is therefore simple logic that a company will tend to deliver what it measures and that things that go un-measured will not be maximised.

There are important consequences of all of this. Senior managers need to think about how their requests for information will be interpreted and in particular whether the requests will encourage any undesired behaviours.

Consider for example the behaviours that may be encouraged in a company that has a particular focus on working capital.[7] The natural reaction to working capital will be that it is something that should be minimised because it represents a use of funds. Is this what an organisation wants? Yes, all other things being equal, lower working capital is better than higher working capital. If, however, there is a focus on working capital, will all other things be equal? Consider a sale that is due to be made near to the financial year-end. The impact on cash flow will be nil until the customer pays for his purchase. The sale will add to year-end accounts receivable while reducing year-end stocks. The net effect, assuming the sale is profitable, is that the sale will increase working capital.[8] So the WYMIWYG concept will suggest that a focus on working capital could provide an incentive for a profitable

[7] Remember that working capital is the net balance of accounts receivable, accounts payable and inventories.

[8] Recall that stocks are shown in the accounts at cost whereas the receivable will be the amount owed to the company by the customer. So the immediate effect of a sale on working capital will be to increase it by an amount equal to the incremental profit on the sale. It is only when a customer pays for the goods that the company gains a benefit.

sale being delayed to the following year. This is a risk which needs to be avoided.

WYMIWYG should not be taken to extremes. If one accepts that the aim of a company is to maximise value then WYMIWYG thinking could be misinterpreted to suggest that the only item to measure should be value. This would be a nonsense. Many things should be measured and WYMIWYG simply warns that the choice is important as it will influence behaviours and that a focus on just a single measure may result in undesirable consequences.

Setting appropriate targets

Targets are the specific deliverables that are chosen to define performance. For a company these should define the rules of the game. The overall objective will probably be maximising shareholder value but in order to make this more relevant to the entire organisation this will usually be converted into a number of specific measurable goals. These become, in effect, the goals of the company. It is vital, therefore, that they are appropriate.

Targets should not only refer to financial items. They should cover operational issues such as safety, environmental performance and reliability. They should also consider strategic development issues such as research projects, staff development or reorganisations. Targets can be brought together into a single summary page.

A company is then faced with a choice. Suppose there are 20 targets. Should each be awarded marks on a 0–5 scale such that a single overall mark out of 100 can be awarded? This has the advantage of clarity. It does, however, create the risk that different items may be seen to have clear financial trade offs. For example, could slightly better cash generation offset a poor accident record? A better approach is to rely on judgement to interpret overall performance in the light of the various targets that were set. This is referred to as a balanced scorecard approach. A balanced scorecard will identify a small number of key areas and set a few measurable deliverables for each area.

How should targets be set? I have been told that it might have been Stalin who invented the idea of setting tough targets because it makes people achieve more. I am sure, though, that the idea must be older than that. Irrespective of whose idea it was, there does appear to be some merit in setting challenging targets because of the way that these will encourage people to deliver more. The idea must not, however, be pushed too far. If targets become unreachable they will either cease to motivate or will encourage people to take excessive risks in order to achieve them.

Stage gate processes

Individual projects can be thought of as having their own time lines. Different tasks have to be undertaken at different points on this line. These tasks usually need to be done in the right order and the concept of a stage gate approach has been developed in order to make this process more efficient. A typical stage gate approach could involve four or five stages as follows:

1. Options identification and selection.
2. Detailed design.
3. Implementation.
4. Operation.

A fifth stage is invoked in situations where detailed design needs to be subdivided into two stages.[9]

This concept of stage gate processes can best be illustrated through the example of a hypothetical project to build a new distribution depot. The project follows from a recent strategy review which highlighted high distribution costs as a significant impediment to profitable growth.

The first stage will concern identification of various options to solve the strategic issue. These options will obviously include a new depot but there will be other options as well. For example, the best solution may not involve a new depot at all. It might perhaps concern a need to modernise existing depots or to invest in larger delivery vehicles or to switch from an owned and operated distribution operation to one where this is subcontracted to a third-party specialist. The first stage ends when agreement is reached on the chosen means of moving forward. This wide range of options is typical of the options stage of a project. The purpose of the options stage is to identify the alternatives and select the best approach. This choice is often the most important choice for any project.

Having chosen the right project to be working on (in this case the right project is to build a new depot) the focus must now switch to detailed design. There is often an initial step which involves selection of the exact project. This can be treated as a stage in its own right. I would call this the selection stage. In our example this would concern selection of the location for the depot. Issues related to detailed design should only then be started. The detailed design stage would end with the approval of the project. A project manager would be appointed to implement the construction phase of the project. The final stage would be to operate the depot successfully.

[9] These stages would be called selection and design. Selection would concern higher level choices such as location while design would concern the real detail.

This approach may seem obvious but the temptation to move ahead too fast with a project can be very great and can lead to considerable financial inefficiencies. In a worst-case scenario a company could simply implement the wrong project because the best option was not even considered. Even if the right project is identified, a lot of redesign costs can be incurred if project design is initiated before the big decisions about, say, the size of the depot, are confirmed.

The stage gate approach also makes it clear when work on some issues should cease. It is often the case that individuals will support different options. Under a stage gate approach those who had supported an option which is rejected are, in effect, then instructed to stop pressing for their preferred route and to line up in support of what has been chosen.

Cost control and risk management

These issues are not always considered in the context of strategy. They can often be left for consideration at the time of the annual plan. My view is that some costs and some risks should be considered as part of the strategy discussion. This is because it is only at this stage that all costs and all risks can be controlled.

One can think of the various layers of a company as adding layers of costs. It is therefore perfectly possible for a company to find that it is being outperformed by a competitor even though its actual operations are every bit as efficient as its competitor. It may just be suffering from excessive overheads. Corporate overheads tend to be a function of corporate strategy[10] and so excessive overheads may only be correctable by a change in the way that a company operates. So one function of a corporate strategy discussion should be to confirm that the various layers of overheads are affordable. We will see how overheads can impact on the valuation of a company in the following section when we consider how to value a plan.

Risk can work in a similar way. If a company does not like the risks that it faces then one way to reduce risk is to eliminate it by choosing not to operate the business that creates the excessive exposure. In simple terms, if you don't like the risks associated with a business you can always avoid them by selling the business. Risks can also be reduced by operating in a joint venture or by ensuring that the company is involved in a wide range of activities so that individual risks are reduced by the portfolio effect. This will be explained in the next building block.

[10] Remember that corporate strategy concerns the questions of what businesses to be in and how to organise and manage them. Choices about organisation and management are inherently choices about costs.

The growth 'imperative'

Many companies operate as though growth were an imperative. They do this because successful companies almost always grow. Growth is good in that it creates more opportunities for employees within a company. Growth is also good if it means that the company is investing in more positive NPV projects. The world economy grows each year and so any company that does not grow is losing market share. Can you imagine a chief executive wanting to stand up and tell investors that they had shrunk the dividend by 5% a year during the tenure of their leadership?

Despite all of the above arguments, it is my view that growth should never be treated as an imperative. Growth should generally be an outcome of a successful strategy but not an objective in its own right. This is because once it becomes an objective it will dominate behaviours within a company. The objective should be value maximisation. However, as we will see when we start to consider how the numbers work, value maximisation may well be achieved through following a path which involves a steady decline in value.

Part 3: Key planning techniques

In this next part I will describe four techniques that are of particular importance to the understanding of Sources of Value. They are mainly the work of Professor Michael Porter from Harvard.[11] I will provide short summaries of these now. I do recommend that readers who aspire to great things in the area of strategic planning should devote some additional time to reading some of his works. My strongest recommendations are for two of his older books. I have included these summaries in the main text rather than as a footnote in order to emphasise the books' importance:

- Competitive Strategy – Techniques for Analysing Industries and Competitors. *This book covers what I treat in this book as two separate techniques. It introduces the five forces model for analysing sector attractiveness and also proposes the three generic strategies which can be used to create competitive advantage. It gives a lot of detailed consideration of industry structure and how to compete in different stages of the product life cycle.*

[11] Michael E. Porter is the Bishop William Laurence University Professor based at Harvard Business School. A read of his personal description at the Harvard Business School website (www.hbs.edu) will point readers towards his many publications. I consider his work on strategy to be seminal. So, for example, my assertion that corporate strategy concerns the questions of what businesses and how to organise and manage them was inspired by his writings.

- Competitive Advantage. *This book starts with a summary of the earlier book Competitive Strategy so if your time or book-buying budget is limited then read just this one. The book then goes on to explain the value chain approach in full detail. My recommendation is that you do not take the one-book short cut and that you read both*!

The value chain model

Although it is only introduced in the second book, I prefer to start my Michael Porter section with the value chain model. This provides a structure for the consideration of the various activities of any business and is shown in the chart below.

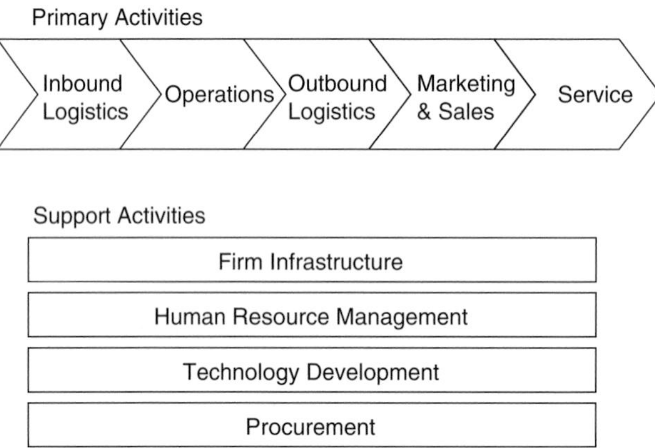

Fig. 4.3 The value chain model

The value chain concerns how raw material inputs are transformed into finished products which can be sold to customers. The idea is that the activities involved can be broken down into five separate categories which together represent the primary activity of the business. The firm does also require four vital support activities. The five primary and four support activities when taken together provide a structure for any analysis of a business. It is this structured approach which I particularly like.

The areas to study are:

Primary activities

- **Inbound logistics:** deliveries of raw materials and inventory control.
- **Operations:** manufacturing operations that convert raw materials into assembled and packaged end-products.

- **Outbound logistics:** all activities related to getting the finished product to customers including storage of finished product, transport and distribution management.
- **Marketing and sales:** everything related to persuading the customer to purchase the product.
- **Service:** activities related to aftersale care offered to the customer.

Support activities

- **Firm infrastructure:** a catch-all category for the overhead activities of a firm such as accounting, management, planning, etc.
- **Human resource management:** activities related to recruiting, training and paying employees.
- **Technology development:** improving current and developing new technologies.
- **Procurement:** all purchases of all raw materials, spare parts and support services.

For each of the nine areas you need to know how your company compares with the competition. The relative importance of the nine areas will change from business to business. For example, inbound logistics may be vital for a business such as a supermarket but insignificant for one selling branded spectacle frames. Or for a supermarket, outbound logistics can be limited to providing trolleys and a car park whereas for a dairy making daily doorstep deliveries of milk, this is the crucial area.

Each business needs to decide where it is going to compete. If it could win in all nine areas at once this would be fantastic, but this would be very unusual. It will be more typical for a business to try to win in, say, one or two key areas while leaving the others with a task of matching the competition without diverting too much of the company's limited senior management attention time. The nine headings and in particular the five primary activities provide good guidance as to where the company should aim to win. Competitor benchmarking can be directed along these lines. If a company cannot point to at least one area where it expects to win then it is in severe strategic difficulties.

The five forces model

The five forces model provides a structure for considering the inherent profitability of any industry. The idea is that industries have different structures and these lead to different levels of profitability. The five forces model explains why this happens.

To illustrate the point about different levels of profitability one only has to think about airlines and pharmaceutical companies. Airlines have a notorious profitability record. An entry of the two words 'airline losses' into Google will produce a stream of hits including a report that the USA's airlines were expected to lose over $30bn during the period 2000–2004. By contrast, enter 'pharmaceutical profits' and you will soon learn that pharmaceuticals is among the most profitable industries in the world.[12]

The five forces model proposes that sector profitability is set through the overall impact of just five forces. These are explained in the following chart:

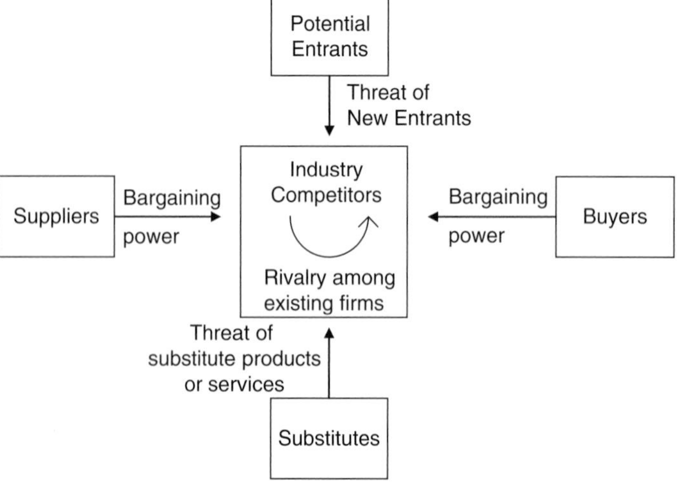

Fig. 4.4 The five forces model

The five forces are:

- the rivalry among existing firms in the industry;
- the bargaining power of suppliers;
- the bargaining power of buyers;
- the threat of substitute products or services; and
- the threat of new entrants.

I will consider each of these in turn, starting with the level of rivalry among existing firms in an industry. It can be taken as a given that firms will compete with each other but quite how hard do they fight? In some sectors it

[12] For example, a report to the US House of Representatives stated that profits by the ten largest US manufacturers rose by $8bn in the first six months of 2006.

would be unthinkable to hear of a joint venture being formed between two competing firms. In others these may be quite natural. For example, supermarkets tend to belong to just one chain whereas a new oil field may well be jointly owned. The growth rate of a sector and the number of competitors will also impact on the degree of rivalry. When a sector is growing fast there can be room for several companies to achieve their strategic ambitions whereas in a slow-growth or static-sales-growth sector, growth in one company will probably mean lower sales in another. This is much more likely to provoke a competitive response.

The relative differences between companies can have an important bearing on this rivalry. The more similar the individual companies are, the stronger the competition is likely to be. By this I mean, in effect, the more that companies will be prepared to remain in business despite short-term losses. This is because if all players are the same then each will think that if only one of the others would close they would be better off while at the same time the competition authorities are most likely to outlaw any deal that saw the companies collaborate in a managed closure programme. By contrast, a situation where no two players were alike would create a better structure because companies would, in effect 'know their place'.

We are starting to venture into areas where competition lawyers earn their fees! I do not want to go there but I will note at this stage that governments and the regulations they impose can have a very important impact on industry structure. This does need to be reflected in the five forces model either as part of the consideration of rivalry or as, in effect, a sixth force representing the regulatory environment on which the other five forces play out.

The bargaining power of suppliers is much simpler to describe. Today, the requirements of business ethics are such that one cannot simply say that bargaining power is demonstrated by who pays for lunch. The idea, however, is explained in this question. Who needs who the most?

Supplier and buyer both need each other but there is usually a gap between the supplier's minimum acceptable selling price[13] and the buyer's highest acceptable purchase price. Supplier power sets where the price will be along this spectrum. In some situations it will bounce between one level and the other. A more long-term relationship will probably result in some form of sharing of the difference between the two prices. The factors that influence the power that a supplier has over a company include things like the number

[13] This will equal their marginal cost if they are not operating at full capacity or their next-worst price if they are currently operating at full capacity.

of potential suppliers, the number of other customers that each supplier could supply, the relative importance of one to the other and the cost of switching from one supplier to another. Big supermarket chains are often cited as having high power over their suppliers because they purchase so much that a supplier may not be able to survive the cancellation of a contract. So this would represent low bargaining power of suppliers to supermarkets.

The bargaining power of buyers is a very similar concept and the same factors come into play. One can then think of the three forces that lie along the horizontal axis of the five forces diagram in a similar way to thinking about the value chain. The day-to-day competitive battles within an industry certainly happen within this domain.

There are, however, still two forces to go. One concerns the threat of substitutes. In particular, at what price will existing substitutes come into play and what potential new substitutes might there be? In my view there is always a substitute because one can always simply say 'No' to a product because it is too expensive. Existing substitutes can set limits on how high prices can rise. New substitutes always represent the potential threat of transforming or even wiping a sector out altogether. It is unrealistic to expect planners to allow for the unknown change that might come about. It is, however, reasonable to expect any plan to reflect what is currently known and so the economics of known substitutes should be considered as part of the analysis of this force.

The final force concerns the threat of new entrants. New entrants are likely if existing players are seen to be earning excessive profits. There can, however, be barriers to entry that can help to keep new entrants out. These barriers may be due to regulations (for example the issue of licences to operate mobile phone networks) or to the industry's requiring difficult technologies or patented processes.

Let us finish this summary of the five forces model with a simple case study. Why are airlines likely to lose money while pharmaceuticals appear to be a sure-fire way of making money?

Well, there are a lot of airlines with similar cost structures and the rivalry among the players is intense. It is very hard for an airline to create a substantial and sustainable performance gap between itself and its competitors. The suppliers of jet fuel charge a take-it-or-leave-it price. The suppliers of planes keep pushing new ones into the market which initially may seem good for the sector but too many planes mean too much capacity and hence an incentive to offer cheap seats. Customers can switch airlines with almost no cost (airline frequent-flyer points and executive clubs are the industry's response to this). Amazingly, however, new airlines are often formed so there is a threat from new entrants as well. Recently, prices have risen owing to additional security costs and the high oil price but this is not the root cause of the industry's problems. This was, in my view, a poor industry to invest in long before 9/11 and the oil price surge.

In the case of pharmaceuticals you can start by asking the question 'How much would you be prepared to pay for something that would save your life or relieve some pain?' I will not bother to give an answer but I guess I have made my point. Now there are many things that will save your life including food. Food, however, is easy to produce. Pharmaceutical drugs are not. This is an industry that is regulated, but because society wants it to succeed, society allows it to do well by, for example, allowing long patents. The availability of patents facilitates strong differentiation between companies and serves to limit rivalry. So regulation is beneficial. Buyers do not exercise too much power because although they are big, the pharmaceutical companies are also big and can stand up to them. Supplier power is not an important issue either. The key to maintaining pharmaceutical profitability is often said to be how long it would take a new company to develop a new drug, gain approval for it and then market it. These represent huge barriers to entry and so the lack of the threat of new entrants completes the case for this being a classic good sector to be in.[14]

Competitive advantage

This is the third technique in my list which was originated by Professor Porter. The idea is that business is about beating the competition and that there are just three generic ways of doing this. These generic strategies are:

- cost leadership;
- differentiation; and
- focus.

[14] There is, I believe, also a degree of myth behind the pharmaceutical story. Yes, it is a good sector and it is true that the big companies are making a lot of money. They are, in my view however, being rewarded for past successes. This does not guarantee future success. Although I have not worked in this industry I often think that it will not feel as cosy inside it as it might look from outside. Unless a continued stream of new drugs is discovered, the huge research cost base could become a millstone. Regulation risk is considerable because it is regulation that is so important to maintaining profitability. Favourable regulation is probably dependent on continued research success.

Professor Porter maintains that companies need to be very clear about the basis of their strategy and that attempts to blend them are doomed to below-average returns compared with the industry overall. He refers to these blends as being 'stuck in the middle'.

Cost leadership is very easy to explain. A firm sets out to achieve the lowest overall costs in the industry. With these cost structures in place the leader can then aim to sell the maximum possible volume using price cuts as a tool to achieve this. If prices are driven down then so be it. The cost leader will, by definition, be the last company to make a loss. The cost leader will be helped by economies of scale which can help reduce manufacturing costs. The more successful the leader is in driving down costs the more it can afford to sell for lower and lower prices. The more it sells, the greater will be its buyer power with its suppliers.

A potential problem with cost leadership is when two or more companies try to achieve it and there is no clear winner. The result can be a price war, with the customer being the only beneficiary.

Differentiation depends on identifying some feature other than price that customers will value highly. If customers are prepared to pay more than this feature costs to deliver, there is a potential for a sustainable advantage. The great thing about differentiation is that there can be many ways to achieve it. An illustration of this can be seen in branded goods. Brands depend on differentiation and we know that there can be more than one winning brand in any market and each will have its own unique features.

The third generic strategy is called focus. This requires that a firm should set out to win in a limited market. Again, winning can be via low cost or differentiation. The simplest illustrations of the focus approach are local shops in a small village or town. They do not have to be as cheap as the supermarket if it is ten miles away. Focus strategies depend on barriers to entry. Location provides an obvious potential barrier. Lack of scale can also work. An opportunity might simply be too small for a national company to bother with.

Companies must understand the basis of their strategy and must stick to it. They cannot, however, afford to ignore the other two approaches that competitors may be using in order to win. So a cost leader must still offer at least an acceptable level of service. A differentiator must still take care with its costs although some luxury brands do suggest that some costs can almost be ignored. A focus strategy must be careful when it tries to grow lest it lose its focus.

What we can learn from the competitive advantage approach is that more than one company can earn above its CoC. For example, there may be one cost leadership winner, two or three differentiation winners and also some small focus winners. Others, however, will lose. If everybody is winning, one or both of two things will probably happen. New entrants will be attracted to the sector and existing players will all try to grow in order to exploit their advantage. As soon as a sector becomes over-supplied the potential returns will fall.

The McKinsey/GE matrix

The McKinsey/GE matrix is a two-dimensional matrix that plots business unit strength against market attractiveness. These two concepts match the Porter frameworks in that business unit strength is another way of expressing how well a unit has done in creating competitive advantage while market attractiveness is a reflection of how the five forces are expected to play out. I have used the two-dimensional matrix a lot and recommend it.[15]

The matrix will look like this:

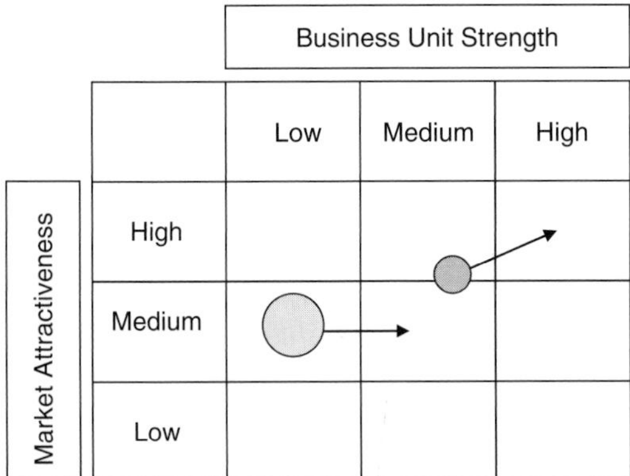

Fig. 4.5 The McKinsey/GE matrix

In the example chart I have shown the positioning of two hypothetical business units. These are shown as circles with the size of the circle being proportional to business unit value. The arrow represents where the unit is

[15] When I first used the technique I was not aware that it was called the McKinsey/GE matrix. I became used to it under the title SACP analysis. SA stood for sector attractiveness while CP stood for competitive position. The technique itself and the 3 × 3 grid was the same. I prefer the title SACP, perhaps just because it is shorter, but will use the more common external name in this book in order to avoid confusion.

expected to get to if the recommended strategy is followed. The larger unit is expecting to improve its relative position within an unchanged sector while the smaller one is claiming that both its own standing within the sector and the sector itself will improve.

Market attractiveness is assessed via the Porter five forces model. This is either done by directly rating each of the five forces or by assessing a checklist of factors that will influence one or more of the forces. A checklist could look like this (with all items marked on a scale between unfavourable and favourable):

- market growth rate;
- number of competitors;
- existing profitability;
- slope of cost curve;
- entry barriers;
- exit barriers;
- buyer power;
- supplier power;
- effect of regulation;
- risk of new entrants; and
- effect of substitutes.

One then processes the initial list via one of two approaches. The mathematical approach is to give each heading a numerical score and a weighting and then calculate a weighted average ranking. The subjective approach is to allow judgement to be made in the light of the analysis. Although intellectually I prefer to use judgement, in a big company it is probably best to use a numerical approach in order to reduce the inevitable arguments which will come about as business units all want to be presented in a favourable light.

Business unit strength is easiest to assess in a business sector where most competition is via price and quality differences between competing companies are small. Strength is then simply a reflection of the unit's position on the industry cost curve. The best unit in the industry has the lowest costs. If, however, quality factors are important as well then these must be included via subjective judgement. A high business unit strength would be awarded where customers perceive high quality but the cost to the company that supplies it is not great. If high quality has high associated costs the unit would rate medium or even low. The difficulty in defining this axis is a key reason why it needs to remain subjective.

The approach is useful as a portfolio screening tool. Business operations positioned on the bottom left must propose strategies that will move them upwards and to the right or else be divested or liquidated. Businesses already in the top right sector must be supported at all costs. This portfolio screening tool is also useful in resource allocation. Competing bids, for example for investment capital, can be shown plotted on the matrix and priority given to those that are more favourably placed. This can allow a strategic view to be added to what can otherwise become simply a numbers battle with the money going to the highest incremental NPV.

The problem with the approach is with practical application. The framework ought to catalyse a quality strategic debate but there is always a potential danger that discussion can degenerate into pointless arguments about the exact positioning of business units on the grid.

Part 4: Words and music

Introduction

We are now ready to see how the numbers fit together. I use the expression 'words and music' to emphasise the relationship which should exist between a strategy and the financial numbers that appear in the accounts. When I read a strategy and then look at the numbers in a long-term plan I expect to see a coherent picture emerging. For example, if the strategy describes a rosy future then the financial numbers should look good. If they don't then something is wrong. The same should be true for a project. If the financial projections for a new project do not line up with the overall financial outlook for the company then, again, the strategy had better have forewarned me that this was to be expected.

At this stage, however, I would not expect readers to know what relationships to expect between projects and overall company performance. We have learned how to analyse projects by using the economic value model and how to calculate indicators such as NPV, IRR and discounted payback. Plans and actual performance, however, tend to be stated in accounting terms. What we need to discover is how the two apparently separate concepts of accountancy and economic value are linked together. I will deal with this question now.

I believe that a good starting point is to demonstrate how a company can be considered to be the sum of a series of projects. We will then see how this approach can allow us to put together plans for businesses. These plans will contain in particular the key financial ratio called ROCE or ROACE[16] which was briefly introduced in the previous building block. We will see how this ratio can provide what I term the 'ROCE bridge' between accounts and value.

We will finish this part by taking a first look at how to estimate the value of a business.

The company as a series of projects

In the previous building block we worked on a case study for a project to set up a scaffolding business.[17] An extract of the AFS for this project follows below:

Scaffolding example: AFS

	2007	2008	2009	2010	2011	2012	2013
Income statement							
Sales revenue		1.7	1.8	1.9	2.0	2.1	
Variable costs		−0.4	−0.4	−0.4	−0.4	−0.4	
Contribution		1.4	1.4	1.5	1.6	1.6	
Fixed costs		−0.2	−0.2	−0.2	−0.2	−0.2	
Amortisation		−0.6	−0.6	−0.6	−0.6	−0.6	
Pre-tax profit		0.6	0.6	0.7	0.8	0.8	
Tax		−0.2	−0.2	−0.2	−0.2	−0.3	
Profit		0.4	0.4	0.5	0.5	0.6	
Balance sheet							
Fixed assets	4	3.4	2.8	2.2	1.6	1.0	
Accounts receivable	0	0.2	0.2	0.2	0.2	0.3	
Inventories	0	0.1	0.1	0.1	0.1	0.1	
Accounts payable	0	−0.2	−0.2	−0.2	−0.3	−0.3	
Working capital	0	0.1	0.1	0.1	0.1	0.1	
Capital employed	4	3.5	2.9	2.3	1.7	1.1	
ROACE		10.2%	13.4%	18.5%	26.8%	42.6%	
Funds flow							
Profit		0.4	0.4	0.5	0.5	0.6	0.0
Amortisation		0.6	0.6	0.6	0.6	0.6	0.0
Working capital		−0.1	0.0	0.0	0.0	0.0	0.1
Capital investment	−4.0	0.0	0.0	0.0	0.0	0.0	1.0
Funds flow	−4.0	0.9	1.0	1.1	1.1	1.2	1.1

[16] Remember that ROCE is the return on capital employed while ROACE is the return on average capital employed. The calculation is profit after tax but before any finance charges as a percentage of capital employed.

[17] At this stage we will ignore the additional factors which were introduced in the individual work assignment and focus just on the numbers that were shown in the main section.

Now remember that this was the financial outlook for a single project. We noted when we first reviewed the ROACE line that there was not a lot which we could do with this number. It started at zero and then rose to well over 40%, but so what?

Now some businesses are, in effect, just a single project.[18] The majority of companies, however, are built from a series of projects. So a more typical situation might be of a scaffolding company that started one new scaffolding rental outlet each year. If each individual project was exactly like the one shown above and if one new project was started each year then eventually the company would reach a steady-state position. What would its accounts look like at this time?

The first step towards answering this question is to change the column titles from the calendar years 2007–2013 to project years 1–7. Next one thinks of the company as reaching steady-state in its seventh year. This is because in year 8, although it would once again be starting a new project, the original project started in year 1 would no longer feature at all.

From year 7 onwards the company would own one project in each year of its project life. This means that it would have a set of accounts which was equal to the sum of the seven project years above. The accounts would therefore look like the table which follows. In this table each dollar number is simply the sum of the numbers in the relevant row of the project spreadsheet. The only complication concerns ROACE. This needs to be worked out rather than simply be obtained by summing the project year ROACE numbers.[19]

Sum of all projects – No growth $m

Income Statement	
Sales Revenue	9.4
Variable Costs	−1.9

[18] The company running the Channel Tunnel which links France and England is an example.

[19] Remember that ROACE is post-tax profit divided by average capital employed. The profit number is easy but obtaining average capital employed requires an additional calculation since at this stage we only have the closing balance sheet and not the opening one. The opening capital employed must be back-calculated given the capital investment, amortisation and working capital change. The formula becomes ROACE = two times profit divided by two times capital employed plus capital investment, amortisation and working capital change. This may well seem strange but it is right as long as cash inflows are always shown as positive numbers with outflows such as capital investment being negative.

Table (*cont.*)

Contribution	7.5
Fixed costs	−1.0
Amortisation	−3.0
Pre-tax profit	3.5
Tax	−1.0
Profit	2.4
Balance sheet	
Fixed assets	15.0
Accounts receivable	1.2
Inventories	0.5
Accounts payable	−1.2
Working capital	0.5
Capital employed	15.5
ROACE	15.6%
Funds flow	
Profit	2.4
Amortisation	3.0
Working capital	0.0
Capital investment	−3.0
Funds flow	2.4

We should note first that for this business which has reached a steady-state situation, the funds flow is equal to the profit. This is exactly what we should expect since we know that funds flow is equal to profit less growth in capital employed and at steady-state, capital employed remains the same.

Consider now the ROACE of 15.6%. When we first introduced this scaffolding example I showed in a footnote how the IRR could be calculated as 18.1% or 14.8% depending on the exact timing of the initial capital investment and the receipt of the residual value. The figure of 18.1% corresponded to the capital investment being incurred at the very end of 2007 and the residual value coming at the start of 2013. The figure of 14.8% was for when the capital spend was in the middle of 2007 and the residual value in the middle of 2013.

This latter IRR figure is the one which I would quote for our steady-state example which shows a total of seven years' worth of cash flows with it taking in effect a full year to 'build' the project and a year to terminate it. So we can see that the IRR of 14.8% is quite close to the ROACE of 15.6%.

If we now 'play' with our assumptions we can investigate the relationship between steady-state ROACE and individual project IRR. For example, a selling price of $1,500[20] gives an IRR of 10.1% and a ROACE of 10.5% while selling for $1,900 gives an IRR of 19.5% and a ROACE of 20.9%. Changing the sales growth rate from 5% to 15% increases IRR to 20.4% and ROACE to 23.4%.

What we observe is that steady-state ROACE is a reasonable first order approximation for IRR. The relationship is not as good for high IRRs as it is for low IRRs but the normal situation is that if ROACE is greater than the CoC then a project has an IRR of above its CoC and so must have a positive NPV.[21]

There are good reasons why this should be the case and these will be explained later in this building block. For the present, however, we can simply note the empirical evidence that steady-state ROACE calculated in the manner above is a reasonable estimate for IRR, particularly if IRR is close to the CoC.

Here, then, is a way of testing for consistency of words and music. If the words describe a good business that is staying about the same size then the ROACE should, over time, be above the CoC.

What would the effect of growth be? Do you think that growth would increase or decrease ROACE compared with my simple steady-state calculation? Suppose the scaffolding company gradually got bigger and each year it invested in a project which was 5% larger than the one before. What do you think would happen to its ROACE?

You might think that because increasing ROACE is good and investing in a positive NPV project is good[22] then growth would increase ROACE. Well, the exact opposite happens. Growth lowers ROACE. This is because the growth that we are referring to is growth in the size of our project and not the growth rate of sales within the project. A bigger project means bigger capital investment. This adds to capital employed which is the denominator of the ROACE calculation. The numerator is profit and this is the profit that is being earned by the smaller projects which were started in earlier years.

If growth is at a constant rate we can model its effect by taking each column in the AFS and dividing it by a growth factor. The project year 1 column is unchanged but a company that is starting a project of this size and that

[20] The base case assumption was an average selling price of $1,700.

[21] I am ignoring special situations where projects are in effect divestments with initial cash inflows followed by subsequent cash outflows.

[22] Growth is good since the individual projects have a positive NPV. Hence growth means that the NPVs that will be earned are always getting bigger.

is growing must have started a smaller project the previous year and even smaller ones in the years before that. We can model this by taking the figures for year two and dividing them all by one plus the growth rate and the year three numbers by one plus the growth rate squared and so on. The adjusted numbers are then added up. We finish up with a new set of numbers as illustrated below which assumes 5% growth:

Sum of all projects – 5% growth $m

Income statement	
Sales revenue	8.1
Variable costs	–1.7
Contribution	6.4
Fixed costs	–0.9
Amortisation	–2.6
Pre-tax profit	3.0
Tax	–0.9
Profit	2.1
Balance sheet	
Fixed assets	13.8
Accounts receivable	1.0
Inventories	0.4
Accounts payable	–1.0
Working capital	0.4
Capital employed	14.2
ROACE	15.0%
Funds flow	
Profit	2.1
Amortisation	2.6
Working capital	0.0
Capital investment	–3.3
Funds flow	1.4

All of the numbers in the income statement[23] are lower than those in the previous table. Why is this?

[23] Note that a careful comparison of the balance sheet will also show that fixed assets are lower in the growing company but that the capital investment is higher. This is a function of the particular profile of capital investment in this example. The investment in the first year is partially offset by the scrap value of the scaffolding in the final year. There is no capital investment in the intervening years. So in the growth case the much lower scrap value coming from the smaller project started several years ago means that overall investment is higher. This situation is not typical.

The methodology is such that the initial year's investment is maintained. If growth is, say, 5% then the previous year the project that was started must have been 5% smaller and so on. So a company that is growing at a steady rate and that implements a project of a given size this year will be smaller overall than a company that implements the same size project but is not growing. Each project that the growing company has invested in will offer the same relative return but they will all have been smaller.

The impact of growth has two important effects. First, ROACE falls a little. In this case it falls to 15.0%.[24] Second, the funds flow is no longer equal to profit. It is now substantially less than profit. This is because growth needs to be funded.

So now we have two more ways to aid our words and music understanding of company performance. A company that is growing will have a small reduction in ROACE and a much larger decrease in the extent to which it can afford to pay out its profit as a dividend.

Here then is a further big advantage of adopting the AFS approach to project evaluation. We can easily see the implications for the accounting performance of the company of implementing projects that are like a particular project that is under consideration. Furthermore, we can see what the impact of growth will be. All that we need to do is add up the lines in our project spreadsheet. I call this approach 'the company as Σ projects' in recognition of the Σ operator from mathematics.[25]

Overheads and sunk costs

The above approach, which treats a company as a series of projects, has, I believe, intuitive appeal but it is missing two features which serve to distort the way that we look at projects. These concern the impact of fixed overheads and sunk costs.

When a project is presented for approval its economic indicators should be calculated by comparing a 'with project' world with a 'without project' world. The NPV is based on incremental cash flows. This means that any overheads which are unaffected by the project will not be included in the cash flow

[24] I should stress again that ROACE is the only number in this table which is not simply calculated by adding up the lines in the project spreadsheet. ROACE is specifically calculated given the accounting data and in particular includes back-calculating what the opening capital employed will be given the change in capital employed inferred by the capital investment, the amortisation and the working capital change.

[25] For the non-mathematical, the Greek letter Σ (pronounced sigma) means 'the sum of'.

projections. This will include, for example, the cost of the chief executive who will, presumably, be running the company irrespective of the particular project. Also excluded from the project NPV calculation will be any sunk costs. Sunk costs are money that has already been spent on the project, for example on the initial design work that was necessary in order to prepare the financial estimates.

So it is unlikely that a company will look as favourable as would be implied by the simple extrapolation from a single project. A better model would treat the company as a series of projects plus overheads and sunk costs. The overheads number would be the sum of all of the costs in a company that were not project costs. The sunk costs would be the project costs incurred on a project prior to its approval.

Suppose that in our scaffolding example with 5% growth there were corporate overheads of $300,000 per annum. This covered the cost of the board of directors, the finance department, etc. Suppose also that the pre-sanction costs on a typical project were $100,000. This covered the cost of the project development team and the specific pre-sanction analysis. Overall then, $400,000 of costs would be excluded in the simple company as the sum of its projects model. A full company model would allow for these. In principle one would allow for all consequent effects including not only the tax relief associated with costs but also working capital impacts. In practice one might simply model the costs and their associated tax relief but not any working capital effects.

The effect of including these assumptions is shown here:

Including overheads & sunk costs $m

Income statement	
Sales revenue	8.1
Variable costs	–1.7
Contribution	6.4
Fixed costs	–1.3
Amortisation	–2.6
Pre-tax profit	2.6
Tax	–0.8
Profit	1.8
Balance sheet	
Fixed assets	13.8
Accounts receivable	1.0
Inventories	0.4

Table (*cont.*)

Accounts payable	−1.0
Working capital	0.4
Capital employed	14.2
ROACE	12.9%
Funds flow	
Profit	1.8
Amortisation	2.6
Working capital	0.0
Capital investment	−3.3
Funds flow	1.1

Capital employed remains unchanged but the overheads and sunk costs serve to lower the overall profit of the company such that ROCE falls by about two percentage points.

This approach of modelling a company as the sum of a series of projects plus central overheads and sunk costs is, in my view, a good way to look at companies that are project based. Not all companies will fit this model, for example a fashion shop is not a series of projects, it is a series of choices about what the public will consider to be fashionable. Many companies, however, are project based. This would include natural resource companies, the auto industry and even film-makers. If a consistent picture of 'words and music' exists it should be possible to see a reasonable relationship between the company's actual results and the results which would be implied by its typical projects given a sensible allowance for growth, overheads and sunk costs. These can serve, in effect, as a reality check on forecast project performance.

The ROCE bridge

We can now turn to the question of why the accounting ratio of ROCE is a first-order approximation for the economic value indicator of IRR. The relationship is not the result of a coincidence. It exists because of the way that accounts are prepared.

We know the accounting relationships are such that funds flow is equal to profit less growth in capital employed. This means that profit is equal to funds flow plus growth in capital employed. Now since return on capital is profit divided by capital employed we therefore know that:

$$\text{Return on Capital Employed} = \frac{\text{Funds Flow} + \text{Growth in Capital Employed}}{\text{Capital Employed}}$$

From a value perspective the IRR earned over a year is equal to the cash paid out plus the growth in value divided by the initial value. Now if capital employed were equal to value this equation would be the same as the accounting equation for return on capital. Now although capital employed is not usually equal to value it is equal to value when an asset is expected to earn exactly its CoC.[26] This is because book value is based on what you spent to buy an asset and the asset is worth exactly what you spent on it if it is earning exactly its CoC.

This illustrates why IRR and ROACE are related. In my view, it is not vital to understand why the relationship holds. What matters is that the existence of the relationship is both understood and distrusted to an almost equal extent.

This may seem a strange statement but it is simply another illustration of the WYMIWYG effect. If companies and analysts did not bother about ROACE then it would be quite a good indicator. The problem is that once people start to target ROACE they will most likely act on the easiest ways to improve the ratio. Most of these destroy value. We will consider an exercise which illustrates this as part of the individual work assignments at the end of the building block.

Valuing a plan

So far although we have talked about the value of companies, we have calculated value mainly in the context of individual projects. We now need to learn how to calculate the economic value of a company. As before, all we need to do is to work out the present value of future after-tax cash flows. The particular difficulty concerns how far into the future one has to make financial projections.

It seems reasonable to make a set of projections for what one might think of as the economic life of a particular asset. A copper mine, for example, would be valued based on the amount of copper ore that was present. What, however, is the economic life of a company? Does one have to make assumptions about what the financial prospects will be many years into the future?

[26] This is true in simple cases where all of the costs of building an asset are included in its book value. In situations where there are material costs spent searching for an opportunity (for example, drilling several oil wells in the expectation of finding just one oil field) the relationship does not work and book value will be lower than economic value even when assets are earning the cost of capital. This is because all of the unsuccessful exploration costs are written off straight away and not carried on the balance sheet as assets. In such cases it is necessary to earn a return on capital of above the cost of capital in order to avoid destroying value.

This approach is recommended by some authors but my view is that one cannot justify the apparent precision which is given by carrying out, say, 15 year valuations. What I recommend is that a plan for, say, five years is prepared and assumptions are then made about how the final-year funds flow will grow (or shrink) into the future. These assumptions are then turned into what is called a terminal value using the perpetuity valuation formula.[27] I will explain more about why I consider this approach to be more appropriate later in this book in the chapter on what sets the share price.

We will illustrate the valuation of a plan through the following example. Suppose that it is almost the end of 2007 and the following LTP has just been agreed for Fence Treatment Inc, a company that manufactures weather-proofing paint for use on garden fences. The company is about to embark on a significant expansion project that will take two years to complete. This will then provide it with sufficient manufacturing capacity to satisfy anticipated demand for at least the next ten years.

Fence Treatment Inc: agreed long-term plan $m

	2008	2009	2010	2011	2012
Sales revenue	22.8	23.8	24.9	26.1	27.2
Variable costs	−6.7	−7.0	−7.0	−7.4	−7.9
Contribution	16.2	16.8	17.9	18.6	19.4
Fixed costs	−5.0	−5.3	−6.9	−7.1	−7.3
Amortisation	−3.5	−3.6	−4.4	−4.4	−4.3
Pre-tax profit	7.7	8.0	6.6	7.1	7.8
Tax	−2.3	−2.4	−2.0	−2.1	−2.3
Net profit	5.4	5.6	4.6	5.0	5.5
Fixed assets	44.0	52.4	49.8	47.5	45.5
Accounts receivable	4.8	5.0	5.2	5.4	5.7
Accounts payable	−1.4	−1.2	−2.5	−2.6	−2.8
Inventories	−1.9	−2.0	−2.3	−2.4	−2.5
Net working capital	4.2	4.2	5.4	5.6	5.9
Capital employed	48.2	56.5	55.2	53.1	51.4
ROACE	12.1%	10.7%	8.3%	9.2%	10.4%
Profit	5.4	5.6	4.6	5.0	5.5
Amortisation	3.5	3.6	4.4	4.4	4.3
Working capital	−1.7	0.1	−1.2	−0.3	−0.3
Capital investment	−9.5	−11.9	−1.8	−2.0	−2.3
Funds flow	−2.4	−2.7	6.0	7.1	7.1

[27] Remember that the perpetuity formula is value = (funds flow x (1 + growth)) ÷ (CoC − growth).

We can now calculate the economic value of this business. This value will be equal to the present value of the plan period cash flows plus the present value of the terminal value. We will calculate the terminal value based on an assumption that the final-year funds flow will remain constant into the indefinite future and using a CoC of 9%. The calculation will be as follows:

Valuation of Fence Treatment Inc

	2008	2009	2010	2011	2012	Terminal value
Funds flow – $m	−2.4	−2.7	6.0	7.1	7.1	79.1
Discount factor	0.958	0.879	0.806	0.740	0.679	0.679
PV Funds flow – $m	−2.3	−2.4	4.8	5.2	4.8	53.7
Cumulative PV – $m	−2.3	−4.7	0.2	5.4	10.2	63.9

Note first that I have used mid-year discount factors in recognition of the fact that cash flows occur on average at the middle of each year while I am aiming to calculate value as at the start of 2008. The biggest contributor to value is the terminal value (TV). This is the final-year funds flow divided by 0.09. Remember, though, that this is the value as at the end of the plan period and so this number must then be discounted to the present.

All valuations are only ever as good as the assumptions on which they are based. One should always test assumptions in order to understand how important they are. Had I, for example, assumed a 2% pa decline for my TV calculation the overall value would have fallen to $53.3m.

One words and music test that I always apply is to compare economic value with accounting value (i.e. capital employed). A business should always be worth at least its book value.[28] As long as the ROCE is close to the CoC this should be the case. If the return is well above the CoC then the business will be worth well above book value. We will see in a later part of this book how we can calculate exactly what relationship to expect between book value and economic value. For the present, however, we can simply observe that words and music appear to be in order as the value is above book value but not by a huge amount. Our 2% decline case would reduce value to a figure that was still above book value.

[28] Accountants require this or they insist that a so-called asset impairment adjustment be made that reduces capital employed to economic value.

Present value and value through time

This plan valuation exercise provides a good opportunity to explain one more important value concept. This concerns the difference between *present* value and the value profile of a business or a project *over time*. Present value is the value of a business today. The value profile is the value a business will have at different points in the future. These are two different but related concepts. The way that they are related is through the combination of annual cash flow and the CoC.

So far we have explained the value calculation as being the sum of future cash flows each times the relevant discount rate. This is the same as saying that the value at the start of a year is equal to the value at the end of the year discounted by one year plus the cash flow during the year also discounted to the start of the year.[29] This is best illustrated by some numbers.

In the Fence Treatment Inc case study the value of the business as at 1 January 2008 is $63.9m. What is the value as at 1 January 2009? Well, first we no longer have to allow for the negative funds flow during 2008 because value is a forward-looking calculation and 2008 is then in the past. Second, the remaining future funds are all one year nearer. So the value at the start of 2009 is all of the remaining future cash flows discounted to this new point.

Actually it is easier to work out value profiles backwards starting with the terminal value. The terminal value is, by definition, the value of cash flows beyond the plan period. The value one year earlier than this will equal the funds flow during that year discounted to the start of the year plus the terminal value discounted for a year.

If we look at the exact numbers, the terminal value of $79.1m which we calculated was as at mid 2012. So in order to convert this to end 2012 we need to divide it by the half-year discount factor of 0.958. So the end plan value is $82.6m. With this as the starting point it is now easy to work out the value profile over time for Fence Treatment Inc. The calculation is shown below. This table also shows the calculation of what I term the value return. This is the sum of value growth plus annual funds flow divided by opening value.[30]

[29] One has to be very careful to allow for the correct timing of cash flows. If we have been assuming mid-year cash flows then the year-end value has to be discounted by one year to get its contribution to opening year value while the annual cash flow is only discounted for half a year.

[30] Once again, one has to be careful about the exact timing of cash flows. The calculation of value return assumes year-end cash flow and the full year value growth. In our case the cash flows are mid-year and so need to be increased in value by half a year's worth of discount factor to get their exact value effect.

Fence Treatment Inc, value profile

Year-end	2007	2008	2009	2010	2011	2012
Value profile	63.9	72.1	81.5	82.5	82.6	82.6
Value growth		8.2	9.3	1.1	0.1	0.0
Funds flow		−2.4	−2.7	6.0	7.1	7.1
Value return		9.00%	9.00%	9.00%	9.00%	9.00%

What we can now see is that although value grows from $63.9m to $82.6m over the five year period, the value return is always 9% which is exactly equal to the CoC.[31] So we finish this section about how the numbers work with what I consider to be a hugely important insight:

In a plan, value growth does not really matter.[32] What matters is present value

Value growth in a plan is simply a function of the extent to which the plan is generating or requiring funds. Value growth is zero when funds flow is exactly equal to the CoC times value. Value growth is –100% when a company sells its assets and returns all the cash to its owners.

So it is possible to have a plan that shows good value growth but that is a bad one because the plan is destroying value. A business that is investing in negative NPV projects will do this. It should stop the projects. The result will be that its present value will rise by an amount equal to the avoided NPV loss.[33]

Value growth matters only after the passage of time. As time passes, new information becomes available. This information may concern actual cash flows or the prospects for what remains of the future. If either or both of these change, then the calculation of value return will become meaningful. If the return is above the CoC then the investment has been good; if the return

[31] I have shown the value return calculation to two significant decimal places in order to make this point.

[32] One cannot say that it does not matter at all because a fast rate of value growth will imply a need for future cash injections which particular investors may not wish to see while a big value decline may imply a greater generation of cash than the investor would have preferred. I experienced this recently when a property fund that I had invested in sold its buildings at a big profit, passed all its money back to its investors and ceased to exist. I was pleased with the high return that I earned but in all honesty would have preferred it if they could have invested the money for me elsewhere. I did not need the cash at the time and so had to find another place to invest. Investors tend, rightly or wrongly, to like continuing to invest with managers who have a track record of success.

[33] Remember the principle of value additivity.

is below the CoC then what we tend to say is that value has been destroyed. What we mean is that present value has been destroyed.

This distinction between value growth over time and value creation or destruction at a point in time is a most important concept. We will return to it in a later part of this book.

Part 5: Individual work assignments

1. Here are some extracts from strategy statements from hypothetical companies. Some are what I would expect to see in a communication of strategy to staff while others are not. Which is which, and why?
   a. Our strategy can be summarised in three words: China, China and China. We will invest in China because it will be the biggest market in the world within a generation and we intend to be part of that.
   b. Our strategy is to earn a ROCE of 15%. It is only by doing this that we can satisfy the needs of our shareholders.
   c. Our strategy is to enhance the already substantial skills of our staff and become the recognised leader in innovation in our fast-changing industry.
   d. Our strategy for 2008 is to grow sales by 10% while holding costs flat in money-of-the-day terms.
   e. Our strategy for 2008 will depend on our ability to find a buyer for our ailing Industrial Products division. If we cannot sell by year-end we will bite the bullet and close it down.
   f. Our strategy remains unchanged from the day our founder set up this great company 50 years ago. We are and we will remain the best company in our business.
2. The management of Fence Treatment Inc has just reviewed its long-term plan and is concerned with the decline in return on capital in the initial years. It has decided that it must target an improvement in ROCE. Several options have been proposed. Classify each of the following as being good or bad for ROACE over 2008–2010 and also good or bad for economic value:
   a. Cancel the major capital investment project scheduled for 2008/2009.
   b. Continue with the capital investment project but require that its size (i.e. the quantity of fence treatment product that it will produce) be reduced by a half.

c. Improve stock control procedures so as to halve the inventory.
d. Cancel the 2008 staff Christmas party.
e. Cancel the 2008 board Christmas lunch in Bermuda.
f. Cancel all training planned for 2008.
g. Invest in a pre-treatment machine costing $1m which will reduce all variable costs by 3%. The investment would be made in 2008 and the full benefit would be gained from 2009 onwards.

3. A company is operating with the simple 4 stage gate process for project development. The project we are dealing with concerns building a new chemical plant. Place the following activities within the appropriate stage:
   a. Placing an order for the reactor vessel.
   b. Negotiating a long-term sale for some of the output to a major purchaser.
   c. Setting up a project development team to prepare and implement detailed plans.
   d. Deciding the design capacity of the plant.
   e. Reviewing competitor plans to avoid overcapacity.
   f. Buying the land on which the plant will be built.
   g. Purchase of feedstock for the plant.
   h. Health and safety checks to ensure the product is not carcinogenic.
4. Return to the AFS which was prepared for the Depot example in the individual work assignments in the previous building block. Use these cash flows as the basis to prepare the plan for a company that builds depots such as this. This company is being started from scratch at the start of year 1. From year 2 onwards it expects to start one new project each year. Each project will be the same as outlined in the Work Assignment. The projects take two years to build and then operate for 25 years. At present you only have the financial projections for the first three years of operation. You should assume that the remaining 22 years generate exactly the same funds flow and that there is no residual value.

   The individual projects are very attractive when viewed on an incremental cost basis; however, the company anticipates incurring the following costs in its head office and project development teams:
   - A head office building will be required. The rental on this will be $5m per year. The rental is payable quarterly at the start of each quarter.
   - Overhead costs of $5m per year will be incurred. All of this cost is paid out during the year.
   - A success bonus will be paid to the project development team each time a new project is approved. This bonus will be $4m.

For ease of reference the project AFS is as follows:

Depot example: AFS $m

	2004	2005	2006	2007	2008	2009
Sales revenue		0.0	0.0	25.0	26.8	28.7
Variable costs		0.0	0.0	–10.0	–10.7	–11.5
Contribution		0.0	0.0	15.0	16.1	17.2
Fixed costs		0.0	0.0	–10.0	–10.2	–10.4
Amortisation		0.0	0.0	–0.6	–0.6	–0.6
Pre-tax profit		0.0	0.0	4.4	5.2	6.2
Tax		0.0	0.0	–1.3	–1.6	–1.8
Profit		0.0	0.0	3.1	3.7	4.3
Balance sheets						
Fixed assets	0.0	10.0	16.0	15.4	14.7	14.1
Accounts receivable	0.0	0.0	0.0	3.1	3.3	3.5
Inventories	0.0	0.0	0.0	2.5	2.7	2.9
Accounts payable	0.0	0.0	0.0	–1.9	–2.1	–2.4
Working capital	0.0	0.0	0.0	3.7	3.8	4.0
Capital employed	0.0	10.0	16.0	19.1	18.6	18.0
ROACE		0.0%	0.0%	17.4%	19.4%	23.6%
Funds flow						
Profit		0.0	0.0	3.1	3.7	4.3
Amortisation		0.0	0.0	0.6	0.6	0.6
Working capital		0.0	0.0	–3.7	–0.1	–0.1
Capital investment		–10.0	–6.0	0.0	0.0	0.0
Funds flow		–10.0	–6.0	0.0	4.2	4.8

You are in charge of the planning activities for this company. Complete the following tasks:

a. Calculate the incremental NPV for the first project that will be put forward for approval. Assume a CoC of 10%.
b. Prepare the financial projections for the first five-year long-term plan. These should be shown in AFS format covering income statements, balance sheets and funds flow. Comment briefly on the different messages which emerge from the project analysis and the overall business plan.
c. Calculate the value of the business as at the date of formation based on the assumptions outlined above.

CHAPTER

5

Building block 5: Risk

Summary

This final element of the financial foundation part of the book concerns the subject of risk. Unlike the previous sections on accounting, economic value, etc. I will assume that readers already know a fair amount about risk.[1] After all, risk is part of life and so we all grow up with it. Risk, however, is something where our own intuition can be very misleading should we need to take decisions on behalf of our companies. Growing up has taught us to cope with risk to ourselves and our close families. We need to learn a new set of skills when it comes to dealing with risk in the context of big publicly owned companies. This building block will introduce this new way of looking at risk. It is called portfolio theory and it provides one of the cornerstones of modern corporate finance.

It is portfolio theory that will allow us to return to the question of how it is that risk must influence the way we choose the appropriate CoC for our valuations. This theory will also help us decide what makes a good assumption to plug into our economic models. The building block, therefore, serves as a crucial integrator of the preceding four.

I must start off by defining what I mean by risk. My dictionary defines risk with words to the effect that it is a nasty event or outcome. This, I believe, is the view of risk that we have grown up with. Unfortunately, in the context of corporate finance, risk means something different. It means what I think would more properly be called uncertainty. I wish corporate finance had not used the word risk as it theorised about what it terms 'risk and reward' and about the 'equity risk premium'. I am, however, stuck with what has gone

[1] In particular I will assume that readers are familiar with concepts such as the odds of something happening and of the probability of something happening. Readers will know that if you list all of the possible outcomes the sum of their individual probabilities will be 100%. Readers should also be able to calculate probabilities of two or more things happening together.

before me. Since this is a book about corporate finance I too have to use the term risk when I really mean uncertainty.[2] The building block is called risk but it is about how we deal with uncertainty.

The building block has five parts. In the first part I will introduce some key techniques and terminologies. The particular focus at this stage will be on what makes a good assumption and the concept of expected values. In the second part I will introduce the portfolio effect. This has some implications which can be hard to grasp but is actually simply an embodiment of the old adage of not putting all your eggs in one basket. In the third section I will introduce the idea of risk monetisation which gives us a means of taking rational decisions in relation to risk. I will then be ready to discuss various ways of categorising risk in the fourth section. Between them these will help to provide checklists which we can use when trying to identify risks before they hit our projects. The final section will contain plenty of questions so that readers can practise what they have learned.

Part 1: Techniques and terminology

What sets market price?

Up to now this book has focused on how to carry out financial calculations given a particular set of assumptions. We have described the idea of presenting particular sensitivities to decision-makers so that they will have a better feel for the range of outcomes that might come about. We have also seen how to turn the approach round and find what particular assumptions will, for example, give a zero NPV.

We have learned that in principle the value of something is given by its NPV, but which NPV? If NPVs are simply a function of what assumptions are made, what assumptions should we make when deciding what something is worth? Take, for example the question of the value of a producing oil well. The most important assumption here is likely to be the oil price, but what

[2] To illustrate the difference between risk and uncertainty you can consider a popular game show that gives money to its lucky contestants. Whatever happens, a contestant will win some money. What makes the show so gripping is the way the exact amount varies between the smallest coin in the realm and a life-changing sum. To the man in the street this show has no risk because a contestant can only win. From the perspective of corporate finance there is uncertainty because the range of winnings is so large. Corporate finance refers to this uncertainty as risk.

price should we use? There is a wide range. Here are ten possible assumptions just for starters!

- the lowest possible number (e.g. lowest price in the previous 20 years);
- a realistic worst case (e.g. lowest annual average in the previous 20 years);
- a slightly pessimistic case;
- the average price over the last 20 years;
- the average price adjusting for inflation;
- a respected consultant's forecast;
- a different but equally respected consultant's forecast;
- the forward market price;
- today's price; and
- your estimate of the most likely price.

If we were to carry out ten valuations using the above assumptions we would gain ten insights but we would still not know what to expect the market value of the oil well to be.

Would it be sensible to assume that market value was set by a pessimistic oil price assumption? Surely the answer must be 'no'. Although one could imagine a buyer wanting to buy an oil field for a price that allowed their company a high chance of profit, why should a seller sell in such a situation? The concept of a market price is such that it requires willing buyers and willing sellers. A fair market price does not allow a buyer an unfair profit because at that price another buyer would offer to buy for a slightly higher price.

We will now investigate what the fair market price should be for a simple situation where possible outcomes and their associated probabilities are known. We will then gradually make the situation more complex until it becomes clear that there is one particular basis for setting assumptions which should allow the fair market price to be established.

Our situation concerns the roll of a dice. If the result is a 1 then the payout is zero. If it is a 2, a 3, a 4 or a 5 then the result is a payout of $2. If the result is a 6 then the payout is a magnificent $4. If all payments are immediate, what would be the fair market price of the right to play this game? The answer, I suggest, is clearly $2. If you pay $2 to play then you have one chance in six of losing $2 but four chances in six of breaking even and one chance in six of winning $2. Is it 'fair' that somebody playing the game on these terms should have a chance of losing money? The answer is 'yes' because they have an exactly equal chance of winning.[3]

[3] It is quite common to hear the argument made that the market price for playing a game such as this just once should be lower than the price for playing the game several times (obviously in the several

But did we choose $2 because it was the most likely payout or because it was the middle of the range between the best and the worst outcomes or because it was the average of all possible outcomes? A price of $2 meets all three of these criteria.

We can change the game and quickly see that the most likely outcome is not what is setting the market price. Suppose the payouts were nil if a 1, a 2 or a 3 were rolled and $4 if the result was 4, 5 or 6. Once again, $2 would be the fair market price but this time it is not the most likely outcome, it is an impossible outcome to achieve on a single roll. It is, however, the middle of the range and also the average outcome.

A further twist will allow us to see whether it is the middle of a range or the average which we should be prepared to pay. Suppose the payout was nil if the outcome was not a 6 and $12 if the outcome was a 6. Again our intuition tells us the answer is a fair value of $2. We simply know to take a sixth of $12. It is the average outcome which sets value, not the most likely or the middle of the range.

Now with the roll of a dice the individual outcomes are equally likely. We can add one final twist to our hypothetical game to see that it is the weighted average outcome that we are using to set value and not simply the average. The weighted average is the sum of the individual outcomes times their probabilities. With a simple roll of a dice the probabilities are all the same and we can just add up the answers and divide by six. To calculate a weighted average, each possible outcome is multiplied by its probability and the weighted average is then the sum of these numbers.

We will now illustrate this effect by changing our dice game to the drawing of lots. Suppose a box contains 600 tokens. The tokens are marked 1, 2, 3, 4, 5 or 6. The payouts are as in our dice-rolling game but instead of having 100 of each number in the box, we now have 80 each of the 1 to 5 numbers and 200 6s. We will now play the first game using the box rather than dice. The payouts are still zero (for a 1), $2 (for 2–5) and $4 (for a 6). The most likely payout[4] is $2 but we know not to take the simple arithmetic average of the payouts because the $4 will have a greater chance of occurring. If the game is

tries example I am referring to the price paid divided by the number of dice that are rolled). This approach is suggested because people understand that it is more likely that the answer will end up close to the average if you have lots of tries. Markets, however, give people the opportunity to invest in lots of risky ventures. You do not have to invest in exactly the same game to spread your bets, you just have to invest in a range of games, each with their own risks. We will return to this when we consider the portfolio effect in the next part.

[4] This payout will happen on average in 320 out of every 600 times the game is played. This simplifies to eight out of every 15 times.

played lots of times we know that we get a payout of $4 one third of the time[5] and a payout of zero, two fifteenths of the time. For the remaining occasions the payout is $2. The fair market value of this game is five fifteenths of $4 plus eight fifteenths of $2 plus two fifteenths of nil. This is $2.40.

Now what happens if you do pay $2.40 to play this final game? The most likely outcome is that you will lose $0.40 and there is a small chance that you will lose the lot. The thing, though, is that you do not mind risking these outcomes because of the one chance in three of winning $1.60. The price is exactly at the margin of what a rational person would be prepared to pay. A rational person would *rather* pay less and, on balance, feel that they were winning but at least they would not feel that, over time, they were losing if this was typical of the decisions that they would take. The rational person would know that if they set their bid to play the game at a level that gave them a profit then they would probably be outbid.

One can think of this price as being an equilibrium price. If there were a market in the right to play this game the equilibrium price is the price at which it would be reasonable to believe that buyers and sellers would balance out. If the price was a little higher then buyers would go away and other people who were about to play the game would rather sell their rights. If the price were lower then sellers would go away and more buyers would arrive.

So we have seen that what sets fair market value is the probability-weighted outcome. Fair market value is the sum of the possible outcomes times their individual probabilities. This probability-weighted outcome has been given a special name. It is called the expected value. Once again, I have to say that I do not like the name that has been chosen but I am stuck with the jargon of my subject. In the context of statistical calculations the expected value is the name for the probability-weighted value.[6] So, fair market value is the expected value, i.e. probability-weighted outcome given the possible outcomes.

There is one minor and one major condition to attach to this rule. The minor condition concerns transaction costs. If for any reason it costs money simply to make a purchase or a sale then this must be factored into the calculation. We will ignore this effect at this time. The major condition concerns an availability of money that people are prepared to risk. Suppose

[5] $200 \div 600 = ⅓$.

[6] I cannot escape the thought that, to the general public, an expected value will mean what you expect to happen and what you expect to happen is the most likely outcome. I understand why statisticians used the term expected value. It is because they think in a particular way, but I do wish that the term was not used! I always worry about a possible misunderstanding by those who are not aware of the definition of the term expected value. It is for this reason that I recommend when using the term expected value it should always be qualified by the expression, i.e. probability-weighted outcome, until it is clear that all are aware of its meaning.

that the sums of money in our game were not measured in dollars but were measured in millions of dollars. Very few individuals would be willing to pay $2.4m to play a game where they would lose at least $400,000 two thirds of the time. Individuals simply cannot afford risks as big as this. The logic that they would do OK over time would not apply if they lost all their money (and more!) on the first throw.

So our expected value rule does depend on the availability of a suitably large pool of risk capital. We will return to this question in the second part of this building block. For the present we will simply assume that decisions are being taken by investors that are financially strong enough to take the implicit downside risks. In this situation it is the expected (i.e. probability-weighted) NPV that sets the fair market value of an asset and that should be used as the decision rule for deciding on investment opportunities.

Probability distributions

We have now learned that we want to establish expected value NPVs. This was easy for simple situations such as the rolling of dice. It is more difficult in most real-life situations. We can, however, gain some useful clues as regards what an expected value will be if we understand a little about probability distributions.

I assume that the concept of a probability distribution is already familiar to readers. It gives a depiction of the range of possible outcomes for an event and of the relative likelihood of different outcomes. One way to depict this information is called a frequency distribution. This plots the range of outcomes on the x axis and the probability of the outcome on the y axis. An example is given below.

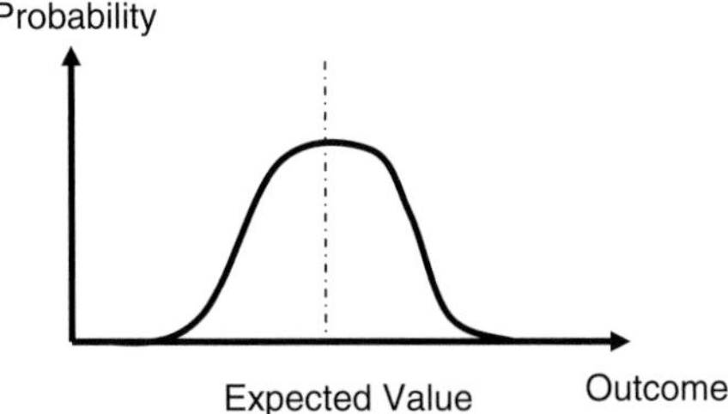

Fig. 5.1 Example of a frequency distribution

The area under the curve is, by definition, equal to 1 because all the possible outcomes have been depicted. The curve is my freehand version of what is called a normal distribution. The distribution of many outcomes fits this particular shape. Of particular importance is the fact that the shape of the curve is symmetrical about its mid-point. This means the expected value of a normal distribution is the same as the mid-point in the full range and also the most likely outcome.[7]

Frequency distributions for actual events will have different shapes depending on what is causing the underlying variability in outcomes. So, for example, the frequency distribution for the throw of a dice will be flat because each of the six possible outcomes is equally likely. Some distributions will cover a wide range while others will be closely bunched around the mid-point. There are also what are called bi-modal distributions where there are two main possibilities, each subject to its own minor uncertainties. The easiest distribution to draw is the so-called triangular distribution. This will comprise two straight lines, one joining the lowest point and the most likely outcome and the second joining the most likely outcome to the highest possible outcome. This may be easy to draw but is very unusual in real-life situations.

In my opinion there is one particular feature of probability distributions that is of the greatest importance to the calculation of economic value. This concerns the question of skews. A distribution is said to be skewed when it is not symmetrical. An example follows. This could well be a plot of the range

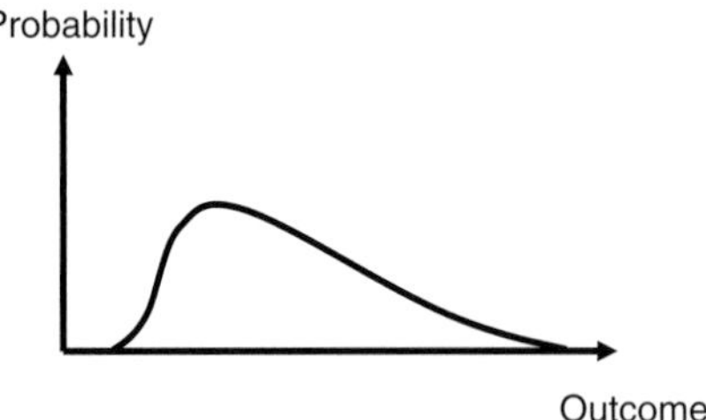

Fig. 5.2 Example of a skewed distribution

of possible capital costs for a major project. Experience tells us that cost overruns are very likely but that there is little chance of the project coming in under budget.[8] With this distribution the most likely outcome and also the mid-point of the range are both lower than the expected value.

[7] Those who have studied statistics should remember the three terms mean, median and mode. The mean is another term for the expected value. The median is the mid-point in the range with half of the possible outcomes above it and half below. The mode is the single most likely outcome.

[8] Unless, of course, the budget has been padded in order to allow for this effect.

Clearly it is a lot easier to estimate expected values when distributions are not skewed. All that is needed is the most likely outcome or the outcome that will be exceeded half the time and you have your expected value. Unfortunately, many of the real life situations that we need to model as we calculate economic value are subject to skews of one type or another and this makes our work that much harder. In fact the difficulty in establishing good expected value assumptions goes to the heart of this book and we will need to work through it all as we seek to build our ability to calculate an expected value NPV.

For the present, and as a good place to start, we will simply note that we should seek to make our valuation assumptions *expected values*. In doing this we should take due account of the shape of a distribution and allow for any anticipated skews. The greater the skew, the greater the difference between the expected value and the most likely value. We should avoid excessive analysis as we seek to estimate expected values and should usually be satisfied just with the application of informed judgement. So, for example, informed judgement for a capital investment estimate would be that the cost would be greater than the most likely outcome because of the upside skew.

Cumulative probability curves

There is a second way that probability distributions can be presented. This is in the form of a cumulative probability distribution. An example is shown below. This is based on the same capital investment estimate. Instead of plotting the probability distribution we plot the chance that the capital cost will be no more than the specified number. This chart will start at the bottom left with no chance of the cost being lower than the minimum possible number. It then rises quite steeply for a while then slowly all the way to the highest possible cost.

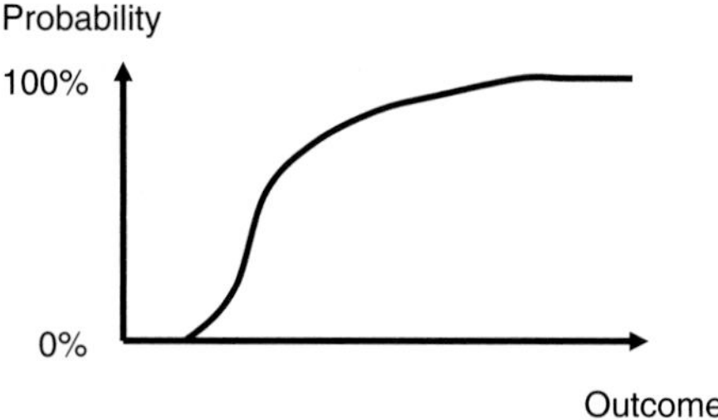

Fig. 5.3 Example of a cumulative probability distribution

The advantage of this presentation style is that it is easy to use it to support statements like 'There is a 90% chance that the cost will be no more than dollars x million.' Or 'There is a fifty-fifty chance of the cost being less than dollars y million'.

The jargon that is used for conveying information such as this is as follows. We say that a P50 number has a 50% probability of being exceeded. We also use terms such as P10, P80, etc. These correspond to the 10% and 80% points on the curve. These points, however, can be ambiguous. Do we mean only a 10% chance of being bigger than the quoted number or a 10% chance of being smaller? The problem is that some people will draw the curve one way (starting at the lowest number and working upwards) while others will draw it the other way (starting high and working down). A third approach involves making the judgement about what is good or bad and plotting that way. Regrettably, there is no agreed convention here so all I can do is warn readers to beware and always make it clear what they mean when they use terms such as P10.

We will return to the concept of P10s and P90s when discussing which sensitivities to show later in this part.

Doing calculations with expected values

Expected values have one hugely useful property. In what are termed linear functions they behave in a linear manner. If you add up the expected value of one outcome and the expected value of a second outcome then the result will be the expected value of the sum of the two outcomes. The same is true for the product of two variables. The expected value of *a* times *b* is equal to the expected value of *a* times the expected value of *b*.

Take for example the roll of a dice. Roll once and the expected value is three and a half. Roll twice and the expected score is seven. That is easy! Now what is the expected value of the product of the number on the first roll and the number on the second roll? This is more complicated. The long way to do the calculation is to calculate all 36 possible answers,[9] add them up (you will get 441), and divide by 36. The answer is 12.25. The simple way is to square 3.5 to get 12.25.

In most financial situations where we are simply adding, subtracting, multiplying and dividing, if we make expected value assumptions then our NPV

[9] The possible outcomes are 1,2,3,4,5,6,2,4,6,8,10,12,3,6,9,12,15,18,4,8,12,16,20,24,5,10,15,20,25,30,6, 12,18,24,30 and 36.

will also be an expected value. This gives us a much simpler way of calculating value. Instead of having to calculate all possible outcomes, if we simply want to know the expected value NPV we only need to do one calculation with all individual assumptions set at their expected value.

We can contrast this way that expected values 'work' with the way other parameters such as the P10 or the P50 work. With these numbers you cannot assume that, for example, a set of P10 assumptions plugged into a financial model will produce a P10 NPV. I can illustrate this through a few examples.

We know, for example, that the chance of getting two 1s when rolling a dice is just one in 36. So if you make two assumptions, each of which have a one in six chance of happening, your result has only a one in 36 chance of happening. As a second example consider our dice rolling and multiplying game developed above. The P50 outcome for this game is ten. This can be established by looking at the full range of possible outcomes.[10] The square root of ten is 3.16 but 3.16 is not the P50 assumption for a single dice.

What this means is that if we prepare our financial evaluations with expected value assumptions our calculated NPV will also be an expected value. If we use any other way of setting assumptions we will not be able to say for sure what the statistical meaning of the result is. So this serves as a big reason to try to use assumptions that are expected values. This is not, however, a 'knockout blow' in favour of expected value assumptions for various reasons including the practical difficulty of establishing what a correct expected value is.

Decision trees

The previous few sections have focussed on dealing with variables where outcomes will typically fall within a range. These techniques are ideal for dealing with things like the uncertainty associated with cost estimates or selling prices/volumes. Another type of risk concerns what can be termed all-or-nothing events; for example, you win an auction or you don't. These are best dealt with via what are called decision trees. A decision tree will have one or more nodes and at each node there is the potential to follow more than one path into the future. A very simple decision tree concerning a sealed bid property action follows.

[10] There are 17 ways of getting a number lower than ten and 17 ways of being higher. Ten is the score in just two of the 36 possible cases.

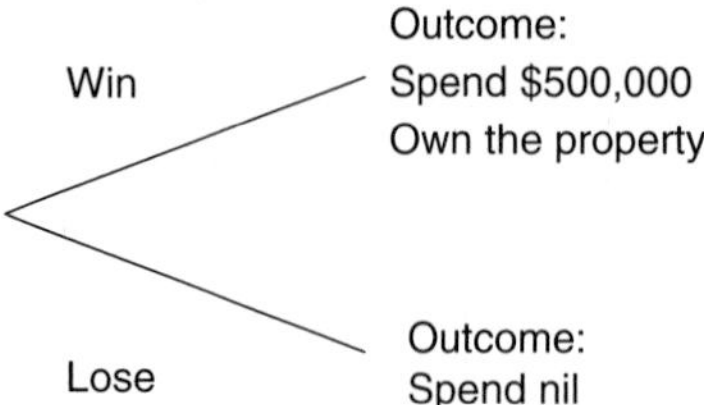

Fig. 5.4 Example of a simple decision tree

A single decision node is hardly worth drawing but multiple decisions can justify the effort. Let us complicate the auction situation. Suppose that we want to decide whether it is worth spending $50,000 on initial design work prior to attending the sealed-bid auction of a unique plot of land with great potential for redevelopment. We have decided that we will submit a bid of $500,000 and with this bid we consider that we have an evens chance of being the winning bidder. If we buy the land we will first have to apply for permission to redevelop. We think there is an 80% chance that this will be forthcoming. If we fail to gain permission we anticipate being able to sell the plot for $400,000. Having gained permission, we estimate that we will need to spend a further $500,000 to renovate the buildings. After that we anticipate being able to sell the redeveloped site for $1.2m. For the purposes of simplicity we will assume that all of the financial numbers are already stated in present value terms. Given the above assumptions, what is the NPV of our proposed strategy?

The following chart shows the decision tree for this situation. The first node covers the auction and the second the granting of planning permission.

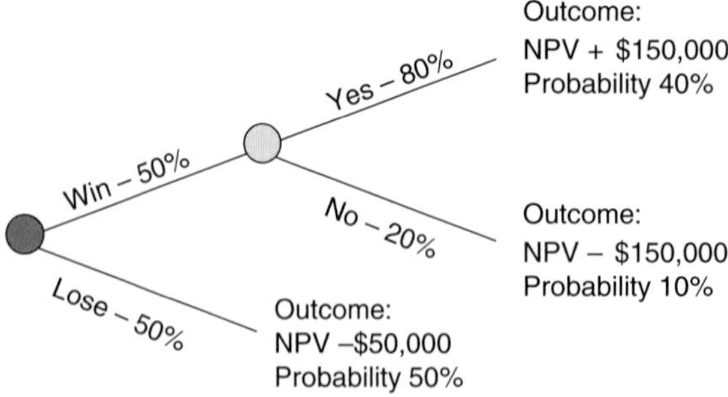

Fig. 5.5 Property development decision tree

The way to calculate the value given a decision tree is first to value each of the individual outcomes. Next we must calculate the probability of each outcome occurring. To do this one multiplies across. So we are successful in our venture in 80% of the times we win the auction. Since we only win the auction 50% of the time we are successful just 40% of the time. Success brings a value gain of $150,000. 40% of this is $60,000. Winning the auction but not getting permission happens just 10% of the time and has an associated value loss of $150,000. 10% of this is minus $15,000. Failing to win the property in the sealed bid auction results in a value loss of $50,000 owing to our initial design work. This happens 50% of the time so the contribution to overall expected value is a value loss of $25,000. Overall, our strategy has a value of just $20,000.

In this case we can also use our model to investigate changes in the assumptions. Suppose that we decided that the initial design work could be delayed until after we gained permission to develop. What would this do to value? The NPV would now be 50% of zero plus 10% of minus $100,000 plus 40% of $150,000. This is $50,000. So now we know that the impact on value of doing the initial design before we know for sure that it is needed is $30,000.

Success values

A related concept to decision trees is the idea of success values. A success value is the value assuming that a successful outcome is achieved. It is easiest to explain this through a simple example.

I swim a lot and I keep detailed records of how often I swim and how far I manage each time. These records show that in 2005 I covered a total distance of 572.5 km whereas in 2006 I only did 546.0 km. How should I explain the approximately 5% decline in distance covered? Was age finally taking its toll? I suggest that to think about my swimming it would be best to distinguish between days when I did swim (we can call this success) and the days when I did not (failure). A check of the records shows that in 2005 I swam 285 times with an average distance per swim of 2,009 m while in 2006 I only swam 263 times but each swim averaged 2,076 m. This gives a much more informative picture. The reduction in overall distance was due to a cut in the number of times that I swam.

The idea of a success value can be very useful when dealing with situations where there is a sharp distinction between success and failure. It is not simply a question of building a better model of what is going on. Some parts of an organisation need to plan for a successful outcome while other parts need to know what will happen after allowing for the failures. In my swimming example, I must clearly plan for individual swimming sets that are about 2 km long. If, however, I am seeking sponsorship per km swum in a year I must allow for all those days when I don't even start.

The business analogy might be with a property development company. Suppose a company had 50 separate property development teams each looking at opportunities like the one we developed above. Each team is invited to submit its budget to the corporate head office. The likelihood is that each team will submit a budget based on success because it will want to reserve the necessary capital should its sealed bid be successful and should planning permission be granted. So 50 plans will come to head office showing a total initial design spend of $2.5m, a total property purchase spend of $25m and a redevelopment budget also of $25m. The sales estimate will be a wonderful $60m. This is clearly unrealistic. Each team is right to be thinking about the consequences of success but at the corporate level it is appropriate to allow for the impact of failure. The corporate budget needs to be for initial design of $2.5m, land purchase of $12.5m, land sales of $2m, redevelopment costs of $10m and property sales of $24m.[11]

The key thing to be aware of when dealing with success values is that different teams within an organisation will need to deal with different sets of assumptions. Some will need to deal with data that are based on the presumption of success. The higher up the organisational pyramid you look, however, the more important it will be to allow for both success and failure. This applies to valuations as well as to simple business planning and target setting.

Making appropriate assumptions

Now that we have a better understanding of how risk works we can return to the question of what makes a good assumption for the purposes of economic evaluation. It should be clear that the best basis for assumptions is that they be expected values. The advantage of this would be that the resultant NPV would also be an expected value and so would be the technically correct basis for assessing whether or not the project created value for shareholders. The calculated NPV would also be suitable for direct comparison with other expected value NPVs from competing projects if capital investment was being rationed.

One does, however, need to be aware of the danger of believing too much in the quality of your assumptions. Expected values are not easy to estimate. We know in principle what is needed, but the evidence is that people find it very hard to produce good quality estimates. With one individual estimate it is hard to prove that a particular assumption was wrong unless the

[11] The overall gain is just $1m which is the same as 50 times our individual project NPV of $20,000.

assumption was accompanied by a maximum range and the actual outcome was outside the range. One can only judge the overall quality of a considerable number of estimates because it is only then that one can expect the result to be close to the forecast.[12]

An alternative to adopting expected value assumptions is to go for most-likely assumptions. This can have the advantage that each assumption will appear reasonable and will require less work to assess. Decision-makers tend to prefer this approach because they can apply their experiences and decide if they believe that the assumptions can come about. The problem with using most-likely assumptions is that one cannot give a particular statistical meaning to the calculated NPV. We know that expected value assumptions should produce an expected value NPV which in turn is the appropriate basis for decision-taking. We have no such rules for most-likely assumptions. One does not even know for sure if a most likely set of assumptions will produce a high or a low estimate of NPV although my personal bias is that most-likely estimates are generally too optimistic.[13]

We will learn later in this book that there is a technique which can help us to understand the result of our assumptions better. The technique is called Sources of Value and it does give some ability to calibrate assumptions for optimism or pessimism.

For the present, however, we must concentrate on what practical steps can be taken to improve decision-making quality without invoking a new and more sophisticated approach to understanding economic forces. With this in mind I will suggest three particular things which can help improve the quality of assumptions:

1. The Plan, Do, Measure, Learn approach that was set out in the Planning and Control building block can allow us to learn from our experiences. If one monitors the quality of estimates it is possible to learn lessons and, hopefully, improve the quality of future assumptions. One should not expect all assumptions to turn out 'right'. One should, however, expect actual outcomes to be reasonable in the light of what was estimated. Lessons can be learned not just about expected values but also about the ranges that are associated with key variables. We will return to the question of ranges in the next section which deals with sensitivities. When looking for lessons it

[12] I have always assumed that this is the reason why statisticians say that the value is expected. It is what you expect to see on average when you do something lots of times.

[13] I make this assertion because the effect of skews is so much more often against a company than for it. Also, there are so many more big impact but low-probability downside events than there are upside events.

usually pays to look deeply into the underlying causes of deviations from anticipated outcomes. If one understands the root causes rather than the superficial explanations the lessons can be all the more powerful. It can also be helpful to split assumptions into those which are uncontrollable and those which are mainly controllable. There can be different lessons to learn. It is not unusual, for example, for people to overestimate what they can achieve themselves while still being pessimistic about uncontrollable variables.

2. It is always worthwhile to keep a register of assumptions. A register is in effect a simple list of what the assumptions are (i.e. the actual number and a comment about whether it is supposed to be a most likely outcome or an expected value or whatever); when the assumptions were made; and who accepts responsibility for them. This register can then be reviewed with the manager with overall responsibility for the project to ensure that they are content. By noting the date of assumptions it is also easy to flag any assumptions that may have become out-of-date.
3. Finally, beware of always being conservative or always being optimistic. A small degree of conservatism on one assumption probably does not matter but if it is repeated many times the analysis can finish up showing a highly unlikely outcome. The danger of this is that if an investment is portrayed in an unrealistic light the wrong decisions may be taken. A well-meaning attempt to be conservative may mean that a good investment is turned down. As an illustration of how conservative estimates can be compounded, consider the roll of a dice. The score can be 1, 2, 3, 4, 5 or 6. The expected value is 3½. A conservative approach would be to assume that each score was 3. This could also be called 'realistic' because at least 3 is a possible outcome from a single roll. Suppose somebody offered to pay 12 for the score on the roll of four dice. How conservative are they being? Well, although on a single throw there is a 50% chance of a score of 3 or less, the chances of 12 or less from four dice is only about one in three.[14] A bid of 12 to play a game with an expected value prize of 14 is probably so low that you would be sure to lose.

Sensitivities

I define a sensitivity as a calculation to show the impact on a given case of changing one or more specific assumptions. Appropriate use of sensitivities

[14] There are 1,296 different ways that four dice can land (6 x 6 x 6 x 6 = 1,296). Only 435 of these result in a score of 12 or less.

can provide another good way to cope with the uncertainty that surrounds the assumptions which have to be made as part of any investment evaluation.

The assumptions will fuel an economic model and allow the calculation of a set of economic indicators[15] for what I typically call a base case. The sensitivities can then provide answers to the vital 'what if?' questions which are almost bound to follow.

The danger with sensitivities is of information overload. In a major evaluation there may well be hundreds of important assumptions. So a single base case and its four economic indicators can be swamped by sensitivity data.

An initial decision about sensitivities concerns how they should be reported. At one extreme one could present a fully worked set of financials for each sensitivity. My view is that this would be overkill and that this information should remain within our computer spreadsheets for inspection only if requested by senior managers. The real choice is between reporting the impact on all four economic indicators or just one. If just one is chosen that should be either NPV or IRR. Senior decision-makers are likely to decide what they want to be shown. If asked, I would recommend use of NPV. This is because of the way that NPVs align with shareholder value and also because they can be added up. IRRs may be preferred because of the way that they provide an automatic scaling for size.

The benefit of NPVs over IRRs as the means of conveying sensitivity data is not great but it can be illustrated via an example based on the scaffolding case study. Imagine we were presenting the data for a sensitivity on the scrap value of the scaffolding at the end of the project. In the base case the assumed value was \$1m. If this is reduced to zero then NPV falls by \$0.36m. If the scrap value is increased to \$2m then not surprisingly the value rises by \$0.36m. So a ±\$1m sensitivity on scrap value would be reported as ±\$0.36m of NPV. The effect on IRR is not, however, symmetrical. The reduction in scrap value reduces IRR by 2.6% points while the increase adds only 2.1% points. The simple ± approach cannot be used unless one sacrifices some accuracy and quotes a figure like ±2.3% points.

I will adopt my preferred approach of presenting sensitivity data as the impact on NPV for the remainder of this book.

Having decided how to present the data we must now decide on what sensitivities to show. My view is that it is the responsibility of the analyst who

[15] Remember that in the first building block I suggested four economic indicators for a project. These were NPV, IRR, discounted payback and an efficiency measure such as NPV per unit of capital investment.

prepares a case to report the relevant sensitivities to the project sponsor. The sponsor then assumes responsibility for further reporting these up the management chain to those who are to approve the project. The analyst therefore has a key role. They should carry out a lot of sensitivity analysis and select just the key results for presentation.

Sensitivity analysis can be greatly improved if some standardised approaches are adopted. Individual companies will develop their own conventions in relation to what sensitivities are required to be shown. My recommendations are that three types of sensitivity should be computed. I give these sensitivities the imaginative labels of Type 1, Type 2 and Type 3! This may sound boring but a deliberately codified approach to cutting through what can be a plethora of data can be a great help.

Type 1 sensitivities show the impact of a change in a single variable or perhaps the impact of a change in variables that are obviously related. A choice needs to be made as regards what change to illustrate. One could either adopt a fixed percentage such as ±10% or changes to an agreed level of statistical confidence. For example, one could show changes to the P10/P90 range for a particular variable. I strongly recommend this latter approach. The ±10% approach may be easy to do but it leaves the decision-maker to make the vital judgement as to how likely the specified change is. For some variables a 10% change is pretty large while for others it is very small.[16] I suggest the P10/P90 range because this is a fairly wide range but it does not take us to extreme outcomes. What we can say about the P10/P90 range is that the result should be within this range 80% of the time.

Type 2 sensitivities are specifically designed to illustrate what change in a single variable (or obvious combination of variables) would result in a zero NPV. These are often reported as being break-even assumptions. The reference is, however, to economic value break-even and not accounting profit break-even. An accounting break-even is a much worse result because accounting does not automatically include the time value of money.

Type 3 sensitivities are the way to convey any other relevant sensitivity data. By giving them a specific title of Type 3 we can differentiate from the other two types. The sort of thing that is covered by a Type 3 sensitivity would be the result of a failure in a case where the base case assumed success. So, for example, in the property development case described above a base case

[16] For example, in the 12 months prior to writing this footnote the highest oil price has been about 50% above the lowest oil price. For gold, however, the highest price has only been about 23% higher than the lowest. So showing a ±10% sensitivity for both gold and oil would potentially understate the relative impact on value of the oil price uncertainty by a factor of about 2.

may well assume success in both the initial sealed bid auction and in the granting of the necessary permission to redevelop. If this were done then two Type 3 sensitivities could be reported. One would show what the loss was if the sealed bid was lost. The second would show the impact of failure to gain redevelopment permission and the sale of the property at a loss.

These sensitivities can all be shown on a single chart as illustrated in the scaffolding project sensitivity chart which follows. This is based on the scaffolding project example from earlier in this book. The data refer to the initial exercise where we considered a single project expected to operate for just five years with the scaffolding sold for scrap at the end of this period. We had calculated the NPV to be $0.6m but what were the main sensitivities? The following chart shows how these can be presented.

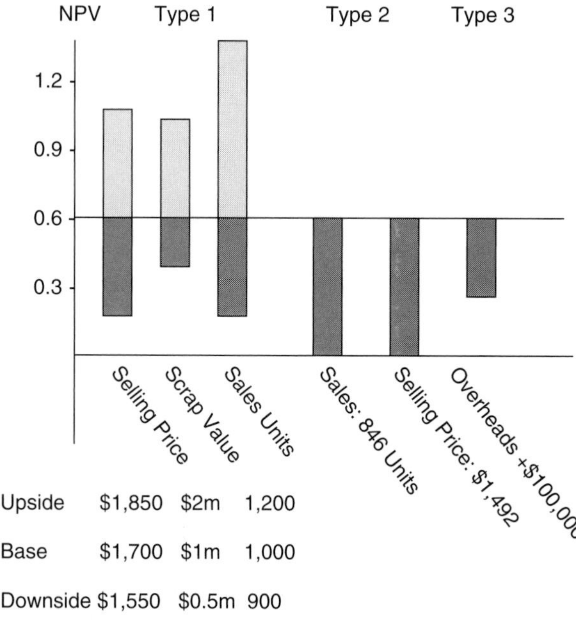

Fig. 5.6 Sensitivities: scaffolding project

The horizontal line across the chart represents the base case NPV of $0.6m. There are three Type 1 sensitivities. Each of these is shown to the P10/P90 probability range. The numbers for each are listed on the chart. In the case of the selling price the base case assumption was $1,700. The judgement of the project sponsor is that the P10/P90 range is symmetrical around this number with the range being ±$150. The impact on NPV is shown as the top of the light-coloured block and the bottom of the dark block. The second Type 1 sensitivity concerned the scrap value of the scaffolding. In this case the range was not symmetrical as the low estimate was \$0.5m while the upside sensitivity was \$2m. The chart shows that the most important sensitivity concerns the sales volume. Once again, there was more upside than downside. None of the individual Type 1 sensitivities was sufficient to force the NPV below zero.

Two zero NPV cases are shown. These were for sales of 846 units in the first year or a selling price of \$1,492. In each case all other assumptions are as per the base case.

A single Type 3 sensitivity is shown. This is for a \$100,000 increase in overheads. This could, for example, represent a calculation of the benefit on the project of not having to pay any rental for the land. The fact that this is not shown as a Type 1 sensitivity suggests that special attention is to be paid to this sensitivity. It is clearly not just a usual degree of uncertainty that surrounds the overheads or else it would be shown as Type 1.

Part 2: Portfolio effects

Spreading your bets

Now we must turn to what I consider to be the almost magical way that financial uncertainty can be made to disappear.[17] In the realm of finance the effect is referred to as portfolio diversification. Once again this is something that I believe is best illustrated via a simple example.

We know that if you toss a coin once the result can be heads or tails. Suppose that heads resulted in a payout of \$1 while tails gave nothing. A single throw will pay out either \$1 or \$0. The range in relation to the average outcome is very great. Now consider two throws each paying out half the

[17] As a rational person, I do not believe in magic. I do, however, believe that it is possible to exploit an individual's perceptions to make them think something 'must' be magic because the outcome appears to defy rational explanation. The usual cause is that there is something the individual is not aware of or some perception of how things work that does not apply in this instance. In the case of financial uncertainty what people do not perceive is the vast pool of money that is available to take risk and the willingness of financial investors to offset a win on one investment against a loss on another. This works in the case of money but not in the case of serious accidents because people are not prepared to tolerate these at all.

amount. We know that three different scores are possible and that there are four possible ways that the tosses can turn out. We should also know that half the time we will get $0.50. So the range remains the same but now we have a good chance of a result in the middle. If there are ten tosses each for one tenth of the prize there are 1,024 different combinations of heads and tails and 11 possible scores. The full range of outcomes remains zero to one but now each extreme only has less than a one-in-a-thousand chance of coming about. The exact mid point comes up 252 times while the middle of the range ($0.40–$0.60) comes up 672 times.

What we have seen in this example is that spreading your bets does not ensure that you will achieve exactly the mid-point but it does more or less ensure that you will avoid the extremes. Put another way, the range around the mid-point within which it is reasonable to assume an answer will lie will gradually decline as one increases the number of times a risk is taken.

Statisticians define a term called standard deviation to represent the variability of a set of data. The smaller the standard deviation, the lower the variability. I do not propose to prove it, but the standard deviation will fall with the square root of the number of items considered. This means that by taking a tenth of ten coin tosses one can reduce the variability by an amount equal to the square root of 10.[18] Spread your bets across 100 coin tosses and variability is down by a factor of 10. A million small bets gives a thousand-fold reduction. This is the sort of level where we can say that risk has been effectively removed.

Now one might think that there are few games which are played a million times over and which can benefit from the portfolio effect and create the one-thousand-fold reduction in variability that I have just described. This would be a misguided thought. Life is absolutely full of uncertainties and one does not have to play the same game in order to spread risks. You could, for example, mix the tossing of a coin with the rolling of a dice. The way that chance works is such that it does not matter whether or not the games are the same, you just need to play lots of games-of-chance to spread your bets.

Readers might think that they do not play many games-of-chance. A game of chance does not have to involve obvious risks like the toss of a coin. Anything that is subject to financial uncertainty is, as far as I am concerned, a game-of-chance. Investing in a range of companies provides a great way of allowing individuals to spread their bets. Each company will be taking lots of small risks each day and a shareholder can gain exposure to lots of

[18] The square root of ten is about 3.16.

companies by buying a few shares in each or by investing in a fund that owns many different shares.

Now before we get too excited and think that risk can be defeated through the portfolio effect there are three points that must be considered. These concern correlations, ability to take risk and transaction costs. We will deal with each of these in the following sections.

The effect of correlations

A correlation exists when one variable is related to another. In the coin-tossing example, suppose that instead of having a million tosses with the resultant thousand-fold reduction in volatility, there were a million separate games each with a payout of 1 for heads and zero for tails but that there was just one coin-tossing shown in a grand televised event. If heads came up there everybody playing a game would win while tails would mean that everybody lost. All of the games are exactly correlated and we would get no risk reduction if we spread our bets.

So we have identified an important condition to the way that the portfolio effect works. Risks can be reduced as long as they are not correlated. The stronger the correlation between outcomes the lower will be the portfolio effect.

What can cause a correlation? In our coin toss TV extravaganza we have an obvious cause of the link. Other links can be caused by the weather.[19] In the world of commerce there are some more subtle links. The world economy tends to suffer from cycles. When the economy is booming most companies will do well. When it is in recession, most companies suffer a decline in profits. This means that the results of companies will tend to be correlated. There will be a few exceptions such as debt collectors who will have more business during a recession but there will be a general relationship for the majority of companies. If this is the case then one would expect that spreading bets across companies would not remove all of the variability. If companies were totally independent of each other we would expect to see variability more or less disappear if we spread our bets across many companies.

We can put this hypothesis to the test. There is a vast array of data on the performance of company shares. A key factor for a share is the return that it gives over a year. Readers should recall that the return is equal to the dividend

[19] On a hot day sales of both sun-screen products and ice cream will do well. On a freezing cold day it could be ski wear and warm drinks that sell better.

plus the growth in share price expressed as a percentage of the opening share price. Over the period 1926–2003 the average annual return on the US stock market was about 12%.[20] The standard deviation of this return was 20.4%.[21] If the market overall gave a return of 12% then the average return on each individual share must also have been 12%. The same is not true for the standard deviation of the returns. Individual companies were on average about twice as volatile.

The following chart illustrates how holding an ever broader portfolio of shares can reduce the risks inherent in owning shares. The chart is illustrative rather than absolutely accurate. The exact shape will depend on which stocks are chosen to make up the portfolio and also on the period under consideration. What matters is not the exact numbers but rather the general picture.

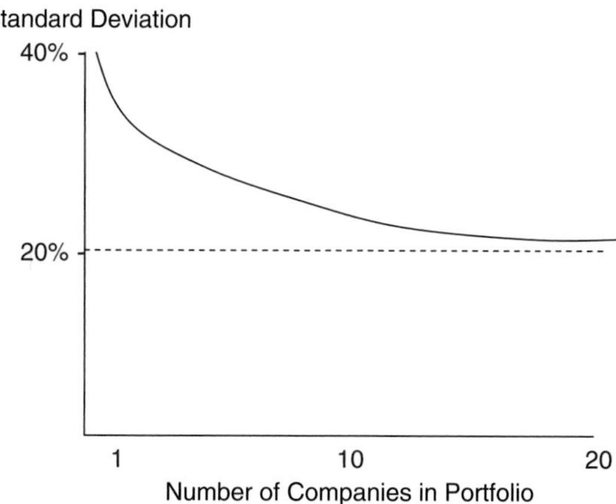

Fig. 5.7 How diversification reduces volatility

The message from the chart is that holding a range of shares allows investors to reduce but not to eliminate risk. If the returns on shares were uncorrelated then holding a wide portfolio would have allowed risk to be reduced to a much greater extent. In the limit, uncorrelated shares could have been effectively

[20] It was 12.4% to be exact. Source Ibbotson Associates: *Stocks, Bonds, Bills and Inflation Annual Yearbook*. This yearbook is a good read for anybody with a deep interest in this subject. Even reading an old edition will teach you a lot.

[21] The standard deviation was 20.4% not 20.4% of 12.4%. The variability of returns on shares is considerable and, as the financial health warnings say, the value of a share may fall as well as rise. Roughly speaking, there was one year with a negative return for each two years with a positive one.

risk free. This does not happen because of the way that shares tend to move together and this in turn is caused by the effect of the economic cycle.

The ability to take risk

The benefit of portfolio diversification is there because people are able to take a long-term view. If, however, an individual loss could be so damaging as to stop you having the money to make subsequent investments you would not then be able to benefit from the portfolio effect. The portfolio effect is only available to investors who can afford to stay in the game long enough to see the numbers gradually trend towards the expected value outcome.

Some risks can be so serious that they obviously threaten the financial viability of the company that is exposed to them. Companies that are subject to risks like this quite clearly cannot afford to take a long-term view. If they get hit they are out of business. In the jargon of corporate finance we would call this 'financial distress'. Companies that are financially stretched start to suffer long before they are in financial distress. They will start to do things like missing good investment opportunities or delaying vital maintenance of equipment. If a company becomes even close to financial distress owing to risks it will feel a financial penalty. This penalty will be such that they should only take the risk if they think they will get a particularly good reward.

The financial markets are such that plenty of money can be made available for good investments. There will be so much competition for good investments that these will normally be taken up by investors who are strong enough to cope with the inherent risks. This market-based competition will not normally allow investors to gain an extra reward for taking risks that bigger players can diversify away. There is a saying 'If you can't stand the heat then get out of the kitchen'. Well, in my view, this definitely applies to financial risks.

In effect, the portfolio effect only works to reduce risks that are relatively small in relation to a company or an investor. If a risk is large in relation to the company or investor that is taking it then they will not be able to assume that the portfolio effect will reduce its impact. They would be forced either to take steps (such as getting insurance) to protect against the risk or to avoid taking the risk altogether. The term 'risk capacity' is sometimes used to describe the ability of an investor to cope with the risks inherent in their portfolio. Wise investors only invest where they have sufficient risk capacity or where they consider the potential reward to be so big as to justify an extraordinary risk. One of the key purposes of sensitivity analysis is to confirm that a project under consideration does not go beyond the risk capacity of the firm.

As an example of this risk capacity effect consider two relatively small businesses each with an annual turnover of $10m. One of these businesses sells to about a thousand different customers while another sells just to one. The customers are all of about the same financial strength, namely a rating of B+ on the Standard & Poor's scale.[22] The first business could probably[23] afford to plan on the basis of a statistical allowance for losses caused by customers defaulting on their payments. The allowance would be informed by several factors, starting with the one-year-average default rate for such companies. As explained in the footnote this is about 3%. Two other key elements of the calculation would be the average loss if a customer did go into default and the average amount of money that is owed to the company at any time. Overall, a relatively modest allowance for what are called bad debts would be required.

Contrast this situation with the single-customer company. There would be little point in making a token allowance for bad debts. This company faces an all-or-nothing situation as it would be wiped out if its customer went into default even if the customer was able, eventually, to pay all of its debts. This is because the company would have lost its one and only customer.

So should a company allow itself to have just a single customer? Well, there is an expression 'beggars cannot be choosers'. If the company had no choice then it might have to accept the situation. There are many small companies that depend, substantially, on just a single major customer for their continued survival. These companies are just much riskier than other companies with broad customer bases. As long as their investors are aware of the risk and consider the potential reward to be good enough, there need be no problem. This is an issue that tends to face small companies and is one of the reasons why they tend to be riskier than large ones.

The effect of transaction costs

The third barrier that limits the benefits of portfolio diversification is that of transaction costs. Transaction costs are the costs involved in sharing risks.

[22] The scale is explained in part 1 of Building Block 2. The B+ rating would be at the upper end of the range that S&P describe as: 'More vulnerable to adverse business, financial and economic conditions but currently has the capacity to meet financial commitments'. The average default rate for such companies over a one year period is about 3% compared with just 0.2% for companies at the bottom of the so-called investment grade credit rating.

[23] I can only say 'probably' because if all of the customers operate in the same line of business they might all get into financial difficulty at the same time. This is an illustration of the potential danger of correlations.

In the coin-tossing example I described how taking a one-millionth share of a million coin tosses would reduce risk by a factor of 1,000. Can you imagine the job of collecting your winnings! The risk reduction would not be worth the inevitable transaction costs.

The more that transaction costs can be driven down, the greater the extent to which investors can benefit from the portfolio diversification effect. Things like shares have quite low costs associated with buying and selling or receiving dividends. By contrast, some major insurance claims create huge associated legal bills. Every dollar of legal expense serves to reduce the overall benefit that the portfolio effect could otherwise have brought.

Overall, the effects of correlations, risk capacity and transaction costs are such as to reduce but not eliminate the potential benefits of the portfolio effect. For individuals, the potential benefit is very significantly reduced because risk capacity is so much lower. Large companies, however, can benefit a lot because they pool together so many risks and they have greater financial strength. At the top of the tree of those that benefit from the portfolio effect are investors who invest in shares in large companies. This fact that individuals will benefit from portfolio diversification to a much lower extent than companies is, in my view, likely to be the main driving force behind the problem that risk decisions within the corporate environment are not intuitive.

The risk/reward trade off

The capital asset pricing model was introduced earlier in this book. At the time we had to leave the question of exactly how risk was defined to a later stage. We did, though, learn about the idea of risk being characterised by the term β.[24] We are now ready to learn what β should represent.

We have previously simply referred to risk and asserted that taking extra risk needed to be compensated for by the prospect of additional reward. We had not defined risk and the natural assumption would have been that risk meant uncertainty. The greater the uncertainty, the greater the required return, one might have thought. Well, this would have been wrong.

Our chart of how diversification reduces volatility has shown how easy it is to reduce some of the volatility inherent in owning a share. All an investor has to do is hold a portfolio of shares and something like half of the volatility is removed thanks to portfolio diversification. This is not magic, it is just the way life works. It is so easy to achieve this benefit that it surely cannot be such as to command an additional return. I would put it another way. I would say

[24] This is the Greek letter β, pronounced 'beta'.

that stupidity does not deserve a return and it would be stupid to invest all your money in a single company.[25]

The facts are that you can get the same return with much lower risk if you invest in a wide portfolio of shares rather than just one or two. This is so easy to do that virtually everybody does exactly that. So when deciding what reward is necessary in order to entice investors to take risk we need to think about risk not as it being the total uncertainty associated with the return but with the contribution to uncertainty that cannot be removed by portfolio diversification.

If we consider first the risks associated with investing in shares, the measure of unavoidable risk is a function of the correlation between the returns on a particular company's shares and the returns on the market overall. The jargon of corporate finance requires that we call this correlation β. If a 1% rise on the market is, on average, associated with a 1% rise in the share price of a particular firm then it is said to have a β of 1. If the 1% rise in market prices is associated on average with a 2% rise in the company's share price then that is a much riskier company and we say it has a β of 2.

A β of 0 does not mean that a share is not volatile. It simply means that it is entirely uncorrelated with the overall stock market. It is risk-free to a well diversified shareholder.

We can therefore return to our chart which depicts the relationship between risk and required return. For shares we will have a chart that looks like this:

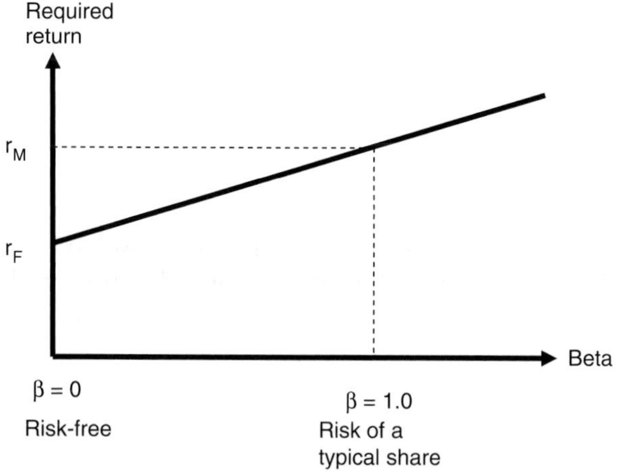

Fig. 5.8 A second look at the capital asset pricing model

[25] Unless of course you had some very good reasons for doing so, such as a desire to control a company or some inside information. Even then, you would still have to think very hard before you did so (and also watch out for the police if you are trading on inside information!).

We can now explain all the parameters of the model as follows:

- the risk-free rate is referred to as r_F;
- the return required by investors who invest in a portfolio of all the shares on the stock market is referred to as r_M;
- the line linking these two points is referred to as the security market line; and
- risk is characterised by the term β which indicates the correlation between the shares of the company under consideration and the market overall.

This model was postulated as a means for understanding how markets value shares. It can also help to understand how a company should look at the individual investment that it makes. If we assume that the company is simply a means of allowing investors to invest in projects then we can translate the CAPM model directly to projects and use it to set the appropriate discount rate for these as well.

In principle, each project has its own β which is a reflection of its degree of undiversifiable risk. Undiversifiable risk is the kind of risk that impacts on everything. Any risk that is unique or purely random can be diversified away and so does not impact on the required return.[26]

We will consider how to set the required return on a project in a lot more detail in one of the final chapters of this book. For the time being we have delved deeply enough into this subject to allow readers to make some good progress and in particular to understand why financial risks may not appear to take as crucial a role in decision making as one might have expected.

Part 3: Monetising risk

'Risk is impact times probability'

In this third part we will learn about a particular technique for making rational decisions concerning risk. The technique is called risk monetisation. It involves use of the fact that the financial impact of a risk on value is calculated by taking the impact of the risk should it come about and multiplying it by the probability of this happening. It is so useful an approach that many people actually define risk as being equal to impact times probability.[27]

[26] Note, however, that although unique risks do not impact on the required return they do impact on the calculation of the expected value cash flows.

[27] Personally I prefer to think of risk as being synonymous with uncertainty, which is why I placed the title of this section in quotation marks.

The statement 'risk is impact times probability' is another way to explain the expected value principle. The expected value of something is the outcome after all the possible outcomes have been considered and the weighted value of all possible outcomes has been calculated. So if we had a base case which reflected what we thought was the expected value outcome but then realised that we had forgotten about one particular risk, we could establish the revised 'correct' expected value by adjusting the old base case by impact times probability for this new factor.

A simple example will show how the approach works. Suppose we are considering a project with a base case value of $100. Suppose further that this will come about 90% of the time. A risk is identified which may cause the project to fail. The risk could happen 10% of the time and when it does, the outcome is –$100. What is the correct expected value? The answer is $80. This is because the impact of the risk is to lower the result by $200 but it only has a 10% chance of occurring. The expected value is equal to the original $100 less $20 equals $80.[28]

The power of the technique is not just in the way it allows the calculation of a correct expected value. It is in how it allows the full impact of a risk to be assessed. This impact can then serve as a budget limit for what can be done to mitigate the risk. In our example above the impact of the risk was calculated to be $20. This means that it is worth spending up to $20 to make the risk go away. This could be done either by eliminating the impact or by reducing the probability of occurrence to zero.

Furthermore, efforts that only partially solve the potential problem can also be easily valued. Some work which reduced the probability of occurrence from 10% to 8% would be worth $4 (i.e. 2% of $200). Work that reduced the impact from $200 to $160 would also be worth $4 (10% of $40). Work that did both would not be worth $8, it would be worth just $7.20. This is because the new impact is $160 and the probability is 8%, so the risk now has an impact of $12.80 which is $7.20 lower than the risk prior to the mitigating actions.

Now the risks that we have been dealing with are typically thought of as being the nasty type of risks. The technique applies equally well to upside risks. Suppose that we thought that demand for a new product would be 100 units per day. If we design our business to sell a maximum of 100 units we will be able to cope with the anticipated demand but not with any upside. If we thought there was a 25% chance of demand being 120 units we might want to build a larger production unit. We could decide whether this was

[28] This is the same as calculating the expected value in the usual manner, which is to take 90% of 100 and add 10% of minus 100. It is just a slightly easier way of doing the numbers by focusing just on the impact of the risk that is being considered and its probability.

worthwhile by taking 25% of the extra profit we would make if we had the additional capacity and comparing this with the incremental cost of building a larger unit.

Managing risks

The usual way to look at the economic prospects of a project is to start with a simple base case that is based on most-likely assumptions. This will produce what I would call a 'first-cut' NPV. That is to say it is a rough estimate of NPV suitable for initial screening of alternatives but not normally accurate enough to justify a final go/no-go decision on a major project. Risk is something that can impact on everything to do with a project. It is not therefore something that should be handled as a specific step in the overall process of project development. It needs to be dealt with throughout the entire stage gate process.

As work progresses with a project it is vital that the risks (both upside and downside) be considered. There are four reasons for this:

1. To ensure that we understand the expected value NPV since it is the correct basis for taking the go/no-go decision.
2. To ensure that the project is not exposing the investor to an unacceptable degree of downside risk.
3. To understand the nature of all the risks faced so that the appropriate trade-off between risk and reward can be made.[29]
4. To ensure that the project's value has been optimised in relation to the risks.

We have already dealt with the first three of these. From the perspective of economic value they are all essential. The fourth step, in my view, is optional but strongly recommended.

I say that it is optional because, arguably, there is nothing wrong in going ahead with a good project. It is strongly recommended because one should always seek to go ahead with the project in the best possible way. It is for this fourth reason of project optimisation that the risk monetisation technique is of particular benefit. This is because it provides an easy way for allowing for risk mitigation actions to be considered. Risk mitigation actions are things that are done in advance of a risk in order to reduce or even eliminate the risk altogether. We will consider an example of how the calculations are done in the individual assignments section which follows.

[29] The trade-off can either be done by calculating the 'correct' cost of capital to reflect the undiversifiable risks inherent in the project or by executive judgement.

The U-shaped valley

The way that risks are gradually incorporated into our economic evaluation can be summarised through a chart that I call 'the U-shaped valley'. My idea is that the initial view of a project that we have will be based just on a single view of the future. The individual assumptions will be most-likely values and it will certainly be a success case. This is the right way to start our analysis but we should never consider this to be an unbiased estimate of value. We need to work through each risk not just so that we understand them but in order to ensure that the project has been optimised with respect to them.

This task of risk identification and quantification will typically result in a reduction in the calculated NPV. The risk optimisation stage should aim to recover some of this lost value. If one is only dealing with 'bad' risks it is unlikely that the mitigation activities will be sufficient to return the outcome to where the original 'un-risked' NPV had been. If, however, additional ways can be identified which serve to increase the benefit from upside risks it is quite possible for the risk mitigation exercise to increase the value of a project to above its original first cut estimate.

This chart depicts how this approach might work.[30]

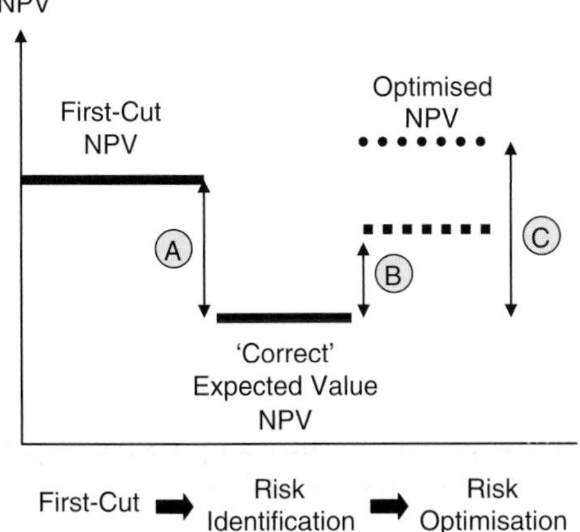

Fig. 5.9 The U-shaped valley of risk

From the perspective of the first-cut NPV it may well appear that the initial work on identifying risks has served to reduce the overall project NPV. On

[30] Readers will probably have to have seen a glaciated valley before they really understand why I use the term 'U-shaped valley'. The sides are almost vertical and the floor is flat.

the chart the apparent value loss is shown as the distance A. In my view this is not a value loss. This value was never there, it was simply that until the risk identification stage the effect had not been quantified. The level titled 'correct' expected value NPV should serve as the point from which the value of risk mitigation should be measured.

The fully optimised project may recover some of the apparent value loss (i.e. the line of small squares on the chart and distance B) and may even push value above the first-cut level (the line of small circles and the distance C). The value associated with risk optimisation is the distance B or C.

The importance of the U-shaped valley concept is felt in two ways. First there is the calculation of the 'correct' NPV after allowing for all risks. The NPV which should be used in assessing whether or not a project creates value for shareholders is the expected value NPV which can only be properly assessed after all risks are considered. Second, the U-shaped valley concept encourages work to be done at the design stage of a project to mitigate risks. A key management judgement will concern the effort to be put into this work. This is because although avoiding large downside effects can save a lot of money, there is the potential to spend a lot of money attempting to optimise the risks on a project and there can be no certainty that this effort will earn a sufficient reward to cover its cost.

Part 4: Categorising risk

I will now introduce a number of ways of categorising risk. My aim in this section is two-fold. First, I will provide the foundations which are necessary when I address questions of risk and reward later in the book. Second, I will aim to improve your ability to identify risks and incorporate them in your analysis of investment decisions.

One of the practical problems when dealing with risk concerns the way that it can impact on any aspect of a project. A requirement for a project analyst to consider 'all risks' and report anything of significance to the project sponsor sets the analyst a very onerous task. Some checklists can help aid what might otherwise appear to be almost impossible. The checklists will indicate where an analyst needs to look and also will allow some areas of risk to be ignored on the grounds that they are beyond the scope of what a project analyst is expected to consider or not of great relevance.

Financial risks and operational risks

The economic value model has two components – cash flows and a discount rate. These two components suggest a first way to think about risk which will usually allow people working on a project to ignore some risks. My first categorisation is to suggest we think of risks as being either financial or operational. Under this scheme one would then think of operational risks as concerning everything to do with a project from the moment it takes money out of the company's bank account until the moment it puts money back in. Financial risks would concern what happens to the money once it is in the banking system until the company pays it out as a dividend to shareholders and also the risk that the CoC might change through, for example, a change in the prevailing level of interest rates.

This book will be looking at what sets the CoC at a later stage but at this point all that is necessary is to state that there is considerable uncertainty concerning this number and the best view of it will probably change over time. Companies will usually adopt a CoC which they think is a good reflection of what the average will be over the period of any investment that is being considered. This means that a company's CoC need not be changed each time interest rates move but nevertheless, over the life of a project, the view of what is the right average to use will probably change. There may also be periods when free movement of capital is restricted for whatever reason or when new borrowing is difficult or perhaps even impossible to secure.

The normal approach would be not to hold project teams accountable for these changes. This is consistent with the approach of separating investment decisions from financing decisions and does serve to remove at least some risks from the long list of items that project people must consider. The organisational picture that I use is that the top management accept responsibility for financial risk and pass this to their finance function to manage. This leaves the project development teams in companies 'just' operational risks to consider.[31] As we will see in the remaining parts of this section, this is a long enough list as it is.

Internal and external risks

This way of thinking about operational risks is a good way of generating checklists. Risks can be categorised as being either internal or external.

[31] There will be some situations where project teams are expected to consider financial risk. An example would be on a very large project where finance was being raised in a way that was specifically linked to the project. These situations should, however, be viewed as exceptions to the general rule that project teams are not expected to consider financial risk.

Internal risks are things within the remit of the company while external are not. Internal risks tend to be more controllable. All internal risks will result in changes to one or more of the five primary and four support activities described in Michael Porter's value chain model.

By contrast, external risks concern the overall environment within which a company operates. These can be thought of through Porter's five forces model.[32] So the value chain model and the five forces model can be used to provide a structure for identifying risks. This does not in any way reduce the number of risks that need to be thought about but it does reduce the chance that some risks are overlooked.

Since the value chain model has nine activities and the five forces model adds a further six categories when regulation is included we finish up with a 15 point checklist for risk. The consideration of risk starts with a single point estimate and then covers each of the 15 points, asking the question 'What else could happen?'.

Company checklists

The previous categorisation is a generic approach which will work in any company situation. It does, however, utilise a 15 point checklist which cannot be described as short. Individual companies have their own unique characteristics and so are likely to have their own experiences of previous risks which can guide their risk evaluation. These company-specific risk checklists can be shorter, particularly if they just focus on the big and bad things that might have happened to a company in the past few years. Using past experience to generate a list such as this is an example of the Plan, Do, Measure, Learn approach in action.

Now although it is always a good idea to be guided by past experiences these do not protect companies from new risks or from risks that may have hit other companies. My experience tells me that projects which are different in nature or just very unusual will be exposed to multiple risks and an individual company's past experience will not be sufficient to prepare it for what might happen. Simply relying on internal checklists is unlikely to be sufficient for any radically new or unusual projects.

I suggest, therefore, that checklists which are based on past experiences should be limited to use on routine projects. Fundamentally new projects

[32] The best way is to use the version of the model where there are five forces plus a sixth that represents the effect of government regulation.

and also projects which are particularly large should always be assessed from the widest possible perspective. If the Porter based framework is not liked then I can offer an alternative 'comprehensive risk framework' as summarised in the following chart:

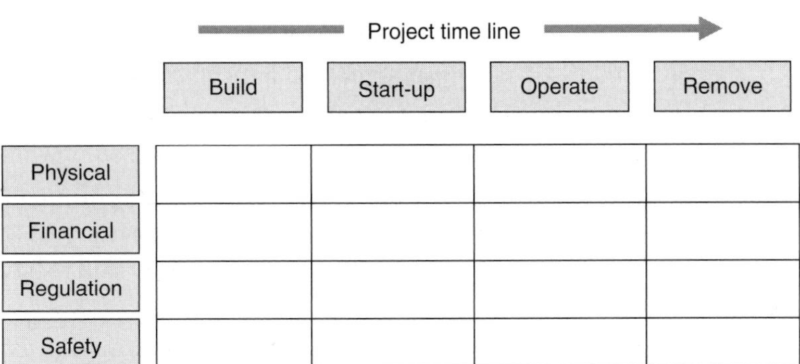

Fig. 5.10 Comprehensive risk framework

This approach utilises the idea of the four steps on a project's time line and suggests four categories of risk for each step. The categories of risk which I suggest are that one must consider the physical things that must happen, the financial consequences, the effect of regulation, and, of course, safety. In this approach, competitor reaction is not shown as a separate category and so must be covered implicitly in the four categories. The result is 16 separate areas to consider but on major projects doing analysis such as this in advance is well worthwhile.

Finally, for companies where structure and lists are not popular, I should mention the brainstorm approach to identifying risks. This simply requires that a major project should be subject to a brainstorm session on risk where a range of people are encouraged to suggest what the risks can be. A good group of people and a good facilitator can make this approach work but my own view is that risk is too important not to provide a clear and comprehensive framework for analysis.

Three types of risks

I will complete this foundation section on risk by explaining briefly how risks can be set into three different types. Readers will need to understand these ideas later in the book when we consider risk and reward in more detail.

- **All-or-nothing and plus-or-minus risks.** Some risks are of the type where an outcome may be within a range. In these situations it is generally meaningful to think about an outcome as being the mid-point plus or minus a certain amount. There are, however, some risks where it is more meaningful to think of it either happening or not happening. The difference between these risks is important because when one considers expected value, with the plus-or-minus risks there is a plus to offset the minus whereas with all-or-nothing there is no natural offset. So a plus-or-minus risk can usually be thought of as being equivalent to simply the mid-point whereas the all-or-nothing is equivalent to a point somewhere between the two possible outcomes. The simple division into all-or-nothing and plus-or-minus is probably an over-simplification. Many uncertainties fall somewhere between the two extremes and are simply said to have a skewed distribution.
- **Diversifiable and non-diversifiable risks.** This distinction is important because it should impact on the return which is required from a project. Risks which can be diversified by shareholders holding a portfolio of shares and which are not so great as to subject the company to the risk of financial distress do not add to the return which a project must earn in order to satisfy its shareholders. By contrast, non-diversifiable risks do need to be considered when setting the appropriate CoC. As an example of this I suggest readers reflect on how the impact of the general economic cycle on a project is clearly not diversifiable whereas the effect of a particular new technology's not working is diversifiable. This means that when decision-makers are studying the list of sensitivities to a project's base case some of these should be thought of as being more important than others because they are adding to the project's non-diversifiable risk.
- **Fat-tailed or thin-tailed.** The idea here is that some risks are subject to a very wide uncertainty range whereas others are subject to a small range. Furthermore, in some cases the extremes are more likely than in others. A fat-tailed distribution means having relatively more outcomes at the extremes.[33] It is clear that the range of uncertainty matters for non-diversifiable risks. It can also be important for diversifiable risks. This is because a wide range is more likely to introduce the potential for financial distress and also because with wide ranges the idea of upsides offsetting downsides might not apply and the expected value may well be harder to establish.

[33] The idea of having so-called fat-tailed distributions is referred to as 'kurtosis' but so few people will know this that I prefer to stick with the more descriptive term of fat-tailed.

The point to remember in relation to these three types of risk is that non-diversifiable, skewed or fat-tailed risks are all relatively more important than their opposites because of the way they complicate the making of good investment decisions.

Part 5: Individual work assignments

1. What would be the fair market price for the right to play a dice-rolling game where the payout is the square of the number shown?
2. A game is played that involves rolling two dice. Competitors pay $1 to play. They are paid $5 if the combined score is 7 but nothing if the score is any other amount. What is the expected value of playing the game once?
3. A casino allows players to play the game from question 2. The casino has annual overheads of $1m and local gambling regulations limit its opening hours to just 12 hours per week while the fire regulations limit the number of gamblers in the building to 500. What would be the minimum number of games per hour that each gambler must play if the casino is just to cover its costs? What conclusions would you draw from this calculation?
4. Here are six different types of probability distribution and ten situations. Match the situations to the distributions.

   Distributions
   a. Symmetrical, narrow range
   b. Symmetrical, wide range
   c. Skewed with heavy upside
   d. Skewed with heavy downside
   e. Bimodal
   f. Substantially flat

   Situations
   1. The quantity of cash being carried by an individual selected at random at a shopping centre.
   2. The height of the people present at an infants' school.
   3. The price of a particular share tomorrow in relation to its price today (ignoring complications such as days when the markets are not open or the effect of any dividends that are paid).
   4. The corporate tax rate in your home country in five years' time compared with the current rate.

5. The price of a TV set in ten years' time.
6. The exchange rate between US dollars and the euro in one year's time.
7. The cost of building the stadia required for the London Olympics compared with the initial estimate made when the Olympic bid was submitted.
8. The amount of rainfall in London on a particular day in July relative to the average daily rainfall for July.
9. The closing price of gold on the London futures market relative to the closing price on the US market on the same day.
10. The average wage rate in the USA in five years' time.

5. A business opportunity exists to sell replica sports shirts outside a stadium. You have two choices. You can go for the minimal overheads approach and carry 50 shirts to the ground for each home game, held over your arm and in a large holdall bag. You would expect to sell at least 40 of these every game for \$20 each while the cost to you is just \$10 per shirt. There are 20 home games in a season. The alternative is to rent a small lock-up stall by the entrance to the ground. This would then allow you to hold a more substantial stock of shirts and win many more sales. The stall costs \$2,000 to rent for the season and you would hold a stock of 400 shirts. Your best estimate of sales would then be 150 per game again at a price of \$20 per shirt and with a variable cost to you of \$10 per shirt. Which would be the best thing to do and how might a risk review make you change this view?
6. Rank the following risks in order of importance to a major corporation.
   a. An uncertainty of ±\$10m on sales revenue.
   b. A 10% chance that a pump will break down and lower sales in the pipeline division by \$10m.
   c. A 0.1% chance of a rupture in a pipeline that would cost \$1bn to clean up should it happen.
   d. A one-third chance that the legal staff will win a law suit against a competitor for breach of copyright and gain a payout of \$200m.
   e. A one-in-ten chance that the legal staff will lose a separate case and a fine of \$500m will be imposed.
   f. A 5% chance that a customer will default on a \$1m payment.
7. Now consider the same risks from the perspective of: (a) a small startup company engaged in just this one business activity; and (b) a medium-sized company engaged in several lines of business with an overall market value of \$500m.
8. You are in charge of the evaluation of a research project. The route to market for the research can be characterised as having six steps. Step 1

is research. Step 2 is safety evaluation. Step 3 is pilot plant scale evaluation. Step 4 concerns gaining the relevant government permits while Step 5 involves obtaining board sanction. The final step is to sell the product. If the project fails at any stage the financial outcome is nil. Build a simple decision tree model that will allow you to investigate the following variables for each stage: probability of success; cost of progressing through this stage; length of this stage; and finally value of a research success that makes it successfully to market. Then use the model to test the viability of the following proposal given a 10% CoC and assuming that money is all spent at the end of the relevant period.

Stage	Cost/ benefit	Duration	Success rate
1. Research	$4m	1 year	50%
2. Safety	$4m	1 year	85%
3. Pilot	$10m	1 year	75%
4. Permits	$10m	2 years	50%
5. Sanction	$1m	0.5 year	95%
6. Sales	Construction cost $50m. Overall value $1bn when sales start.	Construction time 1 year	90%

9. Use your judgement to place the following risks in the categories of 1–5 on a diversifiability scale where 1 means fully diversifiable risks while 5 means no diversification benefit.
   a. Building damaged by a tornado.
   b. Costs rise owing to inflation.
   c. Costs rise owing to failure of new computer system.
   d. Cost over-run on new factory owing to strikes delaying construction.
   e. Shop sales rise owing to demand for very popular children's toy.
   f. Loss of a legal case for copyright infringement.
   g. Computer systems need replacing owing to technology changes.
   h. Production equipment for a specialised product needs replacement owing to technology changes.
10. Describe possible mechanisms that might cause some degree of correlation between the following variables.
    a. Construction time and construction cost.
    b. Capacity utilisation and average selling prices.
    c. Low oil prices and number of people travelling by plane.
    d. Hotel occupancy rates and theatre bookings.
    e. Economic growth and the cost of advertising slots on TV.

f. Sales of baby-clothes and share prices.
g. A coin's landing heads six times in a row and then landing tails.

11. You are evaluating a project to mine iron ore. The first-cut economics show a substantial NPV of $1,500m. There are, however, risks concerning the ore body. The first risk concerns its size because as yet a full geological survey has not been carried out. The second risk concerns the presence of certain trace elements in the ore. If these are present the cost of purification would rise very substantially.

    As regards the first risk of the ore body size, your first-cut economics are based on a most likely quantity of ore in place. Should you go ahead and construct the mine in the usual way, the uncertainty band around the $1,500m NPV is from a worst case of zero (10% chance) to the most likely (75% chance) of $1,500m to an upside case with a value of $2,000 (15% chance). You have three choices. (1) Do nothing and accept the risks. (2) Build the facilities in two stages with the second stage adjusted to suit the quantity of ore in place which will be obvious once the mine comes on stream. This would lower both the most-likely case NPV and the upside NPV by $100m. However, the downside case would improve to $800m. (3) Carry out a traditional geological survey at a cost (stated in present-value-equivalent terms) of $50m. This survey would warn of the downside case and allow you to lower the construction costs such that the new downside NPV was $1,000m. This NPV is excluding the cost of the survey and would occur two years later than the NPV in the do-nothing case.

    The trace elements are assessed only to have a 5% chance of being present. If they are present it would be necessary to construct an additional purification stage. This would cost $500m (stated in present-value terms) and would delay the NPV by three years. We could build the purification unit as part of the main project. If we did so its cost would be reduced by a half and the build would not delay the project at all. We could delay the entire project for two years to carry out the necessary sample tests to see if the trace elements were present. The sample tests would cost $40m to carry out. If they showed that unacceptable quantities of trace elements were present we would then build the purification unit as part of the project.

    What recommendations would you make to the project team in relation to these risks? What value would you put on this opportunity at this time? You should assume a CoC of 9%.

Section II

The three pillars of financial analysis

CHAPTER

6 Overview

Where have we got to so far?

Those who started as beginners and who have worked through the first section of this book should have laid down a firm foundation of financial skills. They are now going to be joined by the existing practitioners who only needed to study a few specific parts of the financial foundation section. From now on I will consider all readers as practitioners.

We have in the economic value model a rational means of making trade-offs between money now and money later. We know, though, that financial decision-making is not a pure science. Our answers are always limited by the assumptions that we make; by the models that we use; and by the context within which we apply them.

This book is primarily about value but the foundations have been spread quite widely. In particular we have been introduced to the main principles of accounting because the financial results of companies are published in this way. We have also looked at planning and control in order to see how financial decisions about projects fit into the wider picture of a company's management processes and strategy.

We have been introduced to the expression 'words and music' which should encourage us to seek consistency between the words in our strategy and the financial numbers that we use. Put another way, we have learned that a good decision is a subtle blend of judgement and rational analysis. When a financial model gives a conflicting signal compared with what our intuition tells us or what a consistent track record of performance has told us, or what our strategy tells us, we know to take note of this important warning sign.

We have seen also how important it is to exercise judgement on behalf of the investing company and not ourselves. We understand how it is that big companies can take a very different view of risk and also how it can be reasonable to assume that money will always be available to fund a good project. We also know how important it is to distinguish between the decision to progress with a project and what should usually be the subsidiary decision concerning how to finance it. These presumptions about the context within which big companies make their decisions mean that we must all learn to leave our personal decision-making approaches behind when we head to work each morning.

From now onwards I will be assuming that readers can, thanks either to the five building block chapters or their past experiences, contribute to teams that are working on financial analysis questions and join in the general discussions that will take place. Put another way, I will assume all readers can now speak 'the language of business'. This means we are ready to build the three pillars which between them will support a platform of rational economic value-based analysis.

Where next?

Most of what I have covered so far has been traditional but now is the time to change that! The rest of this book sets out what I consider to be an approach that adds up to a substantially different way to make good economic value-based financial decisions.

I have at the side of my desk three textbooks which I think set out the current state-of-the-art in relation to economic value. Existing practitioners will probably own or at least have seen one or more of these. Beginners who have worked through my financial foundation section in the first part of this book and who want to deepen their understanding in any areas could achieve this through reading any or all of these books, which are:

- ***Principles of Corporate Finance*** by Brealey, Myers and Allen. I am now using the ninth edition and the book was originally published in 1981. Corporate finance practitioners, perhaps irreverently, refer to it as 'the bible' and the book describes its objective as to describe the theory and practice of corporate finance. It does exactly this and I learned a lot of my valuation skills from it.
- ***Valuation – Measuring and Managing the Value of Companies*** by Koller, Goedhart and Wessels, all of McKinsey & Company. I now have the fourth edition although I started with the first edition back in 1990. This book seeks to do what its title suggests and it does it very well. It describes valuation as being at the crossroads of corporate strategy and finance and I totally agree with this philosophy.

- ***Financial Statement Analysis and Security Valuation*** by Stephen Penman. I have the third edition published in 2007. The book, and the author, specialises in the role of accounting information in what he calls security analysis but I would call company valuation. The book has won an American Accounting Association medal and I particularly like the way that it emphasises the links between accounting results and value and how it describes in detail the task of disentangling financing and operational activities within published results.

Now I apologise to the authors of other books on the subject if I have offended them by leaving their works off my list. It is, however, a list which considers value from a range of perspectives. I agree with the vast majority of what is written in these books but in some important ways I disagree. These differences will, when taken together, add up to a subtly new way of making financial decisions within companies. This way places emphasis on a three-way link between valuation, accounts and strategy.

The key to understanding my approach lies in the bridges which I will build between these three topics. I will stress these differences at the appropriate points as the following chapters progress. In summary, though, I will be:

- arguing for strategic analysis to become more quantified while financial analysis must accept that it currently seeks what I consider to be excessive accuracy;
- placing my main emphasis on forecasting cash flows rather than the discount rate;
- warning of how traditional project evaluation can become pointless unless it is made a part of some different processes;
- showing how the Sources of Value technique offers an answer to the first of Brealey and Myers's famous list of ten unsolved problems in finance which asks about how to find positive NPVs.[1]

These differences rely on two key techniques. One of these is what I call Sources of Value and since it is new it should be no surprise that it offers new insights. The second, however, is the apparently simple approach of structuring project analysis in an accounting format that I call the abbreviated financial summary

[1] The book *Principles of Corporate Finance* finishes with a list of what it calls 'ten unsolved problems in finance'. In the current list, item number one is 'what determines project risk and present value?'. In 1996 this was question number two but the previous question one ('how are major financial decisions made?') has left the list to be replaced with a new number ten which concerns international differences in financial architecture. The main question that Brealey and Myers seem to be asking in their current question number one concerns where positive NPVs come from and whether they can be anticipated and planned for. I would like to think that this book will create the space on the list for a new problem!

(AFS). This should help to highlight the fact that even if a company is simply the sum of a series of projects, the incremental NPVs that are usually studied at time of sanction will not add up to a picture of the company overall. The incremental economics will exclude past costs and also what would be a fair share of future overheads. These costs, in aggregate, create a potentially huge gap in value between the stream of apparently value-creating projects that the board regularly approves and the overall performance of the company. I will argue that decisions concerning these costs need to be taken as a part of the strategy debate and will show how to make this more numerate.

The three pillars

In order to start on these ambitious tasks we need first to look into the topic of economic value in much more detail and with a particular focus on the calculation of value. We need to do this for two main reasons. The first concerns the implementation of valuation within a company. My experience warns me that there are many practical difficulties in taking the simple idea of discounting projected future cash flows and applying it in real-life situations. The second concerns the need to ensure consistency of treatment. Consistency is essential when a decision is of the type 'Do I make this investment or that one?' Decisions like this are often taken within companies and they rely heavily on the alternatives being analysed in a consistent manner. We need what I like to call a 'level playing field' on which we can carry out our investment appraisal.

It is only when we have robust financial models in place that it is worthwhile introducing the second pillar which is the idea of Sources of Value. This will provide answers to several problems including in particular how to make better assumptions and how to identify the best strategy. This second pillar will, in effect, give guidance about where to look for positive NPVs.

The third pillar will concern the question 'What sets the share price?'. The theory will be covered briefly and the main focus will be on how to use economic value to calculate a share price and the implications of the conclusion that it is economic value which underpins share prices. The implications are very wide and should go to the heart of how companies are managed.

An important change in this section is that there are no more individual work assignments. This is not because I believe that readers need no more practice. I will include some significant worked examples in the text and I expect that readers will work through these in some detail. My suggestion is that instead of my setting hypothetical studies, readers should be devising their own applications relevant to themselves and their companies. This is consistent with my aim that this financial pillars section will leave readers ready to lead the financial analysis of opportunities within the companies where they work. A major distinguishing feature of leadership is the ability to set work priorities for oneself rather than simply to follow orders.

So please now, as you start the main section of the book, commit to test your learning and understanding as you go and to a depth that you feel is appropriate.

CHAPTER

7

The first pillar: Modelling economic value

Summary

In the financial foundations section we have learned to build some simple financial models and to use these to gain insights as we strive to maximise value. The purpose of this first pillar is to add a lot of practical detail to our ability to build financial models which will calculate economic value. In effect, this chapter is concerned with the design and operation of spreadsheet models to solve 'real-life' issues.

We must start our thinking about spreadsheet design with a clear understanding of the purpose of economic evaluation. It can be easy to fall into the trap of thinking that evaluation is done in order to demonstrate that an investment has a positive NPV and hence should be approved. My view is that evaluation should be done in order to identify the right thing to do and only then to gain approval for this.

So if evaluation is about finding the right thing to do, it must start early in the process since this is when the most important decisions are taken. This means the initial focus of evaluation must be on the consideration of alternatives. It should only be after the right project is chosen from the alternatives that the focus of evaluation should switch to optimisation as we seek to develop the project in the best possible way. Gaining approval should simply be the third step as opposed to the main driver of the evaluation.

The reference to the choice between alternatives provides an insight into one of the main purposes of this first pillar. This is to provide a so-called 'level playing field' on which alternative investment opportunities can be compared. A level playing field will allow opportunities to be compared on their merits and stop any spurious differences emerging as a result of inconsistent or erroneous financial modelling.

Our starting point for this section is model design. This clearly has to be dealt with first because all of our subsequent work will depend on our ability to build a good spreadsheet model. The focus will be on the financial aspects of a good model and not on spreadsheet skills per se.

After this there will be several more parts, each dealing with different aspects of modelling value. These are as follows:

2. Case optimisation.
3. Sustaining investments.
4. Full-cycle economics.
5. Inflation and forex effects.
6. Project life and other modelling issues.
7. Modelling financed cases.
8. Suggested standard methodology.

These parts are presented in what I consider to be a logical order. They are, however, largely self contained and can be read in any order.

Examples and case studies are developed within each part. A significant case study of a fictitious company called Yellow Moon Chemical Company is developed at the end of part 7. Although this deals mainly with the modelling of financing issues it should also serve as a progress test for readers who joined this book as beginners. Readers who follow the logic of the case study will be able to take great comfort in the progress they have made since starting the book.

This is an important chapter, particularly for practitioners who wish to build financial models for real-life application in business. The majority of the content, particularly in parts 3–7, is, however, devoted to a series of 'how-to-do-it' descriptions. I can imagine that if a reader has not come across a particular situation, then learning how to deal with it when it does come up may not make for riveting reading. I suggest therefore that some readers might want simply to skim-read these sections in order to be aware of the issues that are covered but not necessarily so that they can remember in full detail how to deal with them. These readers should then return to the relevant pages as and when they need to apply the technique in those particular situations.

Part 1: Model design

Initial analysis: what sort of model is needed?

The simplest financial model involves just a few finger taps on a calculating machine or perhaps even just a piece of mental arithmetic coupled with a set of discount factor tables. I accept that this may seem old-fashioned but there are times when this is all that is necessary.[1]

At the other extreme, perhaps the most complex models that I have worked on have involved the detailed re-optimisation of a global supply chain. In models such as this a change, say, in manufacturing capacity in the UK could impact on output from a plant in Asia. Additional demand in the USA could have a knock-on effect on prices in Europe.

The big message from these two extremes is that when it comes to financial models, one size should not be made to fit all. I suggest that before any modelling is carried out the first step should be a fit-for-purpose review that addresses three questions:

- What do I need to know?
- Is this a one-off question or will it be asked many times?
- Is there something already available?

The more that you are dealing with questions that will be repeated, the more thought should go into model design. A well-designed model may save a lot of time later but model design should be considered like any investment. It needs to give a payback. Many companies will use a standard template model to evaluate all of their investment options. In principle this should allow many mistakes to be avoided. The problem, however, is that the model may be too sophisticated in some aspects while it may miss other aspects all together. A standard template model is not always the right answer, particularly at the early stages of a project.

Although this first pillar is concerned with issues related to detailed and complex financial models, I must start with a warning. There are times, particularly at the early stages of a project's life, when the proverbial 'back-of-an-envelope' is the right analytical approach and I encourage readers to adopt the simplest approach that will give a good enough answer for the particular situation that they face.

For the remainder of this part I will assume that we have already decided that a spreadsheet model is required because calculations will be complex and/or will be repeated. Furthermore I will assume that we are dealing with a generically new situation such that we cannot simply copy a previous model or, even better, use an off-the-shelf template model.

[1] These times happen often enough for me always to have available my laminated A4 sheet of discount factors and annuity factors.

Incremental and absolute NPVs

Think back to the initial summary. I explained that the purpose of evaluation is to find the right thing to do. I wrote that evaluation must start early in the process and that evaluation must consider alternatives. The reference to alternatives is very important.

The economic indicators that we calculate should normally compare a 'what-if-we-do' case with a 'what-if-we-don't' case. The NPV and the other indicators would thus all be incremental indicators showing the decision-maker the effect of their decision. These incremental figures can be compared with what I refer to as absolute figures. The absolute figures represent the actual cash flow that will be generated.

We can illustrate this absolute and incremental presentation of results by thinking back to one of the first examples in this book. In the 'Uncle Norman's birthday treat' example[2] I considered how one could choose in a situation where one was offered three options. On your 16th, 18th or 21st birthday you could receive a large present but on the other birthdays you were given a much smaller sum. Furthermore, the large present which you could receive on your 16th birthday was smaller than what you would receive if you waited longer. The value of the three options was:

16th birthday option: NPV $10,813
18th birthday option: NPV $11,190
21st birthday option: NPV $10,920

These are all what I would call 'absolute values'. An absolute value is the value of the cash flows that will arise if you follow a particular path. The highest value option was to take the big present on your 18th birthday and so this was the recommended course of action.

I then showed how you could, if you wanted to, also deem taking the present on, say, your 16th birthday to be the base case and then consider the incremental economics for switching to your 18th or 21st birthday. Either of these decisions could be considered as investments as they represented an initial negative cash flow (i.e. the much lower present on your 16th birthday) invested with a view to gaining a greater sum of money some time in the future. The incremental benefit of switching to your 18th birthday was $377 while that for your 21st birthday was $107.

[2] See Building Block 1 pages 18–21.

My suggestion is that you should allow the circumstances to dictate whether you calculate incremental or absolute economic models. Most models should show incremental cash flows so that decision-makers are given a clear picture of the impact of their decisions. This is because in most situations there should already be a clear status quo that exists prior to a new project's being approved. As long as it is already clear what path will be followed if an investment proposal is turned down, incremental economics should be quoted. Absolute economics are reserved for situations where there is no agreed alternative path. The typical time that this happens is when strategy is being considered. So for a strategy review you should model the absolute value of the alternative courses of action.

Whatever you do, the most important thing is to ensure that any other individuals who will see your economic analysis will know whether the analysis is based on incremental or absolute cash flow. If the analysis is based on incremental cash flows then the assumptions underpinning the alternative case become every bit as important as the assumptions that support the investment case. These assumptions must be made clear as well as the assumptions that underpin the investment case.

This distinction between incremental and absolute NPVs is not something which is given great priority in my three standard textbooks. They tend to adopt a convention that projects are always valued on an incremental basis while companies are valued from an absolute perspective. I imagine that the authors would argue that the distinction does not really matter as long as everyone concerned knows the basis which is being used. This would be true. There are, however, two reasons why I suggest the difference can be important and hence is worth highlighting.

First, it would introduce a huge error if incremental NPVs were compared with absolute NPVs. This is probably unlikely to happen. What is likely is that my second reason will apply. This reason is that for incremental NPVs the devil lies in the detail of the assumptions about what happens in the 'what-if-you-don't invest' case.

In order to compute an incremental NPV one must have some agreed conventions about what happens in the 'what-if-you-don't' world. I usually base these on a series of assumptions that correspond to the world moving on and the market growing as you would expect but your own operations only continuing to grow to the extent that there is already spare capacity in your systems to allow for growth. In other words my 'what-if-you-don't' world is usually a minimum future investment case. Furthermore, I would usually specify that the 'what-if-you-don't' world would not consider the option of selling a business or, for that matter, selling a partly developed project, if you do not go ahead. These conventions might well be important to decisions about which one of several potentially value creating options should be followed. The highest reported NPV might not be the right answer if our method of calculation of NPV is excluding some factors and in particular is excluding the possibility of early divestment.

What is the purpose of an economic model?

The purpose of a model is, in my view, to convert a set of input assumptions faithfully into an NPV and usually also into a fuller set of economic indicators. What I mean by the word 'faithfully' is that another analyst, given the same assumptions but building a new model of his or her own, would produce exactly the same set of economic indicators. This would represent the level playing field which can then facilitate fair comparisons between alternatives which have been analysed by different teams.

Managers and senior decision-makers should be able to focus on assumptions and their resultant economic indicators without having to worry about whether the economic model itself has introduced any additional 'noise' into the system. A well-built model will do exactly this. For economic appraisal to work well within a company, *all* financial models must meet the required standard of faithfully converting assumptions into economic indicators.

It can surprise many people how many different NPVs can be arrived at for a given set of assumptions. First one must always be aware of the danger of downright errors. More subtly, though, are the often unstated methodological assumptions concerning things like the exact point in time that NPV is stated, whether cash flows are mid-year or end-year and the treatment of residual working capital. My three suggested standard textbooks do not give much emphasis to these factors and yet they can result in significant differences.

To illustrate this effect please consider this situation. Imagine you were offered the chance of investing a lump sum of $400 in a project that lasts for just one year and that your CoC is 10%. If the project will generate $430 over the year, is it worthwhile? I suggest that it all depends on whether you assume mid-year or end-year cash flows. If the cash flow all happens at the end of the year then the project is $10 short of earning its CoC. If, however, the cash flows are earned evenly over the year, the project will generate a good NPV.

A clear implication of the need to convert assumptions 'faithfully' into NPV is that each company must develop its own conventions about exactly what elements of the calculation are considered to be assumptions and what are treated as part of the common company-wide methodology. I have included a suggested common methodology in the final part of this pillar. I suggest that this be applied in situations where a company policy has not already been established.

Three spreadsheets or one?

This may seem a strange question but it is very important. The point that I am making is that the incremental effect of some investments can be quite easy to model while for other investments the 'what-if-I-do' and the 'what-if-I-don't' cases can be so complex that each requires their own spreadsheet. In these more complex situations the incremental cash flows can only emerge in a third sheet which is the difference between the first two.

I will now give some examples. A simple case requiring just one model would be consideration of a project to expand into a new country where there were no interactions with the existing business; for example if a company runs a successful chain of coffee shops in Western Europe and then decides to expand into Russia. The cash flows for the new Russian business unit could be built up line by line and would (I am assuming) have no impact on the existing business. The answer to the 'three spreadsheets or one?' question would be 'one'. The alternative to investing in Russia would be what I call 'a line of noughts'.

Suppose, though, that our coffee chain sold a particular blend of coffee that was in very limited supply and that extra sales in Russia would mean lower sales growth in our existing outlets in Western Europe. Suppose also that the new business in Russia would need to take some key managers away from the existing operation and that this too would impact on performance. One would then need to model the Western European operations on their own and also after the Russian expansion took place with the resulting lower performance and sales growth. One would clearly then need three spreadsheets – one showing Western Europe on its own, one with both operations and the third showing the incremental cash flows.

The spreadsheet that covered Western European activities with restricted coffee supply and key managers would require a lot of work because it would be important to identify the best way to react to the new circumstances. It might, for example, be better to close a marginal outlet and reallocate its coffee supply rather than simply impose an across-the-board restriction on the rate of sales growth at each outlet. What is interesting to note is that this optimisation of Western European operations would impact the reported NPV for expansion into the new market in Russia.

Another common situation where three sheets are required concerns when a new manufacturing plant is added to an existing operation. The new plant will usually be the most efficient and so will be run flat out once it comes on stream. This means that the absolute NPV of the new plant should look very good. It would, however, be wrong to use these cash flows on their own. The older plant in the portfolio will suffer from lower throughput and the full effect of this would need to be correctly modelled in order to arrive at the true incremental NPV. A similar situation would also occur if a new retail outlet was added to a large existing chain. Its sales would, in part, have been 'stolen' from existing outlets and this needs to be allowed for when calculating incremental economics.

My third example comes from the oil industry. The NPV for developing a new oil field will normally be stated relative to a 'do-nothing' alternative rather than a 'divest-the-field' alternative. A single spreadsheet will yield the necessary answer. By contrast, however, an option to invest additional capital in order to accelerate production would normally allow for the fact that in the alternative case the oil would simply be produced a few years later and so a three spreadsheets approach is necessary. A decision-maker who was presented with the choice of investing in a new field in one country or investing additional money to advance production elsewhere would not be able to reach a good decision simply by comparing the stated project NPVs. This is because the new oil field NPV is not a true incremental NPV. The true incremental NPV would measure field development against its divestment.

So we can see how the potentially hidden subtleties of methodology and things like the question of one spreadsheet or three could completely change what ought to be the right decision. This is another reason why a standard methodology is so important.

Spreadsheet layout

Spreadsheets should always follow a similar generic style with three sections. The sections should be: data input; calculations; and reports.

The first section should be reserved for data input. This should be the only place in the spreadsheet that data are entered. Any subsequent use of data items should be done by reference to the relevant cell. Hard-wiring should be avoided.[3] The first section can also serve as an assumptions register if

[3] 'Hard-wiring' refers to writing spreadsheet formulas with numbers included where it would be better to include a reference to a data cell. A common piece of hard-wiring is incorporation of the cost of

additional information is stored alongside each data item. By placing all of the data in one place, subsequent auditing of a case is made much easier.

Any item that you will subsequently want to change as part of your sensitivity analysis must be input as part of the data. This is usually a simple exercise. Significant exceptions are questions related to build time and project life. Many models will hard-wire the assumed build period and operating life by, for example, fixing the point in time when a new plant comes on stream. If you want to investigate the effect of changes in build time or operating life then this needs to be allowed for in the model design or else you will be forced to build a new model for each change in assumption.

I cannot say that it is easy to build a model that allows build time and operating life to be assumptions. One suggestion is that you should rely on the principle of value additivity and build your model in three stages. Stage one simply models the build stage, stage two covers operation and stage three is just for the closure effects. Stage one transfers to stage two the cumulative present value of all the build costs and also the date at which stage one ends. Stage two can be given an economic life that fits within a range. The range is fixed with a minimum operating life which is hard-wired into the model. Any years of operating life beyond this are allowed for via a terminal value assumption based on an annuity factor for the extra number of years times the final year's funds flow.[4] The cumulative present value and date at the end of stage two is transferred to stage three to complete the calculation.

A further piece of practical advice is that the data input section should also contain a small section that repeats the key economic indicators for the case under consideration. This will greatly speed up the subsequent sense checking and analysis since this typically involves changing assumptions and seeing the consequential impact on NPV, IRR, etc. If the input cell and the answers are visible on the same screen, analysis can be much faster.

The second section should be where all of the calculations are carried out. My view is that the layout on the screen should be easy to follow. Calculations should be shown step-by-step so that another person reviewing the model can clearly see what is going on. Individual cell formulae should never be too long, again so that a newcomer can quickly understand what is being done. The calculation section can be as big as is necessary and is absolutely crucial.

capital in a calculation as a formula such as = b52/1.1 as opposed to = b52/(1 + B10) where cell B10 is the data cell where the cost of capital of 10% is input.

[4] Terminal values will be considered in considerable depth later in this book as part of the consideration of 'What sets the share price?'.

It will, however, typically only be looked at by the model's author and by anybody who is asked to audit the model.

The final section is called reports. This is where all of the output should be collated. There will obviously be a clear table showing the main economic indicators. There should also be a summary of the important sensitivities and any charts that are required should be shown.

Individual senior managers will have their own particular requirements regarding the amount of information they require to see. At one extreme some will want only to be told what the headline economic indicators are. At the other extreme some managers will want to study the actual spreadsheet in order to convince themselves that it is correct.[5] The usual situation would be that the most detail that a decision-maker would expect to see would be just the reports section. This would contain more detail than just the economic indicators but would not show the calculations in all of their gory detail! As has already been stressed above, this position can only be achieved when decision-makers have confidence that all spreadsheets are of the required quality faithfully to convert assumptions into economic indicators.

My recommendation is that the reports section should always contain the AFS for the base case as well as quoting the economic indicators.

Model audit

It is very hard to get a spreadsheet model right first time. Indeed the only safe assumption about a model is that it will contain errors unless and until it has been thoroughly audited.

The model designer should carry out the initial checking through a process that I call 'working the case'. This involves changing assumptions, seeing what the effect is on the answer and testing this against your intuition of what the impact should be. This work can serve two purposes, namely auditing the model and an initial screening of what sensitivities need to be reported.

Once you think a model is correct it should be audited. I recommend that all models should be checked by a skilled practitioner who is not a member of the project team. The amount of effort devoted to this should be commensurate with the importance of the case and the complexity of the model.

I would go outside of the team for two reasons. Firstly somebody from outside might challenge what items are regarded as givens and hence

[5] I have to admit that when I had the role in BP Chemicals of approving all investment cases as being fit for sanction I required to see actual spreadsheets. I was told that I was the first general manager ever to ask to see such detail but this did not in any way put me off always asking to see the full detail!

hard-wired into a model and what items are assumptions. The second reason is that it is likely that the best financial modeller in the team is already the author of the model and so one needs to look outside the team to ensure a good challenge.

Even after an audit the possibility of errors remains. The most likely cause is incorrect assumption entry. It is also possible that some errors will only become apparent when extreme conditions are encountered. The lesson to learn from this is always to balance what the model is telling you against what your intuition is saying. Do the words and music paint a coherent picture? Treat a negative answer here as a warning sign that there might be an error in the model no matter how long the model might have been in use.

We will learn later how to use the Sources of Value technique to test the credibility of our NPV. This will provide a further way to test the words and music of our finance case. Even this, however, will not prove that the model is right. It will just demonstrate that it is not obviously wrong. Eventually, however, one can have used a model enough times to conclude that since it has always been 'not obviously wrong' it should therefore be right.

Part 2: Case optimisation

The aim of evaluation

Imagine that you are the chief executive of your company. Three investment cases are presented to you for approval. They each involve about the same amount of capital expenditure. The first project is claiming an NPV of about 25% of the capital cost, the second an NPV of 50% of the capital cost while the third is claiming an NPV of 150% of the capital cost. You have checked all of the numbers and are happy that they are correct. What should you do?

One possible answer would be to approve the third project and shout at the managers of the first two asking why their projects were not as good! Another possible answer would be to approve all three projects because they all offer positive NPVs.

Supposing I said that in the event the chief executive approved the first two projects and sent the third project back to the development team. Suppose also that this was not owing to any factors related to downside risk. Why might this be the right thing to do? Why might it be right to reject what is by far the biggest NPV even though you know that the quoted NPV is 'correct'?

My suggested answer is that the chief executive discovered that the first two projects had been through a thorough process of optimisation using the company's established stage gate procedures. The third project looked so good that it had been fast tracked. The chief executive rejected the project because he thought that an extra few months' work on it would result in an even higher NPV.

We should always remember that the aim of evaluation is to find the best thing to do. It is not simply to win approval for a predetermined course of action.

The danger of excess optimisation

When you think about it, it should be self-evident that all projects need to be optimised. Just because a project already offers a positive NPV why should you go ahead if this might mean missing an opportunity for an even better NPV? The danger with optimisation is that of analysis paralysis. There are so many variables to consider that one could become locked into an endless round of analysis which only finishes when you realise, with certainty, that you have waited too long and that others have seized the opportunity that you thought could be your own.

The optimisation of a project is not like the optimisation of a mathematical formula. Project optimisation requires analysis and assumptions and therefore takes time, costs money and tends to involve many people.

For example, you might need to ask your engineers to tell you what it might cost to build a new plant one way (say with a capacity of 100,000 units per year) and also what it might cost to build it another (this time with a capacity of, say, 120,000 units per year). Then when you know the cost, you must approach your marketers to discover when they anticipated they could sell the additional output and at what price. This will be no trivial exercise. In fact, you should expect optimisation to be harder than the overall go/no-go decision on the plant. Why do I suggest this?

The answer to this question is as follows. A project will only rarely be approved if its economics are marginal. Most projects will offer good positive money-forward economics. This will be explained further in part 4 when we consider full-cycle economics. Optimisation decisions, however, will involve some questions which, almost by definition, are marginal. This is because at an optimum the change in value for any extra spend is going to be close to zero. Optimisation is therefore all about making good close calls.

Managing the optimisation effort

My suggested approach is to recognise that it costs money to consider an option. Options analysis is therefore an investment decision in its own right. These decisions about how much effort to devote to optimisation can be aided by three things. These are experience, the stage gate approach and widely held financial skills.

It is experience that allows a manager to have an idea of what the result of a study might be and then to test whether this result would be worth the effort required to achieve it. This is where a proverbial 'back-of-the-envelope' calculation is needed. Experienced managers know how to make good assumptions and so have a huge advantage over those who are new to this particular game.

Stage gate processes provide a formal way of ensuring that optimisation questions are considered in a logical order. They were described in the Planning and Control building block on pages 113–114.

The basic idea is to lock down the big decisions first and only then to move on to optimisation of the chosen approach. The mantra is 'choose the right project then do it right'. All of these choices need to be considered as questions which require economic analysis. This means that financial analysis must start before a project team is set up.

The point about widely held financial skills is less obvious. One could simply tell the originators of any optimisation ideas to submit them to the financial analysis expert who will decide what is worth pursuing. This approach would only require, in the limit, one financial expert. The problem with it is that the idea-generators would not know what sort of things to look for and so would have to pass each and every idea to the financial analyst for consideration. Five answers of 'no' later they would probably give up putting forward ideas. It would be so much better if the idea-generator was able to carry out the initial screening.

One approach that may be adopted involves breaking the optimisation task down into subcomponents. For example, the design team may be told to build a new plant for the lowest possible capital cost. The operations team would be told that their objective was to run the plant with the lowest possible costs and the lowest possible inventory. Finally, sales would be instructed to maximise what I call 'tonnes times price', i.e. sales revenue. This is simple and does not require much in the way of financial skills. It does, however, more or less guarantee that the optimal solution will be missed and so I do not recommend that it should be followed.

Why do I say this? Surely it is good, for example, to lower capital cost. My view is that all other things being equal, lower capital costs are good. However, the means by which we achieve lower capital costs are such that all other things are only very rarely equal. There will almost always be some increases in capital cost which are justified by, for example, lower operating costs. The same applies for other simple objectives such as 'run for the lowest possible operating costs'. The lowest possible operating costs may result in an unacceptable level of service for customers.

Optimisation involves a series of subtle judgements that should be tested via the project's financial model. The aim is to seek the overall optimum. That is to say that the aim is to seek the set of assumptions that give the best overall financial outcome. It is certainly not just about minimising capital cost. It is to do with maximising NPV in relation to the risks involved and the resources required to achieve it. The final decision is a blend of words and music and our financial model can provide the music.

Case study: Selecting optimisation studies

Let us consider, as an example of the optimisation investment decision, a manager who must decide whether to progress immediately with a project that is expected, based on today's numbers, to cost \$30m and yield an NPV of \$15m. Four possible optimisation options have been identified. Should we go ahead now or follow up on one or more of the following possibilities?

- The first option is to work harder at the capital cost. It is estimated that a further year of work on this at a cost of \$2m might reduce the cost by \$5m.
- The second option concerns site layout. A separate one-year study of site layout might enable you to reduce operating costs slightly. The study would cost \$1.2m and you estimate that it could lower operating costs by at least \$0.15m pa for each of the 15 years of operation.
- The third option concerns working harder to reduce a downside risk which has been identified and which has already been allowed for in the expected-value NPV which has been quoted. The risk concerned feedstock shortages. There was a 10% chance of this happening, and if it did come about, the NPV impact was \$20m. The solution which has been identified would require an extra six months for obtaining planning consents. It would be to build an additional tank at a cost of about \$1m. The supplier has agreed to keep the tank full at his expense and building the tank would not extend the projected build time.

- Finally, a one-year delay might allow time for an external manufacturer to complete its tests of a new generation of filter presses. Should these new filters pass the tests the capital cost would fall by \$2m. You estimate that there is a 40% chance of this happening.

For our analysis we will use a 9% CoC and for simplicity we will ignore any tax effects.

The first option involves spending \$2m to save \$5m shortly thereafter but also suffer a one-year delay in the NPV of \$15m. The value impact of the one-year delay is about \$1.2m.[6] We need to add this to the value impact of the cost which is \$1.9m.[7] The capital cost savings will be realised, say, in years 2 and 3. The present value of this is:

$$\left(2.5^{8} \times 0.879 + 2.5 \times 0.806\right) = \$4.2\text{m}$$

So this option offers value benefits of \$4.2m and costs of just \$3.1m. We can clearly justify doing the first study. This has important implications for the other options because once we have decided to incur the one-year delay we do not need to allocate its impact to any other options.

The second option in isolation does not look too good. The 15-year annuity factor with mid-year flows and a CoC of 9% is 8.416. Multiply this by the annual benefit of \$0.15 and you get \$1.26m. The operating cost benefits, however, do not start immediately. They start after the one-year study period and the anticipated construction period (which we will assume is two years). We therefore need to apply a further three-year delay to the benefit flows. This reduces the \$1.26m to just below \$1.0m. This is well below the present cost of the study and so we cannot justify doing this second study.

The third option involves spending \$1m to remove a risk that has a 10% chance of happening and will lower NPV by \$20m if it does. The impact times probability technique makes it clear that this is well worth doing. The choice is between spending \$1m over years 2 and 3 to boost expected value NPV by \$2m and accepting the risk. There is no need to allow for the planning delay because we have already decided to incur a one-year delay because of the first option.

The final option is outside of our control. We would analyse it by applying the impact times probability technique. The impact of success is \$2m but the probability is only 40%. The resultant \$0.8m of risked benefit would not on

[6] Calculated by subtracting \$15m ÷ 1.09 from \$15m.

[7] Calculated as \$2m × 0.958 (the mid year discount factor for one year at 9%).

[8] I have assumed that the capital spend saving is \$2.5m in each of build years 1 and 2.

its own justify a one-year delay. However, since we have already decided to accept the delay, the benefit is, in effect, free.

The conclusion is that it is worth doing the capital cost study and because of this we can justify building the tank. An additional benefit of doing these studies would be that we could wait to see if the filter manufacturers bring out the new generation of filter presses in time. We should not do the site layout study.

Note that if the first two options had been offered *together* as a single option called project optimisation we would have recommended acceptance of this option. This would not have been an optimal answer to the problem. I refer to the lumping together of separate options as 'bundling'. Bundling of different options always creates the risk of suboptimisation and should be avoided.

Summary: Optimising our optimisation efforts

So, in conclusion, economic evaluation provides us with the financial technique to allow a project to be optimised. A stage gate approach should be adopted. The big decisions about the overall nature of the project itself must be taken first and the subsequent optimisation of the selected project follows as a subsidiary exercise. All decisions are taken based on maximising value in relation to risk.

Optimisation itself needs to be thought of as an investment decision. The overall approach to optimisation is that each individual optimisation study must always be expected to cover its own costs while the aggregate value benefit of the studies must be sufficient to justify the cost of the delay. So a great optimisation study can, in effect, provide some subsidy to a less good optimisation study in that it would cover the effect of the delay. We should not, however, allow cross subsidisation to the extent that a truly poor study is funded out of the benefits from the worthwhile studies.

Part 3: Sustaining investments

What is sustaining investment?

I define sustaining investment as any relatively small spend that is necessary to protect against a substantial drop in output from an existing operation.

The simplest example is with a manufacturing site where a pump might need to be replaced. If no pump means no output, then the decision to replace the pump must be the proverbial 'no-brainer'.[9] I call any spend such as this 'sustaining investment'. The required spend must be 'relatively' small so as to ensure that the decision whether or not to incur the expenditure is obvious.

The word 'substantial' is an important qualification in my definition of sustaining investment. Suppose that the loss of a pump might result in the loss of peak manufacturing output of, say, 5%. This would not count as substantial, the logic being that a decision to replace would not be a 'no-brainer' situation because loss of peak manufacturing output might have only a limited impact. It could, for example, easily be mitigated through holding a small additional level of finished products in your inventory. Or as a second example, the plant may only occasionally be operated at full throughput.

The standard texts do not appear to me to pay much attention to sustaining investments yet my experience from working in industry is that there are a lot of sustaining investments that have to be made. This is why I have included this section.

Justifying sustaining investment

How would you justify the new pump that I referred to above? Would it have a negative NPV because it cost some money yet the overall output would not rise?

My answer is that if you consider the 'correct' incremental NPV of the investment, it must be high. The entire value of the operation should be set against this single purchase of a pump. The trouble is that the following week a different pump might also need to be replaced. Does this claim the same NPV? Or should we assume that a pump breaks every week and allow just one week of operation to justify the investment in the first pump?

In my view neither of these approaches makes a lot of sense. Sustaining investments need to be considered in a different way from the usual discretionary investments which we consider. This is why I have devoted a separate section to the topic.

Sustaining investments should be treated as though they were simply a part of the overall operating cost of an activity. We include fixed and variable costs in our financial models. We should also include any necessary

[9] For those for whom English is not their first language, a 'no-brainer' decision is one where the answer is so obvious you do not even have to think about it.

sustaining capital expenditure. The aim should be that our overall financial model presents a viable projection of future cash flow. In simple terms, if pumps have a chance of breaking during the assumed economic life of an overall activity then the cost of replacing them should be included in the numbers.

So sustaining investments are justified as part of the overall decision to be in a particular line of business. This decision is taken either as part of a strategy review or as part of an individual finance case. In a strategy review we say, in effect, that we have a business that can operate in a particular way and that overall has an absolute NPV that is greater than the absolute NPV of the generic alternatives including divestment. Once we have done this we have, in effect, justified an ongoing programme of sustaining capital investment. We should not need to review it again unless/until the passage of time has shown that the assumptions that underpinned the decision need to be reviewed.

Likewise, in an investment case we justify a particular major investment including its associated sustaining investment. Provided the investment remains on track overall, it should not be necessary to justify individual items of sustaining investment as and when they need to be spent. There is, in effect, an overall budget for sustaining spend that has already been justified.

The need to control sustaining investment

The idea of a pot of money that does not require formal sanction before it is spent would always cause a good controller some severe concerns. I would share these concerns. In some types of business the sustaining investment spend can become very material. If this were to be spent without challenge, the discretionary spend can be squeezed. Any of the following might happen:

- Small capital spends which should be treated as discretionary could be classified as being sustaining and then not subject to the usual degree of rigorous assessment.
- Poor businesses may be kept going because of lack of focus on the sustaining spend which, if properly allowed for, might lead to an alternative strategy such as exit.
- Poor new business investments may be made if insufficient allowance is made at the time of sanction for future sustaining investment. Then, once the project has been built, the company would be, in effect, forced to fund the necessary sustaining investment.

What is necessary is to ensure that adequate allowance is made for sustaining investments in original investment cases and in strategy reviews. These must justify the proposed course of action despite the need to fund the sustaining investment. A Plan, Do, Measure, Learn approach should then be followed. Even though sustaining investment has already been justified, it is important to monitor actual spends as time progresses. These actual results should then inform subsequent decisions.

The feedback loop should work like this. Suppose, for example, overall sustaining investment is consistently below the assumed level. In this case it might be appropriate to assume a lower level in the future. The result might be that more investments were made. If spends are above the anticipated level then strategy reviews and future investment/divestment cases should reflect this. The end result might be that poor businesses would be divested.

The way that sustaining investment should be controlled should therefore be through the setting of a budget for the annual sustaining spend. The budget total should be in line with the assumed spend in the strategy review or the investment case that justified the activity. Individual items of spend that are put forward for treatment as sustaining expenditure should be reviewed to ensure that they were indeed sustaining spends and not discretionary spends. If they passed this test then they should be considered to have been justified, provided they remained within the level that could be considered to be consistent with the budgeted amount. Individual items should not be considered on their own merits because this should always be a waste of time.

Dealing with changes in legislation

It is quite common for changes in legislation to require additional capital expenditure. For example, enhanced waste product treatment may be required in order to remain within ever-tightening environmental legislation. The definition that I have proposed would allow such a spend to be treated as sustaining investment provided it was relatively small.

Small spends would be treated as having been already justified if, and only if, they remained within the broad scope of the overall allowance that was made for sustaining spend. There would be a clear need to adopt a broad-brush view to what counted as being within the overall scope of an allowance because changes in legislation tend to be less frequent.

Major mandatory spends on environmental improvements or even minor spends that had not been anticipated should serve as a trigger for a review of the strategy of the affected business. There may well, for example, be lessons to learn about the frequency of legislative changes.

There are two possible ways to model the impact of potential but as yet unconfirmed legislative changes. The first way would be to reduce the assumed economic life of an asset down to your estimate of the expected value of the time when the legislation might force you otherwise to close down. This approach would be appropriate for anticipated major changes which could be so severe as to require closure as the alternative to investment. Potential changes with a more minor impact would be allowed for in our economic models through including a one-off spend at roughly the time when the spend might be needed.

Part 4: Full-cycle economics

Introduction: Defining full-cycle economics

Full-cycle economics is a concept that is concerned with the overall impact of an activity on shareholder value. It can be contrasted with the more typical money-forward economics which are used for traditional project appraisal. Money-forward economics may also be referred to as incremental economics. A positive full-cycle NPV should mean that shareholders are glad that the activity was started. A negative full-cycle NPV will mean that shareholders would wish that the activity had never been started even if today they may well be prepared to go ahead because it had a positive money-forward NPV.

The usual NPVs that are quoted at the time of sanction of a project are incremental NPVs. These show the decision-maker the impact of the decision that he or she is being asked to take at that time. If the incremental NPV is positive then in principle it is worth going ahead with the project.[10] There can, however, be times when this feels very unfair. In particular, a project that overspends its budget and comes back for approval for an overspend may well claim a high NPV on the necessary incremental spend. It would be benefiting from large what we call 'sunk costs'.

The concept of full-cycle economics requires that one goes back to when an activity was first started and tracks all of the costs and benefits that either have already happened, or will in the future happen, as a result of the activity.

[10] Subject of course to a check that the project does not expose the company to unacceptable risks.

There are two key differences which need to be allowed for. Full-cycle economics include both past sunk costs and a fair share of future non-incremental fixed costs.

I will consider first sunk costs. At the time a project is put forward for formal sanction all projects will already have incurred some design costs which, because they happened in the past, will be excluded from the incremental economics. Some projects will have benefited from very substantial sunk costs. An example of this would be the cost of the exploration well which found an oil field. So all projects receive a benefit from sunk costs but some receive a bigger benefit than others. A statement of full-cycle economics would deduct the value impact of these pre-sanction costs from the claimed NPV.

Think now about the overhead costs within a company. If you think about one incremental project it is hard to see that there will be any connection. Irrespective of whether your company progresses with the project it will still occupy the same head office and have the same level of overheads. So, quite correctly, non-incremental overheads are not allocated against a project. If, however, a company were to cease investing in projects it would soon decide to reduce its overheads. Also, somebody has to pay these costs, so it is fair to consider a share of future overheads as part of the full-cycle picture.

Why consider full-cycle economics?

Theory suggests that full-cycle economics should not be relevant to incremental decisions. The book *Principles of Corporate Finance*, for example, makes a strong point about the need to estimate cash flows on an incremental basis and hence to ignore sunk costs and to beware of allocated overhead costs, the logic being that neither the amount of money that you spent in getting to where you are today nor future costs which will not change should impact today's decision about whether or not to go ahead.

So why consider full-cycle economics? Well, there are several reasons that can be put forward but they all boil down to the fact that a good choice of strategy will yield positive full-cycle economics which in turn will impress shareholders. The computation of full-cycle economics facilitates the learning of lessons about this most important of topics. The Plan, Do, Measure, Learn approach needs to consider full-cycle economics to ensure that successes and failures are identified and appropriate lessons learned and acted upon.

Take for example a request for sanction of $500m of capital that will result in an incremental NPV of, say, $3,000m. Should this project be highlighted as a great corporate success? The incremental economics certainly look stunning. So should the chief executive say that they want more projects like this? Should they seek for the lessons of success or should they perhaps be considering the equally important lessons of failure? My answer is that I don't know yet. I need first to understand the full-cycle perspective. I will postulate four generic situations that span the range of alternative possibilities:

- Suppose that the request was for an overspend necessary to complete a long and expensive oil pipeline. Let us say that the pipeline had already cost $3,500m and the full-cycle NPV was about minus $1,000m. In this situation the chief executive should be feeling pretty sick about the project but will have no realistic alternative other than to continue. The concern will not just be with the capital cost since $3,500m increasing to $4,000m is hardly an unheard-of cost over-run. The concern will also be with the anticipated future pipeline throughput fees. These have clearly fallen since the current money-forward NPV is less than the sunk cost. What the chief executive can do is ensure that the lessons of failure are learned. Plan, Do, Measure, Learn must be all about ensuring that mistakes are not repeated.
- Suppose now that the project concerned a new drug launch. A big prize might be necessary to offset the huge R&D, approval and marketing costs which a drug company will incur.[11] The specific R&D and approval costs associated with this particular drug will be known but will not make a material change in the $3,000m NPV. A 'fair' allocation of future marketing costs will also make only a small reduction in NPV. The question that could turn this high incremental NPV into a negative full-cycle one concerns the treatment of other failures at the R&D and approval stages. There will certainly be a celebration of this particular success but the chief executive may know that they need, say, one of these each year just to stand still against the ticking clock of patent expiry on the existing portfolio of drugs and to cover all sunk costs. We will look at this topic in more detail later in this part.
- Suppose that the request was for the funds to build a new chemical plant following an *unexpected* breakthrough in manufacturing technology. Let us assume that the full-cycle NPV was only slightly lower than the

[11] My simple mental model of the drugs industry is that there are three key stages. First, many potential drugs are scanned to find possible winners. The second stage concerns gaining approval for a drug that appears to work. Once again, there will be a substantial failure rate at this stage. Finally, having been approved, the company's sales force must persuade doctors to prescribe it and patients to request it.

incremental NPV. The chief executive should be ecstatic about the NPV but should be questioning the strategy if the company had received no advance warning of a possibility of this magnitude. So although this scenario may represent the best news so far it also represents a very big failure of a company's planning system.[12]

- Finally, consider what I would call the genuine success. The NPV could be the result of finding a new opencast coal resource close to an existing under-utilised coal export terminal. If the terminal belonged to a third party company which was prepared to offer a competitive price to win new business then there would be no issues here concerning allocation of a fair share of export terminal fixed costs. If the terminal were owned by the coal company then its fixed costs would have to be allowed for in the full-cycle calculation. Let us suppose that in this case the terminal was owned by the same company. If the allocation of future non-incremental fixed costs simply lowered the NPV to $2,000m we would know that we had a great success to understand. There was some luck involved but it was the business strategy that created the luck. The lessons to learn are the lessons of success.

Defining sunk costs

Some sunk costs are self-evidently allocable to a project. Examples would include the cost of engineering design of a plant or the cost of a project development team that had been set up with exactly this outcome in mind. A company's accounting systems will treat some of these costs as part of the capital cost. There will, however, almost always be some costs that have been treated as operating costs in the past. These will have lowered profit in the year in which they were incurred. Development team costs will usually be treated like this.

From the perspective of economic value, the accounting treatment is of little consequence. What matters is the actual cash flows. The only extent to which the categorisation of cash flow does matter is the extent to which it impacts on any tax either already paid or to be paid in the future. The tax aspects are complex but largely factual. Many project-related sunk costs will already have resulted in lower tax payments and even if they have not

[12] The chief executive could easily find they were embarrassed when they announced the new plan to their shareholders and analysts. It would not surprise me if a small delay in approval of the project was brought in so that an initial announcement could be made of some secret but high-potential-impact R&D projects which were under way. The subsequent success could then be presented as a brilliant strategy!

done so now, they will do so in the future. It is important to incorporate the impact of these tax effects in the calculation of the economic impact of sunk costs. The calculation is rarely simple and will almost always require specialist input from tax professionals. There is almost always a lag between expenditure and the consequential reduction in tax paid. This is illustrated in a case study later in this part.

In some cases projects may be 'ring-fenced' by tax authorities. This means the project is taxed simply on its own merits. The result can be that no effective tax relief is received for expenditure until the project generates sufficient revenues to become tax-paying. Projects that are like this will receive what can be thought of as a double benefit from sunk costs at time of sanction. Past sunk costs are excluded from the incremental economic analysis but the associated tax relief is included in the numbers since the only way to achieve this benefit is through progressing with the project.

Judgement needs to be applied when there are what can be described as project search costs such as exploration or R&D. A company will typically undertake a search programme in the anticipation of a statistical degree of success. How much of the failed search cost should be allocated against the successes? My answer to this question is that it all depends on the use to which you will put the answer. Some costs self-evidently belong to the full-cycle analysis of a particular project. Many other costs depend on judgement as regards how far back one goes when allocating costs. Reference to how far back refers both to time and to the ever-enlarging, what I think of as a 'cone of costs'[13] that ultimately lead to a successful project.

Defining future fixed but non-incremental costs

A similar set of issues emerge in relation to future fixed costs. We covered this briefly in the Planning and Control building block on pages 131–133. The mental model that I use is one of layer upon layer of additional fixed costs.

[13] I use the term 'cone' because in my mind I am picturing a decision tree. A company decides to explore: it goes to, say, three countries and in each one it buys some exploration rights, it tests all of the acreage and some projects emerge. The decision tree will now have grown quite wide and will look more like a cone. How far back do you go when allocating costs to a successful project? Do you look just to the individual exploration block or the country or all three countries? The further back you look the greater will be the costs. Sometimes the 'cone' may refer to the way that a number of generic alternatives was developed before the final choice emerged. Each of these generic alternatives will have cost money to analyse. Should all of their costs be counted towards the chosen project's full-cycle picture? My view is that it is purely judgemental how much of the early option evaluation costs should be allocated against today's project.

Most projects will result in their own incremental fixed costs. These should always be included in the incremental analysis of the project. Then what usually will happen is that the bigger the company, and in particular the greater the number of organisational layers, the more there will be fixed costs which are being incurred for the benefit, albeit only in part, of the new project. The full-cycle economic performance of the project should take into account a fair share of these costs.

The purpose of allocating non-incremental fixed costs is to gain insights and learn lessons. The sort of lesson one is looking for concerns things like what the necessary surplus needs to be at the project level on average in order to cover unallocated costs. These questions start whenever two or more operations share any common overheads. There is immediately a risk that each individual operation will assume that some other operation will fund the overheads and that they can be treated as an incremental activity which does not have to 'pay' its full share.

The ultimate test is to consider the company's overall ROCE. As we have already learned, if the company can be thought of as being the sum of a series of projects, then its ROACE gives a rough indication of the full-cycle IRR that is being earned by these projects. If the incremental NPVs on the projects within a division are high while the return overall is low, this is simply a sign of what is a common problem. This problem is excess fixed costs.

The approach that I recommend is that all fixed costs should be identified as part of the overall planning and control effort. The beneficiary of costs should also be identified. Cost allocations to individual projects in order to calculate project full-cycle economics should only be done where fairly clear links exist. For example, if a site acts as host for, say, three projects then site-level costs should be allocated. Anything that is broadly shared across a company should not be allocated to an individual project's full-cycle performance.

The most important examples of an overhead that is narrowly shared are the common services at a site or in a building. Consider for example the reception desk at a large office block. A project team that wished to occupy, say, half a floor would be able to argue that the reception cost was fixed and so should not be included in its incremental analysis.

At a site level, a similar argument could apply to the fixed costs associated with the steam and water supplies. Unless a project took the site beyond its currently installed capacity it would be correct only to include the marginal costs of steam and water supplies and no fixed costs should be allocated to the incremental analysis. Costs such as these would clearly, however, be included as part of the full-cycle analysis.

Calculating full-cycle economics

The calculation of the full-cycle economics involves three steps. First, identify the actual costs, then identify the associated tax effects and finally compute the NPV impact, remembering that money spent in the past must be multiplied by one plus the CoC for each year rather than divided. Future costs are simpler to handle from a computational point of view than sunk costs because the financial model will already go into the future and so will usually easily accommodate a few extra fixed costs. Indeed, the model will usually handle the tax aspects automatically.

The following example will illustrate a simple way of including sunk costs through their present value impact.

It is 1 July 2008 and a project is being put forward for approval. The following sunk costs have been identified. What is their NPV impact as at the date of project sanction if the CoC is 9%?

1. In 2005 there were development team operating costs of $0.2m. These generated associated tax savings in the tax payment due in the middle of 2006. The tax rate was 35%.
2. In 2006 the development team costs had grown to $1.5m. Tax treatment on this was as above.
3. In 2007 development team costs were $1.5m again. In addition the first capital expenditure was incurred. It amounted to $3m and was for third party design work. The tax authorities allow the recovery of capital costs based on a straight-line amortisation of the spend over ten years starting in the current year.
4. During the first half of 2008 the development team cost was $1m and capital expenditure was $4m.

We are fortunate in that tax rates and the CoC are the same throughout. We can therefore use a simple short-cut approach to calculate the after-tax value impact of any operating or capital spends.

One million dollars of operating costs will create an associated tax reduction in the middle of the following year of $0.35m. This needs to be subjected to one year of discounting at 9% to come up with a present value of the tax offset of $0.32m. So if all operating costs are multiplied by 68% we will allow for the value impact of tax.

Capital expenditures gain their tax relief over a longer period. We need to use our ten-year annuity factor tables with year end flows to do this calculation. The factor with a 9% CoC is 6.418.

The tax that is saved in each year owing to capital expenditure is 3.5% (i.e. 35% of 10%). The present value of this is obtained by multiplying 3.5% by 6.418. This gives us roughly 22%. So $1 of capital expenditure has to be multiplied by 78% to allow for the value impact of tax. Note that this higher percentage number compared with operation costs is a reflection of the economic cost caused by the tax authorities forcing the capital spend to be amortised over ten years rather than allowing immediate offset as they do for operating costs.

Armed now with these two value-multiplication factors we can easily calculate the value impact of all of the sunk costs by multiplying the annual cost by the relevant factor. This is illustrated in the following table:

Value impact of sunk costs $m

Year	2005	2006	2007	2008
Operating cost	0.2	1.5	1.5	1
Capital cost	0	0	3	4
Value impact op cost	0.14	1.02	1.02	0.68
Value impact cap cost	0.00	0.00	2.33	3.10
Annual value impact	0.14	1.02	3.34	3.78
Discount factor	1.30	1.19	1.09	1.00
Present value costs	0.18	1.21	3.65	3.78
Cumulative present cost	0.18	1.39	5.03	8.81

Our final answer to the problem is that the value impact of sunk costs is $8.81m.

It does take a little getting used to the way that the present value of sunk costs works. Increasing the tax rate decreases the present cost while increasing the CoC increases the present cost. The final number of $8.81m is the amount by which the NPV should be lowered in order to calculate the full-cycle impact of sunk costs.

Put another way, if the incremental NPV is at least $9m we could draw some comfort that our project had covered all of its past costs and we were not finishing it simply because we had gone past the point of no return.

Once again we have relied on value's principle of additivity. Had we been asked to work out the full-cycle IRR we would have needed to create a spreadsheet that looked back as far as 2005 and also with columns going up to ten years into the future simply to capture the timing effect of tax relief.

Interpreting full-cycle economics

I have, over the years, had discussions on the topic of full-cycle economics that have started with questions between the two extremes of:

- Why does anybody look at anything other than full-cycle economics because this is the only true way to measure project performance from a shareholder's perspective?
- Why does anybody ever bother to look at full-cycle economics at all because the numbers are so arbitrary and in any case should not impact project level decision-making?

My belief is that full-cycle analysis can self-evidently give some very useful insights into strategy but is of potential relevance to an individual project decision as well. I will explain the strategy point first because it should be the easiest to grasp.

Suppose that the strategic insights provided by a major project are such that strategy itself may well be brought into question. Perhaps we have learned that the projects are not good enough to cover all of their sunk costs. This should, in my view, catalyse a strategy review. Something must be changed because we have learned that the previous way of doing things was resulting in value being destroyed.

This change in strategy could well be that we exit the business. If you are going to exit, do you want to start a new project? Well, only if the potential buyer will pay more for the business as a result to generate a positive NPV on the incremental spend. Some projects will do this but others will not. This should be thought about explicitly before the project is approved.

Let us now turn to how full-cycle analysis might change an individual project decision. Suppose that you have a project that shows good incremental economic indicators. All logic therefore appears to be saying that it would be acceptable to approve this project. Suppose, however, that if a fair share of future non-incremental overheads were allocated to the project its full-cycle NPV would fall below zero. You can still justify going ahead with the project but this is subject to an important condition. The condition is that there must not be a further project likely to come along later that will also utilise the overheads but that offers better financial returns overall. If only one of the projects can be accommodated then the choice should be to go with the project with the best NPV, not simply the first project to present itself for approval.

As a final example of interpreting full-cycle economic data we will consider again our hypothetical drugs company from page 209. Let us suppose that this company is researching in the areas of drugs to treat heart problems, cancer and HIV. Should it seek strategic insights by thinking about how its overall R&D and drug approval costs match up against its successes or should it consider success area by area or individual drug tested by drug tested?[14]

My answer to this question is that it all depends. It depends crucially on the chances of success. In anything involving chance one needs a big enough sample before any conclusions can safely be drawn. So looking at simply the costs associated with an individual successful drug will yield a pretty meaningless answer. Meaningless, that is, unless the analysis were to show that the drug did not even cover its own R&D costs. Were this to be the case one would have a strong signal that strategy was wrong.

My analysis of this particular situation would be as follows. First I would note that the NPV was large even in relation to a major drugs company. On the day I wrote this page the market capitalisation of the top five healthcare companies (to use their usual stock exchange name) averaged about $150bn. Even a $150bn company is clearly not expected to produce a lot of $3bn NPVs each year. Any analysis of just one large event would therefore have great danger of being spurious. If a large company could expect only a few such successes per year a smaller company could know for certain that a $3bn NPV was good news.

One could think of lessons needing to be learned in relation to three key issues. These are the size of the prize; the direct cost of achieving it; and the probability of success. A single success will almost certainly allow no conclusions to be drawn as regards the probability question.

What I would do with the success is test it against the previous models of success that had been used to justify the strategy in the first place. I may not be able to draw many conclusions concerning assumed probabilities of success but the scale of the financial prize if there was a success and the direct costs of the drug might well offer lessons.

Summary: How important are full-cycle economics?

In my view the difference between incremental and full-cycle costs is the biggest reason why the simple 'invest-in-all-positive-NPV-projects' decision

[14] A generically similar problem would concern exploration by major oil companies. Should they think about exploration performance well by well, geographic basin by basin or just globally?

rule is not a good way to manage a company's resource allocation. The book by Brealey and Myers refers to two reasons why NPVs can be positive.[15] These are because the company can really expect to earn economic rents or because the project has been analysed in a biased way. These two reasons are true but I believe one should add a comment that all companies should really be expected to earn economic rents when these are measured on an incremental cost basis. This is because the overall effect of sunk costs and future fixed costs will almost always be large. So any company that deals with resource allocation at the point of project sanction should find that it is approving all of its major projects. This is because unless the strategy is really bad, the incremental NPV on its projects should always be positive thanks to the benefit of sunk costs and future overheads.

Instead of continuing to carry out resource allocation by studying projects at the traditional point of sanction, one needs to move the point at which projects are analysed much earlier into their time line to the point when their strategy is considered. At present, however, we lack the ability to make the analysis of a strategy sufficiently numerate for this to be meaningful. I will, however, deal with this problem when I introduce the Sources of Value technique in the next pillar.

For the present all that I suggest is that readers note how for any particular case the full-cycle economics may be fundamentally important but they may equally be irrelevant. They are fundamentally important when they cause a company to change its strategy despite a positive incremental NPV on a marginal project. They can become irrelevant when so many judgements have to be made to decide what number to quote that the number ceases to have any real meaning. They can also be irrelevant when the message that they convey has already been learned by the company.

My view is that full-cycle economics offer the potential of what I call a 'free strategic health check' at the time a project is being considered for approval. We tend to receive many so-called free offers and should have learned that some are indeed free but others have hidden costs. Senior-level judgement needs to be applied. Full-cycle economics should neither always be required nor never be required. Like optimisation studies, they should be done only to an appropriate extent. The ability to distinguish what is appropriate is what can separate the good leaders from the bad.

[15] See page 319 of my cited ninth edition.

Part 5: Inflation and forex effects

Inflation impacts on everything and usually 'hurts' a project

Inflation is the tendency of prices to rise over time. Politicians often can become fixated with headline inflation rates. These refer to the average change in prices for a defined set of purchases. For example, there might be an index set by the price of typical household purchases. There could also be another index just for fuel costs.

I take the view that a good economic value model will be based on both an assumed general level of inflation and also a series of specific price rises for the more important data items. This means that a good model will make specific assumptions about the rate of change of important items and will not simply assume that everything changes at the same rate.

Even if inflation impacts on every cost and every revenue item in the same way, increasing the rate of inflation is likely to lower the NPV of a project. I will explain this effect below. Its primary causes are working capital and tax effects.

This part will consider the main modelling implications of inflation. These issues remain of some concern even when inflation is 'under control'. They are, however, of fundamental importance in countries that are unfortunate enough to suffer from high inflation.

Inflation and the cost of capital

The first point to note in relation to inflation is that it is not sensible to think of changes in inflation independently from changes in the CoC. The idea that nominal interest rates are a combination of a real rate and the anticipated future level of inflation was put forward on page 33 in Building Block 2 on Financial Markets. The CoC can also be thought about in a similar way with a nominal CoC set as follows:

$$(1+\text{inflation})\times(1+\text{real IRR})=(1+\text{nominal IRR})$$

It would be spurious to adjust the CoC for very small changes in the assumed general rate of inflation. In my view the best approach is to make an assumption concerning the general level of inflation at the time the CoC assumption is made. The assumed general level of inflation would then be held constant unless and until the CoC was reviewed. For example, one could say that a

CoC of 9% post-tax was assumed and that implicit in this was an inflation rate of 2.5%. The inflation rate assumption would not then be changed without also reviewing the CoC assumption.

With this approach our financial models would always assume the same rate of inflation each year into the future. Small changes in assumed inflation year by year in our model would, in effect, not be permitted. Large changes would need to be accompanied by changes in the CoC or by switching to an approach that models so-called 'real cash flows'. This is explained below and is my recommended approach for countries that do suffer from high inflation.

Modelling specific prices

Just because the general level of inflation is held constant does not mean that all items need change at the same rate. It can be perfectly appropriate to make separate assumptions about, for example, wage rates, feedstock prices and selling prices as long as they remain broadly consistent with the assumed general rate of inflation. These specific assumptions do not have to be held constant across the full time span of the model. They just have to be clearly defined and explainable if they are challenged.

The more specific a particular cost or revenue assumption may be, the greater the potential for its own inflation rate to diverge from the general rate of inflation. Individual commodity prices have changed by huge amounts over recent years while the overall level of inflation has, the politicians assure us, hardly changed. So a good financial model will make several different assumptions about how costs and/or prices are changing for different items.

Modelling when inflation is high

When the general level of inflation is high (say 10% or more) and we want to be able to model the effect of changes in inflation rates over the period covered by the model we are forced to adopt an alternative approach. The approach I recommend is to adopt a so-called 'real terms' convention.

The expression 'real terms' refers to sums of money that have been converted into equivalent purchasing power terms. So if inflation is 20%, something that costs 1 unit today will cost 1.2 units in a year's time and 1.44 units in two years' time and so on. So if all sums of money in the second year are divided by 1.2 and all sums in year 3 are divided by 1.44 they would then be said to be stated in real (year 1) terms. These so-called real cash flows would then be converted into present values by discounting at the real CoC.

We will now study how inflation might impact on one of the earlier cases that we studied during the first building block. This is the paving slabs example that was considered on pages 24–26. In the initial analysis of this case the inflation assumption was set to zero and the project had an NPV of \$6.9m and a reported IRR of 18%.[16] We will now study the effect of changing the assumed rate of inflation to 10% while holding all other assumptions (including the 10% CoC) unchanged.

The numbers with no inflation are shown in table 7.1. If inflation is set at 10% the numbers change as shown in table 7.2. All of the cash flows are simply 10% higher for each year. This is because I chose a particularly simple set of assumptions with no tax or working capital effects to model. We will study what might happen to tax and working capital later but for the present, focus please on the economic indicators.

The project appears to have got a lot better. The NPV and IRR are higher. Note in particular how the IRR change can be explained through the formula:

$$(1+\text{inflation})\times(1+\text{real IRR})=(1+\text{nominal IRR})$$

In this case:

$$1.1\times1.177=1.295$$

The increase in IRR is purely due to the effect of inflation because all future cash flow numbers have been increased by the same percentage figure each year. The increase in NPV is simply a reflection of the fact that we left the CoC unchanged when we changed the inflation rate. It is not realistic to assume 10% inflation and at the same time assume a 10% CoC. We should convert the cash flows into real terms and then apply a real CoC. In this case the real CoC to apply is 10% because this was the CoC that we assumed when the inflation rate was zero.

We can now illustrate the methodology that should be used when inflation is high. We need to insert an additional line into our spreadsheet that converts the forecast money-of-the-day cash flow into real terms.[17] The sheet becomes as shown in table 7.3 (the key lines are shown in bold).

[16] The exact number was 17.7%.

[17] The real cash flow is equal to the money-of-the-day cash flow divided by an inflation index. The index starts at 1 in the first year and then increases by the rate of inflation each year.

Table 7.1 The numbers with no inflation.

Year	0	1	2	3	4	5	6	7	8	9	10	11	12	13
Sales				5.3	5.6	6.0	6.4	6.8	6.8	6.8	6.8	6.8	6.8	0.0
Fixed costs				0.8	0.8	0.8	0.8	0.8	0.8	0.8	0.8	0.8	0.8	0.0
Variable costs				0.8	0.8	0.9	1.0	1.0	1.0	1.0	1.0	1.0	1.0	0.0
Capex		10.0	8.0											
Close-down cost														2.0
Cash flow		−10.0	−8.0	3.7	4.0	4.3	4.6	4.9	4.9	4.9	4.9	4.9	4.9	−2.0
Discount factor	1	0.953	0.867	0.788	0.716	0.651	0.592	0.538	0.489	0.445	0.404	0.368	0.334	0.304
Present value cash flow		−9.5	−6.9	2.9	2.9	2.8	2.7	2.7	2.4	2.2	2.0	1.8	1.7	−0.6
Cumulative present value	0.0	−9.5	−16.5	−13.6	−10.7	−7.9	−5.2	−2.5	−0.1	2.1	4.1	5.9	7.5	6.9
NPV	6.9													
IRR	17.7%													
Discounted payback year	9													
Efficiency	38%													

Table 7.2 The numbers with inflation set at 10%.

Year	0	1	2	3	4	5	6	7	8	9	10	11	12	13
Sales				6.4	7.5	8.8	10.3	12.0	13.2	14.5	15.9	17.5	19.3	0.0
Fixed costs				1.0	1.1	1.2	1.3	1.4	1.6	1.7	1.9	2.1	2.3	0.0
Variable costs				1.0	1.1	1.3	1.5	1.8	2.0	2.2	2.4	2.6	2.9	0.0
Capex		10.0	8.8											
Close-down cost														6.3
Cash flow		−10.0	−8.8	4.4	5.3	6.3	7.4	8.7	9.6	10.6	11.6	12.8	14.1	−6.3
Discount factor	1	0.953	0.867	0.788	0.716	0.651	0.592	0.538	0.489	0.445	0.404	0.368	0.334	0.304
Present value cash flow		−9.5	−7.6	3.5	3.8	4.1	4.4	4.7	4.7	4.7	4.7	4.7	4.7	−1.9
Cumulative present value	0.0	−9.5	−17.2	−13.7	−9.9	−5.8	−1.4	3.3	8.0	12.8	17.5	22.2	26.9	25.0
NPV	25.0													
IRR	29.5													
Discounted payback year	7													
Efficiency	133%													

Table 7.3 The numbers when inflation is high.

Year	0	1	2	3	4	5	6	7	8	9	10	11	12	13
Sales		0.0	0.0	6.4	7.5	8.8	10.3	12.0	13.2	14.5	15.9	17.5	19.3	0.0
Fixed costs		0.0	0.0	1.0	1.1	1.2	1.3	1.4	1.6	1.7	1.9	2.1	2.3	0.0
Variable costs		0.0	0.0	1.0	1.1	1.3	1.5	1.8	2.0	2.2	2.4	2.6	2.9	0.0
Capex		10.0	8.8	0.0	0.0	0.0	0.0	0.0	0.0	0.0	0.0	0.0	0.0	0.0
Close-down cost		0.0	0.0	0.0	0.0	0.0	0.0	0.0	0.0	0.0	0.0	0.0	0.0	6.3
Cash flow		**−10.0**	**−8.8**	**4.4**	**5.3**	**6.3**	**7.4**	**8.7**	**9.6**	**10.6**	**11.6**	**12.8**	**14.1**	**−6.3**
Real cash flow		**−10.0**	**−8.0**	**3.7**	**4.0**	**4.3**	**4.6**	**4.9**	**4.9**	**4.9**	**4.9**	**4.9**	**4.9**	**−2.0**
Discount factor	1.000	0.953	0.867	0.788	0.716	0.651	0.592	0.538	0.489	0.445	0.404	0.368	0.334	0.304
Present value cash flow	0.0	−9.5	−6.9	2.9	2.9	2.8	2.7	2.7	2.4	2.2	2.0	1.8	1.7	−0.6
Cumulative present value	0.0	−9.5	−16.5	−13.6	−10.7	−7.9	−5.2	−2.5	−0.1	2.1	4.1	5.9	7.5	6.9
NPV	6.9													
IRR	17.7%													
Discounted payback year	9													
Efficiency	37%													

NPV, IRR and discounted payback have now all returned to exactly what they were before inflation was increased to 10%. The only change is the small decrease in the efficiency number. This has reduced because it is calculated by dividing NPV by capex and not the inflation-adjusted capex.

How tax and working capital make inflation 'hurt'

There are two more or less unavoidable facts of business life that make inflation 'hurt'. That is to say that inflation lowers NPV, unlike the calculation above where we saw that NPV was unchanged.

The first effect to allow for is that of taxation. The tax rules usually work in such a way that the tax offset for capital costs is spread over a number of years but is set based on the original capital spend. This means that the purchasing power of the tax offsets is reduced as inflation rises. The higher the rate of inflation the lower the value of the tax offsets for capital expenditure.

The second effect concerns working capital. In simple terms the working capital balance at the end of a year will rise in line with inflation. So if there is no inflation there is no need to fund an increase in working capital. If, however, there is some inflation then this serves to lower cash flow by an amount equal to inflation times the opening working capital balance every year. The best way to see this is through an example.

We will take the paving slabs example from above and add two further complications to it. First we will assume that there is a working capital balance equal to two months of sales revenue at the end of each year. Inventories and payables will be assumed to be nil and tax will be paid in the year it is incurred. Second, we will include a tax charge based on a tax rate of 30% and with the tax allowance for capital investment based on a ten-year straight-line amortisation of the cost. The closure cost will be treated as though it is already net of any tax relief and so the cost will be shown as though it were a fixed cost in the final-year column but it will not attract any tax relief.

With these additional items it will pay to show the model output in AFS format. This was not done when we first met this case study because at that stage we had not learned about the AFS approach.

The first thing we should do is confirm that the new model is working correctly. To do this we set the assumed rate of inflation to zero, the tax rate to zero and the receivables to zero. The economic indicators are indeed identical to what we have before so this helps to confirm that the new model is 'faithfully' converting assumptions into economic indicators (table 7.4).

Table 7.4 Paving Business: Abbreviated Financial Summary including impact of inflation

	Inflation Rate 0%													
Year	0	1	2	3	4	5	6	7	8	9	10	11	12	13
Sales revenue		0.0	0.0	5.3	5.6	6.0	6.4	6.8	6.8	6.8	6.8	6.8	6.8	0.0
Variable costs		0.0	0.0	−0.8	−0.8	−0.9	−1.0	−1.0	−1.0	−1.0	−1.0	−1.0	−1.0	0.0
Contribution		0.0	0.0	4.5	4.8	5.1	5.4	5.7	5.7	5.7	5.7	5.7	5.7	0.0
Fixed costs		0.0	0.0	−0.8	−0.8	−0.8	−0.8	−0.8	−0.8	−0.8	−0.8	−0.8	−0.8	−2.0
Amortisation		0.0	0.0	−1.8	−1.8	−1.8	−1.8	−1.8	−1.8	−1.8	−1.8	−1.8	−1.8	0.0
Pre tax profit		0.0	0.0	1.9	2.2	2.5	2.8	3.1	3.1	3.1	3.1	3.1	3.1	−2.0
Tax		0.0	0.0	0.0	0.0	0.0	0.0	0.0	0.0	0.0	0.0	0.0	0.0	0.0
Net profit		0.0	0.0	1.9	2.2	2.5	2.8	3.1	3.1	3.1	3.1	3.1	3.1	−2.0
Fixed assets	0.0	10.0	18.0	16.2	14.4	12.6	10.8	9.0	7.2	5.4	3.6	1.8	0.0	0.0
Working capital	0.0	0.0	0.0	0.0	0.0	0.0	0.0	0.0	0.0	0.0	0.0	0.0	0.0	0.0
Capital employed	0.0	10.0	18.0	16.2	14.4	12.6	10.8	9.0	7.2	5.4	3.6	1.8	0.0	0.0
ROACE		0.0%	0.0%	10.9%	14.3%	18.5%	24.1%	31.7%	38.7%	49.8%	69.7%	116.2%	348.6%	
Profit		0.0	0.0	1.9	2.2	2.5	2.8	3.1	3.1	3.1	3.1	3.1	3.1	−2.0
Amortisation		0.0	0.0	1.8	1.8	1.8	1.8	1.8	1.8	1.8	1.8	1.8	1.8	0
Working capital change		0	0	0	0	0	0	0	0	0	0	0	0	0
Capital investment		−10.0	−8.0	0.0	0.0	0.0	0.0	0.0	0.0	0.0	0.0	0.0	0.0	0.0
Funds flow		−10.0	−8.0	3.7	4.0	4.3	4.6	4.9	4.9	4.9	4.9	4.9	4.9	−2.0
Value calculation														
Funds flow		−10.0	−8.0	3.7	4.0	4.3	4.6	4.9	4.9	4.9	4.9	4.9	4.9	−2.0
Real funds flow		−10.0	−8.0	3.7	4.0	4.3	4.6	4.9	4.9	4.9	4.9	4.9	4.9	−2.0
Discount factor		0.953	0.867	0.788	0.716	0.651	0.592	0.538	0.489	0.445	0.404	0.368	0.334	0.304
Present value		−9.5	−6.9	2.9	2.9	2.8	2.7	2.7	2.4	2.2	2.0	1.8	1.7	−0.6
Cumulative present value		−9.5	−16.5	−13.6	−10.7	−7.9	−5.2	−2.5	−0.1	2.1	4.1	5.9	7.5	6.9
NPV	6.9													
IRR	17.7%													
Discounted payback year	9													
Efficiency	38%													

The next step is to introduce inflation. As before we will assume 10% pa. All costs and revenues will be increased by the same amount. The new AFS is shown in table 7.5.

Again the economic indicators are exactly as before. Thanks to the AFS format we can study one new indicator. This is ROACE. What we can see is that this is massively increased, particularly in the later years. One of the many impacts of inflation is that it does boost ROACE. We can use the company-as-a-series-of-projects approach[18] to see what the impact is overall. With zero inflation the steady state ROACE for a company starting one project each year would be 24%. This rises to 58% with inflation of 10%. The lesson here is simply that ROACE loses its usefulness as an indicator when there is high inflation.

Now we will study what happens when we introduce tax and working capital. Obviously all of the cases will get worse. The original no-tax or working capital NPV of \$6.9m falls to \$2.6m when tax is charged at 30%. It falls to \$2.1m when working capital is also included. Remember also that the original NPV was unaffected by inflation as long as we used the correct methodology of converting cash flows to real terms and applying a real discount rate.

The financial results for the 10% inflation case with tax and working capital are shown in table 7.6.

The NPV is now a mere \$0.6m. The steps between the initial NPV of \$6.9m with 10% inflation but no tax or working capital are that the NPV of \$6.9m falls to \$1.5m when tax is charged and to \$0.6m when working capital is included. So 10% inflation has increased the NPV impact of tax from \$4.3m to \$5.4m and the impact of working capital from \$0.5m to \$0.9m.

I encourage readers either to build this model and use it to investigate for themselves how inflation impacts on the results or to test a model of their own with high rates of inflation.

Inflation and 'stock profits'

Up to now the modelling approach that we have adopted has been simply to increase items in our model by an inflation index. So if inflation is, say, 10% we compute a cost index that goes 1.0, 1.1, 1.21 and so on. We then multiply our costs expressed in initial year terms by this index to get the money-of-the-day cost in the later years. This approach is fine if we hold no inventory.

[18] This approach is explained in the Planning and Control building block on page 126.

Table 7.5 Paving Business: Abbreviated Financial Summary including impact of inflation

	Inflation Rate 10%													
Year	0	1	2	3	4	5	6	7	8	9	10	11	12	13
Sales revenue		0.0	0.0	6.4	7.5	8.8	10.3	12.0	13.2	14.5	15.9	17.5	19.3	0.0
Variable costs		0.0	0.0	−1.0	−1.1	−1.3	−1.5	−1.8	−2.0	−2.2	−2.4	−2.6	−2.9	0.0
Contribution		0.0	0.0	5.4	6.4	7.5	8.7	10.22	11.2	12.3	13.5	14.9	16.4	0.0
Fixed costs		0.0	0.0	−1.0	−1.1	−1.2	−1.3	−1.4	−1.6	−1.7	−1.9	−2.1	−2.3	−6.3
Amortisation		0.0	0.0	−1.9	−1.9	−1.9	−1.9	−1.9	−1.9	−1.9	−1.9	−1.9	−1.9	0.0
Pre-tax profit		0.0	0.0	2.6	3.4	4.4	5.6	6.9	7.7	8.7	9.8	10.9	12.2	−6.3
Tax		0.0	0.0	0.0	0.0	0.0	0.0	0.0	0.0	0.0	0.0	0.0	0.0	0.0
Net profit		0.0	0.0	2.6	3.4	4.4	5.6	6.9	7.7	8.7	9.8	10.9	12.2	−6.3
Fixed assets	0.0	10.0	18.8	16.9	15.0	13.2	11.3	9.4	7.5	5.6	3.8	1.9	0.0	0.0
Working capital	0.0	0.0	0.0	0.0	0.0	0.0	0.0	0.0	0.0	0.0	0.0	0.0	0.0	0.0
Capital employed	0.0	10.0	18.8	16.9	15.0	13.2	11.3	9.4	7.5	5.6	3.8	1.9	0.0	0.0
ROACE		0.0%	0.0%	14.3%	21.4%	31.3%	45.5%	66.4%	91.5%	132.3%	207.7%	387.5%	1299%	
Profit		0.0	0.0	2.6	3.4	4.4	5.6	6.9	7.7	8.7	9.8	10.9	12.2	−6.3
Amortisation		0.0	0.0	1.9	1.9	1.9	1.9	1.9	1.9	1.9	1.9	1.9	1.9	0
Working capital change		0	0	0	0	0	0	0	0	0	0	0	0	0
Capital investment		−10.0	−8.8	0.0	0.0	0.0	0.0	0.0	0.0	0.0	0.0	0.0	0.0	0.0
Funds flow		−10.0	−8.8	4.4	5.3	6.3	7.4	8.7	9.6	10.6	11.6	12.8	14.1	−6.3
Value calculation														
Funds flow		−10.0	−8.8	4.4	5.3	6.3	7.4	8.7	96	10.6	11.6	12.8	14.1	−6.3
Real funds flow		−10.0	−8.0	3.7	4.0	4.3	4.6	4.9	4.9	4.9	4.9	4.9	4.9	−2.0
Discount factor		0.953	0.867	0.788	0.716	0.651	0.592	0.538	0.489	0.445	0.404	0.368	0.334	0.304
Present value		−9.5	−6.9	2.9	2.9	2.8	2.7	2.7	2.4	2.2	2.0	1.8	1.7	−0.6
Cumulative present value		−9.5	−16.5	−13.6	−10.7	−7.9	−5.2	−2.5	−0.1	2.1	4.1	5.9	7.5	6.9
NPV	6.9													
IRR	17.7%													
Discounted Payback year	9													
Efficiency	37%													

Table 7.6 Paving Business: Abbreviated Financial Summary including impact of inflation

	Inflation Rate 10%													
Year	0	1	2	3	4	5	6	7	8	9	10	11	12	13
Sales revenue		0.0	0.0	6.4	7.5	8.8	10.3	12.0	13.2	14.5	15.9	17.5	19.3	0.0
Variable costs		0.0	0.0	−1.0	−1.1	−1.3	−1.5	−1.8	−2.0	−2.2	−2.4	−2.6	−2.9	0.0
Contribution		0.0	0.0	5.4	6.4	7.5	8.7	10.2	11.2	12.3	13.5	14.9	16.4	0.0
Fixed costs		0.0	0.0	−1.0	−1.1	−1.2	−1.3	−1.4	−1.6	−1.7	−1.9	−2.1	−2.3	−6.3
Amortisation		0.0	0.0	−1.9	−1.9	−1.9	−1.9	−1.9	−1.9	−1.9	−1.9	−1.9	−1.9	0.0
Pre-tax profit		0.0	0.0	2.6	3.4	4.4	5.6	6.9	7.7	8.7	9.8	10.9	12.2	−6.3
Tax		0.0	0.0	−0.8	−1.0	−1.3	−1.7	−2.1	−2.3	−2.6	−2.9	−3.3	−3.7	0.0
Net profit		0.0	0.0	1.8	2.4	3.1	3.9	4.8	5.4	6.1	6.8	7.6	8.5	−6.3
Fixed assets	0.0	10.0	18.8	16.9	15.0	13.2	11.3	9.4	7.5	5.6	3.8	1.9	0.0	0.0
Working capital	0.0	0.0	0.0	1.1	1.2	1.5	1.7	2.0	2.2	2.4	2.7	2.9	3.2	0.0
Capital employed	0.0	10.0	18.8	18.0	16.3	14.6	13.0	11.4	9.7	8.1	6.4	4.8	3.2	0.0
ROACE		0.0%	0.0%	9.7%	14.0%	20.0%	28.2%	39.4%	51.4%	68.6%	94.5%	136.5%	213	
Profit		0.0	0.0	1.8	2.4	3.1	3.9	4.8	5.4	6.1	6.8	7.6	8.5	−6.3
Amortisation		0.0	0.0	1.9	1.9	1.9	1.9	1.9	1.9	1.9	1.9	1.9	1.9	0
Working capital change		0	0	−1.1	−0.2	−0.2	−0.2	−0.3	−0.2	−0.2	−0.2	−0.3	−0.3	3.2
Capital investment		−10.0	−8.8	0.0	0.0	0.0	0.0	0.0	0.0	0.0	0.0	0.0	0.0	0.0
Funds flow		−10.0	−8.8	2.6	4.1	4.8	5.5	6.4	7.1	7.8	8.5	9.3	10.1	−3.1
Value calculation														
Funds flow		−10.0	−8.8	2.6	4.1	4.8	5.5	6.4	7.1	7.8	8.5	9.3	10.1	−3.1
Real funds flow		−10.0	−8.0	2.2	3.1	3.2	3.4	3.6	3.6	3.6	3.6	3.6	3.6	−1.0
Discount factor		0.953	0.867	0.788	0.716	0.651	0.592	0.538	0.489	0.445	0.404	0.368	0.334	0.304
Present value		−9.5	−6.9	1.7	2.2	2.1	2.0	1.9	1.8	1.6	1.5	1.3	1.2	−0.3
Cumulative present value		−9.5	−16.5	−14.8	−12.6	−10.5	−8.4	−6.4	−4.7	−3.1	−1.6	−0.3	−0.9	0.6
NPV	0.6													
IRR	10.7%													
Discounted payback year	12													
Efficiency	3%													

If, however, we sell an item that we held in our inventory we will encounter the problem of what are called 'stock profits'.

A stock profit arises when there is a rise in prices between when raw materials are purchased for inventory and subsequently sold to customers. Take for example a business that sells heating oil. It might have a general policy that it holds a stock equal to one month of anticipated sales. If oil prices rise by $10/tonne during that month it should expect to make a profit of at least this amount in order to cover the cost that it will incur when it buys oil to replace what it has sold. This profit is called a stock profit. It is given its own name since it is rather illusory because it is necessary to invest at least that amount extra to purchase its replacement if inventory levels are to be held constant.

A model where all costs, revenues and balance sheet items like inventory values are increased with a simple inflation index will omit the stock profit that should be earned. The way that we can estimate what the stock profit will be is to make an assumption about when selling prices will be increased in response to increases in input costs. If prices are put up after one month and the company holds three months of stock then it will make a stock profit over the year equal to two thirds of the value increase in stock caused by the rise in prices.

This stock profit effect needs to be incorporated in financial models if it is material. It will be material only when the combination of inflation, inventory levels and early passing on of price rises is sufficient to make it so. Models that leave out this effect are making the implicit assumption that prices are increased with a lag against raw material price increases that is exactly equivalent to the inventory holding period.

Inflation and forex effects

Many financial models will need to cope with the impact of changes in foreign exchange rates. We can be pretty sure that exchange rates will change in the future and so in principle any situation that involves more than one currency will need to allow for a forex effect. My recommended approach to dealing with this complication is to do one's best to ignore it when this is reasonable and certainly to avoid wasting time trying to forecast accurately what future exchange rates will be. This approach does not mean that forex is left out of models all together. It means that it is included in a model but that I would hope to conclude that forex issues were not going to change a decision and so they would not need to be agonised about too much.

The justification for this approach goes as follows. We know that forex rates will change but we don't know what the change will be. If we did know

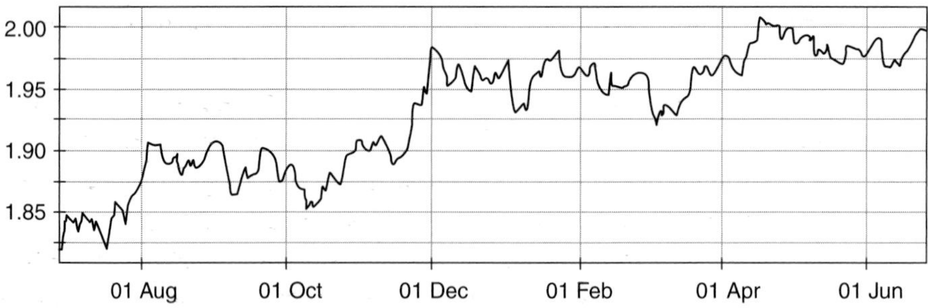

Fig. 7.1 US$ to GB£ exchange rate July 2006–June 2007

or if we even only had a slightly better view than knowing nothing, we would not be financial analysts, we would trade in foreign exchange, make our fortunes and soon be able to retire rich and famous.

If we consider the US dollar to GB pound exchange rate over a 12-month period we can see material changes.

Hindsight, however, is a wonderful thing. What is the exchange rate going to do in the future? We could use forward rates as an indicator but these simply reflect the spot rate and interest rate differentials and they are always changing.[19] The changes happen too often to make forward rates any use in an economic value model which will be used over several months and perhaps several years to help us optimise a project. If we have no useful basis for predicting future exchange rates then why not assume no change?

One possible answer to this question is that you might want to assume a change because it may help or hinder the project and you need to understand the risks that you face. I would agree with this view.

My recommended approach is as follows. We should build a model that allows for different exchange rates each year but usually run it with a fixed exchange rate throughout. We should then use the model to test the effect of exchange rate variations. We should only worry about exchange rates if they look to have an important impact that might change our decision.

There is one situation when we do have a good basis for predicting future exchange rates. This is when there is a material difference in anticipated inflation between two countries. An assumption of purchasing-power parity[20] is reasonable and so could be applied if there are big inflation differences.

[19] The mechanism has been explained on pages 34–35 in the Financial Markets building block.
[20] See the Financial Markets building block page 33.

Purchasing-power parity is quite easy to model and so one could make this automatic so that all that is necessary is that an opening exchange rate is entered as an assumption along with country-by-country inflation rates. A table of implied forward exchange rates based on purchasing-power parity could then be computed. A final simplification would be to ensure that inflation rates were only set at different levels if there were strong grounds for doing this. All inflation rate assumptions, say of between 1½% and 3½%, could be forced to adopt a standardised assumption of 2½%. In this way most currencies would appear to have a fixed exchange rate.

Short-term decisions are largely outside the scope of this chapter as our current focus is on modelling economic value and this is primarily a long-term issue. However, it is important to be aware that the approach I have just recommended is not suitable for short-term decision-making. These decisions should be based on the current market exchange rates even though these change all the time.

A final word of warning is needed concerning the currency in which accounts are prepared and/or the currency in which an economic model is written. These are usually the same but this does not always have to be the case. It can be tempting to impose an implicit assumption on a model that it is prepared in, say, the reporting currency of the parent company in a group. For example, a US multinational might carry out all of its analysis in US dollars.

The first point to note about this is that the local tax authorities will usually require that accounts are prepared in local currency units. This means that tax offsets for things like capital expenditure are set in local currency terms. So if the local currency devalues against the dollar the effective value of tax offsets will fall. A model that was written in US dollars would not pick up this effect.

My recommendation is that analysis should be carried out in the most important currency for the project in question. This will usually be the currency in which the goods or services on offer are denominated. I refer to this currency as a project's 'functional currency'. This will not necessarily be the home currency. A North Sea oil field, for example, will sell its output on the international oil markets in US dollars. So it will have a functional currency of US dollars. If however output is sold for pounds sterling (as may well happen for a North Sea gas field) then the functional currency will be pounds sterling and models should be written in this currency.

Part 6: Project life and other modelling issues

Project life

The assumption concerning project life can have a significant impact on a project's NPV. There will be some occasions when project life is quite clear.[21] Usually, however, project life will be very uncertain. It will be the shorter of the physical life of an asset or its economic life, the physical life being when an asset is actually worn out while the economic life refers to when it ceases to be economic to run an asset even though it still works.

As with all assumptions, one should seek to understand not only the expected value outcome but also the range of possible outcomes. In some industries asset life will be a variable which is well understood. Road vehicles are a good example. Statistics are available on how second-hand vehicles retain their value such that one make of vehicle can be compared with another. As a general rule, however, the more expensive an asset is and the longer its life, the more difficult it will become to justify the assumed project life and the more significant will be the range of uncertainty.

The effect of discounting is such that the longer the project life assumption, the less important a few extra years will be. It can be tempting to rely on this fact and ignore the impact of different project life assumptions. This would be wrong if the different lives were purely the result of an arbitrary decision rather than real differences. The logic behind this can be illustrated by looking at annuity factor tables.

At a 9% discount rate the annuity factors for ten, 15, 20 and 25 years are: 6.7, 8.4, 9.5 and 10.3. The increase between 15 and 20 years is 13.2%. This may not appear great but we should remember that the NPV is the difference between the present value of the inflows and the outflows. Now the NPV for a typical project could be, say, 20% of the present value of the cash outflows. If this were the case an increase of 13.2% in the present value of the inflows would increase the NPV by almost 80%.[22]

If I were working on a single project in isolation I would happily treat project life as just another assumption. In reality, however, it is only very rarely that a project can be considered just on its own merits. Projects exist in companies

[21] For example, a refit on a leased property with three years left on its lease.

[22] If NPV is 20% of cash inflows then 100 of outflows would be associated with 120 of inflows. Increasing 120 by 13.2% gives 135.8. Hence the NPV of 20 has increased to 35.8. This is an increase of 79%.

and single-project companies are rare. Within a company, projects need to be compared with other projects as companies seek to identify the best overall course of action. If we are to compare projects it is important to ensure that any differences in assumed project life are driven by real factors and not simply arbitrary assumptions about project life. Some degree of central guidance is therefore necessary.

Project life should always be consistent with the other assumptions that are made in a financial case. Of particular importance are assumptions about the cost of maintenance and any necessary sustaining capital investment. If a short project life is assumed it may be reasonable to assume low annual maintenance and perhaps even no sustaining capital investment. The greater the asset life, the more costs one would expect to see included in the assumptions. Some assets are required by law to undergo major maintenance checks on a regular basis. Clearly the cost of these must be allowed for and it will be sensible to set the assumed project life to end just before a major check would otherwise be necessary.

The need to ensure consistency between project life assumptions and cost assumptions is often greatest when one is trying to model a company as opposed to an individual project. Individual projects tend to have finite lives and tend only to carry with them costs that are directly related to the project. When one models an entire company the situation is very different. The general overheads of a company will fall into one of two categories. First, there will be the minimum costs that are necessary to maintain the company at its current size. Second, there will be costs which are incurred with an objective of facilitating future growth. This second category will include things like R&D, project development teams and even some of the recruitment and training spend.

I think of these extra costs as being growth costs and have already highlighted their impact on value in the Planning and Control building block on pages 131–133. Now a typical terminal value assumption to include at the end of a five-year LTP would be that the company continued to grow but at a reduced rate from that which was planned during the plan period. If these growth costs are going to be assumed to continue into the future then it would be reasonable to assume they do contribute either a longer life after the plan period and/or a faster rate of continued growth to perpetuity. It would be wrong in my view to value a business on the assumption of high growth costs but low continued growth. There should, in effect, be a direct link between the sustainable funds flow and its duration and/or growth rate.

This idea is developed further in this book as part of the chapter on What Sets the Share Price?

My recommendation as regards project life is that if there is a good reason to assume a particular figure then this should be used. Examples would include:

- where statistical data on asset life were available such as for road transport fleets;
- where we were dealing with, say, a mine with a known quantity of ore in place;
- where a specific project termination date is set by regulation or patent expiry date;
- where an important lease was due to expire on a known date with no right of renewal.

The difficulty tends to be with things like factories and industrial plant where there may well be a big difference between physical and economic life and there may be no obvious 'right' answer. It is here that, in my view, individual companies need to impose some arbitrary but reasonable rules.

Company rules should not normally go as far as specifying a single project life for all projects. This is because some projects will have longer lives than others. The approach that I recommend is that individual companies should set standard project life assumptions for similar types of investment. These project life assumptions should be specified as being 'not-to-be-exceeded' periods since there can always be times when a project might know that it should adopt a shorter period. Project life assumptions for generic categories of investment should also have an associated maintenance and sustaining capital investment allowance. These allowances should be minimum levels.

Experience has shown me how different companies can adopt very different project lives. There can be the potential to waste a huge amount of time debating, say, whether an asset life of 15 or 20 years should be assumed for a refinery. Fortunately, there is one technique which should allow us neatly to avoid any real concerns about project life assumptions. This is the Sources of Value approach which will be dealt with in the next financial pillar.

Residual and terminal values

I need first to explain my nomenclature.

- Residual value is the term that I give to the allowance at the end of the assumed project life for any remaining costs or revenues that will happen.

These costs will typically involve clean-up costs, working capital recovery and scrap/resale value.
- Terminal value is the term I use for when project life is deliberately set at less than the real economic life, with the value from cash flows beyond the planned period being accounted for through a single figure called a terminal value (TV). TVs are usually calculated through formulae like the perpetuity valuation equation.

The two concepts are related but one should not incorporate both into a model. Any discussion of residual or terminal value should also be related to discussion of the assumed project life and also to the assumed level of costs incurred for both maintenance and to generate future growth.

The approach that I recommend for residual value is to include a final column in the spreadsheet representing the year after the end of the project. This will then pick up a whole series of factors as outlined in the following table. In most situations I would assume that all of these costs and benefits occur, in effect, one year later than the final year of the project. The only exception to this would be if a long-term clean-up programme was necessary. If this was the case I would allow specifically for the phasing of this spend (table 7.7).

Residual values are used at the end of the assumed life of an individual project. Terminal values, by contrast, are associated with value calculations for plans or entire businesses when we do not want to forecast cash flow for the full economic life of the asset or business concerned. The idea of a TV is that one should prepare a detailed business plan for, say, five to ten years and then approximate the value from cash flow beyond this point through a single figure.

The TV will usually represent a very significant percentage of the overall value of a business and this often causes some concerns. Some people might think that a plan should be extended for a longer period in order to reduce the dependence on the TV. The McKinsey book *Valuation*, for example, suggests that 10–15 years is a normal period to be covered by an explicit plan. My view is that it is better and more honest to reduce the long term to just a few parameters which between them set the TV.

The fundamental problem that is encountered when plans are extended for many years is that the plan will most likely show a success case because, realistically, no manager will submit a plan showing failure. Consider, however, how unlikely it will be that a business will succeed for, say, ten years without any setback. At any point in time there is usually something going wrong in a big business as well as something going right. So in the early years of a business plan there will be a realistic reflection of this. By year 5, however,

Table 7.7 Items to include in residual value calculation

Item	Calculation method
Working capital recovery	The usual assumption would be that working capital is recovered based on its book value as at the end of the final year. It might be necessary to reduce the recovery if a significant component of the working capital represented spare parts for what would by the end of the assumed project life be an out-of-date plant. These items of stores will probably have no value.
Land values	This can be very material in projects that involve land. I would usually assume that land values remain constant in real terms. So there would be an element of profit here. The tax impact of this would be covered as part of the tax calculation described below.
Scrap/resale value of assets	This would need to be addressed on a case-by-case basis. The default assumption would be for no scrap/resale value because the assets would be at the end of their economic life. It is possible, however, that this may not be appropriate, for example with a chemical plant that used a very expensive catalyst that would be sold to others.
Decommissioning and clean-up costs	It usually costs a lot simply to shut down an industrial operation and clean up the site. Assumptions would need to be guided by experience of the specific situation.
Redundancy and other closure costs	It may be necessary to allow for redundancy and other closure costs. In a big company, however, it may be reasonable to assume that staff can be reallocated to other projects. There may also be other costs to allow for. An example would be if some contracts were not aligned with the assumed project life such that they would need to be terminated in advance of the contractual date.
Tax effects	There will be two tax effects to allow for. First there will be the need to pay any outstanding tax charges related to the final year of operation. This will usually form a part of the working capital adjustment because the tax payable will simply be a part of the overall accounts payable figure. Second, all of the above allowances could create a tax effect that will need to be allowed for. As is usual in the case of taxation, expert advice is needed. Note also that if tax is paid in the year following the year in which the liability is incurred it might be necessary for the sake of accuracy to introduce an additional year to the model over and above the first additional year. This would usually be spurious in my view and I would recommend including all the residual value cash flows as just a single number unless they were really significant.

managers have always promised to sort out the current problems and new problems are not there because few managers will admit that a new problem will occur. This is because if they can see it coming they will always be able to mitigate it by taking action now. Ten-year plans tend therefore to suffer from what I call the 'gold bars' problem. Businesses tend to project such success that the plan appears to be paved with gold and the only problem the business faces is what to do with all the gold. I claim from over 35 years of experience that reality is never that good!

TV assumptions need to be tailored to the specific situation of the business that is being valued. If the business plan contains only minimal expenditure designed to ensure long-term growth then the TV should reflect this by assuming either a steady decline in cash generation beyond the plan period or by assuming only a limited number of further years. If, however, substantial costs are being incurred then some growth beyond the plan period may be appropriate.

A typical TV assumption if a business has good prospects well beyond the period of the plan is to use the perpetuity valuation equation:

$$TV = \frac{\text{Funds Flow} \times (1 + \text{Growth})}{(\text{Cost of Capital} - \text{Growth})}$$

In this case funds flow is the figure from the final year of the plan and growth is the sustained rate of growth to perpetuity. Note also that the valuation is as at the point in time when the final year's funds flow is deemed to occur. So since we usually assume mid-year flows in a plan, the valuation is as at the middle of the final year of the plan. This means that we should apply the same discount factor to the TV as is applied to the final year of the plan.

The formula is arithmetically correct but the answer it gives is only as good as the assumptions that underpin it. I will consider the question of TVs in considerable detail later in this book as a part of the practical applications part of the chapter on What Sets the Share Price? Here I will introduce several means of calculating TV and in particular I will address a key shortcoming of the growth-to-perpetuity approach.[23] I will also consider further the question of how accurate any valuation can be.

Additional complications with joint ventures

There are two additional complications which will occur when economic analysis is being carried out in a company with joint ownership. These complications concern how different owners may have different methodologies and also how some costs within a joint venture may well be revenues to the parent company.

[23] This is that the formula appears to require there to be no link between growth rate and funds flow as each are separate assumptions whereas in reality the two should be linked.

Up to now the presumption has been that analysis is carried out on behalf of the company that is making the investment. This company will have its own board of directors that will make decisions. These decisions will include things like approving the methodology that is used to test investments and setting the CoC that is to be used. With multiple shareholders the directors will have an obligation to work on behalf of the company overall.

The situation can be different when a company is owned, say, by two or three other companies. In a situation such as this a specific joint-venture agreement is likely to have been drawn up. This will specify things like how major investments are to be approved. Each owner may nominate one or two directors and it could, for example, be necessary to have unanimous approval of major investment cases. The joint-venture agreement may, in effect, say, that directors are permitted to act in the interests of their own employing company rather than always for all shareholders.

The first complication to consider concerns methodology. A company with many owners will need to have just one methodology which its directors are happy represents a good way to test its investments on behalf of its shareholders. A joint venture may need to consider investments in different ways in order to satisfy its different owners.

One particular aspect of methodology that might cause differences could concern cash flow. Within a single company, cash is deemed to have been received when it reaches the company's bank account. If, however, analysis is carried out by parent companies, they may want to focus on cash flows into their own bank accounts. This might be limited to annual dividend payments. The different parent companies of a JV might also want to adopt different costs of capital.

There could be real problems if the methodologies are materially different but small differences such as, for example, a one percentage point difference in CoC, are usually irrelevant. This is because it is rare for decisions to be so marginal as to be changed by a single point swing in the CoC.

The point to realise is that the parent companies simply have to learn how to live with each other or accept that the alternative is to break up the JV. Issues concerning methodology should be addressed at the formation stage of the JV so that the company can make good decisions in the future.

The second complication concerns modelling. An additional layer of financial modelling is usually required in joint venture-economic models. This is because what might be seen as a cost by the joint venture might well be a revenue to one of the parent companies. Joint ventures are usually formed when two companies feel that they can both contribute to the success of the venture. This means that material cash flows between parent and JV company are to be expected. Examples of the sorts of flows that might be involved would include payment of licence fees for technology, purchase of feedstock, provision of staff or support services.

The approach to model economic value is first to model the JV as a standalone entity. This analysis will usually be done within the JV. Each parent will then need to prepare an additional model that adjusts for cash flows between themselves and the JV.

Any cash flow will need to be checked to see if it creates an additional contribution at parent company level. For example, are feedstock supplies charged at cost or market price? If they are at market price, is there an element of profit to strip out? It may or may not be necessary to correct for the profit on a feedstock supply. It would be necessary to correct if the parent company could not otherwise have made the sale but if a third party sale was a realistic alternative then there would be no correction to apply. The correction need not always serve to increase value from the perspective of the parent. A formula price for feedstock supplies may be below the anticipated market price.

This analysis should be done within each parent company because it will require access to confidential information concerning profitability. One parent may well be getting a better deal than another and it would not be appropriate for the JV staff to be given access to such information. So in effect a shareholder's economic model is required which can sit on top of the basic cash flow model which the JV company should supply.

Monte Carlo analysis

Monte Carlo analysis is a simulation technique that allows one to investigate the impact of uncertainty. Basically, one builds a model and then instead of running it just once with a single set of assumptions, one sets assumptions as ranges and/or statistical distributions and runs the model, say, a few thousand times in order to investigate the range of possibilities. Each individual case makes a separate 'dip' into the statistical distribution for the variables and produces a possible outcome. The range of possible outcomes can then be tested to find the expected value and also to draw cumulative probability distributions and probability density functions.

The technique has great intellectual appeal because it does allow one to go beyond single-point analysis and to take account of the range of possible outcomes in a statistically justifiable way. The analysis is facilitated via add-ins to the Excel spreadsheet model.[24] A typical financial spreadsheet model is an ideal candidate for Monte Carlo analysis as there are many input assumptions and just a few key economic indicators to focus on.

There are, however, significant drawbacks to the approach. It appears to give scientific precision but is this justified? As usual, the analysis is only as good as the assumptions but these can tend to be hidden from decision-makers. It is always important to assess not just the range for each individual variable but also any correlations that exist between variables. An example of this could be sales volume and price. Correlations will tend to increase the range of possible outcomes. Even if the assumptions are good there can be a feeling of loss of control because one can never say exactly what the answer corresponds to.

My recommendation is that Monte Carlo analysis should only be used in special circumstances. These could include two generic situations:

- where there is an important non-linearity that needs to be investigated;
- where it is important to study the full range of a statistical distribution as opposed to focus on just the expected value.

A non-linearity is where an expected value input assumption will not produce an expected value output. An example might be where the government levies a tax charge based on, say, the higher of two methods in order to ensure that it always receives some tax. I will be considering how to deal with this kind of situation in more detail later in the book when I deal with how to value flexibility. In simple terms, however, one needs to use a Monte Carlo simulation approach that allows for the variability of key variables if one needs to obtain the most accurate estimate of expected value NPV when there is a non-linearity.

The second generic situation where we tend to need to use Monte Carlo simulation concerns when we need to focus on the full range of a statistical distribution. Suppose, for example, a decision-maker wanted to know not only what the expected value NPV was but what the probability was that it would be at least zero or that cash flows would at least reach some specified threshold. Calculating the probability of achieving at least a zero NPV would require all variables to be given probability ranges and then a Monte Carlo simulation would have to be run. A second example of focussing on the full range of possible outcomes would be where a decision-maker was not happy

[24] The two most popular add-ins are called Crystal Ball and @Risk. Both are very good and are easy to use. They are also quite expensive! There are cheaper add-ins available as well. My suggestion is that potential users should first test any product before making a purchase.

simply to characterise the possible outcomes as being just, say, three possible capital costs each with a probability that between them added to 100%. This approach would tend to ignore many low-probability but high-impact outcomes.

My experience is that Monte Carlo analysis is only very occasionally required and I suggest that readers do not learn the skill unless/until they need it. The computational side is very easy if one has a good Excel model and one of the proprietary add-in packages. The difficulty is in establishing good distributions for all of the variables and any associated correlations. Our lack of ability to do this well is such that we will always need to view any Monte Carlo-produced results with considerable caution despite its appeal.

Part 7: Modelling financed cases

Introduction

Although the approach to valuation that is proposed in this book is to exclude finance effects, there are times when it is necessary to build a model which does incorporate finance. A brief summary of the additional issues that are raised is provided in this part. We will also take the opportunity to develop a financial model of a company that will allow us to review and recap several of the issues that have been covered in this book.

One thing that we will learn from this part is that we should be very pleased that the normal approach to finance is to exclude it from investment evaluation. This is because it creates additional difficulties compared with financial analysis carried out in the conventional manner.

We need to learn how to incorporate finance because valuation is not the only thing that we will use our financial models for. The real world operates through debt and equity. Whenever we want to know how our company will look from the outside we will need to build a financed model that distinguishes between debt and equity. The outside is rarely concerned with the overall value of a company. The outside is concerned either with debt and how secure it is or with equity and what the share price will be. So a financed model is going to be necessary when a project is big enough to influence how a company will be perceived from the outside.[25]

[25] A financed model of a project is also necessary if the project is taking on debt directly.

Putting finance into a model

We have learned so far how to exclude finance from a set of results in order to produce what are termed 'asset-based cash flows'. This was quite easy because all of the numbers are provided and all we need to do is decide for each item whether or not it is related to the asset or to the financing of the asset. We know, for example, to ignore interest charges and that the tax charge needs to be adjusted to add back the tax relief that interest charges will have created.[26] We also know about the difference between cash flow (the net movement in cash) and funds flow (the generation of cash before financing effects).

What has perhaps not been apparent is how simple the calculations are when all you have to do is calculate the amount of cash that is available and then simply use this number to value the activity. Finance becomes more difficult when, rather than stripping it out, we are calculating from basic principles what it will look like in the first place. The two key difficulties with this are as follows:

- We have to deal with a circularity in the logic. At the most basic level, the interest charge for a year is a function of the opening debt and the annual increase in debt. The annual increase, however, is affected by the interest charge and so a circular logic is created.
- We have to deal with too many variables. Companies do not simply balance their books with borrowing; they need also to decide what dividend to pay and whether to issue new shares or perhaps even whether to buy back some shares.

The circularity is dealt with by iteration. You guess the correct interest charge, plug this into your model and use this to calculate what the correct interest charge would be. When the two results are very close you stop. In pre-spreadsheet days this took a long time and put those who were adept at mental arithmetic at a great advantage. Spreadsheets nowadays will solve the problem automatically as long as you switch on the iteration option. This is explained shortly in the worked example.

Dealing with financing choices is more complex as it requires judgement. Even at the very simplest level a company needs to have finance in place such that capital employed is equal to debt plus equity. It can, in principle, balance its books with any combination of debt and equity. So what

[26] This is explained on page 74 of the Understanding Accounts building block and also in the Corus example on pages 88–97.

algorithm does one put into a spreadsheet? For example, one could set a fixed debt profile and balance on equity or set a fixed ratio of debt to equity and, in effect, balance on both. There are also many options in relation to equity.[27]

The view that I take is that companies employ highly paid CFOs to recommend the balance between debt and equity. We should not therefore expect to be able to write a simple formula that will always tell us the right answer. All that we can do is build a model that will work within a 'normal' range of results and know that we must always overview the results to ensure they are sensible. We must never trust a simple spreadsheet model to give us a viable financed plan for any set of assumptions.

The main finance decision concerns whether to balance on debt or equity. The computations are much simpler if you decide to balance on equity. If this is what you do then all that is necessary is to set out the assumed profile of debt. No iterations are necessary because the interest charge will be known with certainty. Any cash surplus must be assumed to be paid out as a dividend while any cash requirement is funded by new equity injections from shareholders. The modelling is very simple but in the real world shareholders are almost never happy to receive such a variable stream of dividends or to contribute to new equity issues at a moment's notice. The only time that such a situation would be viable would be if the company concerned was owned by a limited number of financially strong parents all of which were content to fund on this basis.

The more common situation is where a company plans as though it had a fixed commitment to pay a dividend which might well grow at a predetermined rate. Finances are then balanced on debt. Any additional cash is used to pay down existing borrowings while any shortfalls are assumed to be funded out of new borrowings. This is fine as long as the overall level of debt remains within a sensible band within which banks would be happy to lend.

In reality what is done is that you start with an expectation of the overall result and then decide what is a reasonable dividend in view of this outlook.[28] Debt is then treated as the marginal source of funds. Some overviews are essential in order to ensure that if assumptions are changed the overall financial picture remains viable.

[27] The choices that surround equity concern the dividend per share, the issue of new shares and also the buyback of existing shares.

[28] You will also decide whether or not new equity is necessary or if share buybacks are required.

Case study: Yellow Moon Chemical Company Inc

The approach to incorporating financing into a financial model will be illustrated through the following case study. The study concerns a fictitious chemical company called Yellow Moon Chemical Company Inc or YMCC for short. We should imagine that it operates in the USA and that it makes a range of yellow colouring pigments. These pigments are used in many industries including printing, paints and, because they are edible, foodstuffs and even children's face paints.

YMCC is about to embark on a major expansion programme which will see it build substantial additional new capacity. This new build project, codenamed Project Claire, is expected to deliver additional capacity just in time as the company is already having to limit its sales growth owing to impending capacity constraints. When Project Claire comes on stream the company will have enough capacity to cover sales growth of about 5% per annum for the coming four to five years. YMCC's five-year long-term plan is set out in table 7.8 and the current date is December 2008.

Readers should note that this is a particularly important case study. It will serve, in effect, as a test of your understanding of the subject. It will also be referred to on several further occasions in this book. I do, therefore, recommend that great attention be paid to it and that readers should ensure that they are able to follow through the numbers.

I will first give an overview of the plan so that readers understand the context within which YMCC is operating. I will then explain how the model is constructed. Next, I will show how finance can be stripped out of the plan and the economic value of the company can be calculated. Finally I will 'play' with the model to investigate various issues and recap on some previous issues.

The company is anticipating good top-line sales growth but this does not translate into such a healthy picture when one looks at net profit. Indeed, profit falls in the early years of the plan owing to increases in fixed costs, amortisation and interest charges. The unusually large change in working capital in 2011 is due to the accounts payable related to capital investment falling. So all of the noteworthy factors are related to the implementation of Project Claire and once one gets to the final two years the company is back on a healthy track. Overall, the plan is viable.

Table 7.8 Yellow Moon Chemical Company Inc: long-term plan $m

Income statements	2009	2010	2011	2012	2013
Sales revenue	76.1	78.7	82.7	87.7	93.0
Variable costs	–21.5	–22.5	–23.5	–25.3	–27.3
Contribution	54.6	56.2	59.2	62.4	65.7
Fixed costs	–30.0	–31.8	–35.7	–36.6	–37.5
Amortisation	–6.0	–5.7	–7.6	–7.7	–7.8
Pre-tax profit	18.6	18.8	15.9	18.1	20.4
Interest charge	–2.1	–3.0	–3.6	–3.2	–2.6
Tax	–5.8	–5.5	–4.3	–5.2	–6.2
Net profit	10.7	10.2	8.0	9.7	11.6
Balance sheets					
Fixed assets	67.0	90.1	86.2	82.7	79.5
Accounts receivable	19.0	19.7	20.7	21.9	23.3
Accounts payable	–12.2	–13.1	–10.0	–10.9	–11.8
Inventories	8.6	9.1	9.9	10.3	10.8
Net working capital	15.4	15.6	20.5	21.4	22.3
Capital employed	82.4	105.7	106.7	104.0	101.7
Debt	34.8	52.2	49.7	42.1	33.1
Equity	47.6	53.5	57.0	62.0	68.7
Capital employed	82.4	105.7	106.7	104.0	101.7
Cash flow					
Profit	10.7	10.2	8.0	9.7	11.6
Amortisation	6.0	5.7	7.6	7.7	7.8
Working capital change	0.6	–0.2	–4.9	–0.9	–0.9
Capital investment	–23.0	–28.7	–3.7	–4.1	–4.6
Dividends paid	–4.2	–4.3	–4.5	–4.7	–4.9
Cash flow	-9.8	–17.4	2.5	7.7	9.0
Key ratios					
Return on capital employed	16.3%	13.0%	9.7%	11.2%	12.9%
Return on equity	24.2%	20.2%	14.5%	16.3%	17.7%
Gearing	42.3%	49.4%	46.6%	40.4%	32.5%

The model is based on the assumptions made in table 7.9, most of which should be self-explanatory. The new capacity that is being built for Project Claire will increase fixed costs but has lower variable costs than the existing capacity. Costs rise at a different rate from the assumed increase in selling prices. The reference to tax paid in year means that 50% of the tax charge for the year is paid during the year with the remainder paid the following year. This means that the tax relief associated with interest payments is spread over two years.

Table 7.9

Year	2009	2010	2011	2012	2013
Capex – Project Claire – $m	20	25	0	0	0
Capex – sustaining $m	3	3	3.5	3.7	3.9
New capacity – Project Claire – tonnes	0	0	50,000	50,000	50,000
Existing capacity – tonnes	200,000	200,000	200,000	200,000	200,000
Sales yr 1 tonnes	195,000				
Sales growth potential	0.0%	2.5%	4.0%	5.0%	5.0%
Sales price $/te yr 1 money	390				
Variable cost – existing capacity $/te	110				
Fixed costs $m	30				
Extra fixed costs due to Project Claire	0	1	4	4	4
Variable cost saving on Project Claire	10				
Sales price inflation	1.0%				
Cost inflation	2.5%				
Amortisation rate	5.0%				
Receivables months	3				
Payables months	1.5				
Tax paid in year	50.0%				
Inventories months	2				
Cost of capital	9.0%				
Tax rate	35.0%				
Cost of debt	7.0%				
TV perpetuity growth rate (MOD)	0.0%				
Opening fixed assets – $m	50				
Amortisation existing assets – $m	6	5.5	5	4.9	4.8
Opening receivables – $m	19				
Opening inventories – $m	7				
Opening payables – $m	10				
Year 1 dividend – $m	4				
Year 3 step-up in dividend $m	0				
Dividend growth rate	4.0%				
Opening debt – $m	25				

The model allows the potential for a step-up in dividend in year 3 of the plan but the current assumption is that this will not happen. The model also allows for the calculation of a terminal value based on a fixed growth rate to perpetuity although the current assumption is for zero growth.

The next section of the spreadsheet (table 7.10) carries out the necessary calculations:

Table 7.10

CALCULATIONS						
Price index	1.000	1.010	1.020	1.030	1.041	
Cost index	1.000	1.025	1.051	1.077	1.104	
Sales index	1.000	1.025	1.066	1.119	1.175	
Discount factor	0.958	0.879	0.806	0.740	0.679	0.623
Money-of-the-day capex Project Claire	20.0	25.6	0.0	0.0	0.0	
Money-of-the-day sust capex	3.0	3.1	3.7	4.1	4.6	
Amortisation Project Claire capex	0.0	0.0	2.3	2.3	2.3	
Amortisation sust capex	0.0	0.2	0.3	0.5	0.7	
Total amortisation	6.0	5.7	7.6	7.7	7.8	
TV factor						11.11
Sales potential	195,000	199,875	207,870	218,264	229,177	
Actual sales	195,000	199,875	207,870	218,264	229,177	
Production on Project Claire plant	0	0	50,000	50,000	50,000	
Production existing plant	195,000	199,875	157,870	168,264	179,177	
Variable costs	21.5	22.5	23.5	25.3	27.3	
Total fixed costs money-of-the-day	30.0	31.8	35.7	36.6	37.5	
Variable & fixed cost payable	−6.4	−6.8	−7.4	−7.7	−8.1	
Capex payable	−2.9	−3.6	−0.5	−0.5	−0.6	
Tax payable	−2.9	−2.8	−2.2	−2.6	−3.1	
Total payables	−12.2	−13.1	−10.0	−10.9	−11.8	
Opening working capital	16.0					
Opening equity	41.0					
Dividend	4.2	4.3	4.5	4.7	4.9	
Opening debt	25.0	34.8	52.2	49.7	42.1	
Cash flow	−9.8	−17.4	2.5	7.7	9.0	
Interest	−2.1	−3.0	−3.6	−3.2	−2.6	
Closing debt	34.8	52.2	49.7	42.1	33.1	
Opening payable re int tax relief	−0.3					
Interest tax relief	−0.7	−1.1	−1.2	−1.1	−0.9	
Tax on pre-tax profit	−6.5	−6.6	−5.6	−6.3	−7.1	
Profit post-tax pre-interest	12.1	12.2	10.3	11.8	13.3	
Terminal value calculation						
Final year funds flow	15.5					
TV factor	11.1					
Terminal value	172.1					

Once again, these should be fairly self explanatory. Note in particular how the model allocates as much production as possible to the new Project Claire plant because it has lower variable costs. The result is, however, that existing capacity is underutilised.

The cash flow calculation does need to be explained. Opening debt plus cash flow equals the closing debt. The interest charge is explicitly shown here and is calculated as the interest rate times the opening debt plus half of the interest rate times the cash flow (the cash flow is mid-year). This is where the circularity arises because interest is part of cash flow. When I inputted the coding for this calculation I got an error message warning of the circularity. The solution was also suggested and it concerned switching on an iterative calculation mode. In Excel you can switch on iterations via the **Tools**; **Options**; menu. Then select the **Calculation Tab** and check the iterations box.

Note also the terminal-value calculation. This uses the growth-to-perpetuity formula. Calculation of the necessary funds flow figure is explained below.

We have already seen YMCC's LTP. We can now strip the financing items out of it to produce an AFS (table 7.11) in the traditional format and use this to calculate the economic value of YMCC.

Notice that in the profit-and-loss account the change from the LTP is to exclude the interest charge and also to increase the tax charge to reflect just tax on operations and not also tax relief on interest. The balance sheets are changed to remove the element of tax relief on interest from the accounts-payable figure. This causes a slight change in capital employed. We also show only one side of the balance sheet in the AFS while the financed plan must show both. The third section of the AFS shows the calculation of funds flow as opposed to cash flow. Finally, the AFS shows the value calculation.

The main element of value is the terminal value. This is always the case when one values a five-year plan. The calculated value of YMCC as at 1 January 2008 is \$132.4m. Since the opening level of debt was \$25m (see final line of assumptions), the value of the equity in YMCC is \$107.4m. Note that a spurious level of accuracy is implied in quoting the value to the nearest \$0.1m but this is what one would do as the aim is 'faithfully' to convert assumptions into a valuation.

The plan as presented is, if one believes the numbers, credible. Gearing does rise substantially but not to a level that would fundamentally threaten the viability of YMCC.

When one is dealing with a plan that includes financing effects it is always essential to carry out a sense check to ensure that it looks credible. Suppose that we were to change the assumed selling price by about 10% from \$390/te to \$350/te. The spreadsheet will automatically produce a new long-term plan as shown in table 7.12.

Table 7.11 Yellow Moon Chemical Company Inc: Abbreviated Financial Summary $m

	2009	2010	2011	2012	2013	
Sales revenue	76.1	78.7	82.7	87.7	93.0	
Variable costs	−21.5	−22.5	−23.5	−25.3	−27.3	
Contribution	54.6	56.2	59.2	62.4	65.7	
Fixed costs	−30.0	−31.8	−35.7	−36.6	−37.5	
Amortisation	−6.0	−5.7	−7.6	−7.7	−7.8	
Pre-tax profit	18.6	18.8	15.9	18.1	20.4	
Tax	−6.5	−6.6	−5.6	−6.3	−7.1	
Net profit	12.1	12.2	10.3	11.8	13.3	
Fixed assets	67.0	90.1	86.2	82.7	79.5	
Accounts receivable	19.0	19.7	20.7	21.9	23.3	
Accounts payable	−12.6	−13.7	−10.7	−11.4	−12.2	
Inventories	8.6	9.1	9.9	10.3	10.8	
Net working capital	15.0	15.1	19.9	20.8	21.8	
Capital employed	82.0	105.1	106.1	103.5	101.3	
ROACE	17.4%	13.0%	9.8%	11.2%	13.0%	
Profit	12.1	12.2	10.3	11.8	13.3	
Amortisation	6.0	5.7	7.6	7.7	7.8	
Working cap	1.3	0.0	−4.8	−0.9	−1.0	
Capital investment	−23.0	−28.7	−3.7	−4.1	−4.6	
Funds flow	−3.6	−10.9	9.4	14.4	15.5	
						TV
Funds flow	−3.6	−10.9	9.4	14.4	15.5	172.1
Discount factor	0.958	0.879	0.806	0.740	0.679	0.679
PV funds flows	−3.5	−9.6	7.5	10.6	10.5	116.8
Cumulative PV	−3.5	−13.1	−5.5	5.1	15.6	132.4

This LTP is not viable. Several observations lead me to this conclusion. To start with, the dividend in the final three years is greater than the profit. Now take a look at the gearing and also the interest charge as a percentage of pre-tax profit. It is unlikely that a bank would want to lend money to a company in this state. The first thing one would need to do is reduce the dividend since the company clearly could not afford to pay this level of dividend if the selling price of its products were to be as low as $350/te. If one reduces the first-year dividend from $4m to $1m the numbers in the LTP would then be as in table 7.13.

Table 7.12 Yellow Moon Chemical Company Inc: revised LTP with $350/te selling price

					$m
Income statements	2009	2010	2011	2012	2013
Sales revenue	68.3	70.7	74.2	78.7	83.5
Variable costs	–21.5	–22.5	–23.5	–25.3	–27.3
Contribution	46.8	48.1	50.7	53.4	56.2
Fixed costs	–30.0	–31.8	–35.7	–36.6	–37.5
Amortisation	–6.0	–5.7	–7.6	–7.7	–7.8
Pre-tax profit	10.8	10.7	7.4	9.1	10.9
Interest charge	–2.3	–3.6	–4.5	–4.6	–4.5
Tax	–3.0	–2.5	–1.0	–1.6	–2.2
Net profit	5.6	4.6	1.9	2.9	4.1
Balance sheets					
Fixed assets	67.0	90.1	86.2	82.7	79.5
Accounts receivable	17.1	17.7	18.6	19.7	20.9
Accounts payable	–10.8	–11.6	–8.4	–9.0	–9.8
Inventories	8.6	9.1	9.9	10.3	10.8
Net Working capital	14.8	15.1	20.0	21.0	21.9
Capital employed	81.8	105.1	106.2	103.6	101.4
Debt	39.4	62.4	66.1	65.3	63.7
Equity	42.4	42.7	40.1	38.3	37.6
Capital employed	81.8	105.1	106.2	103.6	101.4
Cash flow					
Profit	5.6	4.6	1.9	2.9	4.1
Amortisation	6.0	5.7	7.6	7.7	7.8
Working capital change	1.2	–0.3	–5.0	–0.9	–0.9
Capital investment	–23.0	–28.7	–3.7	–4.1	–4.6
Dividends paid	–4.2	–4.3	–4.5	–4.7	–4.9
Cash flow	–14.4	–23.0	–3.7	0.9	1.5
Key ratios					
Return on capital employed	9.5%	7.4%	4.6%	5.6%	6.9%
Return on equity	13.3%	10.9%	4.6%	7.5%	10.9%
Gearing	48.2%	59.4%	62.3%	63.0%	62.9%

Table 7.13 Yellow Moon Chemical Company Inc: revised LTP with $350/te selling price & reduced dividend

Income statements	2009	2010	2011	2012	2013
Sales revenue	68.3	70.7	74.2	78.7	83.5
Variable costs	−21.5	−22.5	−23.5	−25.3	−27.3
Contribution	46.8	48.1	50.7	53.4	56.2
Fixed costs	−30.0	−31.8	−35.7	−36.6	−37.5
Amortisation	−6.0	−5.7	−7.6	−7.7	−7.8
Pre-tax profit	10.8	10.7	7.4	9.1	10.9
Interest charge	−2.1	−3.2	−3.9	−3.7	−3.3
Tax	−3.0	−2.6	−1.2	−1.9	−2.6
Net profit	5.6	4.9	2.3	3.5	4.9
Balance sheets					
Fixed assets	67.0	90.1	86.2	82.7	79.5
Accounts receivable	17.1	17.7	18.6	19.7	20.9
Accounts payable	−10.8	−11.7	−8.5	−9.2	−10.0
Inventories	8.6	9.1	9.9	10.3	10.8
Net working capital	14.8	15.0	19.9	20.8	21.7
Capital employed	81.8	105.1	106.1	103.5	101.1
Debt	36.2	55.7	55.6	50.6	44.6
Equity	45.6	49.4	50.5	52.9	56.6
Capital employed	81.8	105.1	106.1	103.5	101.1
Cash flow					
Profit	5.6	4.9	2.3	3.5	4.9
Amortisation	6.0	5.7	7.6	7.7	7.8
Working capital change	1.2	−0.2	−4.9	−0.9	−0.9
Capital investment	−23.0	−28.7	−3.7	−4.1	−4.6
Dividends paid	−1.0	−1.1	−1.1	−1.2	−1.2
Cash flow	−11.2	−19.5	0.1	5.0	6.0
Key ratios					
Return on capital employed	9.5%	7.4%	4.6%	5.6%	6.9%
Return on equity	13.0%	10.2%	4.6%	6.8%	9.0%
Gearing	44.3%	53.0%	52.4%	48.9%	44.1%

This plan is more reasonable as at least YMCC is able to start repaying its large level of debt shortly after the new plant comes on stream.

Hopefully these last two financial sensitivities will have served to illustrate the point about how the inclusion of finance introduces too many variables and how a visual sense check of the numbers is always necessary each time a sensitivity is run.

We can also use this sensitivity analysis to emphasise one of the key implicit assumptions of an economic value calculation. This concerns a company's ability to take downside risk. A 10% reduction in selling prices is a fairly small change. We are not dealing with a real company so I cannot provide any actual data to suggest what the probability might be that prices fall by this much but my intuition is that 10% is a relatively modest change.

When one does a valuation and considers risks, the usual assumption is that a company is big enough to take the risk. If this is the case we have learned that we can justify looking at the expected value outcome and trusting that, over time, downsides will be offset by upsides. So if $390/te was the expected value of future selling prices we would focus on this case and consider that, statistically, the $350/te case could be offset by equivalent upsides.

If YMCC was a division of a major corporation with a range of activities so that the selling price of yellow pigment was not correlated with the other selling prices, we could justify adopting this expected value approach to risk. The case study has, however, been set up with YMCC as a stand-alone company that plans to fund its growth primarily from external borrowings. The 10% selling price sensitivity has showed that its financial outlook is very risky. As a stand-alone company there would need to be a much stronger focus on downside risk than would be necessary in a major corporation. This focus would certainly want to consider credible combinations of downside risks such as lower sales volume happening at the same time as lower prices.

I suggest that readers should consider this case study as a mid-term test. Readers should ensure they understand the calculations. They should also confirm that they too can see which plans were viable and which were not. Finally, readers should confirm they understand the point about being big enough to take risk. **If readers believe they have passed the test, they should congratulate themselves on their progress so far and can look forward with confidence to the remainder of this book.**

Part 8: Suggested standard methodology

Why a standard methodology is required

The case for a standard methodology which specifies a level playing field for investment appraisal was set out in part 1 of this pillar. Companies will have to make choices and these will typically be taken by busy senior executives. We should not underestimate how hard their task can be. Imagine how tough it must be choosing between competing projects, each of which will be championed by an enthusiastic project sponsor.

One service which a culture of sound financial analysis can provide to a company is to remove spurious number noise caused by arbitrary differences in the way that numbers are processed. Consider things like:

- the date which is used as the basis for NPV calculation;
- whether cash flows are assumed to be mid-year or end-year;
- whether payback is quoted based on discounted or undiscounted cash flows;
- whether the alternative to investment is 'do nothing' or 'divest'.

There are not necessarily right answers to these questions. There is, however, certainly the potential for material apparent differences if one just looks at the headline numbers and does not dig into exactly how the calculations were done. Senior executives should not be required to do such digging. They should be left free to focus on the important issues which concern the real differences between competing projects and not the methodological differences.

Companies therefore need a set of rules about how calculations should be undertaken. The rules need to be developed within companies to suit their particular circumstances. It would be wrong for an author such as myself to try to impose a standard. I can, however, suggest what a set of rules might look like and I can propose that these be used unless and until companies develop their own versions which are better suited to their particular needs.

My suggested standard methodology follows. The advantage of adopting a standard methodology is that senior executives would then be entitled to assume that stated assumptions would faithfully be converted into their associated economic indicators. They could therefore focus their attention on the assumptions and the resultant economic indicators without needing to delve into questions of methodology.

Suggested standard economic evaluation methodology

1. Applicability

This methodology will apply to all calculations of economic value that are carried out within the company. This will include analysis of investments, divestments and strategic choices.

2. Incremental analysis

The methodology requires that after-tax money-of-the-day cash flows be discounted in order to calculate the prescribed economic indicators. The presumption will be that, unless stated to the contrary, cash flows will be incremental cash flows measured against a deemed alternative case.

For existing sites and/or operations this deemed alternative case will represent a minimum investment stay-in business case with future investment limited to sustaining investment and any other spend that has already been approved. For new sites the alternative case will be no investment. Note that divestment will not be taken as the alternative case.

Two accepted situations where incremental cash flows will not be used are as follows:

a. The term 'absolute value' will be used to distinguish situations where the value of a strategy or course of action is quoted.
b. The term 'full-cycle' will be used when sunk costs and/or future non-incremental fixed costs are included in the analysis in order to assess the overall strategic health of an activity.

3. The stated assumptions

All cases will be based on a series of stated assumptions. The responsibility for making assumptions rests normally with the project sponsor. The assumptions and their basis will be made clear and will be available for inspection via an assumptions register.

The default presumption about assumptions will be that they are reasonable estimates of the expected value outcome. That is to say that they will have a reasonable statistical balance of upside and downside. Assumptions can be set in other ways such as on the presumption of success but when this is done, the decision to do so must be highlighted to decision-makers.

One assumption should concern the project life. However, if the project is similar to other projects that have recently been approved or are currently being considered then a common project life must be utilised unless a clear basis exists for adopting a different figure and this assumption is made clear to decision-makers.

Assumptions must also be made about any necessary sustaining capital expenditure required and also any decommissioning/remediation costs.

The company will determine certain key assumptions which it will publish regularly in a Planning Assumptions Document. Where an assumption is covered by the company's Planning Assumptions Document, it must be followed. The sponsor of a project may show the impact of alternative assumptions as a type 3 sensitivity case.

4. Cash flow model

A cash flow model will be used to convert the stated assumptions into a projection of future money-of-the-day after-tax cash flow. This model will have been audited by a skilled practitioner from outside the project team. The cash flows will have been projected on an asset basis and will not take into account specific finance assumptions.

The model will project cash flows for each year given the company's financial reporting cycle.[29] The usual assumption will be that cash flows occur mid-year. However, major cash flows that are expected at materially different times should be allowed for in the financial modelling. Particular attention should be paid to modelling correctly the timing of cash flows at the start of a project.

The model should operate in the currency that is deemed to be the functional currency of the project. If this currency is subject to high inflation the model will operate by applying a real CoC to the real (i.e. inflation adjusted) after-tax cash flows. Exchange rate assumptions will normally be included in the company's Planning Assumptions Document. These will usually show no change in exchange rates except where high inflation is forecast.

The cash flow model should incorporate working capital effects. Any residual working capital at the end of the project life should be assumed to be recovered at the book value amount in the middle of the following year.

The cash flow model of a business may be truncated from what would be the full economic life by the adoption of a terminal value assumption. Any assumptions required to justify the terminal value calculation must be made clear in the assumptions register. These assumptions will include an implied level of future capital investment and overheads necessary to allow the business to deliver the assumed growth beyond the plan period.

In situations where a project will comprise a number of stages, only those cash flows which will result from the investment for which sanction is being sought should be included in the cash flow model. The economic impact of further stages of the investment may be illustrated through the use of a type 3 sensitivity.

The accounting presentation of the cash flow forecasts and the value calculation will be summarised by the preparation of the standard AFS report.

[29] Remember that company years and calendar years are not necessarily the same. I am assuming that the company's planning calendar follows its financial reporting timetable.

5. Cost of capital

The CoC to be adopted will be specified by the company's finance department. In the absence of any other agreed figures, 8% post-tax should be used.[30] All uncertain cash flows should be discounted at the specified after-tax CoC. Debt like cash flows that are fixed in both quantity and timing should be discounted at the assumed after-tax cost of debt. This rate will also be provided by the finance department. In the absence of any other agreed figures a figure of 4% post-tax should be used as the after-tax cost of debt.

6. The four economic indicators

Each case will normally be characterised by four economic indicators. These are:

1. Net present value (NPV). This is to be calculated as at the beginning of the company's current year. The only exception to this rule would be in the analysis of acquisitions and divestments. In such situations valuations should be stated as at the date of the transaction rather than the start of the year.
2. Internal rate of return (IRR). This is the discount rate that would result in a zero NPV.[31]
3. Investment efficiency (IE). This is the NPV as a percentage of the headline capital investment amount. The headline capital investment amount is the total capital cost in money-of-the-day terms required to bring the project on stream at its full assumed throughput. Subsequent sustaining investment is not included in this total.
4. Discounted payback (DP). This is the point in time when the cumulative present value is projected to return to zero. DP should be stated as a calendar date. In cases where there are no initial negative cash flows (such as divestments and absolute valuations of strategic options for established businesses), only the first indicator should be stated.

In cases concerning only sustaining capital investment no economic indicators need to be stated. The economic justification of sustaining capital investment should be via either or both of the original investment case or a subsequent strategy review which demonstrated that continued operation of

[30] The topic of estimating the cost of capital is considered in great detail at a later stage in this book. This analysis will include consideration of whether a single company-wide cost of capital should be used or whether divisional or project-level costs of capital should be used. The figures quoted for cost of capital and cost of debt in this section of the proposed standard methodology should simply be viewed as placeholders pending specific decisions taken company by company.

[31] In the unlikely event that multiple solutions exist to the question of which discount rate will yield a zero NPV, the discount rate that is closest to the cost of capital should be quoted.

the asset was appropriate in the light of, among other aspects, the required level of sustaining investment. Where sustaining investment is substantially above the average level which has already been justified a new strategy review should be undertaken in order to justify the higher spend.

7. Sensitivity analysis

Three types of sensitivity should be reported.

Type 1 sensitivities should report the impact of a change to an individual variable or an obvious combination of variables to the P10/P90 range.

Type 2 sensitivities should show what change in an individual variable or obvious combination of variables would produce a zero NPV.

Type 3 sensitivities are used to convey any other relevant sensitivity data. This would include illustrating the so-called growth value associated with any future investment which is excluded from the base case NPV as the necessary capital investment is not covered by the current sanction request.

The choice of which sensitivities to show should be made by the project sponsor. All significant sensitivities must be reported.

8. Sources of Value analysis[32]

Sources of Value logic should normally be used to explain and quantify the rationale behind any proposal. The following conventions should be applied:

1. If the company has specified a standard list of sources of value then these must be used and the order of calculation of sources of value shall be as set out in the list.
2. Care should be taken to ensure that any negative sources of value are included in the overall analysis and not just the positive ones.
3. The return implied for a 'me too' player should be stated as a difference in IRR relative to the CoC. If an assumption has been adjusted in order to achieve a desired 'me too' return this should be made clear.
4. If Sources of Value analysis is not used a brief explanation of why should be given. An example would be that sustaining investments would not normally need to apply this approach.
5. It would be permissible for economic evaluation that is carried out at the early stages of a project's life to utilise a Sources of Value building block approach to assessing the anticipated NPV as opposed to a traditional cash flow model.

[32] First-time readers should note that this section is included in this suggested Standard Economic Evaluation Methodology for completeness. The technique is explained in the following pillar.

CHAPTER

8

The second pillar: Sources of Value

Introduction

We are now at about the halfway stage in this book and it is the right time to introduce the eponymous Sources of Value technique. The wait has been necessary for those who started as beginners because the technique can only be properly applied by people with a good understanding of both strategy and valuation. For those who started as practitioners the wait has been short and has simply concerned the need to ensure that we are working with a well-built economic model. For both groups we have now acquired the necessary skills and so can look at the new insights that Sources of Value offers to us. This technique will:

- allow us to explain an investment's value through its underlying strategic rationale;
- help us to make better assumptions in our investment cases and then explain the implications of these assumptions to senior decision-takers;
- guide us as to where to look for positive NPVs and how large we should expect these to be.

My approach will be to start with an overview of the technique. I will then look in more detail first at its theoretical underpinnings and then at its practical application. Finally, I will review some of the lessons that you can learn when you apply Sources of Value thinking. Although the approach has its foundations in some of the heavily used strategic concepts described by Michael Porter it does raise questions about some of the apparently accepted wisdoms that surround business strategy thinking.

In effect, therefore, this pillar will describe Sources of Value under the headings:

- what?
- why?

- how? and
- so what?

It has been my experience when I teach the technique in a class, that different people 'get it' at different stages of the lecture. I am advised that this is probably due to individuals having different learning styles. These four questions should appeal to different learning styles and so readers should, hopefully, find that at least one of them works particularly well for them. I do, though, recommend that readers should read all four, as the full Sources of Value story will only be found in that way since I have tried to minimise overlap between the sections.

If the initial picture which emerges for you is a little unclear then please persevere. My experience has been that the answer will come later, when, for you the individual reader, the focus suddenly becomes sharp. Readers may well want to cycle back to one of the earlier sections when they have this better picture in their mind of what Sources of Value can contribute to their understanding of business.

Part 1: What is the Sources of Value technique?

Suppose that you were the sponsor of an investment project. You have put forward an investment proposal using all the skills that you have learned so far in this book. You have built a detailed economic model which has been well audited and is based on assumptions all of which you are comfortable with. At your presentation to the board, however, you are asked this question:

Where does the NPV come from?

How would you answer?

I can think of two generically different ways of answering this very relevant question. The obvious approach would be to describe the calculations that supported the claimed NPV. So your answer could be to the effect that the NPV arises as a result of the way that assumptions lead to a cash flow projection and those cash flows have a particular value. Furthermore, you could list all of the assumptions and indeed, the most important ones would already be highlighted in your finance case. You could even point to many sensitivities that showed how the NPV would change if the assumptions were changed.

Your answer would be true in every respect, but would it satisfy the board member? Surely, the decision-maker already knew the mechanistic answer to the question. Were they, in reality, looking for something deeper when they asked the question? Were they really asking why they should be expected to believe the NPV that had been presented? The mechanistic approach could lead you down what is often called a 'rat hole' as you seek to justify every single assumption as being reasonable. On a major investment case this can be very difficult and the end result would probably be a reduction in confidence concerning your project because the sensitivities show so many different, but possible, NPVs. I suggest the problem is related to the fact that each individual assumption is likely to be considered on its own and it is difficult to explain the overall implications of the assumptions in aggregate other than to point to the calculated base case.

There is a deeper way to answer the question and I will explain this now. This way would neatly sidestep the many assumptions that underpin your DCF model and would focus on the key strategic issues. The best answer to the question '*Where does the NPV come from?*' would come from saying that the NPV arrives as a result of how competitive forces will play out over the coming years.

Suppose that your reply was that the NPV arose because you believed you could beat the competition in a few very specific and well-understood ways. These ways of beating the competition would not be new. You would have written about them in your strategy review and they would already form the basis of the strategy that led you to propose this project. Furthermore, the organisation of your company would have been selected with a view to maintaining and enhancing these advantages.

Suppose further that you were able to say as part of this investment case, that you knew how far ahead of the competition you were and that you knew how much value this lead over the competition would give you. Imagine your confidence when you say that the NPV you claim for your project is slightly less than the NPV benefit you can see that you should earn through beating the competition. This means that, thanks to the additivity of NPVs, your company should be able to earn a positive NPV when your competitors were not. So you could tell the decision-maker that your NPV was not the result of apparently optimistic assumptions. It was purely a function of your strategy and your being ahead in the competitive battle. So instead of having to justify perhaps hundreds of assumptions, you would simply justify your lead over the competition and the return that they would earn if they evaluated an investment based on your assumptions.

This second approach is using the logic of the Sources of Value technique. Using this logic to justify an investment is just one of the things that can be done once an organisation starts to think in this way. Clearly, you'd need to work in an organisation that understood Sources of Value. I am sure that readers will find by reading this pillar that understanding it is not difficult, provided you already have a basic understanding of the principles of economic value and of strategy.

In this initial overview I will first show how the Sources of Value approach would be applied to an individual project. There are benefits even at this stage as one is, in effect, able to calibrate the assumptions which underpin the investment case. More important benefits are, however, there for the taking when companies act on the new strategic insights which are available and implement better strategies which are more likely to create value.

The Sources of Value analysis of a single investment case will start with a well-built spreadsheet model. This would produce the NPV which was claimed by the project. If one wanted to, one could apply the mechanistic approach to this case and show how the NPV was based on a long series of assumptions, all of which you could justify. Instead of doing this we put the NPV into a competitive context. The Sources of Value technique starts by asking what advantages this project is expected to have compared with a typical competitor. For reasons which will become apparent later, we will call this typical competitor the 'me too' player. In this case please accept that three key advantages have been identified. I will call these A, B and C. They are the project's sources of value.

We will learn later on exactly what sort of things these sources of value could be but for the present we will just call them A, B and C because it does not matter yet what they are.[1] The value impact of each source of value is calculated and a Sources of Value diagram can then be drawn. It should look like this:

[1] If you do need to have something concrete to help you to envisage the situation then I suggest you think of advantage A being the fact that you can sell a greater volume of your product per year than the typical competitor. Think of advantage B as being the fact that you could also achieve higher prices. Finally, advantage C could be lower capital investment costs.

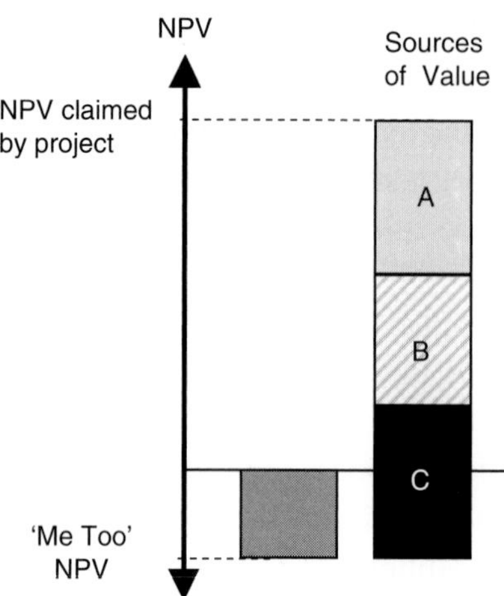

Fig. 8.1 Example of a Sources of Value diagram

The calculation is done by first adjusting the spreadsheet to exclude the effect of the benefit A.[2] The NPV would fall by an amount and this fall would quantify the source of value ascribed to cause A. The next step would be to take the adjusted spreadsheet and make a second adjustment, this time to exclude the effect of the advantage labelled B. Once again, the fall in value would be the source of value attributed to B. Finally, the third source of value would be removed and the reduction in value is observed. This is the numerical value of source of value C.

I have heard of Sources of Value being described as a sort of sensitivity analysis. This is not strictly true because sensitivities are usually done separately, with each sensitivity showing the effect on the base case if that one change were made. In the Sources of Value approach one gradually removes the identified sources of value from the spreadsheet assumptions one at a time until they have all been removed. If, for example, the first advantage referred to sales volume and the second to sales price, the order of calculation would matter because the second step would apply the price advantage to the lower sales volume.

When the final source of value has been removed one has a spreadsheet that shows what the project would look like to the so-called 'me too' player that lacks any of the advantages which our company has. If we have identified

[2] To exclude the effect we simply set the assumption to the figure that we think would be achieved by our typical competitor.

three reasons why we are better than a competitor then a spreadsheet with these three advantages removed must be the same as a spreadsheet that was built specifically to analyse the 'me too' player's investment. In the diagram the 'me too' player is shown as having a small but negative NPV. This is the box on the left which I traditionally show in the colour red.

At this stage we do not know what the NPV should look like for a 'me too' player. Think, though, about the implications of having a 'me too' player with a positive NPV. If this was a typical competitor who lacked any particular advantages wouldn't it seem too optimistic to assume that such a player could earn a positive NPV? If it saw the world in this way, wouldn't it seem reasonable to assume that lots of competitors would invest and that overcapacity would result which would push down prices? So perhaps it can only be reasonable to believe that the 'me too' NPV is either zero or negative.

Later in this pillar I will devote more attention to justifying what at present is purely an assertion that the reasonable assumption is for a 'me too' player to suffer a small negative NPV. For the present, however, please reflect on the added belief in the reasonableness of your assumptions which you would gain if you were able to show that these were such that a typical competitor would not earn a positive NPV.

If this were to be the case you could prove that the answer to the question '*Where does the NPV come from?*' was that it came purely because you expected to be able to beat the competition. Your answer would be that your project can create value even when your competitors cannot. Instead of having to justify lots of individual assumptions about your project, you simply point to their aggregate impact on this typical competitor. In this way you could demonstrate quantitatively that the overall effect of your assumptions was not obviously over-optimistic.

Let us now develop the Sources of Value idea a little further. In our chart we can see that we can explain our NPV as being the sum of two components. It is the sum of our sources of value and of what a typical 'me too' player would earn. Our sources of value are another way of describing our competitive advantages. The value that would be earned by a typical player is a measure of the attractiveness of the sector in which we are operating. The better the return earned by a 'me too' player, the more attractive the sector must be.

Now we have already come across the idea of combining sector attractiveness and competitive position in the description of the McKinsey/GE matrix on page 123 in the pillar concerned with planning and control. We have seen that sector attractiveness is best understood through application of Professor Porter's five forces model and that his concepts of competitive advantage explain how businesses can get ahead of their competitors. What we now see is a way to combine and, crucially, to quantify the two effects. The financial calculations embodied in a value spreadsheet can be linked directly to two key strategic concepts put forward by Porter and to the framework of the McKinsey/GE matrix.

So in a company that applied the Sources of Value technique you would come across it not just in the investment cases for individual projects. It would, in effect, start with the strategic analysis. The sector attractiveness part of a strategy review would go one step further and consider the 'me too' players. This consideration would identify them, consider how they might evolve over time, and consider what sort of return it would be reasonable to assume they would earn if and when they were to make an investment.

The competitive position part of a strategy review would identify the potential sources of value that the company could exploit. Strategies would be designed to leverage the benefit in the most efficient way possible. The organisation of the company would be aligned with the sources of value to ensure that they were sustained and enhanced. Finally, by quantifying the sources of value, the potential NPV which could be expected from future investment projects could be estimated even at this early stage of strategic analysis. This information would allow a more rigorous justification of things like the cost of project development teams.

The point about leveraging sources of value is of particular importance. There can often be more than one way to turn an advantage into value. Suppose a business identified its key source of value as the ability to build new plant for a lower capital cost than any other player in the industry. What should its strategy be?

It could build and operate new plant and this could well allow it to come up with a stream of positive NPV projects. This strategy would not, however, be maximising the leverage of the identified source of value. This is because no additional value will be created once the plant is built. A better strategy might be to build plant for others in the industry and let them act as operators. Suppose that another company operating in the same industry identified that its source of value was its ability to obtain feedstock for a cheaper price than any other player. Should it build a new plant? Again, it is possible that cheap feedstock would give it enough of an advantage to earn a positive NPV but a better strategy would probably be to sell feedstock to the entire industry and create value this way.

So a picture should now be emerging of the Sources of Value technique and its potential power:

- It builds on key strategic concepts and can help our strategy formulation by suggesting where the business's focus should be.
- It allows us to calibrate the overall effect of our assumptions and thus to take a more informed view about their reasonableness or otherwise.
- It links the normally qualitative strategic concepts with the quantitative approach of an NPV calculation and thus creates a bridge between two schools of thought, bringing more strength to both.

With this picture in mind we can now turn to the theory behind Sources of Value and consider this in more detail.

Part 2: Why the Sources of Value technique works

The supporting theory for Sources of Value draws mainly on many of the concepts that have already been introduced in this book. Indeed, there are so many supporting links that I take the view that the Sources of Value approach does not have to be 'proved' because if you accept what has been written so far, then Sources of Value logic should, once it has been introduced, be self-evident.

There is one new piece of thinking that I will need to introduce but this is left to the end of this part and it is only necessary to introduce it to deal with the special case where governments and/or regulators have a controlling role in determining how value is shared between suppliers and customers. This role will often involve tailoring taxes and other sums that are payable directly or indirectly to the government, to the specific situation of each project. For the main body of this second part there is an implicit assumption that things like tax rates are fixed and that competition takes place through the usual free-market mechanisms of price and quality.

The key steps in the Sources of Value technique's 'discovery' came from the combination of the simple thought that value could be analysed in this way[3] with the identification of the many insights and benefits that this approach

[3] The initial suggestion about analysing value this way and the term Sources of Value were ideas of my late colleague Ray McGrath. My contribution has been to champion the idea since about 1990 through codifying how Sources of Value can be applied; showing where Sources of Value logic challenges the existing approaches; and now through publishing the work in this book.

would then facilitate. I will turn to the insights later. For the present I will go over all of the supporting theory. My claim that the approach should be self-evident is based on the sheer number of links that I am now going to describe.

The links are as follows:

1. The principle of additivity of value.
2. Economic value underpins the share price.
3. The ROCE bridge and actual returns.
4. Sector attractiveness and competitive position.
5. Cost curves and what sets prices.
6. Experience curves and the product life-cycle.
7. Point-forward and full-cycle economics.
8. Governments and regulators.

My analysis of most of these points will be conventional and I will point out where I diverge from the current accepted approaches. The only new piece of theory in this part concerns the role of governments and regulators.

Supporting link 1: The principle of additivity of value

The first piece of theory is the principle of additivity of value. This principle states that any value calculation can be subdivided into components and the overall value will be equal to the sum of the values of its component parts. Values can be broken down in any way that you like and the principle of value additivity will still hold.[4] The trick is to think of a good ways of subdividing value and to use this to gain insights.

The principle of additivity of value provides a good reason to focus on value as the primary economic indicator for a project. I will be returning to the primacy of value over the other economic indicators in the final pillar. For the present it is simply worth noting that if one were to focus on the return that a project offered (i.e. its IRR) then the equivalent technique which might have been called 'Sources of Return' would not work because returns are not additive and in some situations it is even possible

[4] I introduced this principle quite early in this book as part of Building Block 1 on page 21. I wrote there that the trick of good financial analysis is to identify good ways of dividing up the value numbers. I had in my mind at the time the Sources of Value approach and also some of the company valuation approaches which will be explained in the final pillar. The point to be aware of is that there are any number of poor ways to analyse value. So you could, for example, and if you really wanted to, analyse value by whether the cash flows occurred on even-dated days or odd-dated days. I cannot think why you would want to do this and it would probably be difficult to obtain accurate data, but once completed, you would know that the even-day value plus the odd-day value would equal the total value.

to have something that enhances value while at the same time reducing the return.[5]

The simplest way to subdivide value is into the individual rows on a spreadsheet model. I call this type of analysis 'components of value' analysis. I gave it its own name in order to distinguish it from Sources of Value analysis because I used to find that so many people who had heard about Sources of Value, but not been trained in its use, would make the error of confusing the two approaches. The components of value approach requires that one calculates the present value of each line in an AFS. The NPV will then equal the sum of the present values of each line.

This components of value approach can be illustrated via any of the previous spreadsheet models that have been built. I have chosen the scaffolding example which, readers will recall from page 87, had an NPV of $0.6m.

The components of value can be calculated via the original spreadsheet model by including a final column which shows the present value of the numbers in each row. This is shown below:

Scaffolding Example: Abbreviated Financial Summary

	2007	2008	2009	2010	2011	2012	2013	Present Value
Income statement								
Sales revenue		1.7	1.8	1.9	2.0	2.1		7.1
Variable costs		−0.4	−0.4	−0.4	−0.4	−0.4		−1.5
Contribution		1.4	1.4	1.5	1.6	1.6		5.6
Fixed costs		−0.2	−0.2	−0.2	−0.2	−0.2		−0.8
Amortisation		−0.6	−0.6	−0.6	−0.6	−0.6		−2.3
Pre-tax profit		0.6	0.6	0.7	0.8	0.8		2.6
Tax		−0.2	−0.2	−0.2	−0.2	−0.3		−0.8
Profit		0.4	0.4	0.5	0.5	0.6		1.8
Balance sheet								
Fixed assets	4	3.4	2.8	2.2	1.6	1.0		
Accounts receivable	0	0.2	0.2	0.2	0.2	0.3		
Inventories	0	0.1	0.1	0.1	0.1	0.1		
Accounts payable	0	−0.2	−0.2	−0.2	−0.3	−0.3		
Working capital	0	0.1	0.1	0.1	0.1	0.1		
Capital employed	4	3.5	2.9	2.3	1.7	1.1		
ROACE		10.2%	13.4%	18.5%	26.8%	42.6%		

[5] This will be explained in more detail later. For the present, and to satisfy any current curiosity, think of the example of a capital spend which would increase the economic life of an asset. This could well increase NPV while at the same time lowering IRR.

Table (*cont.*)

Funds Flow								
Profit		0.4	0.4	0.5	0.5	0.6	0.0	1.8
Amortisation		0.6	0.6	0.6	0.6	0.6	0.0	2.3
Working Capital		−0.1	0.0	0.0	0.0	0.0	0.1	0.0
Capital Investment	−4.0	0.0	0.0	0.0	0.0	0.0	1.0	−3.4
Funds Flow	−4.0	0.9	1.0	1.1	1.1	1.2	1.1	0.6
Value Calculation								
	Set up						Close down	
Funds Flow	−4.0	0.9	1.0	1.1	1.1	1.2	1.1	
Discount Factor	1.000	0.945	0.844	0.753	0.673	0.601	0.567	
Present Value Funds Flow	−4.0	0.8	0.9	0.8	0.8	0.7	0.6	
Cumulative Present Value	−4.0	−3.2	−2.3	−1.5	−0.7	0.0	0.6	

The right hand column shows the components of value starting with sales revenue, which has a present value of $7.1. One has to subtract the present value of variable costs, fixed costs, tax and capital investment[6] to arrive at the NPV of $0.6m. This 'picture' of the components of value can be quite useful in understanding where value comes from and in portraying this information to wider audiences. An example will be shown later in this pillar as part of the implications section.

Now components of value is useful from time to time but Sources of Value is useful most of the time. It works in my view as a direct consequence of the principle of additivity of value. An implication of value additivity is the fact that value of the things that make you different from a competitor must, when subtracted from the value of your project overall, give the value that would be earned by a competitor.

Supporting link 2: Economic value underpins the share price

It is a fundamental presumption of this book that share prices are underpinned by economic value and that economic value can be calculated via the economic value model. I use the term 'underpinned' rather than 'set' to reflect the fact that share prices do not have to line up with economic value every day. They just have to be subject to what I would call mean-reverting forces which tend to push the share price back towards value if/when they diverge.

[6] Amortisation is a non-cash charge and does not impact on value. In arithmetical terms, although it lowers profit it is added back in the funds flow statement. Working capital should be included in the sums but in this case the net impact is zero (or to be exact −$0.04m which rounds down to zero).

So if share prices tend to revert towards their calculated value according to the economic value model, we can use that model as the proxy for what will set the share price. I will be dealing with this relationship in a lot more detail in the final pillar.

A key feature of Sources of Value is that it is a quantitative technique. The AFS approach shows us how to quantify economic value. Thanks to components of value we know that the NPV of the various lines in the AFS shows how much value a project is expected to create. The clear implication of this is that value can only be realised[7] if it impacts on one or more of the lines in the AFS. The spreadsheet model of an AFS is a picture of how value will be realised and, in order to allow valuations to be carried out, all sources of value must be specified in such a way that a clear link to the AFS is established.

This rather mechanistic view of value is very helpful when trying to identify sources of value. A source of value must be something that has a direct impact on the AFS. So concepts like 'technology' or 'reputation' should not, in my view, be used to define sources of value. This does not mean that having a leading technology or having a great reputation does not matter and cannot lead to the creation of superior value. What it does mean is that, in order to facilitate the quantification of value, things like 'technology' or 'reputation' must be defined in terms of how they impact on the AFS.

An example of this would be to move from the concept of 'technology' to the concrete suggestion that through a leading technology a plant will achieve a greater yield than those operated by competitors. In the case of reputation, the mechanism for this impacting value could be something like a company's achieving premium prices or a company's gaining planning permission faster than a competitor.

In all cases the Sources of Value approach is founded on the specific quantification of value through the numerical algorithms that make up an AFS. All value effects are recognised through their impact on one or more of the assumptions that drive the spreadsheet. Value is, therefore, a number rather than simply a concept.

Supporting link 3: The ROCE bridge and actual returns

What I call 'the ROCE bridge' was explained on page 133. The idea is that the ROCE of a company is a first-order approximation for the average IRR that

[7] The realisation of value means the actual appearance of value as cash in the bank. So a plan has a value and that value is realised if and when the plan becomes reality. The realisation of value takes place over a project's entire life even though the value itself is just a single number.

it is earning on all of its investments. This is not a new concept. It is accepted wisdom and is one of the main reasons why there is so much focus on return on capital. Now although this relationship is not always very good, any errors are usually such that ROCE overstates the average IRR. The simple reason for this is that companies are required to reduce the book value of their assets if this is above their true economic value but they do not increase the book value if it is below economic value. This must mean that if a company's return on capital averages out over time to a figure that is less than its CoC then it must have destroyed value.[8]

So we can use ROCE data to see if there is any evidence that companies earn below their CoC. I know that some people think that a company which fails to earn its CoC will be bound to get into financial difficulties. In reality, however, the evidence suggests that many companies fail to earn their CoC and although this subjects them to corrective economic forces it does not stop the poor returns from happening! Although companies do not publish information on the value earned from their projects they do publish ROCE data and we can use this to provide a rough check on how they are doing.

Market data does appear to illustrate the fact that many companies are earning less than their CoC. If we use my rough estimate of the CoC of 9%[9] then it would be clear that companies earning a ROCE of 7% or less must be considered to be earning below their CoC. I have used a cut-off figure of 7% rather than 9% partly to ensure that my assessment of how many companies fail to earn their CoC is conservative and partly to offset the small effect that growth will have in depressing reported returns on capital. Well, based on a ROCE data base that I have reviewed, about 16% of the top 1,000 European companies earned a return of 7% or less in the year 2006. Furthermore, 2006 was not simply a bad year. The figure for 2005 was just over 18%.

What I find stunning is that these returns are returns earned by entire companies, not simply the returns earned on individual projects which happen to have failed. They are also the returns of the top 1,000 companies in Europe and so one might have expected some form of survivor bias to show through with only the best companies becoming very big. No! Even big companies can and do destroy value. So it does appear entirely reasonable to plan

[8] The converse, i.e. the suggestion that earning a return on capital of above the cost of capital means that a company must have created value, is not necessarily true. This is because ROCE can often overstate the average IRR that is earned.

[9] As explained on pages 57–58.

for the future based on assumptions that some members of an industry are likely to invest and yet earn below their CoC. Indeed, I take the view that this statement should be worded differently. I would say that it was unreasonable to plan on the basis that all significant players in an industry earn at least their CoC unless a clear reason for this can be put forward.

I fully accept that the data on individual companies might be subject to question. I also accept that there may be some very good sectors. The overall conclusion, however, does appear to be that it is not safe to make an assumption that the 'me too' player can earn the CoC unless strong evidence is put forward to support this. I do not consider this to be unreasonable or deliberately conservative.[10] I simply view it as evidence of generally strong competition and a position that is supported by the facts of the poor returns earned by so many companies.

Supporting link 4: Sector attractiveness and competitive position

The first three links have dealt with what is treated as part of traditional 'finance' thinking. We will now turn to some strategy techniques in order to create the bridge between the disciplines. In the Sources of Value approach, value is explained as being the sum of the values of a project's specific advantages and the value earned by the typical 'me too' player. Now a project's specific advantages refer to its competitive position while the 'me too' player's value is a quantified measure of sector attractiveness. So the value earned by a project can be explained via the two axes of the McKinsey/GE matrix which in turn refer to two of Professor Porter's techniques, namely competitive advantage and the five forces model.

In a very good sector it may be rational to believe that a 'me too' player will earn its CoC and hence have a zero NPV. In most sectors, however, this player is likely to suffer a small but negative NPV. What we now can see is that we can use the five forces model to analyse the potential return that a 'me too' player will earn. Furthermore, we can now see that a project's value is a function of this value and the competitive advantages measured against the 'me too' player.

[10] I remember one senior manager during my time in the Chemicals division of BP who initially referred to the assumption that 'me too' players earn less than the cost of capital as 'Simon Woolley's hair shirt'. His meaning was that it was deliberately conservative. He subsequently accepted the assumption and became an ardent supporter of the Sources of Value approach. After this, any case which was presented to him based on 'me too' earning the cost of capital or more would be rejected out of hand.

We can illustrate this via the Sources of Value diagram as illustrated below:

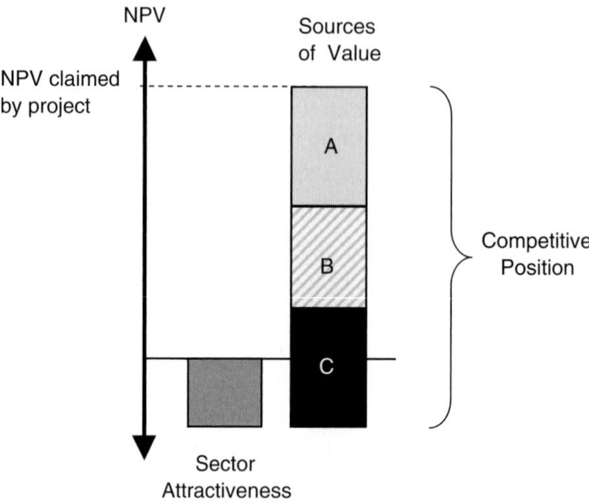

Fig. 8.2 Linking Sources of Value to strategic thinking

In the diagram the left-hand bar is a reflection of sector attractiveness while the right-hand bar in total describes the competitive position of a company.

There are some subtle but very important features of this diagram. These concern the way that the competitive position is defined. First, instead of having a single ranking of competitive position, it is shown broken down into its component parts. Second, in the McKinsey/GE matrix approach one tends to plot the absolute ranking of a company. So the number one player is shown as being top. In the Sources of Value approach all advantages are measured relative to a defined 'me too' player. Being best does help value creation but the key is not simply about being number one, it is how far ahead of the 'me too' player you are and how bad things are for them. It is quite possible, therefore, for a number three position in one sector to offer greater value potential than, say, a number one position in another.

Supporting link 5: Cost curves and what sets prices

The next supporting principle comes from the theories of micro economics. These theories describe the mechanisms that set prices. They will help us to understand one of the two elements of the value-creation potential of a project. The element concerned is the gap between the particular project and the 'me too' project. It is the logic of cost curves that tells us to look towards the poorly placed players in an industry if one wants to understand future prices. This logic is so important to the development of the Sources of Value technique that I will first remind all readers of it and of the conventional wisdom which it inspires in relation to future prices.

Microeconomic analysis suggests that prices are set by the marginal supplier. Economists therefore prepare cost curves which tend to look like this:

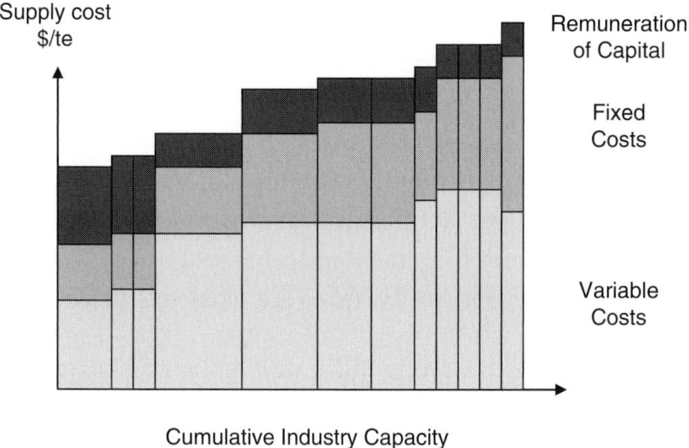

Fig. 8.3 Example of a cost curve

In this hypothetical example, the market is at present supplied by 12 plants. For each plant I have shown the cost to supply the local market broken down into variable costs, fixed costs and the remuneration of capital.[11] The plant with the lowest total cost to supply is shown on the left while the most expensive is on the right. The width of each bar is proportional to the capacity of the plant.

Ideally cost curves will show the above three categories separately because the different categories are used to gain different insights. In some cases,

[11] Remuneration of capital is calculated via an annuity factor. If a plant had a 15 year economic life and we assume a 10% CoC then because the relevant annuity factor is more or less equal to eight we know that the cash necessary to remunerate the capital is one eighth of the capital cost. We can then express this as a $/tonne figure by dividing the overall sum by the estimated annual production.

however, it is either not meaningful to show all three categories or simply not possible owing to lack of data. In these situations costs should be shown in two categories – cash costs and remuneration of capital. An example of when it might not be meaningful to consider variable costs could be when there are significant co-product credits[12] which may mean that the variable cost of production goes negative in some situations.

We can learn a lot about industry structure by studying its cost curve. In principle three equilibrium positions can be identified. Short run equilibrium is where the selling price is equal just to the marginal producer's marginal costs. There is a medium-run equilibrium when prices cover the marginal producer's full cash costs and a long-run equilibrium where marginal suppliers to a market can earn just their CoC. At any higher price there will be too great an incentive for further capacity to be built and so prices cannot logically be assumed to remain so high. It is this logic which encourages the use of things like fade diagrams where high margins are assumed to fade towards the CoC as time progresses.

The first piece of support that this thinking gives for the Sources of Value approach comes from the fact that we are told to look to the high-cost end of the cost curve in order to understand what sets prices. We do not look to the winners in the competitive battle to see what sets prices, we look at the laggards.

All that we can learn from looking at winners is that their profit potential is a function of how far ahead of the laggards they are. There is a direct parallel here with the Sources of Value approach. We are considering value rather than short-run profitability but the approach is the same. If the key determinant of profitability is a company's lead over the marginal price-setter then surely a key determinant of a project's ability to create value should also be its lead over the price-setter.

In my analysis of cost curves above I described equilibrium levels in relation to the marginal producer. Now in the short-run this must be the supplier at the point where the supply and demand curves cross, but who is the marginal supplier in the medium and long term? Whose costs should we study when we try to decide what will be the equilibrium price? I don't believe that this question can be answered with any precision. I think that the answer depends on a judgement. If all companies were the same the

[12] A co-product credit refers to when two or more products are produced at the same time. This often happens in the minerals and the chemicals industries. The sales value of the co-product reduces the effective variable cost of producing the main product and can even make this negative.

answer would be easy, but since in reality suppliers will have different costs it is hard to define who will be the marginal supplier over the long run. All one can suggest is that the long-run equilibrium should be somewhere between the fully built-up costs of the best supplier and the worst but this is not very helpful.

The Sources of Value technique hinges on a simple way of avoiding having to answer a difficult question. Instead of assessing who will earn the CoC I will consider a different but related question. I will define a player and then ask if it is reasonable to believe that it should, over the life of an asset, be able to earn a return of above the CoC.

First, I will consider a situation where there exists a normal level of competition and also a standard way of supplying a market through technologies, supply chains, knowhow, etc. that are available to any reasonably skilled player in the market. I will call companies that make such investments 'me too' players. They are in a growing sector; they decide that they would like to expand and they say 'me too'. They copy what is generally available but lack any particular advantages. Should it be reasonable to believe that they would be able to earn a positive NPV?

My answer to this question is a clear 'no'. If a player with no particular advantages can earn above the CoC, what is to stop others investing in order to gain their share of this supposed 'golden goose'? Once too many players invest the result will be severe overcapacity in the industry and prices must fall. The key to this answer lies in how I defined the situation. I stated that there had to be a standard way of supplying the market that was available to any reasonable player in the market. I also stated that competition was normal which means that there must be several players capable of supplying the market in this way. Finally, I stated that the player was to earn above its CoC. If several companies all considered that they would earn above their CoC, supply would, in effect, be more or less limitless and so, very clearly, this price must be unsustainably high.

Consider next a situation where there was a standard way of supplying the market but where all existing players had at least one way of doing something better than standard. Could this allow everybody to make money?[13] Again, I suggest that the answer should be 'no'. This is because if all players thought they could earn above the CoC then supply would be too great and prices would have to fall.

[13] When I use the term 'make money' I mean in more precise terms 'invest and earn above their cost of capital over the life of the investment'.

Consider finally a competitive market[14] where there is no 'standard' way of creating new supply. Consider a market where there are many ways of supplying a growing demand such that if all potential new supply sources were invested in there would clearly be overcapacity. Would it be reasonable to assume value creation by an investment that was placed at the bottom of the third quartile of those that could be made?

One again I would say 'no'. This time I might be a little less confident but my logic would include an assumption that a player at the bottom of the third quartile would create quite a lot less value than one in the middle of the pack. If players all the way down to the bottom of the third quartile at least earned above the CoC then the sector overall must be earning well above the CoC and so must be considered to be highly attractive. This situation could only be credible into the long run if it was clear that the players in the top three quarters of the industry could not expand their market share sufficiently to squeeze out the laggards. I think I would only accept this in a situation where there was some form of regulation which served to limit competition.

So cost curve logic tells us that where there is a standard way of adding new capacity it must be unsafe to assume that this will earn above the CoC and we can use this as our benchmark for measuring our own sources of value. I call such capacity 'me too' and it would appear reasonable to assume that in most situations it will be associated with value destruction. In situations where there is no 'me too' way of supplying the market or where many players can beat the 'me too' way in at least one way, we should substitute the bottom of the third quartile as the competitive benchmark and use this to assess our sources of value. The benchmark sets a level where the best return that can reasonably be believed is a return equal to the CoC. A more typical situation must be where this 'me too' player invests but destroys some value.

Cost curve logic also points us towards another very important factor. This concerns how important the shape of the cost curve can be. The example chart that I used earlier in this pillar is reproduced below in order to illustrate how it can be used to assess the implications of 'me too' economics for leading players. In the cost curve that I used there was one clear laggard at the high-cost end of the cost curve and then three similar blocks representing what I take to be 'me too' players. These plants are the same size and have the same cost structure. If we define them as 'me too' we can measure the value potential of the better plants.

[14] A competitive market has a normal level of competition. Some markets, for example in the area of utility supplies, are controlled by a regulator and so do not have what I would call a normal level of competition.

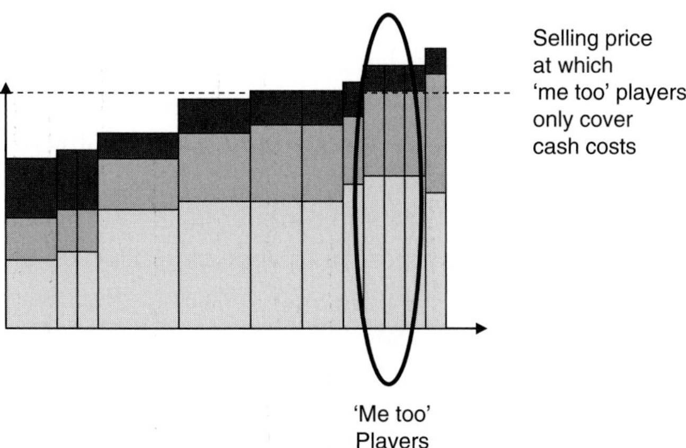

Fig. 8.4 The shape of cost curves

A pessimistic assumption might be that the 'me too' players only cover their cash costs on average over the life of their assets. The dotted line shows this and how the top five plants in the industry could still earn well above their CoC if prices were at this level.[15] It would appear very pessimistic to assume that prices could remain below cash costs for the worst four plants in the industry for a long period. Equally, it would be too optimistic to assume that 'me too' players could earn above their CoC. So we therefore have, for this cost curve at least, a fairly narrow band of prices which it would seem reasonable to assume.

One obvious message from the curve concerns the importance of its slope. The value potential of any project is heavily influenced by the steepness of the cost curve in the sector in which the project will operate. The steeper the slope, the more value an advantaged player can earn. Likewise, a flat curve may mean that most players are condemned to earn poor returns.

A further message about sector attractiveness can come from the relative balance between my three suggested categories of cost. Producers who have very low or even negative[16] variable costs will always have a great incentive to run their plant flat out. In such a situation if potential supply exceeds demand any reductions in output will have to be concentrated on the remaining producers with higher variable costs. This will then provide the effective price floor. The key question for the better-placed players will concern the extent to which they can cover cash costs and also the cost of remunerating capital

[15] Remember that the curve shows full cost to supply including remuneration of capital. So the gap between full cost and the dotted line would highlight the value potential.

[16] Remember that when there are co-product credits variable costs can become effectively negative.

while poorly placed players are only covering their variable costs. Note, though, that if a company does have a lead as big as this compared with an existing competitor there will most likely be pressures on the competitor to quit the business. This may cause a structural change in the industry if the new price-setter has much lower costs.

There is one final piece of theory to consider in relation to cost curves and what sets prices. This concerns companies' abilities to achieve premium prices. The implicit assumption so far in this section has been that the product concerned is sold for a single price. Some extra thinking is required where prices are not always the same, for example where brand and/or quality considerations start to come into play. Simply studying the cost of a branded product in relation to the cost of a non-branded one will not help to understand where value is created. For example, the inclusion of a picture of a Disney character on a set of children's bedclothes may add a couple of dollars to the price but only a few cents to the variable cost of production. There may well be higher fixed costs to consider but, to be honest, these will be hard to understand via a cost curve because they will have been spread over many years.[17]

What I would suggest is that cost curve thinking can help our understanding of situations where there are small price differences driven by quality effects. In such situations the cost curves could be normalised to treat the price premium as a negative variable cost. This could work, say, in relation to understanding the differences between supermarkets. Where brand effects are bigger, cost curves are only of limited use. We will return to the topic of Sources of Value and brands in the last section of this pillar when we consider the strategic implications of the technique.

Now since this has been quite a lengthy exploration of the importance of cost curves it is worthwhile including a short summary of what I have suggested so far. I have proposed that our investment project should be compared with the investment project of a so-called 'me too' investor. I have defined 'me too' in such a way that it should be unreasonable to believe that a project such as this would earn above the CoC. Since we know what makes us different from 'me too' we can check that the implied result for 'me too' is indeed not a positive NPV. Thinking in this way can give us insights as regards what might be reasonable and is potentially much easier than having to make the much more difficult forecast of what the future price-setter will look like.

[17] I understand that Mickey Mouse is said to have been born on 18 November 1928. It would be pointless to try to understand the costs associated with him since then but I am sure that overall he has created value for Walt Disney!

Supporting link 6: How markets evolve over time

Industries do not stand still and their cost curves evolve over time. The driving forces behind these changes are described by two concepts which are referred to as the product life cycle and the experience curve. The product life cycle suggests that all products can be described through an analogy with four stages of life. The stages are Introduction; Growth; Maturity; and Decline and the terms describe what happens to the overall level of demand. The experience curve is a related concept that suggests that as industries build their overall experience of producing a product, the industry learns how to lower its costs. Furthermore, this lowering of costs happens at a reasonably steady rate, with each doubling of the industry's cumulative production leading to the same percentage reduction in costs. The pace of evolution within an industry is therefore heavily influenced by the stage which it is in. This means the rate of change will be particularly great when a sector is in its growth stage and that change will be less pronounced during maturity. The new plants which are built during the growth phase of the product life cycle will often drive through changes in the selling price of the product. The changes might, for example, be sufficient to drive the price-setting 'battle' down to a new and much lower variable cost benchmark.

If one considers the cost curve from above one can see how things might evolve over time. What is important is the continued survival of the deemed 'me too' players. New plants will be built either to meet growing demand or because players want to expand their market share. Now plants that are needed to cover growing demand will not force existing plants to close and so need not have too big an influence on selling prices. If, however, more new capacity is introduced than is needed there will be a period of overcapacity during which prices will fall. These lower prices may encourage the current higher-cost producers to leave the market. The result could be that fairly soon the benchmark for 'me too' has switched.

I can illustrate this effect through the following hypothetical example. I will once again use the same cost curve but now I will show not only the current version but also what I expect it to be like in five years' time. I have assumed that the industry is growing and that two new plants will be built. These are both large and will be the new cost leaders. The plants, however, add more capacity than is necessary to cover demand growth and so the only way that overcapacity can be avoided is through the closure of some existing capacity. The assumption which I have made is that the current bottom two plants will be closed. The following chart illustrates the evolution of the cost curve.

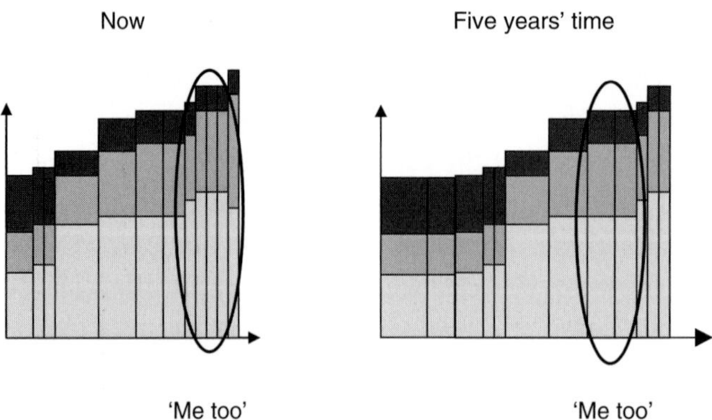

Fig. 8.5 The evolution of a cost curve

One key point to note is that I have assumed the closure of the worst plant in the industry and also one of the former 'me too' plants. Since 'me too' does not refer to the worst player in the industry we need to move the benchmark to the left as shown.

What would be a reasonable price assumption to make during this period? If no plants were closed one could expect prices to fall to about the marginal cost of the inefficient producers. At this level it is probable that all players in the industry would be making accounting losses and no players would be earning enough to remunerate their capital investment.[18]

If there were no exit barriers, inefficient producers would probably close capacity if they thought that prices would only average about their full cash costs. If there were costs associated with exit, the owners of each plant would have an incentive to wait and hope that another producer would close. During the period until capacity was closed, prices could be expected to remain close to variable costs. So a reasonable price assumption must be somewhere between the laggards' variable and full cash costs. One could use the full cash costs of the plant which is expected to be third worst in five years' time as the answer to the question concerning prices during this transitional period.

We can cross check this price for what it means for the new 'me too' players. These have fully built-up costs that are about equal to the cash costs of the industry laggards. I would suggest that this was slightly too high to be sustainable into the long run because eventually these two remaining laggard

[18] Remember that the dark grey block that represents the remuneration of capital covers what in accounting terms would be called amortisation and profit. The exact split between the two will depend on the circumstances but one can guess that about half of the block represents amortisation.

plants would also go the way of the one similar plant that we have already assumed will be closed. If prices were equal to the full cash costs of the third worst plant we would have the situation where the 'me too' players were able to recover some contribution towards their sunk capital costs but nowhere near enough to earn their CoC. This could well be sustainable and so passes the test of being a suitable equilibrium assumption.

So what we have seen through this example is that we can combine concepts such as the product life cycle with approaches like cost curves to gain insights about the future selling price for products. Furthermore, we have seen that an assumption about the return that will be earned by the 'me too' player can set a useful benchmark. If the 'me too' player is earning something slightly less than its full CoC this might well be sustainable into the long run.

The choice of the deemed 'me too' player and of the return that it will earn is judgemental but the cost curve, coupled with the understanding of how sectors will evolve over time, can give considerable insights about what the future might turn out to be. This, I suggest, is an improvement compared with current approaches, which seem to be dominated by the idea that returns will fade towards the CoC with an industry structure where all players are trending towards similar costs. Sources of Value thinking suggests first that value creation can continue for as long as players can differentiate themselves from the 'me too' player. Second, it suggests that value creation potential is a function of how large the difference is between your project and the 'me too' project less the value loss which we should usually assume the 'me too' project will suffer.

Supporting link 7: Point-forward and full-cycle economics

Up to now I have implied that the third element in the build-up of costs shown in my cost curves has been the remuneration of all capital. I have not yet considered exactly what should be meant by this and there are some important issues to consider in relation to the difference between point-forward economics and full-cycle economics.

The usual way to present the analysis of a project is to allow only for incremental costs in the calculation of the project's NPV. However, when one considers a company's overall performance through its return on capital, the focus has switched to full-cycle returns, the differences being that sunk costs and future costs which will not change as a result of the decision about this particular project are both excluded from the point-forward sums.

My consideration of what it is reasonable to believe will form an equilibrium has, by contrast, referred implicitly to fully built-up costs. It cannot be logical, I have argued, to assume that a 'me too' player would earn above the CoC. Well, I would say that it could perhaps be logical to assume that such players earned above the CoC on a purely point-forward basis. They might face a situation where they had to decide whether or not to continue in the face of analysis that said that, on a money-forward basis, they would be better off and the only reason for the overall negative NPV on the full-cycle consideration was something that was unavoidable. I would fully understand a decision to go ahead in such a situation and so it must, in principle, be possible for the 'me too' player's incremental NPV to be positive.

We will see when we come to the application section that it is left to the sponsor of a project to decide what they consider to be a reasonable basis for representing 'me too' players. This consideration must cover not only who they are but also whether we include in their costs, those which are either sunk or are allocable but are in the future and will not change as a result of this decision.

Just because it is possible to believe that a positive 'me too' incremental NPV *can* represent equilibrium does not mean that one *has* to assume this. My own bias is to assume that in most sectors 'me too' players will not earn a positive point-forward NPV. I would only depart from this if there were particular reasons to believe the opposite; for example, if there were very substantial 'search costs' for a project[19] and only some players will succeed. In such a situation it can be reasonable to assume that all players who succeed in the search will earn a positive money-forward return. If this were not to be the case then too few companies would start the search in the first place.

One implication of this consideration of sunk costs is that when one considers a project through the lens of point-forward economics, one can expect sunk costs to be a potential source of value. The magnitude of the source of value is not set by what has already been spent. It is set by what the 'me too' player would have to spend in order to reach the equivalent position to that which you are in now. This requires that one defines not just a 'me too' player but also exactly where it is on its project's time line.[20]

[19] 'Search costs' refer to the cost of finding the opportunity. In the pharmaceutical business, for example, this will cover the costs of screening potential new drugs, while in the oil industry it will cover all exploration. All projects will involve some search costs but it is only when they are really large that I would maintain that it cannot be reasonable to assume that because they are sunk they cannot contribute to the long-run equilibrium price.

[20] For example a 'me too' assumption might be specified as, say, 'me too' earns 3% less than the cost of capital on a full-cycle basis. In this instance the source of value calculation would involve calculating

The sunk cost benefit will not be equal to the total of all sunk costs. It will be equal to the beneficial impact of sunk costs compared with the deemed 'me too' player.

Supporting link 8: Governments and regulators

There are many situations where governments and/or regulators tend to intervene from time to time in order to adjust how the economic rent that may exist in a market gets divided among the various players. An obvious example might be where an industry is subject to control by a regulator who is required to set new rules of the game every few years. A second example would be where governments tailor the tax take on a project to the prevailing level of profitability through imposing things like windfall profits taxes or through setting special taxes that apply just to the sector in question. This is very common in natural resource industries like oil.

In such situations one needs to apply an adjusted version of the Sources of Value technique. This still involves the idea of a 'me too' player but this time 'me too' is defined in a different way and should be expected to earn just above the CoC. I will explain the logic behind this now through a practical illustration.

Imagine that you were the minister responsible for natural resources in a particular country. Your country is lucky enough to have some substantial mineral reserves and, as the minister in charge, it is your responsibility to ensure that these are developed in a way that maximises the benefits that flow to your country. You will, though, have to involve one or more major companies from outside your country because you need to access their technical skills and their ability to fund the high upfront costs of exploration and development.

You will have various policy levers that you can pull which should enable you to ensure that development takes place at exactly the rate which you require and that your country gets the maximum possible benefit from the resource. These policy levers will include:

- the right to grant exploration licences;
- the right to approve development plans for any minerals that are discovered;

the value impact of the costs (both past and future) that the 'me too' player would have to incur in order to reach the position that we are currently at. If, however, 'me too' was specified as, say, 'me too' earns 1% less than the cost of capital on a money-forward basis the comparison would only be between what the 'me too' player had to spend in the future to get to where we are now.

- the right to grant many other approvals that will be required by any foreign company that decides to invest in your country;
- the right to set tax rates and to devise new taxes if you so wish.

Furthermore, because you are the minister of a sovereign state, you will:

- not be bound by any previous decisions (so if you decide that a previously set tax rate needs to be increased, it is your legal right to do so);
- have access to all the necessary information including the profitability of existing projects (because you levy taxes on them) and the potential profitability of new developments (because you have to approve them).

With all of those powers at your disposal, what would you do?

I suggest that you would recognise that perhaps the only limits to what you could do arise because your country still needs to attract outside companies to develop its minerals industry. You would have to be careful to ensure that your actions were such that they did not frighten away potential new investors.

The implication is that if you wanted to encourage companies to carry out exploration for new mineral reserves, you would have to be good enough to existing mineral projects to make potential new ones look attractive. Indeed, because exploration is not guaranteed to succeed, you would have to make sure that those who had been lucky enough to succeed in the past were earning good positive NPVs on their projects.[21] As minister you could tailor any tax changes on existing projects (for example a tax increase in response to a rise in commodity prices) to ensure that you did not frighten away the potential new investors. So before you changed any tax rates you would investigate the impact on the various projects that you were responsible for and you would pay particular attention to the future projects that you wanted to encourage.

The implication is that in a situation such as this the host government will tailor its overall tax take to ensure that existing projects secure sufficient returns to encourage new exploration. Once the future prospects for the new developments look good enough at one commodity price level, any windfalls that a developing company might expect should the underlying commodity price rise would most probably be largely taxed away because the host government would not see the need to give that much economic reward to a foreign company. Should the basic commodity price rise, then foreign

[21] Think of the positive NPV on the development project as the prize and the cost of exploration as the stake that you pay in order to play the game. If the game has only a one-in-four chance of success you would only play it if the NPV was more than four times the cost of exploration.

companies would be encouraged to invest even though tax rates were a little higher as long as they could see that existing players were earning a good enough return.

Now imagine how you could afford to behave as minister for natural resources when you reach the point when all necessary exploration for minerals has been carried out. There may still remain some ore bodies to have their development plans approved but assume that the days of your country's being a key new supplier to the world market have gone. You would be able to be much tougher with your existing companies because you would not need to encourage new exploration. So, existing companies would not need to be offered any much more than a zero NPV on new developments.

Finally, in this review of what the minister can do, move yourself forward to the final years of your industry. You could then afford to threaten the big producers in your country with higher taxes if they did not agree to develop the small remaining ore bodies that still needed to be brought into production.

I would conclude that as minister for natural resources I would always want to have a clear picture in my mind of what was the marginal activity I wished to encourage. I would then try to make it look as though this marginal activity would earn a return that was just acceptable. In the language of Sources of Value one could think of this marginal activity as setting the 'me too' benchmark. In this case 'me too' would earn a small positive NPV, always assuming the project went according to plan. The value potential of other projects would largely be set by how much they could differentiate themselves from the 'me too' benchmark.

'Me too' would not be guaranteed a return because if things went wrong the host government could, in all reasonableness, say this was the fault of the individual company. So a reasonable benchmark would be a small positive NPV based on a success case set of assumptions. As minister for natural resources I would have all the information available to ensure that this was the case.

A further thing I would do as minister for natural resources is always be searching for ways of distinguishing between the big existing projects that look as though they will create huge amounts of value and today's smaller 'me too' opportunities. If I could convince the foreign companies that these were different I could then tax them more without frightening away the potential developers of the small projects. I would try to bring in special allowances for new projects while taxing the existing projects as much as I felt I could. I would, though, be aware that even if I could differentiate between new players and existing players, I would need to be seen to be 'fair' to existing players in order to avoid new players thinking that this treatment would be handed out to them in the future.

Now think about how companies might react to this. I will cover this in more detail in the final section on implications. In simple terms, though, the clear strategic aim must be to stay ahead of the industry. You must always aim to be the company that host governments point towards as the incentive to others to invest in their country. As long as others are needed to follow in your footsteps, you can expect to be allowed to earn attractive returns.

I suggest that this way of thinking about how governments will set their overall take from projects will apply in many situations. The illustration referred to a mineral resource and I must admit that I had copper in my mind when I was writing it. I could, though, have been writing about the oil industry and the logic would have been identical. In both of these situations prices are set globally and governments limit profitability by adjusting taxes.

A similar but slightly different situation exists for those industries which are controlled by a regulator. The economic outcome for the investor is the same but the means of achieving it are different. With regulated industries, control is usually placed on the selling price and the economic benefit of this is passed directly to consumers. The economic impact on investing companies is virtually the same. They must expect that through some form of tax or price control, returns on investment will be limited so as to provide the marginal player with just enough economic rent for it to carry on.

Logically, the dynamics behind government thinking in all of these cases will be the same:

- identify the 'me too' player that you need to encourage;
- only allow better placed players to earn higher returns to the extent that this is necessary as an encouragement to 'me too' players;
- seek to differentiate between existing players and new players in order to maximise the share of the economic cake that the government can take, either directly through taxes or indirectly through holding down prices.

I suggest that the only limits to where this logic can apply are the limits of where governments are prepared to act because of what they consider to be acceptable. In effect, what will the electorate vote for?

In my view, this form of control by government is very common. I have referred so far both to the setting of taxes and to the regulation of selling prices. Governments can also intervene in more subtle ways such as requiring companies to contribute towards the cost of infrastructure or to undertake some social programmes. They can also 'twist arms' with the implied threat of the appointment of a regulator or the launch of an investigation. In all cases what happens is that the potential economic rent which can reasonably be anticipated from a new investment is limited by the extent to which a company can differentiate itself from the benchmark 'me too' player. This differentiation is caused by what I term 'sources of value' and the benchmark is the 'me too return'.

The implication of this distinction between free market competition and government regulation can be seen when we look at the road map for the application of the Sources of Value technique in the following section. An early question is asked concerning the nature of competition. We need always to distinguish between those areas where competition is mainly between players who can decide on the price they charge and those where governments have a role in adjusting how the economic cake is divided between players.

The effect, though, is largely the same. Value potential can be understood as being the sum of two components. These are an element set by the nature of the sector and an element set by the extent of the sources of value relative to 'me too'. Where competition is left to the markets, the 'me too' return will usually be a small negative NPV whereas a small positive may be possible where governments step in, albeit that this might then refer to a success case.

Whatever the situation, the fundamental aim of strategy should be to seek to avoid being 'me too' and to aim to maximise your sources of value relative to this unfortunate player. Furthermore, this 'me too' player which companies must avoid being like is not a hypothetical company, it is a real player. In all sectors the reasonable assumption must be for somebody to be losing out. It does not matter how attractive a sector is, from the perspective of Sources of Value, somebody will always be 'me too' and they should not expect to earn a positive NPV on a fully risked full-cycle basis. In government controlled or regulated sectors the 'me too' player may well be the worst player but in free competition sectors it will not be the worst, it will be about three quarters of the way down the overall cost curve.

My advice to those setting strategies in regulated sectors is therefore the same as I'd give to those in free competition sectors. Think about what makes your company different from other real players. Your potential to create value is a function of how much better than 'me too' you are. So the interesting conclusion for regulated sectors is that you want competitors as long as they are not as good as you.

Part 3: How to apply the Sources of Value technique

I will start this part with an example that is based on one of the earlier case studies. I will then provide a short road map for implementation of the technique with activities identified for the various steps on the stage gate time line. Next, each of these stages will be covered in detail.

This approach should provide a comprehensive guide to the implementation of Sources of Value within a company. This implementation could well, however, appear rather daunting for a reader from a company that has never used the technique. I would fully understand this and do not suggest that companies follow a 'big bang' approach to implementation. It would be more advisable to start with some more limited pilot studies. I have provided some guidance on getting started as the final section of this part.

Initial case study: Sources of Value and the scaffolding project

This project was first introduced in the Understanding Accounts building block and we considered it from a components of value perspective earlier in this pillar. We will now look at it from the perspective of Sources of Value.

We already have a spreadsheet model which shows an NPV of $0.6m following an initial investment of $4m. Once again, let's ask the question '*where does this NPV come from?*'. Why should the decision-maker, who in this instance will also be the owner and manager of the project, believe the numbers?

Let us assume that on first inspection each individual assumption does indeed look reasonable when compared with the current situation in the scaffolding market in this region. Indeed, let us now assume that the current price for an average scaffolding contract is $1,800, compared with the $1,700 which has been assumed for the base case. This was justified on the grounds that a slightly cheaper offer would have to be made in order quickly to win business away from the existing suppliers.

Let us also now reintroduce the additional information from Question 5 at the end of Building Block 3. This indicated that:

- insurance (paid in advance of each year) of $125,000 pa had been omitted;
- no allowance for a salary for the owner had been included and that this salary should have been $100,000 pa (paid monthly);
- no rental was charged for the land that was being used and a charge of $25,000 pa was being considered (paid quarterly at the start of each quarter).

Let us see what would happen if we were to treat each of these factors as a source of value. Remember that the base case NPV was $0.6m and the IRR was 18.1%. To do the calculation one must start with the base case spreadsheet and remove the sources of value one at a time. Including the insurance charge lowers the NPV to $0.2m, suggesting that the value effect is $0.4m. Next we include the salary cost and find that NPV has fallen to –$0.1m. The value impact is $0.3m. Finally, including the land rental still leaves the NPV as –$0.1m. Clearly the effect is not actually zero; we have a rounding problem! If the values are all quoted to two decimal places the sources of value are:

Our project	$0.62m (an IRR of 18.1%)
Insurance	$0.39m
Salary	$0.28m
Rent	$0.07m
Implied 'me too'	–$0.12m (an IRR of 10.8%)

The Sources of Value diagram would look like this:

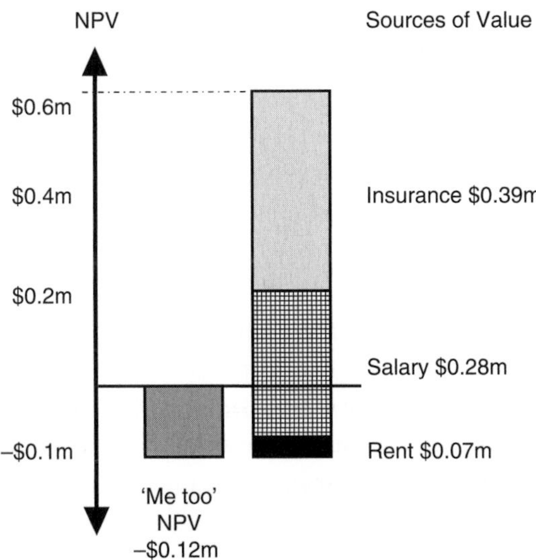

Fig. 8.6 Scaffolding project: initial Sources of Value analysis

Note that I have given the chart the title 'Initial Sources of Value analysis'. In my view the first analysis must always be viewed as just the first stab. This is because the Sources of Value technique should usually provoke an iterative approach to project development. You do the first analysis; you see if it looks sensible; you adjust as necessary; you think about the implications of the analysis; you adjust as necessary; etc., etc. Finally you achieve an analysis which makes sense from all perspectives i.e. financial and strategic. Then you are ready to draw the final Sources of Value diagram. I will go through this process with this example.

So far the process has been as follows. We started with a spreadsheet and our first view of the sources of value. We stripped the sources of value out of our base case in order gradually to reveal the position of the 'me too' player. We drew the chart. Next we inspect the chart to see if it looks sensible. By this I mean does the implied return for the 'me too' player look reasonable given our understanding of the sector in which we are operating? In this case the answer could well be 'yes'. We do at least have a small negative NPV for the 'me too' player. This is what we normally expect to find. We can note that the implied IRR for 'me too' is 10.8%, which is 1.2% below the CoC which we were assuming. So if our CoC assumption is OK, the return for 'me too' could be believable albeit that perhaps it is slightly high, suggesting that the sector is reasonably favourable.

So there are no immediate causes for alarm. Can we stop now? My answer is a clear 'no'. Just because we have a picture that looks credible does not mean that it is. It is only credible if the analysis behind it is. Let us think harder about the claimed sources of value. Are they really sources of value? Do they serve to differentiate our financial performance from that of a typical player in the industry who lacks any particular advantages?

Let us think first about the insurance effect. Yes, a 'me too' player will have to insure but why won't we have to as well? I would maintain that the insurance effect is simply an error in the initial analysis. Yes, the original assumptions all looked OK but we simply forgot to include insurance. It is not unusual to find that some things are omitted from the analysis and omissions can be harder to spot than items that are included but based on poor assumptions. Our base case should not be an NPV of $0.62m; it should be $0.23m. We only appear to have two sources of value. The new picture would still be credible (because the 'me too' result is a small negative NPV) but it is much less attractive to a potential investor.

We will put to one side the fact that the reduced NPV may already be sufficient to put us off the project. We need to do two things. These are to test our acceptance of the remaining two sources of value and to check the credibility of the 'me too' player. There is no particular 'correct' order for this analysis. All items need to be tested and the analysis is only finished if and when a credible picture emerges that achieves what I term consistent words and music.

I will consider the sources of value first. I would ask whether $100,000 pa is an appropriate salary. I had written that the owner 'decided she should receive' this amount. Well, she could have 'decided' to pay herself $1m a year but this would not have been the correct way to quantify the source of value. The correct measure would be to compare her salary with what the 'me too' player paid its manager. Personally, I would doubt that this would be as much as $100,000 a year. I would also note that if the source of value was unpaid time, then the owner could easily gain an equivalent benefit by getting a job elsewhere. What I am doing here is testing whether the project is the best way to leverage the source of value. If the source of value is nothing really to do with the project surely the project cannot be the best way to turn it into actual cash.

The remaining source of value comes from not having to pay any rent for the land. I can certainly see how this would benefit the project compared with a 'me too' player. It would, however, benefit any activity that required land. There might also be an opportunity cost to consider back at the farm if the land could have been used for another purpose. All in all, the review of sources of value would have me wondering a lot about the project. It sounds to me as though the potential owner would be better advised simply to get a paid job!

We will, however, also consider the 'me too' player in order to complete the analysis. Just because the analysis that we did first points in one particular way does not mean that we should go this way without first seeing what else we may find by looking at the other half of the picture. I would start the consideration of the 'me too' player by asking whether we were comparing with the right benchmark.

We may have a credible-looking slightly negative NPV but is this really credible? It is only credible if the 'me too' player really does look like this. What is this industry actually like? Now I have to admit that I am not an expert on this business![22] Suppose, though, that the industry did not have lots of companies operating like this one proposes to do. Suppose that the industry was dominated by larger companies all of which employ scaffolders to carry out the installation and dismantling of the scaffolding. These firms will all have much higher fixed costs than our operation and their variable costs will be minimal.[23] This means that our implied 'me too' model is not correct. At this stage we would not know what a typical scaffolding company's cost

[22] I chose it as a case study because I happened to have some scaffolding delivered to my house the day I was writing the chapter on Understanding Accounts. My knowledge of the sector is limited to a brief chat with the people who dismantled it two weeks later. The leader was employed by the scaffolding firm and he told me how expensive insurance was.

[23] Remember that in our case the cost of installation is a variable cost.

structure will be like but we can be sure that it will have high fixed costs and low variable costs.

Now industries with high fixed costs and low variable costs can be dangerous places to operate. If too much new capacity is built or if demand simply falls, then any price cutting may be very severe as companies fight to win what business they can in an oversupplied market. A small new entrant to this market with a very different cost structure might be seen as a threat or might be small enough not to be noticed. I simply do not know which, but if I were asked to advise the potential owner I would suggest great caution about an adverse reaction from the existing players. If the new business was small in relation to the existing market players they would not want to cut prices to match us. They would, however, have a great incentive to challenge our business in other ways. For example, they might question our capability when they spoke with potential customers or perhaps even our right to operate from a farm.

I will stop the analysis at this stage with a presumption that the potential owner has concluded that she was looking at the wrong project. She is, instead, now looking for a job and, if she has a real passion for scaffolding, she should look to the existing scaffolding companies and seek a management position in one of these.

This example where the analysis has pointed us away from the initial project and towards a related but more value-creating alternative is fairly typical of what can be expected when the Sources of Value technique is applied. The example should have given some useful clues about the application of Sources of Value but now I will provide a more structured implementation map.

Sources of Value: Implementation map

I will now show my overall map of what Sources of Value-related activities should be undertaken at the various stages of a project's life. I will then consider each stage in more detail and give examples.

I will use the various steps in a typical stage gate process to set out the different Sources of Value actions that can take place. I will, however, add an additional stage at the start and this concerns the formulation of strategy. Project Stage Gate processes can treat strategy as a given. The Sources of Value approach does not do this. It treats the thinking process that surrounds a typical project as a source of learning about the strategy.

I should stress that this is not a full guide to running a business; it is simply a guide for adding the Sources of Value approach to an already functioning set of business processes.

Sources of Value: implementation map

Stage	Sources of Value actions
Strategy	Analyse sector attractiveness. Confirm the type of competition. Is this primarily via free-market competition or via government regulation? Consider shape of industry cost curve. Identify 'me too' players and assess their likely return. Consider how the sector will evolve over time with a particular focus on possible changes in the 'me too' benchmark. Analyse competitive position. Identify potential sources of value. Quantify these and assess potential for value creation. Test this value creation against potential search costs. Identify any negative sources of value and suggest ways of reducing/eliminating these. Review strategic options and recommend a strategy. The recommended strategy should have a strong Sources of Value story to support it. Confirm the organisational model will support the important sources of value.
Options identification	Look in the right places! Use the identified sources of value to guide the search for options. Look for options which minimise exposure to identified negative sources of value, perhaps by selection of a partner whose skills will complement your own. Be prepared to challenge the strategy. Use the findings of the options identification to create a feedback loop through which strategy can be challenged. Continually seek to update views about your own sources of value and the position of the 'me too' player. Prepare simple financial models of the various options. These can be full spreadsheet models or can just be models of what the Sources of Value diagram will look like. Use the analysis to refine understanding of sector attractiveness and competitive position. Select and recommend the best option. The best option will be supported by a strong set of sources of value which will allow a good 'words and music' confirmation that the recommendation is sound.
Detailed design	Confirm the initial analysis. A detailed financial model must be built at this stage. Firm-up the analysis and use this to confirm that the initial assumptions made at earlier stages were sound. Be prepared to challenge options selection and even the strategy if the detail does not turn out as expected, but recognise that changes should be rare. Seek approval for project. Include a final quantification of sources of value as part of this process. Confirm that the project is robust and that it does indeed create value through optimal leverage of your company's sources of value. State what return your assumptions imply will be earned by a 'me too' player. Justify this return in relation to your strategic analysis and hence calibrate the bulk of your assumptions. Review company-wide lessons. Pass data on anticipated sources of value and project NPV to corporate staff who should monitor the overall anticipated creation of value within the company and compare this with what was anticipated at the time the strategy was approved.

Table (*cont.*)

Stage	Sources of Value actions
Implementation	Sources of Value-related work during this stage is quite limited. Maintain a watching brief on the sector to identify any important changes such as step changes by existing competitors, new entrants or substitutes. Be prepared to respond to changes but recognise that once project construction is well under way it is generally too late to respond to changes which now look as though they would question the actual decision to go ahead. Monitor progress with capital spend to ensure that any sources of value claimed in this area are achieved. If costs are different from estimates made at time of sanction, decide whether these differences will also affect the 'me too' player. Start to track anticipated value delivery compared with estimate made at time of sanction. Use Sources of Value approach to help structure variance analysis. Use this to create a feedback loop to enhance learnings for future projects.
Operation	Continue to track actual performance, seeking in particular to learn lessons about the delivery of value in relation to sources of value and 'me too' returns.

Implementing Sources of Value at the strategy stage

This work fits into four subcategories which are:

- sector attractiveness;
- competitive position;
- strategic options identification;
- strategy selection.

Strategy stage analysis: sector attractiveness

My recommendation is always to start a strategy review with an analysis of the sector in which we operate and of the new sectors that we might consider moving to. In this way we can start with a broad perspective and then at a later stage focus on our own position. There will be several pieces of Sources of Value-related activity to carry out in addition to the normal five forces analysis that would form part of a conventional strategy review.

For a start, more attention should be paid to the industry cost curve. This may already have been studied, but my experience has been that this may well not have been done in a company that does not apply Sources of Value thinking. Even if cost curves are used, they may well simply focus on cash costs and not fully built-up costs including the vital element of capital remuneration.

Where individual plants are large and expensive it can be possible to construct the cost curve unit by unit. In these situations external consulting

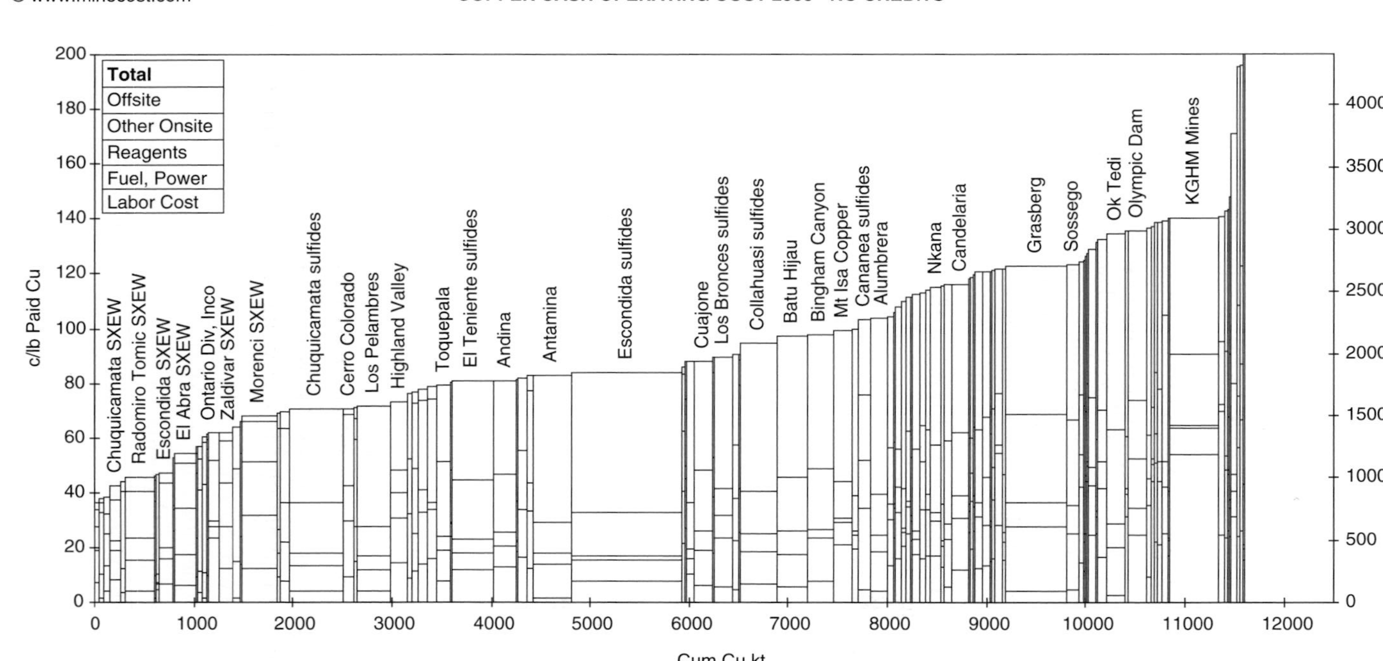

Fig. 8.7 Real example of a cost curve: copper cash operating cost 2006 – no credits

companies often have the data and will provide it for a fee. Figure 8.7 shows an example taken from the minerals industry.

The chart was provided by a US-based firm called World Mine Cost Data Exchange Inc. It illustrates the wealth of detail which can be obtained. One does, though, always have to understand the basis of the chart. In this particular example, costs are analysed into the various categories such as fuel and power. An alternative version of the chart will show costs analysed into the stages along the copper value chain such as mining and milling. This chart also ignores any co-product credits but, again, this information is available. Finally, note that the chart shows just cash costs. The cost of remunerating capital is excluded. If I were leading a strategy review in this area I would want to include estimates of this in my overall cost curve.

At this stage of reading this book, the exact detail of the cost curve for copper does not matter. What does matter is the evidence that the data are available and can be worked on in full detail if and when a real strategy review is under way.

If full cost data are not available it is often possible to produce rough estimates for categories of supplier to the market in question. The key is to fill in as much detail as is possible. The ideal is to know the total potential supply to the sector concerned and to have an estimate of variable costs, cash fixed cost and the cost of remunerating capital. When you are already operating in an industry you will at least know what the figures look like for your company. Armed with this information you will have to use a lot of skilled judgement to fill in the gaps. The approach to take is, I suggest, to assume competitors' costs are similar to your own unless you have reasons to believe otherwise. A dialogue with the key functional experts within your company should soon reveal where competitors are ahead of, or behind, your cost level.

Judgement will have to be used regarding the scale of the exercise which is undertaken in order to prepare the cost curve. Care, and probably also legal advice, will also be needed in order to ensure that competition laws are not broken. For example, some competition laws may mean that companies cannot simply swap cost data with other companies.

The next question concerns the type of competition. By this I mean whether we are dealing with 'normal' free-market competition or regulated competition. I put the word normal in inverted commas because, to be honest, there are so many sectors where governments take on an important regulatory role that I am not sure whether classic price-based competition through market forces is indeed normal. Nevertheless, I will retain the presumption that competition is between companies and via the price mechanism unless we conclude to the contrary.

It should usually be quite obvious where governments already have taken on a regulatory role. The evidence could be in the form of additional taxes or royalties that are levied. Or it could be in the appointment of industry regulators who can set the rules of the game[24] for defined periods and then reset them again later. The more that a government or a regulator has a track record of adjusting the rules of the game, the more important it is to recognise this in your analysis of sector attractiveness.

Large industries are most likely to attract government regulation because the profits that they earn will attract public attention. Even small ones, however, can attract the attention of government's competition authorities. These often have wide powers to intervene when they consider that market forces are, for some reason, not producing what they consider to be a 'fair' outcome for consumers.

A switch from 'normal' to regulated competition is not necessarily bad or good. It simply serves to change the way that a company should think about a sector and about its ability to make money in that sector. The good feature of regulation tends to be that it will usually recognise the need of investors to make a return. The bad feature relates to the way that it tends to limit the upside value potential. The more a company is able to differentiate itself from 'me too' competitors and hence create large amounts of value, the more likely it is the regulation will be specifically tailored to limit value creation potential of individual companies.

Now we are ready to move to the important step of identifying the 'me too' player. This does depend on judgement but this judgement should be led by the facts of the industry and in particular, its cost curve. Different approaches are needed for 'normal' and regulated competition.

When competition is 'normal', the 'me too' player will be operating below the middle of the industry cost curve. If there is a standard way of supplying the market that any existing player can follow then this would set the 'me too' benchmark as long as some companies were doing this. If there is no standard or if virtually all players can beat the standard in one way or another, then I recommend simply taking the position of the bottom of the third quartile player as the 'me too' benchmark. The benchmark must be a real company and not a hypothetical one.[25]

[24] I use the term 'rules of the game' to refer to the full range of powers that regulators may have. This will include setting prices but will cover other aspects such as required service levels as well.

[25] This means that if there is a standard way of supplying the market but nobody does this (because everybody is better than standard in at least one way) then the standard way does not set the 'me too' benchmark. The 'me too' benchmark will be a company with a better cost structure than the standard.

When competition is regulated the 'me too' player should represent the marginal player the regulator wishes to encourage to invest. This may well be a new entrant from outside the current set of industry players and could, therefore, at the point when your investment is being considered, be hypothetical rather than real. In due course, however, you and the regulator must anticipate the 'me too' players investing. In the case of the oil industry, for example, the marginal player may well be an independent exploration company the host government wants to encourage to drill an exploration well. If this is what the government wants to encourage then it must make it look as though this will be an attractive investment.

There are two remaining tasks before we have completed the Sources of Value review of sector attractiveness. These concern assessing the likely 'me too' return and how 'me too' might change in the future.

With normal competition the 'me too' return will usually be slightly below the CoC. This is one of the few occasions where I recommend the use of IRR rather than NPV. The 'me too' benchmark should be set as a return of a given number of percentage points below the CoC. Exactly how many points is decided upon by judgement based on analysis of the relative attractiveness of the sector. This analysis can be based on consideration of the five forces identified by Porter and also on benchmarking data on average returns on capital over prior years.

The following table illustrates the relationship between IRR, value and return on capital for a particular set of assumptions. The table and the approaches which support it should help to aid this judgement of what represents a reasonable return for the 'me too' player. Ideally the numbers for a table such as this would be generated via a spreadsheet model of a typical project in the sector.[26] A key variable such as the selling price is then altered in order to check how much value was created or destroyed for different IRRs and also to see what the average return on capital would be for a company which invested in one project such as this every year. The table uses such a model. The project life was 20 years and the CoC was 8%. So I have investigated a range of CoC +1% to CoC –5%.

[26] One can use a short-cut approach that does not involve a spreadsheet. If we assume the capital spend is immediate and that it generates an equal cash flow for each year of its life, we can use our mid-year annuity factor tables to tell us what cash flow is necessary to give a specified return. The 20 year 8% annuity factor is 10.20. Hence capex of $10m earning 8% would generate an annual cash flow of $0.98m pa. The depreciation charge would be $0.5m pa hence the annual profit would be $0.48m. The average capital employed across all of the years will be $5.25m. So the average ROCE of a company investing in one such project each year will be 9.1%. This is almost exactly the same as the figure I derived from my full spreadsheet analysis.

IRR	9%	8%	7%	6%	5%	4%	3%
NPV as % capex	8%	0%	−8%	−15%	−22%	−28%	−34%
Return on capital	11%	9%	8%	7%	5%	4%	3%

Readers should recall from the benchmarking data I quoted for the top 1,000 European companies that approximately 15–20% of these suffer returns on capital employed of 7% or less. The above table shows how, at this cut-off level and assuming a CoC of 8%, a company would be earning something like two percentage points below its CoC and would destroy perhaps 15 cents for each euro of capital they spend.

This table coupled with the European benchmarking data does provide good evidence that 'me too' players earn less than their CoC. It goes further and suggests the rough magnitude of value destruction which can be anticipated. A reasonable assumption would be that in a typical sector the 'me too' player earns a full-cycle return of about two percentage points below the CoC and destroys value at a rate of about 15 cents per dollar spent. A reasonable range around this to account for the differences between good and bad sectors might be +2 to −3 percentage points on the IRR. At the top end of the range, value destruction by a 'me too' player in a good sector (such as one subject to favourable government control) might be nil while at the bad end, value destruction could be as much as about one third of the total capital spend.

The final element of sector attractiveness that must be considered is how the 'me too' player might evolve over time. Key determinants of change will be the growth rate of the sector and also the possibility of technological breakthroughs creating new lower-cost ways of manufacturing the product. The mental picture that I use is of new plants being added at or near the low-cost end of the cost curve. Provided the new capacity still leaves room for the existing players, change in the industry can be quite slow. There is, however, typically a strong incentive to build new low-cost capacity and this tends to push the higher-cost plant out of business. Eventually the 'me too' benchmark will need to be changed.

Strategy stage analysis: competitive position

Now we are ready to move on and review our competitive position. What are our strengths and what are our weaknesses? Note in particular the reference to understanding weaknesses. Sources of value are not always positive. They are simply the differences between our company's cost structure and those of the 'me too' benchmark. A source of value can be anything but it must be expressed in a way which can be quantified in an NPV calculation. So a simple way to look for sources of value is to check each line of the AFS and see if it is thought it could be materially different from what would be experienced by the defined 'me too' competitor.

Another approach is to define a standard set of sources of value. These would be specifically designed for a company in order to match the important elements of its business. So, for example, in some situations such as pharmaceuticals, search costs are very important. In others such as food retailing, they are not.

I will set out below a suggested set which would, I believe, work quite well in a range of businesses. My suggestion is that companies needing assistance in defining their standard categories of sources of value should select several, but not all, from the list and then perhaps refine it after a few years of actual experience.

Suggested standard categories of Sources of Value

Category	Definition[27]
Existing infrastructure	Access to existing assets, for example spare capacity in an export terminal or pipeline.
Other productive sunk costs	Other benefits related to sunk costs such as where our company has already incurred costs that 'me too' players will have to spend in the future.
Search costs	Low research or exploration costs or higher success rates. Also a discovery of enhanced value such as large ore body or oil field rather than average size.
Capital cost	Low capital cost per unit of capacity.
Time to market	Sales revenues are earned earlier owing to reduced search, approval or build times.
Supply chain	Lower supply costs owing, for example, to integration or location.
Operating costs	Lower manufacturing and/or operating costs per unit of output. Could be caused by manufacturing excellence, economies of scale or location (reducing logistics costs).
Overheads	Lower overheads.

[27] Definitions are all relative to the defined 'me too' benchmark. Note also that although the definitions are worded for positive Sources of Value negative factors are also possible.

Table (cont.)

Category	Definition
Flexibility and trading	Ability to respond to changes or capitalise on related trading opportunities. Could refer to any aspect of the business.
Premium pricing	Where customers are prepared to pay premium prices for our products for example owing to a brand or quality premium.
Other	Any other benefits not specifically listed.
Tax	Lower effective tax rate.
CoC	Lower CoC.

Detailed quantification of sources of value is usually done only when a specific project has been identified. At the strategy review stage one is only looking to identify what the main sources of value will be and to get a rough quantification of how great the benefit can be. This will provide an important input to the impending strategy selection stage.

At the review stage the focus will be on what steps are necessary to enhance identified advantages and mitigate identified disadvantages. The above list can serve as a checklist if previous strategy reviews have lacked this degree of rigour.

Strategy stage analysis: strategic options identification

A good strategy review should always identify a range of potential options. The contribution to this which Sources of Value thinking can give is to suggest where to look and where to avoid. This assistance can be very important as witnessed by Brealey and Myers' inclusion of the lack of guidance about how to find positive NPVs on their list of ten unanswered problems in finance.

If an advantage is identified it should automatically generate the question '*How can we capitalise on this advantage?*' Furthermore, if a particular area is not considered to be advantaged it should automatically generate the question '*How can we avoid investing in this area?*'

A good idea can be to study the value map of a typical project which might be invested in if our company were to build a new plant in the traditional way. A value map is simply a picture of the value of a project based on its components of value. Costs are shown based on useful categories such as distribution costs, manufacturing costs, etc. Then for each cost area one can show the extent to which the present value of our costs is in line with 'me too' or better than 'me too'. Any area with significant costs which are not advantaged should provoke a thorough process about how the company can avoid carrying out this work which brings burden but no advantage. This is because if our abilities are simply in line with 'me too' we must assume we too will destroy value in this area.

Some activities have to be undertaken even if they are not advantaged, but by raising the question a different strategic alternative may be identified.

Examples of the sorts of insights that might emerge include:

- If the main Source of Value concerns only existing infrastructure: look for strategic options to involve selling up!
- If the benefits are all at the search stage: investigate the potential to sell research breakthroughs.
- If the benefits are from low capital cost: consider constructing capacity for others or licensing your technology to others.
- If benefits come from operating cost effects that could be transferred to existing third party companies: consider growth via acquisition of existing competitors.
- If benefits come from premium pricing via branding: consider applying the brand elsewhere, for example into a wider geographic market or a related sector which might also place value on your brand attributes.

Strategy stage analysis: strategy selection

The recommended strategy should have a strong value story behind it. Sources of Value thinking will greatly assist in achieving this. It will, for example, facilitate the rough scoping out of what future NPVs might be earned for new growth projects. These possible future NPVs can be set against the necessary search costs of, for example, the required project development teams and thus allow a proper justification of these costs.

In principle each strategic option should be valued and the highest value option should be recommended provided its risk characteristics are acceptable. In practice this valuation can be very hard to do. What can be done is apply Sources of Value thinking to value particular parts of a strategy and then rely on the principle of value additivity to add up only the differences between strategies and use this to find the highest value option.

An example could concern the strategic choice between growth by new build and acquisition. Suppose a company was operating in a market that was still in its growth phase but where its advantages compared with 'me too' were not particularly great. The approach would be to quantify the value benefit of the identified sources of value and compare this with our 'guesstimate' of the 'me too' negative return. If we were to apply my rule of thumb that a typical 'me too' negative NPV on a full-cycle basis was about 15% of the capital cost we could then decide only to recommend the growth strategy if the identified sources of value had a value benefit of at least, say, 20% of the capital cost so that positive NPVs could reasonably be anticipated.

As a further example I will consider a situation with high search costs. In this instance please consider a strategy that was led by a new R&D programme aimed at lowering manufacturing costs. We would need to estimate the potential prize success might bring and then consider this on an impact times probability basis compared with the known costs of the initial R&D. So if the chance of success was judged to be no more than one in four we would need an anticipated value prize from success of at least four times the after-tax cost of the initial research programme. It would be in the estimation of the potential future prize should the research succeed that we could use Sources of Value thinking. I will demonstrate this via a detailed example using my hypothetical YMCC case study later in the pillar.

Finally, one should consider questions related to organisation and management, given the selected business approach. The organisational structure of the company and the way it operates needs to be supportive of the identified sources of value. The sorts of challenges which might arise could include, for example, 'Do the main functions in a company directly support the sources of value?' and 'What plans are in place to sustain and enhance the key skills necessary to deliver the sources of value?'

Some challenges can also arise concerning the absence of sources of value. If, for example, a company has what is considered to be an important function which has a large budget, then the lack of sources of value flowing from this would be an indicator of the need to focus on why this should be.

Implementing Sources of Value at the options identification stage

We now should have in place an approved strategy. This should have used Sources of Value logic to suggest good places to look in order to create value. It will, typically, have recommended the formation of a project development team to search for and implement growth projects. My view is that it is only now that things become real. Previously, growth projects were what might be thought of simply as 'planners' dreams'. Now they must become reality. It is only now that the presumptions on which they were based can be tested against what third parties are prepared to do.

The danger at this stage is, in my view, for the first potentially viable project to become the only project to be followed up. The development team will almost always be under pressure to move quickly and so will be tempted to push hard for the first project which looks suitable. This project will be good (or else it will not be progressed), but is it the best option? The only way to prove that the proposed project is the best project is to consider a wide range and demonstrate that the selected one is best.

The first thing to do is to make sure that the search for actual growth options is guided by the expected sources of value. Without the benefit of Sources of Value thinking, our strategy might simply have said words to the effect of 'grow in this sector'. Now it should say something like 'grow in this sector through capitalising on our ability to transfer manufacturing excellence'. Or it might say 'grow in this sector through capitalising on our brand strength'. These two statements should point the development teams in different directions, albeit in the same sector. The first will have us looking for existing companies to buy while the second will be all about looking for marketing opportunities.

Each identified option will require a simple financial model. These can be full spreadsheet models but this degree of detail is often spurious at an early stage. It tends to be better to rely just on models of what the Sources of Value diagram will look like. This approach is illustrated in the following example which is based on my hypothetical company Yellow Moon Chemical Company (YMCC).

Suppose that YMCC has chosen a strategy of growth in the Asia Pacific region. The key source of value is YMCC's new patented manufacturing technology.[28] This gives lower capital costs than the alternative manufacturing route and also lower operating cost because it works at a lower pressure and produces a more concentrated final product at the end of the initial reaction stage.

Four different ways of exploiting these advantages have been identified. All of the options require a new plant to be built because the technology is of no use to existing old technology plants. The options are:

1. YMCC could license the technology to companies wishing to build. It is estimated that a single licence fee would net YMCC about $10m after allowing for the necessary support costs but before allowing for any tax.

[28] Please consider this technology to be the result of a research breakthrough that followed from the strategy to search for a breakthrough that was briefly referred to on the previous page.

The total growth potential in the world market might require up to ten new plants over the next five years.

2. YMCC could expand its US manufacturing capacity by building a new technology plant.[29] The plant would be 100% owned and would benefit from capital and operating cost sources of value. It would, however, suffer some negative sources of value compared with a 'me too' plant that was built using the old technology but located in the Asia Pacific region close to the main demand growth. These would relate to higher distribution costs when selling to the Asia Pacific market and higher staff costs because of the US base.
3. YMCC could form a 50/50 JV with a Chinese partner and build a plant in China. YMCC would be able to charge this JV a licence fee and, because the plant was in China, it would avoid the two negative sources of value mentioned in option 2. The partner would, however, not accept YMCC's selling of licences to third party companies. Finally, YMCC would have to open a branch office in China and this would mean its overhead costs would rise.
4. YMCC could build a wholly owned plant elsewhere in the region. This would again avoid the negative sources of value mentioned above in relation to distribution and labour costs. It would still suffer from the overhead problem.

We will now apply Sources of Value logic to analyse these options without simply building large spreadsheet models of each.

Option 1

It is stated that licensing is expected to bring in a net $10m pre-tax per licence sold. This is $6.5m after tax. If YMCC was fortunate enough to sell its technology to all new plants it would receive $13m after tax per year for the next five years. Our annuity factor table tells us to multiply this by four to get to a present value. So the maximum value potential is $52m. Realistically, though, YMCC would be unlikely to win a 100% market share. Before we can make a judgement about how many licences will be sold we need first to understand the potential value to a licensor in order to understand just how good our licence offer might be. We will gain insights on this as we complete the analysis of the remaining three options.

[29] Think of this project as being Project Claire from the YMCC case study in the first pillar on Modelling Economic Value. We are, however, at an earlier point in time *before* the decision is taken to select Claire as the means of implementing our growth strategy.

Option 2

The project has a capital cost of $45m. Let us make the following assumptions. The alternative plant built using the old technology would cost $60m. The plant capacity is 50,000 tonnes pa. Variable costs are $110/te on this plant but say $120/te on an old technology 'me too' plant. Fixed operating costs are $4m pa compared with $6m pa for 'me too'. The negative sources of value for building in the USA but supplying the Asia Pacific region are $20/te distribution cost and $1m pa additional fixed costs. The tax rate is 35% and the CoC is 9%.

We will start with an assumption that 'me too' is an old technology plant built in the Asia Pacific region. It has a capital cost of $60m and, because we don't think chemicals is a particularly good sector, we assume it generates an NPV of –$12m (i.e. 20% of capital cost). The capital cost advantage of a new technology plant is $15m. The value impact of this would allow for the fact that capital costs bring with them a stream of tax offsets. Hence the value impact will be less than $15m. With a 20-year project life the tax offset is an allowance of $0.75m pa. Multiply this by the tax rate of 35% and one gets to a figure of $0.26m pa. Multiply this by the 20 year 9% annuity factor of 9.5 and one arrives at the value of the associated tax relief as $2.5m. So the value benefit of the lower capital cost is $12.5m.

The variable cost benefit is $10/te or $0.5m pa but this amount will be subject to tax. After tax this is $0.325m pa or $3.1m of value.

The operating cost benefit is $2m pa pre tax. The value impact of this is four times the above figure, i.e. $12.4m.

Finally, we must allow for the two negative sources of value. The distribution cost effect is $20/te which is twice as big as the variable cost saving. Hence its value impact is $6.2m. The extra fixed costs are $1m pa with a value impact also of $6.2m.

The anticipated value of our new project in the USA should therefore be:

'Me too' value	-$12.0m
Plus	
Capital cost value	$12.5m
Variable cost value	$3.1m
Operating cost value	$12.4m
Less	
Distribution cost effect	-$6.2m
Fixed cost effect	-$6.2m
Anticipated NPV	$3.6m

Now in due course we would want to build a detailed model of this route should we decide to follow it. For the initial screening, however, we are probably safe in using this estimate of value.

Option 3

This is a joint venture and so we need to value both YMCC's share of it and also the impact directly felt by YMCC. In this case the direct impacts are the receipt of a licence fee and the need to fund an office in China.

The plant's economics would be worked out as follows. It will have an overall capital cost of $55m, being the reduced capital cost plus the licence fee. The value benefit of this $5m reduction compared with 'me too' is one third of the benefit we calculated for Option 2 (because this benefit did not need to allow for the licence fee). So this is $4.2m. The variable and operating cost benefits would be as calculated for Option 2. By building in China the two negative sources of value would be avoided. So the JV's value calculation would look like this:

'Me too' value	-$12.0m
Plus	
Capital cost value	$4.2m
Variable cost value	$3.1m
Operating cost value	$12.4m
Anticipated NPV	$7.7m

YMCC's share of this would be $3.8m. (I am ignoring any additional tax that might be payable when YMCC's profits were remitted to the USA.)

YMCC would also receive the licence fee which is worth $6.5m after tax. The problem, however, would be with the need to open a branch office in China. If we assume this would cost $2m pa pre tax, its value impact would be –$12.4m. Hence the overall value of the China JV option is $3.8 + $6.5 – $12.4m = –$2.1m.

Note also that with this option YMCC would not be able to sell licences to other companies. The other three options would all allow YMCC to market its technology. All in all, it is no wonder that a potential partner might be very keen to progress with a JV on these terms because it would gain its share of the JV NPV and also restrict future competition by limiting licence sales to other companies.

Option 4

This can be analysed in a similar way as follows:

'Me too' value	-$12.0m
Plus	
Capital cost value	$12.5m
Variable cost value	$ 3.1m
Operating cost value	$12.4m
Less	
Overhead cost effect	-$12.4m
Anticipated NPV	$3.6m

The clear conclusion is that of the four options the best means to leverage the combination of Asia Pacific demand growth and YMCC's technology breakthrough is to license it to companies with existing operations in the region. The driving force behind this is YMCC's lack of an existing base in the region which means that any investments there will be burdened with too much overhead. Provided the licence selling is limited this need not threaten the existing manufacturing operation in the US home market.

We can also confirm that our assumed licence fee of $10m is not unreasonable. This is because the value benefits owing to capital, variable and operating costs which would go to the purchaser of a licence would be worth a total of $28m of value after tax. Clearly we would not need to alert the company purchasing a licence that we considered the starting point to be a 'me too' NPV of –$12m. This judgement would be left to the individual company. Our marketing would focus on the $28m value benefit per licence.[30]

Readers should have been able to see from this example how Sources of Value thinking can provide a simple building-block approach to assessing the value potential of strategic options. These building blocks greatly assist in creating a 'words and music' confirmation that the overall approach appears to be coherent and that it is reasonable to believe that the selected course of action is the best way to create value. I should stress that we have not proved that the strategy will create value; we have simply demonstrated that it is reasonable to believe that it will and that the chosen option looks best. This is, however, a significantly better approach than simply following a strategy

[30] We can also now look back to the previous issue of what a technology breakthrough might be worth. If an individual licence sale would create $6.5m of value and sales to every potential new build would be worth $52m, the breakthrough success value would be somewhere between these two figures, say $20m as an order of magnitude estimate.

because of a senior executive's judgement. It is judgement based on rational analysis.

Finally, at this options identification stage, one should always remain aware of the need, when necessary, to challenge the strategy. In the example there was no need to do this because several potential value-creating means of implementing the strategy were identified. If, however, this had not been the case, the cause might be an inappropriate strategy and not simply the fact that the development team had not yet looked hard enough to find the right thing to do.

My recommended approach is to use the findings of the options identification stage to create a feedback loop through which strategy can, if necessary, be challenged. During options identification you should be continually seeking to update the understanding of your own sources of value and the position of the 'me too' player. Hopefully, this will serve to confirm that the strategy remains viable but, if this is not the case, an early warning signal can be obtained.

Implementing Sources of Value at the detailed design stage

A detailed financial model must be built at this stage. In this model all assumptions should be labelled as being either related to specific sources of value or a part of the 'me too' picture. The model will allow one to firm up the analysis and is then used to confirm that the initial assumptions made at earlier stages were sound. If this is the case, the amount of new Sources of Value-related work at this time will be quite limited. One does, however, have to be prepared to do some work to make the financial model align with earlier strategic analysis.

The reason why some work is often required in order to ensure alignment is that the model will usually be the first time a detailed study of the project from the perspective of the 'me too' player is carried out. Now it is quite a task to complete a fully detailed spreadsheet model for the first time and many assumptions have to be made. If the only prior analysis of 'me too' has been based on assumptions like, for example, that the NPV will be minus 20% of the capital cost, then there is a great likelihood that the calculated 'me too' NPV will not equal this number. It will have depended on a large number of individual assumptions and unless at least one of these was specifically set in order to generate the required 'me too' return it would be a great fluke if the anticipated negative NPV were to emerge. This is a classic example of a 'words and music' test. The strategic 'words' will have said, for example, that a negative 'me too' NPV of about this magnitude was anticipated. The 'music' will be the NPV that actually emerges from the spreadsheet.

Small differences, say a percent or so difference between the anticipated and the actual 'me too' IRR, can be ignored. If the IRR difference is greater then the task is either to find a good reason to change one or more of the 'me too' assumptions or to revise the strategic analysis. The more normal thing to do is change the assumptions, typically by adjusting the selling price assumption to the level necessary in order to generate the required 'me too' return.[31]

There is a practical implication of my suggestion that the selling price assumption should be adjusted in order to ensure that our model produces the required 'me too' return. This is that our price assumption should be fairly simple, i.e. either a fixed number or a number that starts at one figure and then changes by a set percentage each year into the future. If we had tried to estimate selling prices each year into the future we would then find it hard to change the assumptions to produce a desired result. There would, in principle, be any number of possible profiles of selling price over time that would result in a required NPV. This would be no help for our analysis. There will, however, be only one selling price that gives the desired 'me too' return as long as it is modelled as a starting point and then a specified percentage change in subsequent years.

It has been my experience that senior managers prefer to deal with simple assumptions such as a single selling price rather than an assumed selling price profile. It is a lot easier for them to consider the implications of such analysis even if it is bound to be different from what turns out in reality. Since nobody can predict with any certainty what the actual price profile will be, it makes sense in my view to base long-term project evaluation on a simple point estimate of price rather than a well-researched, but probably still wrong, price profile.

It is important, though, not to make this adjusting of the selling price assumption a purely mechanical task. It is possible that strategic analysis can be wrong! If the 'me too' spreadsheet appears to be based on a series of reasonable assumptions then it might be right and the presumptions about 'me too' return might be wrong. Should a disconnect occur between words and

[31] In principle one could adjust any of the 'me too' assumptions in order to ensure that the required negative NPV is obtained. Price is usually by far the most intuitive assumption to change. If there was another important assumption that 'felt' better to change there would be no problem with choosing this to act as the balancing item. I could envisage the number of years of operation being used, for example, or the tax take if there is government control.

music this should be treated as an important signal that something is wrong. Every effort should be devoted to further analysis in order to surface what was wrong with previous perceptions. A project should not go ahead until it does present coherent words and music.

It is not simply the assumptions surrounding the 'me too' player that need to be checked. The specific sources of value also need to be confirmed and this can generally only be done in the context of real data on a project. One needs to remain prepared, in principle, to challenge options selection and even the strategy if the detail does not turn out as expected. Changes should, however, be rare and can be difficult to effect.[32] This is why it is so important to have made the right decisions at the earlier stages. The more likely outcome when words and music do not look coherent is that the spreadsheet assumptions will need to be changed.

There are also some practical issues to consider when quantifying sources of value. These relate to the definition of sources of value and the way they are calculated. If we consider first the subject of definition, one has to decide exactly what to call a source of value and what factors to include in each category.

For example, consider a manufacturing business where 'me too' players have to pay a delivery charge for their feedstock but we have located our factory adjacent to the main supplier and receive our feedstock via a direct pipe link. There is clearly a source of value, but do we call this 'location' or 'supply chain' or 'operating costs'? The answer does not matter in the least in the context of the individual project. As long as all are aware of exactly what the source of value is, a good decision can be taken. If, however, this project is looked at in a wider context the answer might matter. What might happen is that the description may be taken out of context and considered alongside other sources of value from other projects within a company. So, for example, the purchasing function in a company may claim this benefit as 'theirs' if it is called 'supply chain' whereas it might be very different in nature from the other benefits which they generate through using their strong buyer power with suppliers.

Having some standard company-wide categories of sources of value can help. Even with these, however, a good amount of common sense needs to be

[32] I would suggest two key reasons to support this statement. First, the longer a company has worked on a selected option the more money will have been spent on it. This means that even if it was the wrong way to go it might now be acceptable simply because enough of the cost has been sunk. Projects also tend to develop their own momentum once they move into the detailed design stage and it is hard to overcome this.

applied. A single book such as this should not seek to dictate all of the answers because each company needs to tailor the approach to its own situation.

Having defined the sources of value the exact calculation method can raise some minor concerns. This is because in some instances the order of calculations matters. Suppose, for example, a company had two sources of value. It sells its product for a premium price and its manufacturing facility produces more units per production line than 'me too'. Does the marketing source of value include the premium price on all units sold or just the premium price on 'me too' volume? I take the view that Rhett Butler had it right![33] Tensions can, however, be created if one part of a company feels that another is taking 'its' value and some pre-set rules will help avoid this. These rules would include a convention on the order of calculation.[34]

One important issue to consider at this stage concerns sunk costs. These always increase as a project progresses and will often lead to a source of value. The headline NPV for a project will be calculated on a money-forward basis but the full-cycle picture may allow a better understanding of the overall value that is created by the strategy which is being followed. The aim is always to be able to show that the money-forward economics may well benefit from a considerable sunk-cost effect but that the project overall does cover all of its costs and yields a positive full-cycle NPV. If it does not then one might want to see if any strategic lessons should be learned since the shareholder would, with hindsight, have preferred it if the company had not started with the strategy in the first place.

This is just one illustration of an overall lessons-learned exercise that should always be under way in a company. Sources of Value thinking can help the Plan, Do, Measure, Learn approach by pointing out useful ways to think about performance. A company may decide to monitor value creation and use Sources of Value logic to set up the various categories that can be studied. If this is being done then the project staff would pass data on anticipated sources of value and project NPV to corporate staff who should monitor the overall anticipated creation of value within the company and compare this with what was anticipated at the time the strategy was approved. This monitoring of the overall value creation by source of value category will be greatly assisted if a company has already adopted a standard set of sources of

[33] Rhett famously said to Scarlett in *Gone with the Wind*, 'Frankly my dear, I don't give a damn!'

[34] The simplest approach is to use a defined set of sources of value and then quantify them by gradually removing them from the initial base case in the order in which they appear in the list. If this is done it is important to put any sources of value attributed to tax effects either first or last on the list so that all of the others are calculated at the same tax rate.

value. Indeed, some standardisation is essential if company-wide totals are to be calculated and used as input to the strategic review process.

The end of the detailed design stage will usually be marked by formal approval of the project. The presentation should include a final quantification of sources of value. The analysis will confirm that the project is robust and that it does indeed create value through optimal leverage of the company's sources of value. The claimed NPV can be calibrated by showing what return the assumptions imply will be earned by a 'me too' player. This return should be justified in relation to strategic analysis of the sector if this has not already been done before.

Implementing Sources of Value at the implementation stage

The Sources of Value action during this stage is to maintain a watching brief on the sector to identify any important changes, such as step changes by existing competitors, the emergence of new entrants or the arrival of new substitutes. The company should be prepared to respond to changes but should recognise that, once project construction is well under way, it is generally too late to respond even to severe changes which now look as though they would raise doubts about the actual decision to go ahead. Money-forward economics should dominate decision-taking on this particular project and the more that has been spent, the less likely it is that the project should be stopped.

The company should monitor progress with capital spend in order to ensure that any sources of value claimed in this area are achieved. If costs are different from estimates made at time of sanction, it will be necessary to decide whether these differences will also affect the 'me too' player. This needs to be done because the financial models need to be kept up to date and this means not only updating data on your own company but also updating the view of 'me too' economics.

Companies should also start to track anticipated value delivery compared with the estimate made at time of sanction. The identified sources of value can provide a structure for any variance analysis. It is not necessary to wait for actual results or even for a project to come on stream before this tracking can be started. Tracking does include consideration of actual results but it also includes updating future estimates given the latest information and views about what will happen in the future.

If we take the YMCC example and suppose that a decision had been taken to build a 100% owned plant in the Asia Pacific region, what lessons could we look to learn during the construction phase? We would obviously be tracking the capital cost. We would also now have a much better estimate of what our local branch office was going to cost. We had previously estimated this would cost $2m pa. We should have a more accurate figure by now. We will also have more up-to-date estimates of the likely selling price for the product. Even though the construction side of the project might now be unstoppable we might be able to react to other changes if we saw them coming. Just because the operation is not up and running from a commercial point of view does not mean that its future activities cannot be managed to respond to changes.

This forward-looking management should be taking place in any case. The extra insights that will come from applying Sources of Value thinking will concern whether changes impact on the sector overall (i.e. they impact on the 'me too' player) or whether they are more focused on our own company (i.e. they impact on a source of value). A cost increase which hits just our own company will be more serious than a change that hits the 'me too' player. This is because we would normally expect extra 'me too' costs to be passed on to customers through higher prices while extra costs concerning our sources of value will hit the company's bottom line to the full extent.

Implementing Sources of Value at the operation stage

During this stage companies should continue to track actual performance as outlined above. The understanding of what is common to the sector and what is unique to our own company will give some new insights. For example, if the market price of our product rises, how should we think about this? Sources of Value logic would suggest that the answer should be assessed by considering the impact on the 'me too' player. The rise may be necessary simply to allow the 'me too' player to reduce its negative NPV to a less painful figure. In this case the rise may well not provoke other responses. If, however, the rise is sufficient to increase the 'me too' return to a positive NPV, one can anticipate corrective economic forces coming in to play. So, for example, new capacity may be built; suppliers will increase their prices; substitutes will be encouraged. It may take several years, but sooner or later the windfall will probably disappear and the company should plan on this basis. In effect the Sources of Value approach should suggest a price band within which prices could remain without provoking strong corrective forces.

The current high oil prices provide a good example of how to think about the impact of price changes. Sources of Value logic suggests to me that the producing governments will adjust their tax take in order to secure most of the additional economic rent. This is clearly what has happened. The consequence is that the oil companies will not quickly move to expand oil production. Instead, there will be a build-up of energy production by other means. The lead time for this will be quite long and so high prices might well be sustained for some time. If and when prices start to fall it is quite possible that the consuming countries' governments will increase taxes on energy under the guise of the need to be 'green' and limit energy-demand growth. So consumers may well have to face permanently higher energy prices than had been anticipated say five years ago. The oil companies will gain from this but not greatly. The main winners will be the producing governments. The share price performance of the oil companies is consistent with this.

A change to a source of value is less likely to impact on the market overall. It is important to note, however, that sources of value are not necessarily unique advantages to one company. They are advantages that a company has over 'me too' players. If other companies also have access to the advantage this might over time change the 'me too' benchmark. The greater the source of value the greater will be the incentive to act in order to realise it. If the only way to realise the advantage is to make a new investment then a large source of value can catalyse a cycle of heavy building followed by low prices which squeeze out higher cost producers, and then stabilisation at a new and lower price level.

An example of this would be our recent YMCC case study. The study uses as the 'me too' benchmark the old technology production route. We assumed that a small number of new plants using YMCC's advantaged technology will not alter the price-setting mechanism. Suppose, however, that the gap between 'me too' and YMCC's technology was found to be much greater. The initial impact would be very favourable for YMCC. If, however, it followed a licensing strategy and this allowed too many new plants to be built, the old 'me too' benchmark may become outdated. The new benchmark may become a YMCC licensed plant and this would fail to earn its CoC. The implications of this for YMCC's existing capacity in the USA are severe and Sources of Value logic would bring this point to the fore.

Getting started with Sources of Value

We have now considered all of the activities which can be undertaken once a company fully accepts Sources of Value logic. It would be unrealistic to expect a 'big bang' style implementation with everybody coming to work one day and doing things differently. A phased roll-out is, in my view, the more suitable way to go.

It should be clear from the above that this phased roll-out should not start with a pilot test on a single project at the sanction stage. This is too late in the project life cycle to introduce a new concept, one of the key benefits of which might well be to challenge the strategy and question the very basis of the project. The project team is likely to feel it has been unfairly picked out for challenge. If projects are to be the starting point then at least it is necessary to consider several in the first tests in order to avoid this issue.

My recommendation is for Sources of Value logic first to be introduced to the strategy review process and/or the initial screening of strategic options. The focus at this stage should not be on things like standard categories of Sources of Value and the order of calculations. It should be on the more strategic insights which can be obtained, such as, for example, the over-riding importance of avoiding being a 'me too' player and the importance of making sure that strategies have a firm grounding in economic value. Since, in my view, strategy includes the answer to the question '*How organised and managed?*', this early work should include ensuring the company's organisational model is well aligned with its main sources of value.

Getting started will require some initial 'bottom-up' work within the planning function but support from senior management will be necessary before much progress can be made. Sources of Value provides the bridge between strategy and finance but the strategists and the financiers will only walk the bridge and meet each other if they are helped to do so. The language which is used, and the back-of-the-envelope calculations which Sources of Value logic allow one to carry out, simply will not fly within a company where decision-makers are unfamiliar with the approach.

So the first important hurdle is to review the technique with senior decision-makers and win their support. This will take a while and may cause some organisational pain. This could occur because unless and until Sources of Value thinking changes an important decision, it will not be considered to have had any impact. The 'proposer' of the decision which gets changed is quite likely to resist because he or she may appear to have been shown to be 'wrong'. An organisation that was attuned to learning, however, would be more likely to respond positively from the outset.

I would suggest telling senior managers that the Sources of Value approach does three key things. It:

- helps guide where companies should look in order to find positive NPVs;
- allows assumptions to be calibrated such that one can focus on their overall effect rather than each individual number;
- encourages a building-block approach to value calculations that can be started much earlier in the process and hence companies can avoid the

trap of not starting analysis until it is too late to stop all but the most obviously wrong strategies.

Once senior management agrees, Sources of Value implementation will need to become a corporate initiative that follows an agreed roll-out plan. This will probably last a few years before some steady state is reached, with the techniques embodied in the way a company thinks and acts.

Part 4: So what!: The implications of the Sources of Value technique

The Sources of Value philosophy

The basic idea of Sources of Value is that it provides a good way of thinking about value creation. The technique started with the answer to the question '*where does the NPV come from*?'. The answer was that NPV came from the combination of sector attractiveness and competitive position as long as one approached both of these concepts from the new perspective of a 'me too' player. It is this new perspective which in turn facilitates the construction of a bridge between strategy and finance. NPV, with its quantitative roots in finance, could be directly related to what would otherwise be simply qualitative strategic concepts.

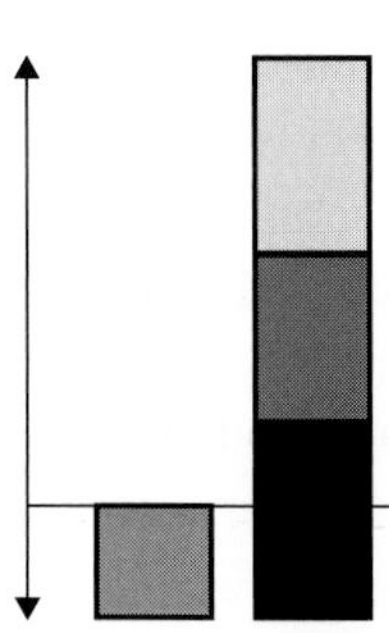

Readers should now understand the approach and be capable of carrying out the necessary calculations. The Sources of Value diagram, with no numbers or words attached, is intended to convey the meaning of the approach. The diagram tells us how NPV comes from beating somebody and should immediately suggest the words 'me too'. It reminds us how important it is to know who this 'me too' player is and to have a view as regards how much value it will lose. The diagram should also invoke the words 'Sources of Value'. These are the reasons why we can be better than 'me too'. There will usually be more than one way to beat 'me too' and the strategies which offer the greatest value are the best to follow.

This fourth section of the Sources of Value pillar will consider some of the implications of what I refer to as Sources of Value thinking. It will look in particular at places where thinking in this new way might change the outcome. It will not, however, go so far as to provide a list of things which are currently being done wrong! In most cases somebody is already winning and so it is likely that they will be acting in a way that is fully consistent with Sources of Value. The insights will be of most obvious use to companies that are not winning. Winners too, however, may well be missing opportunities to win by even more and so I encourage all to consider these implications and to test them for relevance to their own situation.

My focus, for this current section, will be on the use of Sources of Value in business situations. I do, though, want to plant an idea at this stage which I will return to later. I believe Sources of Value thinking can be applied in a much wider way than simply to the calculation of economic value in 'big business'. It is a part of the human condition, I suggest, to compete. If this is true there will be winners and losers. Unless the game is simply one of chance, the winners will win because they are better than the losers. It will always pay to know what a loser looks like and to have an idea of what it costs to lose. We could consider pop bands, corner shops or sports teams; in my view it would not matter. Sources of Value thinking should still apply. If a player is simply copying what others can do, they are 'me too'. 'Me too' players are perfectly competent and they are not the worst in the industry but before they set out on their path, they should never feel that they will be satisfied with what they will get.

Strategic implication 1: How to win

I define winning in business as creating value. We will be devoting more attention to the question of how to measure this in the next pillar. For the present, however, please simply accept my definition of winning. What the Sources of Value technique tells us about creating value is that there are plenty of ways of doing it. Why do I claim this? The answer is because there are so many different potential sources of value which a company can exploit.

This initial implication is quite a positive one for businesses. There can be many sources of value and hence there can be many ways to beat the 'me too' benchmark. Provided the aggregate value of the identified sources of value is more than enough to recover the initial negative NPV that will be suffered by the 'me too' player, a company can anticipate creating value from its investment. This, to me, is a more positive view of what is possible than the suggestion that there are only three generic strategies and that, in particular, only one company can be the least-cost supplier.

Now of course it must be true that only one company can be the least-cost supplier. Furthermore, it certainly can be a disaster for sector profitability if two companies fight for least-cost status with economies of scale as their primary means of achieving these. This is because they will be forced to keep cutting prices and adding capacity in order to get ahead. Lower prices may encourage additional demand but if two or more companies are fighting for the largest share because they think that it is only by being the very lowest-cost supplier that they can win, there is bound to be overcapacity. The Sources of Value view is that there can be room for several low-cost suppliers all of which can create value as long as they do not drive 'me too' out of business. Absolute 'cut-throat' competition is not necessary once it is accepted that there should be room for more than one winner.

A way of thinking about the different ways to win in business is to start with a value map of the business which is drawn from the perspective of the 'me too' player. This value map can start as a simple components of value picture that explains the small negative NPV which we expect the 'me too' player to earn. This could look like this:

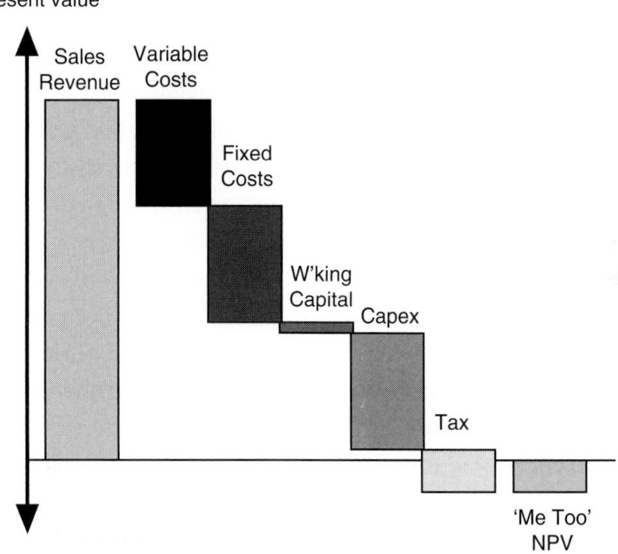

Fig. 8.8 Components of value map: 'me too' player's project

In the chart the present value of all of the sales revenue is shown as the left hand bar. There then follow the various deductions from this in order, ultimately, to get to the NPV. In this case the 'me too' player is suffering a negative NPV which is shown as the box on the right hand side. Note that in this particular chart the effect of working capital is quite small. This is fairly typical in a project because it is usual to assume that any working capital requirements are recovered at the end of the project. Note also the negative impact of tax. The project is paying tax even though it has a negative NPV. This too is quite normal. Governments tend to tax profits[35] and these start as soon as the project generates an IRR of greater than 0%. Value, however, is only created when the IRR is above the CoC. Finally, the chart shows just the value impact of fixed and variable costs but these could be further analysed into their main categories if this was wanted.[36]

The picture can then give us clues as regards how our project could create value while 'me too' does not. The simple message is that the bigger a box, the smaller the required percentage change in order, say, to eliminate half of the 'me too' negative. Three such changes would be necessary in order to achieve a small positive NPV and give the project even a chance of being worth approving in a typical capital-constrained environment. The approach I recommend is the obvious one of starting with the biggest box and gradually working down the priority list.

So first we consider how to make the sales revenue box larger. This can be done by any combination of three things: sales volume; sales price; and sales timing. We can see that because the sales revenue box is so large, a small percentage change in price or volume will allow a good change in value. To create value via favourable variable costs we need either lower unit costs or perhaps higher costs that in turn generate even higher revenue. Fixed costs and capital investment (shortened to capex on the chart) can contribute value if they are lowered. Again, however, one would have to consider also the impact of reductions in sales revenue. If reduced costs impact on the quality and/or service associated with the product there will almost certainly be a knock-on effect on the sales revenue value box. Remember also that with all value improvements we should not forget about the effect of tax. Our project is almost bound to pay more tax than the 'me too' player does because we want to be more successful.[37]

I would suggest that the main messages from this Sources of Value-driven thinking about how to win are that there are many ways to create value and

[35] Note that although governments usually give tax relief for interest paid this is not included in this chart because the value calculation is carried out on a basis that ignores the specific financing route that is chosen. The way that I suggest readers should think about this is that the effect of tax relief on interest is already included in the cost of capital.

[36] Fixed costs, for example, could be broken down into manufacturing fixed costs, marketing costs and other costs.

[37] Although the basic diagram is drawn with tax as a specific deduction it usually pays to think about Sources of Value on a post-tax basis.

that one should always start with the sales revenue box. This is the biggest box on the chart and so must give the biggest value boost per percentage point change in input assumption. There are also three ways of making it better – volume, price and timing. If you cannot get to a positive NPV through the sales route then you must turn to cost reduction. The big cost areas of variable cost, fixed costs and capital investment can all help, but pretty big percentage improvements are needed, particularly after the tax man takes his share of the gain and one allows for possible reduced sales associated with lower quality.

A final comment on this approach is that it looks at all of the contributions to value. In my experience the typical approach for managers who want to improve their business's performance is to focus just on the profit and loss account. This misses two vital aspects. These are, first, the need to allow for the funding implications of changes in capital employed and, second, the need to allow for the impact of changes over time and not just in a single year.

Strategic implication 2: Look downwards

The tendency in business is always to look upwards; that is, to pay attention almost exclusively to the leaders of your industry. This is understandable. For many companies, being best is what they are striving to do. There are certainly lessons to be learned from studying the best companies. The best companies are often also the biggest threat since they may well have plans to grow at your expense. So companies should certainly pay attention to the leaders. Sources of Value logic, however, points to a strong reason to look also at the laggards.[38] Furthermore, it suggests it is your company's lead over the 'me too' player that sets its potential to create value.

Sources of Value logic suggests that laggards have an important role in setting prices. We use the benchmark of the 'me too' player in order to anchor our assumptions in the reality of competition. This means that the continued survival of our assumed 'me too' player is important. If competition forces players (usually laggards) out of our industry then our assumed 'me too' benchmark must be moved. If this happens there is only one implication for our assumptions; we will have to make them more pessimistic in order to reflect the new 'me too', which is almost bound to have lower costs.

The 'me too' player does not have to be forced out of business before the benchmark should be changed. Remember the definition of 'me too' is that

[38] I would define a laggard as a member of the bottom quartile of the industry cost curve. So laggards are usually just below our 'me too' benchmark.

it will be operating at about the bottom of the third quartile of the industry cost curve. Players such as this will not be on the point of extinction! Players on the point of extinction will be earning much less than their CoC. They will probably be reporting losses as they are unable to cover all of their fixed cash costs, let alone depreciation. By contrast, 'me too' players will be struggling along. Yes, they will be earning profits but not high enough to cover the full CoC. The loss of the highest-cost producer moves every player closer to the new highest-cost producer and so should have us thinking about where the new 'me too' benchmark lies.

This is not an exact science but since 'me too' should be operating at about the bottom of the third quartile one should expect to find, say, 20–25% of the installed capacity of the industry below the 'me too' benchmark. The loss of poorly placed competitors and indeed, even simple expansion of the industry through construction of large low cost plants, can change what would be the suitable benchmark.

In my view even the industry leader should understand who is 'me too' in its industry and understand what it must be like to be that company. The temptation, as leader, is to exploit your lead and to grow market share. If this growth is able to remunerate its fully built-up costs and earn above the CoC then surely, the logic might appear to suggest, the leader should grow? Why should leaders bother about laggards?

The Sources of Value logic goes like this. If capacity growth is so great as to force existing players out of a market this must be through a period of particularly low prices. There will usually be some costs associated with market exit. Companies will only bite the bullet and incur these when the alternative looks worse. So if a leader forces a player out of the market through growing its market share, it forces a period of relative pain on all of the industry. Then, when the player has left, a new and lower price level will become the norm because the new 'me too' will be better placed than before.

Remember that the assumption of a typical 'me too' player's earning less than the CoC is not a deliberately pessimistic assumption. In my view it represents a fairly favourable situation for the industry as a whole because it means the average position, probably, is for value to be created. Things can be massively worse than this!

Consider how a 'price war' works. The aim is to lower prices such that, ultimately, inefficient producers will quit the business. This means prices must be below cash cost for the worst players. Unless the cost curve is very steep it is most unlikely that a price which will drive players out of the bottom quartile will allow a player at the bottom of the third quartile to recover depreciation and a modest return on capital. So a typical Sources of Value-inspired long-run equilibrium price assumption that 'me too' will earn a few percentage points below their CoC is not the price which will be sustained while companies are being driven out of business. It is quite a lot higher than this.

So my suggestion to 'look downwards' is a suggestion to pay attention to the tail of the industry's cost curve. It is companies operating down here that will set prices. I recommend that approval of any significant expansion of capacity should be conditional on explicit consideration of the future prospects for the tail of the industry. In particular this needs to cover the implications of the expansion for the companies at the wrong end of the cost curve. If the analysis suggests laggards are required to leave the industry then this is a reflection of poor sector attractiveness and the long-run price assumption should be consistent with this reality. This might mean, for example, assuming 'me too' players will earn well below their CoC.

One way of testing the impact of a leader's actions on the sector overall is to state what share of the growth in an industry a proposed expansion will be taking. So if an industry has a capacity of 1m units and is growing at 5% pa, the annual growth will be 50,000 units. An expansion that adds, say, 10,000 units of capacity, will be taking 20% of the potential growth. If that company already has a 20% market share, this is not an overly aggressive strategy. If, however, its market share is lower than 20% then it is 'stealing' share from other players and this will lower prices unless sufficient of the other players decide not to maintain their market share. So in our example the question to address concerns what other new capacity will be built. If the answer is that only a further 35,000 units of capacity are expected to be built then the industry will look more favourable because the remaining 5,000 units of demand can be taken by the companies that are not currently running to full capacity. If, however, a further 45,000 units of capacity are expected to be built then some players will have to lower throughput which will cause pain within the industry.

It sometimes looks to me as an observer as though some players must believe that by squeezing the laggards out of an industry a golden period of higher profitability will result. It also can look as though some companies assume that if future supply/demand projections show a shortfall of supply then prices must rise to the level that is required to justify the new build. Sources of Value logic suggests that these rosy-tinted future outlooks will not come about. Competitive forces will not let it happen. It may still be the right thing for a leading company to build capacity with a view to forcing weaker companies out of business but only if the alternative would see the leader unable to capitalise on its advantages because laggards were taking too much of the market.[39] In most situations leaders will be able gradually to grow their market share without knocking the 'me too' players out of business.

This thinking may perhaps seem like heresy to a competition authority. Is the implication that companies should collude in keeping inefficient players in business in order to support excessive industry profitability? I am definitely not suggesting that! The usual Sources of Value assumption is that many players will remain in an industry despite the fact they will not earn their CoC on a full-cycle basis. What I am suggesting is that companies need to beware of things becoming a lot worse than this. Armed with this more realistic view of what is likely to happen in the future it then becomes less logical for individual companies to decide to embark on strategies predicated on fast growth driving so-called inefficient producers out of business.

Strategic implication 3: Can you buy success?

This next implication deals mainly with acquisitions. It does, though, also refer to situations where companies aim to build their own businesses through the so-called organic growth route. The basic message is that if all that a company brings is money then it should not expect to create value. Indeed, if all that a company brings is money then it should think of itself as the 'me too' player and anticipate a negative NPV. So if success is the creation of value, you cannot simply buy it. You have to win it through the application of one or more sources of value.

Let us consider a company that is put up for sale. It will have a plan and its current owners will have an idea about what this plan is worth. In logic, the existing owners should not sell the business for less than the present value of its future after-tax cash flows. Provided a good merchant bank is engaged, any sale of a business should always achieve at the very least the fair value of a company. In reality a higher price should be expected, for two good reasons.

The first reason is that potential purchasers that want to buy the company will often have in mind things they can do to make it more profitable. They would not bother to bid for a company unless they thought they could do something better with it. As soon as more than one potential purchaser identifies additional value it can create if it buys the company, it becomes logical for it to allow for some of this value in its initial bid in order to secure the

[39] For example, if the leader can have advantaged costs but only if he builds a very large plant. It may be that this plant will simply have to force existing players out of business.

purchase. So the seller's merchant bank simply has to drum up potential purchasers and they in turn will then force the price up to above what it is worth to the current owner.

The second reason is referred to as 'the winner's curse'. This is a reflection of what happens when there is uncertainty surrounding the fair value of an asset being sold at auction. If we accept that the average estimate of value by all potential buyers is the fair value of an asset and that buyers will bid up to what they think an asset is worth then, by definition, the winner in an auction will have to pay more than the fair value because the winner is the company that places the highest value on the asset.

Now if the only factor was the winner's curse one could argue that bidders should be aware of its existence and so should allow for it as they develop their bidding strategy. Once, however, one introduces the idea of several potential buyers believing they can create more value with the business than the current owners, one has to accept that businesses which are sold will be sold for more than their fair value to the current owner. This also means a potential owner who buys a company and yet who has no plans to create additional value, must expect to destroy value.

In the language of Sources of Value, a potential owner who brings nothing but money is a 'me too' player and must expect to destroy value. So although it is easy enough to buy a successful company, you cannot buy success.

The Sources of Value chart for a typical acquisition will look like this:

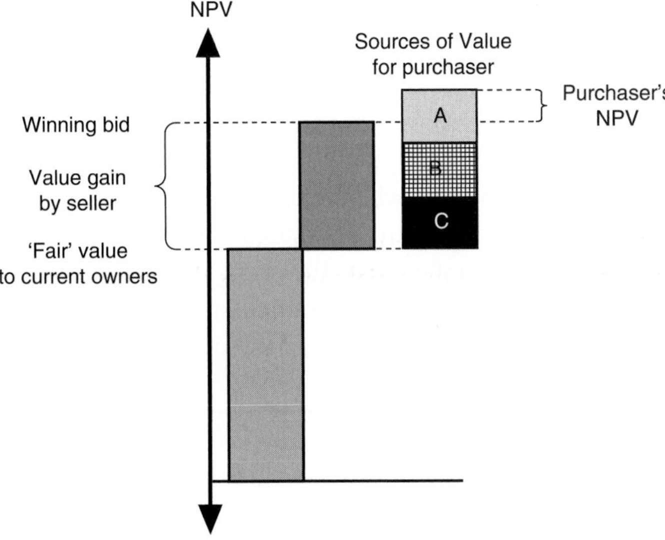

Fig. 8.9 Sources of Value chart for a typical acquisition

In the chart the value block on the left represents the stand-alone value to the current owner. The next block represents the 'overpayment' by the purchaser relative to this value.[40] The purchaser can afford to pay this amount and still create value because of the things it plans to do with the company to enhance its value after the acquisition goes through. I have labelled these sources of value A, B and C. It does not matter for the present what these might be; it just matters that they are quantified improvements in future prospects either within the company being sold or in the existing operations of the purchaser's company.

Now the price of the sale is set through a competitive auction organised by the seller's merchant bank. If a purchaser was bidding for the company simply on the grounds that it was a very good company, what NPV should the purchaser anticipate? Well, Sources of Value logic suggests that unless you bring significant sources of value you should anticipate a negative NPV. A well organised sale will usually result in a sales price that is well over the holding value to the current owner[41] and so unless the winning purchaser has large sources of value it must, in logic, anticipate a negative NPV.

So now we should understand why the answer to the original question for this section: '*can you buy success*?' must be '*no*'. It does not matter how well a company is currently doing, if a purchaser buys it and then does nothing differently, it will have overpaid. With my definition of success being the creation of value, buying a successful company simply to own its success is a fundamentally flawed strategy. The purchaser must have substantial plans to create additional value after the acquisition or else the acquisition will destroy value.

I believe this line of logic goes a long way towards explaining why so many acquisitions are considered with hindsight to have failed. The focus in acquisitions can tend to be on the quality of the assets being purchased rather than on the sources of value which will be exploited. One could argue that the quality of the business being purchased simply does not matter because whatever it is, it will be reflected in the price. What does matter is the magnitude of the sources of value because these must be the drivers of the final NPV. The only extent to which existing asset quality contributes to the deal's

[40] Note that I have not allowed for any tax effects in this example in order to simplify the picture. In reality the winning bid would be taxed and so the value gain to the seller would be lower.

[41] There have been many studies of the outcomes of purchases and sales. The general conclusion of this is that a company that announces an asset sale will see its value rise to reflect the anticipated additional value. By contrast the general view is that something like half of all acquisitions are considered to be failures.

NPV is the extent to which it might limit the life of the assets being purchased and hence the life of some of the sources of value.[42]

The difficulty of buying success is most clearly shown when acquisitions are involved. This is partly because the auction arena makes acquisitions so risky for potential purchasers. It is also because acquisitions are so high profile they get studied a lot. They are big, they can be very good, but they often are not and the evidence of this regularly smacks us in the face! I believe, though, that there are many other situations where companies may bring only money to the search for business success. In these situations the logical conclusion at the start of the venture should be an assumption of a small but negative NPV because, by definition, a company that only brings money is a 'me too' player.

The sort of business activity that I am thinking of is business or brand development teams or R&D where the inspiration is mainly anticipated future growth rather than the way that a company's current talents give it inherent sources of value. Suppose the conventional wisdom was for a particular sector to grow a lot in the coming years. Many companies could see this and would embark on a search for success. This search may be led by a development team or it may start in a company's R&D department. What would it be logical to assume at the outset of such an activity? The Sources of Value philosophy would give a clear answer. Unless a company was advantaged it should not assume it will earn above its CoC. If your company can make money then why can't all companies make money? We know that it is foolish to assume that all companies can make money so we should not assume that we can unless we know why.

What tends to happen with the search for success is that those who find it do well. What one should think about, however, is how many companies looked but did not find. It is only when one factors in the failed searches that the true picture emerges. The time when this needs to be done is at the outset of a strategy. At this point in time, however, one simply cannot know what the probability of success will be. So any company which wanted to justify a search-led strategy could do so. All it would need to do in order to

[42] As (almost) always in business, there is an exception to this rule! In this case the exception refers to new industries. I believe that the acquisition of a company in a sector which is about to take off might well create value even if the purchaser was considered to be bringing nothing but money. Value could come subsequently if and when the industry grows and the purchaser was then already an established player. I would, however, maintain that a situation such as this is exploiting a source of value. In this case the source of value is the knowledge that the sector is about to grow and that as yet there are no players with clear sources of value. So the early arriver can perhaps anticipate creating value.

demonstrate a positive NPV is 'cheat' a little with the assumed success rate and/or the size of the prize.

This 'cheating' can take place with risky or even with almost certain searches. Consider first a risky search. It can be very difficult to argue whether such a search has, say, a 10% or a 15% chance of success. The effect, though, is such as to increase the expected value of the prize by 50%.[43] Now consider a low-risk search. It might be said that it is 'almost bound to succeed'. Consider, however, the impact of incurring all of the up-front costs and then taking only 90% of the assumed prize because there is actually a 10% chance of failure. Again, this can have a big impact on the anticipated NPV[44] which appears to be the consequence of an assumption which is very hard to get exactly right.

Contrast this with a Sources of Value-led analysis. This would simply start with an assertion that the expected value of a search programme was negative and only approve it if specific reasons were put forwards regarding why the search by the company would be more successful than a search by others. Furthermore, the scale of the benefits would need to be calculated in order to demonstrate a quantified source of value. This, to me, would be a much more fruitful line of analysis and would allow better decisions to be made. Yes, a difficult judgement will still have to be made, but is it not more useful to debate why you are better than your competitors rather than whether the chance of success is 10% or 15%?

As a final example, consider the question of developing a new brand. Suppose your company has an existing successful brand but its name means something very unpleasant in the language of a developing country which is experiencing fast growth. So you decide to invest to develop a new brand just for this country. I would suggest you would need to identify sources of value to justify this approach. The fact of your current success would not be relevant because you would need a new brand. So you would need to know how you could beat other companies which also wanted to develop a new brand for this country. It would be illogical to assume that any company that wanted to develop a brand could win. The starting assumption should be a small negative NPV based on expected value assumptions. Examples of possible sources of value could be superior market research capability or lower distribution costs if the product does succeed.

[43] Because effect = impact × probability. So increase probability by 50% and you increase the expected value outcome by 50%.

[44] For example, suppose the present value of the search costs was $20m and the present value of the prize was thought to be $25m. If the prize was certain the NPV would be $5m. If there was a 10% chance that the prize would be zero the expected value NPV would fall by $2.5m.

Strategic implication 4: Having 'quality' investment decision debates

The above example has given a clear pointer regarding how to ensure that investment decisions are taken after what could be termed a 'quality' discussion. I would define this as having the senior decision-makers spend their time discussing the things that really matter.

The Sources of Value approach will always focus attention on the 'me too' return and on the specific sources of value. Now time spent discussing sources of value should self-evidently be time well spent. Even without the technique it is quite likely that decision-makers will spend some time discussing what makes the project good. There will, however, in all likelihood be no systematic quantification. Qualitative expressions like 'relationship' will be used. These will be true but will not yield the same insights. Finally, the investment decision's discussion of sources of value should not be the first time these will have been considered by the company's leadership. The sources of value will already be familiar thanks to the earlier discussion of the strategy.

There can be many different insights from knowing exactly what the sources of value on a new project are expected to be. For example:

- A simple ranking may show that one or more of the stated qualitative advantages are actually substantially irrelevant because their value impact is very low. Quantification will allow enhanced focus on the things which really matter.
- Overdependence on sunk costs will signal how, although the project might be OK on a money-forward basis, the strategy was wrong. So the focus needs to shift to learning lessons so that future projects are not approved simply because it is now too late to stop them.
- The nature of the sources of value may point to a situation where the project was not the best way to exploit the identified advantage. This can lead to new projects being identified or to changes in strategy.
- The sources of value should never be a surprise because they should have inspired the strategy that led to the project. If any major sources of value are a surprise then the strategy might need reviewing.
- Identifying sources of value encourages a focus on whether the company is doing enough to sustain and enhance them so they can remain as sources of value into the future.
- Identifying sources of value also encourages a focus on whether the company is doing enough to exploit them. The bigger a source of value, the more a company should be seeking to utilise it in more ways than just the project under consideration.

- Any negative source of value can be highlighted and means of mitigating them considered.

Now we can turn to the question of the 'me too' return. The huge advantage here is in the way a vast list of individual assumptions can be condensed into a single number. This is the IRR a 'me too' player would earn if it was to adopt this forward view of the world. Senior decision-makers can test this against their overall intuition for the business in which they operate. I strongly take the view that, once they become used to the technique, senior managers will feel more comfortable deciding what the 'me too' return will be than deciding what a huge list[45] of individual assumptions should be.

There will always be a range around any individual assumption which must be considered to be 'normal' uncertainty. By that I mean an expert with full knowledge would have to say that it was perfectly possible this was a reasonable assumption. The trouble with the NPV calculation, however, is how NPV is the small difference between two big numbers – namely the present value of revenues and the present value of costs. So small and apparently reasonable differences in individual assumptions can make big differences in NPV.

This means a sponsor of a project which was, say, marginal, but who wanted to get it approved could always choose assumptions that made it appear acceptable. Even if one assumes that all project sponsors are entirely unbiased there will be a random element to any claimed NPV which makes it a pretty inaccurate way of deciding whether or not to progress with a project. Introducing the Sources of Value technique allows the overall effect of assumptions to be calibrated in such a way that the uncertainty range around what should be considered to be a reasonable estimate of NPV should be significantly reduced.

This conclusion about needing to invoke Sources of Value logic in order to calculate a reasonably accurate NPV is at odds with the approaches set out in the books by Penman and the McKinsey consultants. McKinsey accept that valuation is an art but claim to aim for a valuation range of ±15% which is similar, they state, to the range used by many investment bankers. I consider this to be an unrealistically low range. McKinsey even point out that a 0.5% increase in the CoC will typically lower value by 10%. Penman has a different philosophy. He writes about the need to distinguish between what one knows and 'speculation'. He suggests that by forcing the analyst to forecast in an orderly manner his approach 'disciplines speculative tendencies'. My

[45] Typical 'me too' assumptions will include things like the project life, exchange rates, inflation rates, GDP growth rates, tax rates, feedstock costs and selling prices (for commodity products).

experience is that one cannot 'know' what assumptions to make and hence that some 'speculation' is unavoidable when one makes a major investment decision.

Readers will learn later in this book about the considerable uncertainty which exists in relation to the CoC. In my view, however, even greater uncertainties usually exist in relation to future cash flows. Hence the need for a fundamentally different approach. Instead of claiming an answer is accurate to within ±15% or that the answer is based on fundamental analysis and not speculation, why not claim that your analysis is based on assumptions which are demonstrably reasonable and which can be explained in a way that allows direct comparison with other projects? This way is to state the implied 'me too' return in relation to the CoC.

The key, I suggest, is in the word 'reasonable'. One of the things Sources of Value thinking does is help to decide what might be a reasonable view of the future. It does not, however, tell us what the future *will* be like. The idea of a 'reasonable' view of the future is that it is one which, if others held it as well, could still in logic come about. So, for example, if a lot of people believe that prices of a particular product will be very high in the future then so much new capacity will be built that the price will have to fall. Therefore it is not reasonable to plan on the basis that prices will be so high. If, however, everybody plans on much lower prices then no new capacity might be built and so in the event prices may indeed finish up very high. In the middle there is a range which could be sustained if that was what people thought would happen. Sources of Value thinking helps identify the range. Reality does not have to turn out this way but at least you are dealing with a view of the future which could represent a stable equilibrium.

Overall, the discussion of an individual project should become much more strategic in nature while the numbers can, in my view, be considered to be more accurate as well. A decision that is based on Sources of Value analysis can truly be said to have been judgement based on rational analysis.

Strategic implication 5: How to understand governments

We have already seen how governments and regulators can have an important role in some sectors. These are where taxes, regulations, permits, etc. are used to control profitability in some way. The more I have thought about this topic the more situations I have identified where understanding the implications of government-based control as opposed to free market control should have an important bearing on strategy formulation.

The sorts of situations where government-based control occurs include:

- Utilities, where it is inefficient to have more than one supplier. The monopoly supplier must be regulated to stop it exploiting its power over buyers.
- Natural resources, where the state will consider it owns the resource and will want to charge extra taxes and royalties to maximise the economic benefit which flows to it.
- Vital supplies and services, where a state will want to purchase from the private sector but will use its powers to limit what otherwise would be overly strong supplier power.
- Market domination, where a small number of companies have large market shares and might otherwise exploit this strength to the detriment of customers.

The Sources of Value view of these situations is to define the 'me too' player as the player the government wants to encourage. Then one can calibrate assumptions by checking the aggregate set of taxes, rules, prices, etc. which the government imposes to give 'me too' players a return which is just adequate to make them want to progress with their investment.

There are two key implications of this. The first is to be better than 'me too' and the second is to be ahead of them in time. The ideal situation is to be better than 'me too' and several years ahead such that the government needs to permit your success as encouragement to the players who have still to invest. The worst situation is to have sunk your capital and then discover the government no longer needs you to succeed.

Of the two strategic imperatives of being good and being early, I would suggest being early is the most important. This is because the key risk with governments is for them to change the rules after you have sunk your money. The best defence against this is to have a 'me too' player some years behind you which has yet to commit its capital. The government will then see an incentive to allow your company to profit as an encouragement to others to follow in your footsteps. If, however, you have the best opportunity in the country but are the last to go ahead, you will be badly exposed to a subsequent change in tax take or selling price once it is too late for you to go back.

Now, governments do not always use all of the powers that they have so it is always possible to assume that they will treat your industry in a favourable manner. This would correspond either to not exercising control when they could or to assuming that despite exercising control they would allow 'me too' players to earn above the CoC when all risks are considered.

Experience shows how even the bastions of free market economics permit many situations where companies are subject to controls on profitability. So, for example, all four of my suggested generic situations where control can be imposed can be observed in both the USA and the UK. My experience of well over 30 years in the oil industry has included time spent working in government and in dealing with various competition authorities. This time has encouraged me to take what might be thought of as the highly cynical view of governments, namely that their usual behaviour is to maximise their own revenues subject to only fairly short-term constraints of what they can get away with. The Sources of Value approach fits this perfectly. With only a few exceptions, once governments start to limit profitability what they appear to do is cap the maximum level of profitability and limit the typical level of profitability to the CoC while leaving the downside risk fully with shareholders. On a full-cycle basis and taking proper account of risk, this is a recipe for 'me too' players earning less than their CoC.

It does therefore make sense to allow for Sources of Value thinking in relation to governments when strategies are formulated. This would mean devoting a lot of attention to understanding what the government would consider to be the 'me too' player. If governments are, or might in the future become, involved then this thinking would cover who is the 'me too', what its costs were and, crucially, how it would evolve over time.[46]

The view of the evolution of 'me too' over time should have an important influence on the choice of one country over another. Sources of Value analysis might point towards it being reasonable to believe that one country will be much more stable than another. This would apply in particular to natural resources where countries which are nearing the end of their reserves will be less favourable places in which to invest.

One thing to be aware of is the incentive which governments must have to treat each project as a special case. If it is able to do this, a government can then limit all projects to earning just what it considers to be a 'fair' return. If economic rent is simply divided between the state and the companies, then limiting all projects to just the 'fair' return should maximise the state's share of the pie.

The superior returns earned by well-placed projects that Sources of Value logic suggests are necessary to encourage other companies to risk their capital can be seen by governments as a wasted tax-raising opportunity. All a government needs to do in order to grab this slug of economic rent is to justify

[46] I am referring to how the actual 'me too' players will change, not to changes within today's 'me too'. This evolution is particularly important as industries mature and then decline. In a declining industry, 'me too' may well have surplus capacity whereas in a growing industry 'me too' may need to invest new capital. Clearly the prospective returns will be very different in these two situations.

treating each company on an individual basis. The sorts of things governments can do are tailor permitted prices to allow only a set return on capital or they can set taxes which only apply in specific situations. An example of this might include making a distinction between a project started before a particular date and a project started after that date. This may appear to favour your project today but I would suggest that in some years' time a similar approach may work against you.

Another implication of Sources of Value thinking concerns who gets any particular benefit. Suppose a country is rich in natural resources and also very close to the end market. This will undoubtedly create an opportunity for somebody to generate economic rent in the form of positive NPVs or large streams of tax revenue. Who will be the main beneficiary of this location benefit? Sources of Value gives a very clear answer. The location is available to the 'me too' player and so will not contribute to NPV. As long as 'me too' can earn a positive NPV the host government will take the rest of the economic rent. So location is only useful to the extent it differentiates your opportunity from 'me too' or is necessary to give 'me too' a positive NPV before any government take is considered.

This line of logic should lead the thinking to the final point that I will make in this section. This is how benchmarking of opportunities and the determination of who is the 'me too' player in sectors that are subject to government control needs to be undertaken government by government or in even more disaggregated ways if governments treat things differently within their countries. In the USA, for example, if individual states are free to set royalty rates on natural resources then each state will have its own 'me too' player it wants to encourage.

So, for example, consider what can be learned from a global cost curve for a commodity such as copper or oil. This will typically be prepared on a pre-tax basis although it may well also include any royalties that are levied. In my view, a curve such as this is of little help in understanding the value potential of an opportunity. All the curve can do is set out marginal costs and help you analyse who will continue producing when things get very bad. Now this is certainly relevant in some situations but, as I have already explained, if an industry is suffering from prices that are this low then new investments are unlikely to be looking attractive. Cost curves become useful only when they show just the relevant players. So although the market for a commodity may be global, the value potential for commodity projects is set mainly by local considerations. Each location will have its own 'me too' benchmark and this can mean many opportunities need to be considered as being just 'me too'.

There are potentially immense implications for this. A company may be sitting on an opportunity which 'the man from Mars'[47] thought was one of the best opportunities in the world. The same company may have a competing opportunity that was nowhere near as good yet it might select this one ahead of the apparently better one. Why might this be? Well, the great opportunity may be in a country which does not need to encourage other less good projects to go ahead while the less good opportunity that your company has may well be one of the best in a different country. This situation will only become clear when both are viewed from the perspective of the 'me too' opportunity. Each and every area which is regulated by a government will have its own 'me too' player that is the marginal opportunity which the government wishes to encourage. Our great project may actually only be 'me too' in the country where it happens to be situated whereas the poor project may be the best in its home country. So there can be much more value potential in a project which, on a global basis is poor, than one which on a global basis looks much better.

A simple proof of this can come from the oil industry with a consideration of the development of projects in, say, Saudi Arabia and the North Sea. The man from Mars must still be wondering why we Earthlings developed the oil in the North Sea when we could have simply produced more from the Middle East. Well, Sources of Value can help explain why.

Strategic implication 6: Don't go out alone!

How can Sources of Value be applied if a company is the only operator in a sector? The basic answer is that it cannot. With only one company there cannot be a 'me too' player. The problem here is that if you are the only player, the opportunity is either so large the government will want to regulate it, or so small it does not matter.

My advice about not going out alone is addressed to large companies. They will not be interested in the small opportunities which I will consider later. Their concerns will be with major projects because these might be thought to offer big potential rewards. Sources of Value logic, however, suggests a need for real caution. This is because very large projects are most likely to be regulated.

[47] I use the term 'the man from Mars' to refer to the view of the world that would be taken by an outsider who could not tell the difference between its many inhabitants. They are all just 'Earthlings' coming from the planet Earth. The man from Mars would not understand how nationality and politics would get in the way of what he would consider to be 'rational' economic management of the world's economic resources.

For very large one-off projects the government will, in one way or another, take away most if not all of any anticipated economic rent. It may let you earn the CoC but in an environment where the rules of the game dictate that winning is a function of earning more than that, you will not win. Furthermore, if things go wrong on the project you can expect to be left carrying the resultant losses. It is a case of heads you break even, tails you lose. The expected value here is negative. The bigger the project, the greater will be the public scrutiny of any financial gains made and so the greater will be the risk of subsequent value creation being taken back by governments subsequently changing the rules of the game. This may sound cynical, but it does, I suggest, match reality.

Let us consider now very small and unique opportunities. Governments will only 'not notice' a true monopoly when the project is very small and the behaviour of the monopoly supplier remains reasonable. Being 'alone' in this situation would be where Professor Porter's niche strategy could come into play and it can be perfectly reasonable to anticipate earning a positive NPV. The qualitative source of value would be the niche but the key questions would concern the threat of substitutes and the threat of new entrants. Your NPV potential would be set by considering what your customers were prepared to pay and what it would take to encourage others to enter the sector. You would also always be worried about being accused of exploiting a monopoly position. So I suggest that whatever happened, you would need to stay small. This may satisfy the aspirations of a small privately owned business but otherwise I suggest that in the long run it would not be a worthwhile strategy.

Strategic implication 7: Don't be 'me too'

At the superficial level this should be self-evident. After all, this pillar has been all about the way Sources of Value thinking means a 'me too' player should never assume it will be able to beat its CoC. The implications I am looking at are more subtle. For big companies these implications concern the way a company defines its business and its competitors. There are also implications for individuals, which I will cover briefly.

I will start with the advice "don't be 'me too'" from the perspective of big companies. In relation to how a company defines its business, my example would concern whether a supermarket should also own the farms which make the food or the delivery systems which allow internet shoppers to order their groceries on line? In relation to how it defines its competitors, for a supermarket, is 'me too' another supermarket or a local sole trader?

I will deal with defining the business first. Porter's value chain model reminds us that industries have suppliers and customers. Companies have to draw a line somewhere and distinguish between what is their business and what is not. This line must involve both suppliers and customers and its formulation can be aided by applying Sources of Value logic. This logic suggests if you do something and are not positively advantaged then the only safe assumption should be that doing it means value destruction.

A two-stage test needs to be applied to all activities currently within a company. These two stages concern whether the company has sources of value in relation to the activity and whether, if it does not have sources of value, the value impact of exiting the activity is less than the implied value destruction caused by being 'me too' or perhaps worse. A similar test can be applied to activities which are currently outside the company. This relates to whether potential sources of value exceed the cost of bringing that activity in-house.

Note the emphasis in both cases on the value impact of bringing about change. If there is already a clear market in an intermediate product then the cost of disaggregating a business will most likely be low. So, in the case of a supermarket, if it did own a farm, it would not find it expensive to exit. If, however, a company tries to unravel all of the links between, say, distribution and manufacturing, it may find this harder.[48]

Now this line of logic would appear to be leading towards what is called 'the outsourcing debate'. Sources of Value can certainly help here but there are some simpler and more fundamental messages to be had. In particular, Sources of Value logic can help a company decide when to exit a business.

Most projects can be thought of as operating along a time line that will look something like this:

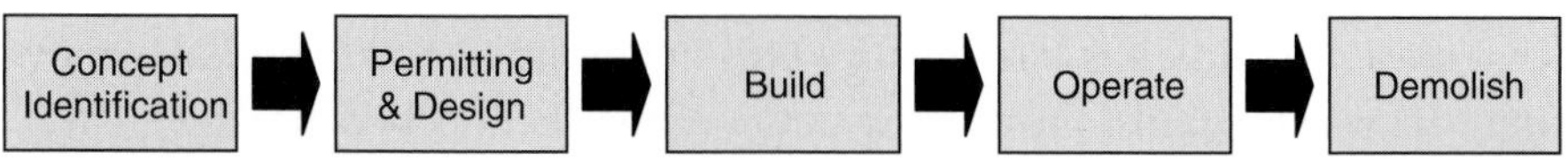

Fig. 8.10 The project life cycle

The length of time spent in each box will not be the same, but from a strategic point of view this need not matter. What does matter is whether or

[48] For example, who carries the cost if a delayed lorry causes the manufacturing plant to be shut down? At first sight the answer would be to make the distribution side pay. But if they do pay, then how much, and how much incentive would there be to build storage capacity to cope with distribution problems? Furthermore, if distribution is excluded from a company, how does the interface with marketing work? It can all get very difficult and so companies end up being involved in full value chains just because they are too difficult to break down.

not a company has sources of value at each stage of the life cycle. So, for example, if a company looks ahead from any point in the project life cycle and observes there are no remaining sources of value to be exploited, then it should consider divesting the activity at that stage. Alternatively, should a company identify sources of value only at the later stages, then it should seek to purchase existing businesses and concentrate just on what it is good at.

The benefit of this approach compared with outsourcing is that buying whole businesses can be easier than breaking an existing business up into its component parts. To an extent this approach is already under way. There are design consultancies, construction companies and even companies specialising in purchasing old assets from major companies. Sources of Value thinking simply salutes these companies and suggests to any company, large or small, which has a cradle-to-grave approach to projects, that it should think hard about whether this is an optimal strategy. This is particularly the case when one couples this logic with the earlier logic that selling should usually create value for the seller.

The second issue to consider concerns who, exactly, is 'me too'. If we continue with the supermarket example, do supermarkets simply compete with other supermarkets or is it possible for them all to earn above the CoC because 'me too' is the thousands of independent shops? Well, I would suggest the answer all depends on the extent to which there is real competition. So, when the very first supermarket opened[49] it did compete with independent shops. However, once there were enough supermarkets, the time would have come to think of them as a sector in their own right. When this is the case one would be forced to assume at least one chain and perhaps more would fail to earn the CoC over time. So one is reminded of the way 'me too' will evolve over time and how this has implications for strategy. A company that does not think it is moving forwards in absolute terms is probably moving backwards against the moving target of the 'me too' benchmark.

The advice about avoiding being 'me too' applies very well to individuals who are considering investments. If all that you are doing is something which can easily be copied by others, then do not expect to earn above the CoC. I can illustrate this by returning to one of the questions which I set as an individual work assignment in the building block on Risk on page 178. This question described an opportunity to sell replica shirts outside a sports stadium. The first option was to carry shirts to the ground each week and sell them from a holdall bag. The second was to rent a stall and sell from

[49] Wikipedia tells me this was in Memphis, Tennessee, in 1916.

there. Both options appeared to offer large positive NPVs. The Sources of Value challenge would be this: what would make either opportunity different from 'me too'? I can think of nothing more 'me too'-like than selling shirts from a holdall bag. If you can make a lot of money in this way then why would others not try to copy you? As regards renting a stall, surely the owner of the site on which the stall was located would know what profits could be earned and would set the rental accordingly. Both approaches could have been ruled out straight away if Sources of Value logic had been applied. There would be no need to do any financial calculations. Unless you could describe in quantitative terms your sources of value a project should not even be investigated.

A final look at Sources of Value

Readers should be almost ready now to leave this topic. If, however, this is just their first reading of this chapter can I remind them of my suggestion that they return to the early sections now they have a better understanding of what Sources of Value thinking is and what it can offer. This may seem a strange comment, but Sources of Value is easier to understand once you understand it and so readers may well learn something new if they return to the start of the pillar and go through it again.

For readers who feel ready to move on, please can I suggest a final action. This is to apply Sources of Value thinking to their own situation. As far as I am aware, Sources of Value represents a new way of thinking about business. I am convinced that its wide acceptance could encourage some significant strategic shifts.

So reader, please think first about the implications of Sources of Value for the company where you work or, failing that, a company you know well. Consider mainly a specific business unit within this company and answer the following questions. When you reach the final two questions on my list, think also about the company's overall corporate strategy and in particular how it is organised and managed.

- Is the business in a government-controlled or free-market environment?
- Who is the 'me too' player?
- Roughly what return would you expect 'me too' to earn?
- What sources of value does your business have?
- Can you quantify these?
- What has recent financial performance looked like?
- How do these results stack up against the sources of value picture?

- If the results do not stack up, is the picture wrong or are we just in an unusual time?
- What is the current strategy of the business?
- How does the strategy relate to the sources of value?

My guess is that somewhere along the line of these ten questions most readers will raise some very interesting issues.

Also in relation to Sources of Value thinking and your own situation, please think about your personal sources of value.

- What are your positive sources of value?
- What are you 'me too' at?
- What are your negative sources of value?

As I suggested at the start of this 'so what?' section, Sources of Value can be applied in many places. Is your own strategy optimal? Is there something you should do more of or something you should avoid? Do you manage your time to make best use of your positive sources of value?

CHAPTER

9

The third pillar: What sets the share price?

Summary

This third pillar is in three parts. I will start with a short consideration of the theory underpinning what sets the share price. This section builds on what was introduced at an early stage in this book in the Financial Markets building block on pages 41–46. Here we learned how the conventional wisdom is that share prices are set by the present value of a company's future dividends. I will return to this idea, work with it a little more and test it by considering some of the problems that exist with the theories.

The two main parts of the pillar will be devoted to the practical topic of calculating share prices and to the more cerebral topic of the implications for understanding and targeting performance of the conclusion that value does underpin the share price. I will deal with how to calculate a share price first but since these two sections can be read on their own, readers can switch the order if they so wish.

My suggested practical approach to company valuation will start with a plan. I will explain that this should typically cover a period of three to five years but that a valuation can be carried out with just a single year's worth of data if that is all one has available. The next step requires the calculation of a terminal value. I will set out several ways of doing this and point out some potential errors to avoid. These two steps will give the so-called asset valuation of a company. The equity value, which is what sets the share price, is calculated through a third step which involves subtracting all other liabilities such as debt. The share price is derived by dividing the equity value by the number of shares.

In the final part I will consider the implications of all of this theory for understanding performance under three headings:

1. **Understanding performance.** There are some strange conclusions to get to grips with, including the way that a plan will offer the same return

in each year and the fact that the best performing share may have just reported a loss.

2. **Continuous good surprises.** This is what companies have to offer their shareholders if they want to remain as 'the darlings of the stock market'. This concept has been described to me as being 'worse than a treadmill' but it does help to explain the apparent never-ending change within quoted companies.
3. **Focus on value.** It is important to place value at the heart of a company's management processes. This may seem obvious but there are many very reasonable-sounding ideas which can, in reality, lead to value destruction if they take the place of the value objective. In particular there are two 'seductive sirens' that will try to tempt managers away from this path. These are the searches for growth and for returns.

Part 1: The theory

The basic principle: value = present value of future dividends

The simplest approach to deciding upon what sets the share price is just to assert that the answer is the present value of future dividends.[1] Risk-free cash flows are valued via the application of the compound interest formula so, it is asserted, risky cash flows can be valued in this way as well. All one needs to do is to set a higher discount rate in order to compensate for the risk. In this case, because we will be discounting equity cash flows, the appropriate discount rate will be the cost of equity and not the CoC. I have always been prepared to accept this logic of discounting future dividends to the present as it stands because it feels right and it appears relatively easy to apply.

We should first remind ourselves why we discount future dividends when the owner of a share will receive a combination of dividends plus the value of the share when they sell it. The logic is that although the initial owner is not going to own the share for its full period, they will know that a stream of owners will, and that the intermediate selling prices must cancel out because they will equal the next owner's purchasing price. Therefore the

[1] Strictly speaking I should have said the stream of all future dividends plus the capital redemption if/when the company is finally wound up.

share is worth the present value of the dividends that it gives rights to. The value of a share should be independent of the holding period of the current owner.

Now the present value approach has a lot more going for it than just the fact that most people agree with it. First and foremost, to me at least, it 'feels right'. I place a lot of emphasis on combining judgement with rational analysis. Well, if the rational analysis is to calculate present values then my judgement says that this seems like a very good thing to do. My judgement is founded upon my own experiences. Included in these are reading many studies of how share prices behave and the bulk of the evidence that I have seen is fully consistent with the value approach.

The present value approach has another key factor on its side. This is the principle of value additivity. It is incredibly useful having a valuation method that allows values simply to be added up. We are all used to going to a shop and buying several items. The price at the checkout is the sum of the individual prices. This is an illustration of price additivity. If share prices 'add up' and they are set by value then value must 'add up' as well. The fact that economic values add up does not prove that they must set the share price. If, however, they did not add up it would prove that they could not set share prices.

There is, however, an important concern with calculating share prices via the present value of future dividends. This concerns assessing the cost of equity. I explained in the Financial Markets building block how risk is carried on equity.[2] This means that the cost of equity is heavily influenced by the level of debt that a company has. So unless a company expects to have the same economic gearing[3] throughout the years into the future, the cost of equity to apply will, in logic, change over time. This will make the calculation very difficult to do because of a circularity in the logic. This is that you need to know the value of a company to calculate its cost of equity but you are calculating the cost of equity as one of the inputs in order to calculate equity value.

Fortunately there is an easy way out of our valuation problem. This involves applying the CoC to anticipated asset cash flows and then deducting the value of any liabilities from this in order to arrive at the equity value as the residual figure. This may sound complicated but it is actually quite simple

[2] See pages 50–53.

[3] Economic gearing is the ratio of the market value of debt to the market value of debt plus the market value of equity. If debt is floating rate then its market value should equal its book value. The market value of equity, however, is unlikely to be equal to its book value and it should usually be higher.

and is well supported by theory. I will explain the theory next and I will demonstrate the approach via practical examples in the following section.

The theory is based on the so called Modigliani Miller proposition 1[4] which states that the CoC does not change as the company changes its gearing. This means we can apply the same CoC to all years in our financial model as long as we are discounting cash flows which have been calculated before any finance effects. The cost of equity, by contrast, changes every time the gearing level changes.

What I propose to do in the rest of this review of the theory is explain some potential concerns with the approach and show how these can all be squared with the view that using a value-based approach is a good way to assess the value of a share. My aim will be to build sufficient confidence in the economic value model such that we should therefore trust ourselves to it when we seek for the rational analysis answer to what investments a company should make. My reason for stressing the doubts that do exist is to emphasise the need to combine judgement with this analysis and to avoid what I consider to be spurious precision.

Problem number 1: The relationship between cash flow and dividends

If the value of a share is set by its dividends, why do we value a project or an entire company by its after-tax cash flow? I have already explained that we need to do this in order to get around the problem of not knowing what cost of equity to apply to future dividends. There are, however, more substantive reasons for doing this which go to the heart of how we carry out valuations. The approach is right, not simply necessary!

The primary reason is explained by thinking of any company as having a pool of finance that it can use. Paying dividends is just one thing the company can do with money in this pool. It can also invest in projects or repay debt. The pool is usually filled with cash flow generated by the business but, when necessary, it is added to by borrowings or cash raised from the sale of new shares. Now if a company is wound up, any money that is left over after third party claims are settled belongs to shareholders. This means that the marginal dollar in the finance pool, in effect, already belongs to the shareholder.

This is the vital point to understand. Money within a company should be thought of as though it already belongs to the shareholders. The decision to

[4] This was explained on page 53.

pay some of this money out as a dividend is, from a shareholder's perspective, simply a transfer of money from one pocket to another.

The shareholder trusts that any money invested by the company will earn at least the relevant CoC.[5] So if money is not paid out by the company, it is invested and earns at least the CoC. Now the present value of the future cash flows generated from a dollar that is invested, and that will earn the CoC, is exactly a dollar. So shareholders should be indifferent between receiving a dollar in dividend today and having that dollar invested by the company if the investment earns the CoC.

The presumption regarding dividends is that companies only pay them if this does not restrict the availability of funds to invest in projects that would earn above the CoC. Dividends are therefore considered to be an alternative to the company's investing and earning just the CoC. So a company either pays a dividend or invests in such a way that the present value of the future cash flows is exactly equal to the dividend that would otherwise have been paid. So a company can be valued by either its future cash flows or its future dividends. The same answer should be obtained either way.

Once the idea of a finance pool *within* a company but, in terms of its economic effect, already belonging to shareholders is accepted, the rest falls easily into place. The value calculation first becomes possible and then it becomes logical.

The logic goes like this:

- We value projects through their cash flows.
- A company can be thought of as being simply the sum of its projects.
- All cash flows can be thought of as flowing into and out of the company's pool of finance.
- So the sum of the values of its current and future projects should equal the value of the company.
- The additivity of value must therefore mean that a company is worth the sum of the cash flows from all of its projects.
- This in turn will be equal to its full future cash flow.
- So long as dividends are not paid out at the expense of investing in what would have been positive NPV projects, the valuation of the company via either its future dividend stream or its future cash flow stream should give the same result.

[5] The relevant cost of capital is the appropriate return in relation to the risks inherent in the particular investment.

Problem number 2: Prices are set in the market

What I am referring to here is that prices are actually set by the balance between buy orders and sell orders. So, an order to sell is given but it can only be executed if a matching buyer can be found. An unmatched sell order will push down the price until a buyer emerges who will buy at that new lower price. Likewise, an unmatched buy order will push up the share price. This suggests that it is supply and demand that sets the share price.

Consider, for example, a situation that is based on what was happening to share prices on the day I wrote this. Within about half an hour of the market opening the quoted price of the British bank Alliance & Leicester had risen by about 1.7%. Could its future cash flows really have changed by this much in just 30 minutes? Strict adherents to the economic value model would say that yes, this is possible. They would argue that new information had become available and that this is why the share price had risen. The fact that we started first thing in the morning means that actually there was a longer period in which the information could come to light. Well, my view is that it might be down to new information but it is more likely to be what some people call 'market noise'. It was just that on the day there were plenty of buyers and the price had to rise in order to tempt some new sellers into the market.

The view that I take is that you do not have to believe that a strict application of the economic value model is always behind what sets the share price. The economic value model can be of great use as long as one is prepared to accept that it underpins the share price. The value approach does not always have to be applied for it to be of use. Indeed, I suggest that it usually is not. I base this on a simple experiment which I have repeated many times. I ask people who have just bought or sold a share whether they carried out a valuation or whether they simply trusted the market and paid or received the going rate per share. The overwhelming majority of answers are to the effect that people simply trust the market. So why should anybody believe a model that almost nobody appears to use?

My answer is that the model works because of a tendency called 'mean reversion'. This refers to a situation where something that is not in line with where it 'should' be is subject to forces that will push it back towards this 'correct' figure. This, I suggest, is the best way to think about what sets the share price. The economic value model simply sets where share prices should be and they fluctuate around this in response to buy and sell orders. The value model depends on assumptions even if you do use it and we know that many people in the market do not. So it would not, in my view, be logical to assume that it always applied. Is it, though, logical to assume that economic value can provide the 'mean' in a 'mean reverting' model? The answer here is a resounding 'yes'.

To illustrate this effect consider what may happen following a series of favourable reports about a particular company. If lots of people read the reports the price could rise without limit because there would be many more potential buyers than sellers. Two things can limit the movement. First, smart financial traders who have read the same reports might anticipate an over-reaction and so sell shares into the rising market in anticipation of buying them back later when people realised that the price had risen too high and the price trend was reversed. Second, sooner or later the people who write the influential reports must take an objective view and question whether the price premium that has opened up compared with a similar company is justified even given the favourable outlook.[6]

Now if individual shares become overvalued they will fairly quickly stand out. What, however, stops the market overall getting too high or too low? Again I suggest that sooner or later the situation will become apparent and the consensus will change and reversion to the mean will come about. When the market gets too high the overall price-to-cash flow can only be justified if one makes more and more optimistic assumptions. With the perpetuity model there are, after all, only two variables that set the required value to cash flow ratio. These are growth and CoC. High multiples mean either high growth, which ultimately must become unbelievable, or low CoC, which ultimately must become unacceptable in relation to the risks. So, sooner or later, investors will react to this and the market will fall. Markets have seen many bubbles but they always burst![7] This, to me, is the evidence that I need to convince me that market prices are not always set by value but they cannot stay too far away for too long.

I have not 'proved' in these few pages that share prices are subject to mean-reverting forces based on the economic value model setting the mean. I simply state that this is conventional thinking and that my experiences strongly support this view. I will therefore act as though it is true.

[6] A price premium would be when a share price offered a greater multiple of cash flow than a peer company. So with a CoC of say 9% and an anticipated growth rate for the sector of 3%, one would anticipate a value-to-cash flow ratio of $1 \div 0.06 = 16.7$. If the favourable prospects for our company were such as to add 1% to its future growth potential its cash flow multiple should rise to $1 \div 0.05 = 20$. So a share price rise of 20% would be justified, but anything greater should cause a subsequent downward revision when the influential writers suggest the share is overvalued.

[7] If you are not aware of the many bubbles that have risen and then burst I suggest you read about them, for example in the book *Manias, Panics and Crashes* by Charles Kindleberger.

Problem number 3: Uncertainty

One of the apparent biggest problems with the economic value approach is the way that it deals with uncertainty. My initial concern was that the approach was not intuitive and hence caused problems when I tried to blend judgement with rational analysis. Any accusation of being 'non-intuitive' is to me of huge importance because the method of judgement based on rational analysis places so much importance on human intuition. I do, though, now have two answers to this problem. I also have a minor concern about uncertainty itself and the fact that we do not know for sure how uncertain our estimates of cash flow are. I have an answer to this concern as well and will give this in the final paragraph of this subsection.

First, it is important to remind ourselves what the economic value model says about uncertainty and to test these conclusions against our intuition. There are four main elements to this:

1. The model uses the term risk but it really means uncertainty because so many people associate risk only with nasty outcomes.
2. The approach presumes that the company concerned is sufficiently strong to take the potential downside financial risks without being diverted in its course. Any losses caused in the project being considered must not be such as to interfere with other value-creating opportunities elsewhere in the company.
3. The future cash flows that should be discounted to the present in order to calculate NPV must be expected-value cash flows; that is to say, they are probability weighted numbers.
4. Risk is reflected in the use of an appropriate CoC. This increases as risk increases but only to the extent that the risk is not diversifiable when viewed through the eyes of a diversified shareholder. So, as far as the value model is concerned, and in relation to setting the CoC, some uncertain events are risk free.

I know from many conversations that item 4 is what makes risk appear to be non-intuitive. 'How can it be', I am asked, 'that 100 ± 10 might be considered to be more risky than 100 ± 150 just because the 150 was fully diversifiable but the ten was not?'. It is items 1–3 that point towards the answer. We are not just thinking about the downside, we are allowing for upsides as well. Furthermore, we are doing this on the assumption that those exposed to the risks are financially strong enough to live with the downside consequences for long enough for the smoothing effect of a portfolio to work its magic. So a fully diversifiable ±150 will gradually go away as bets are spread whereas the ±10 will not if it is undiversifiable.

This is not intuitive to many individuals because intuition is based on our personal ability to take risk. We have to leave these personal views behind when we consider risk within a company environment. Once one can become accustomed to four steps, one can accept that portfolio diversification benefits should inform our intuition. The four steps are:

1. Companies take decisions on behalf of shareholders;
2. Shareholders invest in many companies;
3. Each company takes many risks;
4. One does not have to take exactly the same type of risk to spread one's bets.

The scale of the non-intuitive nature of risk in the corporate environment can be illustrated via many TV game shows. In one particular show a contestant was asked to choose between two boxes, one of which contained £3,000 while the other contained £250,000.[8] At this point the 'banker' calls the show and offers the contestant £45,000 in return for not progressing. This figure is £81,500 less than the contestant's expected value outcome. It does, however, create enormous drama because, to the viewers and more importantly to the contestant, the chance of losing money has now come in. The wrong choice could 'cost' the contestant £42,000 because she would leave the show with just £3,000, as opposed to the certain £45,000 if she had accepted the offer. The banker is well aware of this and knows that most people would never dare take a 50% chance of losing £42,000. If £42,000 was already a life-changing amount, your intuition would scream at you to take it. In the event the contestant said 'no deal', she chose the right box and so scooped the top prize.

Talk about this situation with friends and many will say that they would not have dared to reject the banker's offer. They are right, because they are thinking about playing the game as an individual. It would be so different if they played it on behalf of a large corporation. For a start, there would be no show! The show is all about human emotion and not big companies grinding out efficiency.

So the first answer to the 'non-intuitive' challenge is that it is intuitive once you accept that the full risk story within a company context has four steps. There is also a second answer which I think works on its own.

[8] The exchange rate when I wrote this section was about $2 = £1. The contestant was called Laura Pearce.

To explain this I must ask readers to return to the checkout example from earlier in this section. Imagine turning up at a checkout and discovering that every time a new item was rung up on the till the price of the previous purchases changed and furthermore the prices did not fall as you bought more, they increased! How could this possibly be justified? Well, let us say that you are purchasing shares and that the till, knowing what the future dividend prospects were and the volatility of these prospects, was charging you a fair price. When you purchase just one share the volatility is high and so the till, which is programmed to charge you value, would assume that your purchase is very risky. A risky purchase demands a high discount rate. The future prospects are fixed, so the selling price must be low. If you were foolish enough to present, say, ten different shares to the till operator, the volatility of your shopping basket would have gone down thanks to the portfolio effect. So you would have to pay more! Now people would pretty soon work this out and buy just one share at a time.

It is, to me at least, self-evident that life cannot work out like that. Looking at volatility in isolation must be wrong even though it may seem intuitive. So perhaps we must recognise that sometimes, when it comes to risk, our initial intuition is wrong. So when we exercise judgement based on rational analysis in relation to risk, we need to do so with great care.

Finally I will turn to my 'uncertain uncertainty' concern. I start from a position that maintains that I do not accept that anybody can know what the uncertainty is that surrounds future cash flows. History does not have to repeat itself and we should not consider that we know what future uncertainty will be. I take the view that part of what the risk element of the CoC is rewarding is the uncertainty about risk itself. So there need be no problem with unknown risk as long as we accept that it is allowed for in the way that the CoC is set. I will be giving a more thorough review of how we incorporate risk in the discount rate at the start of the final section of this book.

Problem number 4: I know a professor with a better idea!

There are competing explanations regarding what sets the share price. Some of these simply concern how the CoC is set. Others concern how risk should be incorporated into cash flows. At least these explanations might accept the basic application of discounted cash flow. Yet further approaches suggest treating equity as an option and valuing it via sophisticated options evaluation techniques that do not use DCF at all. Yes indeed, there are many professors with 'better ideas'!

Why, though, did I place 'better ideas' in inverted commas? My answer is that I doubt that many are indeed 'better'; they are often, in my opinion, just different. Now I do not hold the economic value model in such high regard as to suggest that it cannot ever be replaced with a better approach. I do, though, believe that any replacement must be practical and must mimic many of the key features of the economic value model. This is because the value model seems to work so well. Finally, any new approach must, I suggest, recognise the uncertainty that exists about uncertainty.

In my view far too much focus is placed by some academics on the mathematical derivation of approaches which only give enhanced accuracy if we know what future uncertainty will be. Since this is, in my view, unknowable in relation to financial markets that respond to human buy and sell orders, any additional accuracy claimed for new models is, once again, in my opinion, specious.

What is always possible is that new approaches will give different views on particular situations. We will see later in this book how the approach to valuing financial options has been widely accepted and as a result has seen a huge growth in application in that arena. Other techniques may arise that will work in some new areas. It is possible that these will one day replace the economic value model. At present, however, the value model has what could be termed a huge market share when it comes to making major financial decisions. This means that we are safe in using it. No individual or company that acted on the presumption that value was set by the present value of future dividends would be open to criticism for so doing if at some future time a better approach emerged.

What I am trying to convey is that perhaps we should never expect to gain a fully accurate answer. We are dealing with the actions of people and so it would be foolish to view value as anything other than 'just a model'. We know that people generally do not apply the model to each transaction they carry out; they simply trust market forces to give them a fair price. Even if they did apply the model each time, they would have to make many assumptions and so there would never be a unique right answer as to what the share price should be at any particular moment in time. So some noise surrounding the economic value model is inevitable. It is, however, the best thing that we have at the moment so we should use it and not debate it!

The rest of this pillar will be devoted to this topic. I take the view that a search for absolute accuracy via new approaches is less useful than a search for better insights with the current model. This is what the Sources of Value section of this book is trying to do. It offers new insights from the tried and (I hope) trusted value model.

Part 2: Calculating value

Overview

The usual approach to calculating the implied share price involves four main steps. These are as follows:

1. Calculate the plan period asset value.
2. Calculate the present value of the terminal value.
3. Assess the value of any liabilities.
4. Divide the net value of items 1–3 by the number of shares.

This gives the implied share price. I use the term 'implied' simply to emphasise that the actual share price on the market will not necessary be equal to this number. This will be the number that acts as the mean in my suggested mean-reverting model for share prices. I will use the term 'calculated share price' to represent this value for the remainder of this book.

I will go through each step in some detail and then highlight some short cut approaches. Short cuts are, I believe, highly useful because they can force decision-makers to focus on just a few key assumptions which together account for the calculated share price. This can be more honest than having a long list of assumptions and a large calculation because these can imply a degree of precision which is not always justified. I will finish by introducing a new valuation method that I have devised. I have given this method the snappy title of ABCDE valuation.

I will use two main examples in this section. These are the real life example of Corus PLC and my hypothetical company Yellow Moon Chemical Company Inc. I will use Corus to demonstrate the short cut approach for the very practical reason that I lack any specific detail about this company. YMCC will be used for the more detailed examples because I can always make up any necessary detail here. I suggest that readers familiarise themselves with these two companies at this point.

Corus is covered on pages 88–97. Readers should recall how I started with the full accounting data and then placed this into abbreviated financial summary (AFS) format. I will be referring back to the full data when I work on Step 3 of the share price valuation. All that is available, however, is historical data for the year 2005. This will allow me to demonstrate how, through making assumptions, one can still come up with a valuation. I will eventually show how such assumptions could explain the price that was paid by Tata Steel when it purchased Corus.

YMCC has already made several appearances in this book. It appears first on pages 244–252. At this stage I included a simple value calculation. We will now have the opportunity to study this in more detail and, I believe, to come up with some more justifiable numbers. YMCC also returned during the Sources of Value pillar on pages 304–308. I will draw on this analysis when I consider how to incorporate future growth projects into a company valuation as part of my ABCDE valuation.

The most important step in this section will concern the calculation of terminal value (TV). This is because this almost always contributes the lion's share of the calculated share price and also because it contains a range of new techniques.

Step 1: Calculating plan period asset value

The plan period asset value is equal to the present value of the after-tax funds flows that the company will generate. These funds flows need to exclude the impact of any financing effects and should be expected values. This first part is greatly simplified if our plan is already presented in the format of the AFS because this is specifically designed to highlight the relevant numbers. One of the reasons that I place so much emphasis on the AFS is the way that it makes the value calculation so clear.

A second reason for using the AFS format is the way that it works both for plans and project evaluation. If all of our data are structured in this way it is much easier to do things like exclude a project from a set of plan cash flows. We will come to why we might want to do this shortly.

We have already seen on page 25 how to value a set of plan period cash flows but I will repeat the approach here. This should also remind us once again what the AFS for YMCC looks like:

YMCC Inc: Valuation of plan period cash flows $m

	2009	2010	2011	2012	2013
Sales revenue	76.1	78.7	82.7	87.7	93.0
Variable costs	–21.5	–22.5	–23.5	–25.3	–27.3
Contribution	54.6	56.2	59.2	62.4	65.7
Fixed costs	–30.0	–31.8	–35.7	–36.6	–37.5
Amortisation	–6.0	–5.7	–7.6	–7.7	–7.8
Pre-tax profit	18.6	18.8	15.9	18.1	20.4
Tax	–6.5	–6.6	–5.6	–6.3	–7.1
Net profit	12.1	12.2	10.3	11.8	13.3

Table (*cont.*)

	2009	2010	2011	2012	2013
Fixed assets	67.0	90.1	86.2	82.7	79.5
Accounts receivable	19.0	19.7	20.7	21.9	23.3
Accounts payable	−12.6	−13.7	−10.7	−11.4	−12.2
Inventories	8.6	9.1	9.9	10.3	10.8
Net working capital	15.0	15.1	19.9	20.8	21.8
Capital employed	82.0	105.1	106.1	103.5	101.3
ROACE	17.4%	13.0%	9.8%	11.2%	13.0%
Profit	12.1	12.2	10.3	11.8	13.3
Amortisation	6.0	5.7	7.6	7.7	7.8
Working cap	1.3	0.0	−4.8	−0.9	−1.0
Capital investment	−23.0	−28.7	−3.7	−4.1	−4.6
Funds flow	−3.6	−10.9	9.4	14.4	15.5
Funds flow	−3.6	−10.9	9.4	14.4	15.5
Discount factor	0.958	0.879	0.806	0.740	0.679
PV funds flows	−3.5	−9.6	7.5	10.6	10.5
Cumulative PV	−3.5	−13.1	−5.5	5.1	15.6

The value has been calculated as at the beginning of 2009 and cash flows are all assumed to occur in mid-year. We can deduce this from the first year's discount factor of 0.958 which is the 9% CoC discount factor for first-year cash flows. The cumulative present value is just $15.6m. This low number is due to the initial-year negative funds flows caused by the capital investment programme. This is a typical picture to emerge from a long-term plan.

Now this valuation can be viewed as a purely mechanical exercise. Indeed the numbers will work in this way but the answer is certainly subject to what practitioners call the 'GIGO effect'. GIGO stands for 'garbage in equals garbage out'. If the numbers are based on poor assumptions, or worse are simply wrong, then the value too will be poor or wrong. So the most important part of the valuation of plan period cash flows is to check the assumptions and also to ensure that the model has been audited and is faithfully converting the assumptions into the correct cash flow.

The checking of assumptions covers three aspects. First, confirmation that assumptions are expected values. Second, identification of any considerations that should influence the TV calculation. Finally, confirmation that the starting year of the plan does line up with published accounting data. All of these aspects are important.

As regards the first, the calculated share price needs to be based on expected value assumptions if it is to represent the implied market value of the company. So if, for example, the valuation was deemed to represent a success case rather than an expected value, the answer would need to be adjusted in order to arrive at the right expected value of plan period cash flows. This could be done in one of three ways. Either all of the assumptions would need to be adjusted back to expected value levels. Or an alternative downside case (or cases) would be computed and a probability-weighted approach applied. The expected value would be the probability-weighted outcome of valuing the various success and failure cases.[9] The remaining method would involve use of a Monte Carlo-based approach with all important assumptions assigned probability distributions. My usual recommendation is to adopt the first approach and simply ensure that all assumptions have a reasonable balance of upside and downside.

As regards the second effect, the aim is to identify assumptions which will have a particular impact on the TV. We will see in the next part that the usual input to a TV calculation is the post-tax cash flow in the final year of the plan. So any distortion in the final year will be magnified through the way that we calculate TV. If, for example, there is a heavy spend in the final years of the plan aimed at starting a new project then it would be important to ensure that the TV reflected the benefit of this. The alternative would be to exclude such costs from the plan and to deal with the value of growth projects as a separate calculation. Distortions are not just concerned with excluding significant one-off costs. They can also occur if insufficient allowance is made for sustaining investment, in which case additional costs would need to be included in the assessment of the steady state funds flow figure which will feed into the terminal value calculation.

I will illustrate these adjustments later in this section in Step 2 where I calculate the TV. For the present, however, we will simply assume that the final year of the plan does not contain any unusual or one-off effects that would otherwise distort the valuation.

As regards the check that the plan is consistent with published accounting data, one might well simply have assumed that this would be the case. Experience, however, warns of the fact that this will not always be true. The main reason for this is that a plan is usually agreed close to the end of a year whereas the accounts may not be available until some months into the following

[9] Suppose, for example, that the figure of \$15.6m as the plan period cash flow value was deemed to be a success case and it was considered that this would come about 60% of the time. If two other cases were identified each with a probability of 20% and these had values of \$10m and \$5m then the expected value of the plan period cash flows would be:

$0.6 \times 15.6 + 0.2 \times 10 + 0.2 \times 5 = \$12.4m.$

year. We will almost certainly need to use the accounts to establish the value of any liabilities as part of Step 3. Now my presentation above lacks this anchor in published data and so is deficient. I always recommend that where numbers are being used 'for real' they should be what I call 'anchored' in the reality of published accounting data. We will see how to do this with the Corus example.

One of the typical things that need to be allowed for as part of this third check concerns when a plan is prepared on the assumption that some capital spend will be completed before the plan period starts. If this is not done and the spend carries over into the plan period, the plan must be adjusted. Another item that will very often need to be checked is the working capital level. The difference in working capital between reality and the assumptions made in a plan that is finished a few weeks ahead of the year end can be considerable.

I need to conclude this consideration of Step 1 with a discussion of what time period needs to be covered by the plan. A lot must depend on the amount of detail which is available concerning the anticipated future financial performance of the company. One should only prepare a plan for the period during which it is meaningful to make assumptions about what its component parts will be. The further one looks into the future the more the plan is likely to become simply a series of steady-state assumptions. Once these assumptions are producing a steady trend in the post-tax funds flow one might as well substitute a terminal value for the full plan. To do otherwise would, I believe, be misleading to any decision maker.[10]

What can happen, though, is that although several items are being projected to follow a steady-state path, the overall post-tax funds flow may not do this because, say, one or two items have not yet reached their steady state. A typical example of this would concern a business that was utilising past tax losses and so was paying virtually no tax in the early years of a plan. In such a situation the post-tax funds flow would not follow a steady-state path until the losses were used up. So the plan would ideally cover at least this initial period plus, say, one or two years of steady-state performance at the end of the period. This can lead to pressure to adopt very long plan periods. My general advice is to avoid these because although they may appear to add precision, I become increasingly nervous that the assumptions are success-case outcomes and not expected values. In my view, five years is generally long enough.

[10] Imagine telling a decision-maker that you have included a TV only at the end of a ten-year plan period. This sounds as though you know a lot about the future prospects of the company. If, however, all you have is a one-year plan and you have then assumed that everything stays constant in real terms then the remaining nine years of your ten-year plan are contributing nothing different to the valuation than using a TV after year 1.

I should point out at this stage that this suggestion of the adoption of a relatively short period of specific cash flow forecasts is at odds with the approach recommended by the standard valuation texts. As I have already pointed out, these stress the accuracy of valuation and as a result they do suggest use of longer plan periods such as 10–15 years. My view is that this encourages a misplaced belief in the accuracy of numbers. There are times when a long plan period should be used but my suggestion is that this should be the exception rather than the rule.

Step 2: Calculating the present value of the terminal value

This step involves calculating the TV and then discounting it to the present so that it can subsequently be added into the overall share price valuation. Up to now we have simply assumed that the TV is set through the growth to perpetuity approach. In this part I will consider various variants of the perpetuity approach and then give several other methods as well. The full list of methods which I will cover is:

1. Funds flow to perpetuity
2. Growth adjusted profit
3. Overview adjusted profit
4. Sustainable return on capital
5. Two-stage growth to perpetuity
6. Specified company life
7. Life of asset
8. Trading multiple
9. Book value
10. Liquidation

Clearly the list is very long. The skill is to pick an appropriate method for the circumstances. I have used all of these methods at one time or another in the past and there is no 'right answer'. I will review each method and try to point towards their strengths and weaknesses. Readers who are not likely immediately to become involved in calculating a TV might want to skim read this section in order to become aware of the range of techniques that are available. They could then return at some later date and consider them thoroughly if/when they need to apply them themselves.

The traditional **funds flow to perpetuity** formula is as follows:

$$TV = \frac{\text{Funds Flow} \times (1 + \text{Growth})}{(\text{Cost of Capital} - \text{Growth})}$$

This would give the value as at the end of the plan period where the final year funds flow is expected to grow at a fixed rate of growth to perpetuity. The calculation assumes that the first funds flow in the post-plan period occurs one year after the end of the plan. If the plan has assumed mid-year cash flows the value will be as at the middle of the final year. In either case the discount factor to apply to the TV in order to calculate its present value is the same as the discount rate which is applied to the funds flow in the final year of the plan.

This formula was used in the initial valuation of the YMCC plan shown earlier. The growth assumption was zero and so the TV factor was one divided by the 9% CoC or 11.1. With a final year funds flow of \$15.5m the TV was \$172.1m and the present value of this was \$116.8m. Had the growth assumption been changed to a steady decline of 1% pa the TV would have fallen to \$155.0m. If we had decided for some reason that 4% growth was achievable, the TV would have risen to \$310.0m.

What we must all be aware of is that the TV formula is right only if the assumptions are reasonable. The key, in my view, is to confirm that the assumptions are indeed acceptable and to adjust as necessary.

My greatest concern with this approach is the way that it appears that the growth assumption can be changed independently from the funds flow assumption. This is exactly what I did in the simple illustrations above. To do this, however, would be to defy what I refer to as 'financial gravity'. This is illustrated in the following example.

If we consider the final year of the YMCC plan we can see that capital investment is expected to be \$4.6m whereas amortisation is \$7.8m. The result is that the book value of fixed assets declines from \$82.7m to \$79.5m. Quite clearly this cannot go on for ever, yet a simple perpetuity assumption of zero growth in the post-plan period would assume that it did. I have a better method to offer and this will allow for the investment in fixed assets and working capital that is necessary to facilitate the assumed rate of growth.

I call my method the **growth adjusted profit** method. It depends on the relationship that:

$$\text{Funds Flow} = \text{Profit} - \text{Growth} \times \text{Capital Employed}$$

So, rather than take the final year's funds flow from the plan, we can take the final year's profit and subtract from it growth times capital employed. This will then automatically adjust funds flow for different rates of growth. So, in the YMCC case the approach used in the earlier chapters had calculated the TV from the final year's funds flow of \$15.5m times the TV factor which, thanks to the assumed rate of growth being 0% and the CoC 9%, was 11.1.

So we had a TV of $172.1m. The adjusted profit method would take the final year's profit of $13.3m, subtract nothing for growth[11] and then multiply by the TV factor of 11.1. The TV would have fallen to $147.5m.

An equation such as the growth adjusted profit method can easily be programmed into a spreadsheet model and this is, I believe, better than using the traditional funds flow growth to perpetuity method.

What this method is doing is to allow for the investments in fixed assets and working capital that are necessary in order to facilitate growth. It can also allow for the reductions in fixed assets and working capital that follow from a steady shrinkage in size. This will go a good part of the way towards meeting the concern that I have with the traditional growth to perpetuity method that appears to allow growth rates to be set independently from funds flow.

A related method that I call the **overview adjusted profit** method requires the analyst to make a specific estimate of two further items in order to arrive at an even better estimate of the funds flow figure which is consistent with the assumed rate of growth. The first stage of this requires use of an estimated steady-state capital employed figure to be used in the calculation rather than simply using the capital employed as at the end of the plan period. It is possible, for example, that the final year of a plan has a particularly high capital employed figure and using this as the basis for setting value may be inappropriate. In the YMCC example the final-year capital employed was $101.3m. This is still high owing to the heavy capital investment in the early years of the plan. We might want to decide that the steady-state capital employed figure to use in calculating the adjustment to profit was, say, $90m. If we were to do this the valuation with 1% growth would involve deducting $0.9m from the final-year profit to arrive at the sustainable funds flow of $12.4m.[12]

The second adjustment to profit makes an allowance for any fixed costs which are necessary in order to facilitate the assumed rate of growth. These fixed costs would need to cover, for example, the cost of any project development teams or brand development or R&D effort, all of which will contribute towards growth. I should stress that the adjustment may well serve to increase the steady-state funds flow to above the final year's profit figure. This is because plans often allow for high growth rates and so have built into them the costs

[11] Because the growth assumption was for zero growth. If we had wanted to assume, say, 1% growth we would have subtracted 1% of the $101.3m capital employed from profit, i.e. $1m. The sustainable funds flow would have fallen to $12.3m and the implied TV would be $155.3m.

[12] We would complete the calculation by multiplying this by 1.01 and dividing by 0.08. The TV would be $156.5m.

of the various development activities. If the TV assumption is that growth is reduced to only nominal levels then it can be reasonable to strip quite significant costs out of the plan's final year as we seek to establish a good estimate of sustainable funds flow consistent with the assumed rate of growth. It simply has to be left to the analyst to ensure that the costs which are implicit in the plan are consistent with the assumed rate of growth to perpetuity. The numbers assumed, however, are specifically highlighted as assumptions alongside the steady-state capital employed and so are brought to the attention of senior decision makers rather than left as implicit assumptions.

The problem with this method is that it does require judgement and cannot simply be included as a standard part of the valuation methodology but the assumptions are made explicit to decision-takers and hence overall I believe this is the best method introduced so far.

The **sustainable return on capital** method is another variant on the perpetuity valuation formula that also automatically adjusts for the consequence of having to subtract growth times capital employed from profit in order to arrive at funds flow. It depends on the accounting relationship that:

$$\text{Funds Flow} = \text{Profit} - \text{Growth} \times \text{Capital Employed}$$

If one then substitutes this relationship for funds flow in the original TV formula the logic can be worked through to an equation that I like to call 'the magic formula' because it looks so amazing![13] The formula is:

$$\frac{\text{TV}}{\text{Book Value}} = \frac{(\text{Return on Capital} - \text{Growth})}{(\text{Cost of Capital} - \text{Growth})}$$

Now the terminal value divided by book value is equal to a ratio that is called the market-to-book ratio. If this is greater than 1 a company has created value whereas if it is less than 1 a company must have destroyed value.

We can test this approach on the YMCC plan. The final-year capital employed is \$101.3 and the ROCE in that year was 13.0%. If we assume this is maintained to perpetuity with 1% growth the market-to-book ratio would be 0.12 ÷ 0.08 = 1.5, so the TV would be \$152.0m. This is very close to the figures which I calculated using the two adjusted profit methods.

[13] The derivation goes as follows:

TV = funds flow ÷ (CoC – growth). (I am ignoring the small (1 + growth) part of the numerator.)
But funds flow = profit – growth × capital employed.
Hence funds flow ÷ capital employed = return on capital – growth.
Hence TV ÷ capital employed = (return on capital – growth) ÷ (CoC – growth).

What I particularly like about this approach is the way that the assumptions are explained in ways that are easily tested against benchmarking data. One of my earlier TV calculations had suggested that 4% growth could equate with a TV of \$310m. We can use the sustainable return on capital formula to calculate what return on capital is implied by this TV and then see if this is consistent with what we believe the company's performance might be. The TV is a market-to-book ratio of 3.06. Given that the CoC is 9% and the growth assumption which gave us the \$310m TV was 4% we know that:

$$3.06 \times (9-4) = \text{Return on Capital} - 4\%$$

Hence the implied return on capital to perpetuity is 19.3%. In my opinion senior decision-makers will find it easier to decide whether or not they believe a figure such as this rather than a growth assumption of 4% applied to the final-year funds flow. The danger of the method, in my view, is that it can sometimes make the justification of a high TV too easy. Some companies can achieve high returns on capital by sacrificing growth and so it is possible that benchmarking data may even suggest that a company could sustain the above return on capital of 19.3%. What would be difficult would be achieving the return and growing at 4% pa. The formula is good, in my view, only as long as growth rates are low.

I have called the next TV calculation method the **two-stage growth to perpetuity** method. The title should be self explanatory. Rather than assuming a single growth rate to perpetuity, one assumes a two-stage model with, typically, higher growth in the period immediately following the plan period. A new TV is introduced at the end of the first stage, typically based on a much lower growth rate.[14] The approach is best explained via an example.

I will take the YMCC plan and assume 5% growth in funds flow for five years followed by zero growth thereafter. The final-year funds flow was \$15.5m and I will use this figure in this example. Clearly any of the adjusted numbers could have been used as well.

The first step is to calculate what \$15.5m growing at 5% to perpetuity would have been worth. We will then subtract from this the part of this value which is caused by higher growth beyond the fifth year of the post plan period.

\$15.5m growing at 5% is worth:

$$\$15.5 \times (1.05) \div 0.04 = \$406.9\text{m}$$

[14] The second part can even be one of the other methods such as book value or liquidation.

Now after five years the original $15.5m funds flow will have grown by five lots of 5%. So it will be $19.8m. The value of this amount growing at 5% to perpetuity is $519.3m. We want to adjust the growth down to zero. The value of $19.8m with zero growth is $219.8m. So the extra 5% growth beyond year 5 of the post-plan period is contributing $299.5m of value. This figure is five years into the future so its present value is calculated by discounting it for five years at 9%. The present value effect is $194.7m. We need to subtract this from our original $406.9m in order to arrive at our two-stage valuation of $212.2m.[15]

One useful feature of this calculation is that it is not difficult to programme it into a spreadsheet with the two growth rates and the length of the first post-plan growth stage all set as assumptions. There is a second way of doing the calculation which becomes essential if the growth rate in the first post-plan period is greater than the CoC.[16] I call this second method the longhand way. It simply involves calculating the actual funds flows in each year of the first post-plan period and then using a TV formula at the end of this period. The above calculation would have looked like this:

Year	Plan +1	Plan +2	Plan +3	Plan +4	Plan +5
Funds flow	16.3	17.1	17.9	18.8	19.8
Discount factor	0.917	0.842	0.772	0.708	0.650
Present value	14.9	14.4	13.8	13.3	12.9
Cumulative PV	14.9	29.3	43.1	56.4	69.3
TV factor					11.1
TV					219.8
PV TV					142.9
Total value					212.2

There are a few points to note. First and foremost we get exactly the same answer! Small rounding errors can creep in if one relies, as I did, on discount factor tables. The discount factors are all year-end factors because all of the flows are one year apart. In effect what has been done is prepare a second plan covering a further five year period. This is slotted on to the end of the

[15] We can observe, by the way, that the 5% additional growth for five years is adding exactly $40m to the TV.

[16] The perpetuity valuation formula only holds for growth rates below the cost of capital. Value is infinite if growth rates above this are sustained to perpetuity, which is another way of saying that growth rates that high simply cannot go on for ever. They are, however, perfectly possible for, say, five years.

actual plan and a TV is added at the end of the second period. Once again we have to be thankful for the principle of value additivity which allows us to break the calculation down into individual parts which together add up to the number that we want.

This longhand way of doing the sums has the advantage of being easy to follow and it can cope with growth rates of above the CoC. The drawback is the difficulty of doing the sums if a decision is taken to change the length of the first post-plan period.

The next method to explain is the **specified company life** approach. This does what the name suggests! Instead of assuming a company life that spans out to perpetuity, one assumes that after a set number of years the cash generation simply ceases. If no growth is assumed we can then simply use our annuity factor tables. If growth is assumed we apply a variant of the two-stage growth model, only with no second stage.

So, for example, if YMCC continued to generate its final-year funds flow for a further 20 years after the end of the plan period the TV would be 9.129 times the final-year funds flow because this is the 20 year 9% end-year annuity factor. The TV for YMCC would be $141.5m. We can compare this with the perpetuity valuation of $172.2m and note that about 82% of the perpetuity value is realised in the first 20 years after the end of the plan. The remaining 18% is down to funds flows beyond this point.

This approach is useful when there are concerns about the life of a business. These can be related to factors such as the expiry of patents or operating licences. The concerns can also simply be that a business is not of the type that will last a long time.

A similar approach is the **life-of-asset** technique. In effect this avoids using a TV altogether and extends the plan for the full economic life of an asset. This is used in natural resource businesses such as mines and oil fields. The valuation is carried out for the full life of the asset including the effect of shutdown and remediation costs. The technique only works for situations where full life-of-asset models already exist and where these add up to the total operation of a company. I would only consider building a new life-of-asset model from scratch if this was part of an investigation of a possible purchase of a company or if I was an analyst reviewing a company which had a single very significant asset like a mine or an oil field. Life-of-asset models are, however, usually built as a matter of course in extraction companies as part of the project approval process.

Larger companies may well comprise combinations of businesses, some of which should be valued this way while others are more amenable to the usual plan period plus TV approach. What one does here is break the business down into its component parts and value each in a suitable way. So mines and oil fields might be valued using a life-of-asset approach while the other businesses are valued via one or other of the above approaches.

The **trading multiple** approach is very different from anything considered so far although its roots will still lie in economic value calculations. The idea is to identify the value of similar operations that are either traded on stock exchanges or have recently been sold for a known price. The value is then related to some key parameters such as profit, sales revenue, cash flow or capital employed. The average market multiple for several known situations can then be used to set the TV for the company that is being valued. This method can be said to be rooted in economic value because the assumption is that the valuations of the other companies were set by considerations related to value.

This is quite a common approach but my own view is that it should serve as a check on other valuations and not be the main means of setting a TV. There are several reasons for this. First it assumes that the company being valued is average when it may well not be. Furthermore, it assumes that the current market multiple will still apply at the point in the future when the TV is required. Now growing businesses will attract high current market multiples as a reflection of their high immediate growth prospects. In, say, five years' time, however, the prospects are unlikely still to look as good because five of those years of high growth will already have occurred. So future growth prospects should be lower, which would suggest a lower trading multiple. Once one starts to make adjustments such as this one might as well use one of the other methods which can be tailored to a company's specific situation.

The time to use this technique would be when one had only very limited data on a company and wanted an order-of-magnitude valuation perhaps as part of an initial screening exercise. So, I could envisage using it as part of my evaluation of Corus since I know so little about this company.

Perhaps the simplest TV to use is the accounting **book value**. This can give a good estimate of value for a business that is only earning about its CoC. Accounting conventions are such that companies that are considered by their directors to be worth less than book value should reduce their book value to the estimated value. This means that book value should always serve as a lower limit on the value of companies that are going concerns. In the case of the YMCC example the book value based TV would be \$101.3m which is well below the other values.

My general view is that I would only recommend use of book value in one of two situations. First, where the business was expected to earn returns only about equal to the CoC and second, as a TV at the end of a two-stage growth model where the first stage had lasted for quite a considerable period and I was concerned that going beyond this was questionable.

This is not to suggest that companies cannot be worth less than book value. I have already argued when I introduced the Sources of Value technique that many companies fail to earn their CoC. At least some of these companies will be doing so badly as to be worth less than book value.[17]

The lowest TV to use corresponds to **liquidation**. This can even be negative if there are shutdown and remediation costs to take into account. A liquidation value would assume that a business was terminated and that any remaining assets were, in effect, sold for scrap and that the first use of any inflows of cash would be to pay off the staff and return any land to its pre-investment state. A simple way to model this would be to assume a cash inflow equal to the book value of just working capital. For YMCC this would be just $21.8m. One other asset which will usually have a significant 'scrap' value is land. The liquidation approach already allows for the costs of returning land to its original state and so it should certainly not be considered as scrap. I suggest that the original purchase price of land adjusted for inflation should be used as an estimate of the liquidation value of land.

Having established the TV which is to be used it is then necessary to discount it to the valuation date. This can be either the present, if the aim is to calculate today's share price, or it can be the beginning of the company year if one is valuing a plan. Most of the valuation techniques provide the TV as at the date of the final-year funds flow which would usually be mid-year. The liquidation and book value approaches, however, place the TV at the end of the final year of the plan.

My suggested approach is to double-check the methodology that is used to calculate the TV in order to ensure that the TV is correctly placed in time. This is another example of ensuring that stated assumptions are faithfully converted into value. There will usually be two choices with TV located either in the middle of the final year of the plan or at the end.[18] The difference between the two will usually be half a year's worth of discounting. This

[17] 'Why do they not write down their assets?', one might well ask. I can only assume that their directors and accountants are prepared to believe that things will get better in the future!

[18] I only say 'usually' because liquidation may take some time and so may well be assumed to occur say one year after the end of the plan.

may seem small but given that the TV is usually by far the largest part of the overall value, one does not want to introduce an error of say 4–5% if this can easily be avoided. Although I do not suggest that valuation numbers are this accurate, I do suggest that errors of this magnitude should be avoided when it is easy to do so.

Step 3: Assess the value of any liabilities

We have now learned how to calculate the asset value of a company. This has excluded the effect of financing items such as debt and leases. The calculation will usually have excluded the effect of other liabilities such as, for example, future unfunded pension liabilities. Clean-up costs may also not have been covered in the valuation although they will have been if a liquidation valuation was used.

The necessary information about a company's liabilities is usually found in its published balance sheet. The approach required is simple and methodical. Each liability is identified and then tested for whether it is already incorporated in the asset valuation. If it is incorporated, it is ignored in this step. If it is not, then it is added to the list of liabilities. The sum of all liabilities is then deducted from the asset value.

I will illustrate the calculation using data for Corus PLC. We start with the liabilities section of the balance sheet which I have set out below:

Current liabilities		
Short-term borrowings	**(384)**	(379)
Trade and other payables	**(1,844)**	(1,742)
Current tax liabilities	**(79)**	(117)
Other financial liabilities	**(38)**	—
Retirement benefit obligations	**(5)**	(18)
Short-term provisions and other liabilities	**(117)**	(141)
	(2,467)	(2,397)
Non-current liabilities		
Long-term borrowings	**(1,308)**	(1,063)
Deferred tax liabilities	**(126)**	(137)
Retirement benefit obligations	**(436)**	(455)
Provisions for liabilities and charges	**(116)**	(122)
Other non-current liabilities	**(46)**	(26)
Deferred income	**(65)**	(33)
	(2,097)	(1,836)

We then must go through, line by line, to decide what to do. There are only two options. Liabilities are either already included in the asset valuation, in which case we ignore them at this stage, or excluded, in which case we need to allow for them now. The obvious example of the former would be trade and other payables which form part of working capital. As such they are certainly included in the asset valuation already and so are ignored in this stage. If they are excluded from the asset valuation they are added to our list of liabilities. The obvious example of this is any debt. We applied a very similar approach when we placed the Corus accounts into the AFS format and we should make the same judgements now.

Current liabilities	
Short-term borrowings	Not included
Trade and other payables	Included
Current tax liabilities	Included
Other financial liabilities	Not included
Retirement benefit obligations	Not included
Short-term provisions and other liabilities	Included
Non-current liabilities	
Long-term borrowings	Not included
Deferred tax liabilities	Included
Retirement benefit obligations	Not included
Provisions for liabilities and charges	Not included
Other non-current liabilities	Not included
Deferred income	Not included

Although we are dealing with liabilities, it is necessary to check the remainder of the balance sheet to ensure that there are not any assets that are not included in the asset valuation. Although this may sound strange there should usually be at least one asset that falls into this category and this is any cash which is held. Cash is usually netted off against debts in order to arrive at a net debt figure. In the case of Corus there were also assets which were called retirement benefit assets and other financial assets. These are both related to financing and will not have been accounted for in the asset valuation. This final check should also note whether there are any minority interests in the company. If there are then they too need to be allowed for. If these are small we can get away with assuming their value is equal to their book value. If, however, they are large it is necessary to adjust for the economic value of the minority interest. One does not usually have precise data and so it is usual to assume that the same market-to-book ratio applies as applies for the full company.

We finish up, therefore, with the following liabilities in our list:

Short-term borrowings	**(384)**
Other financial liabilities	**(38)**
Retirement benefit obligations	**(5)**
Long-term borrowings	**(1,308)**
Retirement benefit obligations	**(436)**
Provisions for liabilities and charges	**(116)**
Other non-current liabilities	**(46)**
Deferred income	**(65)**
Short-term investments	—
Cash and short-term deposits	**871**
Retirement benefit assets	**157**
Other financial assets	**85**
Minority interests	**26**

We therefore conclude that the net liabilities to allow for amount to £1,259m.

This list may look daunting but as long as one just works item by item through the published balance sheet it should not be too difficult to complete.

My two final pieces of advice are, first, only worry about numbers that are significant. In this case we would certainly not be looking for better accuracy than ±£100m and even this is probably unrealistically accurate. Anything over £500m must, however, be right! My second piece of advice is: when in doubt, seek advice from an accountant, who will be able to explain what each item represents.

Step 4: Divide the net value by the number of shares

We have now almost reached the share price. The present value of the plan period post-tax funds flows plus the present value of the TV gives what is called the asset value. The equity value is the residual after other liabilities are subtracted. This must be divided by the number of shares in issue in order to arrive at the calculated share price. I will illustrate this final step as part of the Corus valuation which follows.

In some circumstances it is necessary to make a final adjustment for any existing share options which have not yet been exercised. These are often not material but if they are, they are usually dealt with by assuming that options which are 'in the money'[19] are exercised. One then simply assumes that the proceeds from their being exercised are added to the equity value and that the number of new shares that this represents is added to the total number of shares in issue.

A more complex approach does exist. This involves using the equation which can value financial options. I will be introducing this equation in one of the later parts of this book. For the present I ask readers to accept that such an equation does exist. We can then, once again, use value additivity to work out what the impact on the share price should be. We know what the options are worth and that this has been excluded from the valuation. Hence all that we need to do is treat this as another prior claim on the asset value of the company like the other liabilities. So we subtract the implied value of unexercised share options from the calculated equity value and divide this by the number of shares currently in issue.

Short cut approaches

The various terminal value calculations should already have pointed readers towards my suggested short cut approaches. My short cuts simply omit the plan step and move straight to the TV. A TV which is applied as at the present is the ultimate short cut.

Doing so can often be justified because the TV already contributes the bulk of the value even after a five year plan period. For example, the initial valuation of YMCC based on the growth to perpetuity approach had a present value of plan period flows of \$15.6m while the present value of the TV was \$116.8m.

I will illustrate several possible short cut valuations for Corus PLC in this section. We should start with the AFS which was as follows:

Income statement	2004	2005
Sales revenue		10,140
Costs		(9,130)
Amortisation		(329)
Pre-tax profit		681
Tax		(151)
Profit		530

[19] An option is said to be 'in the money' when the current share price is above the price at which the option can be exercised.

Table (*cont.*)

Balance sheet		
Fixed assets	3,092	3,167
Accounts receivable	1,382	1,536
Inventories	1,732	1,954
Accounts payable	(2,000)	(2,040)
Net working capital	1,114	1,450
Capital employed	4,206	4,617
ROACE		12.0%
Funds flow statement		
Profit		530
Amortisation		329
Working capital		(336)
Capital investment		(404)
Funds flow		119

We also need to recall that I have calculated the liabilities of Corus PLC to be £1,259m. So can we use these numbers to understand why Tata Steel paid £6.2bn to purchase the company in April 2007 and why the share price in September 2006 had been one third lower than this?

I will start with trying to understand the September 2006 valuation of about £4bn. This is not difficult. Capital employed at the start of 2006 was £4.6bn and the return on capital in the previous year was 12%. If I assume a 10% CoC[20] and 2% growth, the sustainable return on capital method would work as follows:

$$\frac{\text{Market Value}}{\text{Book Value}} = \frac{(\text{Return on Capital} - \text{Growth})}{(\text{Cost of Capital} - \text{Growth})}$$

$$\begin{aligned}\text{Hence market value} &= 4.6 \times (0.12 - 0.02) \div (0.10 - 0.02)\\ &= £5.8\text{bn}\end{aligned}$$

We must deduct the liabilities figure of £1.3bn to arrive at the equity valuation of £4.5bn. This is quite close to the actual share price valuation of a little over £4bn. (I have to ask readers to believe me when I write that these were my original assumptions and that I did not spend time adjusting the assumptions to arrive at the answer I wanted!)

The reason that I got close to the market value was that I chose the right short cut approach. Consider what might have happened if I had used the funds flow

[20] I have used 10% because I judge that steel manufacturing is highly linked to the general economy and so has a ß of greater than 1.

to perpetuity method. With a funds flow of just £119m I would have arrived at an asset value of just £1,517m.[21] Deduct the liabilities from this and the residual equity value is minute. The reason for this is Corus's growth during 2005. Capital employed grew during the year by £411m which is almost 10%, yet my long-run growth assumption is just 2%. Clearly if growth is reduced the funds flow can increase. This sort of situation is where the growth adjusted profit TV method should be used. The value would have been as follows:

$$\begin{aligned} \text{Value} &= (\text{profit} - \text{growth} \times \text{capital employed}) \times (1 + \text{growth}) \div (\text{CoC} - \text{growth}) \\ &= (530 - 92) \times (1.02) \div (0.08) \\ &= £5.6\text{bn} \end{aligned}$$

I will need to make some further adjustments to explain why Tata had to pay so much more. I also need to introduce some more background context. Tata originally made an unsolicited bid to buy Corus based on a significantly lower valuation. This offer encouraged other companies to think about buying it and eventually a bidding auction ensued. Tata won the auction by bidding the highest price. One has to assume, therefore, that Tata paid a fair percentage of its anticipated synergies in order to win the auction. It may even have suffered from the winner's curse.

So what sort of synergies might Tata have anticipated? One thing that is always possible with a takeover of a company in a related line of business is that overheads can be reduced. In simple terms the combined company can operate with just one head office and not two. I do not have any detail to go on and so will assume that the overhead saving could be £50m pa after tax. Now this will not contribute enough value to reach the takeover price. If we divide it by 0.08[22] we get 'just' £0.6bn of value. We need to find a total of at least £2bn to understand the deal.

I think that what Tata Steel might have been hoping to achieve is what is called transfer of best practice. Suppose that Tata Steel had superior ways of producing steel that could be implemented at the Corus manufacturing facilities. Suppose also that there were instances of where Corus was better than Tata. If the two could share what they did and always implement the best approach then there would be considerable value potential. Corus's total costs were about £9bn pa. A 2% improvement through sharing best practice would lower costs by £180m pa. If a further 1% could be transferred back

[21] The calculation is $119 \times 1.02 \div (0.1 - 0.02) = 1{,}517$.

[22] Dividing by 0.08 is equivalent to assuming that the saving is sustained to perpetuity and that it would grow at 2% pa.

to Tata this would make a total pre-tax synergy of £270m. Tax needs to be allowed for. Readers should recall that the typical rate in Corus was just 22%. I will apply a 30% rate to arrive at a post-tax benefit of about £190m pa. The value of this to perpetuity with 2% growth would be £2.4bn. Now assuming a perpetuity value for a synergy can be too optimistic. If we take just ten years with no growth the present value would be 6.145 times the annual saving.[23] This is £1.1bn.

We are now quite close to explaining the Tata bid. Since I do not have any inside information I will stop at this point. What I trust readers have appreciated is how to use simple TV and annuity factors to derive rough company valuations.

ABCDE valuation

This is a technique which I have devised in order to value companies and also to highlight the importance of full-cycle costs. The name can serve as a mnemonic for remembering what the steps in the technique are. The technique works like this:

- A is for **A**sset value. This is the value of the assets which a company already has.
- B is for **B**usiness development value. This is the value of the future stream of NPVs which the company will generate through its business development activities.
- C is for **C**osts. Business development does not come for free! It requires costs and the present value of these must be deducted from the overall valuation.
- D is for **D**ebt and other liabilities. The value of these must be deducted from the total in order to arrive at our answer.
- E is for **E**quity value. The residual value should be what sets the calculated share price.

The approach is to start with a plan for a company and its existing assets. The only future capital investment that is included is major projects which have already been sanctioned plus an allowance for sustaining investment for the existing assets. Costs are assumed to be held at the level necessary simply to sustain the company at its current state. Expenditure aimed at generating growth beyond that which is necessary in order to utilise existing assets is

[23] 6.145 is the ten year 10% annuity factor for end year flows.

excluded. The resultant plan should offer good cash generation by the end of a five-year plan period. An assumption will need to be made as to how long this cash generation will last. It might, for example, be appropriate to calculate the required TV based on a specified life of assets beyond the plan period. A figure like 15 years could be appropriate. Alternatively, a steady percentage decline could be used coupled with the perpetuity valuation formula.[24]

The next stage is to estimate what the stream of future NPVs will be from all of the development activities which are under way. Suppose, for example, the typical NPV was equal to one third of the capital investment. If the anticipated expenditure on growth projects was $60m pa then the stream of future NPVs would amount to $20m pa. If this was sustained in constant money-of-the-day terms the present value of it would be obtained by dividing the value by the CoC. One does not have to assume that the stream of NPVs goes to perpetuity. What is important, though, is to ensure that the assumption is consistent with the assumption which is made concerning costs.

The costs for the third step are the sum of all business development-related costs after allowing for any tax offsets. Judgement will have to be used in some areas because not all costs are clearly either related to existing assets or to growth. Business development teams are clearly growth costs while the staff operating an existing asset are not. Most of the costs associated with maintaining a brand will also be related to the existing business unless a major growth initiative is under way that is not already captured in the plan for existing assets. In companies that are growing there can be growth-related costs spread all over the place. Areas such as recruitment, planning, corporate advertising, government relations and even main board costs will all be higher in growing companies. One of the by-products of carrying out an ABCDE valuation is that these costs will be highlighted. It is then always useful to check that the costs are justified in relation to the anticipated future NPVs which will be generated.

Readers should also recall the emphasis that I placed on the impact of overheads and sunk costs when I explained how to view a company as the sum of a series of projects in the Planning and Control building block on page 126. It is this same principle that I am applying here.

The assessment of debt and other liabilities is exactly the same as the third step in the usual company valuation approach. So too is how we can move from the equity valuation to the calculated share price.

[24] For example, the 15 year 9% annuity factor for end-year cash flows is 8.061. Had we used a 3½% pa decline to perpetuity the valuation factor would have been 1 ÷ 12½% which is 8.0.

I will illustrate this approach by applying ABCDE to YMCC. First, I need a plan which shows just existing assets and sanctioned new projects. I will assume that the major capital project, called Project Claire, has been sanctioned and that the remaining capital investment is just to sustain the existing asset base. I do, though, need to remove any additional costs which are incurred within YMCC but only because of its growth intentions. These costs will currently form a part of the existing fixed costs which total $30m in the first year of the plan. I will assume that the growth element of this is $5m pa. My existing assets plan therefore looks as follows:

YMCC Inc: Existing assets plan $m

	2009	2010	2011	2012	2013
Sales revenue	76.1	78.7	82.7	87.7	93.0
Variable costs	–21.5	–22.5	–23.5	–25.3	–27.3
Contribution	54.6	56.2	59.2	62.4	65.7
Fixed costs	–25.0	–26.7	–30.5	–31.2	–32.0
Amortisation	–6.0	–5.7	–7.6	–7.7	–7.8
Pre-tax profit	23.6	23.9	21.1	23.5	25.9
Tax	–8.3	–8.4	–7.4	–8.2	–9.1
Net profit	15.3	15.5	13.7	15.3	16.9
Fixed assets	67.0	90.1	86.2	82.7	79.5
Accounts receivable	19.0	19.7	20.7	21.9	23.3
Accounts payable	–12.8	–13.9	–10.9	–11.7	–12.5
Inventories	7.7	8.2	9.0	9.4	9.9
Net working capital	13.9	14.0	18.8	19.7	20.6
Capital employed	80.9	104.0	105.0	102.3	100.1
ROACE	22.2%	16.8%	13.2%	14.7%	16.7%
Profit	15.3	15.5	13.7	15.3	16.9
Amortisation	6.0	5.7	7.6	7.7	7.8
Working cap	2.4	0.0	–4.8	–0.9	–1.0
Capital investment	–23.0	–28.7	–3.7	–4.1	–4.6
Funds flow	0.7	–7.5	12.8	17.9	19.1
Funds flow	0.7	–7.5	12.8	17.9	19.1
Discount factor	0.958	0.879	0.806	0.740	0.679
PV funds flows	0.7	–6.6	10.3	13.2	13.0
Cumulative PV	0.7	–6.0	4.4	17.6	30.6

The removal of the $5m pa of growth costs has served to about double the value of the plan period funds flows. The long-term prospects of the company will, however, go down and I will assess the TV based on 15 more years of the final-year funds flow. So the TV is 8.061 × \$19.1m = \$154m. The present value of this is \$104.5m. So my asset value is \$135.1m. I can cross check that this is above book value.

Now we must assess the value potential from future growth. We considered various routes to growth for YMCC as part of the Sources of Value pillar. We concluded that the best approach appeared to be a licensing strategy targeting the growth market in Asia. An NPV of \$6.5m per licence sold was anticipated. If one licence was sold each year for ten years the present value of this would be:

$$6.418 \times \$6.5\text{m} = \$41.7\text{m}$$

We already know that our business development costs are \$5m pa and that the tax rate is 35%. So the after tax value of these over the same ten year period that we anticipate positive NPVs is:

$$6.418 \times 0.65 \times \$5\text{m} = \$20.9\text{m}$$

This business development cost is accounting for about half of the value that is showing up in our stream of business development NPVs. This is in line with what my intuition would suggest. Had the NPVs been below the present value of the additional costs this would have been a sign that the growth strategy was destroying value. Had the costs been very low relative to the NPVs, I would only have believed this if I knew that we had a very strong Source of Value to exploit. Any value contribution from the net of the B and C amounts would only be credible if there was a Source of Value to exploit.

Step D for YMCC is limited to the impact of debt. The opening level of debt was \$25m.[25]

Hence our equity valuation is:

Assets	135.1
Business development	41.7
Costs	(20.9)
Debt	(25.0)
Equity value	130.9

[25] This was one of the stated assumptions. Note the need to use opening debt and not the debt figure for the end of the first year which appears in the plan. The debt rises by almost \$10m over the first year of the plan owing to the need to fund Project Claire. The full effect of this is, however, already incorporated in the present value calculation and it would be wrong to use any figure for debt other than the opening level.

And finally …

It is important to finish this section on value calculation with another reminder of the fact that valuations are only as good as the assumptions on which they are based. We have seen how a large range of values can be justified if different assumptions are made. This could be viewed as a problem with the methodology but I do not take this attitude. It is certainly an indication of why share prices can be so volatile. Different people will adopt different approaches and the price-setter will change over time. So we should expect the share price to move about quite a lot.

What we must do with any value calculation is the same as with any economic evaluation:

- ensure the assumptions are clearly stated;
- avoid errors in translating them into the calculated share price;
- ensure that decision-makers are comfortable with them and understand their basis (for example that they represent an expected value view of the future);
- ensure that our company can afford any potential downsides.

Part 3: The implications

Understanding performance

In this final section I will consider some of the implications of the share price's being set via a calculation of economic value. I will start with the question of understanding performance. The first message is that we must be very careful how we interpret performance as seen through the eyes of shareholders. There are some apparently strange conclusions to get to grips with in relation to this topic including the way that a plan will offer the same return in each year even if it is anticipating making a loss. The necessary theory for this understanding was provided in the Planning and Control building block on pages 137–139. This is now the right time to consider this topic further.

In this earlier section of the book I calculated the value profile of Fence Treatment Inc over the five-year period of its plan. Value was calculated to have grown in the early years but it levelled out at the end. In each year, however, when one calculated the overall return generated through the funds flow plus the growth in value, we saw that this return was exactly equal to the

CoC. I suggest that readers who are unfamiliar with the idea of the profile of value over time review this section again.

The reason for the return's being exactly equal to the CoC is that there is an obvious circularity in the way that we calculate value. We calculate it by discounting funds flows at the CoC. Calculating the return as value growth plus cash generation divided by opening value is using exactly the same numbers and so must by definition give the same answer. I will illustrate this via a very simple case study.

For this study we will take a business which has only two more years of economic life ahead of it. It is expected to generate \$5m post-tax in one year's time and then \$10m in two years' time. I will use a 10% CoC. I suggest that readers repeat the analysis with a different CoC of their own choosing and confirm to their satisfaction that they will get the equivalent answer that the value return is exactly equal to the CoC.

What is the business worth at different points in time and how should we describe its performance?

The business must currently be worth:

$$\$5\text{m} \div 1.1 + \$10\text{m} \div 1.1^2 = \$12.81\text{m}$$

At the end of the first year, however, just after it has paid out its \$5m, the business will only be worth \$10m ÷ 1.1 i.e. \$9.09m. At the end of the second year, after it has paid out the \$10m, the business will have no value at all.

This means that during the first year the owner of the business starts with something worth \$12.81m. At the end of the year they have \$5m in cash plus a business worth \$9.09m. This is a total of \$14.09m which is \$1.28m more than they had at the start of the year. They have gained a return of exactly 10%. To understand performance in the second year we must ignore the \$5m which was paid out at the end of year 1. We started with a business worth \$9.09 and finish with \$10m in cash and a business with no value. Once again, the return is exactly 10%.

Now we will consider the situation if the company was expected to require a further cash injection of \$5m at the end of year 1 as opposed to generating this amount. This injection would have to come from the owner. The valuation as at the start of the period would look like this:

$$-\$5\text{m} \div 1.1 + \$10\text{m} \div 1.1^2 = \$3.72\text{m}$$

At the end of the first year after a further \$5m had been invested, the company would then be worth \$9.09m. So just before the \$5m was invested the value would have been \$4.09m. The return over the first year would have come just from the value growth during this time. This is \$0.37m which once again is exactly 10%.

So we have seen that it does not matter whether a business's plan is for a profit or a loss. Its performance in that plan, when measured using economic value, is always equal to the CoC.

Now to me it is obvious that in both of the situations the company has improved its performance in the second year. The message that I take from this is that the value profile in a plan is not a way to measure performance. So since value is what sets the share price, one must also be careful when using share prices to understand financial performance. This means that even if share price performance is such that shareholders have earned the CoC, the management of the company is not safe in concluding that its actions have earned the CoC. We will consider what it can conclude next.

Continuous good surprises

Continuous good surprises is an expression which I coined in order to summarise what it is that the management of a company must do if it is to keep its shareholders happy year after year.[26]

We have just seen that in a company's plan, the value calculation will point to a return exactly equal to the CoC in each year. Now if a company is able to follow its plan in every way, the value at each point in time must remain exactly in line with our calculations. So the actual share price will follow our predicted path if the company follows its plan. So this must mean that if a company follows its plan then its shareholders must earn exactly the CoC.

Now I am assuming that the shareholders believed the initial plan and used this to set the initial share price. If they did not use the company plan but rather had some other views of their own we would find that what a company had to do in order to give its shareholders a return equal to their CoC each year would be to follow this other plan. Shareholders will not automatically believe in the truth of the company's plan. The company's management will have to establish its credibility in the eyes of potential shareholders before it can realistically expect its plans to be believed.

[26] The expression also owes a lot to the fact that the initials of a senior manager with whom I was working on this subject were CGS. The planner in me spotted a snappy title that would aid the implementation of a good idea and so I grabbed it! 'We need CGS' was the slogan!

As an example of this effect we can consider the Depot Company valuation which I set as individual work assignment number 4 in the building block on Planning and Control. Here we had a business which planned to start one new project every year. Each project had a positive NPV and overall, even after allowing for the effect of overheads, the value of the company before it actually invested its first dollar was shown to be about $60m. This company was, however, anticipating that for at least its first five years of operation it would make losses. In my view a startup company would not be able to convince the market that such a plan was credible. It might well struggle to convince the market that it was even worth book value until some clear signs emerged which would confirm that the projects were actually going to generate positive NPVs. If I am right about this the initial value (i.e. the value before the first dollar is invested) would be nil.

So here is a way of expressing the rules of the shareholder value 'game'.

- Shareholders invest money in the expectation of earning their CoC.
- At any stage, shareholders have a view of the future prospects for the company. We can call this the shareholders' plan.
- The present value of the shareholders' plan is what sets the share price.
- Companies will earn a return equal to the CoC for their shareholders if they can follow this shareholders' plan.
- Companies will earn above the CoC if shareholders change their future plan for the company such that the plan's present value rises.
- Companies will generate returns of below the CoC if the present value of this implied plan falls.

Now if we think about it, managers will always be expected to work hard to make things better in the future. This, however, will be incorporated by shareholders into their current plan which will have to be delivered simply to satisfy the shareholders. To make them happy, the management of a company must convince them to adopt a more optimistic plan. This is the only way to generate a return of above the CoC.

Let us suppose it takes a year to generate the new ideas and to convince the shareholders that they should adjust their future plan. What happens at that point? Well, it is obvious, the price will rise and shareholders will do very well. New ones will, however, have joined the company and the 'game' starts again. This time the new plan is the starting point. To continue to satisfy shareholders the management must follow this new plan and deliver its enhanced performance. To make the shareholders happy, they must be convinced of a future that is yet more exciting. In theory, the game never stops.

One can picture the stock exchange 'game' like this. The 'game' is all about continuous good surprises or CGS for short:

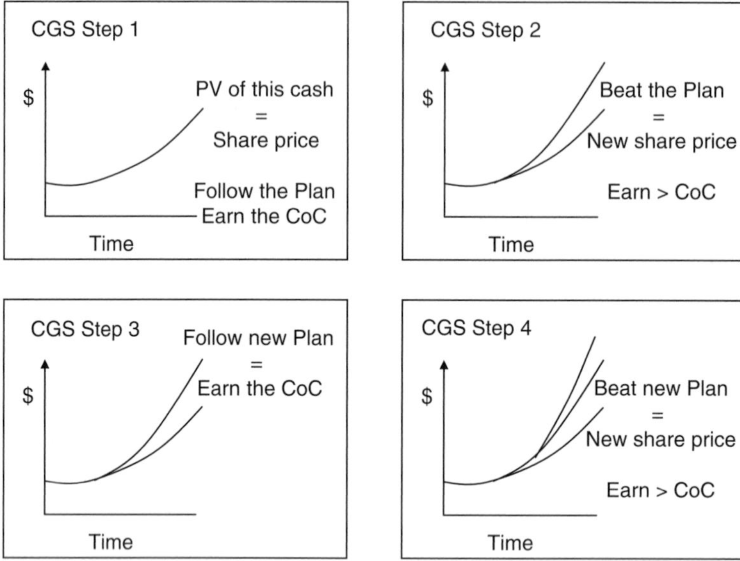

Fig. 9.1 Continuous good surprises

Now after only two revisions the slope of the curve of anticipated future cash flow is looking pretty steep. One could soon imagine its becoming vertical and then crashing down. Some companies do this.

This view of stock market life has been described to me as being 'worse than a treadmill' but it does help to explain the apparent never-ending change within quoted companies. No matter how good and challenging your plan is, once your shareholders believe it they will only earn the CoC in the future if you follow it. To make them happy you have to beat the plan.

The way that I have presented the good surprises steps does contribute to the seeming difficulty of achieving CGS. This does illustrate the power of a picture. If I was a chief executive I would not want to tell my staff that this was what to expect! Many would simply give up now.

There is, though, a better way to look at the challenge and this is to consider the changes as steps. A reorganisation can, for example, offer the prospect of a step change. Follow this with a major merger and this can be the second step change and so on. The pictures would then look like this:

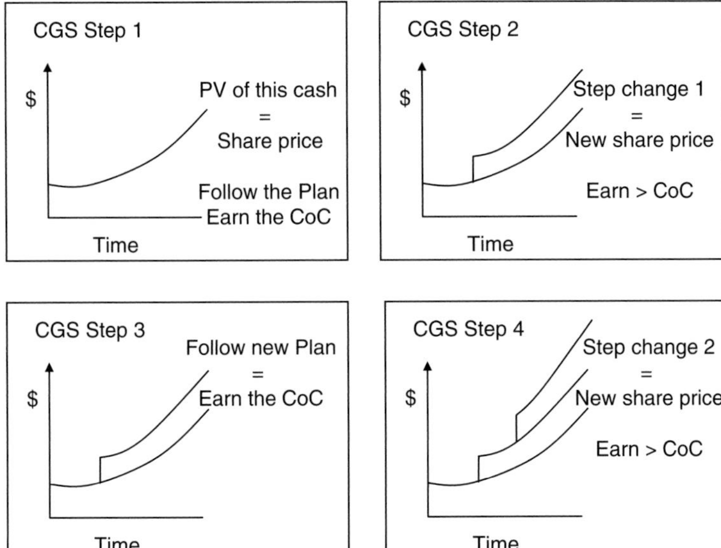

Fig. 9.2 Continuous good surprises achieved via step changes

The overall result may be the same, but, to me at least, this does look to be a lot more achievable. One can link specific initiatives to required step changes in order to suggest what each could do for the share price.

The idea of CGS does now give us a better way to understand what can be learned from a study of the returns which are earned by shareholders. Shareholder returns are caused by two factors. These are actual performance and the present value of changes in anticipated future performance. Of these, it tends to be the present value of changes in anticipated future performance that dominates. This is simply because this is always going to be the larger number.

Now this way of thinking about how markets work does, in my view, go a long way towards rebutting the suggestion that stock markets usually take a short-term view because analysts focus so much on quarterly earnings. I would suggest that big price swings following an unanticipated quarterly announcement were a sign of the market's taking a long-term view. The mechanism could be as follows:

Suppose that a company was expected to generate $100m in the current year[27] and was expected subsequently to grow at 4% pa to perpetuity. With a 9% CoC it would be valued at $2,000m. Its price-to-cash flow ratio is 20.

[27] For simplicity I will assume that during the year the analysts were expecting four equal cash flows and that next year everything would be the same percentage larger.

Now let us suppose that at the time the quarterly results are announced the analysts are able to check their financial models. The analysts do not know for sure that the company will generate $100m and grow at 4%; these are just assumptions. When the quarterly results come out the analysts can use these to recalibrate their assumptions and decide on a new calculated share price. When they do this, analysts will want, in particular, to understand the difference between a one-off event and something that will impact on the cash flow which they are assuming will grow steadily into the future.

For our example we will study what might happen if it was announced that the cash generation during a quarter was $24m rather than the anticipated $25m. A one-off loss of $1m will lower the analysts' overall valuation of the company by exactly that amount. By contrast, a loss which served to reduce their view of the annual cash generation would impact on value by $80m. This is because there are four quarters in the year and the valuation multiple for annual cash flow is 20.

So far I have assumed that the analysts do not change their view about long-term growth as a result of the $1m reduction in cash generation. Suppose, however, that the reduction in cash generation came precisely from where the anticipated growth was expected. What might this do to value? The answer is that it could kill it 'stone dead'. This is because the anticipated growth was 'only' $4m pa. So a loss of $1m might actually be a signal that growth was not going to happen at all. If analysts were to decide on this interpretation the value consequences would be huge. The annual cash flow of $96m with zero growth is worth only $1,067m.

Here, then, is a rational mechanism that can explain why a small change in quarterly results could halve the share price of a company. If a company delivers the opposite of a good surprise, the fact that valuations are based on long-term views of the future can create, in effect, an amplifier. The implications of this view are, I believe, pretty considerable. Companies need to understand what the market is assuming when it sets the share price. These expectations need to be managed so that they remain appropriate and, crucially, so that they remain deliverable by management. If the current management of a company cannot see how to deliver the expectations which appear to be implicit in its share price then it should look forward to one of two possible outcomes: a share price crash or a takeover!

Focus on value

This final implication concerns the need to ensure that economic value is at the heart of all decision-making. If a company adopts as its overall objective the maximisation of shareholder value, one might expect it to make the big decisions in a way that ensures that the objective is achieved and furthermore, one might expect it to reward its staff when it is successful.

One might think that this approach was self-evident. Value sets the share price. A company is supposed to be run for the benefit of its shareholders. So managers should seek to maximise the share price and this means maximising value. There can, however, be some telling reasons why this often does not happen. The first concerns the difficulty with calculating value. We have just learned how different interpretations of the same facts can lead to huge differences in the implied value of a company. We know that companies publish perhaps thousands of numbers but one that they never publish is their internal value calculation. We also know that the stock market value is set by expectations rather than by delivered performance. So the only value number that we do have (i.e. the share price) could be said by some to be a function of spin rather than substance. With this background it is not surprising that value is not the usual key which sets that annual bonus for staff.

The usual response to this uncertainty surrounding value is to adopt what are termed value proxies or value drivers. These are numbers which have a clear link to value but which can be measured. Examples might be the rate of sales growth or the ROCE. Each of these, all other things being equal, offer good ways to enhance value. So, in most financial models, if you increase the growth rate assumption you will find that value rises.[28] These value drivers can serve a useful purpose in bringing a clear and measurable edge to the definition of performance within a company which can be linked in to the annual bonus.

The trouble with this approach can be with the five words 'all other things being equal'. Once an individual value driver becomes set as a target, 'all other things' rarely will be equal. This is due to the WYMIWYG effect.[29] If something is set as a target, the natural reaction is for people in an organisation to pull all possible levers to ensure that it is delivered. The fact that value is hard to create will mean that the easiest ways to deliver a target will be through sacrificing value to achieve it.[30]

In the case of sales growth, for example, make a special offer and sell below cost. It will suddenly become easier to make a sale. Sales will grow

[28] I can only say 'in most cases' because in the sustainable return on capital calculation of market-to-book ratio growth lowers value if the anticipated return is below the cost of capital.

[29] 'What you measure is what you get' is explained on pages 110 and 112.

[30] The logic behind this is as follows. Value is additive, so if your company loses value, some other company must be winning. If all companies are seeking value, any company that in effect says 'here, take some value from me', is likely to achieve this. So it is easy to grow if you are prepared to destroy value!

but value will be destroyed. A second route to value-destroying growth is to embark on growth projects that lack sufficient sources of value to create value on a full-cycle basis. If the initial spend on the project prior to its final sanction and also a fair share of future overheads are both ignored it can be quite easy, even for quite poor projects, to gain approval at time of sanction because they offer a positive incremental NPV. Indeed, senior managers may well not even realise that their growth strategy was destroying value if all that they saw was a stream of positive NPV investment cases. In my language of ABCDE valuation, they would be concentrating on B and ignoring C.

There are two common targets which suffer from the 'all other things being equal' problem. I like to refer to these as being 'seductive sirens' that will try to tempt managers away from the path of value. These are the searches for growth and for returns. I have already explained how growth can easily be achieved through selling for too low a price or by embarking on poor projects and only reviewing their value creation potential at time of sanction through the traditional money-forward NPV. Growth is seductive because so many league tables simply rank companies by size and not for their track record of creating value.[31]

The concern with returns, however, is more subtle but it too can result in a failure to maximise value. I will deal with this second siren now.

First, why do so many people think that the aim of business is to maximise returns? After all, the textbook by Brealey and Myers for example contains a thorough analysis of why NPV is a superior measure to IRR. I think that a part of the cause lies in the typical financial literature. This will usually assert that nobody would take extra risk unless they were promised extra return. It is, I suggest, a small step from here to a belief that more return is always better than less return. The other part of the reason is, I believe, that those who manage investment funds do quite correctly set return as their objective.[32] Now fund managers are a vocal lot and go around talking about returns so much that this quite naturally spreads to company managers!

[31] One could also cynically suggest that growth is seductive because company size is correlated with the pay cheques of senior executives!

[32] It is logical to measure return because the assumption is made that you wish to compare how investors have done over a fixed period. The question that one seeks to answer is 'Would an investment in one fund have performed better than another when measured over a fixed period?'. The answer to this question is given by ranking funds based on the return which they have given over that period with all distributions reinvested in the fund at the time they were paid out. What makes the return a suitable measure is that reinvestment is a realistic option and there are thus no intermediate payments to consider, just an initial investment and a final valuation.

There is, to me at least, a very interesting difference between life as a fund manager and life as a company manager. The fund manager invests in the shares of many companies and measures the return earned by the fund. If more people invest money in his or her fund, the manager simply buys more of all of the shares that the fund currently owns. If people want to withdraw money, the fund simply sells the necessary percentage of all of its shares. The fund can be any size; the skill of the fund manager is to get the right mix of investments. The only extent to which size matters is in economies of scale because of fixed overhead costs. The implicit assumption is always that the fund's actions will not impact on share prices and that shares can be bought or sold to match the exact amount of money that investors wish to invest. The measure of success in this situation has to be the return earned by a dollar invested in the fund compared with a dollar in another fund or a benchmark index. A higher return is always better than a lower return.

The company manager has a different task. This is to find opportunities to invest in physical assets. These opportunities cannot be scaled up and down to match exactly the amount of money that investors wish to invest. Also, positive cash flows which are generated during the life of the project cannot simply be assumed to be reinvested in the project. They are paid out to shareholders. The company becomes whatever size it needs to be and shareholders happily live with this. Opportunities are what set the constraint and the company manager is told to assume that funds will be available if they are needed. If a good project is found then, once the market is made aware of its existence, the existing shareholders reap the reward[33] and, on a money-forward basis, shareholders earn just the CoC through the actual implementation of the project. The measure of success is the value which is created.

If one thinks hard about this situation there is a contradiction. If a company is simply the sum of its projects and the market is the sum of the companies quoted on it, then the market ought to be fixed in size and the individual fund manager's assumption that he or she can buy and sell shares without impacting on the share price looks questionable. The individual fund manager's assumption is usually reasonable because his or her buying and selling is very small in relation to the market. One does, though, understand why the market has the occasional bubble and burst. This is because the actions of individual fund managers tend to be strongly correlated. Share prices,

[33] In this case the reward is the NPV which shareholders expect from the newly announced project. So as long as investors believe in a project they will give credit for all of its NPV to the existing shareholders and the share price will immediately rise to reflect this additional value.

I suggest, are founded on two mutually inconsistent assumptions. These are that companies implicitly assume that the market's overall size will equal the true value of all of the companies quoted on the market while individual investments assume that any investment will not change the overall value of companies.

So I have shown some possible reasons why companies can be tempted to attempt to maximise returns rather than value and I have also shown how the market is likely to be unstable. We now should turn to the 'So what?' question. What is the danger of seeking to maximise returns rather than value? I suggest that this is that some good projects are rejected altogether and that other projects are not appropriately optimised. I will deal with this in some detail later in this book as part of my consideration of the CoC and in particular whether one should add so-called fudge factors to the CoC in order to achieve the desired return. For the present I must simply ask that readers accept that the implications of seeking to maximise returns rather than value can be very considerable.

Now at this stage one might think that the two sirens would tend to offset each other. My concern, however, is that the two effects can survive together. Yes, a search for growth does encourage too many projects to be undertaken while a search for returns might result in some good projects being rejected. So there is an offset in that growth encourages overspending while the search for returns encourages underspending. What can happen, however, is that companies can be misled by the economic signals which they receive from their investment cases. It can be easy to generate high IRRs on projects that have benefited from large sunk costs and which get a free ride from significant future fixed costs. By contrast, major strategic moves that are studied at their initiation may well only offer returns of slightly above the company's CoC because they will be showing an incremental IRR which is much closer to their full cycle IRR. So the pressure to earn high IRRs can result in a bias in favour of one type of project over another and so the two sirens cannot be expected always to offset each other. If a company is performing poorly then raising the required return on projects is not the way to solve the problem as it may simply make it harder to justify the strategic change which might be necessary to solve a company's underlying problems.

CHAPTER

10

Conclusion

This middle section of the book was started with an analysis of where we had come from and where we were going. I propose to finish it in a similar manner. I will use a special diagram that I call a 'fish diagram' to describe the progress that readers should have made to what should now be skilled practitioner status. I will, through this diagram, explain why the numbers behind all projects should be considered as being fishy[1] and how we can then sort out the real fishy numbers from those that just look that way.

This section started with a consideration of how to model economic value. The basic concept was disarmingly simple but the practical application relied on many factors that had to be got right if we were to be able to trust an economic model. I suggested that one key aim for a financial analyst was to remove spurious number noise from the items that senior decision-makers need to consider. A well-specified methodology would then allow a set of assumptions to be converted faithfully into the economic indicators. If a different analyst was given the same assumptions they too would produce the same profile of after-tax funds flows and the same economic indicators.

A typical set of after-tax funds flows can be used to prepare a chart which I believe sums up how most project people will think about their project. This is a graph of cumulative present value. A typical chart for a hypothetical project is depicted overleaf.

This particular project involves a capital spend of $20m. The spend takes place over the first two years and there are then assumed to be 20 years of beneficial operation of the plant. The twenty-third year represents recovery of residual working capital, etc. Overall the project has an NPV of $7.0m.

Project people tend to think of their project as though it starts from nothing but quickly, money is poured into it. This is why the line of cumulative present value starts off by going downwards. It hits –$17.4m after the first

[1] Readers for whom English is not a first language should be made aware that 'fishy' does not just mean fish-like. It also has an informal meaning of being suspicious, doubtful or questionable.

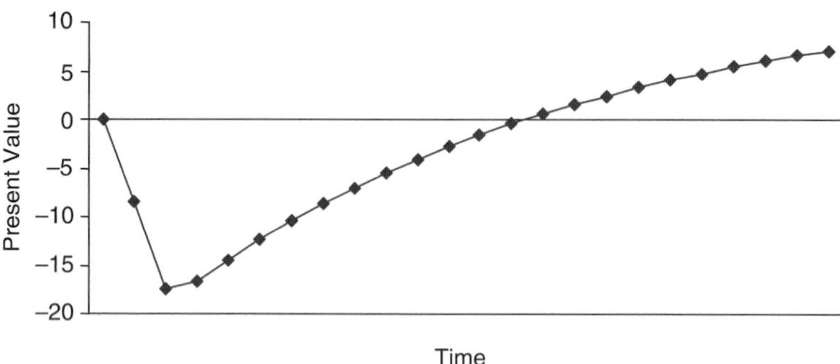

Fig. 10.1 Cumulative present value: the project person's view

two years. It is not the full capital spend of $20m because of the time value of money and the working capital benefit of 45 days of payables on all the spend. Over time the initial investment is gradually recovered and, ultimately a positive NPV of $7m is earned.

The first pillar should have provided the skills to prepare this chart. In effect, it equipped readers to convert assumptions into an NPV. How, though, do readers decide what makes a good assumption? Unless we have something to help us make good assumptions the numbers must be 'suspicious, doubtful or questionable'.

At this stage what a decision-maker who had read the standard texts would probably do is review the assumptions and decide if they were acceptable. The decision-maker would take comfort in the fact that in this instance the project had an IRR of 13.3%. This is well above my assumed 9% CoC. So what might be thought of as the project's 'safety margin' over the fateful zero NPV hurdle would be quite considerable. In this particular case I have calculated that the NPV is the difference between the present value of inflows of $53m and outflows of $46m. The sum of these two numbers is more or less $100m so a change for the worse of 7% would be required in every assumption before the NPV fell to zero. The project's assumptions could be said to have a 7% safety margin.

Imagine, however, the situation where the initial assumptions indicated an NPV of zero. The project would be at risk of not being approved and the sponsor of the project would face a great temptation to see if any of the assumptions could be stretched a bit in order to achieve a token positive NPV while still retaining what seemed to be reasonable assumptions. How easy would it be to fiddle the numbers and improve the IRR by, say, one percentage point?

I have tweaked the numbers a bit in order to investigate such a situation. My new base case had an NPV of –$0.1m and an IRR of 9.0%. The NPV was now the result of cash inflows and cash outflows each with a present value of \$48m. From this I was able to calculate that in order to get the IRR back to 10% one would need on average to enhance each assumption by only about one and a half percent. Changes as small as this would be too small to be resolved by any logical debate. So the reality is that the conventional decision rule of 'invest in all positive NPV projects' when coupled with project sponsors who are bound to exhibit at least some bias in favour of their project will become 'invest in all projects unless they clearly have a negative NPV'.

Furthermore, the standard approach means that this problem is then compounded by the fact that the decision rule refers to incremental NPVs and not full-cycle NPVs. The microeconomic logic of this rule is correct but the strategic implication is that in the case of marginal projects, companies are encouraged to approve them even though their shareholders should either wish they had never been started or would consider they were only going ahead because they were 'free-riding' on future fixed overheads. A situation such as this must be 'suspicious, doubtful or questionable'.

What I have proposed via this book are two key ways of addressing this problem. The first is the simple suggestion that more attention should be paid to full-cycle economics and that a negative full-cycle NPV should be used as a signal that strategy should be reviewed.

The second way is to propose an entirely new approach which I call the Sources of Value technique. This technique enables the NPV to be deconstructed into two components. One component is the 'me too' return, which is a factor of sector attractiveness and which allows the aggregate effect of the assumptions to be calibrated. So instead of having to review every single assumption, decision-makers simply review the overall return which is implied for the 'me too' player. This will remain a judgement call but the call will be an explicit one and one which can be set against similar judgements that have been made on previous projects.

The second component is the value caused by the project's identified sources of value. These should already have been described in the strategy and are the reason that the project can anticipate a positive NPV.

The inclusion of the Sources of Value chart to the right of the cumulative present value curve can explain the NPV and allow the vital 'words and music' test to be applied. Did the numbers appear consistent with the strategy? Yes they did. Indeed, the strategy could be explicitly linked to the NPV. No longer was this 'fishy'.

So why did I suggest that all projects should be considered to be fishy when the correct application of the Sources of Value technique could place a project

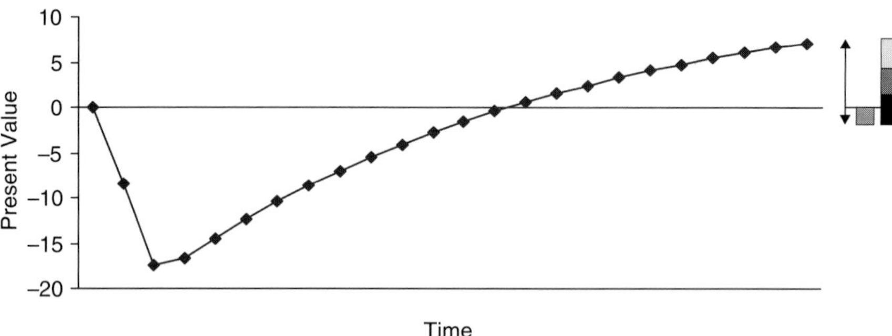

Fig. 10.2 Cumulative present value explained through Sources of Value analysis

as far above suspicion as was possible? The answer to this question is to be found in the third pillar. The chart of cumulative present value might be how project people think about their project but it is not how shareholders think about it. Shareholders think about the present value of future cash flows.

If one took the detail of the above project to a company's merchant bankers and asked: 'What could you sell this for?' or 'How much of the company's share price should this represent?' a different answer would emerge. The answer to both questions would be that a project should always be sellable for its money-forward NPV.[2] This does not start at zero and only gradually move towards NPV as time progresses. It is equal to NPV at the very start of a project and when the project is finished its value is nil.

The shareholder value view of a project is shown as the top line on this chart:

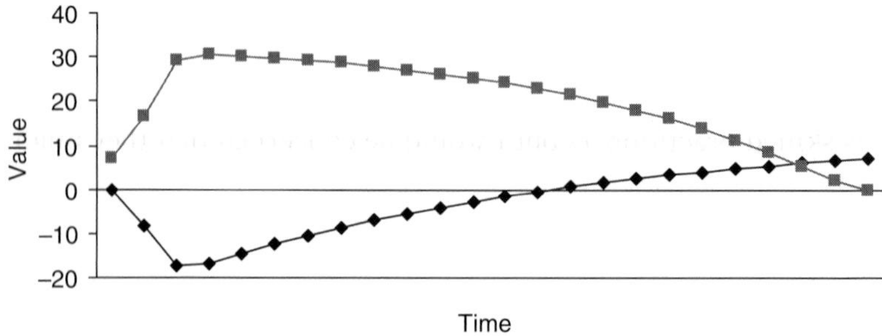

Fig. 10.3 Shareholder value and cumulative present value over a project's life

[2] Assuming that the buyer could also access the various sources of value and ignoring any winner's curse effects.

The project starts off worth $7m before any of the new money is spent. Its value grows to about $30m once the capital is sunk and the future revenues are all that much nearer to hand. The line ends at exactly zero when the project has finished.

The reason why I suggest that this is still a fishy project is perhaps now becoming apparent. Have a further look at the above chart and let your imagination run free. What do you see?

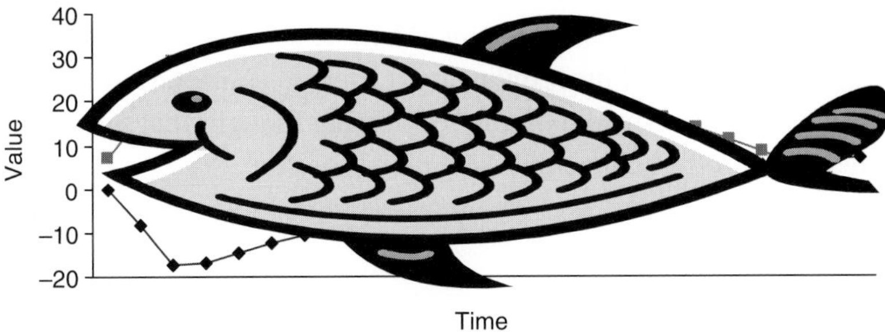

Fig. 10.4 The fish diagram: shareholder value and cumulative present value over a project's life

I see a fish! Project people think about the belly of a fish and then the top of its tail. Shareholders see the top of the fish's body and the bottom of its tail. The wider open the mouth is, the better the NPV. Likewise, the bigger the tail, the better the NPV.

Good techniques should have memorable names. The fish diagram is, I believe, a good way to remind ourselves of the two ways of thinking about a project and yes, all projects, even the good ones, are fishy!

Where next?

It might be tempting to think that we have finished! Readers can stop now as skilled practitioners but I would be concerned that they might think that everything was put in place. My summary of the three pillars may have sounded as though, between them, they provided the key to great decision-taking. Well, I am afraid that although I believe they provide a great platform from which to work, they do not cover everything.

In the final section of the book I will provide what I call three views from the platform. My aim is first to look at what we know about the CoC and to expose some doubts in the model that we use to set it. This is not done to demolish what has gone before but rather to emphasise why it is that judgement is so important. I will then discuss the idea that the path we take into the future is flexible whereas the valuation technique appears to suggest it is not. Again, I do this not to demolish what has been learned but to establish the limit of its accuracy. In this section I will suggest a tool kit of practical ways of placing a value on flexibility. Finally, I will consider how to apply some of these approaches in areas where value is not the primary objective. This can help in two ways. First, it will help to explain the approaches adopted by some organisations that we might have to deal with as customers, suppliers or competitors. Second, it will show that although this is a book about value, it can also give a lot of help to some wider aspects of life itself.

So, once again. I must invite my readers to continue with the journey, this time, however, armed with the comforting thought that the end is now much nearer than the beginning!

Section III

Three views of deeper and broader skills

CHAPTER

11

First view: The cost of capital

Introduction

On 16 October 1990 the Royal Swedish Academy of Sciences issued a press release to announce that the award of the 1990 Nobel Prize in economics had gone to three pioneers in the field of financial economics. The three laureates were:

- **Harry Markowitz** for having developed the theory of portfolio choice;
- **William Sharpe**, for his so-called *capital asset pricing model* (CAPM); and
- **Merton Miller**, for his fundamental contributions to the theory of corporate finance.[1]

I remember this well. To me it represented a very important recognition of the theories which underpinned what I like to call the economic value model. The award of the prize served to elevate these particular theories from being 'just theories' to being the recognised descriptions of how markets can be explained. They remain simply descriptions of how markets can be explained and not absolute laws but, from 1990 onwards, they took on the status of being acknowledged as the best descriptions that were available. The world of economics had, in effect, said that it would use these descriptions of how markets work as the accepted wisdom. From that point onwards, any competing theories had to take on the burden of proof that they were demonstrably better than what was now accepted.

Now I have always liked the theories and been prepared to accept them. I have, though, always been aware of their shortcomings and I used to have a concern that these might be such as to represent fatal flaws. Perhaps it was only a matter of time before the 'right' answer would come along and replace them. I am still prepared to accept that one day this might happen but, since 1990, I have stopped holding my breath in anticipation of their imminent

[1] Merton Miller is the second 'M' in the so-called MM1 proposition. The first 'M' was Franco Modigliani who had already received a Nobel economics prize in 1985.

demise. Now I can simply use the theories with, in effect, the backing of the Nobel brand behind me.

This view of the deeper and broader skills which surround the setting of the cost of capital (CoC) has two parts. In the first I will run through the theory and practice of setting the CoC. I will review the way that we are told to calculate the CoC and also remind readers of some of the implicit assumptions. I will use this review of the theory also to show how the various components of the CoC can be estimated. This will then allow me to show how to compute a CoC and to consider what a reasonable range of uncertainty would be. I will complete this first part with a brief review of some alternative approaches which have been put forward.

The second part of this view will be focused on the question 'so what?'. I will review the implications of the theory which surrounds the economic value model. This will allow me to explain some of the things which can be done with the value model and also warn against some things which should not be done. I will show in particular how a deep understanding of the CoC can provide great insights into how companies should approach the topic of risk. I will also in this section show how one very useful implication of the Sources of Value technique is that it should enable one, in effect, to ignore much of the uncertainty that surrounds the CoC on the grounds that it forms a part of the 'me too' player's return.

The first part will, I imagine, appeal in particular to readers who like theories and technical detail. It may, though, disappoint them somewhat as they will learn that my view of the theories is that they rely for their implementation on huge amounts of judgement. The second part is a contrast to the first. It is of particular relevance to senior managers within companies who are charged with the responsibility of taking the key risk-and-reward decisions on behalf of their shareholders. It proposes some practical approaches to dealing with risk and reward that will allow a company to adopt policies which respect both the theory of economic value and the reality of its limitation in practical situations.

Part 1: The theory and practice of setting the cost of capital

The economic value model

We should first remind ourselves of what the economic value model is; of its obvious components; and of its implicit assumptions.

We can summarise the model through this diagram:

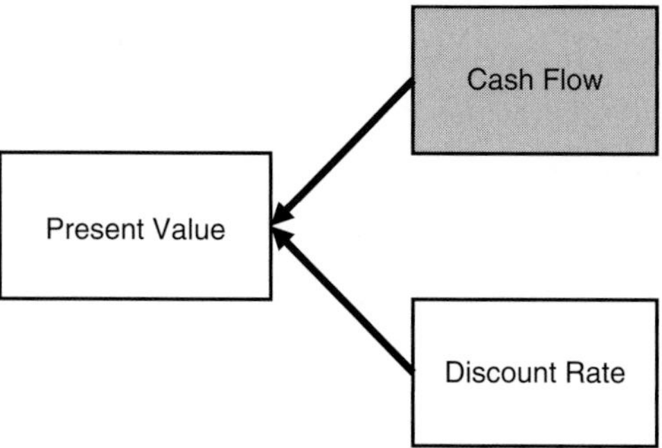

Fig. 11.1 Aide-mémoire: the economic value model

Value is a function of two components: future cash flows and a discount rate.

Cash flows should:

- be assessed on an expected value (i.e. probability weighted) basis;
- reflect the incremental effect of the decision which is being evaluated;
- be after tax; and
- exclude any financing effects.

The discount rate used is the weighted average CoC, that is to say, it is the weighted average cost of debt and equity.[2] The cost of debt is usually self apparent while the cost of equity is calculated via the capital asset pricing model (CAPM). Hence the formula for WACC is as follows:

$$\mathrm{WACC} = \mathrm{CoD} \times (1-\mathrm{t}) \times \frac{\mathrm{Debt}}{\mathrm{Debt}+\mathrm{Equity}} + \left(\mathrm{r_F} + \beta \times \left(\mathrm{r_M} - \mathrm{r_F}\right)\right) \times \frac{\mathrm{Equity}}{\mathrm{Debt}+\mathrm{Equity}}$$

Where:

WACC is the weighted average cost of capital
CoD is the company's cost of borrowing
t is the marginal tax rate
Debt is the market value of the company's debt
Equity is the market value of the company's equity
$\mathbf{r_F}$ is the risk-free interest rate
β is the covariance of the company's equity with the market

[2] I am assuming here that we are dealing with a company with a simple capital structure comprising just debt and equity. If a company is financed by a wider range of funds (for example, preference shares) one would need to include all of these in the calculation of the weighted average.

$\mathbf{r}_M$ is the return required by investors who invest in the market portfolio and ($\mathbf{r}_M - \mathbf{r}_F$) is referred to as the equity risk premium.

Crucially, though, although the formula refers to the ratio of debt and equity, this is assumed not to impact on the WACC in a material way because the cost of equity changes in response to the level of debt such as to maintain a WACC that is substantially independent of gearing.[3] This is a great help to our analysis because it means that financing decisions can be considered as subsidiary to asset decisions. If the CoC was significantly influenced by the balance between debt and equity funding, each project could only be evaluated after one knew how it was to be financed. This would add greatly to the scale of the evaluation task.

I like, therefore, to think of a company's WACC as a highly useful concept. It is intuitive to think of funds coming from a pool of finance but it is not possible directly to observe the cost of funds in the pool. All that can actually be observed is the cost of the two streams of money from which it is formed. Of these, the cost of debt is relatively easy to find, while the cost of equity in principle can be observed even though in practice this is hard.

The implicit assumptions behind our use of the economic value model are:

- that the consideration of the trade-off between risk and reward is done from the perspective of a well-diversified shareholder;
- that the company is strong enough to absorb any risks associated with the project without any material adverse effect on its other activities; and
- that funding will always be found for good projects.

Another important element of the economic value model is that it was designed as a way of describing what sets share prices, but we extend its use to consider the evaluation of projects within companies. This requires that we make the implicit assumption that shareholders see through the company to its underlying projects.

The idea of shareholders seeing through the company to its underlying projects also applies to the way that shareholders consider financing decisions. If shareholders see through a company then the balance that companies have between debt and equity does not really matter because shareholders can tailor the risk of their investment portfolio to exactly the level that they wish by adjusting their own holdings of debt and equity.[4]

[3] The MM1 proposition is that the WACC is independent of gearing; however, this ignores the effect of taxes. These typically give a small benefit to debt over equity and hence I only write that the WACC is substantially independent of gearing and not simply independent of gearing.

[4] So, for example, if a shareholder wished that a company had more debt in order to allow leverage effects to increase the return in a favourable trading situation, he or she could achieve this result by borrowing money himself and using this to purchase further shares in the company.

Now although the idea of shareholders seeing through a company to its underlying assets does have intuitive appeal, I have always had one concern with it. This is with the difference between the liquidity of a share and the liquidity of a project. We generally assume that shareholders can buy and sell shares whenever they so wish and without impacting on the market. Situations where this can always be done are referred to as being highly liquid. The more difficult it is to sell instantly and without impacting on the price, the less liquid the market is said to be. Lack of liquidity creates risk and hence requires an additional return in order to justify investment.

Projects are not liquid. It takes time to divest a project. They are typically all-or-nothing affairs and there are substantial transaction costs associated with exit. If a share were subject to these conditions it would be considered to be much more risky and so would be expected to offer a higher return. This requirement is not factored in to the way that we analyse projects within companies. As I understand it, this is because we assume that there will be an active market in the shares and that the share price will reflect the underlying value of its assets as going concerns.[5] So although the projects are not liquid, liquidity is provided by the financial markets.[6]

So even though projects are not liquid, companies do not need to allow for this when they evaluate them. The CoC which is applied has been derived from a set of assumptions which implicitly include the benefit of liquidity. This is reasonable as long as the project is not capable of causing material adverse effects on other activities.

What I will now do is consider how each of the components of the CoC can be assessed and what the uncertainties are which surround each number.

Estimating the components of the cost of capital

In this section I will consider each of the seven contributors to the CoC. These are traditionally stated as follows:

1. CoD: the company's cost of borrowing;
2. t: its marginal tax rate;
3. *Debt:* the market value of the company's debt;

[5] A going-concern valuation is assessed as the present value of future cash flows. If one becomes forced to sell, then valuations are depressed because the purchaser can strike a tough bargain and there may well also be transaction costs to allow for as well.

[6] There are times when some individuals attack the idea of free market economics. In my view the way that markets, in effect, drive down the cost of capital by creating liquidity is one of their great benefits.

4. *Equity:* the market value of the company's equity;
5. r_F: the risk-free interest rate;
6. β: the covariance of the company's equity with the market; and
7. r_M: the return required by investors who invest in the market portfolio.

This list shows the components in the order in which they appear in the WACC equation. I will now review how each should be set and what the inherent uncertainties are. I will, however, move the risk-free rate to the top of my list of things to consider because it sets the starting point for consideration of both the cost of debt and the cost of equity.

The **risk-free rate** is typically assumed to be the US 90-day T bill rate although some analysts do use a borrowing rate for long-term borrowing by the US government (this is called the bond rate). My view is that one should use the T bill rate because it is clear that one takes inflation risk when lending at a fixed rate for a long period and hence there is a risk premium inherent in the bond rate. In the USA this bond maturity premium averaged about a half a percentage point over the twentieth century but this average figure hides a wider range of year-by-year differences between long- and short-term interest rates.

At any point in time the T bill rate is an observable fact. The trouble, however, is that it changes over time in response to economic events and these changes are really substantial. Many analysts will simply use the current T bill rate as their estimate of the risk-free rate. I believe that when one is taking long-term investment decisions within a company one needs to take a view on what the rate will be on average into the long term and not be dominated by the current rate.

I have prepared the following chart using data on annual averages taken from the Ibbotson Associates 2004 Yearbook called *Stocks, Bonds, Bills and Inflation.* I have shown the basic T bill rate and also the rate adjusted for inflation. This inflation-adjusted number is, I believe, a better way to think about the risk-free rate. It allows a better understanding of historical data. It also allows one to ensure that the CoC is consistent with the other assumptions which underpin any investment case, one of which will need to be the inflation rate. The average T bill rate adjusted for inflation over this 15 year period was 1¾% but the figures, which are already annual averages, cover a range of over four percentage points.

So, what should one assume for the future? Is 1989–2003 a representative period such that it might be safe to extrapolate for the coming, say, 15 to 20 years based on the average which it gives us?

The period does finish with an exceptionally low T bill rate. Indeed between June 2003 and May 2004 the 90-day T bill rate was less than 1%. Is this a

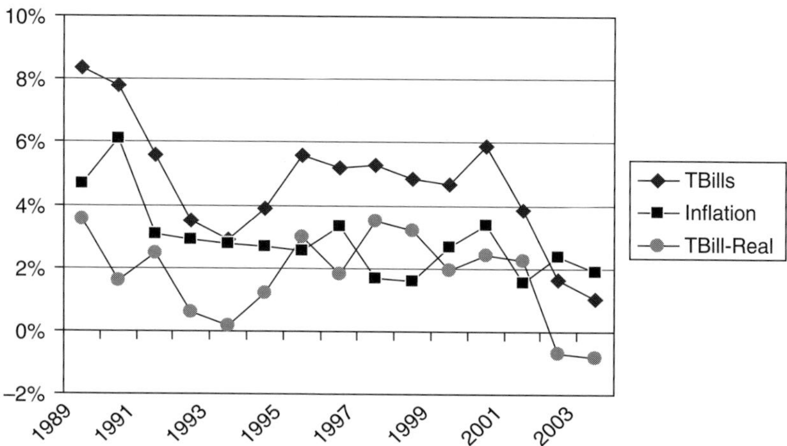

Fig. 11.2 US 90 day T bills and inflation

normal part of the interest rate cycle or was it unusual? Well, I can bring in some extra information and state that after the period covered by the chart the rate then rose steadily to around 5% in the middle of 2006; it remained there for about a year and has since fallen again.

A longer-run perspective gives one a rather different view of the risk-free rate. The data from Ibbotson Associates show an average compound growth rate from investing in T Bills of 3.7% over the period 1926–2003. The inflation rate over this period averaged 3.0%. This indicates a long-run average risk-free rate of just ¾% real. This time period does, however, cover the Great Depression and also a period when inflation was very high and so I take the view that it does not give a good mid-point estimate but rather it sets the lower end of the reasonable range.

So overall perhaps my original 15-year data do give a reasonable mid-point estimate of the risk-free rate being inflation plus 1¾% with a range of ±1% giving a sensible range. We need to convert this real rate back into a nominal rate through making an assumption about the rate of inflation. I will use a range of 2–3½% with 2½% as the mid-point.

With the risk-free rate in place we can now turn to the company's **cost of borrowing**. One could imagine that this at least would be easy. Surely, a phone call to the finance department should reveal it. The phone call would, however, most probably be met with some initial questions such as over what period are we borrowing, what security is being offered, and perhaps also, what currency are we to borrow in? Furthermore, unless the project was to be financed by a fixed-interest-rate loan repayable over its full economic life, there would be a question to answer concerning the future trend in interest rates.

Now I would suggest that if one wanted to respect the idea of separating financing decisions from asset investment decisions, one should really be asking the finance department what it estimated the company's average cost of debt would be over the period of the project and not simply what the cost of debt was now. Unless we are dealing with a single-project company that plans to lock in all of its borrowing requirements now, the finance department could not know what the future interest rate will be. It would know what its average interest rate had been in the past and would have a general idea about its overall future financial policy. This would cover things like its target credit rating,[7] its policy concerning the period over which it would borrow and whether it would borrow on fixed or floating terms. Multinational companies would also consider the currency in which they expected to borrow. With the benefit of all of this background information the finance department should be able to provide a view about what the estimated average cost of debt would be over the life of the project.

If we simplify things by considering just a single currency of borrowing then the component parts of the cost of debt would be the risk-free rate, a premium to reflect the credit status of the company and a premium to reflect the period of borrowing if, as is likely, this is different from what is deemed to set the risk-free rate.

The following chart shows the way that the finance department will probably be looking at interest rates. The chart shows what is called a yield graph. This shows the latest interest rate for borrowing of different periods and for two credit ratings. These ratings are for the strongest companies (AAA rated) and also for companies at the lowest end of the investment grade rating (BBB rated). The majority of large quoted companies will be within this range although some will have a lower credit rating and hence will pay even more for their borrowing.

There is a very steep upward slope on both curves,[8] indicating that in September 2002 the longer the period over which you wanted to borrow, the greater was the return that you had to offer to lenders. At the time the risk-free rate was just 1.6% and so the spread between 20-year borrowing and the risk-free rate for an extremely strong company was about 4%.

I chose September 2002 in order to make the point about the danger of simply assuming that today's interest rates will apply into the long run.

[7] See page 37 for definitions of the various credit ratings.

[8] Note that the borrowing period scale is not linear. The curve starts with three months' borrowing moving out to six months then year by year for 1–5 years and finally ten, 15 and 20 year borrowing.

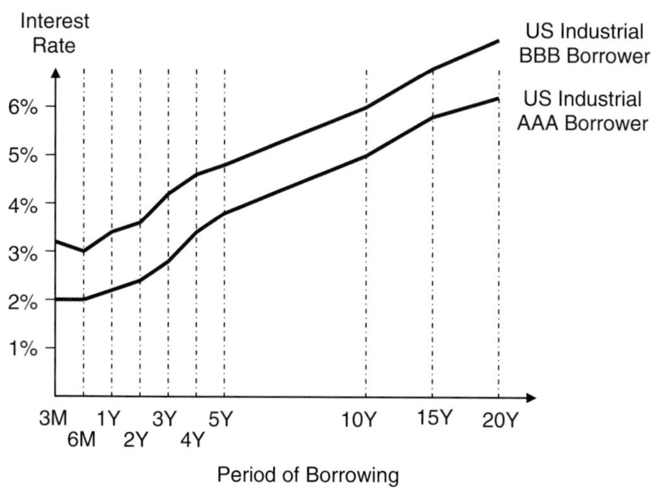

Fig. 11.3 Example yield graph September 2002

September 2002 was not the low point in the interest rate cycle for short-term interest rates but it would still have been considered to be below the trend line. This is why the line slopes upwards so steeply. This is a sign that in September 2002, the market expected short-term interest rates to rise in the future.

In the next chart I will show the picture from September 2006. At this time the T bill rate had risen to about 5%. The market's earlier expectation of a rise in interest rates had been fulfilled. In 2006, the market considered the 5% T bill rate to be unsustainably high and so medium-term interest rates for companies were actually slightly below the short-term rate.

What we now have is a substantially flat yield graph and also a slight reduction in the extra interest rate that BBB-rated companies have to pay compared with the strongest companies. Long-term borrowing rates, however, have hardly changed.

It is currently September 2007 and I am writing this chapter in the middle of what is being termed the US subprime mortgage crisis. In the last month there has been the first run on a major UK bank for over 100 years and, as the Chinese proverb goes, these are certainly 'interesting times'. A notable feature of the latest yield curve is the large gap which has opened up between the T bill rate and the cost at which companies borrow.

I conclude from all of this turbulence that the appropriate assumption concerning the cost of debt will be a rough estimate of what it is likely to be, based on a lot of judgement. Although the data source that I used in order to

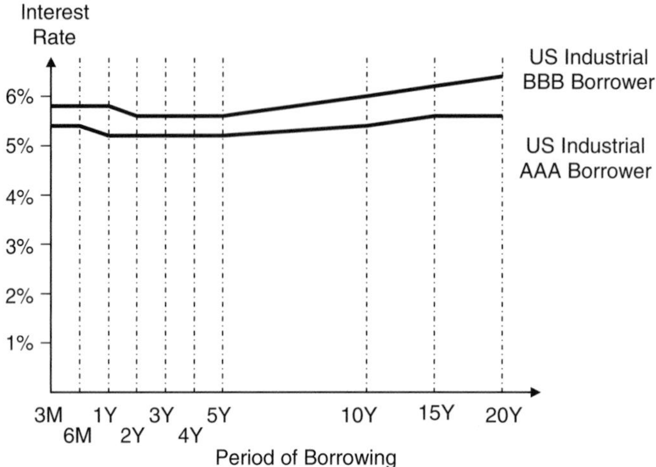

Fig. 11.4 Example yield graph September 2006

prepare the above graphs quoted interest rates to the percentage point plus four figures after this, I deliberately drew it as a PowerPoint chart in order to emphasise what I consider to be the need to view it as a picture and not an accurate statement.

There does appear to be some stability at present in long-term interest rates and if a company adopts a financial policy of borrowing at long-term fixed-interest rates these can be used to set the cost of borrowing component of the WACC. If, however, borrowing is over a shorter period than the WACC will be used for, there is no way of avoiding the need simply to make an educated estimate of what the company's cost of borrowing will be. This could be something like the risk-free rate plus, say, 1–2% for a very strong borrower with a further 1% added if the borrower was only just of investment grade.

The **marginal tax rate** is included in the calculation in order to allow for the benefit of tax relief on interest. At any point in time a company ought to know what tax relief it can gain on any interest payments. In simple situations this will equal the headline corporate tax rate. Tax, however, is rarely simple and does not stand still. My view is that 15-year projects are not unusual but 15-year periods with no changes in tax rates or rules are. So one needs to take a judgement regarding what the rate of tax relief on interest will be over the life of the project. The usual assumption would be that this equalled the current headline corporate tax rate unless one had specific reasons to believe that the rate would be different.

I have encountered many cynics who maintain that tax rates only ever go up. This view is not supported by the facts! The accounting firm KPMG publishes a regular survey of corporate tax rate trends which highlights a steady downward trend in tax rates. This survey shows that between 1993 and 1996 the average tax rate across a range of countries was quite stable at around 38%. In 1997, however, the average fell sharply to about 33% and the rate then followed a fairly steady trend down to about 27% in 2005. The rate was more or less unchanged over 2005–2007.

I am not suggesting that we should extrapolate the future trend based on the past 15 years but this analysis by KPMG certainly does question what is the usual assumption about tax rates, namely that the current rate, whatever it may be, will prevail. This has much wider implications than simply impacting on the CoC. It also questions the assumptions concerning tax in the assessment of cash flow. I do not believe that I can offer a reasoned answer to this question. I do, though, suggest that the government's take in the form of taxation is something that does need to be thought about and be covered by specific assumptions that maintain the internal consistency of the financial case.[9]

The differences between countries are quite significant. In the USA the effective corporate tax rate is said to be about 40% after one allows for federal and state taxes. This is well above the UK's 30% rate and the global average of just below 27%. I will use this US rate when I come to assess the actual CoC later in this section with the 27% figure used as the lower end of the range. Individual companies should make their own assessment of the likely rate at which they will gain tax relief on interest. This could be quite low if a company has a large pool of unutilised tax losses. I have also heard of situations where interest tax relief can be 'double dipped', with relief gained in more than one jurisdiction. This can serve to increase the tax-offset effect and hence reduce the CoC.

The next item to consider is the **market value of the company's debt**. This should usually equal the balance outstanding which will also be the book value. I can, though, think of at least three situations where market value and the outstanding balance should not be the same. These are:

1. If the borrowing had been at a fixed rate and rates have subsequently changed.
2. If the creditworthiness of the company has changed.

[9] Internal consistency requires that any assumed changes in corporate tax rates apply both to the setting of the CoC and to the assessment of the cash flow effect of taxes. There is an offsetting effect in that low tax rates lead to higher future cash flows but also higher costs of capital because the value of the interest tax shield falls.

3. If the market's required premiums for borrower credit rating have changed.

These are all theoretically valid situations but I suggest that they can usually be ignored and so one usually assumes that the market value of debt is the same as its book value.

The **market value of a company's equity** is subject to much greater variability and one should not use book value as the estimate.[10]

As an example of this volatility I selected 50 companies from the *Financial Times* Global 500 share list. This covers the 500 largest quoted companies in the world. I compared the reported high and low share prices over the previous year.[11] The average for my set of 50 companies was that the high was just over 50% greater than the low. The difference was less than 20% in only two of my 50 companies surveyed and the largest difference was well over 150%.

Now we need the market value of equity in order to give the correct weights to debt and equity in the WACC calculation. The fact that equity value is this volatile simply serves to emphasise the relatively inexact nature of the calculation. At any particular point in time we are able to calculate the actual weighting of debt and equity based on market values. We have to recognise, though, that owing to the volatility of equity values this weighting is likely to change significantly over time. Since we want a CoC to apply over a long period, we are forced to apply judgement to decide what figure to use.

Now it is possible that one might think that the economic gearing[12] should not matter when one is calculating the WACC. This would be because the theories tell us that WACC is independent of gearing. The trouble, however, is that one is forced to calculate WACC via its component parts and then take the weighted average because the WACC itself cannot be directly observed. So the relative weightings do matter.[13]

[10] I have seen many studies on the cost of capital that do use the book value of debt and equity. These will almost always underestimate the CoC because the market value of equity should be above the book value and hence using book value gives too low a weighting to the more expensive equity component of the WACC.

[11] The data were taken from the *Financial Times* dated 24 September 2007.

[12] Economic gearing is another name for the ratio of $\frac{Debt}{Debt + Equity}$ where both *Debt* and *Equity* are based on market values. The term book gearing can be used when book values are used although this is often referred to simply as the gearing or the debt equity ratio. The potential for misunderstanding is self-evident and so I always suggest that one should make the meaning of any gearing figures which are quoted absolutely clear.

[13] I have also heard it suggested that one can avoid the problem of not knowing the relative weights for debt and equity by assessing the cost of equity if the company had no debt. It is true that if you know the cost of equity for a company with no debt this will give you the cost of capital directly. The trouble is that in order to assess the cost of equity when there is no debt one has to unlever the equity ß data.

My suggestion is that the market value of equity should be based on a rough average over the past year unless there are strong reasons to use a different figure. These strong reasons could include major share buybacks or issues. They could also include situations where there is confidential data available within the company which, when it becomes public, would have a material impact on the share price. In this situation an internal valuation could be used.

There will be a strong link between the cost of a company's debt and its economic gearing. We have seen above that there is on average a spread in borrowing costs of about 1% just between the top and the bottom of investment grade. There is not a fixed ratio below which companies lose their so-called investment grade status but as a very rough rule of thumb, two parts of equity to one part of debt will serve as a guide. Now the average non-financial company[14] will be somewhat less geared than this, say, 25–30% debt with 70–75% equity. In the oil industry economic gearings of less than 10% are typical.

The next parameter to consider is the so-called β factor, which is the **covariance of the company's equity with the market**. Various data sources will provide this.[15] The data on the β factor will, typically, be calculated based on a series of monthly data for a five-year period. The result will be a figure for the company's β. Many analysts will use the β factor in a rather slavish way. There are several reasons, however, why I suggest that although the calculation is mechanical, my view is that a lot of interpretation is needed.

The first reason for this is that a five-year period may well contain some special external factors. I recall, for example, how the first Gulf War distorted the β for the oil majors. Their share prices rose when the market fell and this appeared to indicate that their correlation with the market was weak. Hence, for a five-year period the oil industry appeared to have a low β. After five years, however, this effect was excluded and the β rose. My view is that judgement needs to be used. To apply the β which was calculated after the end of the five-year period would be the equivalent of assuming that no more events like the first Gulf War would ever happen. By contrast, using the β as calculated during the five-year period to set the WACC is equivalent to assuming that one such event occurs every five years. Perhaps a better assumption might be to average the two figures or simply to apply judgement. My view is

This unlevering requires as an input assumption, the economic gearing, and so one cannot escape without knowing this.

14 Financial companies (i.e. banks) operate with very different business models and have much higher gearing ratios.

15 For example, the London Business School's risk measurement service.

that judgement is necessary because one is trying to take a view about future risk but one only has firm data concerning the past.

There may also be special internal factors to take into account. Suppose, for example, a company suffers some particular setback that drives its share price down. If, by chance, this happens at a time when the market is moving sharply upwards the company will appear to have a low β. If, however, the setback happens when the market is falling the company may appear to have a high β. Unless one thinks that the setbacks and their relationship to movements in the market overall will be regular, it would be best to exclude their impact from the analysis.

This is not just a theoretical point. I recall a study about the two computer companies IBM and Apple. The study showed that Apple appeared to have a lower CoC than IBM. This was because Apple had done badly over a period when the market was doing well. Unless one thought that Apple's performance would always move in the opposite direction to the market it would be wrong implicitly to assume this by using its β as calculated over the particular period.

The usual solution to the internal factors problem is to apply a sector β.[16] This means that rather than using simply the β for the company, one uses the β for the sector in which the company operates.[17] I like this approach but of course it does depend on there being a reasonable number of peer companies available for study. An inherent advantage of the approach is that it would lead one to believe that companies which operate in the same business should have the same CoC. Since this seems right to me,[18] I am intuitively attracted to the approach.

A problem with the sector β approach is that it does assume that all companies which operate within a sector are subject to the same degree of risk. There is an obvious need to adjust for differences in gearing between companies. One can do this by calculating a so-called asset β. This is equal to the equity β times the percentage that equity forms of total market capitalisation.[19]

[16] Calculating the sector ß avoids the internal factors problem, but the external factors problem still remains and can only be solved by the application of judgement.

[17] I can think of several ways of calculating a sector ß. It could, for example, be the arithmetic average of the ß of all of the companies in the sector. Or it could be a weighted average of the ß based on market values. Or one could compute a sector index and assess the ß for this. This final method has the strongest intellectual appeal but will be the most complex to apply unless such an index is already available. The first approach is the simplest and is what I would do 'in real life'.

[18] It seems right because the cost of capital is set by the riskiness of the investment and this should be common across companies that are making similar investments.

[19] The idea is that debt has a ß of zero and equity has the equity ß. The asset ß is the weighted average of the two with the weightings set by the market values of debt and equity. The zero debt ß means that one only needs the equity ß and its weight in order to calculate the overall weighted average.

The real trouble with the sector β approach is not financial leverage, it is with the other risks that companies take on. It would be a huge and often unjustified assumption to assume these risks are the same for all companies that operate within a sector. Some companies operate within a sector but do so with a very different approach to business than their competitors. The balance between fixed and variable costs can be particularly important in setting the volatility of future cash flows. So too can be decisions about selling price such as whether to sell on a cost-plus basis or whether to sell for fixed prices. Companies with relatively high fixed costs should be more volatile than companies with low fixed costs.[20] So what one really needs to compute is a sector β just for companies that are operating to a similar business model to your own company. Yet again, this requires judgement and it also limits the size of the sample of peer companies that is available.

I will be returning to this particular factor later in this view. It goes to the heart of why I believe that questions related to risk and reward need to be decided upon by senior executive judgement and not simply through a calculation of the 'right' CoC.

There is one point concerning β which is nice and precise. This is that, by definition, the average β for quoted companies must be 1.0. So if one is dealing with a quoted company and has no reason to see why it was subject to different risks from other companies then a β of 1 is appropriate. I would describe a β of less than 0.5 for a quoted company as low and more than 1.5 as being high. Unquoted companies tend to cover a wider range and, in particular, can be of much higher risk.

The final component of our WACC calculation is the **equity risk premium**. This is the additional return which equity investors demand in order to be compensated for taking the additional risk that equity investment entails. Now one could simply ask shareholders what this required return was. The problem with this would be that there was no mechanism for testing how realistic the answers would be. I could, for example, say that I wanted a 9% premium whereas another investor might say 10% while a third wanted just 5%. Who is 'right'? The right answer would be where there was a balance between the supply and demand of equity finance for investments. Clearly, therefore, one needs to look at the financial markets in order to find out what the equity risk premium should be.

[20] I made this point as part of the Sources of Value analysis of the scaffolding business case study (page 292). The business model for our example had relatively low fixed costs compared with the typical competitor and so, all other things being equal, was lower risk.

A common approach, therefore, is to look at the returns which have been earned on a stock market over a long period and to assume that the long-run average premium which equities have given compared to risk-free is a good indicator of what the equity risk premium must be. I have, for example, noted on page 40 that the additional return earned on an investment in US equities made at the end of 1925 and held through to 2000 was just over 7%. This, however, represents just a single observation. A better view, I believe, comes from looking at a range of financial markets and a longer period.

A team of researchers at the London Business School has done this and regularly publishes updates to it.[21] It has shown that the range of observed risk premiums across the world is between about 3% and 7% with the world average being about 5%.

Now there is a real problem with trusting historical data to tell us a forward-looking equity risk premium. This problem is that the required equity risk premium may well have changed over the period that we are studying. It is perfectly possible, for example, that the relative risk of companies has changed. It is also perfectly possible that the relative risk of life has changed as well. Either or both of these changes could result in a change in the equity risk premium.

If we consider first the risk within companies, I simply do not know what the business ethos was back in 1900. I certainly have the impression that there was less transparency, which must suggest that risks are now lower. Perhaps also the theories which we now have about business will mean that businesses can be better run and that risks as a result are lower. Perhaps, though, the average level of borrowing is higher, which would serve to increase risk.

We need to consider also what I have termed the risk of life. Perhaps the threat of global war is reduced. There are certainly greater prospects for risk diversification across markets than existed in 1900. These factors would, in logic, suggest a reduction in the required equity risk premium. Global warming threats, increased yearing and terrorism, however, could all suggest a need for a higher risk premium.

One further piece of evidence about the equity risk premium concerns what figures were typically quoted when practitioners attempted to calculate the WACC. Prior to the publication of the LBS study referred to above, the usual assumption, based on my experience, was of a figure in the region of

[21] See for example the *Global Investment Returns Yearbook 2007* by Elroy Dimson, Paul Marsh and Mike Staunton of the London Business School, published by ABN AMRO. This work was first published in 2000 and I remember attending the initial launch at LBS. At this time the markets in 12 countries were covered and the period was 1900–2000. The list is now extended to 17 countries which together account for approaching 90% of the total market capitalisation of all stocks in the world.

6–8½%. This was justified based just on US market data. I remember in the late 1990s having difficulty squaring actual market prices with what I thought the CoC should be. A lower CoC was necessary to explain share prices[22] and this could only be justified if the equity risk premium was lower.

Let us now consider what would happen if the market's required equity risk premium were to change. Suppose that for whatever reason, the market changed its view on the required equity risk premium and decided it was content with a lower figure. What would happen?

I would suggest that share prices should rise to reflect the new lower CoC. Now what does this mean for the actual return which will be observed on the market? Clearly the actual return will go up because the lower CoC would lead to higher valuations. This means that at the end of the year any studies which are published which show actual returns and use these as indicators of investors' required returns will suggest that required returns have increased. This is the exact opposite of what the markets are trying to signal.

I conclude from this that one must be very careful when trying to interpret historical market data in order to set a future equity risk premium. If, as I believe it to be the case, the required equity risk premium has fallen, then the observed equity risk premium should overstate the actual equity risk premium. So even if the long-run world average is about 5%, this might overstate what markets are now requiring.[23]

Once one realises how judgemental the equity risk premium must be, one can return to my initial suggestion about the equity risk premium; namely, that one simply asks investors what they expect. A way of doing this is to study the assumptions being made by analysts when they publish stock market surveys. Another is to study the published investment assumptions which are made by major pension funds. In the UK at least, major pension funds are many of the biggest investors in companies. The parent company that stands behind each pension fund is required to publish the assumptions which it is making when it evaluates its pension liabilities. So their assumptions about investment returns should give some relevant and useful evidence.

For example, the 2006 Annual Report and Accounts for the UK bank HBOS provides as a note to the accounts a summary of the assumed returns

[22] One can explain prices via the simple growth to perpetuity approach. This states that cost of equity = growth + yield. The yield on the market is known. So if you think you know what the cost of equity is you can calculate the implied rate of dividend growth. If this looks unrealistic there must be something wrong. Either share prices are too high or your view of the cost of equity is too high.

[23] I always worry when I see the financial services industry publishing charts of historical performance with just a small footnote to the effect that 'past performance is not necessarily a guide to future performance'. The words are absolutely true but I do not think that the typical person who reads them understands just how poor a guide past performance can be if required returns change.

on investments made by its pension fund. The expected returns are 8.3% for equities and 5.15% for bonds while the associated inflation assumption is 3.0%. Unfortunately bonds are not risk-free because they will embody both a term premium and probably also a credit risk premium. So all that we can conclude is that HBOS is assuming an equity risk premium of above 3.15%.

Another major UK bank, Lloyds TSB, states in its accounts that it is assuming a return of 8.0% for equities, 5.1% for non-government bonds and 3.9% for cash. If we take cash as the risk-free rate this points to an equity risk premium of 4.1%.

The BP PLC accounts provide a similar set of assumptions. The assumed return on equities is 7.5% while bonds give 4.7% and cash just 3.8%. Hence one can infer that the BP pension fund assumption is for an equity risk premium of 3.7%.

Now one always hopes that pension funds will adopt conservative assumptions and so perhaps something round about 4% should represent the low end of the range for the risk premium. I would, though, be nervous because this analysis appears to have shown that the risk premium is subject to a narrow range of uncertainty of just 4–5%. Intuitively this is too narrow for what is an inexact judgement. I prefer to consider a range of 3–6% with 4½% as my best estimate.

Estimating the cost of capital

We are now ready to put the various components together and obtain an estimate of a company's CoC. The components cannot all be considered in isolation because there are a number of important links such as the way that the risk-free rate impacts both the cost of debt and the cost of equity and also the way that high economic gearing leads to a higher company premium and hence a higher overall cost of debt. I will therefore carry out three assessments of the typical WACC. Initially I will study a low case, a mid point and a high case all for a company with a β of 1. I will investigate changes in β at a subsequent stage in my analysis.

Initial cost of capital assessment

	Low	Mid point	High
Cost of debt – %			
Inflation	2.0	2.5	3.5
Real risk-free	0.75	1.75	2.75

Table (*cont.*)

	Low	Mid point	High
Risk-free rate	2.8	4.3	6.3
Company premium	1.0	2.0	3.0
Company CoD	3.8	6.3	9.3
Tax rate	40	40	27
After-tax CoD	2.3	3.8	6.8
Cost of equity – %			
Risk-free rate	2.8	4.3	6.3
Beta factor	1	1	1
Market risk premium	3	4.5	6
Cost of equity	5.8	8.8	12.3
Debt/equity	10/90	25/75	30/70
Weighted average cost of capital	5.4%	7.5%	10.7%

Now although the individual ranges for the various components of the calculation are, I believe, quite reasonable, it is not justified simply to combine a series of 'realistic' downside assumptions and then describe the overall result as realistic.[24] It is highly unlikely that all low-case assumptions will turn out to be good long-run assumptions at the same time. Likewise the high-case estimate is almost certainly too high. I will return to this point in a few pages time. There are, however, two other features of the numbers which I believe require adjustment.

The first feature concerns the approach which this initial assessment has taken in regard to inflation. I have assumed a range of 2–3½%. I believe that it would be better to remove this uncertainty from the initial CoC assessment and to base the assessment on a single assumed rate of inflation. It would then be possible to ensure that the assumptions behind the CoC were consistent with the assumptions behind the assessment of future cash flow. If a different rate of inflation were required, this could be used but the CoC would also need to be changed.[25] So it would be more meaningful to show a table with just a single rate of inflation and accept that if this were to change there would be a need to change the CoC.

There remains a second adjustment to be made to the calculation of the CoC in order to remove one remaining inconsistency. This concerns the β factor.

[24] Remember, for example, that if something has a 20% chance of happening and something else also has a 20% chance of happening, if the two outcomes are uncorrelated the chance of them both happening is just 4%.

[25] When working in a large company the best approach would be for there to be a single company-wide assumption about inflation with this linked into the cost of capital assessment. The inflation assumption would not be changed without reviewing also the cost of capital assumption.

At present I have used a β assumption of 1 in all three columns even though the economic gearings are different. Now the β factor quoted in the table is an equity β. This means that if the gearings are different the implied asset βs are different. It would be better to remove this effect so that we were dealing with the CoC for a set of assets of equal risk in all three columns. My mid point has an equity β of 1 but with 25% debt. Now the asset β is the weighted average of the debt and equity βs. This means that its asset β must be 0.75 since the β for debt should be zero. My low-case column has only 10% economic gearing so if its asset β was 0.75, its equity β would be 0.83. A similar calculation would suggest that the β for the right-hand column should be 1.07.

The updated CoC assessment would then be as follows:

Cost of capital assessment – fixed inflation assumption and constant asset β

	Low	Mid point	High
Cost of debt – %			
Inflation	2.5	2.5	2.5
Real risk-free	0.75	1.75	2.75
Risk-free rate	3.3	4.3	5.3
Company premium	1.0	2.0	3.0
Company CoD	4.3	6.3	8.3
Tax rate	40	40	27
After-tax CoD	2.6	3.8	6.1
Cost of equity – %			
Risk-free rate	3.3	4.3	5.3
Beta factor for equity	0.83	1	1.07
Market risk premium	3	4.5	6
Cost of equity	5.8	8.8	11.7
Debt/equity	10/90	25/75	30/70
Weighted average cost of capital	5.4%	7.5%	10.0%

One should, I suggest, remove the apparent precision of these numbers and call the range 5½%–7½%–10%.

We are now ready to return to the problem that this assessment has combined several low-case assumptions together to arrive at the low estimate. It is my view that it is very unlikely that all of the low or all of the high assumptions will come about together. I therefore suggest that the range needs to be cropped somewhat. This is necessary particularly at the upper end of the range.

Overall, therefore, my assessment of the CoC for a typical set of assets is a range of 6–9% with the mid-point being 7½%. Readers who started as beginners and so read the financial foundation section might recall my earlier very rough estimate of a typical CoC of 9% from page 58. There are several small differences between the way that I derived that number and this revised estimate but it is within my latest range. This one and a half percentage point range for the CoC for a typical company is, in my view, more realistic than the ±0.5% range which other experts claim. Perhaps the one and a half percentage points which I suggest is too great but I cannot see how the reasonable range can be less than ±1%.

Having completed this analysis for a typical company one can then consider the range that is possible between high- and low-risk companies. My mid-point assumptions applied to a low-risk company with an equity β of 0.5 would produce a WACC of about 6%. If the β rose to 1.75, which would be high for a major company, the WACC would be about 10%.

The cost of capital for a project

So far we have been considering how to assess a company's WACC. This is what one should use in order to value the activities of an entire company. The CoC is, however, often used while evaluating individual projects within a company. These projects will have their own unique risk characteristics. So what CoC should we use in these situations?

The theory tells us to assume that shareholders look through the company to its projects. We ought, therefore, to be computing project costs of capital based on the diversified shareholders' views on the risk that accompanies the project. This requirement to take the diversified shareholders' view gives a strong message about one thing that we should not be doing. This is basing our project CoC on the total risk that is inherent in any project. I deliberately referred to projects as having unique risk characteristics. Our portfolio diversification approach tells us that risks which can be diversified should not result in shareholders requiring additional returns. This means that unique risks will not impact on the CoC. What impacts on the CoC is a project's exposure to risks which are held in common with many other companies on the market.

It may well be difficult in practice, but in principle what our theories tell us is that the approach should be that one builds up a project CoC based on a sector β derived from companies that have similar risk characteristics to the project concerned. The trouble, however, is that this is often not possible because there are not enough companies that operate in clear enough ways to comprise the appropriate sector.

My discussions with practitioners over the years suggest that one of three approaches is usually adopted in order to compute project costs of capital. These approaches are:

- applying divisional costs of capital;
- applying 'project types' costs of capital; and
- applying just the company CoC.

The divisional approach is easiest to justify in relation to the theory which calls for a sector β and is most intuitive in companies that operate in different markets. The more different these markets are, and the more quoted companies that operate in them, the greater the justification for using this technique.

So if a company is operating through, say, four business divisions, then each division needs to identify its analogue companies and compute its own sector β. This figure will then be plugged into the WACC calculation, usually with the other parameters such as risk-free rate and company cost of borrowing held constant. In some instances, however, if the typical gearing levels in the sectors are different these effects too may be allowed for.

The 'project types' CoC approach depends on defining types of projects and setting different costs of capital for each type. So, for example, entry into a new market might have a high CoC whereas a cost-saving investment in an existing market may have a low CoC. This approach has strong theoretical foundations because individual projects can be very different and the divisional β approach does not allow for this.

My concern with this approach is that it is hard to find the data to establish the correct β and so the costs of capital are usually fairly arbitrary. I often think that those who set these project types' costs of capital are influenced by their views of total risk rather than the view of non-diversifiable risk. If, however, it is possible to obtain good data on the β factor for comparable projects then the project β approach has a lot to recommend it.

The company CoC approach is often derided by academics but the practical problems with establishing the correct CoC are such that applying a single CoC is often as justifiable as the alternatives.

Now at this stage I propose to introduce a further complication. I need to do this in order to explain how difficult it is to derive a correct CoC and how poor our intuition can often be. This complication concerns looking in even more detail into the individual components of a project's cash flow.

If it is correct to look through a company to its projects, why not look through the projects to the individual elements of cash flow? These elements of cash flow are, after all, subject to very different risks, so why not analyse, for example, each line of our spreadsheet model with its own CoC?

Let us first think a little further about how this would work. Suppose that we were looking at a project which we were happy was typical of the investments that our company made and hence could be valued by discounting its cash flows at the company CoC. We know that, thanks to the principle of additivity of value, we can add up the value of the various parts of the project and get the same overall value. Let us now consider the fixed costs in the project. These are always much more certain than the sales revenue so surely they would justify the application of a lower CoC. Now using a lower CoC for a stream of future costs will serve to lower value compared with what we had previously been doing. So if the principle of additivity of value is to apply what must we do to the CoC for the remaining cash flow streams? This may not seem intuitive, but we must lower it as well. This is because a lower CoC applied to a stream of costs serves to lower value and to offset this with a stream of revenues we must lower the discount rate on these as well.

What I have shown is that the discount rate for the individual lines of a spreadsheet model should, in logic, be lower than the discount rate which is applied to the net cash flow. One has to think quite hard to understand why this effect is correct. The reason is that net cash flow will be more volatile than its individual components. The net cash flow of a project can swing from being positive to being negative. By contrast, however, sales revenues must always be positive and costs must always be negative. So the net cash flow is likely to be the riskiest cash flow line on our spreadsheet.

At this stage I must ask readers simply to hold this thought in their minds. I need to look at some alternative approaches to dealing with risk. I will be doing this with the aim of showing that so far we have nothing better to help us take decisions about the risk/reward trade-off. Once we accept this I will show how we can design a reasonably proactive approach to the question of risk and reward that accepts the general principles of the economic value model without becoming too bogged down in the technical detail of CoC calculations. An important part of this will be the Sources of Value way of thinking about investments. This treats the CoC as usually being a part of the 'me too' player's view of life and hence gives us a way to calibrate what are in aggregate, reasonable assumptions.

Alternative approaches to setting the cost of capital

It should by now have become apparent that the economic value model, supported by CAPM to set the cost of equity, is far from perfect. This is because, although the theories might sound nice, the practical calculation of an appropriate CoC is highly judgemental. It is natural therefore that others have tried to propose their own alternative approaches. Some of these approaches involve relatively minor adjustments to how the CoC is assessed while others involve radically different approaches.

There is a huge incentive to work in this area. The prize of a new breakthrough could involve both fame and fortune. Furthermore, research does not require expensive equipment as is the case for scientific discoveries as there are plenty of readily available data with which to test any new hypothesis. It would be highly surprising therefore if there were not a number of competing approaches available.

One of the lessons from history is that we should know our enemy[26] and so I will not simply ignore all of the competing theories that are available. Now only a few of the theories are, in my view, objectionable enough to be termed enemies but most are, I believe, distractions and it pays to understand why this is.

So to complete this section I will review some of the alternative valuation methods that have been proposed. These approaches usually start off sounding quite attractive. The problem, however, is usually that when one thinks harder about their application one realises they will add complication to the topic of investment evaluation without giving significantly more accuracy. None of them, as far as I am aware, can get round the problem that we do not know what the future will bring. The new approaches also suffer from the disadvantage of being relatively untried by senior managers.

I will deal first with two radically different approaches. These are the certainty equivalent method and the equity-as-an-option approach. I should stress at the outset of this venture into academia that I am not an expert in these topics! I have, however, discussed them with some business school professors who are experts and so I am not a complete amateur.

The certainty equivalent approach depends on adjusting our future cash flow estimates to cash flows that shareholders would consider to be risk free.

[26] I have read that it was the ancient Chinese warrior Sun Tzu who taught his men to 'know your enemy' before going into battle. His view was that if 'you know your enemy and know yourself, you need not fear the result of a hundred battles.' But, he warned, if 'you know yourself but not the enemy, for every victory gained you will also suffer a defeat'.

The advantage of this is that these cash flows can then be discounted at the risk-free rate which means that one avoids having to estimate the CoC and one just needs the risk-free rate.

My problems with this approach fall into two categories. First, nobody has ever been able to explain to my satisfaction how the transformation from estimated future cash flow to certainty-equivalent cash flow can be done without adopting some of the same type of assumptions which we have to make in our usual valuation approach. The certainty-equivalent cash flow is not the expected value cash flow. It appears to me that it is defined as the cash flow which an investor would be prepared to discount at the cost of debt. This transformation is tantamount to estimating the additional premium required to remunerate risk which we do when we set the CoC.

My second problem concerns the risk-free rate. Many academics seem to view this as a given. As I have explained above, however, we do not know what the risk-free rate will be in the future, we only ever know what it is today. Since we are taking long-term decisions we need a long-term estimate of something that is inherently short term in nature. Striving for accuracy in this situation is, I suggest, likely to be pointless.

The equity-as-an-option approach involves deconstructing project cash flows into two components. There are a set of certain cash flows and a set of residual cash flows. These residual cash flows will have many characteristics which make them like options, in particular the fact that they should have limited downside owing to the limited liability nature of equity. Now risk free cash flows can be valued by discounting them at the risk-free rate and options can be valued in a way that will be explained in the next view. So this offers in theory a radically different way to value projects.

My greatest problem with this approach is that it is very much a 'black box' approach. That is to say that one puts numbers into a 'black box' and just has to accept the answer which comes out. It is very hard to relate the input assumptions to the output value in the way that one can for a typical value calculation. This is because the typical value calculation involves calculating cash flow and this is something which can be measured year by year.

A second problem concerns the need to make assumptions about the nature of future volatility. Options valuations depend crucially on the volatility assumption and on the correlation between different components of cash flow. These assumptions, in my view, can only ever be guesses because we cannot be safe in assuming that past volatilities and past correlations are a good predictor of the future. The equity-as-an-option problem also suffers from the risk-free rate problem.

The less radical methods accept the economic value model and concern how the CoC is set. The focus is usually on the β factor. Various alternative approaches have been postulated. The line of logic is usually that a shareholder's required return need not simply be a function of the covariance of a company's stock with the market index.

A generic approach called the arbitrage pricing model (APM) postulates that a number of key parameters can be identified which contribute to a company's β. These factors can be determined by a particular company or a particular analyst. Historical data are then analysed in order to see whether a good correlation can be observed between the factors which are postulated to set required returns and market behaviour. If a good correlation is found in historical data, and if the parameters have a good intuitive feel to them, then perhaps this can provide a better method of setting required returns.

Now the apparent logic of this approach is, to me, irrefutable. The CAPM model for β depends on just a single variable. Surely a more sophisticated model with more variables ought to be better, particularly if one accepts that there are some other factors which intuitively one believes could impact on the required return. The problem with APM is mainly practical. The problems which exist in setting the correct β[27] do not go away when one switches to a multi-variable model, they multiply!

The final alternative approach which I will cover concerns the setting of country-specific costs of capital. This is often done for some developing countries that are considered to be particularly risky, the underlying theory being that activities within a single country are often subject to similar risks and these can be allowed for via a specific CoC. The most common way to calculate the country CoC is to add an additional country risk premium to the established company CoC. This premium may be set at an arbitrary rate determined by the company. Often, however, it is set as the extra cost of borrowing which the host government has to pay compared with borrowing by the US government. I will be explaining why I don't support this approach in the following section.

It is probably apparent for this section that I am not a great supporter of any of these alternative approaches. As a practitioner who has been asked to advise on the appropriate CoC on many occasions, I have to say that I do

[27] The difficulties concern: the need to use a sector ß in order to avoid diversifiable company-specific issues distorting the analysis; the differences in risk between individual projects within the same sector; the need to remove the effect of leverage on each company's ß; the lack of suitable analogue companies; and finally the need to apply judgement in relation to major events which might have distorted observed ß factors during the selected observation period.

not want to have to use a more sophisticated model. Since 1990 I have been very glad to be able to invoke the Nobel Prize argument. If CAPM was good enough for those who awarded that accolade, it is good enough for me.

Conclusions: The choices to be made concerning the cost of capital

My view is that all public companies must have a view about what is their overall CoC. The directors need this in order to justify major financial decisions and in particular to know how to react if and when an offer is made to purchase the company. This decision about a company CoC should be taken in line with the approach which has been outlined above. There will be considerable uncertainties, but the company will need to adopt a figure and will need to have some logical basis behind this. The choice of CoC will be important in some situations but only minor in others. I will be explaining this in the following section on the CoC's implications.

There is, however, a choice to be made regarding whether this rate should be used to assess all decisions within the company or whether a divisional or even a project-based CoC should be applied. The theory in favour of project-specific costs of capital is strong but the practical difficulties of justifying separate costs of capital for each decision are such that I believe that many companies can be justified in sticking to the use of just the one company average rate. I would suggest that companies should only adopt project or divisional costs of capital if each of two tests can be passed. These tests concern practicality and materiality.

As regards practicality, can companies make clear enough distinctions between situations where the various different rates should be applied? Furthermore, can companies justify the differences in CoC by reference to market analogues? There will certainly be companies that do feel able to pass the practicality test. The 'not practical' argument will, however, be strong when there are few analogue companies or when the differences between business areas are hard to define.[28]

My second test concerns materiality. Here I would suggest a threshold of, say, 1% point difference from the company average before it is worthwhile adopting a different CoC for a division or a project.

Two factors which have emerged over recent years are likely to have increased the number of companies that will be able to justify using just a

[28] A signal of this might be if frequent reorganisations move businesses around within the company and this requires changes in cost of capital.

single company-average CoC for all investment decisions. The first factor concerns the general trend away from diversification and towards sticking to a core business. The result of this trend is that nowadays there are fewer widely diversified companies. The second factor concerns the general reduction in the required equity risk premium which has taken place. During the 1980s and 1990s the general consensus was that the premium was in the range 6–8½%. Nowadays, as I have explained above, the range is reduced to about 3–6%. This means that a greater change in β is necessary in order to justify a one point increase in CoC. Whereas it used to be the case that a change in β of 0.1, with the benefit of rounding, was often sufficient to move the CoC by a point, it is now necessary to have a difference in β of about 0.2 before it becomes worthwhile setting a separate CoC.

I will develop my recommended approach to these questions which surround the CoC in the following part.

Part 2: The implications of our cost of capital theory

Overview

This second part is concerned with how we can use the CoC and its surrounding theories. Although these theories may not allow companies to calculate a CoC with precision and accuracy, they do give some strong guidance about how to respond to certain questions. There are also some potential pitfalls to avoid. Accordingly, I have created a list of ten things that you can do with the CoC and its supporting theory and I will deal with each of these over the following pages. The first six are all good things to do while the final four need to be avoided or at the very least, handled with care. As I work through the list I will use the opportunities gradually to spell out my proposed approach to risk and reward. As will become apparent, this is intimately linked to the CoC and its supporting theories.

My list of topics is as follows:

1. Overall approach to risk and reward
2. Treating financing separately
3. Understanding competitors' costs of capital
4. Buying and selling
5. Optimisation
6. Risk archetypes and risk sensitivities

7. Fudge factors
8. Pre- or post-tax?
9. Country risk
10. A cottage industry

Topic 1: An overall approach to risk and reward

I have this topic as the number one on my list because I believe it to be the most important. The CoC is basically concerned with the trade-off between risk and reward. The idea is that a particular amount of anticipated additional reward will compensate an investor for taking additional risks. The first part of this view concentrated mainly on how one should go about assessing exactly how much extra reward was required in order to compensate for extra risk. It did, however, briefly touch on some of the assumptions which underpin the economic value model. I will now explain what the overall approach to risk should be and it will soon become apparent that the numerical trade-off which flows from the particular CoC which we calculate is only a small part of the overall approach.

The economic value approach to risk and reward[29] has, I suggest, four steps, with setting the CoC being a part of the final one. It is necessary to get all four steps right before one can be clear that one is giving the topic its necessary attention.

These four steps in the management of risk and reward are:

1. The recognition that in the context of the value model, **risk is concerned with uncertainty** and not just downside outcomes such as the possibility of making a loss.
2. The need, despite step 1, to apply an **overarching downside risk test** which focuses just on serious downside effects which could lead to value destruction elsewhere in the company.
3. The need to think about the **expected value NPV** when making go/no-go decisions.
4. The need to determine the **correct required return in relation to risk** and to understand that this is done from the perspective of a well-diversified shareholder.

These steps have implications for analysts who have to prepare the necessary data. They also require considerable input from senior management. This is

[29] I should stress that this is a book about financial decision-taking. Other disciplines, and in particular the safety discipline, will have their own approaches to risk. These are very important and can be very different but are not within the scope of this book.

because the treatment of risk and reward is, in my view, one of the key tasks of senior management. It is not something which should be delegated to a technical expert.

The **first step** concerns the definition of risk. The point about the term risk having different meanings to different people was made on the first page of the building block on Risk. The particular difference that concerns me most is the distinction between risk as being concerned with the possibility of loss, and risk as being concerned with uncertainty. The difference between the two is of fundamental importance.

If one treats risk as meaning uncertainty, then one can accept the portfolio effect that an upside outcome on one project can offset a downside elsewhere. If risk is only concerned with downside events then these must be avoided at all costs and cannot be offset by unexpectedly good outcomes elsewhere. Furthermore, if one treats risk as being uncertainty, there can be risk in situations where the only uncertainty concerns how much profit will be earned. If risk were considered to mean the possibility of loss then situations such as these would be considered to be risk-free.

There is a way to deal with the apparent inconsistency between these two philosophies which I believe can help explain why the financial view of risk is appropriate. This way is to think about what represents a loss or a profit from the perspective of a shareholder who owns a fairly priced share in a company. Imagine that a company faces an uncertain future. It only has one year of life left and in that year it will either make \$1m or \$2m. Each of these outcomes is equally likely. From the perspective of the 'risk is bad' person, the company faces no risk at all because the only question concerns how much profit it will generate. Now, however, think about the company's market value. Before it becomes clear which outcome will occur the company's value will be a reflection of the expected value of the range of possible outcomes. This is for a gain of \$1.5m. If there are 1m shares then each will be worth \$1.50.

Now move ahead to when the actual outcome is known. The company will either be worth \$2 per share or \$1 per share. Hence, for a shareholder, a successful outcome will result in a gain of \$0.5 per share whereas an unsuccessful outcome will result in a loss of \$0.5 per share. So although from the perspective of the company, no loss is possible, a loss is possible from the perspective of the shareholder. The fact that we view investments from the perspective of a shareholder and that value reflects the expected value outcome does mean, therefore, that we must recognise that any uncertainty creates the potential of a loss.

The way that an upside can offset a downside within a shareholder's portfolio serves to create a considerable benefit. This is that it allows the impact of risk to be dramatically reduced and hence it drives down the additional reward which risk requires. This is another way of saying that it drives down the CoC, which is something which benefits everybody because a low CoC leads to more goods being available at lower prices.

The only actions required in order to implement the first step concern the need to adopt an open mind and to be prepared to consider all eventualities. In particular, it is the role of senior management to create an environment where upside possibilities are able to offset downsides. This is far from easy and the necessary actions fall beyond the scope of this book. The more concrete actions which should be taken will occur as part of the remaining three steps.

We must now turn to the **second step** which I term the overarching downside risk test. Now it always strikes me as being a little ironic that after a first step which recognises how upsides can offset downsides, the second step is concerned solely with the potential for downside outcomes. The focus of this second step is purely on any really big downsides.

An overarching downside risk is a risk that, should it come about, will have a large enough impact to destroy value elsewhere within the company. The mechanism behind this value destruction could be as simple as a lack of cash to fund good investment opportunities or it may be a more subtle loss of reputation which causes widespread damage to the company. When it comes to financial losses, the bigger the company the higher is the threshold before a risk becomes too large. Reputation, however, may well not be like this and there can even be some situations where more is expected of large companies than small ones.

This step is needed because no allowance for losses beyond the scope of the project being considered is made as part of the normal assessment of that project. The implicit assumption is that the project will be able to progress through to the end of its economic life without causing any impact outside of its boundaries. I like to think about it as though the portfolio approach to risk and reward implicitly assumes that a company will operate for long enough to allow the averaging effect to take place. In effect, the company must be rich enough to play the game many times so that it can eventually count on achieving the mean result.

Now I am not suggesting that companies must not take risks that could cause a material adverse impact on activities elsewhere. What I am suggesting is that companies must be aware when they do this and must be content that the additional risks are justified. This usually means doing two things. These are first to consider explicitly whether the risks should be removed by some form of mitigation. Then, if there remains a residual risk which is still deemed too large, additional reward should be required before the risks are taken on. These decisions should, in my view, always involve the most senior management of a company because they should be the ones who take the key decisions in relation to risks of such great magnitude.

The usual approach to high downside risks is to adopt one of the following:

- Manage their impact and/or probability so that they become acceptable.
- Pass them on to a third party through, for example, insurance.
- Ring-fence them so that they can only impact the project itself.
- Accept them and live with the consequences if they come about.

The first suggestion should always be investigated. This cannot be an exact science because assessing both impact and probability can only be approximate. Companies must, however, always investigate means of mitigating downside risks because this is, in effect, part of the duty of care that they owe to their shareholders.

Passing risks on is usually a good approach as long as the risks are passed to an organisation that is well placed to take the risk. Well placed means, first and foremost, that they are financially strong enough to take the downside. It also tends to be more efficient if the party assuming the downside obligation can also influence either or both impact and probability.

Ring-fencing of a project can reduce the overall impact on the company to a manageable level. In simple terms, all that can be lost is the actual investment in the project itself. There are no additional consequential losses. Ring-fencing can be achieved by some financial structures such as project finance but these will always have a cost.

Finally, companies should also remember that, as far as their shareholders are concerned, they are there to take risks and their shareholders will have spread their risks more widely.[30] The potential for high reward can justify 'betting the ranch' on a project that might bring down a company. The smaller the company, the more likely it is that it might well be justified to take a high risk in order to make a high reward. Small companies, in effect, provide the ultimate ring-fencing for risky projects. Large companies have

[30] One generally makes the assumption that equity shareholders can stand the loss of all of their investment in any one company without hitting financial distress. So decisions about risk and reward are limited to the impact within the company and do not have to go further to cover effects on shareholders beyond the fact that they may lose all of their investment.

a greater ability to absorb high risks and so are less likely to be forced into financial distress. If they are, however, the impact can be greater because they have more to lose.

It is a key role of senior management to decide on the right course of action in relation to any identified overarching risks and on the extra return which must be sought when a company is left carrying some residual risks of this nature. I am not aware of an accepted approach in this area and so the decision will depend heavily on judgement.

I can envisage a wide range of possible actions which could be justified in response to any identified overarching downside risks. At one extreme, I could imagine a situation where a senior manager decided in a highly rational way to accept a major downside risk on the grounds that the same risk would impact on the company in several places in addition to the project currently under consideration. There might, therefore, be little point in protecting one part of the company when one already knows that the company will sink should that event come about. Equally, I could imagine a manager's deciding that a risk was simply not worth taking and so ruling out a potential project. Between these two extremes I could envisage a senior manager's authorising a spend of somewhat more than the amount that was justified purely on a project view of the change in impact times probability. The extra return which is required to justify taking any risks which will still remain after the mitigation efforts have been implemented will also need to be largely judgemental.

Senior managers will, as they exercise their judgement, need to be aware that the overarching risk test will tend to work in a rather strange way. A company which starts its first project is, by definition, immune to the overarching risk effect.[31] When, however, that company has grown, it will become vulnerable to overarching risks because it will have money to lose elsewhere. As a company grows larger it can then tolerate greater financial losses and so the list of overarching risks will decline again. So an important implication of this second step is that very high risks need to be taken either by single-project companies or by very large companies. This, by the way, provides a significant justification for growth by some companies that are insufficiently large to carry the risks inherent in a particular business.

There are many potential ways of managing material risks. Some can be removed simply by adopting an alternative design to a project. For example, if a potentially hazardous raw material has to be transported by road

[31] Because overarching risks cause damage beyond the scope of the project being considered. Any possible losses within the project should already be reflected in the assessment of its expected value NPV.

to a factory and a road traffic accident is identified as having the potential to cause a material risk, one could investigate locating the plant adjacent to the manufacturing site for the raw material. Other risks can be managed through financing means such as insurance, having only a minority stake in the company or through having project finance that is secured only by the cash flows from the project itself.

Further consideration of how to manage material risks is beyond the scope of this book. The key implication, however, is not. This is that the approach to risk and reward is implicitly an approach to cope with manageable uncertainties. Unmanageable uncertainties often exist and dealing with them represents an important task for all levels of any company up to and including its top management.

The **third step** in the economic value approach to risk concerns use of the expected value NPV for go/no-go decisions. This is easy to say but can be difficult to do! It can lead to what I consider to be fruitless exercises designed to assess the accurate answer to what can only ever, in my view, be an approximate piece of analysis.

The logic in support of expected value NPVs is, I consider, irrefutable. In the face of uncertainty, it must, in logic, be the expected value NPV which underpins the share price. NPVs calculated in other ways, for example the NPV based on an assumption of success, will not be what sets the share price. Expected value NPVs can, however, be hard to assess and I will deal with this point shortly. One can, fortunately, often justify ignoring the expected value figure if it is already clear that a decision is worth making based on assumptions which are demonstrably less optimistic than expected value assumptions. When this is true the need to have calculated the 'accurate' expected value NPV is reduced.

The standard 'textbook' approach to calculating an expected value NPV is to use Monte Carlo simulation. Probability distributions are attached to all significant variables and the financial model is run a few thousand times so that a distribution of the possible outcomes is produced. This distribution is then used to calculate the NPV. All of the programming work is done by a software package and the exercise can often feel very easy. The ease of calculation can, however, create a false sense that an accurate calculation has been carried out. In real life application the following problems tend to occur:

- the difficulty of modelling all risks and not just the obvious ones;
- setting appropriate distributions for, and correlations between, each variable;
- gaining management buy-in to the answer.

My point about modelling all risks is that things like the risk to the selling price is obvious. There are, however, thousands of small risks that any project faces including many low-probability but relatively high-impact events. It can be very hard to incorporate these in any way other than by applying a very rough guess.

The point about distributions is that it can be hard to estimate what the range might be on any particular outcome. Studies have shown that familiarity with a particular variable tends to lead people to underestimate the range of outcomes which are possible. Correlations are also important and quite difficult to model. An example of a correlation could come from any natural resource business. Here, when commodity prices are high, service companies can charge higher prices and host governments tend to increase taxes. So the benefit of high prices will always be less than might be anticipated.

The difficulty with management buy-in is, I believe, due to the black box nature of Monte Carlo simulation and the way that the link between individual assumptions and the final NPV is not transparent.

A more simple approach is possible when the financial model which calculates cash flow behaves in a linear manner in relation to realistic changes in assumptions.[32] In this case all that is necessary is to run the model once based on input assumptions which are all expected values. One still faces the problem of estimating the expected value but at least ranges and correlations become less significant and gaining management buy-in is much more simple.

A further simplification is possible if the statistical distributions associated with the assumptions are not skewed. A skew is where there is more upside than downside or vice versa. A typical example concerns the estimated capital cost of a major project. Experience has indicated that overspends are much more likely and can be much greater in magnitude than underspends against the initial best estimate. Where there are not skews the expected value will also be the most likely one and this, in principle, should not be too difficult to estimate. Where there is a skew this simply has to be allowed for in a subjective way by, for example, adding or subtracting an allowance from the most likely value in order to move towards the 'correct answer'.

An example of this effect would be a factory which, if it operates correctly will produce at its peak rate of, say, 50,000 units per day. One might

[32] This means that if, say, a 1% change in an assumption adds \$x to value then a 2% change will add \$2x and so on. Most financial calculations will work in this way but, unfortunately, some things may not. Tax rules, for example, may require that tax be paid on profits but not be repaid if losses are made.

be tempted to assume that the factory will operate correctly and most of the time it will. There can, however, be unexpected reasons why it might have to be shut down or reduce output. So although the most likely output is 50,000 units per day, there is no possible upside to this. Therefore the expected value must be somewhat lower than this in order to allow for the effect of the possibility of reduced output. Companies will have experience of similar factories and the extent to which they can produce to maximum capacity. This can help point towards an appropriate assumption which might in this example be for production of 49,000 units per day.[33]

Some success or failure situations can also be allowed for in this pragmatic way rather than requiring full Monte Carlo analysis. If, for example, permission from government is required but this is granted only at the end of any particular year, one may run a base case with the assumption that permission is granted in the middle of next year. This assumption is a rough expected value estimate of the permission's being granted either at the end of this year or at the end of next year. Although this is not a possible outcome, it could well provide a reasonable estimate of the expected value outcome.

A practical approach which I recommend therefore involves, in effect, making a best guess of the expected value assumptions and using these as the base case assumption. The best guess expected value assumptions are based on judgement, with this judgement allowing for factors such as past experience, skewed distributions and success/failure events. This approach is usually about as accurate as is justified by the quality of one's assumptions. I refer to these estimates of expected value assumptions as being 'reasonable estimates' of expected value to emphasise that they are just estimates.

Obtaining good quality expected value NPV estimates is of most importance when decisions are marginal. This tends to be the case at the early stages in the life of any project[34] and also when one is choosing between alternative strategies. The approach that I recommend is that the sponsor of the project or strategy should make the basis of the assumptions very clear to the decision-maker. The decision-maker then decides if this approach is acceptable given all of the facts which surround the case.

[33] This use of historical reliability data is a good example of the application of the Plan, Do, Measure, Learn approach and it can improve the quality of decision-making.

[34] As a project progresses it will have the benefit of ever-increasing sunk costs. So unless the original decision to start the project was very poor these sunk costs will lead to ever increasing NPVs and hence to a situation where the go/no-go decision should usually be an easy vote in favour of go.

These facts are not just concerned with how the decision-maker will want to take an individual go/no go decision. They concern also the other uses to which the value number will be put. These other uses concern:

- Situations where a choice is being made between options, all of which could pass the go/no go test. In such a situation it is only fair to compare the cases on what might be termed 'a level playing field' and the most relevant 'level playing field' is to use expected value assumptions.
- When the value number forms a material part of the overall value of a company and the company wants to know its view of what the project should contribute to the share price.
- When the company is seeking to learn lessons about its investment decision-making by monitoring its overall achievement of the NPVs associated with its major investment decisions.

It requires decision by senior management to determine how important these factors are and the degree of effort that needs to be put on the establishment of expected value assumptions for all decisions.

We now come to the **fourth step** in the economic value approach to risk. This is where different returns are required in order to compensate for different degrees of risk. The theory suggests that each company will establish its CoC, which is correct on average, and also a CoC for the particular project. I have, however, already suggested that this will often not be done and that the final decision about risk/reward can often be left to senior judgement. I can now explain the logic for this in greater detail.

Project costs of capital are not calculated because the CAPM is simply not accurate enough to facilitate this. It is not accurate because the most detailed estimate of β will be for individual companies. These companies will almost always be combinations of many projects yet their individual β will include company-specific effects which are diversifiable by shareholders. The only way to avoid this is to use sector β data which then means that one is even more removed from the specific risks of an individual project.

Now it is possible to delegate the task of deciding on project β to technical experts. If this is done the senior decision-takers then simply rank project alternatives based on NPV. I believe that this would be wrong because, however good the experts were, it would mean delegating authority to people who had to operate a model which is subject to too much uncertainty. I therefore believe that this is one situation where the final decision should not be delegated.

Companies may choose to apply divisional or 'project types' costs of capital and these can help eliminate some of the bias in favour of high risk projects that might otherwise occur. Senior managers will still, however, need to apply their judgement to decide if the potential return is sufficient in the light of the risks associated with the project under consideration and the alternatives that are available. This is because the projects, even those within a generic 'project type' are all likely to have different risk characteristics. Even an individual project must, in theory, justify different costs of capital if different decisions were taken concerning how it was developed.

I suggest that one of the roles of senior management is to decide on the extent to which differences in risk are allowed for via the CoC and when risk differences are allowed for via judgement. The technical experts can, however, suggest a framework within which, the theory suggests, senior managers should base these decisions. This framework is given by the way that the CoC is calculated and by the things which serve to change the required return.

As regards the way that the calculation is done, we have our estimate of the equity risk premium. Now my estimate of this was that it was in the range 3–6%. Anyone who has observed share price behaviour over the years should be aware of the volatility of share prices. Strictly speaking it would be wrong to call owning shares a roller coaster because roller coasters only go fast when gravity pulls them downwards, whereas shares, on balance, tend to move upwards in value. I am sure, however, that readers will understand why I still want to use the term to describe the ride. Owning shares can be quite frightening at times and one expects to earn just a few percentage points in compensation for all of that risk. So an additional return in the region of 3–6% is sufficient to compensate a shareholder for taking typical equity risk and that level of risk is pretty dramatic. This, to me, gives a major clue about the sort of magnitude of extra return which shareholders require in order to persuade them to take risks. A few additional percentage points on the anticipated return will compensate for a lot of risk.

We can consider now what the CAPM theory tells us about what changes the β factor. The most important point is that diversifiable risk commands no additional premium. So, from a project perspective, many risks have no impact on the required return. They impact on expected value but nothing else. This means that when senior managers study much of the sensitivity data on a project their primary concern should be to establish that the base case is an expected value rather than to establish what extra return is necessary. Things which are unique are diversifiable and hence command no additional risk premium.

By contrast, the point about the β factor is that we have seen how leverage can have a major impact on the equity β. If a business is financed half by debt and half by equity then its equity β will be twice its asset β. So the premium for risk on equity will be twice the premium for risk on the unlevered assets. Debt is not the only way to lever assets and in any case we already exclude its effect from our analysis. Operating leverage, caused by the different balances between fixed and variable costs, also causes leverage and this is not excluded from our analysis.

So to make a good risk/reward decision, senior managers need in their mind a picture of the typical level of operating leverage in what would be a normal project within their company and for which the usual CoC applies. This can set the benchmark for the judgement about relative risk, and hence required return, in other projects.

Topic 2: Treating financing separately

The work required to assess the CoC highlights not one benchmark for assessing financial decisions but three. These are the CoC, the cost of debt and the cost of equity. Now most of the long-term financial decisions which are taken in a company need to be analysed at the CoC. There are, however, some situations, which mainly have to do with financing, that call for the use of one of the other two rates.

The idea of treating financing decisions separately from asset decisions was introduced at an early stage in this book. It can be justified in a fairly simplistic way by saying that the CoC already includes the cost of finance and that it would therefore be wrong to include finance effects in our estimates of project cash flow. We can now look at financing in a more sophisticated way as part of the consideration of a project's overall risk characteristics and the necessary risk/reward trade-off decision. Since we now understand how even individual parts of a project can require the use of a CoC which is correct given their exact risk characteristics, we should be able to understand better why financing is treated separately. If one is faced with a situation with the risk characteristics of debt, or equity for that matter, then one knows that the right discount rate to apply would be the cost of debt or the cost of equity.

Of these two potential situations the need to use the cost of debt for situations which have the risk characteristics of debt will be the most important. This is because most companies will utilise in their finance pool more equity than debt and so the difference between the cost of debt and the CoC will be greater than the difference between the cost of equity and the CoC. This topic will focus mainly on situations where the cost of debt must be used but it will also finish with a short analysis of when the cost of equity is used.

A key characteristic of debt is that it carries no, or very low, risk to the lender.[35] This means that the correct CoC for assessing flows which are risk-free is the cost of debt and not the average CoC. What would be the implication of this for usual project evaluation?

Suppose that included within a set of project cash flows are a set of fixed cash flows. Would this serve to increase or to decrease NPV? Well, the answer depends on whether the flows represent borrowing by the company or lending. Borrowing would be where there was an initial cash inflow followed by subsequent cash outflows. Lending would be the opposite. Since the cost of debt must be lower than the CoC, borrowing by the company will, if it is assessed at the CoC, always appear to have a positive NPV while lending will appear to have a negative value. This is best illustrated via a simple example.

Suppose that at present our overall project cash flows are as follows:

	Yr 1	Yr 2	Yr 3	Yr 4	Yr 5	Yr 6
Cash flow $m	–100	30	30	30	30	20
Discount factor (10% CoC mid-year flows)	0.953	0.867	0.788	0.716	0.651	0.592
Present value cash flow	–95.3	26.0	23.6	21.5	19.5	11.8
Cumulative PV	–95.3	–69.3	–45.7	–24.2	–4.7	6.9

The project appears to have an NPV of $6.9m.

Now, however, suppose that on further analysis of the project cash flows we identified that they included some flows which were completely fixed and not uncertain like those which typically make up project cash flow. I will explain what these flows might be later but for the present, please accept that the finance flows are equivalent to borrowing $11m in year 1 and repaying $2.5m in each of years 2–6. The implied cost[36] of this borrowing is just 4.5%.

If we follow the correct approach to calculating value and exclude financing flows the correct cash flows and the valuation should therefore be as shown in the following table:

[35] The only uncertainties would be if the interest rate was floating and the possibility of default by the borrower.

[36] Note that since the table of cash flows is used to calculate NPV, one should assume that the cash flows are after-tax. The 4.5% cost of borrowing would therefore be the after-tax cost of borrowing.

Cash flows adjusted to exclude finance effects

	Yr 1	Yr 2	Yr 3	Yr 4	Yr 5	Yr 6
Cash flow $m	–111.0	32.5	32.5	32.5	32.5	22.5
Discount factor (10% CoC)	0.953	0.867	0.788	0.716	0.651	0.592
Present value cash flow $m	–105.8	28.2	25.6	23.3	21.2	13.3
Cumulative PV $m	–105.8	–77.6	–52.0	–28.7	–7.5	5.8

The NPV has now fallen to $5.8m. Now for many purposes the difference between an NPV of $6.9m and one of $5.8m on a project involving a capital spend of $111m would not be considered material. If, however, one was trying to get the best possible view of NPV it might be considered to be worth adjusting for. The decisions where the difference of $1.1m would really matter would be where we were considering just the effect which caused us to decide that the small adjustments to cash flow were necessary.

I will now build on this example by giving a detailed illustration of how financing can become intermingled with project cash flows. Suppose that our project involved the construction and subsequent operation of a production facility. The product is sold packed in special containers which could easily be loaded onto trucks. The normal cost of a packing unit is $11m. Our usual distributor has, however, offered to purchase a packing unit for installation at our site for our exclusive use. The deal which the distributor has offered is such that we must pay the cost of operating the packing unit plus a capacity reservation fee of $2.5m per year. Finally, we must give the distributor exclusive rights to distribute our product provided his costs are in line with market rates.[37] Our initial base case (with a cash outflow of $100m in year 1) assumes that we accept this offer.

Were one to analyse this opportunity using a traditional DCF spreadsheet model the temptation would be to compare as shown in the two tables above. The only differences would be in the assumed capital cost of either $100m or $111m and also in the payment of the capacity reservation fee. The operating costs and distribution costs would be the same in either case. Hence, as has been shown above, the offer from our distributor would appear to create $1.1m of value. This, if it were a piece of correct analysis, would give a good reason to accept the offer. The problem with the offer only becomes apparent

[37] Tax is always a complication! For the remainder of this example I propose to ignore tax in order to simplify the numbers. Strictly speaking I should have excluded the after-tax impact of the finance flows.

when one looks just at the incremental cash flows associated with it and with the risks associated with them.

The incremental cash flows are a cash inflow of \$11m in year 1 followed by five annual cash outflows of \$2.5m. The outflows, however, are as secure as the company because the company is committed to pay the fee and it is not dependent in any way on throughput. Even if the new production facility were to be shut down and all of its workforce fired, the company would still have to make the annual capacity reservation fee payments. What, one might ask, is the difference between this set of cash flows and going to our bank and borrowing \$11m to be repaid over the following five years in equal annual instalments? If the bank was going to charge us 4.5% the cash flows would be identical. So although different words have been used to describe the cash flows, the magnitude of each payment and the relative risk associated with them are the same. I would suggest that the 'capacity reservation fee' was a type of borrowing in disguise.

To consider this opportunity as an alternative means of raising debt for the project we would assess it at our cost of debt. So if our marginal cost of finance was also 4.5% the deal with the distributor should not be considered to be creating value at all; it is value-neutral. It is just an alternative means of securing a loan at the same interest rate of 4.5%. Furthermore, this option requires our company to give 100% of its distribution business to just one company for a service provided 'in line with market rates'. A company committing that amount of business to one supplier would often expect to be able to use its strong buyer power to obtain a below market rate deal. So the deal may well destroy value compared with the alternative of purchasing the machine and negotiating a discount from market rates in return for exclusive use of the distributor.

This first example has shown what happens when a company, in effect, borrows from a supplier. A traditional cash flow model which does not separate out the finance cash flows will make the borrowing appear to be a good deal. The opposite would be true when a company decides to lend money in a similar way. Consider the above deal from the perspective of the distributor. If this company knows that our company is financially sound, it could well be prepared to borrow \$11m from its bankers at 4.5%, knowing that the repayments will come from our company. The distributor sees the benefit in the deal as being able to lock in a large amount of business at no cost. Had the distributor looked at the deal using a 10% CoC it would have seen a negative NPV of \$1.1m which might well have made it decline to make the offer.

This example has shown why debt-like cash flows need in some situations to be considered separately and not simply via the main project spreadsheet model's CoC based analysis. Debt-like effects are any cash flows which are subject to similar risks to those involved in 'traditional' borrowing. The overall impact on a project's NPV is often relatively small but when one wants to decide whether or not to follow a specific path which involves financing, the incremental differences will be more significant.

It is difficult to provide a full list of the types of 'hidden' debt which need to be considered separately from their associated projects. I will cover just four key examples here. They all, however, boil down to the same situation which is that a company either directly or indirectly takes on a fixed commitment but does not treat it as though it were debt. My examples are in relation to:

- working capital;
- rental agreements;
- guaranteed payments; and
- when financial markets allow prices to be locked in.

Working capital can be one of the hardest areas to control because it typically comprises a large number of small items rather than a few large items. Payables tend to be the most obvious place for debt to be hidden. A supplier can easily accept late payment in return for a slightly higher sales price. Debt can even be disguised as an agreement to own inventory in return for a fee. In the most extreme case a financing company could agree to purchase inventory from a company for a fee plus an agreement by the company to buy the inventory back at a set price at the end of, say, a year. This is just borrowing but could be 'dressed up' as an operating agreement. Finally, some banks will purchase the entire receivables of a company through a transaction called factoring. This too is a type of finance rather than a usual business operation.

Rental agreements can be for varying periods. If they cover the majority of the life of a particular asset the accounting conventions will already treat them as finance leases which are shown on published balance sheets as debt. Shorter-term rentals, however, can escape this treatment and so provide an opportunity for some debt to be disguised.

Rental payments are not the only area where a company guarantees to pay a fixed amount in the future. Any fixed payment should be treated as though it were a form of financing and it is important to ensure that its valuation does not allow debt to be treated as though it were a typical project cash flow. The test to apply to all fixed commitments is to compare them with the costs associated with operating a normal unit. These costs may appear to be fixed but if a decision is taken to close the operation down, they can be avoided. Costs which need to be treated as though they were debt could not be avoided even if a unit were closed down.

My fourth example concerns where financial markets allow prices to be locked in. In some commodities there is an active forward market and so it is possible to fix a selling price for, say, one year in the future. A company operating, say, a copper mine may need a new piece of machinery and could either buy it for cash or, say, agree to pay for it through a delivery of copper in one year's time. Now the usual way that a company would evaluate copper production would be to discount the estimated sales proceeds to the present at the CoC. This means that the way the company could well evaluate this sale is by assuming a reduction in the future volume of copper that is available to be sold. This, I suggest, would be wrong. If the company's usual approach is to sell the copper when it has been produced it will have, in effect, sold this particular quantity of copper one year early. The company supplying the machinery will have been able to sell the copper for a known price at the moment the deal was done. The future payment is therefore fixed even though the mining company might not see things that way.

In all cases if one wished to assess whether the specific proposal was a good deal or not, one would assess it against the alternative of raising the same amount of money as debt. The effect of the deal which is being offered may create or destroy some value. The overall value of the project if one goes ahead with the deal is derived from the value of the project calculated on the assumption that all funds come from the company's overall pool of funds plus or minus any value created or destroyed by the financing aspects of the deal.

The tendency within the manufacturing sector of the economy is to regard all these actions as ways of borrowing money. My view is that they should also be viewed as ways of lending money. As I have already written, there is nothing wrong with debt-like cash flows. It is only wrong to analyse them as though they were typical project cash flows. If your company assesses these flows in a different way from your counterparty, there is always the potential for the creation of real value, albeit at the counterparty's expense. There can also be tax reasons which sometimes allow value to be created through these activities.

We can now turn briefly to situations where cash flows have similar risk characteristics to equity. An example of this would be if a company owned, say, a 15% share of a private company and was thinking of selling this shareholding. The valuation of the equity could be carried out by discounting the projected dividend stream at the appropriate cost of equity.[38] This would be the cost of equity of the private company and not the cost of equity for the selling company. If the private company being sold and the selling company were operating in the same sector it would be quite likely that both companies had the same CoC. They could, however, have different levels of debt and so have different costs of equity.

The distinction between the CoC and the cost of equity only really becomes worth worrying about when companies have large amounts of debt. By contrast, the less debt a company has the more important it becomes to identify situations where forms of disguised debt are being utilised. For all disguised debt, be it borrowing or lending, the basic message is the same. One of the elements of the economic value model is that financing must be excluded from projections of future cash flow. A broad definition of financing needs to be taken, which includes not only all things that are called debt, but also all things which have the characteristics of debt.

Topic 3: Understanding competitors' costs of capital

This third topic is an area where the Sources of Value technique fits well with the existing theories associated with the economic value model. One of the theories which we normally apply when setting the CoC is to use a sector β in order to set the appropriate CoC. We do this because we want to avoid company-specific effects having an impact on our calculation of the correct CoC if they can be eliminated by portfolio diversification. Now using sector β means that we are implicitly assuming that companies which operate in the sector all have the same CoC.[39]

The traditional logic of the economic value model justifies this common CoC argument by stressing that it is the risk inherent in the underlying assets which sets the required return and these risks should be similar across the sector. If we were to put this view into the language of Sources of Value we would say that the CoC is one of the 'me too' assumptions.

[38] There are two correct ways of doing this valuation. One either values the private company's asset cash flows and subtracts its debt in order to arrive at its equity value or, as I have indicated in the main body of the text, one values its dividend stream at the cost of equity. The apparently obvious valuation approach of discounting the dividend stream at the cost of capital would give too high an answer.

[39] To calculate the sector ß we use unlevered ß data which correspond to the situation where a company is financed with no debt and all equity. Thanks to the MM1 proposition the resultant cost of equity when there is no debt is equal to the cost of capital. Since the cost of equity is made up of a risk-free rate, a ß factor and the market risk premium and none of these vary from company to company, the cost of capital should, in theory, be the same for all companies.

Now readers should by now be aware that an individual 'me too' assumption should not have any significant impact on a project's overall NPV. Remember that a project's NPV is the sum of the assessed 'me too' NPV and the value of individual sources of value. When we study a project we tailor the overall effect of all of the 'me too' assumptions in order to ensure that the resultant 'me too' NPV is credible. Hence, once we have decided what a credible 'me too' NPV is, we should not change this if we subsequently change an individual assumption. This overall view must also encompass the CoC.

What this usually means is that the CoC is a key input in deciding on the assumed selling price for a company's products. So if a decision is taken to change a company's CoC then it would be logical to reassess assumed forward price assumptions in order to allow for this. I will illustrate this in the following example which takes as its basis the project which generated the data for the so-called fish diagram on page 391.

This project involved cash outflows for the first two years followed by 20 years of beneficial operation of a manufacturing plant and then a final year in which working capital was recovered. The capital spend was $20m and the anticipated NPV, assuming a 9% CoC, was $7.0m. The IRR was projected to be 13.3%.

Suppose now that the company's finance department reassessed its CoC and decided that a figure of 7% was more appropriate, with this reduction being due mainly to a reduction in the assumed equity risk premium. If one simply changes the CoC in the spreadsheet model and leaves all other variables as they were, the NPV rises to $11.9m.

Is this 70% improvement in NPV credible? The Sources of Value technique provides us with a means of answering this question. Let us suppose that in our initial analysis the project had three sources of value each of which contribute about $3m to NPV and that we had justified a 'me too' NPV of –$2.2m given our views about the sector.[40] These sources of value were:

- $3.0m from a capital cost saving of $3.6m on the first year's capex;
- $2.9m from a variable cost advantage of $8 per unit produced; and
- $3.2m from a premium selling price of $10 per unit above the normal market price.[41]

[40] The figure of –$2.2m is the exact figure from my spreadsheet. Had the individual Sources of Value each been worth exactly $2m the 'me too' NPV would have been –$2m.

[41] Readers with a deep interest in detail may have questioned why a $10 per unit selling price premium does not contribute 25% more to NPV than a saving of $8 per unit on variable costs. The reason is that I have assumed that costs inflate at a slightly greater rate than selling prices.

Let us now suppose that prior to the change in assumed CoC we were happy with our analysis which indicated that the 'me too' player would earn an IRR of 7.7% which was 1.3% below the CoC.

If we were simply to change just the CoC assumption from 9% to 7% the following picture would emerge:

- The 'me too' NPV would rise to +$1.5m with the same IRR of 7.7%.
- The value of the premium selling price advantage would increase to $4.0m.
- The value of the variable cost advantage would rise to $3.5m.
- The value of the capital cost saving would fall slightly[42] to $2.9m.
- The overall NPV would be $11.9m with the IRR unchanged at 13.3%.

This picture, in my view, is not credible because one should not assume that a 'me too' player earns above the CoC. I suggest that the assumed selling price needs to be reduced in order to return to about the same negative NPV for 'me too' that we had previously assumed or to about the same gap between the 'me too' IRR and the CoC. A $9 per unit reduction in selling price is necessary to return the 'me too' NPV to −$2.2m. The reduction in selling price needs to be $10 per unit if we want to achieve a 'me too' IRR of 5.7%. This is about 10% of the assumed selling price, which is quite a material amount. If we plug the $9 reduced selling price into our model while retaining the assessed sources of value the final NPV which we would claim for our project is $8.3m and the IRR is 11.5%.

So the answer to my question about whether the 70% increase in NPV was credible is a clear 'no'. It would only be credible if one was prepared to accept that either the reduction in CoC was not available to the 'me too' players or the sector had somehow become much better such that 'me too' could now reasonably be assumed to earn a positive NPV. Note that it is not the full change in NPV which is not credible, it is just some of the change. The change in the value of the identified sources of value is credible as long as the annual cash flows are credible. The reduced CoC does mean that the value of the sources of value will change.

Now it is perfectly possible for competitors actually to have different costs of capital. In this situation any difference between your company's CoC and that of a 'me too' player would be a source of value. Like all sources of value,

[42] There is quite an interesting effect to observe here. The value of this particular source of value has fallen as a result of the cost of capital reduction whereas most sources of value will increase in value. A capital cost source of value will result in an immediate saving but some of this will be lost through reduced tax offsets in later years. The fall in value is due to the effect of lower capex meaning lower tax allowances in the later years with the reduced cost of capital increasing the value impact of this.

however, it would be explicitly justified and should have appeared first in the strategy which led to the project under consideration.

Cost of capital differences can be either positive or negative. If your company has a lower CoC this will add to the value of most projects while a higher CoC will usually lower value.[43] Possible causes of CoC differences might include situations where your company has access to the international capital markets whereas the 'me too' player is limited just to accessing the local financial market. I have also heard the amusing suggestion that 'me too' players might have a large CoC advantage if they are front companies for criminal organisations wishing to launder illegal cash. Whatever the actual situation, if a benefit or disadvantage is claimed, it should be justified. The default assumption should be that a competitor's CoC is the same as your own.

The interesting implication of this line of logic is that in many situations the exact CoC does not actually matter too much. This, to me, is a significant 'spin-off benefit' from Sources of Value logic. It means that the uncertainty range around the CoC often does not matter too much because it is simply subsumed within the overall calibration of the 'me too' return. This is a very different conclusion from what would happen if one considered the setting of the CoC to be a separate exercise. This way of thinking through the full implications of changing an assumption is a further example of what I call 'words and music'.

Topic 4: Buying and selling

We now need to consider another of the apparent contradictions which happen in this area. Having just demonstrated that the exact CoC does not really matter I will now explain a situation where it does. I will be dealing with another such situation in the following topic as well. This topic will also give some insights about how our CoC assumptions can be calibrated against the market price of a company's shares.

This first situation when the CoC really matters concerns buying and selling. If a company is trying to decide whether or not to buy or sell an asset then the CoC which it assumes will be of great importance. When one is considering purchasing an asset, a lower CoC would mean that one could justify paying a higher price. So a high CoC will make it harder to justify an acquisition. When one is selling, however, the lower the CoC the higher the

[43] I can only claim that this effect is 'usual' because some projects involve initial cash inflows followed by subsequent cash outflows.

price one must achieve in order to justify the sale. So a high CoC makes it easy to justify selling assets. The overall effect of this can be that companies which use too high a CoC gradually sell themselves off while those with too low a CoC buy some poor businesses. In both situations value is destroyed. The only 'safe' assumption must be to use the correct CoC.

The effect which the CoC can have on value can be quite large. I will demonstrate this in the following example. This example will use the simple growth to perpetuity valuation formula where value is calculated by dividing cash flow by CoC less growth.

Let us now apply my reasonable range for the CoC of 6–9% to a company that is expected to generate $10m of funds flow next year and to maintain this cash generation in inflation-adjusted terms into the future. Remember that my CoC assessment assumed a 2.5% inflation rate. This means that the top end of the valuation range is $286m while the lower end is $154m.[44] Had we allowed for just 0.5% real growth in cash flow the range of values would have been such that the high figure was double the low one.

Now if one was forced to work in a pure vacuum, the fact that values could differ by a factor of two might well encourage one to give up on analysis and to rely simply on judgement. In this situation I could envisage a senior manager using the line of logic that went rather like this. My strategy says I must buy this company therefore I must buy it. If it seems too expensive this is simply because my estimate of the CoC is wrong. So I will pay whatever price I have to pay to buy the company. This line of logic can work in some situations but it can be ruinous if a second company adopts the same tactic and the business which is being sought is being sold by auction.

One can get round the problem by recognising that work on an acquisition or a divestment need not take place in isolation. There are almost always external pieces of information available which can help to assess what the market is indicating a company is worth. This information can come from other similar deals which have taken place recently. It can also come from the share price of companies that operate in the field. Crucially, for quoted companies, it can come from their own share price.

These actual valuations can be used to calculate the implied CoC given a particular growth assumption. The valuation is then undertaken using the same combination of long-term growth rate and CoC or, failing this, using a different growth rate than can be justified given what is known about the business situation.

[44] Because $10 \div 0.035 = 286$ while $10 \div 0.065 = 154$.

This market-based calibration of a company's CoC assumption is, I suggest, a highly useful exercise to carry out. One cannot calculate the CoC from the market price. One can, however, usually find a set of assumptions which include the CoC which, when taken together, explain the share price. If the individual assumptions line up with those which are being taken within your company, then the CoC which goes with them seems to be well aligned with what the market is assuming. This should provide some comfort that the planning efforts within the company are well aligned with the way that shareholders are thinking about the company. If the company then buys or sells assets based on these assumptions it is unlikely that the shareholders will want to disagree with what management have done.

If one cannot find a logical set of assumptions which explain the share price then this should be considered to represent a significant warning sign. Either the company or the market or both may be wrong. Companies can be wrong when they take an overly optimistic or an overly pessimistic view of the world. This need not matter if the view does not impact on the actions of the company. If, however, a pessimistic view results in a business being sold for less than the market thinks it is worth then the share price will fall as a result. If the market is wrong then a company must recognise that some of its actions might well lower the share price even though the company believes that its actions will create value.

The normal situation should be that a company can explain its share price through a series of assumptions which align with how it is planning and making its key financial decisions. These assumptions will include the CoC. We will see in the next topic how this calibration can be of even greater importance in one further area where no external calibration is available and where, again, using the correct CoC can be crucial.

Topic 5: Optimisation

One of the important tasks which needs to be carried out during the detailed design stage of a project concerns optimisation. The main features of a project may well have been chosen but numerous small decisions need to be taken regarding the exact design. These decisions can, in aggregate, have a material impact on the success or failure of a project and even of the strategy on which the project is based. They represent my suggested second area where using the right CoC is important.

There can be any number of optimisation decisions to take in relation to a project. A classic one would concern deciding how thick the insulation should be on a pipe which carries high-pressure steam. The fact that a steam pipe requires some insulation is self-evident, but how thick should it be? Increased thickness of insulation will cost money and there will be a gradual diminution in the amount of energy that is saved by incremental increases in the thickness of the insulation. In principle, therefore, there must be an optimal solution where extra investment on insulation exactly balances the value saved from reduced heat loss. One could envisage a table showing the optimum thickness of insulation given varying future energy prices and costs of capital. The higher the assumed energy price or the lower the CoC, the thicker the insulation should be.

A second example of an optimisation decision might concern mitigating a risk. This is approached using the impact times probability method. When assessing the impact of a risk one needs to use the CoC because the risk will be something that happens in the future. The higher the CoC that is used, the less likely it will be that a particular mitigation activity can be justified because the assessed value impact will go down.

Consider, for example, the risk that demand for our product might be much higher than anticipated in our base case assumption.[45] It is often possible at the design stage of a manufacturing plant to build in easy ways to expand capacity in the future at a relatively low cost. One could also simply build a bigger plant today and accept the downside risk that this might waste some money. Either way, decisions have to be taken now which will impact on future cash flow. The lower the CoC, the greater the incentive will be to spend money now in order to earn more later.

My recommendation is that optimisation should be carried out through the technique which I call unbundling. This involves showing the optimisation decisions as separate investment decisions to be taken alongside the main decision to go or not to go with the project. There are several reasons for this.

The first is that at time of final approval, a good project should always offer a significant positive NPV. The difference between a point of sanction IRR and a full-cycle IRR can, when project search and design costs are high, be considerable. Now projects that do not offer a return at point-of-sanction of well above the CoC should automatically trigger a lessons-learned exercise to identify what went wrong and how any mistakes can be avoided in the future. Most managers want to avoid these reviews and hence there can be considerable pressures on a project to make sure that its anticipated IRR is high

[45] Remember that in the area of financial decision-making, risks can be good as well as bad.

enough to clear any corporate hurdle. The inevitable pressure at time of sanction, therefore, is to deliver projects with IRRs that are as high as possible so that the strategy looks good and the project is more likely to be approved. This can create what I suggest is an unhealthy pressure for incremental optimisation spends to earn equally high IRRs even though these investments are subject to only very small sunk costs at time of sanction and should not, in logic, be subject to such criteria.

I will illustrate the consequences of setting a high hurdle rate for optimisation decisions shortly. Before then, however, I will complete my list of reasons why optimisation decisions should be unbundled and shown as individual decisions to be taken in their own right.

My second reason is that optimisation decisions tend to be much smaller than the overall investment decision and so there is a danger that they will be swamped by the main decision. A very good project with a high NPV may, for example, be so good that several poor optimisation projects can be added to it without a decision-maker's being able to spot that the return is not as good as it should be. The small size of individual optimisation decisions is also such that senior managers might not have enough time to consider them properly. If they are not unbundled then no decision-maker will look at them.

A third reason is that the risk characteristics of an optimisation decision may be very different from the main project. This difference may be such as to justify, in principle, the setting of a different CoC. Even if this is not done, decision-makers should allow for the different returns that would satisfy shareholders through the application of subjective judgement. At the low end of the risk spectrum, some optimisation decisions may concern trade-offs between operating costs and capital cost which are well documented and subject to very low risk. At the other extreme some optimisation projects will only create value if demand is high. This is a classic situation which would justify the use of a high β because demand is usually linked to growth in the general economy, which is an undiversifiable risk.

We can now turn to the question of why optimisation opportunities should not be expected to generate similar returns to those which should be expected from the project overall. The reason lies in one of the implicit assumptions behind the way that we analyse projects. This is that all good projects will be funded. A good project is one with a positive NPV. So if the CoC is 7½% then an optimisation project that offers, say, 8% is worthwhile even if the project overall needs to earn, say, 20% to justify its sunk costs. Optimisation projects need to be accepted right down to the margin if value is to be maximised. So the use of the correct CoC is clearly important.

I can illustrate the importance of this effect by calculating how much money a company should, in principle, be prepared to spend in order to save operating costs of $1m pa over the life of a 20-year project. The 20-year annuity factor with a 7½% CoC is 10.19. If, however, a 20% hurdle rate were set the annuity factor would be just 4.87. This means that by applying the correct 7½% CoC as opposed to the inappropriate 20% hurdle rate one can justify spending more than twice the amount in order to gain the future cash flow saving. The consequence of spending this money will be that future cash flows will be higher and the point at which the asset has to be closed down because it has ceased to be economic will be delayed.

Another way of looking at this effect is to note that the 20 year discount factor at 7½% is 0.235. At 20% the factor is just 0.026. So shareholders who are content with a 7½% return will place almost ten times the importance on what happens in year 20 than a company that sets a 20% hurdle rate. The clear consequence will be that application of high hurdle rates to optimisation decisions will lead to companies with short lives.

Optimisation should in theory be a relatively simple issue to deal with. The key is to unbundle each opportunity and then to assess it on its own merits. If senior decision-makers cannot afford the time to become involved in this amount of detail, they should delegate the task. Projects could then be brought forward and presented as an overall recommended case which includes the optimisation options which the more junior manager has selected. A separate sensitivity can be included which shows the result if all optimisation options were rejected and the minimum capital cost approach was followed. Decisions about whether or not the full-cycle return is good enough to justify the strategy should be based on the overall full-cycle NPV which the project offers.

The senior managers who delegate the decision to optimise projects will need to give clear guidance to their more junior managers concerning what constitutes acceptable returns. These senior managers will need to signal that optimisation decisions should be accepted right down to the margin and that judgement is needed concerning the risk of individual optimisation decisions. A good way to achieve this would be for examples of good optimisation decisions to be made available for the junior managers to follow. Key points to be covered in these examples concern the required return for different risks and the use of expected value assumptions.

Topic 6: Risk archetypes and risk sensitivities

This topic builds on the suggestion which I have just made about senior managers making examples of good optimisation decisions available for junior decision-makers to learn from. Making risk trade-off decisions will always require an element of subjective judgement. In large organisations it can be hard to achieve a consistent approach if decisions are left to individuals. As has been shown, the CAPM theories lack the precision to allow 'correct' application for individual projects. A way to achieve consistent approaches to risk across a company is to document a range of risk archetypes and to specify the required return for these situations.

So a company could adopt a particular CoC and then describe a number of projects that it considers to be typical of its activities and for which this CoC applies. The company could then also describe some low-risk projects and suggest the CoC that should apply to these situations with the difference being derived by judgement about the approximate β. Likewise some high- and some very high-risk projects could be described and their costs of capital specified. It would be important to avoid spurious precision and to ensure that the risk differences were large enough to result in CoC differences that were material. I could envisage companies with an average CoC of, say, 8% documenting a low-risk archetype that used a 6% CoC, a high-risk one that used 10% and a very high-risk archetype that used 12%.

Now I am sure that this approach will have intuitive appeal, particularly to those who accept the logic that projects should be assessed using the 'correct' CoC and not the company's average rate. There is, however, a practical problem of implementation. This problem is that projects will not all fall into one of the clear archetypes. There could be a considerable potential for unhelpful debate about which risk archetype applied to a particular project. In most situations project sponsors will want to apply as low a CoC as is possible since this will give a higher NPV.

A way to reduce the organisational problems which can be caused by having to apply different costs of capital is to relegate the use of different costs of capital to risk sensitivities. This approach would require that all projects be assessed at the company's average CoC. If the project was considered to fall into an unusual risk category, a sensitivity should be produced showing the revised NPV. In many instances this revised NPV would not be sufficiently different to change the decision which is being made. It would only be important to use the right CoC if the risk sensitivity signalled that use of a different and perhaps more appropriate rate would change the decision.

Situations such as this would be the situations where senior-level attention to the question of risk and reward was justified.

My view is that it is up to individual companies to decide whether to use a single CoC or to apply multiple costs of capital. If a company does decide to use multiple costs of capital then I believe that a risk-archetypes approach to setting the CoC is preferable to a divisional approach. Whichever approach is used, however, it will still need to be supported by the exercise of senior-level judgement. This judgement can be aided by the use of risk sensitivities which should illustrate the rough magnitude of value difference which might be expected by shareholders given the assessed risk differences.

Topic 7: Fudge factors

A fudge factor is where the 'pure' CoC is altered by an amount in order to allow, in a pragmatic way, for some particular consideration. In my view fudge factors have both good and bad characteristics. I conclude therefore that they will most likely be used within many companies and the important thing to do is to minimise any problems which might be associated with them. This topic will consider where and why they might be used. It will then consider the implications of using them in inappropriate ways. Finally, I will suggest a way of minimising the problems that will follow from their being used.

I will start with a list of five examples of where and why such factors might be used.

Possible situations where fudge factors might be used:

- A typical fudge factor might arise when senior executives felt that projects were not delivering the returns which were promised. If they felt, for example, that the typical actual return was 3% below what was claimed, they might add 3% to the CoC to compensate for this. Senior executives might prefer this approach to having to tell the sponsor of a project that they simply did not believe its projections.
- A fudge factor might also be used in order to allow for the fact that some expenditure is, in effect, mandatory for environmental reasons. So if some of the capital budget is deemed not to earn a return, then the rest of the budget must earn above the CoC to offset this. So if, in effect, value is only created if a project earns, say, a few points above the CoC, why not add these points to the CoC?
- Fudge factors may also be used simply to make project teams work harder at creating value. There can be a natural tendency to stop trying to improve once one is sure that the project should go ahead. So setting a higher target

might make sure that project teams work harder to maximise the value of their projects.

- Next, fudge factors can serve as good indicators of the return which projects must earn in order to justify sunk costs. If it was calculated that on average a project which at point of sanction offered an IRR of 20% was necessary in order to yield an overall full-cycle IRR of 10%, which was the company's CoC, then a 10% fudge factor could be used to signal the return which was required in order to cover sunk costs.[46] Increasing the CoC from 10% to 20% would be a means of ensuring that only projects which covered their sunk costs were approved.
- Finally, a fudge factor might be used in order to achieve a nice round number as the CoC! In my view 10% is a really nice round number and it is not going to be a long way away from the correct CoC. So why, the logic might go, not use 10% even if the numbers appear to be pointing towards a lower number?

Now these situations could all occur within a company. Most of them have the common feature that companies must do better than earn the CoC at point of sanction if they are, overall, to create value for their shareholders. This is a point which, I believe, is not given enough attention in the theory. The theory can be read as giving dogmatic support for the use only of money-forward economics. The fact is that unless significant positive money-forward NPVs are earned, shareholders will, overall, see their value being destroyed.

A way of incorporating this into a company's resource allocation process is to build a fudge factor into the CoC. This provides an automatic scaling for size which should allow a rough but reasonable target to be set for all projects. The target is also a better benchmark than the CoC to signal when a business unit can at least consider that it is, on a full-cycle basis, earning the company's minimum required return and is hence at least satisfying the zero value criteria.

So if these are the reasons why fudge factors can be justified, why might they be wrong? The answer is that the intentions might be good but the effects can be bad. Fudge factors are almost always increases in the CoC. These may have the desired effect on traditional projects where there is an initial spend followed by several years of cash generation. They do, however, work in entirely the wrong way for divestments as a high CoC means that a business might be sold for less than its true worth.

[46] A difference of this magnitude between full-cycle and point-of-sanction IRR would not, in my experience, be unusual. Indeed, I have regularly worked with even greater differences.

Even on traditional projects there is a very real problem when too high a CoC is used. This is that projects which shareholders would be very happy to invest in might be rejected and that projects which are accepted will be implemented in a suboptimal way. Now one project invested in through a suboptimal design might not matter too much, but over the years the effects can build up as companies which set artificial hurdle rates which are too high will continually invest too little in too few projects. The overall implication of this can be large as I will illustrate via the following example.

My example uses, once again, the basic project cash flows which were used to derive the fish diagram and also the competitor's CoC example in topic 3. This time I will take the basic project and add also two further opportunities. I will call the basic project, Project A. The first new opportunity is the chance to spend additional capital in order to lower future variable costs. The required capital spend is $2.2m and the resultant reduction in variable costs is $5 per unit. Overall this optimisation opportunity gives an IRR of a fraction over the CoC and, to the nearest decimal point of a million dollars, a zero NPV. I will call the combination of this optimisation with the original Project A, Optimised A. The third opportunity is Project B. This is similar to Project A but does not achieve so high a selling price. I chose the numbers such that its IRR would be 9.9% (compared with the CoC of 9%). It has an NPV of $1.3m.

Now Project A creates $7.0m of value. So too does Optimised A. Project B creates just $1.3m. Now it should be clear that Project A is worthwhile but what about the other two options? The optimisation creates only a token amount of value and one might think, therefore, that shareholders would be indifferent to it. Project B is acceptable but hardly exciting.

I will now use the sum of all years approach to show what these projects look like if companies invest in projects like this each year. After 23 years a steady-state situation will be reached and the resultant company will have a set of accounts equal to the sum of all of the years in the project spreadsheet. We can study this company and look at things like its average ROCE and also what it should be worth.[47]

We can see that optimising the project adds profit even though it does not create any additional value. It does add to capital employed. Project B has a much lower profit and a slightly lower capital employed than Project A because the working capital associated with the lower sales price is lower. Funds flow is, as readers should expect, equal to profit because we are dealing

[47] The worth will be equal to the sum of all of the years of funds flow divided by the cost of capital.

Summary of steady state financials

	Project A	Optimised A	Project B	Optimised A + Project B
Profit $m	47.3	50.5	32.3	82.7
Capital employed $m	263.7	287.1	262.5	549.5
ROACE	17.9%	17.6%	12.3%	15.1%
Capital expenditure	24.4	26.6	24.4	51.0
Funds flow $m	47.3	50.5	32.3	82.7
Value $m	525.7	560.6	358.6	919.1

with a steady-state situation with no growth. Finally, look at the respective values of the companies when they reach steady state.[48]

Company A is worth $525m. Optimise it by spending more money on value-neutral projects and, when steady state is reached, the company will be worth $560m. Invest also in a project that creates just $1.3m and, at steady state, the worth of the company will have risen to $919m.

Now readers should be very clear by now that the objective in relation to value is to create it and not to seek to maximise it at some future date. The main driver of the value differences will be the fact that the higher capital spends will all have resulted in lower dividend payouts during the 23-year build-up to steady state. We are, however, encouraged by the CoC theory to accept that shareholders are indifferent between dividends and reinvesting in projects which earn at least the CoC. This means that the growth in the company during the build-up period will not in any way have concerned the shareholders. All that will have happened is that the larger company will form a greater part of typical shareholders' diversified portfolios.

Of the two new decisions which have to be taken, the decision to optimise Project A should have been the most difficult to take. This is because it has a zero NPV. There is, therefore, no margin for error but as long as the shareholders are satisfied that the assumptions which underpin the case are expected values, they will be indifferent to the investment being made. This is, however, the kind of decision which could easily have been swamped within the overall outlook for Optimised A. Had the sponsor of the project not unbundled the optimisation opportunity the decision-makers would not have been aware that they were taking a marginal decision because the average position looks so good.

[48] Remember that this is the value of a company that has achieved steady state by investing in one project every year. It is not simply the present value of the individual project's NPVs.

The decision to invest in Project B should be simple. If the numbers are correct it creates value. The NPV is small and the use of any fudge factor or hurdle rate would serve to rule it out because the IRR is less than one percentage point above the CoC and I am assuming that the fudge factor is always at least one percent.

Let us now reflect on the returns which shareholders will earn at the point at which the choice of projects is announced and believed by the market and also the returns which will be earned in the following 23-year build-up to steady state and finally the return which will be earned by shareholders at steady state.

The return at the point of acceptance by the market of the strategy will equal the present value of future NPVs. If either Project A or Optimised A are announced the value gain will be $7m divided by the CoC of 9%. This is $77.8m. If the decision to invest in A and B is announced the value created will be $92.2m. It is the owner of the company before the announcements are made that will gain this value. Once the announcements are made shareholders will then earn just the CoC if the company implements the plans in line with expectations. This means that throughout the 23-year build-up and then through to perpetuity shareholders will earn just the CoC. The only difference is that more money will have been invested in the larger company. CoC theory tells us that shareholders are happy with this. This is why the company should be content to invest in a project which earns exactly the CoC. This is, on average, all the shareholders ever expect to get.

I hope that this example has helped to explain why investing in a zero-NPV project is quite acceptable. Of course the shareholders would love it if the project were better. If this happens, however, it is the existing shareholders who reap the benefit and not any new shareholders who invest after the new value is reflected in the share price. So the model is that shareholders are investing in the company to earn their CoC. The best way to align company decision-making with this fact is not to incorporate a fudge factor in the CoC.

Within a company, growth can bring some subtle benefits. It may, for example, have created better employment opportunities which could have attracted better quality staff. The increased size might also lower risk, although if Project B is in the same business area as Project A the strong correlation between the two projects will mean that the reduction in risk is only small. The company's status and position in many published league tables will be enhanced and the additional market capitalisation may be enough to cause its inclusion within a stock exchange index. This can enhance the liquidity of the company's shares which should benefit shareholders.

What I have shown is that the inclusion of a fudge factor or a hurdle rate of just 1% over the CoC can cause material effects when they play out over many years. If the company had adopted a hurdle rate of just 1% above the CoC it would reach steady state with a market value of $525m. Without the hurdle rate it reaches $920m.

The solution, in my view, is to have a clear perception of the difference between what is the correct marginal CoC and what projects must earn on average. Fudge factors usually represent what projects need to earn on average if a company is to remain healthy. This is an important number to know. If a company's projects on average fail to deliver a sufficient return to cover things like search costs then its strategy was wrong and it needs to learn lessons. It will not, however, solve its problems by setting an artificially high CoC for marginal decision taking.

Topic 8: Pre- or post-tax?

This topic should, in my view, not merit a mention in this book! It has to, however, thanks to some accounting standards which require asset impairment valuations to be carried out on a pre-tax basis. It is also necessary because I have seen pre-tax value calculations carried out.

The dogma of the economic value model is that the CoC is applied to after-tax cash flows. In this approach tax is, quite correctly in my view, treated as just another cost which serves to lower funds flow. This simple statement of approach is very clear. Now nobody asks that, for example, a valuation should be done based on only variable costs and with fixed costs incorporated in the discount rate. So why might the treatment of tax be different?

The reason, I think, is that in some situations one can ignore tax and work with a pre-tax discount rate. A classic example is with debt. Here the usual approach is that tax is only applied to interest receipts and the lender of money is not taxed on the repayment of the principal. Hence with a loan paying 6% interest in a country with a 33.3% tax rate the valuation numbers on a two year loan would work like this:

Time zero:	lend $100
Year 1:	receive interest of $6
Year 2:	receive interest of $6 plus the principal of $100

If we work pre-tax and use a 6% discount rate the present value of the year 2 flow is $94.34 while the present value of the year 1 flow is $5.66. Overall the loan is worth exactly the amount which is lent.

If we work post-tax the discount rate is reduced by an amount equal to one minus the tax rate. The relationship is:

Pre-tax cost of debt × (1 – tax rate) = Post-tax cost of debt

So in this situation the discount rate is 4%. The post-tax cash flows are $4 in year 1 and $104 in year 2. So once again, the value is exactly $100.

It is this relationship between pre- and post-tax costs of debt which has, I am sure, led to the idea of it being acceptable to have pre- and post-tax costs of capital. This relationship also works with businesses which will endure to perpetuity with no growth. In this situation value is equal to funds flow divided by CoC. Funds flow is, however, also equal to profit. Hence value is equal to profit divided by post tax CoC. Since profit is equal to pre-tax profit times one minus the tax rate the correct pre-tax discount rate is also given by the above formula.

Now the problem is that most valuations do not concern the valuation of debt or of companies that will remain in steady state with no growth to perpetuity. Real life businesses and real life tax are both too complicated to expect this situation to be maintained. My experience is that many taxes start with a set of very simple principles. Then, however, loopholes are found or unfair anomalies emerge. So the tax authorities bring in more complex laws to address these problems. Within a few years, tax is back to its usual complexity. Against this backdrop I find it hard to believe that the effect of tax can be so simple as to multiply by one minus the tax rate.

If one accepts that the right way to calculate value is by discounting post-tax funds flows at the post-tax CoC, what might the necessary rate be in order to achieve the same result when discounting pre-tax funds flows? The answer to this question is that the rate can vary greatly. I will illustrate this through two examples.

At one extreme, some companies have large carried-forward losses such that they do not expect to pay tax for many years. For these companies the pre- and post-tax CoC would need to be the same because pre-tax funds flow is equal to post-tax funds flow.

At the other extreme, consider an asset that has already used up all of its tax allowances and that has just one year left to go before it is wound up. It expects to generate, say, $10m of pre-tax cash and the tax rate is, say, 30%. The post-tax cash flow is $7m. If the CoC is 7.5% the value of the business is $6.5m. Now if we want to arrive at a value of $6.5m but starting with the pre-tax cash flow of $10m, the pre-tax discount rate must be 53.8%.

So in this situation we have a post-tax CoC of 7.5% which would under the usual formula have suggested a pre-tax CoC of 10.7%. In reality, however, the actual rate may be as low as 7.5% or as high as 53.8%!

This is a rather extreme example but in my experience, the requests for pre-tax valuations do tend to be focused on confirming that assets are worth at least book value. This is exactly the sort of situation where there is the greatest uncertainty about what pre-tax discount rate will give the same answer as would come from applying the correct post-tax rate to post-tax cash flows. If the only way to establish the correct rate is to do the valuation post-tax first, then why bother to do it pre-tax I wonder?

My simple message is that one should only use pre-tax discounting for debt. Project cash flows should be assessed after tax and discounted at the after-tax CoC. Tax can be hard to assess, but no harder than other elements of future cash flow.

Topic 9: Country risk

Country risk is something that is often allowed for via an adjustment to the CoC. The usual way of calculating this CoC is to start from the local government's cost of borrowing rather than that of the US government. I have also seen the analysis done using an estimate of the local financial market's equity risk premium. Both of these adjustments are, in my view, quite appropriate for a local company that does not have effective access to international financial markets. The local CoC can, therefore, quite easily be higher than the international CoC for an activity of similar risk. It is also possible in theory that the local CoC could be lower, but in my experience this is unlikely.

I have, however, assumed that typical readers of this book will not be employed by domestic companies in countries with limited access to the main financial markets. A more typical situation where readers will be considering using a country risk premium concerns where their company is considering making an investment in a foreign country. Should this investment be valued using the company's CoC or should it utilise a local CoC?

My conversations with practitioners and academics over the years have indicated that many companies do utilise country costs of capital for investments in selected high-risk countries. The logic in favour of this approach may appear to be quite strong and I have read several articles that set out methodologies to calculate the required rate. The strongest piece of logic is, I think, that if a shareholder were to lend to the foreign government it would do so at the rate at which the foreign government borrows. Surely, therefore, this sets the local risk-free rate and equity returns must be higher.

It is my view that this apparent logic is wrong for international investors. I consider country risk premiums to be just another example of the use of fudge factors which can distort investment appraisal. In this topic I will explain why, in my view, country risk premiums are wrong and what I suggest the approach to country risk should be.

The economic value model has a clear approach to risk. The correct treatment of risk is to apply the right discount rate to expected value cash flows. Using a country risk premium attempts to compensate for some risks via the discount rate alone and not via the combination of the discount rate and cash flows.

As I have already suggested, I think that some people try this approach because they are using the same approach that they would use for borrowing. Investing in a country via debt is fundamentally different from investing via equity. If investors want to lend money to a country the only way that they can be compensated for taking the extra risk is via a higher interest rate. This is why the local government's cost of borrowing in a risky country is higher than the US government's cost.[49] With equity, however, the main compensation for risk is that the equity investor owns the rights to any financial upsides. One is not, therefore, forced to compensate for risk just via the interest rate.

My assessment is that companies tend to use a country risk approach because they find the question of country risk too hard to deal with. The approach is therefore a pragmatic one. The company knows that on balance, country risk effects will lower value but the company does not want to devote the effort to identifying exactly what the effects could be. A simple alternative is to increase the CoC in order, at least roughly, to correct for the risks which have been ignored.

I fully accept that country risk factors are difficult to assess. What, for example, is the chance of a government's being overthrown and what would the impact be on a project should this happen? These are hard questions to answer. It would only be safe to ignore them if it were felt that the impact of a change had a balance of upside and downside risks. If an overthrow is more likely to bring about a deterioration in cash flow then, in theory, this needs to be reflected in the expected value assumptions.

[49] There is an interesting point to note here. Lenders should, in theory, start with their required return from lending to this risky country. This return will be above the risk-free rate. Now the expected value from the debt repayments must give this required return. The expected value will need to allow for the possibility of default and the loss if there is default. The consequence of this must be that the headline interest rate charged is above the cost at which the lender originally required to earn. The premium must be enough such that when it is earned on a portfolio of loans it will cover the losses on the loans which do default. This factor applies in theory to all debt but only becomes material when the probability of default is material.

I would, however, ask why investing in another country should be treated any differently from investing in another project or in another sector. My logic against the use of a country risk premium boils down to just three points:

- If a country risk premium is used it suggests that all projects within a country are subject to equal risk. Is this likely to be the case?
- Surely the specific risks in a particular country are exactly the sort of risks which are diversifiable by international investors. The right treatment for diversifiable risks is to use the expected value outcome.
- If the sponsor of a project in a risky country is, in effect, charged for the average level of risk in the country through the CoC, what incentive does it have for attempting to reduce the impact of risk on the project?

The third point is, in my view, the most important. The objective of economic appraisal is not, I suggest, simply to determine what the NPV is. It is to identify the best course of action in order to maximise value. An economic evaluation approach which set a fixed country risk premium would provide a strong signal that country risks were outside the control of project managers. This would mean that project managers were being encouraged to limit their consideration of the effect of risk just to the dimension of impact. The dimension of probability would be ignored because the evaluation methodology was signalling that it was not controllable.

Now all projects should undertake work to reduce the effect of risk on a project. This work should go ahead irrespective of whether or not a company employs a country risk premium approach to some risks. Once the work is going ahead it can be utilised in order to provide the necessary input to the correct consideration of risk. That is to say, it will provide an assessment of both impact and probability of country risk effects.

So, if we return to the question of what is the effect of the risk of the overthrow of a government, the approach should not be limited to doing a calculation of what the effect is if the company simply and passively accepts the outcome if and when it occurs. The proper response to the risk is to consider whether anything should be done in advance in order to mitigate it. I have termed this the U-shaped valley.[50]

One might start with a simple picture that ignores a risk but one should identify the correct expected value and then consider risk mitigation.[51] This

[50] See page 171.

[51] To complete this example, if one was worried about the effect of a change of government one could initiate some social programmes in the country now. The aim of these should be to win the overall favour of the local population and not just the current rulers. Then, if and when the government is changed,

consideration of mitigation will require that all of the factors which are required in order to assess expected value be identified. So with the data available, why not do the exercise properly?

My recommended approach to country risk would be to treat it in line with other significant risks which might impact on project or a strategy. This approach is to:

- identify the significant risks;
- quantify their potential effect using the impact times probability method;
- identify potential options to mitigate them;
- select the appropriate approach which will be to manage, to accept or to avoid them.

One could use the local government's cost of borrowing compared with that of the US government as a trigger. If the cost for borrowing US dollars was, say, more than 2% above US rates, then I would expect to see an explicit review of country risk factors as part of any material investment proposal or strategy. This review would consider what events could occur and how they could impact on our strategy or our project. I would then expect to see some actions proposed which could reduce downside impacts or position us to benefit more from upsides. The ultimate aim of the study would be to facilitate a fact-based approach to the key decision which concerns whether to manage the identified risk by implementing one or more of the identified mitigation activities, to accept the risk of the event's coming about and only respond if it occurs, or to avoid the risk altogether by rejecting the project.

Topic 10: A cottage industry

A potential danger with the CoC and its associated theories is that it spawns what could be called 'a cottage industry'. A cottage industry is one where the workforce do their work from their own homes using their own equipment. There is no centralisation and no economies of scale. This could happen if each project was encouraged to assess its own CoC. Quite clearly, in my view, this is something to be avoided.

The approach which I recommend is that the CoC should be the responsibility of a central team within each company. This team would usually be based in the finance department. The team would recommend an approach to

one might anticipate that the incoming one would be more likely to look favourably at your company. Whether or not one decides to do this will involve judgements about the scale of social programme which might be necessary in order to have any noticeable effect on a future government and the value hit which might occur if the programme was not undertaken and the government was overthrown.

the CoC to the senior decision-makers. This approach would involve a methodology for dealing with risk, a company CoC and possibly also divisional, project or archetype costs of capital. The methodology and the CoC would need to be designed to work together. The senior decision-takers would have the responsibility for approving the proposed methodology and CoC and then for implementing decisions in the prescribed manner.

This may appear to be a self-evident approach. It does, however, appear to go against what might be interpreted as being the traditional business school approach. This approach seems to me to attach considerable importance to the calculation of the CoC and places less emphasis than I would on issues related to estimating expected value cash flows and mitigating risks.

I recall, for example, being invited to judge a business school competition. All the students were invited to make presentations in support of hypothetical projects which they had devised. Huge amounts of work were done and I was very impressed with the overall reports. I did, however, observe that about 50% of the effort was concerned with assessing the correct CoC, with the rest of the effort devoted to the projects themselves. In my opinion little was gained from the CoC half of the work since all the students arrived at costs of capital which were broadly comparable while most claimed big positive NPVs for their projects. Their efforts to calculate the CoC were, in my view, a cottage industry that I would not wish to see replicated within a company environment.

Conclusions: What the cost of capital can tell us about risk and reward

It should now be clear that the key feature of the CoC is not its exact magnitude. There are times when the exact number does matter. Examples of these are in acquisitions, in optimisation, and in early-stage decision-taking before sunk costs start to dominate the picture. There are many occasions, however, when the CoC can simply be viewed as one of many 'me too' assumptions which, in aggregate, can be calibrated to give a small negative return for these players.

What matters most about the CoC is the way that the theories which support it tell us how to cope with uncertainty. In this view I have described a four-stage approach to managing uncertainty, with setting the CoC appearing only as part of the final step. Thinking about both upsides and downsides, identifying overarching risks and applying expected value logic all come before the need to consider the return which a shareholder would want, given the risks.

Readers should now be under no illusions that the theories can give accurate answers. I have on several occasions stressed the vital role of senior-level judgement concerning risk and reward. The theories can help to aid this judgement, in particular by giving a framework such as the insight that diversifiable risk does not command an additional risk premium and in the magnitude of the equity risk premium.

I have come down quite hard against some short cut approaches which involve adjusting for some difficult factors through additions to the CoC. My general approach is that it is better to address risk specifically through its potential impact on cash flow for the project under consideration. I justify this adherence to the theory rather than to a more pragmatic or rough-and-ready approach to risk because the work on risks should be undertaken in any case. All projects should be assessing the significant risks which they face and ensuring that value is optimised in the light of these risks. This work should provide the necessary data such that rule-of-thumb approximations such as the use of a country risk premium can be avoided.

The greatest benefits from a deep understanding of the CoC and its implications are, in my view, likely to come from:

- Working in advance on risks. Identifying and then implementing early actions to minimise downsides and maximise the impact of upsides.
- Understanding that the goal is to maximise value and not return and that incremental IRRs calculated at point of sanction are poor indicators of whether or not a company's overall strategy is creating value.
- Having a rational framework for taking risk/reward trade-off decisions that will be aligned with how shareholders with well-diversified portfolios would want decisions to be taken.

The CoC and its supporting theories provides the framework within which this work can take place.

CHAPTER

12

Second view: Valuing flexibility

Introduction

This second view of broader and deeper skills also starts with a press release announcing the award of a Nobel Prize in Economics. This time the date was 14 October 1997 and the award went to:

- **Robert C Merton**; and
- **Myron S Scholes**, for devising a new method to determine the value of derivatives.

The press release also recognised the late Fischer Black. He, along with Myron Scholes had, in 1973, published the pioneering formula for the valuation of stock options which takes the name of the Black-Scholes formula. Robert Merton's contribution was to show another way to derive the formula and to generalise it in many directions. The methodology has, to quote from the press release, paved the way for economic valuations in many areas. It has also generated new types of financial instruments and facilitated more efficient risk management in society.

These words hardly do justice to the transformation that has been facilitated by the ability to calculate the worth of a financial option. Although many people, typically those with less financial sophistication, view so-called derivative products with suspicion, I consider them to be fantastic innovations which allow financial risk to be managed in a professional way. In particular they allow various types of risk to be transferred to those who are best placed to cope with them and this, in turn, serves to reduce the overall cost of risk to society.

Now when the Nobel Prize was awarded, other uses for options valuations were expected soon to allow the valuation of insurance contracts, guarantees and the flexibility of physical investment projects. It is this so-called flexibility of physical investment projects that I will deal with in this view. I have to say that although the take up of the valuation of financial options has been overwhelming, the ten years since the award have resulted in a distinctly underwhelming use of the valuation of flexibility in physical investment projects. I will give my perspective of why this is the case and then will propose my own so-called flexibility valuation toolkit which provides a number of more rough-and-ready approaches to evaluate flexibility.

These approaches are mainly ways of applying the traditional economic value approach to cope with flexibility. They have application in both tactical decision-making areas such as project optimisation, and in strategic decision-making such as coping with growth options. When taken together I believe that the components of my flexibility valuation toolkit provide a robust defence to the criticism which is sometimes levelled at the economic value approach, namely that it cannot deal adequately with flexibility.

There are three parts in this view. I will start with a short explanation of how and why flexibility in a project can add value. I will not at this initial stage consider how we can place a numerical value on this flexibility. The main aim of this part will be to introduce the idea that the path into the future is not fixed and that good decision-taking along the route can lead to the realisation of greater value.

In the second part I will consider financial options. This is the realm of the Black-Scholes equation and I will show how it enables the value of financial options to be established. The main purpose of this part is to demonstrate the key characteristics of options. I will finish the consideration of financial options with an explanation of how it has been proposed that financial options valuation can be extended to cover physical flexibility. I will show that this has some appeal but will set out also my concerns with the necessary simplifications which must be made in order to translate the accepted approach to valuing financial options to a methodology for coping with flexibility in real-life projects.

In the third part I will set out my flexibility valuation toolkit. This will provide a number of approaches for quantifying the value impact of flexibility in projects and strategies. These approaches represent what I consider to be the tools of the trade for understanding flexibility. In addition to explaining these tools I will explain when and where I recommend that they be used. One of my key messages will be that the valuation itself is often not the most important thing to do. What is often of more importance is simply the thought process concerning how to structure projects in a way that can maximise their inherent flexibility.

Finally, readers should note that I have deliberately avoided the use of the term ‘real option’ in order to describe the effect of flexibility. The term ‘real options’ is used a lot in the academic and consultancy professions and, in my view, it could be synonymous with flexibility value. The problem, however, is that a number of practitioners prefer to reserve the term 'real options' for situations where sophisticated option valuation techniques are used. To this group of people my rather rough-and-ready valuation approaches are too simplistic to deserve the term real options. I have no wish to become engaged in any debate about exactly what a real option is and is not, and so I have chosen simply to avoid the term altogether.

Part 1: Why flexibility matters

Initial example: The value of flexibility

Sections 1 and 2 of this book have placed considerable emphasis on the AFS as the way to calculate value. It requires that all projects produce a base case which is displayed in accounting terms. This then allows a clear link to be created between projects and a company's planning and control systems. The link is a vital part of the Plan, Do, Measure, Learn performance improvement cycle. It is my belief that creating this clear link enhances the chances that companies will, on balance, at least deliver on the performance that they project at the time individual projects are approved.

My only real concern with the AFS format is that it might be considered to suggest that there is only a single path into the future. This is the path which is depicted by the set of financials which comprises the AFS and which, in turn, are usually derived from a single set of assumptions. Furthermore, I have placed considerable emphasis on the importance of these assumptions being expected values. One could easily understand that a manager could focus on managing just this base case as opposed to managing whatever may come to pass. There could be a number of suboptimal outcomes should this happen. I will shortly give one initial example of this effect. I will then develop a more generic framework for thinking about flexibilities and how they might impact on value.

My initial example is based on the petrochemicals industry. The lessons, however, are generic and will apply widely. I need first to make available a short background description of the chemistry involved so that readers will understand the investment options which are available and also so that when we return to the question of exactly how to value this flexibility, readers will understand why some alternative valuation methods which have been proposed will not, in my view, work. This background is given in the footnote below.[1]

With this background in place we can now consider how flexibility may enable a company to create value. Steam cracker designers face a choice. They can either design their plant to crack a single feedstock and provide it with exactly the right by-product separation facilities such that all items of kit are fully utilised. They face an initial choice concerning which feedstock to use but the methods which have been proposed in this book are fully suited to making such decisions. Their alternative is to design for a range of feedstocks. This opens up the possibility of always purchasing the cheapest one, but means that the design is not optimised against any particular feedstock and the overall capital cost is higher. It is the flexibility that is inherent in this situation that is more difficult to value.

If the cracker can operate with multiple feedstocks then the operator must regularly decide which particular feedstock will give the best overall marginal contribution.[2] This decision will need to be taken before each cargo of feedstock is purchased and perhaps even more regularly if different feedstocks can be resold or kept in stock. A commercial optimisation team will manage this decision over the life of the cracker, which the designers will hope will be more than 20 years. So, unless a single feedstock is always the optimal choice, the marginal contribution from a flexible-feed cracker should always be higher than the marginal contribution from a single-feed cracker. The difficult economic question to answer concerns how much capital it might be worth spending in order to add further flexibility to a cracker.

[1] One of the key building blocks for the petrochemicals industry is a molecule called, in the industry, ethylene. This forms the feedstock for many chemicals and plastics. Ethylene is a fairly simple molecule made of just two atoms of carbon and four of hydrogen. A layman's description of how it is made is that larger hydrocarbon molecules are heated up until they break apart. Some of the output will then be ethylene. This reaction takes place in a large chemical plant called a steam cracker in which the steam provides the heat and the molecules are cracked apart.

Now ethylene can be made by cracking a wide range of feedstock molecules. The simplest approach is to crack the molecule called ethane. This is a gas and it has just two carbon atoms and six hydrogen atoms. If it is cracked, the resultant products are just ethylene and hydrogen. These are fairly inexpensive to separate and so the relative capital cost of an ethane-based ethylene cracker is low. If, however, larger hydrocarbon atoms are cracked one has to deal with feedstocks which are liquid and also more by-products are produced. The resultant cost of separating the products into their component streams is higher but the by-products too have a value and there is a substantial demand for them.

Designers of steam crackers face a choice between at least five different feedstocks. They can design their plant to cope either with just one of these feedstocks or with, in principle, any combination. The greater the feedstock flexibility, the greater will be the capital cost.

[2] Each feedstock will produce different yields of ethylene and the various by-products. At any particular time each product will have its own value to the producer. These product values will be influenced by market prices but will also reflect the exact situation of the company concerned.

Now the usual approach to the economic analysis of a plant that will operate for at least 20 years would be to make a series of annual price assumptions and to plug these into a spreadsheet model that would convert these into annual cash flows. I have implicitly given strong encouragement to this approach in this book through all of my examples and through my emphasis on the use of the AFS. In this approach, each individual assumption would be an expected value and a typical calculation would be of annual average price times annual average volume.

If this approach were followed for a plant which was designed for a single feedstock, the correct answer would be obtained. If, however, it were followed for a plant with feedstock flexibility, the correct answer would not be obtained. This is because the annual average prices would point towards a single feedstock as being the best choice and this choice would then be assumed to be made throughout the year. So use of an annual average must be equivalent to assuming that the commercial optimisation team takes just a single decision for each year. One can only allow for the benefit of the regular optimisation decisions if one uses a different approach.

Now in principle an economic trade-off decision must be made because the added flexibility comes at a cost. So one must balance the incremental capital cost against the anticipated incremental annual contributions. The decision is further complicated by the fact that we are not simply dealing with the question of whether or not to invest in flexibility. There are a number of different flexibilities which need to be considered as at least five different feedstocks are possible, each with their own design requirements, and hence impact on the final capital cost of the steam cracker.

At this stage I must simply ask readers to accept that this represents a difficult series of financial calculations to carry out. There ought, in principle, to be an optimal solution but the economic value approaches which we have used so far in this book will not help us to find this because we have focused simply on an approach which depends on the use of annual average prices. A number of academics tend to suggest that this represents a major flaw in the economic value approach. Some may even say that the economic value approach cannot deal with flexibility and that an alternative is required.

My view is that the problem lies mainly with the way that economic value calculations are usually carried out and not with the technique itself. I will be introducing various ways through which flexibility value can be calculated using economic value-based approaches in the third part of this view. For the present, however, I simply want readers to register the point that flexibility can have value and that a traditional economic model based on annual average prices will miss this.

Where flexibility may affect value

Now this feedstock flexibility case study gives just one example of how flexibility can impact on value. There are many more such situations. I will now provide a wider framework for thinking about how flexibility may impact on value. This framework will utilise the ubiquitous 2 × 2 matrix that planners love so much to show four generically different situations.

These situations concern whether the flexibility impacts on just the project under consideration or the wider activities of the company concerned. I refer to flexibilities which impact on just the project under consideration as tactical while I use the word strategic to refer to flexibilities which impact on the company in a wider way.

The second dimension of my 2 × 2 matrix concerns whether the benefit of the flexibility is received by the company or given by it, typically to one or more third parties. This second dimension is, I suggest, of equal importance to the first. Although the typical view of flexibility is that it is something which benefits a company, it is important to recognise that companies can easily give flexibilities away and thus lower value.

The four possibilities and specific examples of each are given in the following diagram:

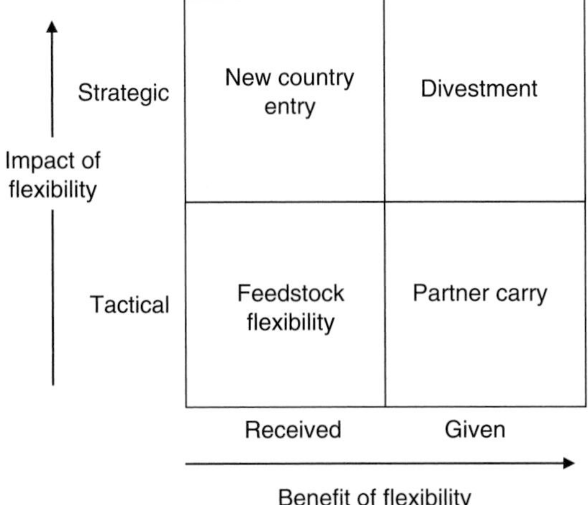

Fig. 12.1 The four types of flexibility

The box on the bottom left is concerned with where the benefit of flexibility is within the scope of the project and it accrues to the company which makes the investment. We have already seen how feedstock flexibility fits this description. A second example would be the ability to cease production on a temporary basis if selling prices fell below marginal costs. This represents a second situation where the use of annual average prices might miss the beneficial impact of being able to respond to whatever circumstances happen to come about. This category would also include the value of the right to choose when to abandon a project.[3]

If we now move one box upwards towards the top left box, at the borderline between tactical and strategic is the option to expand a project. I view the option to expand as a separate decision and hence treat it as a strategic flexibility. This is because I take a fairly hard definition of a project as being something for which sanction is sought and for which an NPV is stated. There are, however, often opportunities at the design stage of a project which can allow subsequent expansion to be lower cost. If these options are implemented and yet value is only claimed in relation to assets that are covered by the current sanction request we would face a situation where it is quite possible that a project will be approved with a lower base case NPV than would have been the case had the pre-investment not been included. The subsequent return on this investment would come if and when the plant was expanded and the best outcome may well not correspond to the highest possible base case NPV.

We should now move fully into the top left-hand box which concerns received strategic flexibility. The classic example of a strategic flexibility received by a company is entry into a new country or new sector. The initial investment will give the company a place in the market and will facilitate the building of a set of skills which might, at a later stage, allow subsequent positive NPV investments to be made. As long as we have a choice concerning the future investment it is fair to assume today that we would only exercise that choice if, at the time, we thought that the follow-on project was good. There can, therefore, be value in a situation where today's perspective of the economic prospects for a future project is bad as long as there is at least some chance that it might subsequently look good. If we will only invest in the subsequent project if it looks good at the time, there must be some implied value now.

[3] There is value in this flexibility because it means that we will tend to run a plant for longer if prices are high compared with if prices are low. If we were to model just the average price and the average project life we would miss this effect.

Now, senior managers often refer to investments as being 'strategic'. I know from my conversations with practitioners that the word 'strategic' is often considered by them to be a euphemism for unprofitable or value-destroying. In many instances, however, I think that what the senior managers are referring to is the way that 'strategic' investments create possibilities well beyond their initial scope, such that an initial negative NPV on the first project may miss the subsequent value that can only follow if the first step is taken.

Further examples of strategic flexibility would come from wide-ranging research work not targeted on a specific outcome but aimed nonetheless at building intellectual property. It will also come as a result of building human capital through training programmes and graduate recruitment. In all of these instances a tightly focused approach to controlling costs could easily result in efforts which would create value for shareholders being cancelled because a clear value case would be hard to make. A framework which provides legitimacy to the calculation of the value which such efforts might bring must be helpful to a company.

My ABCDE valuation methodology gave an initial pointer in this direction. It suggested that the present value of future NPVs will form a part of the current value of a company but that the costs of generating these NPVs must also be allowed for. The B, which stood for business development value was, in the language of this view, a value from received strategic flexibility. The anticipated stream of future positive NPV projects forms part of the overall value of a company.

We can consider now what I term the given strategic flexibility box. If entering a new country creates a strategic flexibility, exiting must close down the possibilities. The implication of this is that if one is considering the divestment of a business, one should value not only the cash flows that are anticipated from the assets already in place but also the cash flows from future projects which might be approved were our company to remain in that area of business.

Companies are also giving away the chance of benefiting from strategic flexibility if they outsource the provision of some activities. The company will lose a set of skills and will pay a third party provider to maintain them. A narrowly focused approach might suggest that this was cost-effective whereas a wider focus might give a different view.

A final example of the given strategic flexibility box would be if a company decided not to patent a discovery which it had made, perhaps because it could not see an immediate use for it, or if it published findings without previously securing the intellectual property rights. I think that the early success of

Microsoft owes a lot to decisions which permitted the value of the computer operating system to go to that company. The rest, as they say, is history. So perhaps one of the largest companies in the world was built on the back of ignored given strategic flexibility.

The fourth box will be given tactical flexibility but before we arrive there we have a second borderline case to consider. This is very similar to the option to expand a specific project which is part tactical, because it relates to the project in hand, and part strategic because it requires capital that is not accounted for in the project base case. The situation to which I am referring concerns things like the use of land or office space which is already owned.

Suppose a company owns a large industrial site and that there are a few spaces left on this land on which expansion projects can be carried out. There may well be no realistic chance of selling this land or renting it to a third party. In such a situation the first project that can utilise the land is likely to obtain its use, in effect free of charge. If one is only considering incremental cash flows for the existing company and for the project under consideration, then the land will indeed be free. It will only have an opportunity cost if at some stage in the future a further project is approved which has to purchase land. I would suggest that the use of the land represents the consumption of flexibility value. It would not impact on a traditional value calculation but it does impact on shareholder value because it is consuming potential flexibility.

I have listed partner carry as a classic example of my fourth category of given tactical flexibility value. Partner carry would happen when a strong company takes a weaker company as a partner. This could well be required in a developing country where strong local contacts might be necessary in order to run a business but where the local companies lack the financial strength to fund their share of the investment. In these situations the strong company could well be forced to 'carry' the weaker company. The 'carry' would mean that the strong company would lend to the weaker one the funds necessary to make its share of the investment. The loan would then be repaid out of the proceeds of the project concerned. The problem with this is that if the project is unsuccessful the local partner loses nothing while if it is a success, it gains a return. Risk and reward is unfairly skewed in favour of the local partner and this represents a transfer of value. Since the overall value of the project is not influenced by how it is shared between the partners, the strong partner must be gaining a lower than fair share of the total prize.

A second example might be if a company gave its customers the right to return goods within an initial window of the sale taking place. Customers could then purchase the goods but if the price fell before they were used, the customer could return them and replace them with purchases at the new lower price. I have also seen situations where customers were given the flexibility to determine the exact load size. The original intention had been to allow customers to collect the exact amount to fill a particular delivery vehicle. This can, however, be exploited such that the smallest possible volume is loaded if prices have fallen while the maximum volume is taken when prices have risen.

Initial conclusions

The common feature of all of these situations where flexibility can create value is that a *subsequent* decision can be made when further facts are known. To create value it must be possible to do either or both of reducing the impact of a downside or enhancing the benefit of an upside compared with the status quo. It is this ability in the face of uncertainty to make the necessary decision later, which creates the value. There are, therefore, two vital components to flexibility value. These are uncertainty and the ability to react to events as they unfold.

The traditional single-case discounted cash flow model which uses annual average expected value assumptions and which is limited in scope just to consideration of the current project does not capture this flexibility value. The value should, however, have an effect on the share price and so we need a means of allowing for it if we are to be able to put forward a rational basis for financial decision-making in companies.

Part 2: Financial options

Introduction: The characteristics and terminology of options

An option is where somebody has the right but not the obligation to do something. A financial option is where that 'something' concerns an item that is traded on a financial market. A classic financial option would be a call option which gives the owner of the option the right to purchase, say, a share or a specified quantity of gold at a specified price (called the strike price) at some date in the future.[4] The second classic example would be a put option which

[4] Just to add a complication there are in fact two generic types of option. So-called European options can only be exercised on a specific day whereas American options can be exercised on any date up to

conveys the right to require a counterparty to purchase an item at a predetermined price and date in the future.

There need to be two parties to any option. These are the writer and the purchaser. The purchaser pays an agreed sum of money, usually called the option premium, to the writer of the option in return for receiving the right to exercise the option if they so wish. Clearly, the purchaser will only exercise this right if it is beneficial so to do. This means that the purchaser knows with certainty what the cost of their action has been and knows that they cannot subsequently lose any money.[5] They may, if events turn out favourably, make a profit and there is, in principle, no limit on how big this profit might be. By contrast, the writer of an option receives a certain amount of money at the outset but then takes on the possibility of a subsequent cost if the option is exercised and they are forced either to buy at above the market price or to sell at below the market price. There is no limit to the writer's potential downside other than the practical limit that most prices will not go negative.

Another characteristic of options is that the value of a put option and the value of a call option must be related. Suppose that one owned both a share in a company and also a put option at some specified share price. On the date at which the option can be exercised one would receive as a minimum the put price plus any premium above this should the share price be higher. The same outcome could be obtained if one were to own instead a call option at that price plus an amount of cash equal to the present value of the exercise price. This is because the cash holding would have grown to exactly the strike price on the strike date and one could either keep this money or use it to purchase a share. This means, therefore, that the following relationship between a put and a call option must always be true:

Put Option + Share Price = Call Option + PV Exercise Price

Financial options are themselves traded on the financial markets. This means that in addition to a market trading, say, the shares in a company, it may also trade specific options on shares in the company.[6] The market trades specific options simply in order to limit the choice that exists because otherwise there might be chaos with a plethora of exercise dates and prices.

the expiry date of the option. I do not, however, propose to look into the differences between the two and will focus just on European options in this section.

[5] The option premium is a sunk cost and so does not count as a loss in this context.

[6] For example, in September 2007 the *Financial Times* reported the prices of put or call options with strike dates of end September, December and March for a number of major UK companies. Some other options with strike dates of end September, October and November were also reported.

My view is that options exist because the world finds them useful. The producers of a commodity find them useful because they provide a good way of protecting against downside while retaining upside. Consumers of a commodity will be interested in the opposite; namely, protecting against future price rises. Producers and consumers can achieve these effects by the appropriate purchase of put or call options. They will, however, have to spend the option premium and so this does serve to increase their costs. There is a way around this which utilises a so-called cap and collar. A producer could give away price upside above a certain price level by writing a call option at this price. This will give the producer some cash but will remove any price upside above the strike price. The producer then uses the cash to purchase a put option at a lower price. The producer can thus ensure that their final price will be within a specific range at no extra cost.

Traders and speculators also find options a useful means of investing. They will typically see the opportunity to apply what they consider to be their superior acumen and make money by coming in between producers and consumers. What is happening in all cases is that risk and reward are being shared. Furthermore, if the result is that risks are taken by those who are better placed to take them, then this does drive down the overall cost of those risks to society.

Valuing financial options

Now until a relatively few years ago there was no agreed means of valuing a financial option. This did not stop people who really wanted to from buying or writing options. It did, however, greatly limit their use because the liquidity of the market in options was limited to those prepared to trade despite having no proven valuation method. Prices were set by supply and demand pressures.

The standard approach of discounting forecast future cash flows was considered not to be suitable, for two reasons. These were that it was very difficult to forecast the expected cash flow associated with an option and it was considered impossible to calculate the correct discount rate because the risk inherent in an option changed over its life in an unpredictable way. The difficulty of forecasting cash flow was caused by the fact that the calculation of expected value cash flow required one to assess the effect of high-impact low-probability events. Whereas with a typical operating project one could often ignore upsides on the grounds that they were offset by downsides, with an option there was always either just an upside or just a downside.

The discount rate represented an even greater problem. There was general agreement that writing an option involved taking on more risks than simply owning the underlying asset. This indicated that the CoC for an option would be higher than the CoC for owning the asset. The problem was that the additional risk associated with an option would be a function of the asset price and the strike price. Now our model for the asset price is that it will vary like a random walk. This must in turn mean that the risk associated with an option must also have a random nature and will change over the period of the option. Hence, it is argued, the risk is not knowable and so the CoC is incalculable.

My view about economic models is that if, for thousands of years, willing buyers and willing sellers have been able to agree on a price yet the economic value model appears not to work, one must simply conclude that the economic value model is not the right approach to apply to this situation. In 1973, Black and Scholes published their way of calculating the value of an option. They approached the valuation problem through the principle of arbitrage. One interpretation of this principle stated that if two courses of action always produced the same result and if the prices of following both courses are traded on the same market, then the price of following those two courses of action must be identical. So if one could show that an option gave exactly the same payout as something else, then the option must be worth the same as that other thing.

Black and Scholes managed to show how, based on some quite realistic assumptions, options on a share could be replicated by holding the right combinations of shares and borrowing. Since both shares and borrowing can be valued, options can be valued.

The reference to 'quite realistic assumptions' is very important. If one were prepared to accept some very simple models of future share price behaviour one could come up with some equally simple options valuation formulae. If, for example, one was prepared to accept that a future share would either trade at one price or another and that the probability of each outcome was known, the valuation would be trivial (our traditional valuation approaches could cope!). Black and Scholes allowed for the fact that share prices were continually changing in a random way and showed how it was still possible to replicate a call option by a combination of share ownership and borrowing, with the exact make-up of shares and borrowing changing continuously in response to the market.

The exact formula looks (and is!) nicely complicated. Fortunately one does not need to remember the formula. There are just five variables and these in turn need to be grouped into just two expressions. One can then either use a preprogrammed computer function or a set of look-up tables to determine the option value. The five variables are:

S	The price of the asset today
E	The exercise price for the option
σ	The standard deviation per period of the rate of return on the asset
t	The time to the exercise date of the option
r	The risk-free interest rate

The two groupings that one calculates are:

$\sigma \times \sqrt{t}$	The standard deviation times the square root of the time to exercise.
$S \div PV(E)$	The asset price divided by the present value of the exercise price.

Look-up tables will then reveal what the call option value is as a percentage of the asset price today. The value of a put option is calculated by adding to the call value the present value of the exercise price and subtracting the current asset price.

Now most of the parameters in the formula are intuitive. What is not immediately intuitive is the use of the risk-free rate and the fact that there is no risk premium anywhere to be seen. The only risk factor is σ, the standard deviation of the rate of return on the asset, and this works in such a way that increased standard deviation increases call option value. This is a complete contrast with the economic value approach where owning an asset that is subject to higher risk lowers value. One can explain this by noting that it is volatility that creates flexibility value. If there is no volatility there is no flexibility and hence no flexibility value. Use of the risk-free rate is explained by the fact that the approach is one which allows all risk to be removed. By continuously updating a portfolio of shares in the asset and borrowing one can create an exact replica of the option. By replicating it one can cancel its risk.

The formula was quickly adopted by market participants and it facilitated a large increase in the trade in so-called derivative products. The formula became almost a self-fulfilling prophecy. People believe in it and so people are willing to price options using it. A large influx of like-minded market players creates exactly the liquidity that is necessary for a market to take off.

These investors are implicitly accepting the assumptions which were made in deriving the formula. There are several, but the three key ones which I would highlight are that investors are prepared to make an estimate of future volatility; to assume that markets are very liquid; and to ignore transaction costs.

The question of volatility is of prime importance because it has a huge impact on option value. It is never really safe simply to assume that past volatility is a good indicator of future volatility and yet I do believe that many investors implicitly do this. The more sophisticated investors certainly do not and they will use anticipated changes in volatility compared with the historic trend as a signal of whether to write or to buy options.

Liquidity is usually relatively unimportant, particularly for small investors. It can, however, become very significant, particularly if one is considering very large positions. My view is that it is unreasonable to believe that there will always be somebody prepared to do the opposite of what you want to do once the scale of your investment becomes in any way material in relation to the market overall. So I take the view that the valuation method becomes more dangerous as the scale of investment increases. This provides quite a dilemma for any individual or company that believes they have found a great trading strategy to make money out of options. They must not overexploit it or else they may become the victims of their own success when, all of a sudden, the market is not prepared to deal when they want to and prices change in an unanticipated way.

Transaction costs need not really matter if investors are prepared to act as though no arbitrage opportunities will exist. This would mean that prices would remain where they 'ought' to be without the need for some investors to act in response to any opportunity. It does, however, cost money to put in place the replicating portfolio which can allow investors to lock in any opportunity and so apparent mis-pricing of financial options can be sustained.

Can financial option valuation methods be used to value flexibility in projects?

The Nobel press release suggested that the answer to this question was 'yes'. The logic behind this was that the flexibility that existed in projects had many of the characteristics of a financial option. In particular there was the fact that flexibility would only be utilised if it was beneficial to do so at the time that the subsequent decision had to be made. This similarity did lead some academics to suggest that the Black-Scholes formula could be used to value some real-life flexibility situations such as the right to make a follow-on investment. The approach was also anticipated to work for situations where flexible production facilities were being considered. Many examples of the possible use of the Black-Scholes equation to value real investment projects were published in the financial journals and textbooks.

Now although I accept that there are some similarities, I have to say that I do not believe that I could keep a straight face and at the same time propose to a senior manager that a real-life decision concerning something such as a follow-on value or flexible production could be valued using the Black-Scholes formula. This is not because these senior managers do not understand how financial options are valued. It is because the similarities between financial options and these real-life situations are, in my view, too tenuous to use to justify any major investment.

There are several reasons why I make this assertion. The first is that the risks which govern the return on these real-life projects are not all traded on financial markets. There is, therefore, no ability to replicate the option through some combination of borrowing and owning an asset. Related to this is the fact that there are usually no data on the volatility of the return on the underlying asset. So the volatility number is usually simply plucked out of the air or deemed to be the same as the volatility of some financial asset. Furthermore, real-life flexibilities are usually much more complex than a simple call option with a specified strike price and exercise date. The flexibility will often, for example, be available for some long period of time, usually going beyond the period for which financial markets provide a real opportunity to trade.

Let us consider the earlier example of feedstock flexibility on a steam cracker. The decision concerning whether to go for a single feedstock or for multiple feedstock capability will need to be taken before construction commences. The cracker will probably not come on stream for at least three years. Even if all of the feedstocks and products were traded on the market, there would not be an active trade in product for delivery in three years' time. So we would not even know for sure which feedstock would be best on day 1 of operation or what the implied options which feedstock flexibility gave us might be worth even during the first month of operation. Yet we need to evaluate the benefit of flexibility that will last for, say, 20 years.

Yet further complications become apparent when one considers that it is not just necessary to identify which is the cheapest feedstock, one needs to identify which feedstock gives the best overall contribution given the particular yield of ethylene and by-products which it gives. The optionality which we need to value concerns multiple feedstocks and products. The calculation would be mind-blowingly complex even if one thought it could be done at all. Then, imagine trying to explain the result to a decision-maker. All that you could do is say words to the effect of 'This is my answer; please trust me'.

As a second example, consider the valuation of a growth opportunity. A typical Black-Scholes approach to this might start with an initial project which had a negative NPV. A follow-on project would be assumed to be the same or perhaps to be the same but larger. A discounted cash flow approach, it would be argued, would place no value on the follow-on project because its expected value was negative. Then we would be told to apply options thinking. Things may change in the future and the follow-on project may turn out to be a good idea. The project would be rejected if it had a negative value and accepted if it had a positive value. Hence, unless it was impossible that the follow-on project had a positive value, it must have some option value.

Up to this stage I am reasonably happy with the logic of what has been suggested. My concern is with the detail of what follows. The exact calculation would be done like this. First, the timing of the follow-on project would be specified. Then the project would be described as an initial investment which was the equivalent of the strike price and the present value of future cash flows once the asset was built. This present value of future cash flows would be treated as the asset price at the future date. Then a volatility assumption would be made. This should represent the volatility of the present value of future cash flows from the project and this would, typically, be assumed to be equal to the volatility of the company's share price.

On the face of it this might sound like a potentially credible argument. One should always be prepared to accept that things may get better and hence there should be some potential for option value. I cannot, though, accept that a project is something which one can treat as being like a share and lock in the value from it in a single action at the moment the project is approved.

Suppose that the project was a gold mine. Yes, at today's gold price the mine may not be economic, and yes, it is possible that, thanks to the random nature of future prices, the gold price will be high enough in, say, four years' time to make a project viable. The problem is that no sensible person will base a long-term project on the current price of the product which will be manufactured on the day on which the project is sanctioned. The analysis will be based on the forecast price over the life of the asset. Hence in my view, what one needs to deal with is not the volatility of the gold price, it is the volatility of your company's view of the gold price over time. This number is likely to be much lower than the volatility of the price itself. Crucially, the number is not traded on any financial market and so all of the logic about being able to create an equivalent instrument cannot apply.

One other simple reason to reject this approach concerns the problem of when the follow on investment might take place. This date has a large impact on option value through the 'sigma root t' parameter. So if your calculated option value is not enough to justify a project, all that you have to do is assume that the option is exercised a few years later and your value will rise. Intuitively, this does not seem right.

It is for all of these reasons that I am forced to the conclusion that financial options valuation approaches do not appear to offer any major benefits for valuing the flexibilities that are inherent in real-life projects.

Part 3: The flexibility valuation toolkit

Introduction: So what should be done about flexibility?

It is easy to demolish a proposal. I believe, however, that since I accept that flexibility does have a value, I must propose a means of assessing this or else go along with whatever is the best approach that others put forward. In this section I will rise to this challenge and suggest how I believe flexibility should be incorporated into financial decision-making. I will use the existing suite of techniques and hence, I trust, disprove the assertion which is too often made that discounted cash flow techniques implicitly assume that companies hold their assets passively and that it is thus not possible to reflect the value of flexibility through this approach.

Like any good toolkit this one will start with a set of operating instructions and a strong recommendation that these should be read before the tools themselves are got out and tried. This is really important because the context within which the tools are used will greatly influence the success of their application. Furthermore, I will show that there are many prizes to be won simply through thinking through the implications of flexibility without ever having to carry out a single valuation. I hope that through doing this I will be able to rebuild the bridges which I may appear to have burned when I rejected the Black-Scholes approach to flexibility valuation. I am a huge fan of incorporating flexibility into the way that we think about strategies and projects; I simply don't like some of the approaches that have been suggested for valuing it.

In this section I will put forward a ten step process for incorporating flexibility into decision-making. These steps are:

1. Life is not a single path into the future.

2. Recognise when flexibility matters.
3. Understand the types of flexibility.
4. Clarify objectives and boundaries.
5. Prepare first guess of the likely path.
6. Identify the important uncertainties and decisions and map them onto the path.
7. Decide whether flexibilities need to be valued.
8. Apply appropriate tool from the toolkit to value the flexibility.
9. Ensure that organisation is equipped to capture flexibility value in the future.
10. Monitor results to facilitate Plan, Do, Measure, Learn approach.

Note in particular that calculations have to wait until Step 8 and that I will propose several ways to calculate flexibility value. I would contrast this approach with one which starts with a particular model and then forces all potential flexibility situations into that way of thinking. Dare I say it, but what I will now propose is a flexible approach to dealing with flexibility!

There are ten steps in the approach but in many situations one will not need to follow the course through to the end. Many important lessons will become apparent early on.

Step 1: Life is not a single path into the future

The first step is fairly simple. It concerns the need to raise awareness about the fact that the future success of a company depends to a considerable extent on decisions yet to be taken. The company may have a plan, but this does not mean that it knows with certainty what it will do.

From a financial perspective, a company's life is described through its AFS. Its history is fixed and, with the hindsight which the present gives us, we know the path that it followed. The future is not fixed. The world around a company is uncertain and the company's response to that world is also uncertain.

The stage gate approach gives us a good way of thinking about these uncertainties and decisions and how they create what can be thought of as a 'cone of uncertainty' for a project. This is depicted in the following diagram.

The stage gate approach for project development starts with strategy as a given. The strategy could be, for example, to grow ethylene production capacity. It then requires that possible projects which could implement the strategy be identified. These projects could concern where a new cracker was located and whether a partner was involved. The choice of project is

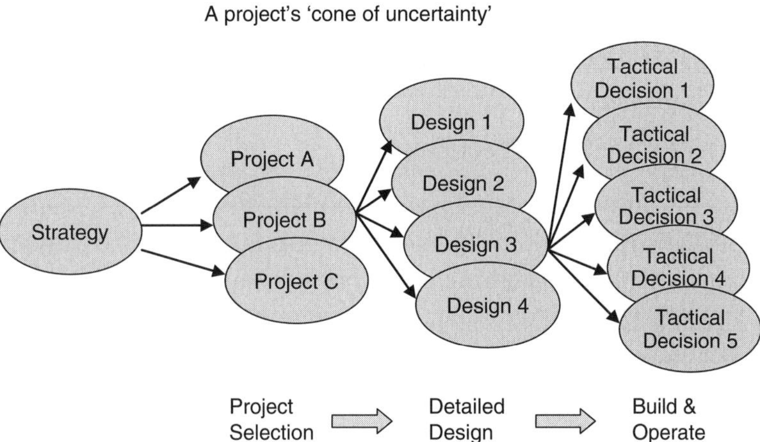

Fig. 12.2 Paths into the future

made at the project selection stage gate review. In my diagram I suggest that there might have been three different projects and that just one, Project B, is selected. Detailed design now takes place. Again, many decisions have to be taken concerning, for example in the case of my flexible feed steam cracker, what flexibility to allow. My diagram suggests that there may have been four design options for this one selected project and that we choose design 3. In reality there will be many more choices. Finally, when the new steam cracker comes on stream, the individual decisions are taken concerning exactly which feedstocks will be cracked. I have depicted just five decisions in the diagram. In reality these are likely to be taken weekly or even daily over the estimated 20-year life of the asset.

Now these are just the decisions that our company will take. What is not shown on the diagram is the fact that we do not know what the external world will do to things like the price of ethylene. So, when one stands at the project selection stage gate, the future looks very uncertain. Indeed, when the future is set out in this way it is perhaps surprising that we even dare to summarise the financial results of these decisions as a single set of numbers, yet this is indeed what we do. We do this on the basis that our numbers do not represent what will happen. They are supposed to represent the expected value of what will happen.

So our analysis of flexibility must start from a recognition of the uncertainty which our company faces and an understanding that, to an extent, a company can influence its future by taking good decisions. What is needed is a means of reflecting these decisions in our decision-taking methodology.

Step 2: Recognise when flexibility matters

The next step is to recognise when flexibility matters. We know that the future is uncertain but there are times when this uncertainty is more important than others. I like to think of any business as being simply a means of transforming inputs into outputs. I am not trying to demean the fantastic efforts that technical people put into designing their machines, etc., but to me they all serve the same purpose. They convert inputs into outputs and these can be summarised via an AFS.

We do not know exactly what the input will be but if it has a linear relationship with the output then this does not matter too much. By linear I mean that if a 1% change in input value produces an x% change in output then a 2% change in input must produce a two times x% change in output. If this is true, and it typically is, then we can obtain the expected value of the output by using a single model that is based on expected value assumptions. So if we cannot do anything about uncertainty and our business model is linear, we don't have to worry too much because we can calculate the correct result through a single calculation of our business model based on a series of expected value assumptions.

Suppose, though, that our company can respond to events. Suppose that if prices fall below marginal cost we can cease production. This would give us the opportunity to do better than would be predicted simply by applying expected value logic. Now if such decisions are within the control of our company, then the flexibility is going to enhance value. If, however, our customers or our suppliers were able to exercise flexibility against our company it is likely that this would lower our value compared with the simple situation of a linear business model. Both of these would be situations where we would need to think further about the impact of flexibility.

So far I have considered flexibility just in the context of how future decisions can influence value. Flexibility can also be present or absent in physical machinery. Any lack of flexibility will usually be bad. Let us think again about our steam cracker and what the demand for ethylene might be. We do not know what this will be but if we can supply whatever the market might require we can run our financial model based on our expected value estimate of ethylene demand. If, however, our cracker has a physical limitation on its output and this is lower than the highest possible level of ethylene demand given the uncertainty then the expected value of ethylene demand is not the right number to use in our calculations. The right number would be somewhat lower.

So this second step requires that we understand the physical constraints within our own business, the flexibilities that others can use against us and the flexibilities which we can use to our benefit. We need to apply our skill and judgement to decide which of these really matter and then devote our further attention to them. This is not to suggest that other uncertainties do not matter. They do, but they can be properly considered through application of the approaches which I have set out earlier in this book.

Step 3: Understand the types of flexibility

The types of flexibility are explained by my 2 × 2 matrix showing the four types categorised as strategic or tactical and given or received. I suggest that the approach should be that a skilled analyst would review what flexibilities came with the project and what flexibilities were given away. The analyst would need to involve corporate staff in order to consider the wider strategic effects but the lead for this should, I suggest, be taken by the project team. Any lack of flexibility caused, for example, by the physical design of our equipment would be classified as being a given flexibility because it represents something where our company cannot make the choices. We would, in effect, have given away the right to produce at above the maximum design capacity by our choice of the size of our manufacturing plant.

A stage gate approach will force attention to the right issues at the right time in the life cycle of a project. In particular, it will direct attention to the wider strategic issues at the options identification and selection stage. This is the time when strategic flexibilities need to be considered. If strategic issues are important then they must be considered at this early stage in the development of a project. The analysis which is made at this stage can then be carried forward for continued use at later stages.

The investments which will create tactical flexibility will be considered fully during the detailed design stage. They will, however, need to be recognised at earlier stages, particularly if they might be great enough to influence the selection of one project compared with another. This means, for example, that a rough estimate of the benefit of feedstock flexibility and of its cost should be incorporated in the early stage decisions concerning which project to select. My example of a flexible feed steam cracker is particularly relevant in this context because the availability and pricing of alternative feedstocks changes greatly from location to location. Other flexibilities may be less relevant if they were equally available to all potential projects.

This options identification and selection stage is the right time to give particular attention to whether there is any significant value in future growth opportunities. I categorise these as being received strategic flexibilities. Senior managers tend to use just the word strategic. There is, however, a danger that I perceive in that almost any project can claim this so-called strategic benefit and use it to justify staying in business despite the current opportunity's having a negative NPV. The logic behind this is that any project might lead to another and the future may be more favourable. Since unfavourable future outcomes have zero value the follow-on value for any project must be positive. I suggest that this is a very poor line of logic because I cannot accept the economic logic that anything might have a positive NPV. I maintain that NPVs are not random events; they are the product, among other things, of sources of value.

Accordingly, I suggest that the following checklist might help to narrow the list down somewhat to those which really do offer the prospect of high future value creation potential. The list is based on the suggestion that there are three critical characteristics of a growth opportunity in order for it to be reasonable to believe that it may provide significant flexibility value. These are:

- sources of value;
- growth; and
- constraints.

These factors work together in such a manner that one must feel confident that all three give positive signs that a situation may subsequently lead to positive value from future growth.

Sources of value refers to the ability of competitors to make similar investments in the market concerned. If competitors can also invest in a similar way to our company, then, in logic, this will limit the return which we can reasonably be expected to earn. Indeed, in this situation we should be considered to be 'me too' and should anticipate destroying value. The ideal situation is a market where we have strong sources of value relative to the relevant competition. Reference to relevant competition is often the key. A company may face a strong competitor in one market but if that competitor is not established in a new market then our company may have a large advantage over the other local competitors. This logic is not attempting to claim that it is impossible for a follow-on investment to have a positive NPV even if it lacks sources of value. It is claiming that it is not reasonable to believe that it would do so at any early stage in its life.

The reference to growth should be self-evident. The flexibility to invest in a further project can only have real value if the market actually grows at a fast enough rate to justify the building of enough plants for both our growth aspirations and also those of our competitors.

There is one possible situation where I believe that future growth potential may even be important enough to overcome a company's current lack of sources of value. This concerns newly emerging markets which are as yet very immature such that the main players and their sources of value have yet to emerge. In this situation it could be reasonable to believe that a company that was currently no worse placed than others, and that was committing significant efforts to building capability for the future, could have a positive follow-on value. I refer to this situation as the nascent industry argument and suggest that there is actually a source of value present. This source of value is the early mover advantage enabled by the strategic vision of the company which is prepared to commit resources to a new sector in advance of others. This will always be a high-risk strategy but it does offer the potential of high reward.

The reference to constraints is less self-evident. The concern addressed by this heading is the need to avoid constraints on our company's ability to implement value-creating projects. The worst type of constraint might be the need to secure government approval which was tailored to each individual project. Here again we would have become 'me too' because we were, in effect, regulated by government. There might also be a need to involve a local partner who could secure an unfair share of any value prize. Next, our company might have a concern about the scale of money at risk within a single country, triggering an overarching risk concern. Finally, there might be human resource limitations, particularly those caused by language and other cultural differences. Overall, any constraints can serve to limit the flexibility value of growth.

So, in summary, my approach at Step 3 concerns understanding and identifying the various types of flexibility which might impact on a project or strategy. It requires that decision-makers should be aware of the limitations of traditional valuation methods and can then require a particular focus on the value of flexibility only when it is really likely to matter. The checklist which I have suggested will limit the study of growth value to situations where sources of value are present.

Step 4: Clarify objectives and boundaries

This next step is included as a direct result of my own experiences and also of conversations with other practitioners. It concerns the need to understand the importance of objectives and boundaries. One might assume that the objective of all analysis was to identify the highest value course of action. This is what I would always assume if I was told nothing to the contrary. There are, however, often different objectives for projects and these may be explicit or implicit.

As an initial example I would cite the way that the headline capital expenditure on a project can often become key, particularly during the detailed design stage if initial approval has been given for a project costing, say, $50m. What can often happen then is that the detailed design will be done to the objective of achieving the highest value within a capital expenditure budget of no more than $50m. The theory may say that value should be paramount but the practical reality may be different.

Time can often also become an objective and when it does it can stand in the way of the capture of flexibility value. This is because flexibilities take time to investigate and if a project is up against a tight deadline the assessment of flexibility value may have to be sacrificed.

My reference to clarity about boundaries is best explained by an example. Suppose that an oil company had struck oil in a particular offshore location. It has made, we will assume, quite a large find such that it might be able to justify building a new platform and pipeline to shore. It could, however, seek to come to an agreement with the owner of an existing platform and pipeline which is nearby and has sufficient spare capacity to allow our field to be developed. The initial options identification exercise could well come up with three possibilities. These are as follows:

1. Develop using third party's platform and pipeline.
2. Build own platform and pipeline sized just for this oil find.
3. Build large platform and pipeline in anticipation of future oil finds by our company or third parties.

Now if the manager of the project was appointed with responsibility just to develop the particular oil find he would choose between options 1 and 2. If, however, he was given wider responsibility option 3 would come into play. Even then, it would be important to understand whether the manager believed he was responsible just for the development of all oil finds by his company or for the wider task of maximising value for the company from all activities in that country, including earning, for example, pipeline throughput fees earned from third parties.

The way that companies are organised will often have a substantial effect on how wide a view is taken of the possibilities for flexibility value. In principle, the wider the view that is taken, the more the chances are that some flexibility value will be encountered.

My point in including this step is to emphasise that if a manager is constrained by either or both objectives or boundaries then it is important either to respect this in any analysis that is carried out or to get the constraints changed. This is something that needs to be done at this relatively early stage if wasted effort is to be avoided and we wish to achieve an overall optimum for the company and not just a local optimum for the current project manager.

Step 5: Prepare first guess of the likely path

It may seem surprising, but I recommend that the way to approach the question of flexibility value is to start with a single view of the likely path into the future. This is necessary in order to obtain a rough idea of the scope and potential value creation associated with a project. The approach will require the use of a simple financial model but this will need to project annual cash flows in AFS format and not simply rely on building up the estimate of value through the sum of a series of sources of value less the assumed 'me too' result.

There is, I am well aware, a considerable temptation, particularly for highly skilled analysts, to build a beautiful and sophisticated model at this stage. An analyst may well already have identified multiple options which will need to be evaluated and so may wish to move directly to a complex model which will facilitate this analysis. My recommendation, however, is to start with a simple model and only move to a more detailed one later on. At some stage the original model will be replaced with a new one but much of the early work will be easier if undertaken on a simple model.

At this early stage the model should be based on what I would refer to as success case assumptions. We would not at this stage want to consider both success and failure and use this to generate expected value assumptions. The aim would be to have a rough idea of what success might look like.

Step 6: Identify the important uncertainties and decisions and map them onto the path

A combination of a company's stage gate approach to project development and the simple AFS picture of what success might look like can now serve as the basis for identifying uncertainties, potential responses and decision points. These should be mapped onto the project's time line so that decisions are taken at the appropriate time.

The uncertainties and the decisions are related but will appear at very different points on a project's time line. There may well be uncertainty concerning demand for the product but decisions relating to the capacity of a manufacturing unit will be taken well in advance of this at the detailed design stage. The approach needs to work like this:

1. Identify what the impact of an uncertainty would be if we simply wait and respond to events as and when they happen.
2. Identify what things could be done in advance in order to reduce any downside or enhance any upside.
3. For each identified action, determine the key decision points.

I will now illustrate this approach for our ethylene steam cracker project. One uncertainty might concern demand. Suppose that we think this will be 500,000 tonnes per annum in the first year of operation and that subsequent growth will be in the range 2–5% pa. Suppose that there is also a possibility that one of our downstream plants that consume ethylene might be closed and that the impact of this would be a reduction in demand of 100,000 tonnes per annum.

The first thing to do is to establish what we would do if we are long or short of ethylene. At one extreme, if there is no third party market where we can buy or sell ethylene, any mismatch between supply and demand will be very serious. Any lack of supply would mean that downstream production would be curtailed. Any potential excess supply would result in throughput having to be reduced below the maximum. At the other extreme, if there was a large local market, surpluses and deficits might not matter at all because they could be sold on the market. A third possibility might be that buying or selling on the market required us to pay a pipeline fee in order to move the ethylene to or from the market.

Let us assume that our initial view of the likely path was based on a 500,000 tonne per annum plant exactly matching the initial demand. Let us further assume that our plant is linked to an ethylene market but that there is a quite substantial cost involved in any product flows in either direction owing to the need to utilise a third party pipeline.

We should quickly identify that we had an early choice to make concerning the size of the plant. We might consider building a 400,000 tonne per annum plant if we were worried about the closure of the downstream plant. We could also consider building larger plants which could then gradually build up to full capacity as demand grew. We should also consider whether there were any other decisions which could be taken now in order to reduce the impact of low demand or increase our ability to benefit from high demand. It is here that we would want to devote quite substantial efforts and to make sure that we thought of a wide range of possibilities.

It would be a good exercise for readers to think of, say, half a dozen potential responses to this demand uncertainty and only then go on and read my list below.

Possible responses to the demand uncertainty could include:

- Are there some initial investments which could be made now which would make a subsequent expansion in capacity quick and cheap to implement?
- Are there any studies which can be done now which might give a better idea about whether or not the downstream plant will have to be closed?
- Are there any deals which can be done now which might make the future of the downstream plant more certain, such as agreeing a long-term supply deal with a customer?
- Is it possible to increase throughput at our other downstream plant?
- Can we negotiate an access right to the pipeline which links our plant to the market at a lower cost than we have anticipated?
- Should we build our own pipeline to the ethylene market and then perhaps build a much larger cracker?
- If we are short of ethylene, can we calculate which downstream product should be cut back and what the exact economic impact would be? Do some downstream plants have, for example, a group of relatively unprofitable customers or are all customers giving the same contribution?

Now with the exception of the final bullet point, all of the above would require a relatively early decision. Even the final suggestion would need to be examined roughly at an early stage in order to ensure that our analysis was based on appropriate data. It is also worth reflecting on the fact that although the usual mantra of options is that 'flexibility is money', my second proposal is aimed simply at reducing the uncertainty surrounding the downside event.

This step in the process is potentially very important because it is where the actual ideas are generated. It does, however, have a cost associated with it and this can be quite substantial. The work will require a skilled team to be assembled to carry out an initial brainstorming exercise. It will then need quite a lot of input in order to follow up the potential ideas. So, for example, it is easy to ask whether we can make a subsequent expansion quick and cheap to implement but it will cost quite a lot in terms of engineering work to establish the answer. Senior judgement about the amount of effort to be devoted to this work is important.

One final thing to consider at this stage is whether there are any relatively small flexibilities which surround this project and which can be picked up for free. The main aim may be to find big things to do, but if there are small things which have no cost associated then one might as well take them. One should also ensure that small flexibilities are not being given away. It may well not be worthwhile having a specific 'free flexibility' brainstorming session but if the project team is aware of how flexibility can enhance value it should be encouraged to collect free flexibility wherever and whenever it can.

Step 7: Decide whether flexibilities need to be valued

Flexibilities do not always have to be valued. This is only necessary when the actual value will affect a decision. There are many examples when this will be the case. For example, the decisions about ethylene demand uncertainty, which would need to be taken in the light of my list of ideas above, would require quantification. So too would my example concerning feedstock flexibility.

There are, however, many instances where flexibility value exists but where it is not necessary to calculate exactly what it might be. I will give three such examples.

The first concerns flexibility which is considered to be part of the 'me too' return. It does not matter how much effort one puts into calculating this if one is only then going to assume that the 'me too' player has a negative NPV equal to 10% of its capex. Second, the value of subsequent growth is not crucial if one already knows that the initial investment will earn at least the CoC. My third example concerns flexible uses for an asset. There is, for example, enhanced value when ordering a new aeroplane if one knows that it can operate on, say, three major routes, not just one. If, however, one is content that it is worth committing to an order just on the basis of the potential demand from one main route then the additional flexibility value may be an interesting fact, but it is not really crucial to know what it is worth.

Even when one is doing flexibility valuations it can pay to manage the effort which is put into them. So, if we return to my ethylene demand example, one might be able to avoid some valuations if one knew the result of another study. If, for example, we decide to build a large cracker and a pipeline to the market, then the study concerning demand for the downstream product would not be necessary.

Step 8: Apply appropriate tool from the toolkit to value the flexibility

We are now ready to meet my suggested list of tools for valuing flexibility. This is as follows:

A. More sophisticated assumptions
B. Risk monetisation
C. Growth value
D. Valuing the tail
E. Monte Carlo simulation
F. Simple decision trees
G. Reverse engineering
H. Black-Scholes
I. Analogy
J. Include any additional costs

I will now explain each of these. In most instances I believe that the description which is provided in this book should allow a practitioner who is skilled in basic economic value techniques to complete a flexibility valuation. I will highlight those limited situations where I believe that additional specialist assistance is needed in order to carry out a flexibility valuation.

Step 8A: More sophisticated assumptions

This first approach is so simple that I sometimes wonder why I have to introduce it as a technique in the advanced section of this book! I need to do this, however, because my experience tells me that many practitioners do not realise the implicit assumption which they are making when they carry out a valuation. The more sophisticated assumptions approach simply involves making more refined assumptions than are usually made in an economic value calculation. In particular the approach requires that one rejects the use of annual averages.

The usual approach in an economic value calculation is to project annual cash flow through a series of calculations which are typically of the form:

sales revenue = sales volume × sales price.

Sales volume and sales price are annual averages. Companies will often, in effect, mandate this approach by specifying a central set of assumptions for their key products and raw materials. There is no problem with this approach if your project is producing a single product that is sold at a steady rate throughout the year. It can, however, miss a lot of potential value creation if your project brings with it the inherent flexibility to change things throughout the year.

Consider any of the following situations:

- you anticipate that there may be times during a year when you will shut down your plant because the marginal contribution would be negative;
- you expect to judge the timing of your purchasing of raw materials in order to buy at a better than average price;
- you expect to judge the timing of your sales such that you sell at a better than the average price;
- you have the flexibility to switch feedstock in response to market movements;
- you have the ability to change the output of your plant.

These will all allow a company to create more value than would be implied by the use of simple annual average assumptions and on some occasions the effect can be quite significant. Now I would suggest that most projects will anticipate doing at least some of the above. In all of these situations, therefore, one will not capture the benefit of the flexibility if one applies a simple annual approach. One can start with the annual average and then, I suggest, add a little sophistication to the assumptions in order to capture more accurately what will, in reality, happen.

I will consider first the ability to shut down production when the marginal contribution goes negative and illustrate the effect with a simple example.

Suppose that a company is investigating the purchase, for $700,000, of a manufacturing machine that makes bathtubs. The company expects to have sales of 10,000 bathtubs per year and each unit sells for $100. Variable costs are $80 per unit and cash fixed costs are $100,000 per annum. We will ignore working capital, inflation and tax and assume a ten-year project life and a CoC of 9%. The financial model which we use can be very simple and is as follows:

$	
Sales revenue	1,000,000
Variable costs	(800,000)
Fixed costs	(100,000)
Annual cash flow	100,000
Annuity factor (mid-yr flows)	6.700
Present value cash inflows	670,000

The project has an NPV of $(30,000). The IRR is almost exactly 8%. Faced with this prospect the logical reaction would be to decline the investment opportunity.

Now let us introduce the potential for shutting down production when the marginal contribution is negative. If the variable costs remain the same but the selling price is variable we would shut down production whenever prices fell below $80 per unit. So if we thought that selling prices would never fall below $80 per unit the flexibility to shut down production would, based on this assumption, have no value.

Suppose, however, we thought that a more realistic set of price assumptions was that the selling price would be in the range $70–130 per unit with the lower figure prevailing for 20% of the time, the mid point for 60% of the time and $130 for 20% of the time. What would be the implications of this for the potential NPV of our project? We would still face the same average selling price over the year of $100 per unit but our company would not sell throughout the year. We would only produce during the period when the price was $100 or $130 per unit. The overall sales volume would be lower but the result would be better. Our revised financial projection would be as follows:

$	
Sales revenue[7]	860,000
Variable costs	(640,000)
Fixed costs	(100,000)
Annual cash flow	120,000
Annuity factor (mid-yr flows)	6.700
Present value cash inflows	804,000

The project now offers a positive NPV of just over $100,000. The source of this additional $134,000 of value is the decision to cease production when prices are low and our assessment of how often this occurs. This flexibility allows us to avoid a negative contribution of $10 per unit on sales of 2,000 bathtubs. The present value of $20,000 per year for ten years is $134,000.

At present these are just a set of assumptions and the answer is only ever as good as the assumptions on which it is based. The decision-maker would need to convince himself that he was content with the assumptions. Was it realistic, for example, for our company to move in and out of the market when we wanted to? This suggests that customer relationships were of no

[7] Calculated as 6,000 × $100 + 2,000 × $130 = $860,000.

importance. Also, was it possible simply to turn production on and off at no cost? If the production machine took a little while to get going properly this might destroy the economic case.

The decision-maker would also want to investigate the assumptions concerning the range in price. If the lower price was to happen only 10% of the time, the value prize from flexibility would be halved to \$67,000 but the project would still have a positive NPV. If the price range was ±\$25 per unit rather than ±\$30, the value prize would also be reduced by a half. A combination of both of these effects would give an NPV of approximately zero.

Now I cannot say for this situation whether or not I believe the assumptions because this is a purely hypothetical case. I hope, however, that readers can see how it is quite possible to look into the detail of a financial model and make a few additional assumptions in order to incorporate the effect of this type of flexibility. The answer depends on the assumptions but then that is always the case. One is already making many assumptions about demand, price and cost, so why not make a few more and model the flexibility to shut down in this way?

Finally, in relation to shutdown flexibility, I need to point out that, in principle, shutdowns do not have to be occasional for this simple technique to be applied. One can apply the same approach to a plant which will only very occasionally be operated. Suppose that a cheap bathtub manufacturing machine was available at a cost of \$50,000. It would require fixed costs of just \$50,000 per annum but it has variable costs of \$100 per unit. This machine would only be operated in our high price situation. It is justified on the assumption we would sell 2,000 units a year and generate a contribution of \$60,000. After paying our fixed costs the annual cash flow would be \$10,000 and the NPV would be \$17,000. So a plant that, based on annual average prices, would never be switched on, turns out to offer a positive NPV.[8]

I will consider now the procurement and sales possibilities which are covered by the second and third bullet points in my list. These are both concerned

[8] This particular example is very closely related to an example which I have often encountered as a supposed illustration of where traditional DCF techniques do not work. This concerns the valuation of a small diesel-driven generator which is operated only when electricity prices are particularly high. Devotees of options thinking claim that this is best valued as a call option on electricity and they will apply the Black-Scholes formula in order to come up with a value. I accept that the DCF valuation depends on some key assumptions about how often the plant will be run over its life and what the average margin will be when it does run. I would, however, point out that the generator cannot be treated as a single option, it gives a series of options over its life and there is no market in the price of electricity that goes that far into the future. So any options-based valuation must equally depend on a set of assumptions and not the 'fact' that the ability exists to replicate the asset through the right combination of financial instruments, all of which are available at a known price today.

with flexibility and I will treat them together because the way that they can be modelled is identical. In these instances most people would say that the flexibility involved the addition of one or two extra types of business to our overall business model. Instead of simply making money out of our ability to produce, we are anticipating making money out of our commercial/trading acumen which will allow us to make good timing calls in relation to market prices and also to make money out of our procurement expertise. Trading and procurement are, in my view, two separate business skills, both of which can augment the more traditional manufacturing and marketing skills.

Once one is prepared to accept these additional elements to a business model it is quite simple to incorporate them through a few extra assumptions. For raw material procurement one could, for example, assume that raw material purchases are made at, say, $1 per unit below the average price and incorporate this assumption in the overall valuation. In our bathtub example, if we return to the original financial model before the flexibility to shut down was incorporated, the impact of a $1 per unit reduction in variable costs is $10,000 per year, which would increase value by $67,000. The flexibility to beat the market on selling prices would have the same impact.

There are some situations when it might be entirely reasonable to believe that a timing benefit could reduce costs compared with paying the annual average. A typical such situation would be where your company holds a substantial stock of raw material and buys it in through a few large purchases. In other situations it might be highly unrealistic to assume a purchasing benefit. An example of this might be an airline that purchases jet fuel a few minutes in advance of when each plane takes off. If a business is run like this then there is no possibility of achieving a raw material purchase timing benefit.

I have stressed this point because of the vital need to ensure that the assumptions which are made are realistic in the specific situation of the project under consideration. Although the examples which I have just shown have highlighted the relevance of a stock holding, this is not always essential. Any situation where it is possible to agree today to a price for delivery in the future creates the possibility of flexibility value. This can be modelled by making some additional assumptions concerning how much benefit this will generate.

Now I imagine that many people would consider that the procurement saving was not really a flexibility at all. Procurement savings are possible when a company has buyer power over its supplier and chooses to organise itself in order to capture this advantage. Most people would, I think, agree that this was just a part of 'normal business'. The reason that I am making this point is that if procurement is part of 'normal business' then most people must be quite happy to incorporate it in a traditional economic value model via a series of assumptions which generate a set of cash flows which are discounted at the CoC. So if this means of saving, say, \$1 per unit on variable costs is acceptable it should also be acceptable to incorporate the impact of \$1 per unit that is achieved through what some people might call 'optionality' in the same way. All that is necessary to make the incorporation of this type of flexibility value an entirely reasonable thing to do is that the decision-maker is prepared to accept the assumptions on which it is based.

The question of whether or not a decision-maker should be prepared to accept an assumption raises what I consider to be one of the most important questions in relation to flexibility value. This concerns whether flexibility is a source of value or a part of the 'me too' return. I have already raised this point but it is so important that I will devote a little more attention to it now.

One should always consider whether the 'me too' players will also gain the benefit of any flexibilities which may be identified. If they do, then it should be considered as part of the 'me too' return and so including it explicitly in the analysis should not have an overall impact on the NPV which is reported. We should always remember that the logic of the Sources of Value approach is that one can calibrate the overall return which it is reasonable to assume a 'me too' player will earn. If one does the analysis using annual average assumptions one will need to ensure that the overall impact of the full set of 'me too' assumptions gives a realistic NPV. Any subsequent change to the assumptions, such as, for example, including a raw material purchase timing benefit, should not increase the NPV of a project as one should presume that an equal and offsetting change is made to something else such as the selling price.

I would suggest that it was up to the sponsor of a project to make the necessary judgement concerning whether procurement or selling will represent a source of value and, if so, to what extent. My view is that in many situations at least some of any apparent flexibility value anticipated from procurement or selling should be considered as part of the 'me too' return and so should not contribute to a project's reported NPV. It is one of the beauties of Sources of Value logic that if a flexibility is considered as part of the 'me too' player's return, then it is only of secondary importance[9] to incorporate it in our analysis. This applies to all of the techniques which I will cover in this view and can, therefore, save a lot of work.

[9] It is of secondary importance because it contributes to the overall 'shape' of an AFS through changing the exact balance of costs and revenues but it should not alter the value.

I will consider now the flexibility to change feedstock. An example of this was my original steam cracker case study. The typical way to model the investment in any long-life asset is to prepare a set of forecasts covering all relevant costs and revenues. My experience tells me that these will be prepared on an annual basis. As we already now realise, this will mean that the true value of flexibility will be ignored. In effect we will be assuming that our commercial optimisation team arrive at work on 1 January each year and agree to purchase the same feedstock as last year and sell the same quantities of product. They may as well be on holiday for the rest of the year!

It should now be obvious that what we should do is make a set of assumptions about the individual feedstocks, the economic benefit they will give, and how many days per year each will be used. This set of assumptions and a slightly more sophisticated financial model will allow an AFS to be prepared. The extent to which the year was broken down into periods of months, weeks, days or even hours would be selected in order to allow a realistic modelling of the reality which the commercial optimisation team will face. The reasonableness of the assumptions could then be justified through some combination of the following:

- Use of historical data which will show what the flexibility would have contributed had it been available in the past.
- A summary of the implied average price for each feedstock and also its volatility. These could be tested against any corporate assumptions and also against historic data.
- A Sources of Value calculation which computes the implied NPV for each potential optimisation step.

These three steps are all important but the third is probably of greatest importance. The usual assumption is that one needs to be different from 'me too' in order to create value. It is always possible, however, to argue that it will take some number of years before the full 'me too' effect works through. So the addition of one cracker with feedstock flexibility to a market that is dominated by fixed feedstock crackers might be expected to earn a positive return as long as it was built quickly, even if the ability to build flexible feed crackers was now generally available. In such a situation the benefit from flexibility should be assumed to reduce as one moves into the future.

The flexibility to change output is modelled in a similar way to the flexibility to change raw material. I include it in my list for completeness and to emphasise the full generic range of situations where flexibilities do exist.

One would usually use the more sophisticated assumptions approach when the flexibility is likely to be used quite often. This is because it is perfectly reasonable to base a valuation on a set of assumptions if the outcomes are quite likely. This is, after all, what is usually done with any valuation. Unlikely switches, such as those involving a major change in the business or flexibilities with a very low probability of being used, will still have a value but the more sophisticated assumptions approach is probably not the best way to estimate it. I will return to the approach that I would use in this situation when I deal with reverse engineering in section 8G.

Step 8B: Risk monetisation

I introduced the risk monetisation technique in part 3 of the building block on Risk on page 168. It depends on the use of the impact times probability technique and is the standard way of dealing with many situations involving risk. When one thinks about many of these situations, however, one realises that they can be described through the language of options.

Let us consider the example of installing a spare pump so that if the primary pump were to break down the spare could immediately be switched on and so no production would be lost. The risk monetisation approach would require that one estimated the probability of the pump's failing and the financial impact if it did so. The product of the two would indicate the maximum amount which could be spent on installing the spare in order to remove the risk. In the language of options, a spare is something which gives the right but not the obligation to utilise it. It is a call option. So a spare pump gives flexibility to respond to a downside event and we already have an economic value-based means of calculating its value.

So risk monetisation can be considered as a type of flexibility valuation. I will explain its primary use in the following section. First, however, I will complete the example of treating a spare pump as a call option.

Let us assume that we are concerned with the potential impact of a particular pump failing. If it were to do so we would lose production on a key item of our plant and I will assume that we have estimated that the financial impact of this would be \$1m. We intend to purchase the most reliable pump on the market at a cost of \$50,000. Reliability data from the manufacturer show that the chance of failure during the first two years of operation is very small indeed. After this, however, the chance of failure during any subsequent year is 2%. The additional piping associated with installing a second pump would cost \$10,000. Our plant has an estimated economic life of ten years and our CoC is 10%. For simplicity we will use just the above assumptions and ignore things like tax.

Should we:

1. install just one pump and accept the risk of failure;
2. install two pumps; or
3. replace the pump every two years and avoid the risk of failure in this way?

Now when one considers this situation, even if one accepts the assumptions, one starts to realise that there are some potential complications in particular related to the possibility of multiple pump failures during the life of the project. One could also think of some quite complex models which consider all possible times when the pump could fail. I would suggest, however, that an initial piece of analysis may well point towards a clear answer and if this were the case one might want to accept this analysis and go ahead on this basis. So first I would recommend that a rough-and-ready calculation should be carried out as follows.

In this initial analysis I will first compare options 2 and 3. These two both offer the potential for risk-free operation. Of the two, it should be self-evident that it is better to go for the backup pump option. In the most likely scenario (i.e. when the pump does not fail), one spends $60,000 up front but then saves $50,000 spent at the end of years 2, 4, 6 and 8. If the pump does fail even twice it is self-evidently better to have gone for the backup option because in return for our early investment of $60,000 we are highly likely to save subsequent spends of $50,000 every two years on pump replacement.

The question, therefore, concerns whether backup is better than accepting the risk. If there is no failure, the incremental cost of the backup option is $60,000. If there is a failure during years 3–8 then cost saved is $1m. If there is a failure during years 9 or 10 then the cost saved could perhaps be increased by a further $50,000 because one could decide not to replace the pump since it would, in theory, still be unused and so have a risk-free operating life of two years. I will, however, ignore this factor which is small in any case. The chance of the pump's not failing during the eight years when it is at risk is 0.98 to the power 8. This is 85%. So the chance of its failing at least once is 15%. If we look at the least bad outcome should the pump fail, this is for failure near the end of year 10. The ten-year discount factor for 10% is 0.386. So the lowest monetised risk that the backup pump would save is:

$$\$1\text{m} \times 15\% \times 0.386 = \$57{,}900.$$

If we had used mid-year discount factors rather than end-year factors the calculation would have shown the backup option to be giving a break-even value relative to taking the risk. Any assumption about the failure's occurring earlier than late in year 10 would have justified investing in the backup. Furthermore, the backup option will also give protection during the supposedly risk-free first two years and also continue to protect against second or subsequent pump failures. So if the other assumptions look reasonable and we have considered all of the possible options I would suggest that the backup route should be recommended.

Step 8C: Growth value

Growth value is one of the most common situations where one might want to attach a value to flexibility. My experience is that senior managers will happily accept the principle that the possibility of future positive NPV projects has a value. What they tend to find harder, however, tends to be attaching a specific value. My suggestion is that one should use the risk monetisation approach, that to say, that growth value is equal to the present value of the growth opportunity that might arise times its probability.

So let us suppose that we are investigating an initial investment for our company in the potentially fast-growing market of India. The problem with this first investment is that it appears to have a small negative NPV. Is there some way that we could justify a strategic value from potential growth beyond the initial project? I suggest that we approach this through the following three-step approach.

First we must produce an estimate of what the subsequent NPV might be. Some sceptics might claim that this was a bit like asking 'How long is a piece of string?'. I suggest, however, that it is reasonable to make a suggestion of what a subsequent NPV might be based on a company's experience of previous projects. Is the project likely to be just a de-bottleneck of the existing plant? If so one can estimate what the economics will look like. Or is the project like one more large project but without all of the set-up costs that the first project has? Or is the project potentially a stream of future projects, say, one every two years for the next ten years?

These should not be questions to be answered in a vacuum. The answers should be guided by the strategy which had your company identifying the initial opportunity in the first place. The strategy should have suggested what the long-term potential was. Crucially, the strategy should also have identified the sources of value which would be exploited in order to gain the value. It is these sources of value which should be used in order to give a reasonable estimate of what the future NPV might be.

The technique of using specific sources of value to obtain a rough estimate of NPV was illustrated in the Yellow Moon Chemical Company example in the pillar on Sources of Value starting on page 304. If one follows the Sources of Value approach, one can create strong links between the strategy and the economic analysis of the subsequent projects that follow from it. A kind of virtuous circle can be created because the early identification of sources of value will make the claims of growth value at the time of initial market entry all the more credible.

The second step in assessing the growth value of market entry is to estimate when the future NPVs might come about. We need to know this because our overall valuation will use the present value of these future NPVs. So, for example, if we decide to model the future growth as five projects, each with an NPV of \$100m at the time of approval, and with approval being at the start of years 7–11, the NPV today (with a 9% CoC) would be:

$$\$100\text{m} \times \left(0.596^{10} + 0.547 + 0.502 + 0.460 + 0.422\right) = \$253\text{m}$$

I would call the final \$3m spurious and say that the growth value was \$250m. The idea is that the estimated growth value should be a reasonable mid-point estimate of what the value might be if the project or projects go ahead.

The final step concerns probability. There is no certainty that these projects will go ahead as planned. One needs to decide on a reasonable probability of the projects' going ahead. When one is dealing with just one project it is not too unreasonable to ask what the probability of making the follow-on investment might be. One could be guided to some extent by the strength of the financial case which can already be assembled. If our Sources of Value analysis is already pointing towards a strong positive NPV then the chance of a follow-on project is quite high. If, by contrast, our current outlook is that the follow-on project has a negative NPV then the chances of its subsequently turning out to look good will be much lower. Companies with a track record of setting up project development teams might even have data on the number of teams that have been set up in the past and their success rate.

With multiple projects it might seem a bit more difficult to come up with a single probability and one might be tempted to reduce the probability of each project's going ahead as one moves into the future. I suggest, however,

[10] 0.596 is the year-end discount factor for six years at 9%. This is appropriate since the NPV quoted will be as at 1 January of year 7.

that since the estimated value prize if the project goes ahead is already, in principle, a mid point of a range, one should aim just to come up with a single probability of this coming about. So, let us assume for our Indian market entry example a 40% chance of success. This would point to an overall flexibility value of $100m.

The advantage of this approach is that the assumptions should have strong links back to the strategy of the business concerned. Furthermore, the methodology has strong links to the established risk monetisation approach. I would contrast this with the approach which utilises a Black-Scholes calculation. This will assume that value comes from volatility and hence that any volatile situation offers the potential for value creation. Although I fully agree that a volatile share will justify a higher value for its options than a stable one, I do not accept that real projects can be assumed to benefit in a similar way. If one accepts that value is rooted in sources of value, then flexibility value too must be justified in this manner and not automatically be available to any project that faces volatility before the final decision to proceed is taken.

So growth value is assessed via the risk monetisation approach with the impact of growth assessed through an extrapolation of Sources of Value logic and the probability too guided by the strength of the sources of value.

Step 8D: Valuing the tail

This is an entirely different technique which I have devised particularly for use in many optimisation situations. It does, though, have many potential uses. It concerns situations when one needs to understand the economic consequences of gaining or losing access to the edge of a statistical distribution. It is easiest to explain via a simple example.

Suppose that an oil company has struck oil. It knows that it has found a large field and the geologists have estimated that annual production will be 100,000 barrels per day (100 kb/d for short). The oil is, however, a long way from the market and so the company will need to build a pipeline in addition to the oil production facilities. How big a pipeline should the oil company build? One might think that the answer was obvious. You have a 100 kb/d oil field so you build a pipeline that will have a throughput of 100 kb/d. Life, however, is more complicated than one might think and there are two particular reasons why it might be worthwhile building a bigger line.

These situations are caused by the uncertainty which surrounds the estimated annual production from the initial oil field and also the possibility that other oil fields may be found that could also use the line. I will deal first with the uncertainty surrounding the initial oil field because this is where the technique of valuing the tail comes into play. I will show how to use the growth value technique to value the possible income from other oil fields after that.

It is always important to question the basis of any number which one is given concerning the future. So, in this case what one should do when told that a 100 kb/d oil field has been found is ask how sure we are about the production forecast. Is it, for example, an expected value, a conservative estimate or the best you can possibly get? Readers will, by now, be used to my preference for the use of expected value estimates. So, let us assume that the figure is indeed an expected value. It is the expected value of what the oil field could produce given a range of uncertainties concerning the size of the oil reservoir, oil recovery rates and the number of production wells which will be drilled. Does this mean that it is safe to use this number in our financial model? The answer is that it is only safe to do so if the pipeline is built big enough to handle the highest possible oil output that the field might produce. If, however, the stated output is subject to a range where the top end cannot flow through the line, the correct expected value of oil which is delivered to market will be lower than 100 kb/d. The oil company will, in effect, lose access to the top end of the statistical distribution of possible oil production rates. This is illustrated in the following diagram:

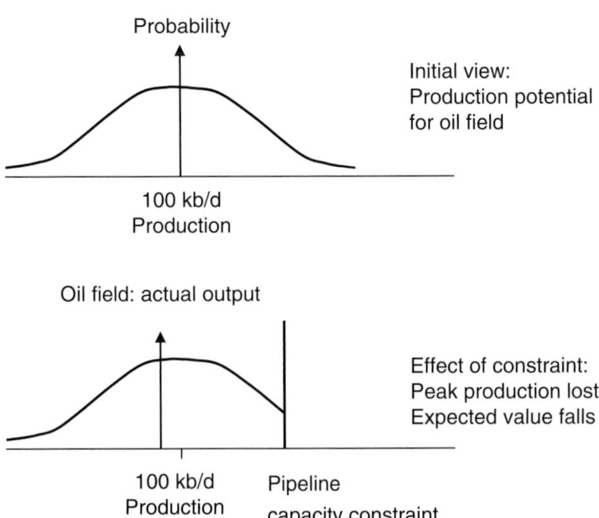

Fig. 12.3 Valuing the tail

What happens is that the company will lose the potential to produce at rates which are above the pipeline's capacity. The probability distribution will contain a spike at this point reflecting the relatively likely outcome that production will be limited by the pipeline's maximum capacity. Indeed, this outcome may well finish up as the highest probability outcome. Now since the higher production was needed, in statistical terms, to offset the possibility of lower production, the overall expected value must fall. What one needs to do is to calculate the effect of losing access to the tail of a statistical distribution and replacing it with the constrained production. I call the technique which does this 'valuing the tail', because this is what it is doing.

What I will do first is develop some rules of thumb for a very simple statistical distribution. I will then show how a more accurate approach can be used if this is felt desirable. For this first stage I will assume that the statistical distribution takes the shape of a triangle. Instead of the usual bell-shaped curve which typifies a normal distribution I will assume a straight line between the absolute maximum and the most likely value. If the distribution is not skewed then the downside triangle will be a mirror image of this.

The following diagram illustrates a triangular distribution for this hypothetical oil field. I have assumed a range of ±20%.

The triangle at the top of the diagram shows what would be the situation if there were no pipeline constraint. This would be the case as long as the

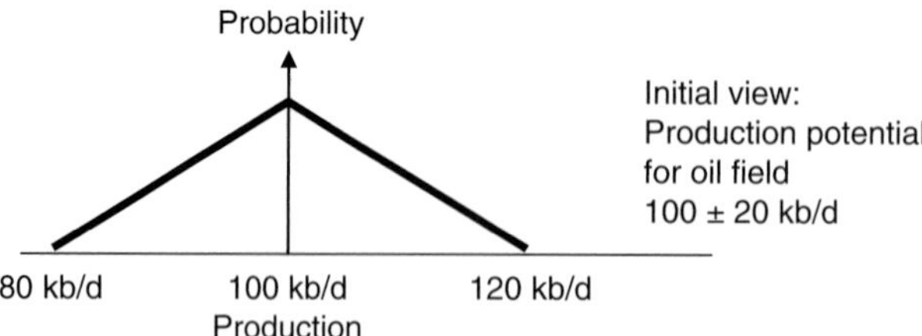

Oil field: effect of 100 kb/d pipeline constraint

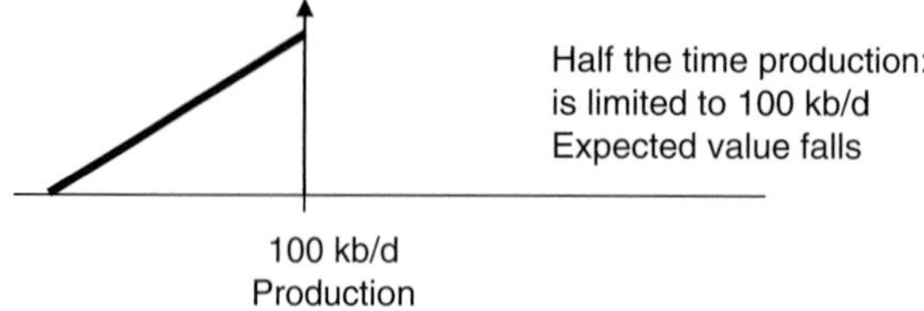

Fig. 12.4 Valuing the tail: triangular distribution

maximum pipeline throughput was at least 120 kb/d. The lower half of the diagram shows what the effect will be if the pipeline has a capacity of only 100 kb/d. I have not shown the distribution on the right-hand side of this lower chart because it would be a vertical line at exactly 100 kb/d.

The key question concerns what the loss of upside potential does to the expected value. The answer can be obtained from the useful fact (which I do not propose to prove here) that a statistical distribution with the shape of a triangle can, for the purposes of calculating expected value, be replaced with a single point one third of the way along the lower axis. In this case, the upside of between 100 and 120 kb/d which happens half of the time can be considered equivalent to a production of 106.67 kb/d also happening half of the time. This is now replaced with a production of just 100 kb/d happening half of the time. So the effect on the overall expected value of losing access to all of the potential upside is that one suffers a reduction in expected value of one sixth of the maximum range. In this particular case, the expected value of the oil volume which will be available to sell will be 96.7 kb/d rather than the original 100 kb/d.

Now up to now I have assumed that the stated range of uncertainty of oil production was the full range. In a lot of instances people do not state the full range because the top and the bottom ends cannot actually happen. It is quite common for ranges to be stated to the P10/P90 range of statistical confidence. This would mean that the range would be exceeded 10% of the time and would be too optimistic 10% of the time. The full range is always much bigger than just the P10/P90 range. For a triangular distribution the range is, in fact, almost doubled. A P10/P90 range of ±20% indicates an absolute maximum range of ±36% (trust me![11]). So if, as I suspect would be the case, the oil reservoir engineer who provided the original 100 kb/d estimate and stated that it was ±20% meant that this covered the P10/P90 range, then the expected value of oil sales that would be lost in the peak year through building a 100 kb/d pipeline would be 6 kb/d. We could, if we wanted to, use this simple rule of thumb to see if the extra cost of building a pipeline with a capacity of 136 kb/d was justified.

[11] If you want to know how to do the maths, read this footnote. This is actually a useful piece of learning should you wish to do any other calculations such as working out the impact of, say, losing production in excess of 110 kb/d. If 120 kb/d has just a 10% chance of being beaten there must be a 40% chance of the result's being in the range 100–120 kb/d. If the actual peak production is p kb/d we know that the area of the triangle with a base that is from 100 to p is 50% while the triangle with a base from 120 to p has an area of 10%. The areas of the two triangles are proportional to the square of the size of the base. We know the length of each base (one is p units long while the smaller triangle is $(p-20)$ units long. This means that p^2 must be five times bigger than $(p-20)^2$. We can solve by trial and error to find that $p = 36.2$ or revert to algebra and the formula to solve quadratic equations if we want to be really clever!

Now so far I have only dealt with a simple situation where the constraint was set at the expected value and where the statistical distribution was triangular. What I hope is evident is that the generic approach can be applied to a wide range of situations where a company gains or loses access to the tail of a statistical distribution. The constraint need not be set at exactly the expected value. It can be set at any level and one then must investigate the economic impact of losing the upside above this constraint while still suffering from the downside.

One could, for example, investigate various sizes of pipeline and also the effect of various shapes of statistical distribution. Then, since a larger pipeline must cost more money, in principle each set of assumptions will have an optimal solution. If pipelines were very expensive in relation to the cost of producing the oil, one could even discover that it paid to build a line that was below the expected value of oil production in order to ensure that there was a high probability that it would be fully utilised. The reality for pipelines, however, is usually that the incremental cost of a slightly larger line is well below the average cost and it is generally beneficial to oversize rather than undersize.

My personal flexibility toolkit contains a spreadsheet model which allows me to specify a range of possible types of statistical distributions, an expected value and a constraint which can be anywhere between the minimum and the maximum possible production. The model then generates for me the revised expected value in view of the constraint. I did, however, need to enrol the assistance of a PhD student in order to build it.

I will leave it to readers to decide whether they wish to build such a model for themselves. It is, I believe, quite useful when one is dealing with the effect of a single constraint and one wants to go beyond simple assumptions concerning triangular distributions. Once multiple constraints are involved, one in any case needs to switch to Monte Carlo simulation, which I will be explaining in the following section.

There are two further steps which I need to cover in order to complete this example. The first is to explain that in the case of an oil field, production that might be lost in one year owing to a pipeline constraint should be recoverable at a later stage once the field's production starts to fall. For most manufacturing plants, however, a sale lost in one year owing to a physical constraint will be lost for good.

The second step is to consider how one might also value the potential for an oversized pipeline's being used on further oil fields. The answer is that one applies the growth value technique as outlined in section 8C above. One makes estimates of when other oil fields might wish to utilise the pipeline, what fee they would pay and what the associated probabilities were.[12]

I have a particular enthusiasm for the valuing the tail technique because I believe that a good case can be made for oversizing many assets. There are two factors which could justify building bigger assets than would be suggested by the simple rule of build to cover expected value demand. The first is that there must be uncertainty about demand. Without this there is clearly no point in oversizing. Most situations, however, have demand uncertainty. The second factor is where there is an opportunity to add incremental volume to a project at a cost which is well below the average cost per unit if it is done at the design stage. If the capacity can be added later at about the same cost then it will not be worthwhile building in advance.

Pipelines are classic examples of where capacity expansion is cheap before you start but expensive later. They are expensive to build and a lot of the cost concerns gaining access to the right of way and digging the trench. Once in place, throughput is capped.[13] This means that at the design stage, increasing throughput is quite cheap. Once the pipeline is in place, however, any expansion would be hugely expensive.

Pipelines are not the only example of where extra capacity can be cheap if it is introduced at the design stage. A sports stadium where plenty of land is available is probably the same and so too would be almost any infrastructure project. My suggestion is that use of valuing the tail and growth value techniques can, hopefully, offset the tendency which otherwise exists which is to seek to minimise the headline capital cost for the initial build of such assets.

Step 8E: Monte Carlo simulation

I introduced this technique in the modelling economic value pillar on page 239. At that stage I rather played down its potential usefulness. This was because in most simple situations I do not believe that its use is justified. When one is dealing with flexibility value, however, it is potentially very useful and it forms an essential part of the flexibility valuation toolkit.

The primary purpose of this particular section is to build awareness of what can be done. This should give enough information to allow a relatively

[12] When one does this analysis, it quickly becomes apparent that having good information about what oil fields might be found can be hugely valuable. This is because of the sums of money at stake when one oversizes an expensive asset like a pipeline. I will be looking at a possible way of justifying the spend necessary in order to gather information in section 8F.

[13] In reality, throughput can be increased by installing more powerful pumps or by adding what is called a drag-reducing agent to the crude oil. There is, however, a limit to what these two steps can achieve.

simple situation to be evaluated through one of the standard Monte Carlo spreadsheet add-ins. More complex situations would probably require specialist assistance.

There are two main situations where Monte Carlo simulation needs to be used. The first of these concerns when decision-makers wish specifically to investigate the impact of different assumptions concerning uncertainty. In such a situation they may well not be happy, for example, with an assumption that the world can be summarised by just three states such as low, medium and high demand, each with a specific probability and value attached to it. This simplification would have been what we often do when we apply the more sophisticated assumptions approach to value a flexibility. We might, for example, have assumed that with a flexible feedstock cracker, when we run with one particular feedstock the resultant margin is a given number. If the decision-maker was not happy with this degree of simplification of what the future might be like, then the next step would be to use a Monte Carlo simulation approach to test a larger range of possible assumptions.[14]

The second situation concerns when non-linearities exist and these are influenced by more than one uncertainty. The valuing the tail approach only really works for a single uncertainty. If one needs to investigate multiple uncertainties in a non-linear situation then a Monte Carlo approach is required.

A good example of this would be the evaluation of partner carry. If a strong company has a weak partner and has to lend the partner its share of the initial investment then what interest rate should the strong company charge in order at least to earn the CoC on the loan? If there is any chance of the loan's not being repaid then the actual interest rate must be higher than the CoC. The sophisticated assumptions combined with risk monetisation approach might be to assume that in, say, 10% of the time the partner does not repay at least some of the loan and that the average loss when this happens is a particular amount. Armed with these assumptions it would be quite simple to calculate what premium over the CoC needed to be earned in that percentage of the time when the loan was repaid. A Monte Carlo approach would allow ranges and probabilities to be attached to all important variables such that all possible outcomes could be evaluated. Partner default would not then be treated as being a single outcome with a fixed probability. It would be studied

[14] I have, for example, worked with a model which enabled one to investigate the effect of volatility and also mean reversion on a plant which had some inherent flexibility. The full details of this were published in the *Journal of Applied Corporate Finance* in spring 2005 in an article entitled 'Taking Real Options Beyond the Black Box' which I co-authored with a BP colleague, Fabio Cannizzo.

in more detail and it could result in anything between just the last dollar of partner carry not being repaid and, in principle, none of the carry being repaid.

One can also use Monte Carlo simulation to improve the treatment of growth value. It may just be that a decision-maker was not happy with the simplification implicit in treating growth as being just a single outcome. If the decision-maker wanted to test multiple growth possibilities then Monte Carlo would be used. Testing the potential growth value of an oversized oil pipeline could be evaluated in this way, particularly if there were several potential new oil fields which might use the pipeline if it were built. The oil field and pipeline example, even without growth value, may also need to be solved by simulation because of the need to model the fact that oil which is not produced in one year will be available later in the field life when the oil production would otherwise have fallen below the constraint.

Step 8F: Simple decision trees

A decision tree allows one to depict multiple possible paths into the future. The approach requires that various decision points are identified and, for each decision, a range of possible outcomes is identified. Each new outcome leads to further paths and further decisions. I often recommend the use of simple decision trees to solve some flexibility valuation problems. Typical situations would concern the evaluation of research projects and also the value of information. I will illustrate this through the following example which investigates whether it is worth spending money on a detailed, and hence expensive, market survey.

Let us suppose that our company produces a high quality swimming pool cover. The cover can last for as much as twice as long as a normal cover but costs 25% more. The life of a pool cover is, however, quite variable as it depends on how many times it is taken off, how careful the pool owner is when they do this and how long the cover is exposed to the sun. The result is that a normal cover will last between two and four years while our company's covers will last between four and six years. Take-up of the cover will depend a lot on our company's ability to convey a quite sophisticated economic/environmental message to potential customers for whom the cover will be just one of many costs associated with owning a pool. At present we have developed three possible scenarios of future demand. In two of these it is worthwhile for our company to invest but in the low-demand case we would face a negative NPV.

A detailed survey which investigated the market and tested our proposed advertising campaign would have a present cost of \$1.5m but would give us a more accurate view of what the future might turn out to offer. The initial investment in market entry would have a net present cost of \$20m. The three possible outcomes would generate subsequent cash inflows with present values of \$40m, \$25m or \$10m. At present we consider that the respective probabilities of the three scenarios are 20%, 60%, 20%.

At present, therefore, going ahead without carrying out the survey can be valued via a very simple decision tree as follows:

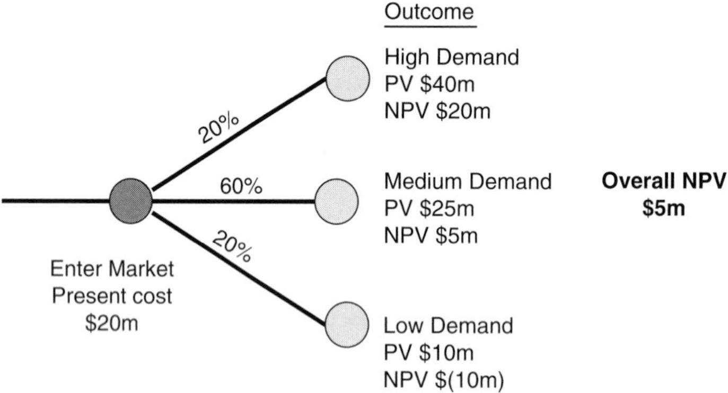

Fig. 12.5 Swimming pool cover project

One hardly even needed a decision tree thanks to the upside and downside's offsetting each other. With no skew, the mid-point outcome was the expected value. It is worth building one, however, because by doing so we can test the impact of different assumptions on the overall economic viability of our project. For example, we could determine that if the respective probabilities for low, medium and high demand were 40%, 40%, 20% then the NPV would fall to \$2m. A zero NPV would be the result if the probabilities were 46⅔%, 40%, 13⅓%.

Now, however, let us introduce the idea of a market survey. The cost, in present value terms is \$1.5m. One could simply subtract this from the initial view of NPV of \$5m and claim an NPV of \$3.5m. The project would still appear worthwhile but our valuation would, however, ignore the entire point of carrying out the survey. This is because we appear to be taking no notice of what it concludes. We need to make some assumptions about how the survey might influence our decision-taking. What we must not do at this stage, however, is assume that the survey can change the likelihood of the three possible outcomes. This information can only become available after the survey is complete and we must take care to respect this fact as we make our assumptions.

The most optimistic assumption which we could make about the survey is that it would always be right and would warn us if the low-demand scenario was going to come about. If we were sure that if the survey indicated low demand, then demand would indeed be low, and that if medium or high demand was indicated then low would not happen, our decision tree would look like this:

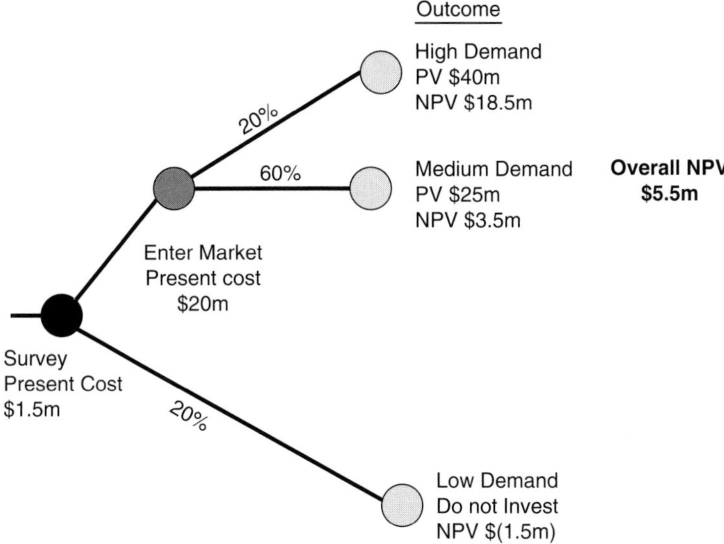

Fig. 12.6 Swimming pool cover project with 'perfect' survey

The 'perfect' survey has added $0.5m to value compared with not carrying it out because the NPV has risen to $5.5m. If we do the survey but then ignore it we would lower value by $1.5m.

Now let us investigate what the result would be if we believed that the survey would be right 80% of the time. We will still assume that we will act on the survey's recommendation but now there will be a probability that, with hindsight, we regret this. We will assume that if the survey indicated low demand then 80% of the time this would be correct but 20% of the time the demand would be medium. If high demand is forecast then we will assume that 80% of the time this is right and 20% of the time demand is medium.

Again, we must be scrupulous about ensuring that we do not change our overall assumption about the balance between low, medium and high demand.

All that we can do is change the success rate for the survey's predictions. This means, for example, that the survey must forecast medium demand with a 60% probability and that, in our view of reality, the overall percentage of medium demand must also remain at 60%. This means that once we have decided upon the accuracy in relation to when the survey indicates high or low demand we must back-calculate what the probabilities must be for when the survey indicates medium demand.

The decision tree will look like this:

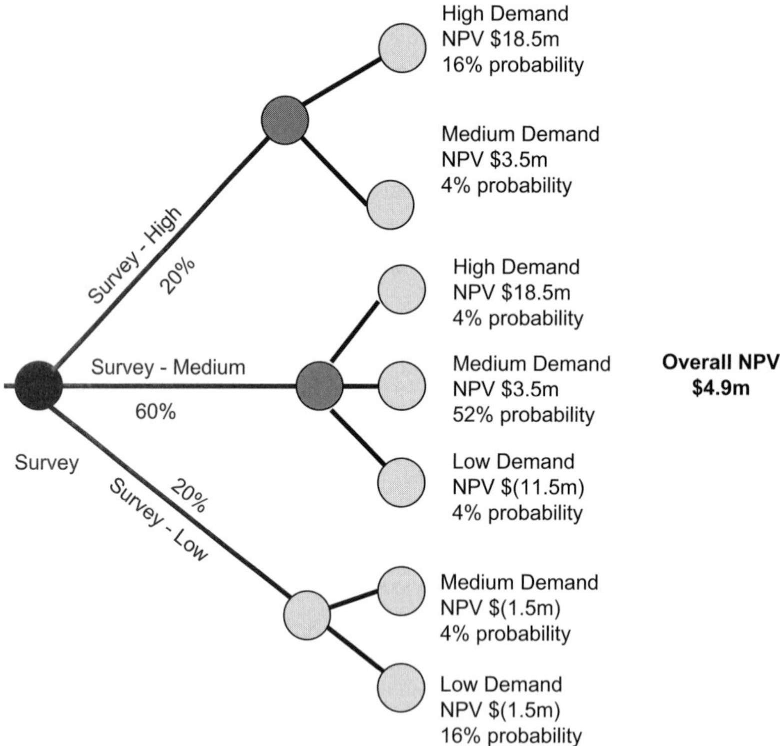

Fig. 12.7 Swimming pool cover project with '80/20' survey

Since the overall value of $4.9m is below the value of $5.0m if we do not carry out the survey, we should conclude that the survey was not worthwhile. The value of the survey is actually quite close to zero and so what we have done here is, by chance, identify roughly what set of assumptions will result in a zero value. We will return to this approach in the following section when we consider the reverse engineering technique.

I think that it is important to reflect on the exact assumptions which I chose to make about the survey and how they have influenced the valuation. I assumed that the survey would provide a specific answer about future demand, in particular whether this was expected to be low, medium or high. This, in turn, would allow us to make a clear decision concerning whether or not to go ahead with market entry. Had I assumed that the survey would simply place probabilities on each of the three possible outcomes then I would not have been able to apply this technique. This is for two reasons. First, there is the generic reason that I cannot know in advance what the outcome will be and so must assume that the survey tells me what I already know. The second reason is specific to this case and is that that unless the survey comes up with an answer that is very different from our initial assessment, we will approve the investment.

The message that I take from this is very clear. This is that if we want to undertake a valuation of a study it would be vital to agree with the author of the study exactly what type of answer they will be giving us. We would then need to think carefully about this and whether, in principle, it would enable us to take an improved decision and also whether, in reality, we would have enough confidence in it to allow it to dictate our decision.[15]

I have illustrated the technique here for a market survey mainly because it presents a fairly simple situation which can be explained in a few pages as part of this book. A similar approach can be used to assess other situations where there are multiple decision points between the present and the ultimate realisation of value. Exploration and research and development are two examples. In each case one is faced with a series of steps and one does not need to justify the full spend at the outset; one just needs to justify the funds which are going to be committed prior to the next decision point. As I have illustrated, one can then use this to assess the value of a particular piece of information and hence take a rational decision about how much money it is worth spending in order to get it.

The usual warning must, however, be given about the quality of the decision's being limited by the quality of the assumptions. One particular concern that I have is that studies are often not as clear-cut as one would like. So, for example, my assumption in the above case study that the recommendation

[15] The approach which I have outlined is what I would do if I had not initially thought that a survey was necessary. If a new and major expense has come to light, it needs to be justified. There is an alternative way of justifying the expense of a survey. This is simply to assert that an investment is too significant to make based on the knowledge that your company has. Expert opinion is required in order to plug a gap in the host company's knowledge. This assertion should be made at the outset when the budget for the development team is first put together. The survey is then considered to be just a part of the overall cost of project development and this is what one must justify.

of a study will always be followed is probably far too optimistic. Any tendency to reject a study would greatly lower its value.

A further concern that I must raise with decision trees is that they can quickly become overly complex. There can be a need to deal with so many nodes that, in my view, one faces a great danger of becoming a slave to a model and never really being able to trust the answer. Special software packages are available which facilitate the building of large decision tree models and, in theory, these can have advantages in allowing one to calculate value and identify optimal courses of action in highly complex situations. The problem with these is that the ease of computation for a skilled user of the software[16] may disguise the need to have quality assumptions. Unless sufficient skilled people will be available to provide the necessary assumptions, a large decision tree cannot be trusted.

Step 8G: Reverse engineering

Reverse engineering is the term which is used to describe a situation where, instead of making assumptions and calculating the implied value, one specifies the required value and then calculates the necessary assumption. The typical calculation is done by specifying a zero NPV and then identifying what assumption, or set of assumptions, would result in that answer. One can then inspect the necessary assumptions, decide how credible they are, and use this to guide a decision. The more difficult it is to make assumptions concerning the impact and probability of a flexibility, the more appropriate it will be to use the reverse engineering approach.

The results of reverse engineering can be presented as a single-point assumption if just one variable is being considered; as a line of possible combinations if two assumptions are considered; or as a series of lines if three assumptions are in doubt. If more than three assumptions were in doubt, then my advice would be to try to identify the three which were of greatest importance and to focus on these.

The decision-maker will be faced with one of three possible outcomes concerning their judgement about the necessary assumptions or combination of assumptions which are necessary to give a zero NPV:

1. They may appear highly conservative. In this case the decision can be approved with some confidence even though its exact value is not known.

[16] My experience is that there are only a few such skilled users of the software and so technical assistance is typically required in order to deal with complex decision trees.

2. They may appear to be roughly what one might think expected value assumptions would be like. One would perhaps investigate a little further to see if any additional insights might make the decision easier to take. In any event, the decision-maker could be content that the decision was marginal and that getting it 'wrong', if they were to do so, would be an understandable error.
3. They may appear to be highly optimistic or perhaps just impossible to believe. In this situation the decision can easily be turned down.

Examples of the reverse engineering approach abound throughout this book. This is because it is not just of use in valuing flexibility. It is of use in considering any financial decision and is very simple to apply. The importance of understanding the conditions which lead to a zero NPV lies behind why I have suggested that a special category of sensitivity, the type 2 sensitivity should be defined.

The more difficult it is to make good assumptions, the more useful the reverse engineering approach becomes. This is why it is so useful in valuing flexibility. It is difficult to make good assumptions in relation to high-impact low-probability events but one often finds that one can be spared the necessity of doing so because a clear-cut decision can be made without knowing its exact value. So, for example, if I was considering whether to purchase a diesel generator to protect against spikes in the electricity price I would first simply ask what set of assumptions would justify a zero NPV and then decide whether I thought these were conservative or optimistic. In either case I would be spared the problem of making a difficult judgement regarding exactly what a good assumption would be.

We can return to the swimming pool cover example that was developed earlier and use this to illustrate how the reverse engineering technique could be applied in practice. Let us recall the decision which we faced. We were trying to decide whether to spend \$1.5m on a survey in a situation where we were fairly confident that we should go ahead and enter a new market. Our initial analysis showed that if we had full trust in the survey it would add \$0.5m to value. We did not find the exact zero value set of assumptions but we did show that if one thought that the survey would correctly identify the low-demand world 80% of the time, the survey would have a small negative value. Had I been a decision-maker I would have felt able to take a decision based just on this additional piece of information and the reverse engineering approach. The information would have told me that I needed to believe that the study would correctly identify the low-demand situation with a better than 80% probability. I would stop the analysis at that point and say that, based on my experience, I would not be inclined to believe that the study's success rate with identifying the low-demand world would be better than 80%, so I would not spend \$1.5m on having it done.

A similar approach would be useful for investigating whether to oversize for potential third party demand. This can often be difficult to assess, whereas reverse engineering will often indicate that there is a fairly clear answer available after even the most simple of calculations.

Step 8H: Black-Scholes

There are some situations where real-life flexibility can be valued using the Black-Scholes approach. These concern where the flexibility is directly related to a financial asset. Any flexibility on a financial asset should, in principle, be tradable and the market price will be set via application of the Black-Scholes equation. One would not normally expect to come across such situations but they do happen from time to time, usually when one of the companies involved in a transaction is not aware of flexibility value.

This book will not be able to devote enough attention to this topic to allow a real-life situation to be valued with any confidence. My aim in relation to this particular part of the flexibility valuation tool kit is to build awareness of what can, in principle, be done. I would recommend that specialist advice be obtained in order to undertake the valuation.

My first example concerns a supplier who makes an offer to supply a major piece of equipment and specifies payment in one of two possible currencies. If the purchaser were given the choice of which currency they paid in and yet the amounts payable in both currencies were fixed by the current exchange rate, then this would, in effect, have given the purchaser a free call option on both currencies at the current exchange rate. A variant of this situation which might be more achievable in a commercial negotiation would be if payment in a second currency was permitted but at an implied exchange rate which is currently very unfavourable. There would be some value in the optionality, particularly if the payment was not due for some long time.

A common variant of this example concerns tendering situations on international projects. In such a situation, a potential purchaser will typically require those who tender to provide a quotation set in just a single currency but which is valid for some long period of time. In this situation the potential supplier may well be giving away flexibility in relation to exchange rate effects. If the underlying costs for a major project are set in different currencies and yet the tender bid is set in one currency, then each potential bidder faces the cost of having to give away some flexibility. The danger to the company running the tender is that all those who tender might build the cost into their bid. This could be avoided if the company permitted those who tender to do so in multiple currencies.[17]

My next example concerns the flexibility to load an exact cargo size. Suppose that one is selling iron ore to be loaded on a ship. Now ships come in different sizes and if one could negotiate a deal to load a specified amount ±10% in order to allow the flexibility to fill the ship that is chartered, one would have gained two free options compared with a simple agreement to purchase a fixed volume of iron ore. You would have gained a put option on 10% of the volume at the current price and also a call option on 10% also at the current price. There would be substantial value in this compared with the no flexibility alternative.

My final example concerns the flexibility to decide when an oil field is finally shut down. One might imagine that an oil field should be shut down when the cash cost of producing the oil is greater than the sales proceeds. There are, however, additional complications. One concerns the fact that when a field is shut down there may well be abandonment costs to pay. I will not consider these in this example. The flexibility which interests me in the context of this situation concerns the flexibility to produce oil in the following year.

At the start of any year one would definitely produce oil for the coming year if it was possible to sell the anticipated production for an amount which covers the cash operating costs. If this was not possible, one could contemplate writing a call option on the oil which you anticipate producing in the following year with a strike price set at the level which is necessary in order to cover your cash operating costs in that year. This price would be higher than the current oil price because future costs are likely to be higher and production on declining oil fields goes down. There would in principle, however, still be some option value in this out of the money call option. If writing this option produces enough cash to cover the current year's costs then you should write the option and stay in business. If at the end of the year the option is exercised then you can stay in business for the following year. If it is not exercised, and if writing a further option on future production will not keep the operation cash positive, then you should shut down.

[17] This would be an example of how understanding about what I term given tactical flexibility can facilitate the creation of value without any need for the exact value to be calculated. If one did want to calculate the value one would apply Black-Scholes.

Step 8I: Analogy

My suggestion of the use of analogies is based on the fact that, in my experience, flexibility valuations are relatively rare. When they are done they are usually subject to some special attention exactly because they are new. This means that unless a company has never undertaken a flexibility valuation, some situations will already have been valued. Furthermore, these valuations will have been the subject of special attention from decision-makers and experienced practitioners. My suggestion is that these valuations should all be logged and should provide analogies which can set the rough bounds for subsequent flexibility valuations.

There should be two parts to this approach. The first part is where the real use of analogy can come into play. A flexibility valuation which has been well studied can provide a benchmark which other flexibilities can be compared with. A new situation may at least be sufficiently clear that the sponsor of one project could say that the value must be at least as much as this number which was agreed in a previous situation. I could imagine that in a company if the chief executive had, in effect, approved growth values of, say, \$10, \$100 and \$1,000m for three particular situations, then almost any growth situation could be slotted somewhere into the scale. I accept that there is virtually no 'science' in this approach but it does have some pragmatic appeal.

The second part concerns the traditional Plan, Do, Measure, Learn approach. If companies wish to build their ability to value flexibility, they should focus attention on learning from previous flexibility valuations. So, for example, if the growth value approach is used, this can be monitored. One does not have to wait for the subsequent growth project to be approved in order to observe its actual NPV and learn lessons. Actual growth projects should start to appear in the long-term plan long before they are approved. One can start to learn lessons as soon as they appear in the plan.

Step 8J: Include any additional costs

The tenth and final part of my suggested flexibility valuation toolkit is not a further valuation technique, it is a reminder about something which needs to be allowed for in all flexibility valuations. The step concerns whether any future costs must be incurred in order to capture the value. The answer will often be 'yes'. Take, for example, growth value. It is almost impossible to believe that subsequent positive NPVs will be earned if no project development teams are set up in order to bring the projects about. Consider also the use of sophisticated assumptions about the actions of a commercial optimisation team. This team will cost money and this must be allowed for in the valuation.

What one needs to do is to ensure that the costs which are necessary in order to realise the value will actually be incurred and remember to deduct their present cost from any calculated flexibility value. This can have quite a significant impact on value if, for example, one is not sure that the growth projects will go ahead. The cost of the project development team would be fixed but the growth projects would be uncertain. Now including the costs need not mean that any necessary project development team must be set up straight away. It does, however, mean that one must recognise that unless a team is set up, the growth value will be zero. So the decision-maker should expect to approve the subsequent request to set up the team.

I will illustrate the potential impact of allowing for future costs by extending the Indian market entry case study which I started in section 8C above. In this study I had simply assumed that a stream of five positive NPV projects would be approved. Each project had an NPV of $100m at the time of approval, and approval was assumed to take place at the start of years 7–11. In reality it would be completely unrealistic to assume a stream of positive NPVs without allowing for the cost of the project development team which would make them happen. I will assume a project development team cost of $10m pa after tax during years 1–9. This development team cost would have a present value of $62.6m.[18] My original growth value had been $100m before costs. So the actual growth value which one could justify using to set against the current project's negative NPV is about $40m. Since I suggested that the initial project had a 'small' negative NPV, I assume that the assessed flexibility value of $40m should still be sufficient to give a rational basis for approving the project. It is, however, a lot lower and might well be low enough to question a very poor initial project.

Step 9: Ensure that organisation is equipped to capture flexibility value in the future

I do not think that it would be right to end my proposed approach to valuing flexibility with a calculation. There are still two important steps to take. These relate in particular to the final two elements of the toolkit and to concerns that I have about ensuring that flexibility value is actually realised.

[18] The nine year mid-year annuity factor at 9% is 6.259.

My first concern is that the value of flexibility will only be realised if and when a company's managers take good decisions in the future and then the company's staff implement them well. An organisation must, therefore, have the necessary capabilities to do this.

One good reason for assessing a rough estimate of flexibility value in all situations, even when the flexibility has no cost, is to use the value as a signal concerning the importance of capturing that value. Values can quite simply be converted into rough annual equivalent sums and the ability of an organisation to deliver such amounts can then be considered.

So, for example, my flexible feedstock cracker may result in a company's spending, say, an additional $40m of capital in the anticipation of an NPV of, say, $10m. This means that when the cracker comes on stream it will be expected to produce additional cash flows with a present value of about $50m. Since the 20-year 8% annuity factor is about ten this means that our feedstock optimisation team for the cracker needs to generate an annual benefit of about $5m after tax. If the investment was in the USA with a federal-plus-state tax rate of about 40% the company will need to earn a pre-tax margin of nearly $10m pa after allowing for its operating costs. For some companies this may be a small additional challenge to a large and well-established commercial team. To others, however, it may represent a step change and may require a new organisation to be set up in order to ensure that the theoretical prize is actually captured.

The overall message from this is that any decision-maker who approves a project that includes flexibility value should previously have contented themselves that their organisation could deliver the necessary performance. They should also have confirmed whether the requirement would result in any incremental costs and, if so, whether these were included in the economic assessment.

Similar assessments need to be done in relation to any growth or follow-on values. If these are material then it would be normal to expect to see also a budget for a project development team which will generate the follow-on project. The cost of this project development team should have been deducted from the calculated flexibility value in accordance with the final part of the flexibility toolkit.

Step 10: Monitor results to facilitate Plan, Do, Measure, Learn approach

My final step concerns the importance of monitoring results. If a material amount of value is associated with flexibility then I believe that this should be monitored in order to allow the vital Plan, Do, Measure, Learn feedback loop to be established. The feedback can help to improve future decisions. This is particularly important for the Analogy approach on my list. If one is valuing one flexibility by relating it to another, it is so much better if that benchmark value is grounded in actual performance rather than hypothetical assumptions.

Conclusions: Flexibility is important but flexibility valuation is less so

What I have tried to demonstrate through my flexibility valuation toolkit is that it is possible to put a rough value on several common types of flexibility. I have, I trust, demonstrated that it is perfectly possible to put together a set of assumptions which can be plugged into a discounted cash flow model and will then allow a quantification of the value of flexibility. I do not, however, believe that this will need to be done as a routine part of project evaluation. This is why I have left this topic for treatment as part of the advanced section of this book and not included it as a fourth pillar in what I consider to be the book's all-important middle section.

What matters most about flexibility is, I believe, that practitioners and decision-takers should be aware of the potential biases that are created in particular by the usual annual average approach to economic evaluation and by the way that we tend to focus just on the project under consideration and not the full outlook for our company overall. There can be times when the bias might be so great that some rough quantification is necessary in order to counteract it. This is when the valuation toolkit should be used.

In most instances, however, the bias should be just another factor which the decision-makers weigh up as they come to a decision. There are plenty of other difficulties to deal with and flexibility is just one more. This, I suggest, is why major financial decision-making is best described as judgement based on rational analysis. If we thought we could do an 'accurate' calculation we would drop the need for judgement and delegate decision-making to a computer. This would be folly.

If one starts the consideration of flexibility from the perspective of a decision scientist one can easily get led down a path that:

- starts with the recognition that almost all projects have flexibilities; and then
- recognises how the traditional DCF method is blind to the effect of these; and hence requires one to

- devise some more advanced techniques which could cope better and so should be adopted.

I suggest, however, that one should start from the perspective of a senior decision-maker who knows that the numbers only form a part of the decision-making process. My well-informed decision-maker will be aware of four key factors which serve to reduce the need for a new approach. These factors are:

1. Many flexibilities form part of the 'me too' player's view of life. As such a company has to have the organisational capability to realise them, but they should not add to one's anticipated NPV at time of sanction.
2. Most projects should have a positive NPV at time of sanction because of the sunk cost effect. So if one needs to rely on flexibility value in order to achieve a zero NPV, this might well be a sign that the underlying strategy itself was wrong.[19]
3. Sophisticated approaches still require assumptions to be made and these remain at least as difficult to make as those which support the economic value approach. Hence, in reality, all that the more sophisticated approaches offer is the opportunity to base a decision on a different set of assumptions.
4. Many projects are small enough to be considered in isolation and so do not create significant follow-on or growth value. Growth value is usually only significant for projects which really do open up entirely new prospects for a company and these decisions are usually taken based to a much greater extent on judgement rather than numerical analysis.

My well-informed decision-makers will know that they should concentrate on flexibility when it is a part of a key source of value or when it is actually setting a negotiating boundary such as the walk-away price in relation to the acquisition of a company. They will also know the difference between needing to understand the value of flexibility, which serves to encourage one to try to keep all options open, and needing to progress down the stage gate path, which does require that, at the key options selection stage gate, many options must be closed down. Finally, my well-informed decision-makers will include consideration of how flexibility effects may serve to increase or decrease the risks associated with a particular project if and when they are forced to make their subjective judgement about the exact trade-off between risk and reward which is appropriate for the project under consideration.

[19] This, I suggest, is why, to some senior managers, 'real options are the last refuge of a poor project'.

CHAPTER

13

Third view: When value is not the objective

Introduction: Why study this question and how it will be covered

This book has, from the outset, been about financial decision-making in companies. It has implicitly assumed that companies are quoted on a stock exchange and hence have as a key objective the maximisation of shareholder value. The book has shown how an approach to financial decision-making that seeks always to maximise present value, calculated via the economic value model, is the accepted means of enabling a company to achieve this objective. In the book so far, therefore, value has been king.

In the first part of this view I will remind readers of just how many situations there are where this is not the case. It will quickly become apparent that there are many organisations where value most definitely is not king. This means that, even if we work in a company that does seek to maximise value, we will often encounter as suppliers, customers or competitors, players that are working to a different rule book.

I propose to call this group 'non-value players' in order to distinguish them from 'value players' who do treat the maximisation of shareholder value as the main objective. I will also use the collective terms 'the value sector' and 'the non-value sector'. I mean nothing derogatory in the placing of a player in either category. I consider the differences simply as a fact of life and as something that we must live with and learn from.

I believe that it must pay to understand the motivations of others with whom we will interact and, in particular, how they will take decisions. There are three main reasons for this. First, differences of perspective will often cause players to act in different ways from what we might have expected had we thought about their using our own implicit mindset. An ability to predict the actions of others is very important as we make our decisions and hence an understanding of how others will make decisions is vital. Second, a wider understanding of how others take decisions may also throw up opportunities to create value that will arise when two parties see the same situation in different ways. Third, there are times when one can learn from what others have developed to help them take decisions.

There is also a fourth reason for studying the non-value sector at this stage in this book. I propose to use the differences between value and non-value decision-taking as a means of recapping on some of the main principles behind the value approach and reviewing some of the underlying philosophies. I will, therefore, be including various 'compare and contrast' sections throughout this view. These will permit me to emphasise what I consider to be several of the really positive features of the concept of shareholder value which tend not, in my view, to get enough publicity. The compare and contrast exercises will also throw up some issues where I believe that the value approach has some inherent problems. An awareness of these is, I believe, a useful skill to have. I will return to these differences and present my overall score card in the final part of this view.

The primary aim of this view is to prepare those who will be working in the value sector for their encounters with those who do not and on seeking lessons from the non-value sector which are of wider use. This is not to suggest that those who will be operating in the non-value sector of the economy will not benefit from reading this book in general and this view in particular. Readers will, for example, learn in the second part of this view that many of my suggestions about the planning infrastructure that should support value maximisation can be used in other circumstances. The need for strategies, plans, stage gate processes, learning loops, etc. remains as great. I will, however, identify four key differences that are likely to arise when value is not the key objective and these will form the subject of parts three through to six. These differences are:

- loss of the single objective of value;
- availability of finance;
- different attitude to risk; and
- escape from continuous good surprises.

It is these differences which are of greatest importance when one seeks to predict future actions and identify win-win situations caused by differences of view.

Readers will discover, as they work through this view, that there are indeed lessons to be learned from non-value operations which will allow better decision-making even by the purest of the pure adherents to the value philosophy. One major example of this concerns the fact that not everything has a price attached to it and some decisions, even in commercial companies, do come down to how we treat non-financial considerations. It is in this area that we, the operators in the value sector, need to learn from our colleagues in the non-value sector how to deal with non-financial items such as the importance of having happy staff. This will be dealt with in part 7.

I will conclude my review of the non-value sector with what I have called my overall scorecard. This will summarise the main differences between the value and the non-value sectors.

Now as an author, I have to enter the non-value sector with care because my experience of it is much more limited than my experience in the value sector. During my career I did, however, practise what I will preach in this view and it hence I tried to incorporate how I thought others would address a situation in my predictions of future actions, rather than treat all as though they took decisions in the same way as my company would. I was greatly helped in this by a two-year secondment to work for the British government. During this time, in addition to working on foreign policy issues, I became specifically involved in designing a resource allocation system for the UK's Foreign and Commonwealth Office. I have also, more recently, had cause to look at a major investment decision in the health service sector. I believe, therefore, that I am sufficiently qualified to express my views.

Finally, by way of introduction, I need to introduce an entirely imaginary charity that I have invented in order to illustrate some of the concepts that I will cover in this view. I have gone for an imaginary situation to add a little amusement and in order to avoid any potential for my being accused of telling a real charity how to manage its business. I call my charity the BGS. This stands for the Bromley Goldfish Sanctuary.

I ask readers to imagine that BGS has just been formed by the bequest of a net £3m from a generous, if slightly barmy, benefactor. The benefactor recognised in his will how, in his final years, his main enjoyment in life came from watching goldfish. He indicated that he had become worried about the treatment of some goldfish and so left his entire estate for the care of goldfish in his home town of Bromley that otherwise might fall upon hard times or risk early death. He appointed a board of four individuals to oversee the carrying out of his wish and gave them full power over his estate.

You, oh reader, are to consider what you would do if you were one of those four! I will return to this study on several occasions throughout the view and build it as a case study in objective-setting and decision-making in the non-value sector.

Part 1: The non-value sector

The basic point that I need to make in this first part is that although this book has devoted all but this view to proposing an approach for value-based decision-making, many financial decisions are taken in the non-value sector. Economists tend to classify the economy as falling into two sectors: the public sector and the private sector. The exact definitions will vary, but the public sector will comprise central and local government plus public corporations while the private sector will comprise financial and non-financial corporations, households and not-for-profit institutions. Of all of these groupings, members of the value sector will only be found among private sector corporations while the non-value sector will comprise the remainder.

There is, in my view, nothing in particular to be gained from knowing the exact split between value and non-value players once one has accepted the general view that there are many non-value players and that they probably dominate financial decision-making. One needs simply to reflect on the following:

- **Governments** form the most obvious non-value players. In the OECD area, tax revenues account for slightly over a third of GDP. This money is all spent on annual operating budgets and also on capital projects.
- **Charities** and not-for-profit organisations are common. For example, the Bill and Melinda Gates Foundation has reported that it has endowment funds of approximately $33bn available for its charitable activities. This is obviously an exceptional case but in the UK alone, donations to charity in 2003 were reported to have exceeded £7bn.
- **Private** individuals are under no obligation to make so-called household decisions based on value and yet they will account for a huge amount of investment in, for example, housing stock, cars and IT equipment.
- **Companies** are not all devoted to maximising shareholder value. Those with restricted ownership, for example owned by families or individuals, will often have specified other objectives and will not be subject to stock exchange rigour. There are also many cooperatives that are owned by members rather than investors.

None of these categories of player are entirely immune from the forces of economic value and many will carry out implicit or explicit value calculations as they make their financial calculations. Most observers would agree, however, that all of the above categories of player will take decisions with a view to achieving broader objectives. Between them, these players must represent substantial numbers of suppliers, customers and competitors of the value players. They are therefore a very important group and one where it would be wrong to try to forecast how they will react based on the simple application of value based logic.

What I find interesting is the fact that not-for-profit companies have not slowly taken over the world. Take for example banking. In the UK, there was a historical legacy of many mutually owned building societies, some of which had transformed into banks. These institutions, collectively called the mutuals, were owned by their members and had no requirement to pay out dividends. One could, perhaps, have imagined that the need faced by the stock exchange-quoted banks to pay a dividend to shareholders would have served to give a sufficient advantage to the mutually owned banks to allow them to win any competitive battle owing to their access to a 'free' source of finance. This advantage has not led to a domination of the sector by the mutuals. There is, perhaps, something special about the value approach which has allowed it to flourish. We will return to consider some of the possible factors which might be offsetting the 'free' capital as this view progresses.

Within the non-value sector I suggest that, for the purposes of understanding how financial decisions are taken, it is useful to make one further subdivision. This is into private individuals and organisations. I accept that I am making a generalisation here, but individuals have no obligation to demonstrate the reasonableness of their decisions other than to other family/household members. This group tends, therefore, to act in an informal way and I do not propose to study them in this book. My focus will be on governments, public corporations, charities and large, but non-quoted, companies. All of these entities have in common the need for formal decision-making processes so that important actions can, if required, be justified. The next part will deal with the main similarities that will exist between these processes while the four which follow will each deal with an important difference.

Part 2: Similarities – the planning infrastructure

I use the term 'planning infrastructure' to refer to the overall set of processes which an organisation implements in order to create formal means of taking major financial decisions. In this section I will deal with the similarities that will exist in the planning infrastructure between value and non-value players. My basic message is that the vast majority of the planning infrastructure can be the same in the non-value sector as it is in the value sector. The key differences are first that the players serve what are different and sometimes unique objectives as opposed to the common goal of shareholder value, and second, the limitations on the assumed availability of funding for good projects.

I summarised the main components and concepts of a planning and control system in parts 1 and 2 of the fourth building block on pages 110–115. I started the list of components with a strategy and moved through long-term plans to accounting results and controls. If one now returns to this list with the idea of applying it to, say, my goldfish charity BGS, it is quickly apparent that something is missing. One cannot simply start with a strategy, one must first have a purpose.

When one is dealing with a quoted company, the purpose is already a given because one has to have a purpose in order to form the company in the first place. The purpose is likely to be to create value, perhaps subject to a condition that specifies the sector in which the company will operate or its means of doing business. These conditions are, however, typically so widely worded that companies can do anything that can reasonably be expected to create value. So, with a quoted company, we already know that we are dealing with a company that, for example, seeks to create shareholder value through the business of property development.

In the non-value sector the first thing that is necessary is a purpose. This could also be called an objective or, more likely, a set of objectives. There are many more choices available here and everything else in the particular organisation's future will flow from these choices. This topic is of such importance that I will devote a full section to it immediately after this one. I will, however, suggest now what my objectives would be for BGS so that I can then follow these through in order to create the BGS case study.

Objectives for the Bromley Goldfish Sanctuary

To promote humane behaviour towards goldfish in the London Borough of Bromley by providing appropriate care and protection for those which are in need of care and attention by reason of sickness, maltreatment, poor circumstances or ill usage and to educate the public in matters pertaining to goldfish welfare.

It is only when a set of objectives is in place that one can put any real flesh on the question of planning infrastructure. So, I can now ask that readers skim through pages 110–115 and think about how these concepts could be applied to the specific situation faced by BGS. Please first think about strategy, what it is and how it might apply to BGS.

My answers to these questions are that readers should recall that a corporate strategy is concerned with the questions of 'What businesses?' and 'How organised and managed?', while business strategy is concerned with how to beat one's competitors. These questions are just as relevant to BGS as they are to a quoted company. Think about the BGS objectives and you should quickly start to identify questions such as:

- What exactly is a goldfish?[1]
- What is the priority between public education and fish care?

The first question is a 'What businesses?' question, the second is a 'How organised and managed?' question.

Now it is easy to pose the questions, but how can they be answered unless the original objectives had made the answer clear? The answer, I suggest, is that if the original objectives were not sufficiently precise, one has to see what is possible and can only say that a strategy is ready for approval when it not only looks acceptable but also can be implemented by the organisation, given the resources to which it has access. It may well be, for example, that BGS simply cannot afford to adopt a wide definition of exactly what a goldfish is along with giving equal priority to education and fish care. The strategy must be affordable before it can be approved.

We have encountered here the second key difference between quoted companies operating in the value sector and organisations operating in the non-value sector. This concerns the assumption that funds will always be available for good projects. This applies in the value sector but not in the non-value sector. I will be covering this topic in more detail in section 4.

I now ask readers to return to the building block on Planning and Control and quickly review the remaining topics covered in sections 1 and 2. For each topic please consider briefly the similarities and any key differences between what would be done in a typical quoted company and what would apply for BGS. Please reach your views before you review the following table which shows my suggested answers:

Applying building block 4 to the non-value sector

Topic	Comments
Strategy	Similar but with the overall goal's needing more attention.
Long-term plan	Similar but vital to test that the LTP is affordable given BGS's anticipated sources of funding. Also no need to calculate a value.

[1] Are we applying a strict definition concerning the colour of the fish or did the benefactor really mean any colourful fish?

Table (*cont.*)

Topic	Comments
Annual plan	Similar, although reference to plan's being price sensitive would not apply to BGS.
Performance reports	Similar, although references to management hierarchy will not be appropriate given the small size of BGS.
Accounting results	The same except, once again, the data are not price-sensitive.
Controls	Similar, although there may be a relatively greater need to ensure that the resources of BGS are not used inappropriately.
Initiatives	May well be required once BGS is up and running. In early years, however, everything will be a new initiative and it will be very important to recognise the sheer difficulty that this will create.
Nomenclature	As suggested, BGS will be free to create its own nomenclature.
The planning cycle	This will apply. The lack of feedback loops in the early years will mean that BGS will have to accept that mistakes are quite likely and so will need to be very open to learning from these.
Top-down and bottom-up	In the initial stages everything will be top-down. BGS will need to adjust in order to facilitate bottom-up planning once it has some staff who have worked for a reasonable period.
WYMIWYG	Applies exactly.
Setting targets	Applies but it will be difficult at the outset of activities to set good targets without knowing what is possible.
Stage gate processes	Applies exactly. It will be crucial to get the initial investment in the sanctuary right because the limits on funding will probably leave little room for a second chance if a major error is made.
Cost control and risk mgt	The need to consider risk and costs as strategic issues is crucial. Excessive overheads will be a great potential risk and BGS will have strictly limited capacity to take downside risks.
The growth 'imperative'	Will not apply to BGS. Steady state is much more likely to be seen as an imperative unless new sources of funding are anticipated.

It is very clear from my table that most of the components and concepts are directly applicable to BGS. Many of the skills that might be learned for use in the value sector can, I suggest, be applied elsewhere. This common approach to planning should serve to make it easier to understand how non-value players will react. A simple request for a copy of the objectives of a non-value organisation may well provide the greatest set of insights that are available into how it will act in the future and what opportunities may exist to exploit differences in order to create value.

Now the similarities shown in the table would have been even greater had BGS not been starting from scratch. I deliberately set up the case study as a startup so that it would provide an opportunity to consider this situation in some more detail and use this to learn lessons which will also apply in the value sector. Learning lessons was, after all, the third of my reasons for writing about the non-value sector. I find it more credible that a charity could be required to start with just a large amount of money and a rather vague objective than would a quoted company. This is because, in the value sector, large amounts of money are not usually pledged until a company and a strategy are in place. BGS can, I believe, help us to see why this is the case and this should throw some light onto the apparently heroic assumption which underpins the value approach, namely that funding is always available for a good project.

At the start all that we know about BGS are its objectives. How does one turn a set of objectives into a functioning operation? The objectives give a few clues as to what must be done. The S stands for sanctuary, which points strongly towards the need to have a place where the fish can be cared for, but do we even know whether this is to be inside or outside? Also, have we got any idea at all about how many fish will need to be brought to this sanctuary? It is very unlikely that there is any information available about our 'market' because this is, as far as I am aware, an entirely new idea. Finally, at the end of the objectives we suddenly come across a second aspect to our business. BGS is to educate the public and this will require a further set of skills that is very different from those needed to care for fish.[2]

At least, one might think, BGS does not need to worry about raising finance and so perhaps it could follow a Do, Learn, Do approach. The problem with this approach, however, would be that the four individuals appointed to the board would face a duty of care to handle the money wisely and so would have to be able to show that they took decisions only after what one might call 'due consideration'. They would, therefore, almost certainly not leap into action, they would start by initiating some studies while placing their £3m on deposit in a safe but interest-bearing account.

Now if it is difficult to start up BGS, I suggest that it must be difficult to start up any new business. The only special thing about BGS is that I made life easy for it by providing a large cash injection to get it going.

Think now about how to start a value sector business. In business, so much of what goes on is guided by what went on before. Even if an initial start was beset by errors and poor judgements, it is usually easier to move ahead from

[2] The public does not take well to being thrown into a pond, protected from herons and given a few flakes of fish food twice a day!

this position than to start entirely from scratch. The only exceptions to this would be if the errors had been funded by debt that still required repayment or if the errors had been so damaging to the reputation of the startup company that it was better to jettison this and start afresh.

If a new business starts up and tries to compete against existing players it must be at a disadvantage because its competitors have already got something to build on. The startup can at least try to copy the best attributes of the existing players and can perhaps recruit some staff with experience in the sector. If this can be done, however, surely others too can do so and hence how can it be rational to believe that a positive NPV will be earned? If the new startup can do it, surely, by definition, the startup is 'me too' and so cannot anticipate a positive NPV. If the startup is in an entirely new sector then it cannot be 'me too' but instead it faces the problems of not knowing what the market is, what customers would be prepared to pay and what it will cost to supply it. Clearly, any startup in a new sector must face huge challenges.[3]

So thinking about how to start up BGS should have helped us to understand that any startup is very difficult and that believing that a startup will offer a positive NPV is probably too optimistic. Now, think about this conclusion in the context of the assertion that funds are always available for a good project. What further conclusion is one pushed towards? I conclude that a startup[4] can never be considered to be 'a good project'. A new but already started up company may, just, be able to persuade investors that it could invest new money and earn above the CoC. It could do this if it could point towards some capability that it already had such as a manager with a proven track record of creating value.[5]

This leads me to a conclusion that if funds are always going to be available for a good project, then a project can only be 'good' if it is to be implemented by a company with the credibility and experience to deliver it. The apparent blank cheque of the assumption that funds are always available to a good

[3] Readers should recall the depot company example that I set as an individual assignment as part of the Planning and Control building block and returned to on page 379 in the pillar on what sets the share price. Here I simply asserted that the market would be very unlikely to accept the high NPV indicated by the initial plan until there was good evidence of its credibility. The claimed NPV of \$60m at the very outset of company formation would not, I suggested, set the initial value of the company. A company would not, I suggested, be valued at \$60m before it had spent a single dollar. The difficulty with starting up which I have just explained was behind this assertion.

[4] I should stress that a startup is, in my view, setting up a new business and not the restructuring of an existing business.

[5] Even this may well not be sufficient because the market may well assume the experienced manager would take a lot of the economic rent which he promised to create through a generous salary/bonus package.

project should not, in my view, be considered to extend to startups. Even when an existing company announces a startup it is likely that the best that the market will do is not reduce the share price to reflect the likely value destruction. The share price will only rise to give a return of above the CoC once sufficient evidence of real sources of value has emerged.

The biggest example of which I am aware of a large sum of money's becoming available to a charity was the $33bn endowment received by the Bill and Melinda Gates Foundation that I mentioned earlier in this view. A visit to the foundation website[6] is, I find, an inspiration. I will use it to provide a real example to augment my hypothetical BGS case study.

I particularly want to focus on the description which the website provides concerning how to decide where to spend the endowment. This represents a classic example of what I have called the Plan, Do, Measure, Learn approach. In this case a five step approach is explained:

1. Define the problem and opportunity.
2. Develop the strategy and agree on a budget.
3. Make grants consistent with strategy.
4. Measure results and learn.
5. Adjust strategy.

The first step serves to remind us that one does not Plan, Do, Measure, Learn in isolation. One does it in order to achieve a goal. Steps 2–5 are the traditional Plan, Do, Measure, Learn with, I suggest, one really important addition. This addition is in step 5. There is a presumption that learning will result in a change to strategy. I think that this is a really good and, dare I say it, humble development.

I would contrast this openness and willingness to admit that one cannot expect to get things right first time with the apparent approach by some senior executives and almost all politicians that suggests that strategies must never be changed. The 'Our strategy is still intact' speech by a leader in response to some great setback is, I suggest, something that cannot be right. Since strategy includes, in my view, the issue of organisation and management, significant failures are usually down to strategy or the lack of it in relation to some key aspect of the business. Since one of the purposes of this view is to learn lessons from examples in the non-value sector, I suggest that this Plan, Do, Measure, Adjust Strategy approach might be one for many others to follow. The implicit purpose of the final Learn step in the conventional improvement

[6] The main website address is www.gatesfoundation.org. The detail on the approach to giving which I have quoted above is found at www.gatesfoundation.org/AboutUs/OurWork/OurApproach/.

cycle is, after all, that one learns with a view to changing things so that the future can turn out better.

I will finish this review of similarities with a consideration of one technique which might well be thought not to apply in the non-value sector but which, suitably adjusted, does offer some insights. This is the Sources of Value technique. Quite clearly the technique does not transfer across in a nice and simple way. I suggest, however, that there is an underlying concept which does. This is the need not simply to copy if one really wants to succeed. If one really wants to stand out as an exemplar, one has to be doing something in a better way than others and this idea applies as much in the non-value sector as it does in the value sector.

There can, in the non-value sector, be a temptation to hide behind the different objectives that one has. These can suggest that one has no competitors and hence that there is no competition. This is not true. A non-value sector organisation may well have no direct competitors but it does face competition. This competition is from the alternative bids for people's time and money that other different organisations put forward.

So, for example, the BGS could well think that it has no competition as there is no other organisation offering a similar service. It is, however, in competition to get the public to visit its sanctuary and watch goldfish as opposed to other ways of spending an hour or so of leisure time. Furthermore, if it hopes to attract new donations it is most certainly in competition with many other worthy causes. BGS will need to do something special if it is to win on either of these two fronts. I suggest that asking the question 'What is our source of value?' would force the idea of competition to the fore and would be of benefit not just to my hypothetical BGS but to many non-value sector organisations as well.

Part 3: Objectives

A great advantage of the value objective is that it can provide a common means of bringing together what would otherwise be separate objectives. It is widely accepted that in order to succeed, a company must satisfy what are termed its key stakeholders. Value provides a means through which these various demands can be balanced against each other.

Many quoted companies appear to me to struggle with the apparent conflict that the shareholder value objective appears to give. Their concern is that satisfying shareholders might be done 'at the expense' of other key stakeholders such as customers, staff and society more generally. The view I take is that there need be no conflict. Companies have to worry about their stakeholders because, without them, there would be no business. The price an investor is prepared to pay for a share in the company is a reflection of the dividends which it will pay in the future and these, in turn, are influenced by the relationships which exist between a company and its stakeholders.

In the case of employees and customers this mutual relationship is self-evident. If customers do not like a company they will buy fewer of its products. If potential employees do not like a company they will choose to work elsewhere. In the case of society more generally, the linkage is through the idea of a widely defined licence to operate. If society likes what a company is doing then, on balance, it will accept it. If society does not like it then it will move to curb it. These moves will happen in subtle ways. For example, as governments regulate and tax they take account of the potential impact on the electorate. Charging extra taxes on unpopular companies is, politically, much more acceptable that doing so against well respected companies.

Hence all stakeholders can influence the value of a company. So when a value calculation is undertaken, in its most simple form it depends on a sustainable cash flow, a growth rate and a CoC which reflects its risk. The value calculation serves to integrate the requirements of all stakeholders. If sufficient resources are not devoted to satisfying a particular stakeholder then they can react and damage value through their impact on cash flow, growth or CoC. In particular, decisions taken today with a view to maximising the current year's cash generation will not necessarily enhance value because they may well reduce the anticipated growth rate. So there need be no conflict between stakeholder needs and shareholder value.

The model of decision-making in a value sector company is actually quite simple. The manager has a dollar left and must decide whether to spend it on:

1. the staff, through increased pay and benefits;
2. the customers, through reduced prices;
3. society at large through, for example, reducing CO_2 emissions below any mandatory limit;
4. additional investment within the company;
5. shareholders as an increased dividend.

The theory is that a manager makes a judgement about the value implication of all of these options and spends the money in the way that creates the most value. In the cases of all of the options except option 5, a judgement is needed concerning the future returns on the investment. Even the voluntary CO_2

emissions reduction is considered as an investment thanks to the mechanism that is called 'enlightened self-interest'.

The model goes further than just telling a manager what to do with a 'spare' dollar. It tells the managers to keep spending money on items 1 to 4 until the marginal return is zero even if this means reducing dividends, borrowing money or issuing more shares. Shareholders will understand that difficult judgements are required in order to decide at what point the marginal return on a further dollar directed towards a particular stakeholder is zero, but the underlying principle remains intact. This is that all decisions are measured against their impact on the single objective of value.

Shareholders, provided they accept the judgements made by their managers on their behalf, will want money to be spent on the wider objectives and will rather that this be done than, for example, receive dividends. They will want this because the money so invested will result in more being available at some later date. Sooner or later, however, the point must be reached where extra money must go back to shareholders because the marginal returns from using it in other ways will have fallen below zero. The value model requires that shareholders get everything that is left over after this. So, yes, shareholders do come first, but only after other stakeholders have been appropriately satisfied.

Now I have just had to devote a fair amount of attention to demonstrating that the value sector need not suffer from a conflict of interests between its stakeholders. I could go no further than this because, in reality, some value sector companies are managed in such a way that there is a conflict. The problem, I suggest, lies with the managers and not the model, but the problem exists nonetheless.

The non-value sector avoids these concerns at a stroke by adopting the right to choose whatever it likes as its objectives. It surely must be a big advantage for an organisation to be able, in principle, to do whatever it likes but this freedom comes with new consequences. The first to consider concerns the way that because the non-value sector lacks this overall value objective, decision-making usually becomes much more complex. This is because there is no ready means of deciding on how to make trade-offs between what are often competing objectives.[7] Decision-makers have to rely on the guidance

[7] I used the word 'usually' because if a non-value player has a single objective then in principle its decision-making can be as simple. Most non-value players will, however, quickly discover that they cannot operate with a single objective for reasons which will soon become apparent. We can therefore conclude that decision-making in the non-value sector is more difficult because it needs to adapt to the problem of multiple objectives.

that their objectives give to them while recognising the reality of any limits that exist on the availability of resources.

This fact needs to be recognised when setting objectives and it means that an iterative process needs to be followed in order to achieve a harmony between objectives and resources. The iteration is greatly aided if a hierarchy of objectives is used with at least two, and perhaps more, levels of objective. As is usually the case with things related to planning, the exact nomenclature used can vary. I can illustrate this via some examples:

- In the UK, the government department HM Treasury specifies an aim, eight objectives and ten performance targets.
- Also in the UK, the Cambridge University Hospital NHS Foundation Trust uses the terms purpose and resolution at the top of its hierarchy and then specifies five priorities which it is working on.
- In my BGS example below I will use the terms overall aim; guiding principles; and performance targets.

The titles do not matter much but the exact words used within each item are of great importance. When taken collectively, they are 'the objectives' to which I refer in the title to this section.

The process of setting objectives needs to be iterative because they must be achievable within the resources that are available. It will work something like this:

- Start with an overall aim. This can be given many different names such as the aim or the main objective. What really matters is that it sets out the basic reason why the organisation exists in a way that allows enough latitude in interpretation to allow resource constraints to be respected.
- Identify the main decisions that will have to be taken and set out some guiding principles which will aid the taking of these decisions. This step needs to consider both strategic and tactical decisions. There will be choices concerning the guiding principles. At the initial stage, start with what would be the preferred choice in the light of the aim without taking much regard to the effect of resource constraints.
- Prepare a plan that will deliver against the aim in a way that is consistent with the guiding principles.
- Confirm that the plan appears to be deliverable given the resources which are available. Recognise at this stage that the resources which will be available may depend on the activities undertaken.
- If the plan appears feasible move ahead to the Do stage of the Plan, Do, Measure, Learn cycle. If the plan is not feasible investigate whether changes to the guiding principles will make it feasible. If no set of guiding principles

can be found which appear to allow achievement of the aim, cycle back to the aim itself and consider whether it can be changed.

- Ultimately one must devise a plan which will implement a set of guiding principles in the light of the resources which are expected to be available. It is only when this is achieved that the plan can be approved and work moves to the Do stage. The plan should consider in more detail what must be achieved in the shorter term and set some specific measurable performance targets that will indicate progress towards the overall aim and the guiding principles.
- Once operations are under way carry out the Measure and Learn steps. Use this to create a feedback loop that may well require changes in the guiding principles in order to ensure that resources are used in the most efficient way possible. The measurable performance targets will be of particular importance in this measurement and learning exercise.

It should already be apparent that this can be a horribly complex task. It can be greatly eased by limiting the number of guiding principles to a few key points that will help determine the resources that are required. It will be further aided if decision-makers accept that the concept of achieving an optimum is unrealistic at the outset. What is needed is a feasible plan that looks reasonable. This can then be implemented and optimisation can follow later.

I will show now how this would apply for BGS. All we have so far is the following:

Objectives for the Bromley Goldfish Sanctuary

To promote humane behaviour towards goldfish in the London Borough of Bromley by providing appropriate care and protection for those which are in need of care and attention by reason of sickness, maltreatment, poor circumstances or ill usage and to educate the public in matters pertaining to goldfish welfare.

The word 'Sanctuary' tells us to think about having a site where goldfish can be cared for. This will cost a lot but, with £3m available, a site with some outdoor ponds and indoor tanks should certainly be possible. An early strategic decision will concern the sanctuary's size, balance between indoor and outdoor accommodation and exact location. Then there will be the tactical decisions to be taken concerning which fish to accept at the sanctuary.

There is, however, a second strategic decision to be taken concerning the need to educate the public. These few words are potentially hugely significant to BGS. Once it has to spread £3m between both fish care and public education it will be forced to make difficult resource allocation choices between two very different things. How can a single organisation choose between alternatives when it is unable to use the value approach?

I will shortly suggest a means of doing this. First, however, I must progress the BGS case study a little so that we can use it to consider resource allocation.

So, for BGS, I ask readers to accept that after due consideration of the alternatives by the board, the following four guiding principles and an associated plan were adopted:

Bromley Goldfish Sanctuary: Guiding Principles

- *A sanctuary will be established at a location within the London Borough of Bromley. The sanctuary will provide ponds and internal tanks. Care and protection for goldfish is only provided at the sanctuary. Grants will not be given for the maintenance of goldfish at other locations.*
- *A goldfish is characterised by its distinctive colour which must cover at least one third of its surface area. For the avoidance of doubt, tropical fish are only considered to be goldfish if they have the distinctive colour.*
- *Care is only provided to goldfish that suffer from sickness, maltreatment, poor circumstances or ill usage while in Bromley. To be eligible for treatment, goldfish must arrive in Bromley in a healthy state.*
- *Public education will be made available to all via a website and via public lectures offered at the sanctuary and elsewhere.*

The key features of the plan will be the setting up of two project teams and a coordination group. One team will work on the sanctuary and fish care, the other on education and the website. The coordination group will ensure that there is mutual cooperation since the sanctuary project will need to provide facilities for public lectures while the website and public lectures will be a major means by which the sanctuary is publicised. The lectures should also help identify some volunteer workers and possible future donors.

Now this initial plan should specify the allocation of resources between the two teams. By definition the plan has been set such that there are considered to be sufficient resources for both to succeed. As time passes, however, things will change and new ideas will emerge. How can these subsequent decisions be taken? In particular, what happens if subsequent developments mean that all aspects of the plan cannot be implemented or it becomes apparent that the plan had omitted something vital? How does one decide if, in six months' time, it becomes clear that a car park is needed at the site but that this will cost more money and will use the space which had been earmarked for a fourth goldfish pond?

Can we use the value approach? We could only do this if we were prepared to place specific values on things like a saved fish or an individual who attends a lecture. This would be very difficult because in each case the service will have been provided free or perhaps just for some nominal charge. Furthermore, the basic idea is that BGS is acting out the wishes of its founder; it is not in the business of making money. Even if one option made more money than the other, we could not be sure that it was right for BGS.

I suggest that instead we should apply a technique that I have devised, which I call the prism approach, as a resource allocation tool. Its foundation is my belief that important resource allocation decisions should never be reduced to a simple formula. Human judgement should always be a necessary component of the decision. I will first justify this assertion and then explain the prism approach, first using an example based in the value sector and then through its application to BGS.

In theory, resource allocation decisions should be all about ensuring that value is maximised. If this was followed to its logical conclusion companies would adopt a simple approach to resource allocation. They would invest in all positive NPV projects. My experience tells me that it is unusual for companies to do this.

There are many reasons for this, including the lack of precision in the calculation of value; the wish to stretch projects to do better; and the need to recognise constraints such as risk capacity and limited numbers of key people. If you accept the 'pure' approach to value there is no resource allocation decision, there is simply a series of resource approval decisions. The decision is simply to confirm the existence of a positive NPV and then to go ahead. Once you accept that a company will not invest in all positive NPV projects yet still maintain an objective of shareholder value, you must also, in my view, accept that judgemental issues were behind this decision and so their importance must be recognised.

The basis of the prism approach is that you should view any important investments from several perspectives in order to ensure that an informed judgement can be made. Companies are free to decide what these perspectives should be but if they want to allocate resources between competing projects, they should at least understand what each project looks like when viewed from the same perspectives. The prism approach is to view competing projects from several different but clearly defined perspectives and then make a judgement in the light of what has been learned.

The analogy is of looking through different facets of a prism. My diagram of the prism approach looks like this:

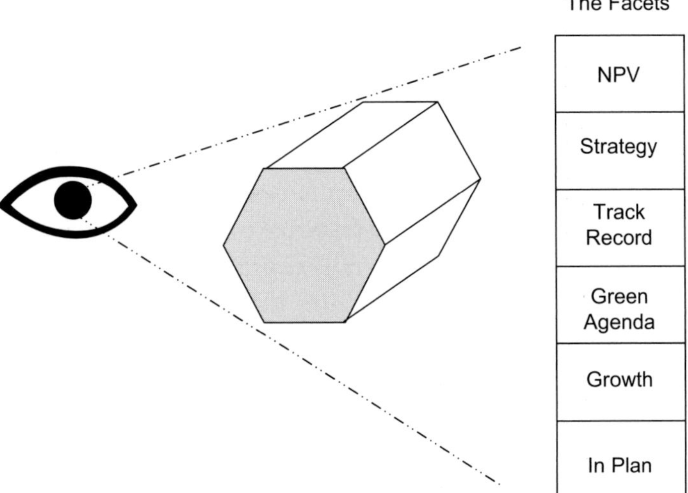

Fig. 13.1 The prism approach

In the diagram I am suggesting that there are six facets. This is simply to illustrate the technique in a hypothetical resource allocation discussion in the value sector. The exact number of facets is up to the model user to define. There must be a few but not too many. They must be agreed by decision-makers as being representative of the factors that they want to weigh in their minds as they decide how to allocate resources. Six, which is the number I use in my example, is probably about as many facets as one would want to use. There should be at least three.

In my example the chosen facets are:

- **NPV.** This would refer to the value prize the project offered.
- **Strategy.** This would refer to how important the project concerned was for the overall strategy. Some projects are vital to strategy while others might be simply 'nice to have'.
- **Track record.** This could be the current performance record of the business that was sponsoring the project or it could refer to the track record of recent similar investment projects.
- **Green agenda.** This could refer to some environmental considerations such as the carbon footprint of the project.
- **Growth.** This could refer to whether or not the project would facilitate further profitable growth that was not reflected in the current case.[8]

[8] It is typical for new plant builds to facilitate additional value in the future when the plant is de-bottlenecked. By contrast, a de-bottleneck may well be the final opportunity to expand a plant.

- **In plan.** This would refer to whether the proposal was allowed for in the current long-term plan. It would be usual to have a bias in favour of such a project unless there was a really good reason why it was not included.

There can be a great temptation to give each facet a score[9] and then to work out an overall average. This should not be done, because the essence of the prism approach is that the decision is based on judgement. What tends to happen is that once the approach is started many of the choices become quite easy. If something clearly wins or fails against a particular facet then that can dictate the decision. If you are not directly involved in a business you might think that some decisions would still be too difficult to take. Once you know a business well, however, it does become possible to make even very close judgements and still feel that you are not just forced to rely on the toss of a coin to make the final decision.

It is the specification of the facets which facilitates the decision. The facets must represent what people will accept are the key objectives of the organisation. By forcing each project to address each facet, one can stop each project's sponsors simply giving a great presentation of why their project should go ahead. Experience tells me that these presentations will always focus on the strengths of the project being supported. What then happens is that, say, two projects produce two great presentations but there is so little overlap that the decision gets made based purely on the quality of the presenter and not the objective quality of the projects.

The prism approach addresses this problem by creating a new level playing field against which all bids for resources can be considered. For BGS I suggest that the facets could be:

1. ***Fundability:*** *cost, potential to generate income and overall impact on agreed plan.*
2. ***Care:*** *impact on the care of goldfish.*
3. ***Education:*** *impact on the education of the public.*
4. ***Integration:*** *extent to which the project links care with education and thus contributes to the overall success of BGS.*
5. ***Founder's vision:*** *fit with what the founder is known to have wanted.*

Although I invented these myself, I can imagine that the people associated with BGS would accept them. Furthermore, they would, I suggest, help the board to reach a decision between a car park and an extra pond. The prism analysis might well have looked like this:

This typically means that lower NPVs per dollar of capital spend are expected on new builds than on de-bottlenecks.

[9] For example, to rate everything on a 1–5 scale.

Prism analysis of BGS car park proposal

	Car park	Additional pond
Fundability	*Goes beyond existing budget and requires spending some of the cash which is currently earmarked for funding ongoing operations. Car parking fees are expected to recover this and repay the overspend versus budget in about five years.*	*Achievable within existing budget. Will not generate additional income.*
Care	*Insignificant positive contribution to care. Might make it easier for people bringing fish to the sanctuary to park close to the fish reception area. Would reduce number of ponds by one but the sanctuary would still be able to manage.*	*Would provide additional capacity for outdoor fish. There would be four ponds as opposed to three if there is a car park. Initial forecast does show that the sanctuary can function with three ponds but growth may be faster than anticipated in which case the lack of the fourth pond might be regretted.*
Education	*Vital to the success of education at the sanctuary. Would allow lectures to be offered to groups requiring up to 20 parking spaces. The alternative to parking at the sanctuary if the fourth pond is built would only cope with up to five cars parked at the sanctuary and a few cars in the road within a reasonable walking distance.*	*Not expected to make a real contribution to education. Might be useful in the context of some lectures which involved an outdoor project.*
Integration	*Will bring people to the site and hence facilitate stronger links between care and education.*	*No significant contribution to integration.*
Founder's Vision	*The founder is known to have wanted people to be able to visit the sanctuary and look at the fish. The car park will make this a much more pleasant experience and will allow more to visit at any one time.*	*The founder is known to have preferred fish to people; that is why he set up the BGS. A pond cares for fish!*

In my view, the telling points are that the car park is essential for integration and education on site while the extra pond is just nice to have. Furthermore, although the founder did like fish more than people, he gained pleasure out of looking at them. Sharing pleasure was part of his aim in setting up BGS and the car park will mean that more people will share the pleasure of looking at the fish.

Now this is just a single example of how the prism approach can work. I have used it in both non-value sector situations and also value situations where it was, for whatever reason, not possible to implement all possible projects. The approach works only if one can select good facets. The advice that I give in relation to this is to test potential facets against known decisions that either have recently been taken or will soon have to be taken and see what insights are gained. If a particular facet gives few insights because all reasonable projects score well against it then perhaps this facet can be dropped.

The most important aspect of the prism approach, in my view, is the way that it rejects the use of a weighted average score. If a weighted average score could be calculated this would become the equivalent to value for the organisation concerned. What tends to happen with the prism approach is that a 'killer reason' tends to emerge in relation to most projects. This reason is either a great reason to say 'No' or a reason that you must say 'Yes'. The reason may well emerge in relation to just a single facet but because all facets are important, this can be enough to dominate the final decision-taking. The decisions that are left after dealing with all 'killer reasons' are less important because the consequences of making the wrong choice are less severe.

So, to conclude this part, in the non-value sector the players have the freedom to specify their own objectives. These will determine what might be called 'the rules of the game' for that particular entity. They will probably start with a fairly broad statement of purpose but will need to provide additional detail in order to help guide the organisation as it seeks to take its key resource allocation decisions. My broadly defined set of objectives will also need to include measurable performance targets so that the Measure step of Plan, Do, Measure, Learn can be carried out. The objectives do not have to be tied back to a financial number but they must not only be consistent with the overall purpose of the organisation, but also be affordable given the resources available. When the organisation has to take difficult resource allocation decisions the more pragmatic prism approach is recommended over any quantitative attempts to derive numerical algorithms to describe the non-financial objectives.

Part 4: Availability of finance

I have already shown how the availability of finance is inextricably linked to the achievement of objectives. This is the second of the key differences between the value and the non-value sectors.

In the value sector we are encouraged to assume that a good project can always be funded. This is because there is such a huge pool of funds searching for opportunities to invest in that it is the availability of good projects and not money which provide the constraint. This means that there is a very clear pecking order. Good projects come first and deciding how to fund them comes second. In the non-value sector, objectives and funding have to be considered hand-in-hand.

It often strikes me as ironic that the value sector is thought of by some as having only limited principles. It is said of the value sector that everything has a price and so there is no room for principles. Yet in the value sector the principle of value is fixed and funding does not get in its way. Contrast this with the non-value sector where objectives are only fixed to the extent to which they can be afforded. In this sector, it is always understood that some principles cannot be afforded and so organisations must be ready to bend under the weight of lack of cash.

I find it hard to believe that a non-value sector player can ever remain for long with its funding in balance. It may, rarely, have too much money[10] but it will usually be working against a funding limit. There are clear reasons for this. The financial markets provide a near-infinite cushion of funding for value players. All good projects can be funded. The same cushion is not available to non-value players. Furthermore, the non-value sector is, almost by definition, providing something for a price which is below its fully built-up economic cost. If it was charging more than a free market price then a free market alternative would spring up to tap into this potential source of positive NPVs. It is natural for something that is underpriced to suffer from excessive demand. As word of a free offer spreads, demand is likely to grow.

There is a further aspect of the availability of finance to consider. This is the task of balancing money over time. In the value sector one has to make just the one judgement about the overall viability of a project. If it is viable, it should be safe to assume that funding will be available throughout the life of the project. Unless an overarching risk from elsewhere in the company triggers a major crisis, once it has started, funding should be virtually automatic provided a project remains broadly on track.

This luxury does not usually exist in the non-value sector. In this sector there is a further complication to consider in relation to the timing of funding. One has to consider not only what is available today but also what will be available in the future.

[10] I have thought of a scenario where the lucky four directors of BGS spend just enough money to put a fish tank in the back room of one of their houses and call this the sanctuary. A plaque saying BGS on the door, a cheap website and a willingness to speak about the evils of eating live goldfish as a dare, and the tasks allotted to the board are done! They could then spend the bulk of the endowment funding lavish monthly dinners for the directors!

So, for example, BGS has a specific endowment of £3m. It has to use this to finance its activities over its entire life. What should it do? Should it, at one extreme, spend the money quickly and then either shut down or hope that further benefactors come along? Or, at the other extreme, should it spend the endowment and purchase an annuity that will pay out, say, £150,000 per annum for ever and then organise itself to spend no more than that amount each year? Even this approach is not particularly conservative owing to inflation. If BGS were to purchase a fixed annuity it would suffer from a gradual erosion of its spending power as inflation gradually put up prices. If it were to buy an index-linked annuity if would receive much less per year in the early years but would, in principle, be able to go on for ever.

For the BGS case study I have assumed that some major projects will be allowed to use the capital and that the remaining capital will be invested to provide a steady annual income to fund operating costs. So what I envisage happening is that the plan and the objectives are tailored to consume the initial resources which will be available. With this approach a sanctuary can be bought outright whereas if all of the endowment was invested in an annuity, it will have to be rented. My view is that only small amounts of income will be generated in the future and that the £3m must, therefore, fund the entire project over its life. My idea was that £1m of capital is spent on the sanctuary and the remaining £2m is invested to produce a regular income to cover operating expenses. So if more money does arrive from, for example, further donations, new ways of spending it will have to be identified.

A real-life example of a fund's having a specified life comes from the Bill and Melinda Gates Foundation. This is required to spend all of its money within 50 years of their deaths. With this objective the endowment can be managed to produce an appropriate stream of cash. At this time the cut-off date will, I imagine, have only a small impact on decisions but as the date nears it will start to dominate what happens. This serves to illustrate how interlinked the questions of objectives and funding must be and also the way that non-value objectives can be tailored to meet the specific wishes of those who set them.

Once again, readers, please contrast this approach with the value sector. In the value sector, good projects get funded. In the non-value sector, funding comes first or at least equal first. Activities are adjusted to fit within the funding constraints. This perhaps helps to explain why the value sector has grown so successfully. Its ability to provide finance for good projects gives it an inherent advantage.

So if the first main clue concerning understanding non-value players will come when you ask to see their objectives, the second will come from enquiring about how they are financed. Many of the opportunities to create value will exist because of funding constraints. If, for example, BGS has spent its capital allocation but still has some remaining scope to incur operating costs, then potential suppliers of fish tanks should offer to rent them to BGS rather than insist on outright purchase.[11] A second example would be if BGS had spent its annual budget yet needed to purchase something vital. BGS would probably be prepared to pay a high implied interest rate in return for extended credit terms that allowed actual payment to be deferred until the following year. This can mean that the same deal offered at different times in the year will be responded to in different ways.

Gaining an understanding of how non-value players are funded is not just necessary in order to identify value-creating opportunities. It is also important in the context of identifying downside risks. It is fair to assume that a quoted company will carry on in business if it has a positive equity value. It may face a liquidity crisis owing to a shortage of cash but, logically, if the firm still has some equity value, it should be able to survive. Non-value players are very different. They will, typically, depend on a regular infusion of money. For government departments this comes in the form of the annual budget set by the Treasury. For charities it will come from donations. There will also often be inflows of cash generated from operations. In most situations, however, internal cash generation will not be enough to sustain the activity. Regular infusions from the sponsor will be needed or else the organisation will have to set itself up to survive on what it already has got. So long-term relationships with these players can only safely be considered to be as long term as is allowed by the availability of finance.

Individuals trained in the economic value model are often tempted to try to interpret the non-value sector through the eyes of value. So value-trained analysts might, for example, try to deduce an implied CoC for a non-value player. This is, I suggest, almost bound to lead to some almost impossible questions to answer. There will, for example, be an implied high opportunity CoC if good projects are turned down for reasons of lack of resources. At the same time, however, another project will be implemented based on an implied low or perhaps even zero CoC. Yet no financial or value-based logic will encourage the non-value player to switch investments in favour of the one which appears to have the higher value. This is because the spend is dedicated to the achievement of wider objectives and not just the one target of value. Non-value sector objectives, simply put, have no need to be consistent

[11] In the UK, a significant new business area called PFI has emerged. This stands for private finance initiative and is where private sector companies, in effect, lend to the public sector in a way that does not appear as debt on the national accounts.

with value. The idea which I have heard expressed, that economic forces create an ultimately unstoppable force, is just wrong.

It can sometimes be easy to think that a non-value sector player has joined the value sector when it declares that it analyses its projects through the discounted cash flow approach. As I have already pointed out, the UK government, for example, requires that government projects carry out a discounted cash flow analysis. This analysis, however, is simply there to provide a minimum return requirement and the government does not seek to maximise value.

Part 5: Attitude to risk

As I have already stressed, one of the first things to do when considering the topic of risk is ensure that all involved in any discussion are using the same definition of risk. For the purposes of the economic value model as applied in the value sector, risk is concerned with uncertainty and is usually considered from the perspective of a diversified shareholder.

I will now contrast this with a non-value sector player. The first thing to do here is to stress that the player's objectives may well specify an attitude to risk and in such a case, clearly, this will apply. It is a safe generalisation, however, to state that non-value players are much more likely to view risk from the perspective that risk is a subject concerned with nasty things, and their avoidance or at least the minimisation of their impact if they should come about.

This is, I believe, the logical response for a non-value player in the light of the fact that it is not able simply to assume that funding will be available for all good projects. If there is a small shortfall in a particular year then there is quite likely to be no simple means of making this up. It will, therefore, have to cut back on its delivery against its objectives. Now I have described debt as the flexible friend of value players that allows them to balance their exact cash requirements. Non-value players usually do not have this option open to them and so, for them, downside risks are potentially much more serious.

I can provide a real-life example here. This is taken from a body called Monitor, which is the independent regulator of NHS foundation trusts.[12]

[12] For those who do not know what an NHS foundation trust is, please simply treat them as a part of the British National Health Service. They have a degree of independence but are funded by the state and provide part of the overall healthcare provision which, in the UK, is basically free of charge at the point of use. The independence is such that the foundation trusts are able to make their own financial and strategic decisions.

Monitor has specified a set of best-practice principles in making investments. These, to me, look very like what I would call a set of stage gate processes. As such they could easily be used in the value sector. There is, however, a vital difference. Risk, as defined by Monitor, 'refers to the probability of an adverse outcome that is different from the expected outcome and the potential impact of such an outcome'. As a consequence, risk management is considered to relate just to the minimisation of the probability and impact of adverse outcomes.

This issue is not just to do with Monitor and the UK's NHS. It is a generic issue faced by non-value players. Non-value players are all less well placed to cope with risk than value players. The fact that uncertainties create both upsides and downsides and that diversified shareholders are exposed to both is not relevant to non-value players because, in this sector, there is no simple mechanism for the sharing of upside and downside to take place.[13]

Now I can fully understand this risk aversion if the consequence of a downside in performance on an investment project is the cancellation of an important operation elsewhere within that hospital owing to the resultant shortage of cash. If one were to apply value sector language, the overarching risk test must apply to any risk that causes an operation to be cancelled. Overarching risks must be avoided.

The most important consequence for value sector players is that risk aversion creates a huge opportunity for so called win-win situations between those that can take risks and those that cannot. Typically this would involve, say, NHS foundation trusts joining together with private sector companies that are working to a value-based set of rules and hence have access to funding that will cushion the inevitable annual fluctuations caused by uncertainty. These companies will be encouraged to see value in upsides and will, in principle, be happy to take a statistical view of these, trusting the good times to offset the bad. The foundation trusts cannot do this and so will be encouraged to sell their risk to the private sector. This need not mean that the trusts will lose out. As long as there is competition among the potential private sector suppliers a fair price for risk should emerge. There is, however, a huge amount of risk aversion and if this outweighs the value sector's ability or appetite to take on risk, a fair price for risk transfer is not guaranteed.

In the BGS example, the car park option might well provide an opportunity for some risk transfer. BGS will be using some of its initial capital in

[13] The stock market provides the value sector with ideal means for sharing of upsides and downsides. Consider, for example, two companies that bid for a contract. One will win and one will lose. Shareholders can simply invest in both and hence ensure that they gain access to the project while sharing the pain of losing the tender as well.

order to fund the initial cost of the car park and is anticipating using the subsequent car parking fees as a source of revenue. The main concern for BGS would be to secure a minimum level of contribution from the car park after allowing for its associated costs. It might be able to do a deal with a car parking company whereby the company guaranteed a minimum fee level in return, say, for 50% of any upside over this amount and for agreeing to install a ticket-issuing machine.

There is, fortunately, a counterbalancing factor which can offset the non-value sector's risk aversion. This is its potential to have low-cost capital. The capital that is provided to the non-value sector, if it has any cost associated with it at all, tends not to have a risk premium built into it. The UK Treasury's guide to Appraisal and Evaluation in Central Government, for example, requires that a 3½% real discount rate be used. If we compare this with my mid-point assessment for a typical set of assets of 7½% given 2½% inflation, the UK government is setting a discount rate that is about 1½% lower than would apply in the value sector. The difference, in this particular instance, is down to the fact that the government is assessing what return society at large requires in order to justify delaying consumption from one year to the next. Risk does not really enter into this assessment at all.[14] Charities are funded by donations and the only cost associated with this is the cost of the fund-raising activity itself.

So the non-value sector probably finishes up with cheap, but not free, capital but significant risk aversion. This creates the potential for value sector players who are prepared to take risks to build businesses based primarily on the transfer of risk.

Part 6: The acceptability of continuous improvement

We are now ready to consider what I have listed as the fourth key difference between value sector and non-value sector players. I have given this the title

[14] The logic behind the UK's 3½% discount rate is that it is the so-called Social Time Preference Rate. It comprises a rate which would be used to discount future consumption over present consumption if there was no change in per capita consumption plus an allowance for the impact of anticipated changes in consumption. The first element, which I would equate with the risk-free rate, contributes 1½% while consumption growth contributes 2%. It is interesting that if HM Treasury achieves its overall aim which is to increase sustainable growth, the government's cost of capital would have to rise. Furthermore, if the approach were applied in China where growth rates are planned to be very high, the cost of capital (if Communists could abide such a thing!) would need to be much higher.

of the acceptability of continuous improvement. I was, however, tempted to refer to it more emotively as the escape from the taskmaster of continuous good surprises.

I introduced the idea of the requirement for value sector companies to deliver continuous good surprises on page 378. In this chapter I adopted a reasonably factual approach to the idea of companies always having to do better than expectations if they want to generate for their shareholders returns of above the CoC. I did not, however, devote much attention to some of the potential downsides of this requirement nor did I suggest that the appearance of short-termism which is often associated with the value sector may really have its origins here.

This requirement to do better than expectations is the entirely logical consequence of value reflecting anticipated future performance. Once one accepts that the value of a company reflects the present value of its expected value future cash flows, the need to deliver continuous good surprises in order to offer shareholders returns of above the CoC becomes inevitable. A consequence of this need is a pressure for continuous change which is not always helpful for the delivery of long-term objectives.

I can illustrate this effect through this hypothetical situation. Please consider these two descriptions of a management board. One is 'sleepy and self-satisfied' while another is 'professional and reliable'. The first offers 'mid-table mediocrity' while the other offers 'solid and reliable performance'. Which board would you rather serve on? This is, however, the same board being described by different people. The board has run a company with great efficiency and has implemented its five-year plan with admirable diligence. The first descriptions are written by a stock market analyst who is commenting on the share price performance over the past five years. The second comments are taken from a professional journal which is writing about the successful implementation of a major transformational project by the company concerned. It was transformational, but it transformed exactly as anticipated!

This situation is just hypothetical but it does illustrate the different perspectives that can be taken. A value sector company that does simply implement its long-term plan should anticipate being at best in the middle of the pack when one considers stock exchange performance. The arguments against it will be that it should have aspired to do more. If it was capable of implementing that plan, why did it not try to use its abilities on a wider arena? This is why its return is only at best in the middle of the pack. If it had been anticipated that, say, halfway through implementation of the plan it would launch something new and even more exciting, it would have disappointed its shareholders.

What we can learn from this is that the value sector is ideal for situations where there is always a potentially wider arena which can be exploited. By contrast, the non-value sector is good for more specific activities with natural boundaries. This does not mean that discrete activities with fixed boundaries cannot survive within the value sector but it does suggest that they will not remain as the total activity of a company.

My BGS example is an ideal example of an activity that fits well in the non-value sector. One can anticipate its future performance quite accurately – it will build the sanctuary and then operate it. A board that achieved this would have met its implied obligations to its founder and would be justified in awarding itself its celebratory annual dinner. Expansion is probably only possible if more donors emerge. If, by some unanticipated chance it turned out that looking after goldfish was a commercial proposition then one could expect value sector operations to copy BGS's lead and start up operations across the country. They would not stand still, they would always try to create yet more value by evolving.

Non-value sector organisations are, in effect, immune from the need to offer continuous good surprises because of the nature of their objectives and their ownership. They do not have to consider what they would be worth if they were put up for sale. Performance cannot therefore be measured in the way that the total shareholder return can be, and the ultimate sanction of takeover is removed. This means that many observers would view the continued efficient delivery of an organisation's objectives as an eminently acceptable level of performance. If an organisation was able to demonstrate continuous improvement against its objectives, this would be the best that could be expected. The overall effect of this is that it should be easier for non-value sector organisations to implement long-term plans without the pressure to make regular improvements to them.

When one is doing the compare and contrast exercise between value and non-value organisations, the pressures for continual change are, to me, one of the worst features of the value sector. I believe that the pressures for change are at the heart of accusations of short-termism which are levelled at the value sector. It is wrong, in my view, to say that the stock exchange is short term because it demonstrably takes a long-term view when it sets share prices that are on average more than 30 times the current dividend.[15]

[15] The dividend yield on the FTSE 100 index was 3.05% on 21 September 2007.

The value sector is, however, subject to a charge of requiring continual change. This can create damage in two ways. The first is if companies attempt change for the sake of change. Of potentially wider and greater significance is the way that continual change can damage the commitment to deliver performance. This is a real danger because it is much harder to monitor performance when plans are consistently updated. The vital flow-through of items from the final year of a plan ultimately into the annual budget is much harder to monitor if, for example, organisations are regularly changed. It is also hard to monitor actual performance through the organisational changes which may occur between, say, the approval of a 20-year project and the ultimate realisation of its value. The value sector's desire for change presupposes that an agreed plan will be delivered and that change is simply a means to make things even better. The danger of change can be that it does more harm than good.

Part 7: Valuing non-financial items

This is a topic where I suggest that the value sector can learn from the non-value sector. There are many situations where the value sector has to make decisions that hinge, at least in part, on judgements about things that do not have an obvious price tag but which do have some kind of link to value. Examples would be an additional spend aimed at enhancing customer satisfaction or the introduction of a new perk for staff. Satisfied customers will, hopefully, buy more of your company's products. Happier staff might work harder or might result in a lower staff turnover rate. How should decisions like this be taken?

The traditional economic value approach would require that some links to the company's cash flow would need to be identified. These, once established, would enable one to carry out a valuation of the action. In this way there are, in effect, no non-financial items to value. Everything ultimately must have an impact on one or more of the numbers in an AFS or else it has no value at all. So one just identifies the mechanism and makes some suitable assumptions. I will illustrate this approach via the following example.

Suppose we wished to investigate the cost of providing coffee and tea facilities aimed at improving staff morale and, ultimately, at reducing staff turnover. These facilities will cost \$50 per month per employee. We employ 600 staff and so the total cost will be \$360,000 per annum. Is this worthwhile?

We would first need to identify some links between staff turnover and the numbers in the company's AFS. In this case we will consider the effect on recruitment costs, training costs and staff salaries. It might, for example, be known that recruiting a new member of staff results in agency fees of $10,000 and that each new member of staff requires additional training costing $2,000. A direct cost of $12,000 could therefore be associated with each person who has to be replaced. So if our current 600 person workforce has an average stay-in-job time of three years we would currently be recruiting 200 new recruits per annum. If the three years were increased to 3½ years as a result of the improved morale, the saving would be about 29 recruits per year which equates to about $350,000 per annum.

The effect on staff salaries could be that by having fewer inexperienced staff the overall workforce size could be reduced. If all new recruits require a month of mentoring time during their first year it might be possible to save 30 months of mentoring. If we round down to the nearest person we could anticipate a net reduction in staffing levels of two people. If salary and benefits average $60,000 per annum the overall salary saving would be $120,000. The total saving of $470,000 is well in excess of the cost and so the proposal looks to be a good idea as long as one was prepared to accept the assumptions.

I have described this as the traditional approach because this is exactly what it is. I will be returning to it later because there is a particular aspect of the calculations concerning the small reduction in staff numbers that I am not really happy with. This specific issue need not, however, change the overall message. This is that the normal way to quantify a non-financial effect is to:

- propose a mechanism;
- make some assumptions;
- plug them into a financial model.

The mechanism and the assumptions should always sound reasonable and the result therefore must also be reasonable since it is simply a mathematical result of what has gone before.

There are, however, two generic issues that I should raise with this approach. My first issue concerns how reasonable the overall approach is. Is it possible to describe via just these three mechanisms the full impact of a subtle change such as providing free beverages to staff? Surely, for example, the full impact of staff morale is felt more widely than just through its impact on staff leaving the company. Also, even if there are just these three mechanisms at work, how good are our assumptions?

In the specific case of my example I could have suggested several other mechanisms. For example, would happier staff take less sick leave? A reduction of only just over one day per year would, on the same logic as the mentoring argument, allow a reduction in staff of three people. There might also be some negative effects. Would staff spend more time away from work? Three ten minute beverage breaks per day could be considered to be equivalent to about a 5% reduction in working time and so, perhaps, could sink the proposal.

What is clear is that there is a lot of potential to debate the mechanism and that even when a mechanism is agreed, the exact assumptions are only ever educated guesses. In principle, however, this first concern cannot overrule the underlying logic; it just suggests that there may well be many opinions. The basic idea of the value model is that everything can be brought back to value and that this is what the stock market would do if it were told about a specific situation. Now clearly the stock market would not be told about a plan to offer free beverages, but I have heard of the markets being told that extra staff are to be recruited to pack customers' shopping at a supermarket and this could well impact on the share price. One has to believe, in principle, that such an announcement can be translated into its impact on value and, as I have stressed, this is what the theories tell one to expect the stock market to do.

Now is the time to introduce my second issue. This concern starts with a strong link to the value approach but has an answer which comes from the non-value sector. The concern is based on an idea that was raised at the very start of the first pillar which considered modelling economic value. Here I stated that the purpose of economic evaluation is to identify the right thing to do and I contrasted this with gaining approval for a decision already taken. The approach which I applied above implicitly makes the mistake which I believe is made time and time again in organisations. It sought, without question, to justify a chosen course of action. It should have first addressed what should be the real question, which should concern identifying the best thing to do. So, in my example, we should not simply have been calculating what the benefit of providing free beverages was, we should be addressing the question of how best to minimise the value impact of staff turnover.

How do we do this? Well, we can learn some lessons from the non-value sector. First, because the value sector is used to having to measure non-financial items, it is much more used to using things like attitude surveys and opinion polls in order to establish the impact of something on a stakeholder. Second, the non-value sector is more attuned to using proxies for what we would like to quantify but do not know how to. An example of this is the idea of using willingness to pay. You can put a financial price on a service if you can identify an equivalent service which is purchased and which has a similar objective.

So, for example, consider the question, 'What is the value of a nice day out?' The answer may well be 'I do not know but it must be quite high'. Surely, a better answer would be 'I know the price of a day ticket to various amusement parks and also the price of a day ticket for an open-topped bus tour of London and these should set good indicators of what we should be prepared to pay for a day out'.

There is a very important question at stake here. What is it that we really want to know? Do we want to know the *value* of a day out or the *cost* of a day out? The value of a day out to the individuals that enjoy it may well be huge but this does not mean that they will pay what it is worth to them in order to experience it. They will weight up the alternatives and choose the best combination of day out and price. In this situation, the purchaser keeps the difference between value and cost.

So a purchaser does not have to pay what something is worth if there are several ways of achieving an overall goal. The purchaser chooses the lowest-cost means of achieving the goal. If we translate this to the free beverages example, the real decision concerns whether free beverages are the best way to reduce staff turnover. In this case the company must be considered to be the purchaser. The company can choose between many ways of reducing staff turnover and should purchase the least-cost one provided always that this cost is below the saving caused by reduced staff turnover. There are many ways of achieving the underlying goal and the best way to address the problem is to work on identifying and ranking these.

The question of calculating an absolute value for the decision only becomes relevant when one has identified the best course of action. One can usually hope that the best course of action is demonstrably worthwhile. This would be proved by reverse engineering what set of assumptions was necessary to make the approach just worthwhile. When this has been done one should hope that the answer is that these assumptions are clearly highly conservative and that hence one should go ahead with the proposal. In effect, we can change the exercise from valuing an outcome to ranking various alternative means of achieving the outcome. This is usually an easier exercise to carry out.

So how do you identify and rank the alternatives? This is a classic non-value sector problem that is dealt with as a matter of routine in such organisations. The starting point will not be that everything has a price. It will be in measuring things that are considered to be important even though they are not easy to quantify and, crucially, listening to what stakeholders such as customers and employees have to say. Surveys of randomly selected people or, even better, of all people who come into contact with an organisation, need to be carried out. Mechanisms also need to be set up to collect the feedback that happens every time a conversation takes place between, for example, a manager and a member of staff. Although excessive attention to recording what is said will overburden an organisation, failure to pass the relevant messages to the right person in the organisation will leave a company, in effect, flying blind.

So, in our free beverages example one could study the problem like this. I would first want to confirm that management thought this was a real problem and wanted to devote some effort to solving it. There is, after all, always a possibility that the idea was simply a result of a speculative marketing pitch which the CEO got from a company that wants to supply the beverages. By confirming that this is considered to be important, one can usually avoid any need to get into detailed value calculations. This is because important issues are clearly worth acting on and the only real decision concerns not whether to do something, but what to do.

The first stage of the task would be to gather facts about people leaving in addition to the basic information that we already have. So we know that in a typical year 200 of our 600 staff will leave. The additional questions to consider would include:

- Is our staff turnover rate good or bad in relation to comparable companies?
- Do our staff naturally fall into just one homogenous group or is it better, for example, to think about them as two subsets?
- What reasons are given by people who decide to leave?
- Has any specific analysis been done concerning why people leave and what might change things?

It is only when this work was done that one would move to the question of identifying and ranking the potential means of addressing the problem. Many of the basic suggestions should, however, already have been identified through approaches suggested by the third and fourth bullet points above. Overall, we would need to find out:

- What are the alternatives?
- What would be the rough impact on a low, medium and high scale?
- What would be the rough costs on a low, medium and high scale?

We should quickly be able to produce a short list from this with the ideal answer being high impact but low cost.

I can now return to my example of the suggestion that free beverages be provided to staff in order to reduce staff turnover. The initial work suggested that a clear economic case could be made for this based on savings in recruitment costs, training costs and staff salaries. What is now clear is that we should not simply try to prove that the proposal is worthwhile, we should find the best thing to do.

First, though, I would challenge a significant part of the analysis. This concerned the two person reduction in staff numbers owing to the time saved in mentoring new staff. It is my belief that small changes in work load spread across large numbers of people do not result in the equivalent reduction of the number of staff employed. It is, however, a tempting mechanism to assume when one is trying to value a non-financial impact on staff or working practices. My view is that people simply readjust their priorities when small changes happen and there is unlikely, therefore, to be any overall reduction in staff numbers from a small change in workload. If the salary saving were removed the entire case becomes break-even, which is a strong warning sign that it is probably a bad idea.

Let us now return to this case study and consider the results of some of the wider questions which I have suggested need to be addressed. Let us suppose that our turnover rate was worse than our competitors and that this was having a negative impact on the company. We were, therefore, right to be carrying out a study. What was wrong was that we were trying to justify an answer before we had considered the alternatives.

Suppose now that it turns out that of the 200 staff that leave each year, 100 have stayed for less than a year while the remaining 100 have stayed for an average of about five years. If this was the case, it would almost be as though our company has both temporary and permanent staff. The solution could then be to take more care at the recruitment stage to select people who display long-term commitment rather than simply concentrating on recruiting staff with the right technical skills. The agency that is being paid $10,000 per recruit that we take on needs, I suggest, to be told to screen the people that it sends along or else we will change to another agency. We could encourage it by saying that its $10,000 fee will be paid in two tranches, $5,000 immediately and, say, $5,500 after the recruit has worked for a year. Or alternatively we could say that if a new recruit leaves within the first year we should be charged only, say, $4,000 to find a replacement. This approach offers the potential for a much more effective solution potentially at no cost.

Should we be providing beverages? Ideas such as this rarely come from nowhere. My guess is that the staff do indeed want this and that a well-meaning manager has linked the two issues together in an attempt to maintain a happy work force. Well, perhaps we should allow a commercial company to install machines at our site. We could require that they charge lower rates than normal as a reflection of our providing the space and water/power supplies free of charge. This would boost morale, stop staff bringing their own kettles to work to make their regular drinks and might even save time wasted waiting for these to boil! Again, we would have achieved this at virtually no cost.

What can we learn from this example? I suggest that there are several things. At a simple level the lesson is not to leap straight to a value calculation to deal with a non-financial item even if we can see a clear mechanism that will allow us to do so. We can, in most situations, avoid doing a value calculation by studying instead the alternative cost of achieving a similar outcome. At a deeper level, the example should have illustrated the value of having good management information. Good management information is not just concerned with financial data. It covers non-financial data as well, in particular in relation to the views of customers and staff. The non-value sector is probably more attuned to collecting this because financial numbers are much more clearly understood to portray only a part of the overall picture.

Things like surveys, focus groups and willingness to pay can all contribute to a structured and more scientific approach to management even where the value model is not directly applied. The non-value sector is managed without always referring back to the yardstick of value and some decisions in the value sector can be done this way as well. One needs to understand in principle how a non-financial item can ultimately impact on cash flow but it is usually possible to avoid having to carry out a specific value calculation. Most non-financial items can be compared with other non-financial items which deliver a similar outcome and then simply be ranked based on cost.

Part 8: The overall scorecard

This is what I would conclude from this view:

Issue	Value sector	Non-value sector
Objectives	In principle all companies in the value sector work to the same overall objective of maximising shareholder value. This is ideal when money is what matters. The objective of value provides a simple yardstick that can be used in many situations. Value need not mean that other stakeholders are not considered but it does mean that,	Individual players have the freedom to specify their own objectives. This is ideal when non-financial objectives are important. The ability to specify anything as an objective and to cope with multiple objectives gives great flexibility. Flexibility is, however, constrained by the availability of funding and hence there

Table (*cont.*)

Issue	Value sector	Non-value sector
	at the margin, all spare cash belongs to shareholders. The common approach to objectives means that skills learned in one industry will also apply in another.	are real practical limitations on the actual ability to set 'anything' as an objective. Furthermore, the flexibility in relation to objective-setting does complicate decision-taking and skills from one area are not so useful in others.
Availability of funding	Funding ceases to be a constraint for any credible project. This represents an enormous advantage for projects and also for investors that wish to invest. It is, however, a barrier for projects that are not credible from an economic value perspective even if society at large would wish the projects to go ahead. There is also a particular barrier against startups. The CoC is, in principle, known, and applies to all projects.	Funding can be made available for anything that can access funds. An individual with money can launch an organisation to do anything that is legal, however mad it may appear to be from a financial perspective. Once launched, however, funding is always a constraint. A base load of funds with low or even no cost is available but the implied marginal cost of finance once this basic allocation is spent is high because it is usual for good opportunities to be turned down owing to funding shortages.
Risk	The ability of investors to spread their bets provides a mechanism for sharing in the upsides as well as the downsides. This substantially reduces the overall impact of downside risks and hence their implied cost to society. Ideally suited for coping with risks that are not 'overarching'.	Tends to encourage risk-averse behaviours with a focus on avoiding downside effects. The implied cost of risk is high.
Stability	A relatively unstable model. The focus on achieving continuous good surprises will encourage change for the sake of change. The difficulty with achieving a balance between supply and demand of finance for investments is likely to cause economic cycles rather than steady growth.	A relatively stable model with the main inherent instability being the shortage of finance.

I am inclined to conclude from this that one should expect both sectors to continue. Neither can deliver a knockout blow to the other and each has its own natural areas of strength. We should not, therefore, seek to solve all problems by providing a market-based solution but we should do so where possible because the value model works so well in the right places.

CHAPTER

14

Overall conclusions

I have now completed my three views of broader and deeper skills. This is the time to draw some conclusions about these three recent views and also about the book overall. The conclusions will deal with the two main sources of value that this book has to offer and then turn to the one area where I believe their application can offer the greatest potential to create value through improving the quality of financial decision-making.

Although the three views are directed in very different directions they do, in my view, help to reinforce a single message. This is that good decisions are a balance between judgement and rational analysis. We have considered three topics but have discovered in each case that deeper skills do not allow us to achieve more accuracy in our calculations. Hopefully, though, the views of deeper and broader skills have contributed to a wiser understanding of the nature of the questions which we try to solve when we calculate value, and to some new ways of thinking about value and how it can be maximised.

In my opinion, the deeper skills simply serve to warn that accuracy in this area is a chimera.[1] There is no point, I suggest, in searching for absolute accuracy when several of the assumptions on which any valuation will have to be based will, at best, only be rough guesses. Now, in direct contrast to the 'accuracy brigade', some decision-makers use this situation as the justification for leaving everything to judgement. This too, should be rejected because, despite the inaccuracy, a structured approach to decision-taking still has a lot to contribute.

The main reason for not relying solely on judgement is that when one does a value calculation in a company, one is not doing so on one's own behalf, one is doing so on behalf of others. These 'others' are the owners of the company and they are not usually happy to hear that a decision was taken simply

[1] A chimera was a fire breathing monster in Greek mythology. It is also now considered to refer to what my dictionary describes as 'a grotesque product of the imagination'. These words are, in my view, an excellent way to describe some attempts to achieve 'accuracy' in financial analysis.

because a particular individual thought it was the right thing to do. They may, just, be prepared to accept this statement from their appointed chief executives, but everybody else must be able to give reasons. Even chief executives will usually be required to say why they did something. We have learned throughout this book how economic value provides the conventional way of doing this.

So value is the basis for financial decision-taking but we have also learned that we must blend judgement with our rational analysis. What this book has done, I trust, is strengthen the contribution that can be made by rational analysis. It has done so by setting out a practical approach in a single book that assumes no prior financial knowledge. To use the language of Sources of Value, however, simply being 'practical' and 'a single book' sounds, to me, dangerously close to a description of the 'me too' finance textbook! A 'me too' book would not be the worst in the world. It would cover the topic in an entirely competent way but it would lack anything that really differentiated it from its competitors. This book has developed two key sources of value that do, I believe, make it different. These are:

- The **Sources of Value** technique; and
- The wide application of the **AFS.**

These are two entirely different ideas and each stands in its own right as a way of improving the quality of decisions. I will, in this conclusion, show how they can work together in a way that will serve to facilitate a significant improvement in the contribution that analytical effort can make to the making of major financial decisions. Overall, they can link together strategy, accounting results and value.

The Sources of Value technique may well have greater academic appeal because of the way that it brings together ideas from two of the key disciplines which are taught at a business school. The technique shows how to link the strategy class to the finance class. There are great benefits in this. Strategies can become more numerate while project evaluation can be linked back to the original strategy in such a way as to strengthen the confidence that the financial projections in a business case will actually be delivered. It is worth reminding ourselves how this can work:

- A business strategy starts by identifying the ways that a company can beat its competitors. These are its sources of value, and the technique requires that the advantages be described in quantitative terms and not just qualitatively.
- The individual business then formulates a forward plan that allows it to exploit its sources of value and hence create value. The financial projections

in the business plan should be consistent with the sources of value and with the return which is anticipated for the 'me too' player.

- If, as is usually the case, the individual business exists within a larger company, the company's organisation is aligned with the sources of value of its main operations to ensure that they are sustained and enhanced. In very simple terms, a senior manager is put in charge of each key source of value. This is a key part of the 'How organised and managed?' part of a corporate strategy.
- The 'What businesses?' part of a corporate strategy can also be helped by understanding sources of value. The businesses which should be put together to form a corporation should not only be strong in their own right, they should be able to reinforce each other's sources of value or perhaps allow new ones to be created.
- The company becomes more confident that it understands its advantages and that they will endure, specifically because it is organised to ensure this outcome will come about.
- As individual projects emerge, these will exploit the sources of value. Each project's NPV is explained as being the sum of its sources of value and the 'me too' player's anticipated value which is usually negative.
- When presented in this way, project economics look more credible and so projects are more likely to be approved. Each project that is approved also serves to confirm that the strategy is on track because it is, as anticipated, producing exactly the kind of projects that were foreseen.
- A project's NPV can be estimated without even having to prepare a full spreadsheet. This is particularly useful at the very early stages when choices need to be made and the costs of project development teams need to be justified.
- A clear understanding of the sources of value should allow a company to focus its attention on exploiting them. Activities that have no inherent sources of value can be challenged and it may be possible to adjust the approach to business to avoid these activities.
- Performance monitoring can also be focused on the sources of value. This can provide early warning signs if things are going wrong so that quick interventions can be made.

This approach has focused on understanding and exploiting sources of value. We have seen in each of the three views how the approach is also useful when one is considering something that is not a source of value. In particular we have seen how the overall calibration of performance means that we do not need to be super-accurate with any individual assumption that applies to the 'me too' player because we will compensate for any inaccuracy when we ensure that the overall 'me too' return is reasonable. A huge amount of effort can be saved by estimating, for example, what the future selling price of our product will be, what CoC to apply and what the effect of operational flexibility will be if, as is often the case, all of these items are deemed 'me too'. We are then spared the burden of forecasting each individual item; we must just forecast the overall effect of all of the 'me too' assumptions.

My two greatest cautions about the Sources of Value approach would be as follows. First, it may encourage companies to ignore their 'me too' activities. This would be wrong. This is because an organisation must be fully competent in order to justify even 'me too' status. Since 'me too' is considered to be at about the bottom of the third quartile there will be, roughly speaking, one player in four that is worse than this. They will suffer from negative sources of value. There is always a danger that by focusing on the advantaged areas a company might leak value through substandard performance elsewhere.

My second caution would be to remember that the Sources of Value approach can only suggest what it is *reasonable* to assume about the future. It cannot tell you what *will* happen. The approach therefore in no way reduces the need to test the range of possible outcomes in order, in particular, to identify overarching risks.

I will turn now to the AFS. This starts off in a way that is far too simple to consider as a technique. The first step is simply to take the financing effects out of an income statement, a balance sheet and a cash flow statement. We must do this because the change in cash, which is what the cash flow statement highlighted, is not really relevant to any company of investment grade status. For such companies, borrowing is usually too easy to make focusing on cash the most important thing to do. One focuses instead on a new bottom line which is funds flow rather than cash flow. Funds flow is the post-tax but pre-financing generation of cash. Now this is a much more meaningful number because it is the number that feeds into the value calculation.

The AFS is 'born' in my view when a value calculation is tacked onto the bottom of the three adjusted accounting statements and a direct link between accounts and value is demonstrated. This link between accounts and value can also, thanks to the Sources of Value technique, be seen as a part of a three-way coming together between strategy, accounting results and value. I have already coined the expression words and music to represent the need for consistency between the words of a strategy and the financial numbers which emerge as a result of actual performance. We therefore have three key concepts linked together as illustrated on the next page.

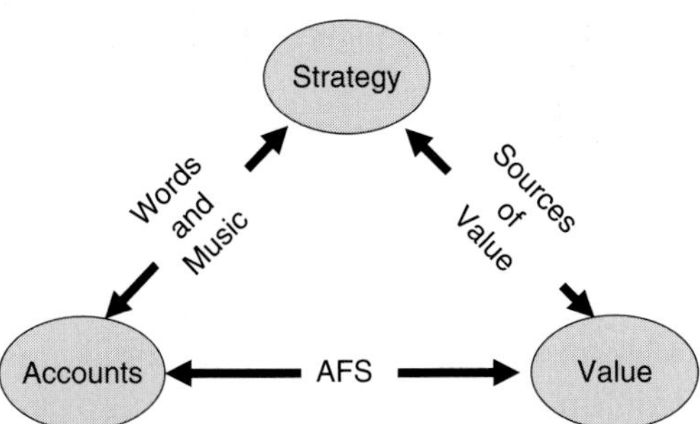

Fig. 14.1 The linkages between strategy, accounts and value

Now, based on what I have written so far in this section, neither words and music nor the AFS have enough substance to them to justify their being referred to as sources of value for a book on financial decision-making. I must now finish my description of the AFS in order to explain why I consider it is fit to be elevated to this status. When I have done this I will be ready to explain why I chose to show strategy at the apex of my triangle.

The AFS gains its importance only when one realises all of the things that can be done with it. If it was born by showing how accounts link to value, the AFS reaches maturity through the following six steps:

1. **Putting conventional project cash flow forecasts into the AFS format.** This makes it possible for a clear link to be established between a project and the effect it will have on the accounts.
2. **Invoking the idea of a company's being the sum of its projects.** By adding up the years in a project's spreadsheet that is prepared in AFS format, one can see what the company should look like if it continues to implement projects like the one that is currently under consideration. If a new project is started every year a company's accounts will look exactly like the sum of each year in the project spreadsheet.
3. **Incorporating growth into this analysis.** This is done by scaling each year in the project's AFS by a growth factor. One can then study the effect of growth on aspects like ROCE and the percentage of funds flow that can be paid out as a dividend.
4. **Recognising the impact of sunk and future fixed costs on the company's full-cycle return.** This is a vital step. A company is not simply the sum of a series of projects. This is because the incremental cash flow forecasts that comprise a project evaluation will exclude sunk costs and also the effect of future costs which will be incurred irrespective of whether the particular project is approved. These costs can be added into an AFS-based

assessment of what a company will look like if it is the sum of its projects plus its extra costs.

5. **Calibrating actual performance against implied performance.** The theoretical picture of a company as the sum of its projects and also their associated sunk costs and the future fixed costs can be tested against the reality of actual performance. One can also calculate, albeit only roughly, what return is necessary on a typical incremental project in order for the company to earn its CoC on a full-cycle basis and hence to be able to claim that it was following a viable strategy.
6. **Facilitating ABCDE valuations.** The idea of a company's market value's being the sum of its past and future projects is the final step in the growing up of the AFS. Accounting results and forward plans can be separated into two components. These are the elements concerned with the existing assets and the elements concerned with future assets. The existing assets are valued as the present value of all of the future cash flows that will be generated after allowing just for those future fixed costs which are necessary to sustain the company at that size. To this one adds the present value of all of the future positive NPVs which are anticipated from new investment proposals (B in my ABCDE equation) and subtracts the present value of the after-tax costs (item C) which will have to be incurred in order to achieve that growth. In a value-creating growth strategy, B will always be larger than C. The difference between B and C gives another view of whether full-cycle returns are above or below the company's CoC.

We can see from these descriptions that both the Sources of Value technique and the AFS approach can allow us to gain insights into the level of growth-related overheads that any company can afford in relation to its anticipated future stream of positive NPV projects. We can also see that both approaches will tell us that if an incremental project is approved with a zero or close-to-zero NPV, there is probably something wrong with the strategy. So the conventional decision rule of 'approve all positive NPV projects' does need a strong safety warning attached to it. Yes, we should approve all positive NPV projects but if the NPV is close to zero then we should certainly first be confirming that the strategy remains appropriate.

So now I have summarised my two key sources of value and there remains just the task of explaining the one place where they can be applied to the greatest effect. In my view this is without doubt in the *formulation of strategy*. The reason for this is that the strategy represents the point of greatest influence and yet it is probably also the place where judgement is given the greatest priority over rational analysis, perhaps because there are so few numerical techniques available.

Strategy formulation is the moment of maximum leverage for any corporation. The strategy gives the organisation a direction and, once implementation starts, it gains an inertia which makes subsequent changes much harder. A simple example of organisational inertia is the setting up of a project development team. This always costs money, which is a sunk cost by the time any subsequent project is put forward for sanction. The original decision to set up the team must have been really bad if the subsequent project has a negative NPV despite the sunk costs. Inertia does not just favour growth. Once divestment is selected as a strategy it too tends to become unstoppable because one will always be biased towards assuming that the sale price is fair and indeed benefits your company because of the winner's curse effect.

If the strategy is wrong, then businesses fight on the wrong corporate battlefields, the wrong businesses get grouped together and the organisation acts as a barrier to efficiency rather than as a facilitator of it. So the most important thing that any company must do is get its strategy right.

The conventional tools for a strategy review are things like sector attractiveness and competitive positioning. These are very useful but in my view they do not go far enough because there is too little quantification, and without quantification decisions are based solely on judgement. If a business is currently doing badly then judgement will inevitably be biased towards sell, while when it is doing well, the bias will be towards growth. If performance data are the only numerical facts available at the time of strategy formulation then performance will assume an overriding influence on strategy. Performance should have an impact, but it should not, I suggest, be overriding.

My proposal is that the Sources of Value approach should be used as a key tool for strategy formulation. The approach tells the company where to look for good value-creating projects. It does this in a way that goes well beyond the qualitative and allows future NPVs to be estimated before the full detail of a project emerges. With estimates of future NPVs, an organisation can ensure that it follows the highest value strategy. We are reminded by the ABCDE approach that growth has a cost and this must be justified in relation to the anticipated future NPVs.

Once Sources of Value thinking becomes embedded in a company's strategic thinking it will flow through to the development of projects, to the shape of the organisation and, ultimately, to the way that performance is analysed and lessons are learned. All of this will strengthen the vital Plan, Do, Measure, Learn approach.

The role of the AFS in strategy formulation rests on the concept of WYMIWYG. If you accept that 'What You Measure Is What You Get', and your objective is to maximise value then it should be obvious that the planning system should allow the measurement of value. The AFS, through its focus on funds flow, gives a simple means to calculate the value of any plan. By tracking value performance over time it will be possible to learn lessons and to benefit from the WYMIWYG effect.

So, the journey is now over. I trust that this book has indeed created great possibilities for you, the reader. I must now leave it to you to move ahead and grasp them. Good luck, and, to parody a film slogan, 'may the Source be with you'.

Appendices

Individual work assignments: Suggested answers

APPENDIX

Building block 1: Economic value

1. *If your CoC is 10%, what is the present value of $100 in one year's time?*
   100 ÷ 1.1 = 90.9
2. *By how much would this change if your CoC was (a) 5% and (b) 15%?*
   100 ÷ 1.05 = 95.2 – an increase in value of $4.3m
   100 ÷ 1.15 = 87.0 – a decrease in value of $3.9m
   Note that although we changed the CoC by ±5% the change in value was not symmetrical.
3. *What is the present value of $100 in ten years' time if your CoC was (a) 5%, (b) 10% or (c) 15%?*
   Discount factors for ten years' time are:
   5% CoC Discount factor = 0.614 so present value is 61.4
   10% CoC Discount factor = 0.386 so present value is 38.6
   15% CoC Discount factor = 0.247 so present value is 24.7
4. *An investment offers the potential to earn $10 per annum for the next five years with the first cash flow being in one year's time. If your CoC is 12% what is the maximum amount you should be prepared to pay for the investment?*
   Discount factors for years 1–5 are: 0.893 0.797 0.712 0.636 0.567
   So present value of cash flows is $10m times the sum of these = 36.05
   This is the maximum you should be prepared to pay unless there are any other factors to consider that are not mentioned in the question.
5. *The discount factor and annuity factor tables given in Tables 1 and 2 only cover a limited range. Extend them to cover a wider range that can still fit on a single sheet of paper. For example, discount rates going from 1% to 15% and a longer time horizon covering say 1–20 years plus also columns for 25, 30 and 40 years. Do this for both mid-year and end-year cash flows. If you are able to, print these tables out on both sides of a sheet of paper and get it laminated as a reference sheet.*
   The year-end discount factors can be checked against the tables shown in the building block. The mid-year factors are a little more complicated. The discount factor for year 1 is calculated via the MS Excel formula 1/(1 + r)^0.5 where r is the cell reference to the appropriate discount rate. For subsequent years the discount factor is the previous year's factor divided by (1 + r). As a check, if your 12 years 12% mid-year factor is 0.272 then your table is probably correct. To check the annuity factors, make sure your mid-year 15 year 15% factor is 6.271.

   These discount factor and annuity factor tables are 'old fashioned' but I find them very useful and have copies to hand whenever I am at work. They save me a lot of time.

6. *An investment of $100 will yield you a cash flow of $15 for every year into the future with the initial cash flow being in one year's time. (a) If your CoC is 12%, how much value does the investment make? (b) How many years will it take before your investment has earned back at least its CoC?*

   The value of a sum to perpetuity is the number divided by the CoC.

   So 15 ÷ 0.12 = 125. Deduct the investment of 100 to reach a net value creation of $25. The investment has earned the CoC when the present value of cash inflows is $100. This is 6.667 times the annual cash flow. Your year-end annuity factor tables should show that payback is somewhere between years 14 and 15. Since the payments are made just once each year the actual payback point will be when the payment is made at the end of the fifteenth year. Alternatively, one could simply start with the 3.605 figure from Q4 and keep adding the discount factor until you reach 6.667.

7. *Your engineering team can only cope with one further investment next year and you have to choose from three possible projects. Project A involves a capital spend during the year of $20m and will then generate cash flows of $8m per annum for the following four years. Project B involves a capital spend of $7.5m and will then generate cash flows of $2m per annum for each of the next ten years. Project C involves a capital spend of $36m and will then generate cash flows of $11m for each of the next five years. Your CoC is 12% and it is now the middle of the present year (so end-year discount tables can be applied). (a) Which project would you recommend; and (b) Are there any circumstances which would make you change this recommendation?*

   Project A – Present value cash inflows is 8 × (.797 + .712 + .636 + .567) = $21.70m

   Present value cash outflow is –20 × .893 = –$17.86m

   So NPV is $3.84m

   Project B – Present value of cash inflows can either be calculated simply by adding up the discount factors for 12% for years 2 through to 11 or through taking the 11 year annuity factor of 5.938 and subtracting the one year discount factor of 0.893. The answer is 5.045. Hence the present value of cash inflows is 2 × 5.045 = $10.09m. Present value cash outflow is –7.5 × .893 = –$6.70m.

   So NPV is $3.39m

   Project C – Present value of cash inflows is 11 × (4.111 – 0.893) = $35.40m

   Present value cash outflow is –36 × 0.893 = –$32.15m

   So NPV is $3.25m

   So I would recommend project A as it has the highest NPV of the three options. However, since project A has a capital cost that is $12.5m higher than project B the extra NPV earned per unit of capital is not great. If the company was capital constrained as opposed to engineering resources constrained I would almost certainly recommend project B.

8. *You own a retail outlet that you expect to generate cash flows of $1m pa for each of the next four years but then you expect sales to fall dramatically when a relief road for the town is opened. Your current expectation is that you will close the site when this happens and that your sales proceeds net of remediation costs will be $0.5m. Your CoC is 12%. It is the beginning of the year and the retail site therefore has four years of economic life left. You have just received an offer of $3.5m for the site. Should you sell? How would your answer change if your CoC was (a) 5% or (b) 15%?*

Cash flows if we retain ownership of the outlet are projected as $1m pa for four years. We need to use our mid-year discount factor tables. From these we find the annuity factor for four years and a discount rate of 12% is 3.214. Hence the present value of cash inflows is $3.21m.

Present value of residual value of $0.5m is 0.5 × 0.636 = $0.32m

Note that an end-year factor has been used on the assumption that the residual value is realised immediately on closure i.e. in four years' time. This may be slightly optimistic as it might take some time to realise the residual value. So if we do assume immediate receipt of the residual value the overall value of continued operation is $3.53m. Hence the sales offer is a marginal call and, based on the assumptions, we would be substantially indifferent between selling or retaining ownership.

If the CoC were reduced to 5% the retain value would rise to 3.63 + 0.41 = $4.04m. Clearly the offer would then be too low. With a 15% CoC you would be pleased to sell.

9. *Build a spreadsheet model to investigate the following project. It is 1 January and your time value of money is 8%. The capital cost of the project is $20m and this will be spent during the current year. There will then be ten years of operation. In the first of these years the cash flow will be $2m, in the second it will be $3m. During years 3 to 9 of operation the annual cash flow will be $4m but in the final year this will fall to $1m. For the initial evaluation assume no closure costs. What is the NPV, IRR, discounted payback and investment efficiency? Investigate also what capital cost increase would cause the project to have a zero NPV. Finally, identify what closure cost incurred at the end of the project life would cause a zero NPV.*

   This exercise requires a very simple spreadsheet model as set out below:

Year	1	2	3	4	5	6	7	8	9	10	11
Cash inflow	0	2	3	4	4	4	4	4	4	4	1
Cash outflow	−20										
Net cash flow	−20	2	3	4	4	4	4	4	4	4	1
Discount factor	0.962	0.891	0.825	0.764	0.707	0.655	0.606	0.561	0.520	0.481	0.446
Present value cash flows	−19.25	1.78	2.47	3.06	2.83	2.62	2.43	2.25	2.08	1.93	0.45
Cumulative PV	−19.25	−17.46	−14.99	−11.93	−9.10	−6.48	−4.06	−1.81	0.27	2.19	2.64

The NPV is $2.64m, discounted payback is during year 9 and the investment efficiency is 13.2%. The IRR can be found either by trial and error or via the IRR function (the cash flows are all one year apart and so this function will work correctly). The IRR is 10.9%.

The maximum tolerable capital cost increase is the NPV divided by the year 1 discount factor. This is $2.74m. (Note that we have not taken any account of tax as this was not mentioned in the assumptions.)

The maximum closure cost is the NPV divided by the year 11 end year discount factor of 0.429. The answer is therefore $6.15m.

APPENDIX

Building block 2: Financial markets

1. *What is the best way to invest if your primary concern is to minimise risk?*
   One should invest in debt rather than equity if the aim is to minimise risk. Furthermore, one should aim only to make low- or even no-risk loans for example by investing in short term government bills. Any long-term loans should be at floating interest rates unless you were completely sure when you needed the loan to be repaid.
2. *Which source of finance should a new company use if it was intending to go into the oil exploration business?*
   The appropriate source of finance here would be equity. Oil exploration involves high risk and the potential loss of all money spent if the so-called wildcat well is dry. Hence it would not be appropriate to take on any debt.
3. *If a 90 day US T bill was sold for $982 what (to the nearest 0.1%) would the US risk-free rate be?*
   90 day US T bills will repay $1,000 at the end of the 90 day period.
   The interest rate over the 90 day period is 1,000 ÷ 982 = 1.833%
   If we work on the basis of there being four 90 day periods in a year (justified because we are only seeking an answer to the nearest 0.1%) then the annual interest rate is:
   $(1 + 0.01833)^4 - 1 = 7.5\%$
4. *If the dividend yield on a share is currently 2% and the market consensus is that this dividend will grow at 5½%, what cost of equity does the market appear to be using for this company?*
   The relevant equation is cost of equity = yield + growth
   So the implied cost of equity is 7½%
5. *A company currently pays a dividend of $3.75 per share. It appears to be subject to the same degree of risk as a typical large US company and so we decide to apply the time value of money that was calculated in the 'Estimating the cost of capital' section above. What would the share price be in the following situations?*
   a. *If the dividend was expected to grow at a steady rate of 4% into the future;*
   b. *If the dividend was expected to decline by 10% pa into the future;*
   c. *If the dividend was expected to grow by 5% a year for the next ten years but then growth would decline to 2.5% pa; and*
   d. *If the dividend was expected to grow by 20% for each of the next five years and then growth was expected to fall to 5% pa.*

We must start by determining the appropriate time value of money. In this instance we are dealing with shares and so we need to apply the cost of equity and not the CoC. Our rough analysis on page 58 suggested a cost of equity for the US market of 10.2%.

The valuation is then obtained by multiplying the dividend by one plus growth (to determine the dividend in one year's time) and dividing this by the cost of equity less growth.

So the answer to (a) is $3.75 ×1.04 ÷ 0.062 = $62.90

The calculation for (b) is similar except that growth is negative. The numbers are: $3.75 × 0.90 ÷ 0.202 = $16.71

Part (c) can be computed in two different ways. I will use the more sophisticated two-stage growth model first. We can also apply what I call the longhand approach which is demonstrated below when I deal with part (d).

We are helped in answering this by the additivity of value. The value of a company growing for ever will be greater than the value of a company growing in this two stage manner. We can determine the difference in value at the point when growth changes and then discount this difference back to the present. This number is then subtracted from the value of the company had it grown at the high rate for ever. The numbers work like this:

Value with 5% growth to perpetuity:

= $3.75 × 1.05 ÷ 0.052
= $3.75 × 20.19
= $75.72.

After five years the dividend will have grown to:

$3.75 \times 1.05^5 = \$4.79$

The values with 5% and 2.5% growth will then be:

5% growth: $4.79 × 1.05 ÷ 0.052 = $96.64
2.5% growth $4.79 × 1.025 ÷ 0.077 = $63.71

So the decline in growth prospects will lower value at a point in five years' time by $32.93.

The present value of this is:

$\$32.93 \div 1.102^5$
= $32.93 ÷ 1.625
= $20.26.

So the share price will be this much lower than $75.72

i.e. $55.46.

The advantage of this approach is that it can be quite simply programmed into a spreadsheet model with the number of years of higher growth treated as an input variable. The alternative approach which I will show as the answer to part (d) is harder to programme if the number of years of higher growth is treated as a variable.

In part (d) we cannot simply replicate the approach used above. This is because the growth rate in the early years is above the cost of equity which we are using. The perpetuity valuation formula does not apply for growth rates that exceed the discount rate. We are forced to adopt what I think of as the longhand approach. We need estimates of annual dividends which are then discounted to the present. We can switch to the perpetuity formula once the sustainable growth rate is below the cost of equity.

The numbers will be as follows. The dividend grows at 20% and the terminal value factor is 20.19 (for calculation see part (c) above) times the year 5 dividend. The discount factors are based on the 10.2% cost of equity and year-end cash flows.

Year	1	2	3	4	5	Terminal value
Dividend	4.50	5.40	6.48	7.78	9.33	188.37
Discount factor	0.907	0.823	0.747	0.678	0.615	0.615
Present value	4.08	4.44	4.84	5.27	5.74	115.91
Cumulative present value	4.08	8.52	13.36	18.63	24.37	140.28

Hence we conclude that the share price in this situation should be $140.28.

This approach is nice and easy to follow but requires quite sophisticated spreadsheet skills if one wants to allow the number of years of high growth to be treated as a variable.

6. *A company takes out a loan of $100m at a fixed interest rate of 6%. It will repay the loan in four equal annual instalments starting at the end of the second year and interest is paid at the end of each year. (a) What will the pre-tax cash flows associated with the loan be? (b) If the corporate tax rate is 33.3%, how will this affect the after-tax cash flows?*
The loan repayments will each be $25m. Thanks to the repayments occurring at the end of each year we can calculate the annual interest charge quite easily. The numbers will look as follows:

Borrower's perspective $m

	Initial loan	Year 1	Year 2	Year 3	Year 4	Year 5
Loan principal	100.0	0.0	–25.0	–25.0	–25.0	–25.0
Loan interest		–6.0	–6.0	–4.5	–3.0	–1.5
Net loan cash flows	100.0	–6.0	–31.0	–29.5	–28.0	–26.5

The loan interest will be allowable for tax relief and so will result in a saving of one third of the interest charge. There may well be a timing difference between the company's having to pay the interest and receiving back the benefit of the associated tax relief but we will ignore this for the purpose of this calculation. So the negative outflows associated with the loan would be reduced by $2m in each of the first two years then $1.5m in year 3, $1.0m in year 4 and $0.5m in year 5.

7. *Now consider the loan described in question 6 from the perspective of the lender.*
   a. *If interest rates remain unchanged what would the loan be worth to the lender just before the end of the first year (i.e. just before the first interest payment has been made)?*
   b. *What would the loan be worth immediately after the first interest payment has been made?*
   c. *If interest rates fell by 1% what impact would this have on the answers to questions (a) and (b)?*

We can answer question (a) in two ways. The simplest approach is to apply the principle of additivity of value. When the interest is paid we have in place what is exactly the same as a loan of $100m that will pay interest at the ruling rate in one year's time. By definition this must be worth $100m. The interest which we are about to receive is $6m. So if we ignore tax, the value of the loan just before this first interest payment is made must be $100m + $6m = $106m.

If we allow for tax (which we should always do!) the value would be $104m.

The other way to approach the valuation is simply to calculate the annual cash flows and discount them to the present. The pre-tax answer would look like this. Note that the loan repayments are shown as positive numbers because they represent cash inflows to the lender:

Lender's perspective (end of first year just prior to interest payment) $m

	Initial loan	Year 1	Year 2	Year 3	Year 4	Year 5
Loan principal		0.0	25.0	25.0	25.0	25.0
Loan interest		6.0	6.0	4.5	3.0	1.5
Net loan cash flows		6.0	31.0	29.5	28.0	26.5
Discount factor		1.000	0.943	0.890	0.840	0.792
Present value cash flows		6.0	29.2	26.3	23.5	21.0
Value loan (pre-tax)	106.0					

After tax the numbers look like this (in this situation we use a discount rate of 4% which is the interest rate net of tax):

Lender's perspective (end of first year just prior to interest payment) $m

	Initial loan	Year 1	Year 2	Year 3	Year 4	Year 5
Loan principal		0	25	25	25	25
Loan interest		4.0	4.0	3.0	2.0	1.0
Net loan cash flows		4.0	29.0	28.0	27.0	26.0
Discount factor		1.000	0.962	0.925	0.889	0.855
Present value cash flows		4.0	27.9	25.9	24.0	22.2
Value loan (post-tax)	104.0					

The answers are exactly the same as those that we got when we simply applied the law of conservation of value. What, however, is the cause of the difference between the $106m pre-tax value and the $104m post-tax value? Well, $106m pre-tax is the amount of money that the bank would want to receive if it sold the loan while $104m is how much it would expect after tax.

We can notice that the loan has gone up in value simply owing to the passage of time. We have moved almost a full year into the future. In present value terms this $106m pre-tax value is worth $100m today if we apply a discount rate of 6%. Similarly the $104m post-tax value is worth $100m today if we apply the post-tax discount rate of 4%.

Part (b) is very simple. Immediately after the interest payment has been made the loan would then be worth $100m. So we can see that the value of a loan will follow a slightly zigzagging path owing to the exact timing of interest payments.

Part (c) will require a spreadsheet model.

If interest rates should fall then the value of the loan would rise. This is because the loan cash flows will be unchanged because we are dealing with a fixed rate loan. The cash flows would, however, now be discounted at the lower rate of 5% pre-tax or 3.33% post-tax. The calculations are being done as at the end of the first year and so the discount factor at this point is 1.000.

The spreadsheet is shown below. Note that the initial loan is ignored because we are trying to calculate the value of the loan after it has been made.

Lender's perspective (end of first year just prior to interest payment) $m

	Initial loan	Year 1	Year 2	Year 3	Year 4	Year 5
Loan principal		0.0	25.0	25.0	25.0	25.0
Loan interest		6.0	6.0	4.5	3.0	1.5
Net loan cash flows		6.0	31.0	29.5	28.0	26.5
Discount factor		1.000	0.952	0.907	0.864	0.823
Present value cash flows		6.0	29.5	26.8	24.2	21.8
Value loan (pre-tax)	108.3					

The value of the loan before tax is $108.3m.

Once again, immediately after the first interest payment of $6m had been made the value of the loan would fall by $6m. So it would now be $102.3. The $2.3m increase in the value of the loan compared with the calculations in part (c) is caused by the decline in interest rates.

The post-tax valuation is as follows:

Lender's perspective (end of first year just prior to interest payment) $m

	Initial loan	Year 1	Year 2	Year 3	Year 4	Year 5
Loan principal		0	25	25	25	25
Loan interest		4.0	4.0	3.0	2.0	1.0
Net loan cash flows		4.0	29.0	28.0	27.0	26.0
Discount factor		1.000	0.968	0.937	0.906	0.877
Present value cash flows		4.0	28.1	26.2	24.5	22.8
Value loan (post-tax)	105.6					

This would actually have been the theoretically correct way to do the numbers because tax represents a real charge on businesses and it should clearly therefore be incorporated into our analysis.

In our post-tax calculations, the value of the loan immediately after the interest payment has been made will be $4m lower. This is $101.6m. The difference between the pre- and post-tax values is equal to the tax rate times the gain in value.

8. *The central bank of the hypothetical country called Lightvia aims to maintain real interest rates of 2.5%.*
   a. *If inflation is averaging 26% what will the nominal interest rate be?*

b. *The Lightvian currency is the dia and the current exchange rate is 235 dia/\$. If the interest rate on US dollars is 5.6% what would the future exchange rate be for dia/\$ in one year's time?*

The formula for part (a) is:

(1+ real interest rate) × (1 + inflation rate) = (1 + nominal rate)

So the numbers are: 1.025 × 1.26 = 1.2915

The nominal interest rate will be 29.15%. Compare this with the figure of 28.5% had we simply, but incorrectly, added inflation to the real rate.

For part (b) we start with equal amounts of dia and dollars and then add one year's local nominal interest. The two amounts of local currency must then equal each other in value. The exchange rate will be the ratio between the two. So the calculations are as follows:

In dia 235 × 1.2915 = 304.91
In dollars 1 × 1.056 = 1.056

The forward exchange rate will be 304.91 ÷ 1.056 = 288.74 dia per dollar.

9. *A company is planning to raise further equity through a rights issue. It has 575m shares in issue and the current share price is \$10.87 per share. The company wishes to raise \$750m of new equity and the decision is taken to launch a 1 for 5 rights issue.*
   a. *What price would the new shares have to be offered at?*
   b. *What would be the anticipated share price after the rights issue if the market thought that the cash raised would be invested in zero NPV projects?*
   c. *How much cash would an investor who owned 1,000 shares expect to receive if they decided to sell their rights in this situation?*
   d. *What would this investor need to do if they wished to maintain the same amount of money invested in the company?*
   e. *What would be the answers to questions (a)–(d) if the market anticipated that each dollar invested by the company would generate an NPV of \$0.40?*

   a. We are told that the rights issue will be 1 for 5. Since there are currently 575m shares in issue it is clear that 115m shares must be sold. If 115m shares are to raise \$750m the issue price must be \$6.52 per share.
   b. Market capitalisation before the rights issue is \$575 × 10.87m = \$6.25bn. The issue raises a further \$0.75bn which the market believes will be invested in zero NPV projects so the total market capitalisation after the rights issue must be \$7bn. There will then be 690m shares in issue so the share price will be \$10.14 per share.
   c. An investor with 1,000 shares would have been awarded rights to purchase 200 shares because the rights issue is 1 for 5. The right is to buy a share for \$6.52 when the anticipated ex-rights price is \$10.14. Hence each right must be worth \$3.62. So the investor's 200 rights would be worth \$724.
   d. Once again, this calculation can be done in two ways. There is a long way and also a shorter way if we invoke the principle of conservation of value. The long way is as follows. In order to maintain the same amount of money invested in the company the investor would want their investment to remain at \$10,870 worth of shares. Since the share price is \$10.14 after the rights issue the investor now needs to hold 1,072 shares. So the investor must purchase 72 shares at a cost of \$730. The shorter way is to apply the principle of conservation of value. To maintain value the investor simply uses the proceeds from selling their rights to purchase new shares. The investor has \$724 and

this would purchase 71 shares with a small remainder of $4. The difference between the two methods is simply a rounding effect.

e. The rights issue strike price of $6.52 per share would be unaffected by the assumed return from the money raised. What would change would be the ex-rights price and all the other things that depend on this. So answer (a) is unchanged but (b)–(d) will be changed. The calculation for these is as follows.

If each dollar invested was expected to generate $0.40 of NPV then the total additional NPV would be $300m. The revised market capitalisation after the rights issue would be $7.3bn. With 690m shares the share price would be $10.58 per share.

The 200 rights would be worth 200 x $4.06 = $812.

To maintain the investment we are no longer able to apply the law of conservation of value because we are now assuming that the company will create value as a result of the announcement of the rights issue and the associated value-creating investment. To maintain the original value invested in the company we must hold shares worth $10,870. Given the share price of $10.58 this means holding 1,027 shares. The 27 additional shares required would cost $286.

So where, one might wonder, has the remaining $526 come from? The answer is that it comes from the $300m value creation that is anticipated from the investments that will be funded by the rights issue. This gain is our hypothetical shareholder's share of this since this shareholder owns 1,000 of the 575m shares in issue. So value is actually conserved provided one allows for this effect (once again subject to very minor rounding effects).

10. *A company is planning to buy a high-temperature moulding machine that will manufacture kitchen utensils. The machine will cost $2.5m and the company is seeking a bank loan of $2.0m to help fund this purchase. The remaining $0.5m will come from a cash injection from the company's owner. How would a bank view the security on this loan and how might it respond to the loan request in the following situations?*
    a. *The company was a new start-up and had no other assets at the present time.*
    b. *The company already had two similar machines and a four year track record of profitable growth. These machines had been purchased thanks to loans which were guaranteed by the founder's rich uncle. Loan repayments were being made on schedule but $1m was still outstanding.*
    c. *The company was as outlined in (b) above but following the recent sudden death of the rich uncle, the owner had inherited $4m.*
    d. *The company owns several similar machines and also a factory building worth $3m and currently has no debt.*
    e. *The company is as outlined in (d) but the lender has just learned that although the facts presented are true, the company only recently repaid a $3m overdraft from another bank.*

Banks would not like the lack of security in situation (a). The bank might consider the second-hand value of the machine as providing some cover provided it held a mortgage on it. The bank would also want to understand the full business plan for this new company. For example, how was it going to finance the necessary working capital?

Situation (b) is more favourable. The bank would want to see the full accounts for the company and may consider there was enough security for a further loan. It is likely, however, that the bank would once again ask for a guarantee from the rich uncle.

Situation (c) illustrates how things can change and the sorts of things that banks will think about. The death of a guarantor is the sort of thing that loan agreements will allow for. The bank may well have the right to request its loans to be repaid on the uncle's death. The bank might well ask the owner to use some of the $4m to fund the machine's purchase. If the bank did give a loan it would probably want to know how the $4m was going to be invested and whether it could gain some kind of financial lien over it. A bank would not simply accept that because the owner of a company was rich then it was safe to lend to a company. This is because the owner has no legal obligation to fund the company's debts.

Situation (d) looks favourable from the perspective of a bank. In particular there is a factory building which on its own is worth more than the total loan that is being requested. The strongest link principle might well mean that the bank would give a loan if it was given a mortgage on the building.

Finally, situation (e) reminds us again of all the things that must be considered before a bank can be sure that a loan is secure. Has the company perhaps simply repaid its bank loans by not paying its suppliers? If so, then perhaps it is not as secure as one might think.

11. *The chief financial officer of a company is contemplating whether to recommend that it should declare its first cash dividend. The company was floated on the stock exchange four years ago and since then has retained all of its profits in order to fund its growth. The company has been very successful and has just paid off the initial overdraft that it had. It has no other debts. The plan for next year, however, shows that the business operations will not generate any cash owing to the capital investment budget's using of all of the anticipated cash flow from operations. Summarise the main pros and cons for declaring a first cash dividend.*

In favour of paying a dividend:

- A good signal to the stock market that the company is confident of its future prospects and can afford to start paying cash dividends.
- Sooner or later, all companies should pay cash dividends. The transition would be taken by the market as a positive sign of success.
- If the company now has no debt this means that it is entirely reasonable for it to borrow some money if only to achieve a more flexible finance pool and the debt tax shield.

Against paying a dividend:

- This may be too early to start paying because it would look bad if, having started paying cash dividends, the company then had to stop. The company might need additional growth funds in the next year or so, and so retaining equity at this time could be sensible.
- The market might interpret the change as a signal that growth prospects were not as good as anticipated and this could lower the share price if the growth had been expected to be value-creating.
- The company might be exposed to downside risks and need a bigger equity cushion before it could afford to pay a dividend.

Overall, as we can see, the answer will depend on how the company presents the situation. If it presents whatever it decides in a positive light the share price may go up. If, however, its presentation is not liked by the market the share price could fall.

APPENDIX

Building block 3: Understanding accounts

1. *A company spends $10m in 2005 and $6m in 2006 building a new depot. It estimates that its useful life will be 25 years. The company starts trading in 2007. What will be the amortisation charge in 2006 and in 2007?*
   The total capital cost is $16m. Amortisation will therefore be $640,000 pa. This will be charged each year the depot is in operation. There would be no charge in 2006 because the depot was under construction during that year and was not in operation. The charge would commence in 2007.
2. *The same company anticipates cash fixed costs in 2007 of $10m and variable costs of $10 per unit sold. It expects to sell 1 million units per year for a price of $25 per unit. It is taxed at 30% and the tax authorities allow fixed assets to be depreciated at the same rate as is used in the accounting books. At this stage assume that all transactions are paid immediately with cash except the tax charge which is paid in the middle of the following year. Prepare an AFS for 2007.*

All financial figures in $000	2006	2007
Income statement		
Sales revenue		25,000
Variable costs		(10,000)
Contribution		15,000
Fixed costs		(10,000)
Amortisation		(640)
Pre-tax profit		4,360
Tax		(1,308)
Profit		3,052
Balance sheet		
Fixed assets	16,000	15,360
Accounts receivable	0	0
Inventories	0	0
Accounts payable	0	(1,380)
Net working capital	0	(1,380)
Capital employed	16,000	13,980

Table (*cont.*)

All financial figures in $000	2006	2007
ROACE		20.4%
Funds flow statement		
Profit		3,052
Amortisation		640
Working capital		1,380
Capital investment		0
Funds flow		5,072

Note that we can check the funds flow calculation. Funds flow does indeed equal profit less the increase in capital employed. In this instance capital employed goes down during the year and so funds flow is greater than profit.

3. *Now allow also for the following working capital effects and show via an AFS what the impact of working capital is on funds flow. Customers pay for their purchases on average 45 days after receipt. Bills are paid on average after just ten days and the depot will hold a stock equivalent to three months of product (which is valued at variable cost).*
We should realise that the income statement will be unchanged. The changes will be to the balance sheet and to funds flow. Forty-five days of sales will mean that year-end accounts receivable will be 45/365 times annual sales which is $3,082,000. The bills will relate to both variable costs and fixed costs. These total $20,000,000. Hence the accounts payable will be $548,000. This is added to the tax bill of $1,308,000 which is already shown as owing at the end of the year. The total accounts payable is therefore $1,856,000. Finally, three months of product valued at variable cost will be equal to a quarter of the variable costs or $2,500,000. The AFS therefore becomes:

All financial figures in $000	2006	2007
Income statement		
Sales revenue		25,000
Variable costs		(10,000)
Contribution		15,000
Fixed costs		(10,000)
Amortisation		(640)
Pre-tax profit		4,360
Tax		(1,308)
Profit		3,052
Balance sheet		
Fixed assets	16,000	15,360
Accounts receivable	0	3,082
Inventories	0	2,500
Accounts payable	0	(1,856)
Net working capital	0	3,726
Capital employed	16,000	19,086
ROACE		17.4%

Table (*cont.*)

All financial figures in $000	**2006**	**2007**
Funds flow statement		
Profit		3,052
Amortisation		640
Working capital		(3,726)
Capital investment		0
Funds flow		(34)

We can observe that the working capital effect is such as to eliminate the entire positive funds flow for the year. Working capital does tend to be a considerable call on funds in the first year of operation of a company and also when it grows fast.

4. *To complete this exercise now produce a financial summary for the years 2005–2009. Assume that in 2008 and 2009 sales volume grows by 5% pa while inflation causes all costs and the product selling price to rise by 2% pa.*

   This is best calculated via a spreadsheet model which can also be used to check your answers to the previous question. The resultant AFS is below. Note that I have shown the figures rounded to the nearest $0.1m. It is usual in a five year projection to avoid spurious precision.

Depot example: Abbreviated Financial Summary $m

	2004	2005	2006	2007	2008	2009
Sales revenue		0.0	0.0	25.0	26.8	28.7
Variable costs		0.0	0.0	−10.0	−10.7	−11.5
Contribution		0.0	0.0	15.0	16.1	17.2
Fixed costs		0.0	0.0	−10.0	−10.2	−10.4
Amortisation		0.0	0.0	−0.6	−0.6	−0.6
Pre-tax profit		0.0	0.0	4.4	5.2	6.2
Tax		0.0	0.0	−1.3	−1.6	−1.8
Profit		0.0	0.0	3.1	3.7	4.3
Balance sheets						
Fixed assets	0.0	10.0	16.0	15.4	14.7	14.1
Accounts receivable	0.0	0.0	0.0	3.1	3.3	3.5
Inventories	0.0	0.0	0.0	2.5	2.7	2.9
Accounts payable	0.0	0.0	0.0	−1.9	−2.1	−2.4
Working capital	0.0	0.0	0.0	3.7	3.8	4.0
Capital employed	0.0	10.0	16.0	19.1	18.6	18.0
ROACE		0.0%	0.0%	17.4%	19.4%	23.6%
Funds flow						
Profit		0.0	0.0	3.1	3.7	4.3
Amortisation		0.0	0.0	0.6	0.6	0.6
Working capital		0.0	0.0	−3.7	−0.1	−0.1
Capital investment		−10.0	−6.0	0.0	0.0	0.0
Funds flow		−10.0	−6.0	0.0	4.2	4.8

5. *Finally, return to the scaffolding example. As a result of further studies the potential owner of the business realises that she has left out the following items:*
   a. *The business will require insurance. This will cost $125,000 pa and will be paid in advance of each year.*
   b. *The initial plan omitted any allowance for a salary for the owner who would run the company. The owner decides she should receive $100,000 a year and that this will be paid monthly at the end of each month.*
   c. *A rental charge of $25,000 pa will be made for the land that will be used. This will be paid in four instalments at the start of each calendar quarter.*

   What is the impact of these changes on the NPV of the project and what selling unit price would be necessary in order exactly to offset the changes and maintain NPV?

   These changes all concern fixed costs but the working capital implications add a further wrinkle. The insurance will be accounted as a prepayment which forms a part of the accounts receivables line in the AFS. The other two charges do not impact on working capital as there is no outstanding balance at the end of each year.

   This kind of analysis is made easy if one has a well-designed spreadsheet. All that is necessary is to add a few further cells with the data on the additional fixed costs. The resulting spreadsheet model follows:

Scaffolding Example revised assumptions: Abbreviated Financial Summay

	2007	2008	2009	2010	2011	2012	2013
Income statement							
Sales revenue		1.7	1.8	1.9	2.0	2.1	
Variable costs		−0.4	−0.4	−0.4	−0.4	−0.4	
Contribution		1.4	1.4	1.5	1.6	1.6	
Fixed costs		−0.5	−0.5	−0.5	−0.5	−0.5	
Amortisation		−0.6	−0.6	−0.6	−0.6	−0.6	
Pre-tax profit		0.3	0.4	0.4	0.5	0.6	
Tax		−0.1	−0.1	−0.1	−0.2	−0.2	
Profit		0.2	0.3	0.3	0.4	0.4	
Balance sheet							
Fixed assets	4.0	3.4	2.8	2.2	1.6	1.0	
Accounts receivable	0.1	0.3	0.3	0.4	0.4	0.3	
Inventories	0.0	0.1	0.1	0.1	0.1	0.1	
Accounts payable	0.0	−0.1	−0.1	−0.2	−0.2	−0.2	
Working capital	0.1	0.3	0.3	0.3	0.3	0.1	
Capital employed	4.1	3.7	3.1	2.5	1.9	1.1	
ROACE		5.4%	7.6%	11.0%	16.4%	27.4%	
Funds flow							
Profit		0.2	0.3	0.3	0.4	0.4	0.0
Amortisation		0.6	0.6	0.6	0.6	0.6	0.0
Working capital	−0.1	−0.2	0.0	0.0	0.0	0.1	0.1
Capital investment	−4.0	0.0	0.0	0.0	0.0	0.0	1.0

Table (*cont.*)

	2007	2008	2009	2010	2011	2012	2013
Funds flow	−4.1	0.6	0.9	0.9	1.0	1.2	1.1
Value calculation	Set Up						
						Close Down	
Funds flow	−4.1	0.6	0.9	0.9	1.0	1.2	1.1
Discount factor	1.000	0.945	0.844	0.753	0.673	0.601	0.567
Present value funds flow	−4.1	0.6	0.7	0.7	0.7	0.7	0.6
Cumulative present value	−4.1	−3.5	−2.8	−2.1	−1.5	−0.8	−0.1

The NPV is now negative although the business does still show a profit each year. It is worth reminding ourselves that there is a big difference between what can be thought of as an economic profit when a project shows a positive NPV and the much easier to earn accounting profit.

To calculate the required selling price to offset these changes one can use the goal-seek function or trial and error. The required selling price is $1,948 compared with the original assumption of $1,700. Clearly the potential investor in this business would want to take a view about whether or not this was achievable. Perhaps the most relevant number is the sales price for a zero NPV of $1,740.

A word of advice in relation to an exercise such as this is always to check that the changes to the spreadsheet have not corrupted the logic. This can be done by setting the input assumptions for the three changes all to zero and then ensuring that the same answer is obtained as before.

APPENDIX

Building block 4: Planning and control

1. *Here are some extracts from strategy statements from hypothetical companies. Some are what I would expect to see in a communication of strategy to staff while others are not. Which is which, and why?*
   a. *Our strategy can be summarised in three words: China, China and China. We will invest in China because it will be the biggest market in the world within a generation and we intend to be part of that.* I would not be surprised to see such a statement in a strategy. I would, however, consider that it lacked a vital element as it gives no indication of how the company expects to win. It is as though the competitive battle would have been won simply by succeeding in investing in China. A good strategy statement would, in my view, include a statement as to what sectors of the Chinese economy were selected for investment and how the company expected to win in these areas.
   b. *Our strategy is to earn a ROCE of 15%. It is only by doing this that we can satisfy the needs of our shareholders.* Once again, I would not be surprised to see this in a strategy. However, in my view the required ROCE is a performance target and should not in itself be called a strategy.
   c. *Our strategy is to enhance the already-substantial skills of our staff and become the recognised leader in innovation in our fast-changing industry.* This is a statement of strategy. I would ideally like to see some more detail as regards what is special about the company concerned.
   d. *Our strategy for 2008 is to grow sales by 10% while holding costs flat in money-of-the-day terms.* This is not strategy! It is a set of short-term performance targets. A slightly different statement to the effect that 'Our strategy is to be the least-cost supplier and we will achieve this by growing our top-line sales while holding down our business expenses' would have been one way to describe the strategy that fits with the targets.
   e. *Our strategy for 2008 will depend on our ability to find a buyer for our ailing Industrial Products division. If we cannot sell by year-end we will bite the bullet and close it down.* This is a strategy but I would certainly not expect to see such openness in a communication to all staff. Potential buyers would doubtless become aware of the strategy and use the closure alternative to drive a very tough bargain.
   f. *Our strategy remains unchanged from the day our founder set up this great company 50 years ago. We are and we will remain the best company in our business.* A strategy

statement might start like this but it would need to give more detail. Simply saying that the aim is to be the best is not good enough. No guidance is given to decision-makers as to how they should focus their activities. The strategy statement would need to state how the company anticipates beating its competitors.

2. *The management of Fence Treatment Inc has just reviewed its long-term plan and is concerned with the decline in return on capital in the initial years. It has decided that it must target an improvement in its ROCE. Several options have been proposed. Classify each of the following as being good or bad for ROACE over 2008–2010 and also good or bad for value:*
   a. *Cancel the major capital investment project scheduled for 2008/2009.* We have to assume that the investment project has a positive NPV, so cancelling it would lower value but it would increase ROACE (because capital employed would fall and there would be no impact on profit until 2010).
   b. *Continue with the capital investment project but require that its size (i.e. the quantity of fence treatment product that it will produce) be reduced by a half.* This would have a significant impact on value. For a start one has to assume that the previous size of plant had been selected because it optimised value. Furthermore, a late change in design of this magnitude would be bound to cause substantial additional costs. There would be a benefit in terms of ROACE but less than that obtained for action (a).
   c. *Improve stock control procedures so as to halve the inventory.* This should be good for both value and ROACE unless stock were reduced to a level where production efficiency was damaged or customers felt there was a reduction in service quality owing to stock of finished product's not being available when required.
   d. *Cancel the 2008 staff Christmas party.* Although this may have a symbolic impact, the effect on ROACE and value should be quite small. The symbolic impact could be positive or negative to value depending on how staff reacted to the announcement. (See also comments about the board's Christmas outing!)
   e. *Cancel the 2008 board Christmas lunch in Bermuda.* Probably good for both value and ROACE. The cost of a board lunch in Bermuda is likely to be excessive in relation to the scale of the company that is only anticipating annual profits of about $5m. Staff would also be aware of board-level extravagance and morale may increase which could enhance overall performance.
   f. *Cancel all training planned for 2008.* One has to assume that training would bring benefits in the long term and hence be value creating. So cancelling it would be bad for value. However, since the cost of training is treated as an expense in the year in which it is incurred, cancelling it will increase ROACE in the year in question unless the payback on it was very fast. Over a three-year period one would expect to see ROACE fall as the impact of the lack of training would impact on performance.
   g. *Invest in a pre-treatment machine costing $1m which will reduce all variable costs by 3%. The investment would be made in 2008 and the full benefit would be gained from 2009 onwards.* A quick check on the numbers shows that the 3% reduction in variable costs would equate with a reduction in costs of about $0.2m pa pre-tax or $0.14m pa post-tax. The investment will clearly be good for value. It will, however, lower ROACE in 2008 while the spend is taking place and no benefit is being earned. The benefit is so great that it will result in an improvement in ROACE from 2009 onwards.

3. *A company is operating with the simple four stage gate process for project development. The project we are dealing with concerns building a new chemical plant. Place the following activities within the appropriate stage:*
   a. *Placing an order for the reactor vessel.* This will normally be an early part of the Implementation stage. In some instances a reactor may take a long time to be manufactured and so it is possible that the order could be placed during the Detailed Design stage but this would be unusual and would require specific approval since it prejudges the normal go/no-go decision which usually marks the end of the Detailed Design stage.
   b. *Negotiating a long term sale for some of the output to a major purchaser.* Selling the product is usually a part of the Operation stage. However, a long-term sale may be negotiated earlier. It could happen during Implementation while the plant is being built, during the Detailed Design stage or even during the Options Identification and Selection stage. The position in the stage gate process would depend on how significant the sale was. If the sale was for, say, half of the total output of the new plant it would be dealt with at a very early stage.
   c. *Setting up a project development team to prepare and implement detailed plans.* This is clearly an early action in the Detailed Design stage.
   d. *Deciding the design capacity of the plant.* This is an early decision during the Detailed Design stage.
   e. *Reviewing competitor plans to avoid overcapacity.* This should be done initially as part of the Options Identification stage. It should, however, be kept under review until the point of final project sanction (i.e. end of Detailed Design) because should a competitor announce its intention to build new capacity this might be of sufficient importance to require the original Options Identification and Selection stage to be reviewed. Stage Gate processes are not simply one-way. The Plan, Do, Measure, Learn approach can still be such as to require a company to think again about earlier decisions.
   f. *Buying the land on which the plant will be built.* This all depends on the exact situation. If plenty of land is available and the precise location is unimportant then the land could be purchased as late as the beginning of Implementation. Land can, however, be so important that it is necessary to purchase it at an earlier stage such as early in Detailed Design. Land could even be purchased ahead of a particular project if the company felt that land would be necessary for some use or other and a suitable plot became available.
   g. *Purchase of feedstock for the plant.* This is usually done only when the project has started its Operation stage. If, however, feedstock is special and hard to obtain then agreements in principle for feedstock supply might well be signed at an earlier stage.
   h. *Health and safety checks to ensure the product is not carcinogenic.* A review such as this which deals with a major generic risk of any chemical plant should be completed during the Options Identification and Selection stage. After that it should be kept under review in case of developments in safety rules, etc.
4. *Return to the AFS which was prepared for the Depot example in the individual work assignments in the previous building block. Use these cash flows as the basis to prepare the plan for a company that builds depots such as this. This company is being started from scratch at the start of year 1. From year 2 onwards it expects to start one new project each year. Each project will be the same as outlined in the Work Assignment. The projects take two years to build and then operate for 25 years. At present you only have the financial projections for*

the first three years of operation. You should assume that the remaining 22 years generate exactly the same funds flow and that there is no residual value. The individual projects are very attractive when viewed on an incremental cost basis; however, the company anticipates incurring the following costs in its head office and project development teams.

- *A head office building will be required. The rental on this will be $5m per year. The rental is payable quarterly at the start of each quarter.*
- *Overhead costs of $5m per year will be incurred. All of this cost is paid out during the year.*
- *A success bonus will be paid to the project development team each time a new project is approved. This bonus will be $4m.*

You are in charge of the planning activities for this company. Complete the following tasks:

a. *Calculate the incremental NPV for the first project that will be put forward for approval. Assume a CoC of 10%.*
b. *Prepare the financial projections for the first five-year long-term plan. These should be shown in AFS format covering income statements, balance sheets and funds flow. Comment briefly on the different messages which emerge from the project analysis and the overall business plan.*
c. *Estimate the value of the business as at the date of formation based on the assumptions outlined above.*

The NPV calculation for the first project is fairly simple. We have the funds flow projections for the two-year Implementation stage and the first three years of operation. We also know that the funds flow will remain constant after that. So we can replace the remaining 22 years of cash flow with a terminal value that is based on the 22-year annuity factor for a CoC of 10%. This factor is 8.772. So by including 8.772 times the final year funds flow as though it were an additional funds flow in the third year of operation we can then compute the correct NPV.

We do need to think about the three additional costs that the company is incurring. The head office cost and the overheads are unchanged by the decision on the project and so can be ignored in the calculation of incremental NPV. The success bonus, however, is an incremental cost and does need to be allowed for. It is an immediate expense and so the discount factor for it will be 1.0. The final twist concerns tax relief on this expense. We know that the company is a new startup and so it will not be paying tax. This means that the tax relief on the bonus will not be available until the project itself is paying tax. An inspection of the tax line in the project spreadsheet shows a charge of $1.3m in the first year of operation. We also know that tax is paid in the year after it is charged. Since the $1.3m is more than the tax relief of $4m (the tax rate is 30%), the full benefit of tax relief will be felt in the second year of operation. The resultant project value calculation is as follows:

Depot NPV Calculation

	Sanction	Build Yr 1	Build Yr 2	Year 1	Year 2	Year 3
Success Fee	−4.0					
Fee tax relief					1.2	
Project Flows	0.0	−10.0	−6.0	0.0	4.2	4.8

Table (*cont.*)

	Sanction	Build Yr 1	Build Yr 2	Year 1	Year 2	Year 3
Terminal Value						42.4
Total Flows	−4.0	−10.0	−6.0	0.0	5.4	47.3
Discount Factor	1.000	0.867	0.788	0.716	0.651	0.592
PV Flows	−4.0	−8.7	−4.7	0.0	3.5	28.0
Cumulative PV	−4.0	−12.7	−17.4	−17.4	−13.9	14.1
NPV – $m	14.1					

So the project shows a healthy NPV of about $14m which is quite high relative to the combined capital and bonus cost of $20m. Note that the fact that we were only asked to calculate NPV has simplified our task a lot. Had we been asked to compute the full set of economic indicators we would have needed to prepare a full year-by-year analysis of the project.

There is a further potential twist in the calculation in relation to tax. We now know that the company will be incurring substantial overhead costs before this project even starts. These overhead costs should mean that it will not have to pay any tax for several years. Strictly speaking the incremental analysis of the first project should allow for this. It would serve to increase the NPV but I have not included this effect in my suggested answer because of the complexity involved in modelling it correctly. Tax calculations can become horribly complex and one quite often has to simplify in order to avoid excessive work in getting the tax 'exactly' right because the accuracy is usually spurious.

We turn now to the plan. Things will not look as good when viewed in this way. Each year the company will incur rental, overhead and bonus costs totalling $14m. In its second year of operation it will start the capital spend on its first project. Its first income will not occur until its fourth year of operation. During this year it will also incur the year 1 and year 2 building costs and also the full $14m of corporate costs. The company will not gain any effective tax relief for these costs until well after its fifth year of operation.

The plan is put together using the sum of projects approach but after adjusting for the full corporate overheads and their impact on tax and the tax element of accounts payable. I have assumed that the additional projects which are started each year have exactly the same cash flows as the original project. I did not include any adjustments to allow for inflation. The numbers are as follows:

Depot Company LTP

	Year 1	Year 2	Year 3	Year 4	Year 5
Sales Revenue	0.0	0.0	0.0	25.0	51.8
Variable Costs	0.0	0.0	0.0	−10.0	−20.7
Contribution	0.0	0.0	0.0	15.0	31.1
Fixed Costs	−14.0	−14.0	−14.0	−24.0	−34.2
Amortisation	0.0	0.0	0.0	−0.6	−1.3
Pre-Tax Profit	−14.0	−14.0	−14.0	−9.6	−4.4

Table (*cont.*)

	Year 1	Year 2	Year 3	Year 4	Year 5
Tax	0.0	0.0	0.0	0.0	0.0
Profit	–14.0	–14.0	–14.0	–9.6	–6.0
Balance Sheets					
Fixed Assets	0.0	10.0	26.0	41.4	56.1
Accounts Receivable	0.0	0.0	0.0	3.1	6.4
Inventories	0.0	0.0	0.0	2.5	5.2
Account Payable	0.0	0.0	0.0	–0.5	–2.4
Working Capital	0.0	0.0	0.0	5.0	9.1
Capital Employed	0.0	10.0	26.0	46.4	65.2
ROACE					
Funds Flow					
Profit	–14.0	–14.0	–14.0	–9.6	–6.0
Amortisation	0.0	0.0	0.0	0.6	1.3
Working Capital	0.0	0.0	0.0	–5.0	–4.1
Capital Investment	0.0	–10.0	–16.0	–16.0	–16.0
Funds Flow	–14.0	–24.0	–30.0	–30.0	–24.8

We see a picture of a company's reporting losses every year (this is why I did not bother to compute ROACE) and with a very significant funding requirement in every year.

If the projects are going to perform as indicated by the assumptions then financial theory suggests that the markets would fund the company. The projects all have NPVs of \$14m or more and this annual NPV is more than enough to justify the \$10m of pre-tax overheads which are incurred as part of the overall business. It is, however, what would be called 'a big ask'. In reality a company with no track record would find it hard to convince the market that its plans were viable if it was still projecting losses after five years of operation.

In my view, the company's problem is that it is trying to grow too fast. If it were to delay its growth plans until the first project was operating profitably it would find it easier to convince the markets of its viability.

This exercise should have served to illustrate how important it is to look at the LTP as well as the project value calculations.

Finally, what might this company be worth if the market believed its plans? It is expected to produce a steady stream of positive NPV projects. Each project has an NPV of \$14m. The present value of this is \$140m if one assumes the stream will continue for ever and the first project will be approved in one year's time.

This analysis has excluded the office rental and overheads of \$10m pa. If these never get any tax relief their present value will be the present value of a mid-year cash flow stream of minus \$10pa which is minus \$105m[1]. The business will eventually get the benefit of tax relief on these costs and so their value impact will not be as bad as \$105m. If tax relief was

[1] If the costs were all incurred at the end of each year their present value would be \$100m. In fact they are all incurred half a year earlier and so their value impact is increased by half a year's worth of the time value of money.

immediate, the impact would be to reduce the value hit by 30%. Without a full model one cannot calculate the exact impact. We were only asked for an estimate of value. So I will use a tax relief factor of about 25% which suggests a value reduction owing to overheads and rental of about \$80m and hence a net after-tax value of the business of about \$60m.

We will return to how the market might actually value this company later in this book. At this stage we simply need to be able to calculate a value based on a given set of assumptions. In this case the value of the business before it has spent any money at all would be \$60m as long as the market believes the financial projections.

APPENDIX

Building block 5: Risk

1. *What would be the fair market price for the right to play a dice rolling game where the payout is the square of the number shown?*
   There are six possible outcomes. These are 1, 4, 9, 16, 25 and 36. The average of these is 91 ÷ 6 = 15.167. This would be the fair market price if we ignore any transaction costs.
2. *A game is played that involves rolling two dice. Competitors pay $1 to play. They are paid $5 if the combined score is seven but nothing if the score is any other amount. What is the expected value of playing the game once?*
   There are 36 different ways that the two dice can come up. Six of these will add to seven. So the player will win one sixth of the time. So if you pay $1 and have an expected payout of one sixth of $5 the expected loss is one sixth of a dollar.
3. *A casino allows players to play the game from question 2. The casino has annual overheads of $1m and local gambling regulations limit its opening hours to just 12 hours per week while the fire regulations limit the number of gamblers in the building to 500. What would be the minimum number of games per hour that each gambler must play if the casino is just to cover its costs? What conclusions would you draw from this calculation?*
   The principle of value additivity means that the value loss to the player must equal the value gain to the casino. In theory, therefore, there is a gain to the casino owner of one sixth of a dollar each time the game is played. However, the casino has to incur high costs and only has limited access to gamblers.

   If we define one unit of gambling capacity as one gambler present for one hour, the casino has a maximum capacity of 12 × 500 × 52 gambling hours per year. This equals 312,000. We know that each individual gamble is worth one sixth of a dollar to the casino operator. The required gain per gambling hour is $1m divided by 312,000, which equals $3.205. Finally we multiply this by six to get to the minimum number of games per hour. The answer is 19.2.

   So simply to break even each and every gambler in the casino must play about one game every three minutes throughout their time in the casino and the casino must always be full. Now I am not a gambler but I doubt that those are good enough conditions to make it worth operating the casino. I would not, however, give up straight away. If the gambling regulations could be relaxed or if the size of bets could be increased it might well be worthwhile opening a casino.
4. *Here are six different types of probability distribution and ten situations. Match the situations to the distributions.*
   Distributions
   - *Symmetrical, narrow range*

- *Symmetrical, wide range*
- *Skewed with heavy upside*
- *Skewed with heavy downside*
- *Bimodal*
- *Substantially flat*

Situations

- *The quantity of cash being carried by an individual selected at random at a shopping centre.* I would suggest skewed with heavy upside. Most people will have some cash but some will have a lot. You cannot have less cash than zero. One could also suggest a bimodal distribution with all very young children having no cash and grown-ups having more.
- *The height of the people present at an infants' school.* This would be bimodal with, in effect, two groups present – the infants and the adults. Each of these two groups would have its own distribution.
- *The price of a particular share tomorrow in relation to its price today (ignoring complications such as days when the markets are not open or the effect of any dividends that are paid).* This would be symmetrical with a narrow range.
- *The corporate tax rate in your home country in five years' time compared with the current rate.* With tax rates there is always a possibility that there might be some major reform within a five year period. One would need to know which country before one guessed whether this could give a downside or an upside skew. If this possibility was ignored one would usually assume a symmetrical distribution with a narrow range.
- *The price of a TV set in ten years' time.* This is difficult to answer because with the pace of technological change, who can be sure exactly what functions will be present in a TV ten years in the future? My perception is that the trend has been that on a like-for-like basis TV prices have come down but technology changes have resulted in substantial overall rises in the headline price of a TV. Lacking any better basis I would suggest a symmetrical distribution with a wide range.
- *The exchange rate between US dollars and the euro in one year's time.* I have no real reason to expect any significant changes or skews and so would go for symmetrical, narrow range.
- *The cost of building the stadia required for the London Olympics compared with the initial estimate made when the Olympic bid was submitted.* This would be a classic skewed distribution with heavy upside (always assuming that the term 'upside' means higher cost and not a better outcome).
- *The amount of rainfall in London on a particular day in July relative to the average daily rainfall for July.* This is a success or failure situation. The way to model rainfall is through whether or not it rains and then the average rain on days when it does rain. Even on the days when it does rain, I would expect a wide range of outcomes.
- *The closing price of gold on the London futures market relative to the closing price on the US market on the same day.* International markets are connected and so the only difference that I would anticipate would be due to the time difference between the two countries. This would drive a small and symmetrical distribution.
- *The average wage rate in the US in five years' time.* It is a fair bet that wages will be higher but even this is not certain because the national average will be affected by several

factors and not just inflation. However, the overall uncertainty is probably not very great. So I would suggest a slight upward skew.

Note that my answers to these questions have tended to be very imprecise. This uncertainty about uncertainty is fairly typical!

5. *A business opportunity exists to sell replica sports shirts outside a stadium. You have two choices. You can go for the minimal overheads approach and carry 50 shirts to the ground for each home game, held over your arm and in a large holdall bag. You would expect to sell at least 40 of these every game for $20 each while the cost to you is just $10 per shirt. There are 20 home games in a season. The alternative is to rent a small lock-up stall by the entrance to the ground. This would then allow you to hold a more substantial stock of shirts and win many more sales. The stall costs $2,000 to rent for the season and you would hold a stock of 400 shirts. Your best estimate of sales would then be 150 per game again at a price of $20 per shirt and with a variable cost to you of $10 per shirt. Which would be the best thing to do and how might a risk review make you change this view?*

The first stage in the analysis is to carry out a first-cut analysis of the economics given the stated assumptions. The so-called minimal overheads approach looks as follows:

The outlay per game is $500 (50 shirts bought for $10 each) and the minimum return is $800 cash plus $100 towards next week's shirt purchases. This is a minimum profit of $400 per game. With 20 home games per season the anticipated profit is $8,000 per year. We should not forget the need to fund the inventory (i.e. any unsold shirts that we own). For our base case assumptions we would finish the year with ten shirts in stock. These would have cost $100. So the overall return is $7,900 of cash and $100 in unsold shirts valued at cost. In addition to this if you are able to sell all 50 shirts each game then the cash gain increases to $10,000 per year and there would be no unsold shirts at the end of the year.

The alternative approach involves an initial outlay on shirts of $4,000 and a commitment to pay rent of $2,000. The contribution to profit per week from shirt sales is $1,500. So the profit per season is $30,000 less $2,000 equals $28,000. The closing inventory would be 250 shirts (I am assuming that we start each match day with 400 shirts and since we sell 150 we must finish with 250). The book value of the unsold shirts would be $2,500. Hence if we start from scratch the cash generation would be $25,500 over the season and we would also have 250 unsold shirts.

If we accept the numbers at face value and if we can afford the initial outlay to purchase shirts then it is clear that the stall approach is preferable.

What might a risk review surface? Well, there are plenty of thoughts that come to mind. I will put to one side the questions of whether it is legal to sell shirts from a holdall bag outside a stadium and whether any tax would be payable.

My risk review on the minimal overheads approach highlights two key factors. First, I do not see how it is reasonable to assume the same selling price for shirts sold from over the arm compared with shirts sold via a well stocked and clearly officially endorsed stall. I would assume that the $20 was a stall price and that the over-the-arm approach would have to be lower. If the selling price was $16 per shirt the profit would fall by $160 per game or $3,200 per season. The second risk would be that of lost or stolen shirts. I think that I would need a partner to help me with the selling and to look after the holdall when I was busy selling. My financial result would be obvious to the partner and so I would assume that I would have to share the profit with him (or her). Even with a partner I would still expect some losses, say two shirts per game which cost $20 per game or $400 per season. So the overall effect of the risk review is to suggest that the profit estimate should be approximately halved and that I would need to share this with a partner.

With the stall approach my big risk questions concern the lack of allowance for other costs. I cannot imagine that a stall selling $3,000 worth of shirts in the period around a game could have no overheads and would not suffer from some degree of theft. At the very least it would need a second person to help run it. There may also be days when the owner was unwell and could not be there. The stock would also need to be taken to and from the stall on match days. If it was left at the stall there would be too big a chance of all the shirts being stolen (perhaps to be sold over the arm at a subsequent game!). I would allow $200 per game for two helpers on the stall and $50 per game to bring the stock to the stadium and then keep it stored safely between games. Other overheads would also have to be allowed for. Even if the owner did the work for no charge there would be an opportunity cost to consider. Overheads would cover things like insurance, accounting costs and stall fitting-out costs. My guess is for something like 10% of turnover or $6,000 per year. Finally, I would also make a guess about how many shirts would still be stolen per game. If I allow for five shirts stolen per game the cost per season is $1,000. The total effect of all of these costs is to lower profit by $12,000 per season.

Provided the potential owner has the capital available to fund the purchase of stock this still looks a very profitable opportunity. So profitable, in fact, that I would still be wondering what I was missing! We will return to this question later in the book when we consider the Sources of Value approach.

Finally, it is worth noting that I did not carry out any value calculations as part of this analysis. It is only worthwhile doing value calculations when the time value of money is an important factor. There are many financial decisions where time and capital are not the key variables. This is an example of one such situation.

6. *Rank the following risks in order of importance to a major corporation.*
   a. *An uncertainty of ±$10m on sales revenue.*
   b. *A 10% chance that a pump will break down and lower sales in the pipeline division by $10m.*
   c. *A 0.1% chance of a rupture in a pipeline that would cost $1bn to clean up should it happen.*
   d. *A one third chance that the legal staff will win a lawsuit against a competitor for breach of copyright and gain a payout of $200m.*
   e. *A one-in-ten chance that the legal staff will lose a separate case and a fine of $500m will be imposed.*
   f. *A 5% chance that a customer will default on a $1m payment.*

I will first review the risks then place them in order of importance.

Item A is what I term a plus or minus risk. Because it is symmetrical the impact times probability calculation shows a zero impact.

Item B has a risk impact of 10% of $10m or $1m.

Item C has the same risk impact but the absolute magnitude of the impact is such that it would need to be considered separately as it could cause financial distress. I will assume that $1bn is sufficient to cause even a 'major' corporation financial distress.

Item D is a risk impact of plus \$66.7m while item E has a risk impact of minus \$50m. With item E it would be important to check the company's ability to take a hit of \$500m should the case go against the company. I will assume that the company can just cope because it is said to be 'major'.

The impact of F is just \$50,000.

A simple ranking of the risk impacts gives the order:

D, E, B, C, F and A. (with B and C ranked third equal).

However, the list needs to be overviewed to allow for possible financial distress effects. This would move item C to the top of the list and item E to second. So the order would be:

C, E, D, B, F, A.

7. *Now consider the same risks from the perspective of: (a) a small startup company engaged in just this one business activity; and (b) a medium-sized company engaged in several lines of business with an overall market value of \$500m.*

   The startup company could probably find that the \$10m downside on sales revenue caused it financial distress. This would mean ranking items A and B equally. Item C has a huge downside but would so clearly wipe out the company that it would tend to ignore it as it suffered from many other downside risks that were much more likely to wipe it out. Item D could represent a huge gain in relation to the scale of a startup company. With an expected value of \$66.7m I would expect this to be the company's largest asset. Item E would be a real concern since if the case was lost, the company would be bankrupt even if it won the law case in item D. Item F is small.

   So my ranking for the startup company is:

   D, E, A, B, C and F.

   The medium-sized company is closer to the major corporation except that the \$500m loss would probably be too big for it to cope with. Since this hit has a much greater probability than the pipeline rupture it would go to the top of my risk list for this company. My order is therefore:

   E, C, D, B, F and A.

   Again I have to stress that there are a number of subjective judgements made in my answers to this question. Risk is not a topic where there are always answers which are unequivocal.

8. *You are in charge of the evaluation of a research project. The route to market for the research can be characterised as having six steps. Step 1 is research. Step 2 is safety evaluation. Step 3 is pilot plant scale evaluation. Step 4 concerns gaining the relevant government permits while Step 5 involves obtaining board sanction. The final step is to sell the product. If the project fails at any stage the financial outcome is nil. Build a simple decision tree model that will allow you to investigate the following variables for each stage: probability of success; cost of progressing through this stage; length of this stage; and finally value of a research success that makes it to market successfully. Then use the model to test the viability of the following proposal given a 10% CoC and assuming that money is all spent at the end of the relevant period.*

Stage	Cost/benefit	Duration	Success rate
1. Research	*$4m*	*1 year*	*50%*
2. Safety	*$4m*	*1 year*	*85%*
3. Pilot	*$10m*	*1 year*	*75%*
4. Permits	*$10m*	*2 years*	*50%*
5. Sanction	*$1m*	*0.5 year*	*95%*
6. Sales	*Construction cost $50m. Overall value $1bn when sales start.*	*Construction time 1 year*	*90%*

The model will show seven possible outcomes. There are six different ways of failing and just one way to succeed. Each stage will have its own discount factor and will add further costs. My model is as follows:

		Probabilities				
	Disc Factor	Fail now	Continue	Cost/Ben	PV	Risked PV
Stage 1	0.909	50.0%	50.0%	−4	−3.6	−1.8
Stage 2	0.826	7.5%	42.5%	−8	−6.6	−0.5
Stage 3	0.751	10.6%	31.9%	−18	−13.5	−1.4
Stage 4	0.621	15.9%	15.9%	−28	−17.4	−2.8
Stage 5	0.592	0.8%	15.1%	−29	−17.2	−0.1
Stage 6	0.538	1.5%	13.6%	−79	−42.5	−0.6
Prize	0.538		13.6%	921	495.7	67.5
check			100.0%			
NPV						60.2

The discount factors are calculated as at the end of the periods. Stage 4 is long but stage 5 is short. The discount factor for the prize is the same as the factor for the construction spend.

The fail now column shows what percentage of the total fail at each stage. So 50% fail at the first stage and 50% continue. Since 15% of those projects that make it to the second stage fail at this time the overall 'fail now' percentage for stage 2 is 15% of 50% equals 7.5%. Hence 42.5% make it through stage 2, and so on. The check calculation confirms that the sum of the fail-now percentages and the probability of winning the prize is equal to 100%.

The costs gradually increase as the project progresses. So to fail after stage 1 only implies a cost of $4m while failing after the plant has been built results in a cost of $79m. Each cost is multiplied by the discount factor to reach a present value.

The final stage is to calculate the expected value. This requires that each outcome is multiplied by its probability. The expected value is the sum of all of these numbers. The answer, given all of the assumptions, is $60m. This suggests that the project is viable as long as the assumptions are reasonable expected value estimates and the company is big enough to take the risks.

The model can also be used to test the impact of the various failure rate assumptions. The project is robust (i.e. continues to show a positive NPV) to very large changes in the failure rate for stage 1. Even a 90% failure rate, for example, still gives an NPV of $9m. This is because the costs incurred up to the end of stage 1 are low. The prize could also be reduced significantly while still retaining a positive NPV.

9. *Use your judgement to place the following risks in the categories of 1–5 on a diversifiability scale where 1 means fully diversifiable risks while 5 means no diversification benefit.*
Building damaged by a tornado. I would assume this was fully diversifiable, i.e. 1 on my scale.
Costs rise owing to inflation. This is a classic undiversifiable risk because it hits all companies in the same way. So it is 5 on the scale.
Costs rise owing to failure of new computer system. This is largely unique to the company concerned but may have some costs in common with other companies so I would rate it as 1 or 2.
Cost over-run on new factory owing to strikes delaying construction. Strikes can be unique to a company but are often also felt by many companies at the same time. So this is probably a 2 or 3.
Shop sales rise owing to demand for very popular children's toy. The particular toy is unique but ours is not the only toy shop. So I would rank this as 3.
Loss of a legal case for copyright infringement. This is presumably unique to the company concerned so the ranking is 1: fully diversifiable.
Computer systems need replacing owing to technology changes. This tends to be a generic problem and so would rank as a 4 or a 5.
Production equipment for a specialised product needs replacement owing to technology changes. Technology changes impact on many companies but this is described as a specialised product so this is about a 3 on my scale.
10. *Describe possible mechanisms that might cause some degree of correlation between the following variables.*
Construction time and construction cost. You would expect a strong link between the two because, as the saying goes, 'Time is money'. If a project is delayed this will almost inevitably mean extra costs compared with budget.
Capacity utilisation and average selling prices. Low capacity utilisation could mean that selling margins would be reduced because companies would be tempted to reduce selling prices in order to win more sales. So there may well be a correlation between capacity utilisation and selling prices. We cannot, however, be sure whether low margins would cause low selling prices. This is because if the raw material prices had risen a lot this may drive down demand for the product.
Low oil prices and number of people travelling by plane. Low oil prices can translate into lower ticket prices which in turn can encourage more people to fly.
Hotel occupancy rates and theatre bookings. More people staying in hotels may indicate more people want to go out in the evening. Some of these people will go to the theatre.
Economic growth and the cost of advertising slots on TV. Greater economic growth will mean companies can afford more advertising spend. Since the number of advertising slots is more or less fixed, this will mean that the price per slot will rise.
Sales of baby-clothes and share prices. Share prices will rise if the economy does better than expected. When the economy does better than expected people may have more

money to spend on baby-clothes. However, since the arrival of babies is probably more or less independent of the stock market the correlation would be weak.

A coin's landing heads six times in a row and then landing tails. Although seven heads in a row is very unlikely and one might therefore think that sooner or later a tail must show, there is no correlation between one coin toss and another.

11. *You are evaluating a project to mine iron ore. The first cut economics show a substantial NPV of $1,500m. There are, however, risks concerning the ore body. The first risk concerns its size because as yet a full geological survey has not been carried out. The second risk concerns the presence of certain trace elements in the ore. If these are present the cost of purification would rise very substantially.*

    As regards the first risk of the ore body size, your first-cut economics are based on a most likely quantity of ore in place. Should you go ahead and construct the mine in the usual way, the uncertainty band around the $1,500m NPV is from a worst-case of zero (10% chance) to the most-likely (75% chance) of $1,500m to an upside case with a value of $2,000 (15% chance). You have three choices. (1) Do nothing and accept the risks. (2) Build the facilities in two stages with the second stage adjusted to suit the quantity of ore in place which will be obvious once the mine comes on stream. This would lower both the most-likely case NPV and the upside NPV by $100m. However, the downside case would improve to $800m. (3) Carry out a traditional geological survey at a cost (stated in present-value-equivalent terms) of $50m. This survey would warn of the downside case and allow you to lower the construction costs such that the new downside NPV was $1,000m. This NPV is excluding the cost of the survey and would occur two years later than the NPV in the do-nothing case.

    The trace elements are assessed only to have a 5% chance of being present. If they are present it would be necessary to construct an additional purification stage. This would cost $500m (stated in present-value terms) and would delay the NPV by three years. We could build the purification unit as part of the main project. If we did so its cost would be reduced by a half and the build would not delay the project at all. We could delay the entire project for two years to carry out the necessary sample tests to see if the trace elements were present. The sample tests would cost $40m to carry out. If they showed that unacceptable quantities of trace elements were present we would then build the purification unit as part of the project.

    What recommendations would you make to the project team in relation to these risks? What value would you put on this opportunity at this time? You should assume a CoC of 9%.

    First we will deal with the ore body risk. The base case NPV is not an expected value. The 'correct' NPV can be calculated in two ways.

    Either 10% × $0m + 75% × $1,500m + 15% × $2,000m = $1,425m
    Or $1,500 – 10% × $1,500 + 15% × $500 = $1,425m

    This is the expected value if we simply accept the ore body risk but before we allow for the trace element risk.

    The expected value of the two stage construction approach is:

    10% × $800m + 75% × $1,400m + 15% × $1,900m = $1,415m

The incremental effect of the approach can also be calculated directly using the impact times probability approach. In this instance there are two impacts and two probabilities which together sum to 100%. The calculation is:

10% × \$800m – 90% × \$100m = –\$10m

This way of mitigating the risk does not add to value and so should not be recommended.

The survey approach would cost \$50m and delay the NPVs by two years. I will first look at the impact of the survey and then study the effect of the delay as a separate step.

The benefit of the survey approach is \$1,000m but this only happens 10% of the time (when we commit to the survey we do not know what the result will be so we must continue to use the same assumption about the likelihood of the downside). Since 10% of \$1,000 is \$100, the net gain of carrying out the survey is \$50m, meaning that the expected value of following this approach is \$1,475m. This, however, is before allowing for the two year delay. This happens irrespective of the outcome. It is quite clear that applying a 9% discount rate for two years will lower the NPV by more than the \$50m gain so this approach should also be rejected. The conclusion in regard to the ore body size is to live with the risk.

Now we turn to the trace element effect. This is anticipated to occur 5% of the time. There is an additional capital cost of \$500m (which, conveniently, was stated in value terms). Also there is a three year delay. With a 9% CoC the discount factor for three years is 0.772. This means that the value loss owing to delay is:

(1–0.772) × \$1,425m = \$325m

So the total value impact of delay is \$825m (i.e. delay cost plus extra capital cost). Since the trace elements are anticipated just 5% of the time the impact is \$41m. The resultant expected value is \$1,384m.

If we built the purification unit as part of the main unit it would cost just \$250m. This is much more than the risked impact of the trace elements so clearly we should not do this either. The second option to mitigate the risk costs \$40m and also delays the project. Once again, we do not need to do all the maths to work out what to do. It is very clear that this proposal would not create value and so it can be rejected.

We can conclude that the value of the opportunity at this time is \$1,384m.

This final exercise should have indicated the particular benefit of the risk monetisation approach. Calculations are greatly simplified if you do not always have to work out the expected value of all possible outcomes. Answers are often obvious and a technique that allows one to focus on the impact of a risk can save a lot of time.

The exercise should also have shown why one starts with a rough-cut NPV calculation. If we had tried to build a model that would allow all possible outcomes to be tested the work involved might have been great. If short cuts exist, then I would suggest you use them!

Glossary

Abbreviated financial summary (AFS)
A simplified way of presenting the three main accounting statements (income statement, balance sheet and cash flow statement) alongside a value calculation such that the link between accounts and value is made very clear. This book suggests adoption of the AFS layout as the standard means of carrying out all valuations.

ABCDE valuation
A method of valuing a company which is explained in the book. In the model, A stands for Asset value; B for Business development value; C is for Costs; D is for Debt and other liabilities; with the result being E the Equity valuation.

Amortisation (also called depreciation in the UK)
An accounting term for the charge which results when the capital cost of a fixed asset is spread out over its estimated useful life. Note that although this charge serves to lower profit, it does not lower the generation of cash in the period.

Assumptions register
A list of all of the assumptions which have been made as part of the preparation of an investment case. The suggestion is that decision-makers review the assumptions and then study the economic indicators that they imply.

Balance sheet
A summary of the assets and liabilities of a company at the end of any financial period. It is said to show what a company owns and what it owes. It is called a balance sheet because a consequence of the conventions which are used to prepare it is that the assets which are owned must equal the sum which has been invested in them. This balancing sum is called the liabilities.

Beta factor (β)
One of the key parameters in the capital asset pricing model (CAPM). Beta (the Greek letter β) is a measure of the risk inherent in any share which cannot be removed through the phenomenon called portfolio diversification. It is calculated via the co-variance of a share price with the market index.

Bundling
This refers to showing the overall effect of two or more related but actually distinct investments as though they were a single investment with a single set of economic indicators. A typical situation would concern, say, including the cost of a new canteen along with the cost

of a new plant on the same site. If the canteen was required irrespective of the new plant it should be shown as a separate investment.

Capital asset pricing model (CAPM)
An approach which allows the cost of equity to be calculated. The cost is calculated via a straight line relationship between risk and required return. Under the CAPM, the cost of equity is equal to the cost of a risk-free investment plus a factor referred to as the Greek letter beta (β) times the average premium which is required by investors for investing in a typical share. β is a function of the risk inherent in the equity which is not diversifiable by holding a wide portfolio of investments.

Capital employed
An accounting term representing the sum of a company's fixed assets and working capital. It represents the money which has been invested in the so-called assets of a company. Note that traditional accounting statements have to be restated in order to highlight this figure.

Capital investment (often shortened to capex)
The initial investment in a project which is required in order to build its physical assets.

Cash flow
The cash which a company generates in a period as measured by its change in cash. Note that because cash holdings can be changed by financing activities such as borrowing money as well as operational activities, cash flow is not as important as one might anticipate and is not the key input into the so-called discounted cash flow model. The discounted cash flow model is actually based on the so-called funds flow which is the generation of cash excluding any financing effects.

Company as Σ projects
A technique proposed in this book which estimates the accounting performance of a company that simply implements a series of projects all similar to the one under consideration. Adjustments for growth, sunk costs and overheads can also be made with the aim being to allow actual company performance to provide a reality check on claimed performance.

Components of value
This is a technique which involves describing the NPV of a project by reference to the sum of the present value of the individual lines in the project's cash flow model.

Continuous good surprises (CGS)
This is what quoted companies have to deliver to their shareholders if they are continually to deliver to shareholders returns of above the cost of equity. It is a very tough challenge and this is due to the way that the share price will already capture anticipated future performance in today's share price.

Cost of capital (CoC)
The average cost of the funds used by a company. The funds will usually comprise a mixture of debt and equity. Our theories suggest that the main determinant of the cost of capital is the risk associated with the use to which the funds are put. The cost of capital can be calculated as the weighted average of the cost of funds raised through debt (referred to as the CoD) and the cost of funds raised through equity (CoE).

Cost of debt (CoD)
The cost of funds raised by a company as debt. This is the interest rate charged on the company's debt.

Cost of equity (CoE)
The cost of funds raised by a company as equity. Unlike the cost of debt, which is observable, the cost of equity is not. It is deduced via various approaches, the most common of which is called the capital asset pricing model (CAPM). Companies must seek to give the required return to equity shareholders through a combination of dividends paid out plus growth in the value of shares owned.

Credit rating agencies
These are companies whose business is assessing the potential risks taken by lenders when they lend to companies. This service helps companies decide whether or not to lend to a company and also to assess what interest rate to charge.

Current assets
An accounting term referring to assets which will be held for less than a year. The main components of current assets are receivables and inventories.

DCF return
Another name for a project's internal rate of return (IRR). That is to say, the discount rate which, when applied to a project, results in a zero NPV.

Debt
One of the two main sources of finance (the other is equity). Debt is characterised by the requirement to pay interest and to repay the sum borrowed (called the principal). Debt can be given many names including borrowing, gearing, leverage, a mortgage, an overdraft, a bond or a note. Debt is a low-risk way of investing money but is high risk to the person or company that borrows because failure to pay interest or repay the principal according to the agreed schedule can allow the lender to force a company into liquidation.

Discounted cash flow (DCF)
A methodology which aids financial decision making by converting sums of money which are anticipated to occur at different points in time into their equivalent in present value terms. The methodology involves two components. These are cash flows generated through the operational activities of the project under consideration and the appropriate discount rate (or cost of capital). Cash flows caused by financing activities are excluded from the calculation. The methodology's alternative name, which is the economic value model, is emphasised in this book because it avoids this potential confusion concerning exactly what is to be discounted.

Discounted payback (DP)
The point in time when a project first recovers its initial investment after allowing for the effect of discounting. It is the point when the graph of cumulative present value first returns to zero after the time below zero which is caused by the initial investment.

Discount rate
The interest rate which is used to convert a sum of money in one year's time into its equivalent now. Other names for this term are the cost of capital and the time value of money.

Economic indicator

A means of characterising the projected financial performance of a project. This book suggests use of four indicators which are net present value, internal rate of return, discounted payback and investment efficiency.

Economic value model

A methodology which aids financial decision-making by converting sums of money which are anticipated to occur at different points in time into their equivalent in present value terms. The methodology involves two components. These are cash flows and the appropriate discount rate (or cost of capital). The methodology is also referred to as discounted cash flow (DCF).

Equity

One of the two main sources of finance (the other is debt). Equity is characterised by the way that it allows investors to take risks in return for the potential of higher rewards than when investing in debt. Equity brings with it ownership rights such as a vote on the appointment of directors.

Equity risk premium

The additional return over the risk-free rate which investors in equity require on average in order to compensate them for taking the risks inherent in investing in a wide portfolio of shares.

Expected value

The probability-weighted outcome. This is the sum of all of the possible outcomes times their respective probability.

Fish diagram

A chart suggested in this book. The fish diagram shows both the traditional project view of the value profile over time and also the market view of what a project is worth. With a typical project the two lines on this chart will form the shape of a fish.

Five forces model

A structured way for considering the inherent profitability of any industry. The model was proposed by Professor Michael Porter and suggests that different levels of profitability can be explained by reference to: industry competitors; supplier power; buyer power; potential entrants and the threat of substitutes.

Fixed assets

An accounting term which describes the long-term assets of a company (contrast these with current assets which will exist for less than one year).

Full-cycle economics

The economic analysis of the full implications of a project on shareholder value. The calculation should include two additional categories of cost on top of the incremental spend which is included in traditional economic analysis. These are sunk cost and also a fair share of future fixed overheads.

Funds flow

The generation of, or requirement for, cash caused by a project before any financing effects are allowed for. Funds flow is one of the two key inputs into the economic value model.

Future value (FV)
A sum of money available at a specified point in the future.

Growth value
The implied value that a project might have because of the way that it might enable future positive NPV projects to be undertaken. Under the usual standard methodology conventions suggested by this book such value would not be included as part of a base case valuation. It could, however, be shown as a type 3 sensitivity.

Income statement
One of the three main accounting statements. This shows the sales made in a period and the related costs, with the difference being the profit. Hence the alternative name of profit and loss account.

Indivisible finance pool
A description of the overall sums of money that a company has available. The term 'indivisible' is included in order to stress that although funds will come from different sources (basically debt and equity), once they go into the pool one should think of them as being perfectly mixed with the other sums of money that are already in the pool.

Inventories (also called stocks in the UK)
An accounting term which describes holdings of raw materials and partly made/finished products. These are all shown based on what they cost the company and not their potential sales value (unless this is lower than their cost).

Internal rate of return (IRR)
The discount rate which, when applied to a project, results in a zero NPV. This is often also referred to as the DCF return.

Investment efficiency (IE)
A 'bangs per buck' economic indicator which relates net present value to a defined measure of the resources used by a project. Typically calculated as NPV per unit of capital expenditure.

Judgement based on rational analysis
The suggestion that good decisions are a subtle blend of analysis and senior executive judgement.

Level playing field
An expression which describes the intention that investment appraisal should be carried out in a consistent manner across a company. A level playing field would ensure that individual analysts who were given a set of assumptions would all report the same economic indicators. (See also Standard methodology.)

Leverage
The way that changes in key economic indicators can be magnified by finance or high fixed costs. Can also be another name for debt.

Market capitalisation
The market value of a company's shares. If one adds the value of debt and other long-term liabilities to this one obtains the overall value of a company's assets.

McKinsey/GE matrix
A two dimensional matrix which plots business unit strength against market attractiveness. The technique is of particular use as input to a study of strategic options.

'Me too' player
A key element of the Sources of Value technique. The 'me too' player is the one which it is reasonable to look to when considering what will be a sustainable set of long-term assumptions. When competition is of the normal free market type, the 'me too' player will be a bottom of the third quartile player. When competition is regulated the 'me too' player will be that player which the government or the regulator wishes to encourage to invest.

Modigliani Miller proposition 1
The suggestion that the value of a company is independent of how it is financed. This proposition greatly simplifies investment evaluation because it allows one to distinguish between the decision to make an investment and what should be the subsidiary decision concerning how it is financed.

Monetising risk
A technique which uses the expected value principle. Under the monetisation approach the impact of a risk is assessed as its impact times its probability of occurrence.

Net present value (NPV)
The sum of the present values of all of the future cash flows which a project is expected to generate. These will usually involve initial negative flows associated with investing in the project followed by positive flows once a project starts to operate. The term NPV does, however, refer to the present value of all flows associated with something irrespective of whether they are positive or negative. If the NPV is positive then the activity being studied can be said to create value for its owner. If it is negative it destroys value. NPVs are usually assumed to be incremental to some defined alternative case unless they are stated not to be. The term absolute NPV can be used to describe a situation where a particular course of action is given a value based on what funds flow will be generated and not the changes in funds flow compared with the deemed alternative.

Options and option value
An option is a situation where somebody has the right but not the obligation to do something. Financial options refer to situations where the option concerns an item which is quoted on a financial market. These options can be valued through the so-called Black-Scholes model. Many investment situations have characteristics similar to financial options and traditional DCF analysis tends to miss the value implicit in these situations. This book, however, suggests a series of ways of estimating option value in investment projects using the economic value approach.

Payables (also called creditors in the UK)
Sums of money owed by the company to its suppliers but not yet paid.

Plan (could also be called a long term plan or a one year plan)
A set of projections for the future which sets out the detailed path which a company intends to take.

Planning cycle and Plan, Do, Measure, Learn
The never-ending cycle which describes how a company starts with consideration of its strategy, then formulates a plan which it implements and subsequently monitors in order to learn lessons for the future. At any time, lessons from past actions are used to improve current decisions.

Portfolio diversification
The phenomenon through which the average volatility of investments in a large number of shares (referred to as a portfolio) is lower than the individual volatility of each of the shares which are in the portfolio. This serves to lower risk for investors but not remove it altogether (which is what would happen in theory if share prices all moved in ways that were independent of one other).

Present value (PV)
The equivalent of a sum of money received now.

Prism approach
A resource allocation technique suggested in this book. It requires that all investment opportunities be considered in a specified number of ways and that these should allow informed judgements to be made about resource allocation.

Profit and loss account (P&L)
One of the three main accounting statements. This explains the profit or loss made in the period as being the difference between the sales made and the related costs. The alternative name for the P&L is the income statement.

Project life
The assumed life of a project. This can have a significant impact on the reported NPV and so some conventions are necessary if companies want to create a level playing field for investment decision-making.

Receivables (also called debtors in the UK)
Sums of money owed to the company by customers who have not yet paid for their purchases.

Residual value
The remaining value of cash flows which will occur when a project is closed down. This will cover things like the recovery of working capital and also any necessary remediation costs. The residual value is usually assumed to occur in the year following the final year of a project's life.

Return on capital employed (ROCE)
An accounting ratio which shows profit as a percentage of capital employed. It is sometimes calculated based on year-end capital employed and sometimes the average over the year. When average capital employed is used the term is adjusted to return on average capital employed or ROACE. The ratio gives a rough indicator of the IRR which the company's projects are earning.

Risk
In the context of this book the word risk usually refers to the fact that uncertainty exists as regards what will happen in the future. Note the contrast with the idea that risk might simply be associated with nasty outcomes.

Risk-free rate
The rate of return which investors require in order to justify investing in a situation where there is no risk.

ROCE bridge
An explanation for the link which exists between the project's IRR and the accounting return on capital employed which a company will earn if it simply invests in a stream of projects like this one. The relationship helps to explain why companies need over time to earn a ROCE of above their cost of capital if they are to create value for shareholders.

Search costs
The cost of, for example, R&D, exploration or a project development team that has searched for and found an opportunity which is now being considered.

Sensitivities or sensitivity analysis
Calculating the financial consequences for a project should different assumptions be made. Sensitivities are usually reported as impacts on one or more of the economic indicators such as NPV or IRR.

Sources of Value
The eponymous technique which allows a project's NPV to be explained by reference to two factors. These are the value calculated for its individual sources of value and the value anticipated for the deemed 'me too' player. The technique creates a bridge between finance and strategy and offers great insights into NPVs.

Stage gate processes
A way of aiding the efficient implementation of a project by breaking it down into key stages. Each stage is characterised by its own key aims and work on one stage should not start until the previous stage has been completed. Various versions of the process exist and typical stages would be: options identification and selection; detailed design; implementation; operation.

Standard methodology
The discounting conventions through which senior decision-makers can be assured that they can compare investments based on their actual merits and not have to worry about spurious methodological differences. This can only be done when all those involved in calculating economic indicators adopt a standard methodology which defines the approach to discounting and makes it clear where assumptions must stop and a standard approach must start. (See also Level playing field.)

Strategy
The overall direction in which a company is trying to go. Note the distinction between a strategy options study which considers the alternatives open to a company and an agreed strategy which describes the chosen course. For most companies corporate strategy will describe the choice of businesses that the company invests in and the way that it organises

and manages itself. Each individual business will have its own strategy which describes how it intends to beat its own competitors.

Success value
The value of a set of financial projections which are based on a presumption of success in relation to some key aspect such as winning an auction. Success values can be contrasted with expected values which incorporate also the possibility and impact of failure.

Sunk costs
At any point in time this refers to money that has already been spent on a project.

Sustaining investment
Relatively small amounts of investment which are necessary in order to protect against a substantial drop in output from an existing plant. The usual analogy is the need to replace a pump should it fail. This might count as capital expenditure but the justification would be different from justifying a major new build. The appropriate approach is to justify a programme of sustaining investment and not each individual item.

Terminal value
A terminal value is used when an economic evaluation is deliberately carried out for a period of less than the full life of an asset. The cash flows beyond this period are replaced with a calculated terminal value which represents the present value as at the end of the period which has been explicitly modelled on cash flows expected beyond this point. Terminal values are usually used when valuing entire companies.

Time value of money
The extra amount of money that is required in order to justify receiving money later rather than now. This is stated as an annual percentage and is also often referred to as the cost of capital or the discount rate.

Types of sensitivity
This book proposes the use of three different types of sensitivity. Type 1 should show the impact of changes in assumptions to the P10/P90 range. Type 2 should show what changes are necessary in order to have a zero NPV. Type 3 should show any other relevant information.

U-shaped valley
A description adopted by this book for the approach of incorporating the consideration of risk into the development of a project. The approach has three steps. First one calculates a first-cut estimate of NPV based on single-point assumptions corresponding to a successful outcome. Then one assesses the risks to this (both upside and downside) on an impact times probability basis. This provides the floor of the so-called U-shaped valley. Then finally one considers actions which can be taken in advance to mitigate the risk.

Value chain model
An approach proposed by Professor Michael Porter under which the activities of any company can be divided into five primary and four support activities. The approach gives a disciplined framework for considering the activities of a company and how it compares with its competitors.

Value creation
The positive NPV caused when a new plan or project is identified.

Value growth
An increase in value that happens over a period of time. This is a potentially dangerous concept because one cannot know whether value growth is good or bad unless one also knows how much money was invested in a company or withdrawn from it between the dates of the two valuations.

Value profile
A graph which depicts the cumulative present value of a project over its anticipated life.

Value sector
That part of the overall economy that is made up of companies that take the maximisation of shareholder value as their primary objective. The individual companies in the sector can be termed value players.

Weighted average cost of capital (WACC)
Another term for cost of capital. The term places emphasis on the fact that the cost of capital is indeed the weighted average cost of the various forms of finance which a company uses.

Words and music
A technique suggested in this book which emphasises the links which should exist between a strategy (the words) and its financial results (the music). These links should be mutually supportive. Any apparent disconnect which exists between the two should be taken as a sign that further analytical work should be carried out before a final decision is taken.

Working capital
An accounting term describing the net value of accounts receivable, inventories and payables. When working capital is added to fixed assets, one arrives at capital employed.

WYMIWYG
Stands for 'What you measure is what you get' and serves to stress the importance of setting the appropriate targets.

Bibliography

Books

Accounts Demystified by Anthony Rice (2008, Pearson Education, Harlow). *Now in its fifth edition, this book is suitable for absolute beginners who need more detail on basic accounting than I provide in the third pillar.*

Against the Gods – The Remarkable Story of Risk by Peter Bernstein (1998, John Wiley & Sons, New Jersey). *A very enjoyable book, well worth reading by those who want to study the topic of risk in greater detail.*

Competitive Advantage by Michael Porter (2004, Free Press, New York). *See page 116 for my comments.*

Competitive Strategy – Techniques for Analysing Industries and Companies by Michael Porter (2004, Free Press, New York). *See page 115 for my comments.*

Financial Statement Analysis and Security Valuation by Stephen Penman (2007, McGraw Hill, New York). *See page 185 for my comments.*

Global Investment Returns Yearbook by Dimson, Marsh and Staunton all from London Business School (2008, ABN Amro, London). *For a widely based and authoritative analysis of long-term returns on investments in debt and equity.*

Manias, Panics and Crashes – A History of Financial Crises by Charles Kindleberger (2005, John Wiley & Sons, New Jersey). *You should read this as a warning if you think that crashes and bubbles are unusual!*

Principles of Corporate Finance by Brealey, Myers and Allen (2008, McGraw Hill, New York). *See page 184 for my comments.*

Stocks, Bonds, Bills and Inflation – an Annual Yearbook (Ibbotson Associates, Chicago). *I have the 2004 edition which gives US data for 1925–2003.*

Valuation – Measuring and Managing the Value of Companies by Koller, Goedhart and Wessels, all of McKinsey and Company (2005, John Wiley & Sons, New Jersey). *See page 184 for my comments.*

Websites

Charities

www.gatesfoundation.org

Cost curve data
www.minecost.com

Credit rating agencies
www.moodys.com
www.standardandpoors.com

Monte Carlo analysis software
www.decisioneering.com (*for Crystal Ball software*)
www.palisade.com (*for @risk software*)

Value based management techniques
www.valuebasedmanagement.net (*for short summaries of hundreds of techniques*)

Harvard Business School (*find Michael Porter's web page here*)
www.hbs.edu

Journal of Applied Corporate Finance (*see spring 2005 edition for the article which I wrote on taking real options beyond the black box*)
www.morganstanley.com/views/jacf/index.html

Judge Business School Cambridge (*I lecture to the MBA and Masters of Finance classes*)
www.jbs.cam.ac.uk

London Business School (*Risk Measurement Service*)
www.london.edu

McKinsey (*register for its quarterly journal here*)
www.mckinsey.com

Index